Safe by a Mile

Charlie Metro with
Tom Altherr

University of
Nebraska Press
Lincoln and
London

All photographs are from the Metro family collection.

⊗

Library of Congress Cataloging-in-Publication Data
Metro, Charlie, 1918–
Safe by a mile / Charlie Metro with Tom Altherr.
p. cm.
Includes index.
ISBN 0-8032-8281-8 (pbk. : alk. paper)
1. Metro, Charlie, 1918– .   2. Baseball managers—United States—Biography.
I. Altherr, Tom.   II. Title.
GV865.M49 A3 2002
796.357'092–dc21
[B]
2001053180

To my wife, Helen Deane Bullock Metro, and my children: my daughter, Elena, and my sons, Bud (Charles Jr.), Steve, and Geoff

Contents

List of Illustrations, ix
Acknowledgments, xi
Introduction, xiii
1 Hookey from High School, 1
2 The Big Leagues Were a Long Way Off, 24
3 Up with Detroit and Philadelphia, 63
4 Go West, Young Man, 106
5 Points South, 157
6 The Road Back to Triple-A, 192
7 Mile High, Here We Come, 227
8 A Car Missing a Wheel, 250
9 Scouting, the Toughest Job in Baseball, 281
10 Putting All the King's Men Together, 316
11 If This Is Tuesday, It Must Be Albuquerque, 345
12 Billy Ball, 378
13 Retirement? What Retirement?, 403
14 My Own Hall of Fame, 441
15 I Dream of Baseball, 469
Appendix: Career Statistics, 499
Index, 503

Illustrations

following page 142

1. Charlie at age two with his father
2. Charlie with third grade friends
3. Charlie as a high school senior, with friends
4. Charlie after his release from Easton, 1937
5. Charlie with the Pennington Gap team, 1938
6. Charlie back home in Nanty-Glo, Pennsylvania, with the mayor and a friend, 1938
7. Charlie and Helen Deane Bullock courting, 1939
8. Charlie with the Mayfield Browns of Kentucky, 1939
9. Helen and Charlie visiting Charlie's mother, Pauline Moreskonich, January 1942
10. Charlie and John Gorsica in Philadelphia, 1943 or 1944
11. Al Simmons, Charlie, and Mr. Mack, 1944
12. Charlie at the batting tee in Twin Falls, Idaho, 1948
13. Charlie at Yankees spring training, Boyes Hot Springs, California, 1948
14. Charlie with Ty Cobb in Twin Falls, Idaho, 1948
15. Charlie after a fight in Twin Falls, Idaho, 1948

following page 300

16. Charlie with his umpire brother, John, at spring training, Montgomery, Alabama, 1952
17. The Metro family, December 1956
18. Charlie as one of three luncheon speakers, Riverside, California, 1957
19. Charlie with sons Steve and Bud, Vancouver dugout, 1957
20. Charlie managing with the Denver Bears, 1960
21. Rival managers Casey Stengel and Charlie, 1962
22. Charlie with his youngest son, Geoff, 1965

23. Charlie in the Tulsa Oilers dugout, 1966
24. Ted Williams and Charlie, 1970
25. Charlie coaching with the Oakland A's, 1982
26. Charlie and Billy Williams with Hitters' Hands sculpture, 1993
27. Helen and Charlie at their ranch, Arvada, Colorado, 1999

Acknowledgments

We would like to thank the editorial staff of the University of Nebraska Press for their invaluable help, which has undoubtedly made this a better book; Joan Foster, the dean of the School of Letters, Arts, and Sciences at Metropolitan State College of Denver, who contributed some funding for the transcription; Steve Gietschier, director of historical records at *The Sporting News*; Jim Gates, Tim Wiles, and the staff of the National Baseball Hall of Fame Library in Cooperstown; Paul White of *Baseball Weekly*; the members of the Society for American Baseball Research (SABR), particularly the Rocky Mountain chapter, of which we have been members; baseball historians, such as Larry Gerlach and Mark Rucker, who have been great encouragers of this project; and Sharon Porter, Chris Hause, and Lisa Haight, who provided invaluable transcription help.

From Charlie Metro: I would particularly like to thank the people of Nanty-Glo and Jenners, Pennsylvania; my major league managers, Mr. Connie Mack and Steve O'Neill, and other baseball people: Casey Stengel, Cedric Tallis, Billy Martin, Jack Fournier, Al Lopez, Al Campanis, Tommy Lasorda, and Bob Howsam, who was there all the time when I needed him, and all the players I played with, managers and coaches I played for, all the players who played for me, all the organizations I worked for, all the sportswriters who wrote about me, all the sportscasters who covered me, all the fans in all the cities where I played, coached, managed, and scouted, and my many friends, especially the late Eddie Newman, and Raelee Frazier and Frank Frazier for their association with Hitters' Hands. And, of course, I would like to thank my wife, Helen, and my children, who followed me around the country all those years, and my brothers and sisters, who were among my biggest boosters, and especially my father, Metro, who encouraged me in baseball, and my mother, Pauline, who got me out of the coal mines.

From Tom Altherr: I would especially like to thank my brothers, Douglas, Paul, and James, and their families; my colleagues in the history department at Metropolitan State College of Denver and at other institutions, particularly Richard Aquila at Ball State University, for their patience and support; and last, but hardly least, Jenny, who has been there all along.

Introduction

My father might as well have put a baseball in my hand when I was born, even before the doctor slapped me into this world. As far back as I can remember, baseball has been a part of my life. I wouldn't trade my career for anything. I have seen about everything imaginable in baseball, but just when I think so, I see something totally new, almost every ball game. The game is always interesting to me; I can't understand people who claim it's boring. For me it's the perfect game, a gift from God that elevated our country's spirit throughout the rough times of this past century. I've said many a time that after I go to that great natural grass diamond in the sky, I want a handful of my ashes spread over a ballpark during the seventh-inning stretch.

Every time I walk into a ballpark, go up a ramp or down the steps, and see that expanse of green, I still get the same goose bumps I did when I was a kid and saw my first major league game at old Forbes Field in Pittsburgh. How could I forget my first glimpse of Yankee Stadium? This was the place where *they*, the ballplayers who were only names on the radio and in the newspapers, were *playing*! In the flesh! Even today, when I go to a game at Coors Field, a true gem of a ballpark if there ever was one, I can hardly wait to enter the stadium, hobnob with the ushers and any Rockies personnel I see, chat with friends from the opposition, and settle into my seat for the game. I don't always stay for every inning anymore, but that hasn't dampened any of my enthusiasm for this greatest of all games.

Someone once asked me what I would do if there were no baseball. He didn't mean like the strikes during 1981 and 1994, which were bad enough. He meant what if baseball disappeared entirely. I told him that I couldn't even imagine a total loss of baseball. What a vacuum! How could you possibly wake up on a summer morning and thumb through a newspaper without box scores? What would a spring evening be without the hum of a radio broadcast of a ball game? What would a September conversation consist of without the tension of the stretch run or the wait-until-next-year resignation of, say, Cubs fans? Baseball fills up our lives as well as our hearts.

Baseball, for me, is akin to a religion. I say that with no trace of sacrilegious intent. It's certainly more important than a pastime. Look at the emotions that the game evokes, the memories that it triggers. Tribes of fans identify strongly with their teams, rooting them on and warding off insults from competitors. Fans wear their colors, regalia, and paraphernalia with intense pride. They recite statistics and conjure up memories, even here in Colorado with the young Rockies franchise. The national anthem before the game and the singing of "Take Me Out to the Ball Game" serve as the hymns—I know all the words to the latter, even the second stanza! Passions fly in the discussions. Debates over the three greatest outfielders of all time or the best left-handed relievers flare up all the time and bring out the true believers. Let a franchise fall apart and the faithful wring their hands over the demise with all the warnings of an Old Testament prophet: What happened to the Tigers? Where did the Mets go? Who can resurrect the Pirates? Players perform rituals on and off the field over and over again with the devotion of longtime parishioners. They adhere to superstitions more fiercely than perhaps even a spiritualist. Older players teach the traditions to the rookies to complete the generational cycle of the religion. The game has changed some of its rules since the 1860s and undergone other transformations, but the religious qualities have only deepened.

Without baseball some of us would be slaves. Personally I would have most likely been trapped working in the coal mines in western Pennsylvania. That was tough dangerous work. Sometime just read a history of coal mining or track down the May 1943 issue of *Life* magazine that documented the struggle in my hometown of Nanty-Glo. I would have been toting a lunchpail like most of my friends and worrying when the next explosion would snuff out some more of us. Baseball gave me hope of a better life and lighted the way up out of those tunnels. I worked hard, dug out a lot of coal, and suffered injuries from a mine blast. I was lucky enough to come out alive.

But there was baseball as a savior, a glorious outdoor game, not just a ticket out of poverty but a chance to run free in the sunshine. At a time when fewer and fewer Americans were working or playing outdoors, I got the chance to play and work at a profession that celebrated the grassy expanses and to escape from the stale air of the mines and factories and offices. Can you begin to guess how refreshing it was to dash about the outfield in pursuit of fly balls? Do you remember that first time you circled under a high fly, the sky a perfectly heartbreaking blue, hardly a cloud around, the air so balmy and the wind so warm, the ball seemed to stay up there forever? I knew, in my bones, what the "Shoeless Joe" Jackson character in *Field of Dreams* meant when he talked about the "thrill of the grass." How could it be anything less than thrilling? Whenever I see people, even ballplayers, sweating away in workout gyms in daylight, in spring, in summer, in the fall, peddling machines and pushing weights, I scratch my head. There isn't a single play in baseball where you ride a stationary bicycle around the bases! I want to say to them, that's all well and good but get out into the sunshine, sweat it out in the grass and dust, run from foul line to foul line, take a hundred ground balls at infield practice, shag a hundred flies in the outfield, play pepper and limber up every muscle in your body, feel the pleasure of good, honest sweat trickle down your face. Exercise should be liberating, not confined torture. And it should come outdoors, even in the cold and even in some rain.

I have had a unique career in baseball. I played for Steve O'Neill with the Detroit Tigers in 1943 and 1944, and for Connie Mack, 'er pardon me, *Mr.* Mack, with the Philadelphia A's in 1944 and 1945, and I coached for Billy Martin with the Oakland A's in 1982. I was a member of the Chicago Cubs "college of coaches," and when my turn to manage came in June 1962, I ended up convincing Mr. Wrigley to not send me down but instead let me stay at the helm the rest of the season. In 1968 I became Director of Player Procurement for the newly forming Kansas City Royals franchise and helped them become the most successful expansion team in that era. In 1970 I also took a turn at managing that club, making me one of several managers to manage in both leagues. I missed the chance to manage the "Big Red Machine" by a week, instead recommending George "Sparky" Anderson for the job. I crossed town in Chicago in 1963 and coached and scouted for Al Lopez's White Sox. I was a scout for Tommy Lasorda's Los Angeles Dodgers. That got me three World Series rings, the last one for winning over the "cursed Yankees" in 1981. I helped secure the signing of Fernando Valenzuela from Mexico. I was the first "eye in the sky" or "spy in the sky," the guy up in the press box or out in the bleachers with a walkie-talkie directing the outfielders where to play certain batters. I scouted for Cincinnati and Detroit, and I was the cross-checker for the National Scouting Bureau.

But it took me a while to make it to the majors. I played hookey from high school in 1937 and attended a St. Louis Browns tryout camp in Johnstown, Pennsylvania, with about 1,500 competitors and was one of fourteen players signed to a minor league contract, one of three to get very far. I had a less-than-promising first year at Easton, Maryland, in the Eastern Shore League in 1937, but in 1938, I recovered and did better at Pennington Gap, Virginia. By 1939 I was at Mayfield, Kentucky, in the Kitty League, where I had the great fortune to meet Helen Deane Bullock, the lady who became my wife of sixty years and mother of our four children. The next stops were at Palestine and Texarkana in the East Texas League in 1940 and then back to Texarkana when it went into the Cotton States League the next year. In 1942 I met up with one of the men I most admired and whom I named one of our sons after, Steve O'Neill, who was the manager at Beaumont in the Texas League.

I had a real good year at Beaumont, so when Steve went up to manage the Detroit Tigers in 1943, he took me with him. I finally made the majors! I didn't play much, because I couldn't get the hang of hitting major league breaking balls. But I did some pinch running and played good defense. In 1944 I made the club again, but by midseason, possibly because I had been active in some players' union business, the Tigers released me. The Philadelphia Athletics picked me up. There I learned a lot more about baseball under the tutelage of Mr. Mack, but the A's were a second-division club, not a contender like Detroit.

After my stay with the Philadelphia A's, I ended up out at Oakland in the Pacific Coast League. The next year I met up with Charles Dillon "Casey" Stengel, a manager who, like Mr. Mack, taught me an immense amount about the game. Never did I dream that one day I would manage against the "Ole Perfesser" and his Mets and even beat them out for ninth place (well, just barely) in 1962. I also made the acquaintance of a scrappy clubhouse boy named Billy Martin, who would pester me into throwing him batting practice in between his duties. The Oaks, however, sent me to the Seattle Rainiers for the last half of 1946.

Seattle released me during spring training the next year, much to my shock and disappointment. I thought I had the club made. It was one of the darkest hours of my life. I was down to $3.75 and had a family to support. As luck would have it, at that moment the Yankee scout Joe Devine got me a spot as playing manager for the Yankees' Class C Bisbee, Arizona, club. I had done Joe a great favor a few years before by giving him scouting information on Texas League players. This new assignment launched me on a minor league managerial career that took me to Twin Falls, Idaho; Montgomery, Alabama; Augusta, Georgia; Durham, North Carolina; Charleston, West Virginia; Terre Haute, Indiana; Idaho Falls, Idaho; Vancouver, British Columbia; and Denver, Colorado (where Helen and I decided to settle down on a small ranch west of the city) with clubs in the Yankees, Tigers, Cardinals, and Orioles organizations.

Much of the time, my teams finished second or third, but in 1960, my Denver Bears went all the way to the championship. Only twice did I have a last-place club, the first at Montgomery in 1953 and then at Charleston in 1956, mainly because the Detroit system stocked it with over-the-hill players. In 1966, after three years with the White Sox, I accepted Bob Howsam's offer to skipper the Tulsa Oilers, a Cardinals farm team in the American Association. We had a fine squad, anchored by future Hall of Famer Steve Carlton, and we won the flag. The next year I went back up to the majors as a scout for the Cincinnati Reds, where I got my first look at Johnny Bench and penned a note to Bob Howsam, then at Cincinnati himself, that that Oklahoma catcher was a "can't miss" superstar. The remainder of my career was with the majors, but I always looked back on my minor league record with a definite sense of pride.

My career had some additional unique aspects. Unless I miss my guess, I'm probably the only Ukrainian-American to have played *and* managed in the big leagues. Out of perhaps 50 million Ukrainians worldwide and who knows how many in America, I was maybe the luckiest. What are the odds on that? In my first three years, I earned more money than Babe Ruth did in his first three! You could look it up, but I'll save you the trouble. The Babe pulled down the paltry sums of $1,900 for 1914 and $3,500 for 1915 and 1916 respectively. The Tigers tossed $3,600 my way for each of 1943 and 1944, and the Athletics raised me to $5,500 for 1945. Imagine outearning the best player ever in baseball! As a manager in the minor leagues, I believe I may have directed the clubs to more wins than virtually any other skipper; if not the one with the most, I'm high on the list.

As a baseball man, I spent a lot of time trying to improve equipment and training methods. In the mid-1930s, I invented the batting tee. Like a lot of kids, we were constantly swinging at stones and bottle caps and, when we could get them, actual balls. I scrounged up a piece of real hard rubber pipe, split one end on it in four pieces, and nailed the bent supports to a board. Just place a ball on top and work on that swing! Ten years later I tried to get a patent but couldn't at that time justify the five hundred dollars or so necessary to complete the legal process. I was the first manager to experiment with batting cages down the left-field line, at the stadium in Kansas City, and have my pinch hitters warm up in them. That caused a dispute with umpire Charlie Berry in 1970.

Since I retired in 1984, I have kept my hand in the game, doing a little bit of bird-dogging and going to meetings and reunions here and there and experimenting with new bats and planning my comeback. In the past few years, I have launched a new project called Hitters' Hands. A Denver sculptor, Raelee Frazier, convinced me to let her make a bronze model of my hands wrapped around a baseball bat. The sculpture came out so incredibly lifelike that I had the brainstorm of persuading Hall of Famers to get their hands molded for posterity, in their favorite batting grip around their favorite bat and with wristbands from the team they played for the most. The bat would be fastened to a home plate base of either walnut or oak with their signature lasered on. We've done some pitcher's hands too. We have placed a Ted Williams sculpture in the Smithsonian Institution, three others in the Arizona Diamondbacks museum, as well as some in other museums, and we hope to sell others to baseball memorabilia collectors and interested museums.

I have seen baseball from every angle imaginable. As my friends say, I'm like horse manure—always around and underfoot. I have played, coached, managed, or scouted in just about every commercial ballpark and stadium in the United States and quite a few in Canada, the Caribbean, and Mexico. I counted up forty-four major league stadiums alone, and I drove by two more, the old Baker Bowl in Philadelphia and Braves Field in Boston. How many times did I stand at third base, coaching, sweating a one-run lead, looking up at my wife while she was having a hot dog and a Coke or the fans were having beers. A Denver exhibition of panoramic photographs of past and present parks a few years ago brought back a flood of memories. With most of the photographs, I could point to the exact spot where I hit a home run or where I first saw a current ballplayer take tentative rookie swings or where I got thrown out of a game for questioning an umpire's ancestry. My "gold card" for forty-plus years of service in baseball nearly always gets me two seats at any ballpark, and on a couple of occasions when it hasn't, I managed to get in anyway by hook or by crook.

Because I didn't have a long and famous playing career, because I wasn't a Joe DiMaggio or a Mickey Mantle, I have been able to observe baseball minus the filter of fame and the excessive distractions of the media. Without hundreds of writers following me around when I was a player or in my early days of managing, I could pay attention to what made those great players superb, what it took to bump a player's skills up a notch or two, what were the overall strategies and finer points of winning a ball game. I was able to communicate the virtues of hard work and the regimen of practice to younger players, to cultivate their burning desire to play, because I saw myself in them. To be sure, I would have loved to have gone on to be a

Hall of Famer, yet I wouldn't trade what I did have for the long career of learning and teaching, for what I was able to impart to hundreds of players.

Nearly fifty years meant a carload of changes. I personally witnessed the days of baseball's racial integration. I saw the fires of Detroit's race riots in 1943. I observed the first wave of African-American minor leaguers to play in the South in the early 1950s, watching their anguish in the face of bigotry and their determination to excel. I handled a baseball tryout for a black athlete for the presidents of Tuskegee Institute and Alabama State University and received thanks personally from Martin Luther King Jr. In 1960, when the Sheraton Seelbach Hotel in Louisville refused to give rooms to three black ballplayers on my Denver Bears—Jake Wood, Bubba Morton, and Ozzie Virgil—I did my small part to force that hotel to integrate. In 1962, when I managed the Cubs, Buck O'Neil, the former star first baseman of the Kansas City Monarchs, became the first African-American to coach in the major leagues. When I became a scout, I was the first to stop marking racial designations on scouting reports. Bill White, the Cardinals star and later president of the National League, was among the first to remark on that switch to racial equality. I helped recruit Latin American players for the Dodgers. And now baseball with its racial diversity is all the better for the steps that Jackie Robinson and Branch Rickey took fifty years ago. For me, a son of immigrant parents, baseball—the sport and the ball itself—has been the great equalizer.

Additionally, I have watched the massive changes in the commercialization of the sport with mixed feelings. On the one hand, the amounts of money involved have spiraled upward so fast, it's almost dizzying. On the other hand, I don't begrudge the players their salaries. Today's players make more great plays in one week than I would have seen in a season in the 1940s. I wish, however, that Major League Baseball would revise the pension rules to include us players who played before 1947. If the major leagues were to restore their image and market the game effectively to its greatest potential worldwide, there would be more than enough money to go around. I don't have the greatest sympathy for small-market franchises who let their scouting systems and minor leagues deteriorate and then come whining for revenue sharing. The best franchises have achieved their greatness by working hard and paying attention to details throughout the system. Sloppiness earns its own miserable rewards. And yet, through all of the bickering, the labor disputes, the strikes, the arrogant players, and the other elements that have detracted from the game, I still see the game I have loved all along, this grand game of baseball, shining through, with the same vibrancy as when I first saw it so many years ago.

ONE

Hookey from High School

Baseball has been my life as far back as I can remember. I don't ever remember when I didn't know anything about baseball, when I wasn't crazy about it. I never thought that I would do anything else but baseball from the day that I was old enough, when I was just a little guy in fourth and fifth grade, when I was a mascot for the town team. I was obsessed with it. And it stayed with me all of my life, for my forty-eight years in the game. I never wanted any other job, never thought for one minute that I would be anything but a ballplayer.

I was born on April 28, 1918, to Metro and Pauline Moreskonich. I was raised in the coal mining country of western Pennsylvania, Heilwood in Indiana County, Jenners in Somerset County, and Nanty-Glo in Cambria County. Baseball—good gosh!— was all over the place. When I got up there in about the third, fourth, fifth grade, Babe Ruth was a household name. People were always talking about the Yankees or the closer Pittsburgh Pirates. Over in Johnstown was a club in the Mid-Atlantic League. Kids played whenever they could, pickup games and the like. Every coal mining town and every steel mill town had a team, and they had leagues, the Somerset County Coal League and so forth. There were some good players. One guy, Rip Engle, who played catcher for Acosta, eventually became a very fine football coach at Penn State University.

My father was crazy about baseball. I don't know where or how he got the love of the game. He came from the Ukraine, so he never saw the sport until he came to the United States. He just had a love of baseball. He liked everything about it, the action of it. He made bats by hand for the town team. Later on I worked one summer and bought him a wood lathe with my earnings, and he made baseball bats. He called them the "Metro Special." He used to walk to see ball games eight or ten miles, every Saturday or Sunday, when the mines didn't work very much, and if there was a game scheduled in the middle of the week, he would walk to those games. I'd go with him when I was just a little guy. He loved it, and he knew all the players by name. I think he played in a baseball game only once. He got hit in the nose by a batted ball, and he left the game frustrated. He used to catch me when I was a young guy in the lower grades. He'd warm me up. One time I threw a ball pretty hard, and even though he had the catcher's mitt, he got hit, just smack, right in the nose. He threw down the mitt and said, "No more. You're throwing too fast for me."

He had great faith in baseball. He once told me, when I was in the second or third grade, "Charlie, you can do anything you want if you play baseball, *anything*." That was his simple way of saying that I could do anything. Baseball would be a means of acquiring a better life. That stuck in my mind and drove me on. And I have passed this on to ballplayers: you can do anything you want to do.

Years later I would read the baseball box scores for my father. He came over from the Ukraine, and he couldn't read or write English. But he loved baseball. When I started playing in the county league, box scores would be printed in the paper. It really pleased him that the writers would drop our name of Moreskonich because it wouldn't fit very well in the box score and replace it with Metro. That was my father's first name. So they called me "Little Metro," and later I became Charlie Metro. I would read the box scores to him, read the names of the players. He would memorize and recognize them. Then when I started playing professionally, I would always take out a subscription to the local paper and send it to him. At first he'd have somebody help him go down the columns of names, but after looking enough at the writing, he learned to read that way.

I had a great boyhood. I played in the woods in the summertime and played baseball and swam in the creek, did about everything there was to do. I never had a bike. We didn't have school buses. We had to run everywhere, walk everywhere we went. I used to trap for muskrats and weasels. You could get twenty cents for a muskrat pelt and a whole dollar for a weasel skin, if it had no holes in it. I'd find a hollow log with a small hole on one end and a big hole on the other, where I'd set the trap and nail the chain. Then I'd bait it with bacon rind. One day I went to check my trapline, and I saw that the chain had been dragged into the hole. For some reason, I thought twice before I bent over to check it. Lucky for me I hesitated, because that skunk let loose a blast, and it didn't hit me. I waited two weeks until the skunk died to get my trap back.

It seemed like there was always a baseball game going on. When you were kids, you picked up a pickup squad, you threw the bat and did the picking up of your team, you played on a sandlot or a vacant lot, always in the country, out in the small schools, little mining towns, little country towns, farming towns, out in the open air. We used to hit bottlecaps with broomsticks. That was a popular thing when I was a young boy. We'd get a handful of bottlecaps, pick them up and save them. Then some guy would get a broomstick, and one guy would pitch the bottlecaps and the other guy would hit. They sure could throw some pretty wicked curve balls with those bottle caps, and it was very good practice. They had caps from the root beer. We'd call it "Ruth Beer." If you got enough of those caps, you could get a Babe Ruth model glove. We used to watch for people at the grocery store to buy a case of that root beer, and we'd stop at their houses to ask for the caps. It wasn't easy to collect the caps. You might get only one Babe Ruth cap from a whole case. It broke my heart because I couldn't get enough caps for a glove, but it was one of the big things among us kids. We didn't have baseball cards, like bubble gum cards later, but we had tobacco cards. In winter, we'd play fox and geese and throw snowballs, have snowball fights, and build forts and snow caves. Even then I was building up my arm by throwing snowballs for accuracy.

We had to scrounge for equipment. We got sticks out of the woods to use as bats, until my father made my first bat. My first ball was one we found in the creek, floating down the creek right by the ballpark. We had come up that creek and somebody said, there's a baseball. In we jumped and got the ball. The team had foul-tipped the ball, and it went into the creek. Before they could get there, we found it. That was my first baseball. Boy, that was a good one. We dried it off and played with it, I think for a whole year. We taped it up over and over again with black tape. And my first glove I made from the tops of those old touring cars. I don't know what the material was, but it was black. I sewed the outside edges of it, but I didn't put the fingers in it, because it was too hard to make them. So I made it a catcher's mitt, and stuffed it with cotton out of an old mattress. That was my first glove. Later on when I needed spikes, my father fashioned a pair. Spikes were expensive. My father was a pretty good shoemaker. He would take a pair of my old shoes, not the high tops but the over-the-ankle ones, and he would put a new sole on the shoe and then rivet the spikes on the sole. Sometimes he'd find an old pair of cleats that somebody discarded, or we'd buy new cleats and he'd rivet them on. We always found ways to play baseball.

When I was a young guy, six years old, I was catching and throwing a baseball, watching baseball games. And when I'd gotten to about sixth grade in Jenners, I was the batboy for the town team. I traveled with the club and took care of the bats and the catcher's equipment. I'd carry the equipment in a sack, lugging and dragging it with me. Around that time we traveled by truck. We'd get the team loaded up on a truck, and I'd get all the equipment and throw it on there. One time we went over to a town named Hooverville. I got into a game with the bigger guys. Only eight of our players showed up. I'd been running around catching fly balls and ground balls and throwing the ball, like all the kids do, especially the little batboy, in a uniform that they'd provided me and a little old pair of spike shoes. Short one player, the older guys finally said, "Well, let's put little Metro out there in right field." I had caught a few balls in my time out there practicing. So I went out in right field and, as my luck would have it, here came a fly ball my way about the second or third inning. I ran in there and caught that fly ball and threw it into second base. Boy, I got a pretty good standing ovation from all the spectators at the ballpark. About the fifth inning, here came another fly ball, and I caught that fly ball too, a difficult catch for me at that time. I'll tell you, I was the hero. I didn't do much hitting. I couldn't hit over the infielders' heads when they threw to me off the mound, but I got a base hit off of soft-toss pitching. But making those catches was a highlight. My father was there, and I guess you've never seen a prouder man, and, of course, I was pretty cocky and pleased with myself. I don't even know who won the game, but afterward, the fans took up a collection and bought me a quart of ice cream right across the street at a grocery store. That was my first big pay as a player! Boy, I said, if this is what you get for playing baseball, I'm going to play forever.

My mom, however, made me do chores. We had a big family and we had a cow. I had to milk that darn thing. I didn't know how to milk a cow. We had to build a little barn for it out on the back of our property. Then I had to get all the firewood for the winter. I had to learn how to saw down those trees, the maple trees and the oak trees. My mother had a garden that had to be spaded early every spring, and that was my job. I couldn't go and play baseball until it was done. My mother loved her garden. She grew Oxheart tomatoes that she was so proud of. They were great big tomatoes, just like two double fists in size. They were wonderful eating tomatoes. I don't know that I've seen them since. Every once in a while, one of the neighbors would come over and want to buy one of those tomatoes. But she knew that they wanted them for the seeds, so she wouldn't sell them or give them away. She would win the prize at the little old fair every year with her Oxheart tomatoes. My mother canned everything. Gosh, we would have a thousand quarts of things. She'd can everything. She never threw anything away. As kids, in August we'd go up to the mountains and pick blackberries. We had blackberries galore. She canned, I guess, hundreds of quarts of blackberries. My father, whose integrity slipped when it came to this, would go into where she had all of her canned things and he'd pull the rubber out of the quart jars. And the blackberries would go sour, and he would come in and look at them and tell my mother that she didn't tighten up those jars well enough. There'd be maybe fifteen or twenty quarts of those berries soured up. There was nothing to do but throw them away, but he'd say, "Well, we won't throw them away. We'll make wine out of them." My mother finally caught on.

My father was a coal miner, and he loved his beer and he loved his wine. He'd take a drink, and sometimes he'd drink too much. Finally my mother would make my father go to the priest and take an oath that he wouldn't drink for three months or six months. My father never broke it . . . while he was at home. Later on, when he would come visit us and watch games in North Carolina or Vancouver, he would take a nip. He always claimed that the oath applied only in the state of Pennsylvania.

So I spaded that garden, and I swear, at that time I thought that doggone thing was about two acres. God, I hated to dig that garden up in the spring instead of playing. Everybody was playing baseball, and I had to dig that garden up. Later on in life, I took my two grown sons back there to Jenners and showed them the home that we lived in. They wanted to know where that big garden was, and there it was, about twenty-five feet wide and about fifty feet long. They said they thought I said that it was two acres. I got out of that pretty easy. I said that I thought it was two acres. It felt like five acres. I thought it was five acres.

We'd have to go to church every Sunday. My father would get me dressed up. Of course all I could think of was baseball. The church was up on top of the hill, and the baseball park was right down below it. I wanted to go down there and watch. There was going to be a game, and I wanted to watch the guys hit, practice, and everything else. We had a priest that was a heck of a guy and a baseball fan, but doggone, his sermons were long. They would go on for three, three and a half hours. We'd start about 9:30 or 10:00 Sunday mornings, and the game would be starting about 12:00. I was the altar boy, gown and everything, so I couldn't get off to get down there early.

But when I was a kid, my nose would bleed at the least little thing. I'd bump my nose and it would bleed. I don't know why, nothing chronic or anything, but it would bleed. So I figured out a way to get to play and watch baseball. When the priest was dragging on and the game was about to get started, I'd reach up and slap myself on the nose. Sure enough, it would start to bleed. And I'd just start a-sniffing. Sniff, sniff, sniffing. Eventually the priest would take a look at me, and he would shake his head, no, no, no, no, and I'd keep sniffing, and all of a sudden, he'd give me the nod to go. I'd rush into the back room, take off that robe, and down that hill I'd go. When the sermon was over and church let out, here would come my father and the priest down to the ballpark. The priest would walk up to me and say, "Little Charlie, how is the nose?" I would say, "Oh, pretty good, but"—then I'd sniff—"still bleeding." And he'd laugh.

Babe Ruth and the Yankees were household words, spoken with reverence. When I was about age twelve, I made up my mind to go to New York to see the Bambino and the Pinstripers. I was peddling grocery flyers, those sale flyers that the grocers put out for the weekend. I conned four grocery stores into letting me distribute their bills for their weekend sales. Each paid me a quarter, so I got a buck all together. I decided to hitchhike to New York. I had a dollar and a dime. I had an older sister living in New York, so I knew I would have a place to stay.

On the way I spent a night in the jail in Gettysburg. I was hitchhiking along U.S. Route 30. It was a cold and rainy evening. When I got to Gettysburg, I saw a house with a porch and a swing, so I sat on it to get out of the rain. The people who lived there were gone, but as they were coming home, they called the cops. The policeman asked me what I was doing. I told him I was going to New York to see Babe Ruth. The officer took me down to the jail and assigned me a bunk in a cell. The door was open, of course. They told me I had to be up and out of there by 6:00 A.M.. I had a good night's sleep. One of the cops did a little cooking in the jail, and he fed me a little breakfast. I sat there and ate breakfast with him. He told me, "Now you be careful. You don't get in trouble." I said, "No, sir, no, sir. But I'm going to see Babe Ruth." I've had great respect for police ever since that day. Rested and a little less hungry, I was off to see the Babe.

When I finally got to New York, I used half of my dime to take a subway and find my sister's place. I told her I was going to see Babe Ruth at Yankee Stadium. She asked, "How much money have you got?" I said, "I've got a dollar and five cents." I didn't know anything about the subways. So she told me where to go, and she gave me two more tokens to get there. I still had my dollar. And I rode that darn subway. I left at 9:00 A.M. to get to an afternoon game. I got lost and went back and forth on that subway. It seemed like I rode all day with that one token. I was going to find my way into that ballpark if it was the last thing I did. I finally took the right subway to the Bronx and came above ground to see it big and bold, Yankee

Stadium. I didn't know how to get into the stadium, but I saw a line of kids about my age by one gate. The police around the stadium were rounding up a bunch of kids and putting them in a line, and they hustled me into that line, which must have been a hundred feet long. I got in line, and I asked the kid in front of me, "What are we doing in this line? Is this where we pay to get in?" He said, "Oh, no. We're going to get in for nothing." I asked, "How? I've got money. I want to pay to see." He said, "Oh, they'll get a ticket for us." Corporations would buy blocks of tickets and send them out to the ballpark. And they'd line up all these kids, and you'd go in. As long as there was a ticket, you'd get into the ballpark, Yankee Stadium, for nothing, with that ticket. We were just about ready to get in, but the line stopped. "Oh, gosh," I said, "they've run out of tickets, haven't they?" The kid said, "Yeah, but there'll be more." And in about five minutes, here came another batch of tickets and in we went. The kid, whose name was Spinelli, was right. The ticket takers herded us in.

We sat above the third base side in the second deck, right even with third base. There I was, finally watching big league ball clubs. Yankee Stadium was a delightful place. This was my first professional game ever, my first American League game. I was watching the Yankees play, and I don't even know who the other club was. I don't remember and didn't care. There they were, the Yankees, players I knew only by name, word of mouth, radio, and newspaper stories and photographs. There were Ruth and Lou Gehrig and Bill Dickey and Tony Lazzeri, all the great ones larger than life, impossibly real. I couldn't talk. The game was beyond my expectations. Ruth, Gehrig, and Dickey each hit home runs that day. Dickey hit a shot into the second deck. Gehrig hit a line drive into the lower right field stands. It just kind of went in there about twenty feet. Babe came up and hit one into the upper deck. If I can tell you one thing, I have never had a thrill like that. He did that pigeon-toed little trot. And he had the stomach on him too. I wondered how he could play with that big belly. My day was complete. I'll never forget it. I said, "That's what I'm going to do. I'm going to play big league baseball." Spinelli, next to me, said, "Yeah, yeah, yeah, sure, yeah."

So when the game was over, Spinelli said, "Come on with me." By this time, I was calling him Tony and he was calling me Chuck. He said, "Chuck, we'll go down here, and we'll see the Babe coming out." So we went down by the players' entrance, and an hour after the game, here came the Babe with his big cigar. He walked out, saying, "Hi, kids, hi, kids." He was the Pied Piper. All the kids hung on his words. I was up there close in front, and he looked down at me. "How are you, kid?" he laughed. I said, "Fine."

He said, "See that one I hit for you?" I said, "Oh, yes." He touched me on the shoulder and asked, "What do you want to do?" I said, "I want to be a ballplayer, Babe." He patted me on the shoulder, and I said, "Oh, boy."

I hitchhiked back home in something of a daze. When I got home to Nanty-Glo, after I stayed with my sister, I told every kid that would listen that Babe Ruth touched that shoulder and I wouldn't let anybody touch it. In fact I doubt that I took a bath for a couple of weeks. I told them the Babe touched that spot, and they all thought I was dreaming. But I know that he touched it. Babe's been an idol of mine all these years. He would be in the Hall of Fame on his pitching career alone. But just marvel at the record and think about those years that he was a pitcher. If he had been converted to an outfielder sooner, five years sooner, he might have hit a thousand home runs.

I played a lot of baseball at Jenners. I probably even subconsciously picked out my future number there. I never did know why I favored number 36. I got it as a manager and for a time as a player. I never could figure it out until here in the later part of my life I took my daughter and my sons back to Jenners, and I stopped by the house to show them the duplex that we had lived in, and there, on the side of that house, was the number 36. I asked the people that were living there if they'd put it up there. "No," they said, "it's been there ever since." Then I recalled my father putting that number up when I was just a little guy. That's where I must have gotten the idea.

Back then I was playing all the time and finally got to play with the bigger kids a time or two, in about the sixth, seventh, and eighth grades or so. I broke a school window before I got to eighth grade. We played in the schoolyard, and we had that taped baseball—you could always get some electrical tape from your father to use. We were hitting toward the schoolhouse, and bang, I hit one through there, and the kids all shouted, "Charlie did it!" I had to sit in the corner for doing that, but I was kind of proud. Nobody else had ever hit that ball that far. And so the schoolteachers made us turn around and hit the ball toward the outfield. This is not a verified record, but I hold the record for the longest ball ever hit, before it hit the ground, in the history of all baseball, maybe even all time. The coal train went by the school from the mines, and one day I hit a ball that landed in a moving coal car that stopped three miles down the track in Boswell. I hit a ball that traveled three miles in the air!

I had some problems with a teacher in fourth grade in Jenners. We played baseball in the spring, and he was always giving me heck. Why, I don't know. I must have been the biggest kid in the class, and he was always on my case. Finally I got tired of it. Once we were reading the stories about the "village smithy stands under the spreading chestnut tree." He asked me what I thought about it. I said, "Heck, I don't know. I wasn't there." He really gave me a good going-over. In fact, he put my name up on the board and gave me marks. I had 1–2–3–4–5 across. I had about four or five of them across there, and he gave it to me. I said, "Well, I'll get him." He was very proud of his Ford car. So I got a potato and put it in the exhaust pipe and took a stick and pounded it up in there. He couldn't get the car started, and he couldn't pry that potato out. Eventually the guys at the garage had to take the exhaust system apart and try to blow air through there to get that potato. Now, mind you, this was in the mid-1930s, when he had one of the first cars in the area. I fixed him good. But I'm glad nobody ever told him. I think he knew that I'd done it. After that, I kind of laid off of him and he didn't give me a bad time.

We got in some typical mischief as kids there in Jenners. We used to try to sneak a carrot or a tomato from this one lady's garden. She'd catch us and whack us with her broom as we tried to scramble over the fence. Once we filled a garbage can with all sorts of tin cans and junk and placed it on top of the slanting shed right outside her back door. Then we attached a string from the garbage can handle to her back door and ran off to hide and watch to see and hear the clatter. She would also bake cookies and pies and put them out back. We never did swipe a pie, because she was too sharp for us, but we did beg and plead about the cookies, and occasionally she'd give us some.

I was quite an athlete in those school days. I had some track-and-field skills ahead of my age. One day the high school track team was practicing at the nearby fairgrounds. This was at Jenners Crossroads, and I was in the spring of seventh grade. I had a pole, which I used to pole vault all the time. When I saw the high school team trying out, I decided to try my luck. They had the bar set at nine feet, six inches, and I saw they had a bamboo pole. I'd never seen one. Boy, it was something. The coach was over there giving his track team a talk or something, so I grabbed the pole, ran down the runway, and cleared the bar. When the team saw me, they all chased after me. I thought that they were going to whip the heck out of me. What they were trying to do, I found out later, was to find out where I was going to school. Nobody had cleared nine foot six at the time, and there I was, a seventh-grader, clearing it with ease. I didn't know one thing about it. The next day I came down, and they were running around the track. It was a half-mile dirt track, a fairgrounds kind of track. When I heard the starter gun go off, I jumped in the race. I was way behind, but then I started really running and I outran them all. But I didn't finish. I thought they were going to come after me again because I beat all of them. I loved to run.

I was an adventurous kid in many ways. In fact I had a brief career as a pilot. This was in Jenners too. I was in about the fifth or sixth grade. We were right in the pathway of the airline going to Pittsburgh. Those old Ford trimotor planes would fly low, and you could hear them buzzing in the fog. I got a hankering to design and build a plane. So I did. I got some nice pine wood from all around the coal mine that they had thrown away. I built a two-wing plane with a fuselage and everything. Every detail was as authentic as I could get it. I covered it with burlap. There was a cockpit in it, and I put front wheels from an old kid's wagon on it. I put on an aileron so I could lift up the tail. I was going to fly that thing. So my friends and I dragged it up the side of a hill. This hill was sloped real well. I was going to fly that son of a gun. Down I came. Oh, gosh, it was a good thing I ducked, because I sheared the wings right off coming down the hill. The plane hit a barbed wire fence. That kind of put a temporary end to my flying days. But I was always building something, tinkering around with something.

Some years later, when I was about to become a junior in high school, I had another flying episode. A friend of mine, who was a senior, called me up one day and said, "Charlie, come on with me." His father had a Ford car. We went up to the airport at Ebensburg. He said, "We're going to fly this glider." I said, "Fly the glider?" I remembered my first flying experience. So we got up to the airport, and there was this glider. Nobody was around. He said, "I'm going to fly this thing, and you're going to drive the car." I didn't know how to drive a car, but he showed me. It was an old Ford model with the throttle on the steering wheel column. "I'll tell you when let her go," he said. "Pull me down to the end. Now don't run off down over the end of the airfield." It was a big field with a woods down below. So he got out of the car and into the glider. I hooked it up to the car, got the Ford started, jerked it a couple of times, and started down the runway. This glider was on skids, not on wheels. And, boy, he was hollering to let her go, and the plane was up, and I released the hook on the glider, and I turn around and he's flying, boy, he got into an updraft. Everything was going real fine. He circled a couple of times and came in and landed the glider real well. I didn't know that he'd been studying all that stuff about airplanes. He was a sharp guy. He said, "Now Chuck, it's your turn." I thought, I'm not going to fly that thing. But he showed me. "Now here's what you do," he said. "If you let go when it gets off the ground, it'll take off." Well, I didn't want to be called chicken or whatever. Kids were always daring one another to do things. He said, "I'll dare you." And I said, "No, you don't."

So I got in the glider and off we went. He was driving, and the first thing you know, he was going faster and the glider went up. I hollered, "Let her go, let her go." I unhooked and up I went. Aw, dang, it was beautiful, quiet and everything else. So I circled the field, found the updraft, and went up higher in elevation. I circled around, and then thought I better try to land. I came down, and oh, boy, that ground was coming up fast. I finally hit the ground and bounced four or five times. What a thrill! I won't mention names, because we kind of swiped the glider, and I don't want people to know that we did that. But we did it. My buddy became a fine Air Force pilot in World War II. But that was my experience as a glider pilot. When you're young, you do a lot of crazy things.

During that period, of course, the country was in the Great Depression. I don't mind telling you that things were rough at the time. My father worked for the WPA. They were fixing roads and buildings and culverts, and there were a lot of springs in that area. They'd clean out the little streams, cut the wood, trim the woods, thin them out. My father had that background back in the Ukraine, when he was a young man, and his father had done that sort of work too. I myself spent a month in what they called the Youth CCC camps. That was great. We did all kinds of cleaning up work on the highways and on the streets. They issued us a kind of military clothing, a pair of boots and some khakis, what the army wore at that time. We worked from morning till night, but, boy, what a dinner we had. Food wasn't exactly plentiful. A lot of food was a luxury to somebody from a big family, and I enjoyed that. We didn't get paid anything, but we got three good meals a day and a clean cot to sleep on and fresh air. Gosh, it was tremendous. I'd like to see them do that again.

As time went on, in the latter part of my eighth-grade year, we moved from Jenners over to Nanty-Glo, over in Cambria County. Nanty-Glo had a pretty good town team. That summer I went out for the baseball team and darned if I didn't make that men's team. I made the left-field position. Boy, I could catch a ball, and I could run and I could throw a ball well enough to get it back into the infield. And I'd swing a bat, but not great. If I'd have known how bad I was going to be as a hitter, I think I would have started a ground-floor movement to outlaw the curve ball. Every spring, it seemed like we had to deal with a flood at the ballpark in Nanty-Glo. We put up the board fence out in right field. It went from center field to the right-field line, and the creek was there, outside the fence. In the spring the flood waters would come along and take all those fence boards out of there. We'd find them two or three miles down the creek, up against the bank. We had to haul them back and rebuild the fence.

In Nanty-Glo, we had a home on Heisley Row. Heisley Coal Company was the name of the company and the town team. I played on that team my freshman year and throughout my high school years. I played left field, and the best ballplayers played center field. One was John Yorkitis—we called him Snorkey. He taught me a lot about the game. He was an older guy and had been around. He eventually became a police chief. Each coal mining town or steel town had a team sponsored by the company. The companies usually bought all the equipment and supplied a company vehicle, a truck, as transportation. We had a superintendent who was a great baseball fan, and Heisley and Nanty-Glo had great sports fans. He saw to it that we had good equipment. Schweinbrenner was his name. I'll never forget him. He would supply us with uniforms and everything, and we had some of the best. We didn't always have the best ball club, but he was our greatest fan. Sometimes there'd be three or four different sections of town that would have their own team, and they would play like they were supposed to be the minor league team. There were great rivalries, and, wow, you would have thought we were the cursed Yankees or the cursed Dodgers. It was wild, and the fans would get rowdy, especially if you were getting beat, even when you had a pretty good team. That's when the fights would break out. But it was a joy, because it was always Sunday and sometimes you'd play a doubleheader on Sunday. It was great. After the game was over, everybody would gather around. They'd have a keg of beer, and somebody would bring sandwiches and food. It was good for the towns and the young people. All sorts of different people—Ukrainians, Poles, Irish, Swedes, and others—associated. I saw these older guys playing and, boy, I wanted to play. My father got a little better job working in the mines or got work when it was scarce. I didn't get much preferential treatment, though, because I worked Friday, Saturday, and Sunday while I was going to school. The players certainly didn't cut me any slack on the ball field. They brushed me back because I was a kid. Once I got beaned. We didn't have helmets then. I became a little shy at that, but then I got over it. Some guys never get over it. I got over it real quickly.

At that time I started my interest in making innovative baseball equipment. I invented the batting tee when I was playing for the Heisley Coal Company team. We had no place to practice hitting, except the baseball park. We had a lot of what we called blowgun weeds, because they were round, hollow, and strong—we used to blow elderberries and stuff through them like a blowgun. We would take these, when they were dry, and use them as supports. We'd get one that was maybe an inch or two across, and I used to put a old baseball on top of that and hit it off that into a bank.

Then when I was out in the coal mine, I found some pipe that was big, thick rubber, about four inches across. I don't know what it was used for, around the boiler house or somewhere. I got hold of some of those pieces. I took a four-foot piece and sliced it down two ways criss-cross the bottom and folded them up and nailed that to a board. Then I put an old taped baseball on top of it and hit that baseball against the side of the house or into a mattress. Or I'd set tin cans on there and hit them off with a hockey stick. I've often thought that if I had had a batting tee in, say, 1939, I might have become a pretty doggone good hitter, because I did hit .300 three or four times later as a playing manager. Later I had the patent pending on it but didn't have the money to secure the patent. Quite a few guys have used the batting tee. It's a great instrument in teaching, far better than some of these gadgets they have nowadays.

The school, Nanty-Glo High, didn't have a baseball team, so I played on the town team. One day in class, I wasn't paying much attention to the geography teacher, "Buns" Moody, and he had me stand up and he gave me a pretty good going-over. I wasn't the greatest student, but I was good in history and geography. I could draw a map of the United States freehand, with all the states in it. But that day I wasn't paying attention. He finally said, "Hey, Charles, why aren't you like that little boy that was out there—that kid that was out there playing on the Heisley Coal Company team? Why aren't you patterning yourself after him? Why don't you make him your idol?" A girl in front of me was snickering. Ann Labosh was her name. We had alphabetical seating. Helen Lamont and Ann were in front of me, and they started laughing. And "Buns" didn't like that. He asked, "Well, what's so funny, Miss Labosh? Stand up!" So she got up. She said, "Mr. Moody, the boy you're talking about is Chuck!" He said, "What?" She said, "Yeah! Chuck has been playing on the town team." It turned out he was a great baseball fan, and I'll tell you one thing, I never failed one of his classes. After that I was his fair-haired boy. From that day on I was A-1. I could do no wrong. To this day, whenever I go back to Nanty-Glo, some of the kids that I went to school with still remember that episode.

I worked in the coal mines right after my sophomore year in the summertime. Then, after my junior year in the coal mines, something happened that made me forever in my mother's debt. We had a big family: my father, my mother, and nine kids. I was the oldest, so I had to work to help support the family. I worked all that summer in the coal mines, right after my junior year, and my father naturally wanted me to go ahead and work. We were indebted to the company store, and if you've ever heard the song "Sixteen Tons"—"load sixteen tons and what do you get? Another day older and deeper in debt"—that's about what we were. We were in the hole all the time, and I was helping work us out of the hole at the company store. The day school was starting, my father got me up and said, "Put your clothes on son. You're going back in and work with me at the mines." Supposedly we could do this and we could do that and we could buy me this and buy us that and get out of the debt. So I got up early in the morning at 4:30 and built a fire. I was putting my clothes on, when my mom put her foot down. She said, "No, Charlie's going to school. He's going to finish his year in school." Pop said, "No, he's not. He's going." And my mom, bless her, stood right up in my father's face and said, "Charlie is going to go to school." Now I had my work clothes on already, ready to go to work. It was about 5:00 in the morning. "If you take him in, if he goes in the mine, you take him in the mine today," she said, "I won't be here when the day's over, when you come home. I will leave you." My father looked at her and said, "Do you mean that?" She answered, "Yes, I do, and if you don't believe me, you take Charlie into the mines. I mean it. I won't be here. I don't care. My clothes will be all gone." "Well," he said, meekly, "all right." I never saw my father back down from anything, but he sure backed down from that tiger. I took my work clothes off, washed up, and went back to school. I had never seen my mother like that. I think she's passed it on to some of my sisters.

The coal mining life my mother helped me get away from was pretty tough. As I look back on it now, I know I didn't realize how tough it was at the time. I worked in the coal mines after my sophomore and junior years in school. We were paid eighty-five cents or so a ton for coal. We worked two days a week in the summertime. We'd get four empty cars a day. Each car would hold about three tons, so if you had four cars, that would be about twelve tons. After you divided that up, you made about five dollars a day, and your partner, my buddy or my father, made five too. But you didn't really take home five dollars. The company deducted for your dynamite and your caps and your battery lamp and for sharpening your tools. They usually took something out for the company doctors, and you probably owed the company store money as well. And there were the union check-off dues. "Tennessee Ernie" Ford had it right, but very seldom would we load sixteen tons. We had to heat our houses with firewood a lot of the time, because we couldn't afford to buy the coal we were digging. Sometimes we picked up coal from the tracks, where the big coal cars would bump each other and the big lumps of coal would fall. You couldn't afford it otherwise. You had to pay eighteen dollars a ton for the coal to buy it, whereas loading coal, you got paid only eighty-five cents a ton or so.

The work was tough going. It was soft coal, bituminous. But it wasn't in the big veins that they have now. They have big seams now, eight to ten feet, some even bigger that they can scoop out with bulldozers or use giant augers. Our coal tunnels were forty-two inches high. The machine would cut it, make a twenty-four-foot cut on the bottom, and then you had to shoot your coal down. A lot of times you had water and seepage. That meant you had what they called water coal, maybe anywhere from six inches to three feet high, and it was just dead labor. You got seventy-five cents a yard. You had to dig wide enough so the cars could get in there. We used battery lamps, with a battery on the back of your belt, for light. It was really a dandy place to work: bad roof, water, everything that you could think of and worse.

And it was dangerous. Guys would get their fingers blown off. One guy they called "Stubby," who'd lost some fingers in a mine accident, was our manager on the local town team. Every once in a while, he'd get out there and throw a little batting practice. He was funny with those short, stubby fingers. But it was a constant reminder of what could happen in the mines. Gas could explode at any time. Indeed I was in a gas explosion that killed several men, and I was lucky enough to come out alive. The company had twenty-one men out in an old digging. Later I testified about the carelessness of management. Then I went back in to work again to see if I had my nerve back. Everybody said you had to go back in so you wouldn't lose your nerve. So I did.

There was always the threat of labor violence. We went on strike for one of the steel mills down at Johnstown, a sympathy strike of sorts to help them out. The steel mills had their own police force. They rode horses. We were helping the steelworkers out one time, and these police had pick handles and, boy, they'd whack you across the shoulders or on the head if you weren't careful. They gave us a pretty good going-over, so we climbed up on a little bank where they couldn't get up at us and we threw bricks at them. We spooked their horses. I got some of my labor union sympathies working in the mines.

I did learn some carpentry skills around the coal mines. You were always doing this and doing that, digging here and digging there, taking the wrecked cars apart and putting the bolts in on the new boards on the cars. Some of the physical work resembled the physical effort in baseball. I found that when I had to work in the coal mine and do the shoveling, the shovel handle was like a bat and you were swinging a pick handle or a sledgehammer just like you were swinging a bat. About the only thing you didn't do was your running. There was no running in this work. And I learned something about teamwork. When you were working, you always had a buddy; whether it was your father, your brother, your friend, or some neighbor, there were always two of you. You really had to have teamwork to be successful in the work. You couldn't fight against each other. That's where teamwork came in, and baseball's the same way. You had to have teamwork, the catcher and the pitcher, the infielder and the first baseman, the outfielder yelling "I got it" or "It's all yours." There was always teamwork involved, similar to your work habits, whether it was working in the coal mine, the steel mills, the lumber yard, or wherever.

But I couldn't wait to get away from the mines, to tell the boss to take the job and shove it. My father worked all of his life in the coal mine, but I was able to get out. Baseball was my means of getting away. I decided that I was going to continue to play baseball, and that's what I did. I have fine memories of working there. A lot of people survived, but a lot didn't. It was a tough life. But I prefer baseball. My brothers worked a little bit, but they got out too. John became an insurance agent and an umpire. Later I hired him as a baseball scout. Joe was a professional schoolboy. He went to school and got all kinds of degrees, and he became a fine teacher and a vice principal of a high school. He also became an auctioneer. Although women didn't work in the mines back then, my sisters all took their chances to leave the area. Two of them married ranchers, and the other two wed fine guys too. So we all left. Both my father and my mother encouraged me to do it, especially my father. My mother didn't want to see me leaving home, but my father said to go for it. I've told my sons and daughter the same thing many a time: go for it.

My brother John would borrow chewing tobacco from John Gustin, the basketball and football coach. My brother would spit on the opposing player's leg when he was a guard or forward. But my brother John would correct me, tell me what to do. I was a little bit afraid of him. He was a little rougher than I was. My family used to follow my exploits in the box scores. Back then you could get *The Sporting News* for a dime or twenty cents. My brother John would buy it so he could read the averages wherever I was playing in the late 1930s and early 1940s. He knew exactly what to look for. He'd recognize my name in the box scores. My sisters would kid him and turn the list upside down, and "Charlie Metro" would be way up there in the averages. Some of those years, my average would be down a bit. But he was always pleased when he'd see my average up around the .300 mark.

We always had baseball to help take our minds off the mines. We knew something about the history of the game. We were vaguely aware of some of the guys like Cap Anson who played back in the 1880s, but more recent players, future Hall of Famers like Sam Rice, Ty Cobb, Tris Speaker, and "Home Run" Baker, were more familiar. I knew about some odd incidents like Fred Merkle's "boner play" of 1908. We heard about the current controversies, such as when Joe Medwick slid into Marv Owen at third base in the 1935 World Series. As for current players, mostly you'd just hear about them. You'd rarely see them. There was no television, so you couldn't watch them and see what they looked like. They were names in the paper, and you could read their stats at that time. You could see that this guy would hit a home run and so forth, and once in a while you would see his name in the All-Star Game.

Occasionally one major leaguer, Rip Collins, came to town. He was from Nanty-Glo, even though the baseball encyclopedias list him as being from Altoona. He had some pretty fair years with the St. Louis Cardinals. He was a power hitter. Rip Collins was the first big league ballplayer that I'd ever seen come in and put on a hitting exhibition at the local ballpark. The right-field fence ran alongside the creek, and he hit the ball clear over the creek in right field, and, boy, we thought that was an awful long way. He'd bring a couple dozen balls and put on a batting practice show. And all we kids would do was get over there across the creek and find the balls, because we'd never seen a big league baseball before.

In the mid-1930s we went into Pittsburgh and saw the Pirates play. Those were my first National League games. I saw all those guys, some of whose names I can't even recall. But they were there. The Waner boys, Lloyd and Paul, were there as well as Pie Traynor and Arky Vaughan. There were a lot of those good ballplayers. I was almost petrified with awe. Our high school graduation trip was to Pittsburgh in 1937. They took us out to the ballpark. Somebody arranged for tickets for us. We went out and saw the ball game. I liked Forbes Field. I was sad when they switched over to Three Rivers. It was a wonderful old sports field, a great old ballpark in a nice setting. It had the longest distance from home plate back to the stands. In fact, you could score a guy from second base on a passed ball. I don't think it's ever been done anywhere else.

About that same time, I saw the Negro League Homestead Grays play in Pittsburgh. One of the mine bosses, Ken Woodrine, who had an automobile, wanted to see this game, and he asked my father if he wanted to see it, and he said to bring me with him. My father had given Ken Woodrine a bat. I think I saw Satchel Paige pitch and Josh Gibson catch. I was amazed at how well they played. I thought, gee whiz, would I ever be that good? I couldn't imagine anybody doing all those things that those black ballplayers did. I was fascinated by them. There were quite a few African-Americans at the steel mills, and we played against some of them. They were really good. I was fascinated by their ability. I'll never forget one outfielder. Man, could he run! Holy cow, every time he got on base he would steal second, steal third, and then dance around with great showmanship. I thought, wow, if I could just run like he could!

In addition to watching the Pirates and the Negro League teams, I got to see some pretty good teams over in Johnstown. My father and I used to walk down there, ten miles away, and watch the game at night. We'd get back in time for him to put on his clothes and go to work, and I'd go to school. Sometimes we would grab a ride with the early bakery delivery trucks going to Johnstown. The Johnstown Johnnies were the St. Louis Browns farm club in the Middle Atlantic League. They had Chuck Stevens, who became the director of the Baseball Professional Ballplayers' Association. Chuck was one of my idols. He was a real good fielder. My father was crazy about him too. He would pick out a favorite and, boy, you couldn't shake him from his choices. Johnny Lucadello was also there, and I thought he was about as good a ballplayer as I'd ever seen. I saw Hank Greenberg's brother, Joe, play there too. And I saw Hugh Alexander and Frank Scalzi, names I remember from different clubs. My father loved Hugh. He was a right-handed hitter. I believe he led the league in just about everything that year. A year later, I read in *The Sporting News* that he had lost his hand in a tractor accident in Oklahoma, and when I told my father, he broke down and cried about that. Hugh became one of the top talent scouts in the history of baseball. He was very knowledgeable, having had a playing background. But there were cheerier things too. We saw them experiment with a yellow baseball, back in the mid-1930s, decades before Charlie Finley thought of the idea.

I was in awe at the Johnstown ballpark, especially at how fast the players were. My father would say, "Well, you can run fast. You can throw the ball. You can hit the ball." He would encourage me. And wouldn't you know it? A couple of years later, I had my first professional baseball tryout in that same stadium.

When I was a senior in high school, in 1937, the Browns announced a tryout camp at Johnstown in the local paper. I decided I was going to go down there to the tryout camp. Prior to hearing about the camp, I had started running. I'd been playing basketball too. As a kid you never got out of shape. And I loved to run. So I got in pretty good condition to attend that trial camp. I had played on the town team in my sophomore and junior years, so I felt ready. But all my friends and teammates ridiculed me and said I wouldn't make it. The guys on the regular team said I'd never make it. They said that guys from the whole area of three or four counties and as far away as Pittsburgh would show up. The more they said that, the more determined I was to prove them wrong.

Because there would be so many guys there, I wanted to be noticed. I had a buck or two saved up, so I went down to the dry goods store and bought myself a pair of those black stockings that the kids, boys and girls, used to wear, that went up above the knee. I was going to be noticed. I was going to wear those black socks. The town team stockings were all half blue and half white, half red and half white, half green, half black and half white. Stripes were kind of standard for the teams up there to have for their stockings. The black socks would set me apart.

I played hookey from high school. I hooked a ride on the early bakery truck that serviced the grocery stores in Nanty-Glo from Johnstown. At the tryout camp, I put on those black socks. I had a uniform, pants and a shirt, a sweatshirt, and I had my glove. We registered, signed a card, listing your full name, your age, and where you were from, your address and everything. They gave you a number to pin on your back. I don't remember except that it was high. The highest was up in the 1,500s.

The tryout camp was at Point Stadium in Johnstown. It was named Point Stadium because it pointed at two rivers right there. It was right near a Pennsylvania Railroad bridge, a big stone bridge, where all the debris piled up during the 1889 Johnstown flood and during the second Johnstown flood too. The field was muddy. It was spring, and the frost hadn't gotten out yet. Jack Fournier, the manager of the Johnstown Johnnies, was one of the scouts there running the camp. He had had a fifteen-year major league career with the White Sox, Yankees, Cardinals, Dodgers, and Braves as a first baseman and occasional outfielder.

The first thing they did was warm up the pitchers. While they were warming up the pitchers, infielders and outfielders were out there warming up your arm. They wanted to try your arm out first. So they had you line up in the outfield in a long line of about 50 to 100 outfielders. The scouts and some of the helpers would hit a ground ball out to you. You'd come in, field it, and throw it home. They were testing your arm. If you couldn't throw, you couldn't play anywhere. I had a pretty good arm. My arm was coming around. I played and was getting stronger. I think I outthrew every guy there, both for accuracy and for distance. To start, we were throwing about 225 to 250 feet. Then we'd move way back to 300 to 325 feet. I was shining and, oh, I had those black socks. Fournier kept calling to me, "Hey, Black Stockings, you got a pretty good arm." I was scared to death. Still all they were doing was hitting a ball out to one of the players, who'd pick it up and bounce it on the dirt or second base.

If you didn't have the skills, if you didn't have the arm, a guy came around and said, "That's it, son, take off your number." Oh, God, guys were crushed. A lot of them couldn't throw. In fact, some threw like a girl and were eliminated. And before that, they'd line you up and take a look at your size. I was about five foot ten or so, and I weighed about 165 or 170 pounds. I had played football and basketball, so I made their cut. They were also letting heavyset guys go as well as guys with gray hair. A lot of guys would get crew cuts to look younger, but if they saw a little gray, they'd say, "Take off your number, son." They also discouraged the kids, the fourteen- or fifteen-year-olds. It took a whole day to thin out some of the players.

The camp went on for five days. It took a long time to get through 1,500 guys. The next thing they did was hold running trials, sixty-yard dashes. They'd line up eight or ten guys on the foul line. Point Stadium was a football stadium too. The football field ran from right field to the third base side. They'd line you up right at the yard markers. They had the two scouts line up seven, eight, ten guys, and then you heard, "On your mark, get set, go" and, boom, the gun. I could run pretty well. I wanted to see how they were doing it, so I waited until about the fourth group and walked in then. I was way out in front. Oh, boy, I felt good. I stood out when they saw those black stockings. This was an all-day affair, because we were all running in elimination heats. As soon as you won one, they took three or four of the winners and ran them together. They didn't want to overlook anything. I think I ran eight or ten heats, and I won practically every one of them. I was beaten by one guy.

Next they hit infielders ground balls to check their hands and watch them throw. Fournier said, "Hey, Black Stockings, get out there." So I went out to shortstop, because I had a fairly decent outfield arm. I didn't field ground balls too well, but I fought them. I fielded some ground balls and threw them over to first base. I threw a couple right up in the seats, which turned out to be a plus, even though I thought it was terrible. Fournier told me my arm was good, a strong arm. Some of the guys were bouncing the ball on throws from third or shortstop, so they got eliminated. After that we started in the outfield. Jack asked me what position I had played, and I said I was an outfielder, so he put me in center field. They started hitting fly balls out to the outfielders. They put some guys in left, some in center, and he was hitting to them. Now I thought I was being favored a little. I thought I was being singled out because I was surviving. This was the second or third day. After Fournier eliminated a whole bunch of guys, he took me by myself and started hitting fly balls to me in center field. I never dropped a one. I could field, still could till the day I quit. I caught everything, and I was watching. He was trying to be clever with me and he'd slice the ball, or he'd swing real hard and hit one underneath and it wouldn't go very far. I'd have to recover and come in. Eventually I caught on, and I caught everything that he hit.

The next big test was hitting. This was the third or fourth day, on which they watched us hit. Fournier sat there behind a little screen with his pad. Some of these kids that had lasted that far would take the bat and hit cross-handed. They got eliminated right away. The scouts had finally selected a group of pitchers, and we had an all-day batting session. The pitchers were showing off their stuff too. So you had two hungry groups competing against each other. They had catchers catching the ball too, sitting right back close to the screen. I had played against pretty good county league pitching, so I felt pretty confident. I watched the pitching for a while to see what was going on. They changed pitchers real quick at one point. The guy they brought in couldn't throw well. He had no control. So I grabbed a bat and jumped in there. I had been hitting off that batting-tee contraption that I had. I had a little bit of a swing down. He started throwing, and I swung and I missed. I cut my eyes to see if the scouts were going to take my number. I swung and missed again. Fournier was sitting there, mumbling something. I swung and missed a third time, and he started to say something, but I said, "No, I'm not, no, I'm not, I'm going to hit one. I'm going to hit some." He looked at me and said, "Well, all right, Black Stockings, if you want to hit, go ahead and hit." Finally I ripped one pretty good. Left field was real short at Point Stadium. It was probably 270 feet, with a big, high screen, and I hit one on top of the screen. I stood in there and they threw me another, and this time I hit it pretty well too, maybe 300 feet. It wasn't a great drive, but I stood in there and hit about eight or ten balls. Fournier asked, "What are you going to do? Take up all the batting practice, Black Stockings?" I said, "You didn't tell me to quit, so I'm hitting."

That was the clincher for me. Out of the 1,500 guys, they chose fourteen for contracts with the Browns organization. I was one of them. Only three of us played any length of time. I never saw eleven of the guys again, but there were two others, Gus Donatelli and Tony Venzon, whom I played with and who went on to become very good National League umpires. They were a couple of years older than I was. Donatelli was a third baseman. Later we played together in Virginia for a while. Venzon was from right in our neck in the woods. He played with a great handicap. On his glove hand, he had no thumb. His thumb had gotten cut off when he was a kid, and he had a glove built real strong to compensate. He was a shortstop, he could run and he could hit, and he had a good arm that never bothered him, but he just didn't quite make it. Fourteen of us made the cut, but what tickled me the most was that some of the guys from my town who kept telling me I wouldn't get selected got dismissed, mostly for age. I was the youngest one chosen.

So finally the time came when Jack Fournier came up to me with a contract to sign for sixty dollars a month. I took it, and he asked how old I was. I told him seventeen. I was actually eighteen, but there had been some confusion about my birth certificate, which the doctor had written out in Ukrainian. He said, "Why don't you go have your mom and dad sign this and bring it back tomorrow?" So I took the contract and went home. But on the third day of the tryout camp, I had looked up in the stands and there was my father sitting there watching me. He had his legs crossed. He was up there with some people and motioning out there. I had let my parents believe I had been going off to school. I said, "Oh, gosh," but I didn't lie. I didn't tell a lie. You wouldn't dare tell a story to my father. He said, "When you're done, son, you'll take your medicine, you'll take a punishment," and I said, "But I'll never lie." So that night he was feeling pretty good, and my mom asked, "What are you feeling so happy about?" And he never said anything, so my mom didn't know it either. The next day he was down there. He missed work, and he wouldn't dare miss a day of work. So when I brought the contract home, he said, "Hmm, you've got a baseball contract." And I said, "Yes, sir, Pop, I do." He asked what I wanted to do. I said, "I want to play." He asked what the contract was for. I said, "Sixty dollars a month, but I'm not going to sign it." He said, "Well, that's up to you."

I took the contract back the next day. Jack Fournier called me into the office there at Point Stadium in Johnstown. He asked, "Charlie, did you bring your contract back?" I said, "Yes, sir," and I handed it to him. He said, "Hey, you didn't sign it." I said that was right, and he asked why I didn't. I replied, "Well, I'm going to have to work in the coal mines, I guess." And he said, "Why, you got a chance to be a ballplayer." I said, "Well, I have to have a hundred dollars." There was some silence. He asked, "What do you mean, a hundred dollars?" I said, "Well, I have to have a hundred." He kind of grinned and asked, "Well, what do you want a hundred dollars for, Charlie?" "I want to buy my mother a washing machine. If I buy my mother a washing machine, then I can go play baseball," I told him. I came from a large family, nine kids, and I had watched my mother wash our clothes by hand all those years. He said, "Well, all right," and called the business manager over. Jack said to him, "Write Charlie out a check for a hundred dollars." So he wrote out a check to Charlie Metro, using my father's first name as my last name. I said, "Oh, I don't want that. I can't take that." He asked, "Why not?" I answered, "I can't take that. I want the money." Hell, I'd never seen a hundred-dollar check, let alone that much money. So he asked, "Well, how do you want it?" I said, "In money." "Well, how do you want it?" I replied, "One-dollar bills." So Fournier had the business manager go down and get a hundred dollars in one-dollar bills for me.

I took the contract home, and my father signed it. He could barely write, but he signed it. A friend of ours, the superintendent, OK'd the signature. I gave my mother the hundred dollars. She wondered if I had stolen it. But she went out and bought a washing machine. Years later, when I was managing the Vancouver club in the late 1950s, I looked up in the stands and saw Jack Fournier there, scouting for another major league club. He waved me over. He was thrilled to see me, and I was also pleased to see him. He said, "Kid, I want to ask you a question. Did you really buy your mother a washing machine?" I answered, "Yes, sir." And he laughed like heck. I also told that story to my Denver banker friend Merlyn Williams, and he got a big kick out of it. "Now, if I give you a check, you are going to have to take it," Merlyn would say.

But that day back in 1937, I jumped at the chance. Boy, if baseball is going to pay this well, I thought, I might as well stick with it. I didn't care that it was the St. Louis Browns, who had had terrible seasons and never been in a World Series. The Yankees were the big team, but the Yankees never came around. I had an opportunity to go to college, but I didn't have the money. I was being recruited as a football athlete and a basketball player. Penn State, for instance, was interested in me for football. But at that time, heck, you couldn't work your way through school, you couldn't get a scholarship, you could get only a little help. From the financial standpoint, I just couldn't go to college. This baseball offer was an opportunity. You had to grasp it. So I chose professional baseball. I've never regretted it since. I would never exchange that for anything in this world, not even the U.S. presidency.

TWO

The Big Leagues Were a Long Way Off

My first minor league club was the Easton Browns in the Eastern Shore League. This was a Class D league. This was where Jimmie Foxx came from. He was a legend, of course. People still pointed out where he had hit home runs in the Easton ballpark. I took a bus down to Easton, Maryland. "Doc" Jacobs was the manager of the club and was also the coach for Villanova College. I played a few games with Easton, but I didn't get to stay long. In my next-to-last game with Easton, at Crisfield, I hit a home run with the bases loaded. I finally hit a curve ball. The fence wasn't very far. I kind of fell away from the pitch and hit it just right. It cleared the fence and drove in the runs, but they released me two days later. I think I had only about three or four hits by then, but I played center field and I could field. I guess they had already made their minds up or had somebody else coming to join the club. So I was the odd man out.

The Salisbury club had a couple of players that stick in my mind. One's name was Fermin Guerra, and the other was Jorge Comellas. They were both Cubans, dark-skinned Cubans. "Mike" Guerra was a catcher. Later he went up and played for Washington for a little while. Comellas was a pitcher, and that was the first time that I had ever seen a curve ball like he threw. When he threw me three curve balls, I was backing out, boy. My heart was in it, but my backside wasn't. Comellas was an older guy, and apparently he didn't make it to the major leagues, even though he went 22-1 for Salisbury that year.

While I was there, we stayed in a boardinghouse and traveled back and forth to the games. We paid a quarter a night for our room and a quarter for a meal, whether it was breakfast, lunch, or dinner. Living in a boardinghouse was wonderful. In Crisfield, I got introduced to crab, crab cakes and soft-shell crabs. A pitcher from up in Pennsylvania, who'd been around a little while, took me out, and we had soft-shell crabs. I didn't know how to eat them. It was quite an experience for me. Seafood was a rarity in the mountains of Pennsylvania.

In the other bed in this big room where we were staying was a guy by the name of Mickey Vernon. Boy, he was my idol. He was from Marcus Hooks, Pennsylvania. He was a left-handed hitter. He was long, tall, and lanky. I had never seen a fielder like he was, so graceful. He just picked everything up one-handed and danced around the bag. He could swing the bat, and boy, he had power. He eventually wound up with the Washington Senators and played a lifetime there. What impressed me most was not his hitting, although he hit real well, but that he came out of Villanova College when he was a freshman and he had those brown-and-white saddle shoes. I thought that was big league. I vowed that if I ever made it good in baseball, I'd buy myself a pair of those brown-and-white saddle shoes. Later I told him this, and he asked, "Don't you remember my hitting or my fielding or anything?" I said, "No, just your brown saddle shoes." The next year, 1938, I was a regular, and the first thing I bought with my first paycheck was a pair of brown-and-white saddle shoes. I figured I had arrived. I was showing professional class.

When I was released from Easton, I was absolutely crushed. I didn't want to go home to face all my friends. I didn't want to face the guys who had told me I couldn't play. My oldest sister, Mary, was in New York, so I hitched a ride there. I was going to stay with her. I worked briefly at a grocery store, keeping the produce fresh, moving the older tomatoes to the front of the shelves. But my mind was still on baseball. I told myself that I was going to make it. I tried to get a tryout with the Yankees. Paul Krichell was the Yankees' head scout in the East. I went out to Yankee Stadium and pestered the heck out of him for a tryout. I was in good shape. He informed me that they never gave tryouts. He said, "You'll have to go out and play somewhere, and then we'll watch you." My comment to him was "You'll be sorry, because I'm going to play in the big leagues. I'm going to be a big league ballplayer." He kind of grinned, patted me on the shoulder, and said, "If you think you will, son, you will." When I made the Detroit club, and Philadelphia later, he came down to the dugout and told me I was right. That really pleased me. And it pleased him too.

So I decided to try the Brooklyn Dodgers. I went over to Ebbets Field and talked my way into the ballpark. It was early in the morning before a day game. I bought my subway tokens and went there with my glove and my old cap and tennis shoes. I put my sneakers on and went in. I talked them into letting me on the field. I was talking to one of the players when they called Cookie Lavagetto over. Cookie said, "Kid, you got your glove?"

I said, "Yes, sir," and he said, "Come on." There I was in my street clothes out at Ebbets Field, working out, and he was hitting me pepper, playing pepper with my back to the grandstand. All I knew was Wow! He was really ripping the ball. He was bouncing the ball off my shins, off my leg, and off my stomach, but I never quit. After a while out there, he said, "Go on in the clubhouse and see if the one I hit you on the shins is bad." So I went in there, and the trainer came over and asked, "What's the matter?" I said, "Well, I was playing pepper, and Cookie hit me on the shins with the ball." He said, "Well, you're supposed to field those." I said, "Yes." But I was limping. I had strawberries on both my hips. Some of those fields that I played on in Maryland were really rough, gravelly in fact almost around the bases. I had two bad strawberries. The Brooklyn trainer told me to let him take a look at them. He looked, and, boy, they were tough. He put some purple stuff on them, which cured them pretty good.

While I was in the training room, the Brooklyn pitcher Van Lingle Mungo came in and saw me. He said, "Boy, kid, what did you do?" I said, "Well, I was sliding." Then he saw my cap and asked, "What kind of a cap is that?" I had a little old baseball cap of sorts. He went over to his locker and brought out a cap. "Here," he said, "try this on for size." I did, and he gave me a Brooklyn Dodgers cap. I wouldn't have cared if it was ten sizes too big. There I was, nineteen years old, getting a Dodgers cap from Van Lingle Mungo in Ebbets Field. When I got home to Nanty-Glo, my brother Joe wanted the cap, so I gave it to him. He grew up with that Brooklyn Dodgers cap. Then my youngest brother, Jim, wore that cap until it came apart. I think one of them still has it.

After that I went home to Nanty-Glo. I tried to talk Jack Fournier at Johnstown into giving me a contract again or letting me stay with the Johnnies. He said, "No, son, I can't give you a contract now. We're going to have another tryout camp next spring. We'll take another look at you then." So the next spring, I tried out again. I made the cut again with the Browns. This time the Browns sent me down to the Lee County Bears at Pennington Gap, Virginia, down near the lonesome pine country, Big Stone Gap. Augie Donatelli was down there at spring training, but he didn't last long because the new playing manager was also a third baseman. Pennington Gap was right near the Kentucky-Virginia line up in the mountains. This was quite an experience. I played center field all season, and I had a pretty good year. I could really roam the outfield. I got to where I was pretty good. But that old bug, the curve ball, got to me again. I should have carried out my campaign to get it abolished. But I did well enough to last the season. I hit a few home runs and led off the lineup. I could drag bunt, and I sure could catch a fly ball and throw. The manager tried to get me to switch-hit when I was leading off, but I was almost getting killed. I was always stepping into the ball.

We didn't have anybody particularly outstanding on that team. Our manager was Ralph Goldsmith, a college ballplayer from one of the Illinois colleges. He was a fine guy. One of the players on another team in the league, Stan Lujack, was the older brother of Notre Dame football star Johnny Lujack. He kept telling us to watch for his brother. We thought he was just bragging until we heard about his brother's rise to stardom.

The Appalachian League was a six-team D league. We played every day, with the exception of rainouts, even Sundays, because there were no restrictions in that area of the country. We played at Kingsport, Elizabethton, Johnson City, Greeneville, and Newport, all over in Tennessee. Kingsport was a very nice town. It had the widest main street I'd ever seen, a big camera factory—Kodak, I think it was—and a very nice ballpark. Elizabethton was also a nice place. It was close to the Virginia-Tennessee line, so we'd get a lot of Pennington Gap fans over there for games. I don't remember much about Greeneville, except one game I lost my favorite bat there. I don't recall much about Johnson City and Newport either. I was too wrapped up in playing and being successful. I was very intense. I didn't have much of a sense of humor while I was playing then.

This was my first real introduction to the South. It was a fine experience, quite an education. Everything there was brand-new to me. I had never been very far down south. Those girls with those southern accents! This was first time I went to a barbecue. I'd been to picnics but never to a barbecue. It was a delight. I was interested in the area, partly because sometime during high school I had read a great novel, *Trail of the Lonesome Pine*, by John Fox Jr., about Big Stone Gap. We played an exhibition game there. I saw some people who were poor, wore bib overalls a lot, were from up in the mountains, and didn't leave much food on their plates. But I could relate to that, having come from a big family myself. The big meals were few and far between, usually on Sunday, the biggest meal of the week. I noticed that also in the South, especially in Pennington Gap. I didn't notice any problems with religion. I was a Ukrainian Catholic, and most of the people there were Protestants, but it never came up as an issue.

The people of Pennington Gap were wonderful. It was a little old town. Gosh, they had one little café. You would eat at the café or be invited for a Sunday dinner by some fan after the game. If you did something outstanding, they'd invite you to dinner at the café. When that happened to me, they'd tell me to order anything I wanted. It was great. I never did take to grits, but I developed quite a hankering, still strong to this day, for biscuits and gravy. We stayed at a boardinghouse. The people just took us in as if we were young kids, as if we were part of the family, especially if there were young ladies there. The ladies were close by, next-door neighbors, and they'd come over and help us with serving the food at the boardinghouse table. We'd always manage to get a second dessert when those young girls were there. The meals were family-style. The lady of the house had us pretty well trained. We had to say, "Pass it, please." So I learned to say, Pass, pass such and such, please. The guys would all laugh at that, especially some of the southern guys. We had a couple of southern boys on our team. The players were scattered all over town. The manager stayed in the hotel himself. We washed at the ballpark, and we'd get a ride after the game. We had no clubhouse, so we dressed at home. We'd load onto a bus of sorts, and we'd get to the park on time, usually. In a couple of the towns in Tennessee, we stayed overnight. We'd go over there, stay one night, and then come back.

Pennington Gap had the most unusual ballpark I've ever seen. It was a great huge ballpark. They used it for a fairgrounds and even as a landing field for airplanes. Center field was about 1,000 feet, left field was about 800, and right field was about 600. It was all enclosed in kind of an "L" shape. They'd mow the grass in the outfield to about 330, 340 feet in right field. Left field and center field would be a little farther, about 360. Then they'd cut another 30 or 40 feet down to eight-inch stubble. The rest was left as tall grass, knee-high. Everything back to the fences was in play. We'd get these incredible rainstorms that would hit the outfield from time to time, just roll right out from the mountains. I'd be in center field, and all of a sudden I'd look up and here would come a sheet of rain. It wouldn't quite reach the infield, but it played heck with us in the outfield. We got drenched, but they kept playing. Years later I went back through Pennington Gap. I went with my boys and sat in the ballpark. There was still a rickety old wooden grandstand that looked like it would seat maybe only a hundred people. The fence was down on the entrance side, and the grass was overgrown real high. The little old wooden dugout was still there, filled up a little bit. I had a lot of warm feelings about that park.

We played a night game at Pennington Gap. The people had brought in this traveling light operation. They set up lights propped up on ladders at first base and third base, ones down the foul lines, about halfway to the fence, and back of home plate. There were cables all the way around from a great big generator that created electricity for the lights. We played the game under those conditions. You could hardly see the ball and, boy, it was tough, but we played. That's the first night game that I ever experienced like that with a makeshift outfit. We won the game, 1–0. One of their guys lost the ball in the outfield. I happened to be the runner, and my teammates had sacrificed me to second base. With two outs, I was running when one of our guys hit a fly ball to right field, and the fielder never did find it. I scored, and we won the ball game. But can you imagine playing a night game with lights on twenty- or twenty-five-foot ladders?

Our right fielder, Cowboy Barker, was a local hero, right from Lee County. I never heard anybody call him anything but Cowboy. He had played semipro ball up at Harlan, Kentucky. Cowboy was in his thirties at the time. He took me under his wing and taught me quite a bit about playing the outfield. I was his protégé. I roomed with him. He was a great guy, but boy was he a fierce competitor! I found out just how fierce one game at Johnson City, Tennessee. In the game the night before, the umpire had called Cowboy out on strikes on what Barker thought was a bad pitch. This had been with the bases loaded, and we didn't win the game. So the next evening, when we were dressing back in the hotel, I looked at him and he was stuffing a gun, a big pistol, in his belt, right by the belt buckle. I said, "Cowboy, what are you doing?" He told me to be quiet and said, "If that son of a bitch calls me out tonight, calls a strike on me, I'll kill him." There I was, a twenty-year-old guy, scared to death. I said, "You can't . . ." He said, "You be quiet, Rookie." So when I was leading off that game, I was standing there wondering what to do. I didn't know if the gun was loaded or not. I couldn't stop trembling. Clyde Kluttz was catching for the Cardinals farm club. I said to the ump, "Mr. Umpire, please don't call a strike on Cowboy Barker." He said, "I'll call a strike any way I want to." I said, "Please sir, don't call a strike on him. He's got a gun, and he'll shoot you." The umpire turned red, and then he turned white. The umpire's name was McNab, if I recall correctly, and he was a pretty good umpire. He never did call a strike on Cowboy, even on pitches right down the middle. Kluttz knew, because he overheard me, but I don't think our manager, Ralph Goldsmith, ever did. I know I didn't tell him. I was too scared. Cowboy told me to keep my mouth shut, and I did. Years later I bumped into Kluttz, when he was scouting, and I asked him if he knew whatever happened to Cowboy. He said, "Oh, he's that wild guy who had the gun." Nobody knew what had happened to Cowboy.

Speaking of guns, one time we played an exhibition game in Harlan, Kentucky, the site of some violent mining strikes during the 1930s. That was the first time I saw fans bearing guns. Fans would have revolvers in their belts. I thought I saw hundreds of guns. Every time you'd look up, one of the fans in Harlan would have a gun. Cowboy Barker certainly would have fit in that league. He told me, "Don't you ever say anything back to them, boy. They'll shoot you." He had me scared to death.

Cowboy Barker also taught me a trick in the outfield in Pennington Gap. If a batter slammed a ball into the higher grass, it was still live, and a center fielder with some speed and gumption, such as myself, could try to track down a fly even into the tall grass. But often a guy would get a home run before you could find the ball. So some veteran outfielders, such as Barker, would stash a ball or two just inside the tall grass and grab it in case a gapper rolled in, rather than hunt around for the original. Now, I was a pretty green rookie and never had done anything like that, but I soon learned the advantages of that angle. It only worked, though, if somebody hit a ball where you'd hidden the other one.

Another time I saw Barker pull a dandy trick. One particular night game, when we were using the auxiliary lights, a guy hit a fly ball with two outs to right field. I could see that it was going over Cowboy's head, but he came running in, waved his glove up as if he were catching the ball, and kept running in. He'd taken a ball out of his back pocket—he often carried one there—put it in his glove, and pretended he caught the ball. He had a ball in his glove, so the umpire called the batter out. When we got into the dugout, I said, "Cowboy, you can't do that." He said, "You shut up. You be quiet." They couldn't tell that he didn't have the original ball, which was way back in the grass where you couldn't see it. I thought that was about one of the funniest things I'd ever seen.

In 1938 at Big Stone Gap, Virginia, I witnessed what may have been one of the shortest home runs ever hit. We were there playing an exhibition game. Sometime right before we came back from a road trip, the town had held a carnival on the field, setting up tents and booths and the like. When they struck the tents, they left a couple of tent-pole holes unfilled. The infield grass was pretty high. I was not playing that day, so I coached third for the manager. Our batter laid down a bunt on the third base side that all of a sudden disappeared. It went down that tent-pole hole and stuck. We had two men on. I couldn't see the ball, and the third baseman couldn't either. So I waved our runners on home. The batter got over to third base with a puzzled look on his face. We still couldn't see the ball, so I sent him on home too, for an inside-the-park homer. Eventually they got the ball unstuck, but we got 3 runs on a fifteen-foot home run bunt!

Something similar happened one time at Greeneville. I drag bunted four times in one game. I got 4 base hits. I was batting leadoff. I pushed 2 on the first-base side and dragged 2 on the left-hand side. I got 4 base hits and never really hit the ball. They didn't go a total of ninety feet, all four of them. I got the biggest razzing from my manager, Ralph Goldsmith, who was then right out of college. He said, "That's the greatest feat of hitting I've ever seen." But then he said, "Yeah, but they didn't total ninety feet, the whole four of them."

In the Appalachian League, I also got to play with an ambidextrous player, Whitey Carr, who was one of our pitchers. He was an older guy, maybe twenty-five, twenty-six years old. You always had a couple of veterans on the team. He had a glove with two big thumbs, a funny glove that he had had specially made. In a game he was pitching against Kingsport, he played a funny cat-and-mouse game with the batters. He started throwing right-handed. In the first inning, we got their first three guys out. When their number-four hitter came up in the second inning, the guy turned around and was hitting left-handed. So Whitey took off his glove and put it on his other hand. He was going to pitch to him left-handed. Then the hitter stepped out and went to the other side. Whitey turned, took the glove off his right hand, and put it on his left hand. This went back and forth, back and forth like that. Finally the umpire got exasperated and asked the batter, "Are you going to hit one way or the other?" And the hitter said, "I can hit any way I want." So he stood there hitting right-handed. Whitey in turn dropped the glove on the mound and held the ball in his bare hands right in front of him. He then got on the rubber, and once he started his motion, the batter couldn't tell which arm Whitey was going to throw with. That broke up that little game. He was even able to hold a runner on first better, because the guy couldn't know if he was pitching left- or right-handed. I thought it was hilarious. They'd play the cat-and-mouse game, and the fans really enjoyed it.

While I was at Pennington Gap, we had a couple of ballplayers who in the later part of the season kept telling me, "Charlie, if you ever get a chance to play at Mayfield, Kentucky, kid, you take it." I asked why, and they said, "It's the fastest D League in the Browns organization." It was another D league. I wanted to play there when I heard all of this. I said, "Heck, yeah, I'll play there." I went back home after the season was over to wait to see where the Browns would send me. When I came home to Nanty-Glo, I was a little bit of a hero by that time. I went back and worked in the coal mines, biding my time until I got another contract. It wasn't long in coming, but I was disappointed to see it was for only sixty dollars a month, the same as my pay at Pennington Gap. I said, "Holy smokes." But they also didn't put the date on it or which club I was assigned to. So I wrote back to the Browns and asked where I was going. They replied that they were going to invite me to Belleville, Illinois, where they'd hold a condensed early camp, and then send me to Paragould, Arkansas. I told them that I wasn't going to Paragould and that I wasn't going to sign for only sixty dollars a month. I was asking for seventy-five dollars a month. They sent me a bus ticket in the spring, in March, and I was through working in the coal mines. I rode out to Belleville, Illinois. Bill DeWitt, who later became the general manager at Cincinnati and Detroit, decided that I was holding out. I was just trying to get another fifteen bucks a month.

When I got to Belleville, DeWitt asked me why I didn't want to go to Paragould. I said that I didn't want to go to Paragould, that I didn't know anything about the league. I said, "Heck, I want to go to that fast Kitty League. I want to go to Mayfield, Kentucky." He said, "You can't make the team." I replied, "Yes, I can." And I said, "Besides, I want seventy-five dollars a month. I'm not going to play for sixty dollars. I'll go back and work in the coal mines." That was kind of a bluff, just a little bit of stuff that you tell the big guy. He said, "Well, let's see how you can play." The Browns had players from the A league, the B league, about three or four C leagues, and three or four D leagues in camp in Belleville. We all played. We dressed at the hotel and drove out to the ballpark and put on our spiked shoes and our gloves and stuff out there. I was ready to play. I had worked out all the time during the winter. I ran like heck, and then I threw in the gym. I always loved to run. I'd run for miles just to stay in condition. We got nice, sunny weather. It was springtime in Belleville. I had just come out of the cold, the ice and snow, in Pennsylvania, and, boy, I was feeling good. After two or three days of practice, the time came to play some intersquad games. So they lined us up for teams. I reminded DeWitt that I was not going to Paragould, Arkansas, that he could forget that. There I was, pretty cocky. He said, "Well, we'll see about that."

DeWitt and a guy by the name of Gilliland, who was also in the Browns front office, put me in center field in a game at 9:00 the next morning. While I was in that game, they made all kinds of changes. They brought in a new first baseman and so forth—all these kids played three or four innings—and I was waiting to be replaced. But I played nine innings, and then I played eighteen innings. I asked what time it was, and somebody said 11:00, and I was still playing. The next time I asked it was 12:00 noon, and I was still playing center field. Boy, by then I was getting mad. Everybody else was being relieved, in and out, but they wouldn't take me out. The madder I got, the better I played. I caught everything that was hit out there, and I was hitting a lot better than I thought I could hit. But I was also getting darn tired. I was really getting mad at that whole situation, when the manager came up to me and asked, "What's the matter, kid, you getting mad?" I said, "No, I'm not mad." He asked, "Don't you want to play ball?" I said, "Yeah." They all knew that I was holding out, so they kept me in there. I played from 9:00 to 4:00 that afternoon. I stayed in the game, and the longer I played, the harder I played, the better I played. Finally they took me out.

When the game was over, Bill DeWitt came over to me and said, "I think we're going to send you to Mayfield. Don't think you can make it, but I think we're going to send you to Mayfield." We stayed in Belleville another four or five days. Then they assembled the club, put us all on the bus, and down to Mayfield we went. It was somewhere about the middle of April. We got down to Mayfield, and we were going to have spring training for about a week or ten days. Then they would form the club and get some extra players. I liked Mayfield as soon as I saw the little western Kentucky town. And the Kitty League, that was the dream. I told a couple of the guys, "You better forget about center field. That's my job. You can forget it." Boy, I was playing well. I was in good shape and played up there. I was hitting against the pitching better than before.

The Mayfield manager was Bennie Tate, who had caught for the Washington Senators years before. His claim to fame was that he had caught the great Walter Johnson in a few games. Like Ralph Goldsmith, Bennie was a great guy. I don't believe I ever played for a manager who wasn't great. I loved them all. Bennie said, "Kid, I think you got the center-field job won on my club." I said, "You mean I don't have it won yet?" He said, "No, not yet." I got riled up and played even harder. If only someone would have made me mad when I finally got to the majors, I might have been a heck of a ballplayer. I did make the Mayfield ball club. I had to sign for $60 again, but they offered me a $15-a-month bonus if I stayed all year. But Bill DeWitt still owes me $67.50 in bonuses! I stayed the whole season, but the Browns didn't make good on the bonuses. We started out the season well. We had a real good team, good enough to take the pennant that year. I had a great year for me. I led off, hit 14 home runs leading off, and drove in 75 runs. I played the living daylights out of center field.

On that Mayfield Browns club, we had Jim Russell, a switch hitter, in right field. Boy, could he run and hit! He had that trademark windmill swing with the bat like Willie Stargell did later. We had Joe Morjoseph in left. He looked something like Joe DiMaggio. He was from out in California, Los Angeles, and was French-Italian or something. He was a pretty good hitter too. He couldn't field very well. He'd miss the cutoff guy and miss the bag and just look terrible. I saw him later in 1947 in Tucson, when he was on his way out. But he made out all right. Years later out in California, I bumped into him and found out he'd gotten rich with a chain of Don José restaurants, serving frosted margaritas. He had a racehorse and a private plane and everything. Gosh, I had thought he was the dumbest son of a gun that ever lived. We had a couple of pitchers, Bennie Knuyper and Bill Scott, who had pitched in Triple-A. The third baseman, Red Lanfersieck, became an umpire in the municipal league in St. Louis. I guess Red was up in his seventies when he finally quit umping. He never got too far in baseball, but he was a tremendous guy and a fine ballplayer. Once, however, the fans were on him something fierce. He was having a hard time in the field and at the plate, and he lost his temper. He jumped on the dugout and climbed up the screen, trying to get at the fans. They really roasted him. The second baseman was Dutch Funderburk, and at shortstop we had Vern Stephens, who later played for the Browns and eventually the Red Sox.

When I had an opportunity to talk to Ted Williams about Hitters' Hands years later, I asked him who was the best hitter they had on the Red Sox, next to him, of course, and he said Vern Stephens. He said he was the toughest hitter to hit behind him in his whole career. I told Ted that I had played with Vern in Mayfield in the Kitty League. He said, "Tell me about him." I said, "Well, you've heard this story about guys rooming with another guy's bag? I roomed with Vern Stephens's bag." He was from California, and he was a bundle of energy. I don't know where he got it. He played hard, and he was a tremendous hitter. In fact he hit .350 something. He hit 28 or 30 home runs, drove in runs, and played a great shortstop. He kind of walked like a duck a little bit, with his toes turned out. I saw him jump up off the ground with both feet and hit a ball out of the park. He holds the record for the most RBI in a season by a major league shortstop. He got mixed up in that Mexican League stuff in 1946, but somebody went down and smuggled him back, so he escaped retaliation from the big leagues. I may be partially responsible for his great career. One night, at Hopkinsville, Kentucky, we were rooming together, and we got into an argument about the light. This led to a wrestling match. I think I was a little bit stronger than he—but not anywhere near the hitter or ballplayer he was—and he got his foot caught under the old rug in the room and twisted his knee. That bad knee kept him out of the service. He wore a brace on his knee, and when he ran he would sling that leg out. I was the cause of that. But it sure didn't slow him up, and it didn't stop him from hitting.

Vern Stephens also taught me a few things about how to stretch my pay. Mind you, I was making $60 a month, and Vern was making $70 or $75. At the time, he was a better prospect than I was, which turned out to be true. We would buy meal tickets for $5 and get a $7.50 value at the eateries in town. The two big clothing factories there, Merit Clothing Company, which made Style Mart clothes, and Curlee Clothing Company, had dining places, and there were a couple of restaurants. We'd have lunch before the games, because mostly we played night games. Vern had played with big league guys out there in California in the wintertime when he was a fifteen-year-old kid. He had heard all sorts of talk and knew his way around. I followed him around like a puppy dog, because he was sharp. He had all the answers. So we were having lunch, and he said, "Rooms, you want some pie à la mode?" I said, "Heck, we can't afford pie à la mode!" It was twenty-five cents for lunch, and we couldn't afford this dessert. He said, "I'll show you how to get it. Do you have a nickel?" I said, "Yeah." He said, "I have one too." He called the waitress over. She was a young woman, and, of course, we were heroes in the little town. Vern asked, "What kind of pie do we have?" She said, "Apple." He said, "Okay, Roomie?" He took his nickel, set it down, and slid it over toward the girl as she was cleaning up, and I put mine down and slid it over too. When she saw us giving her a big tip—can you imagine when a nickel was a big tip?—she said, "À la mode?" We said, "Yes." We got pie à la mode free for a nickel tip apiece! Vern taught me quite a bit.

It was a great time, and we loved it there. The fans took us into their homes and made us feel right at home. We stayed at a private home, at a Kentucky colonel's home. His name was Colonel Brizendine. He was a baseball fan and a magnificent person. His wife's name was Maudie. Four of us, Vern Stephens and I, and Fritz Klann and Bud Williams, stayed there. Fritz and Bud had the big room where the bath was, and Vern and I had the room out over the carport. Maudie would cook a great big country ham—I'd never seen ham like that—on Saturday afternoon for Sunday. The Colonel would invite us into the kitchen to have a little snack. We'd start in on that ham. He'd say, "Boys, have a little slice of ham." We'd pretty damn near eat the whole ham, the four of us, while he'd be drinking hard cider. I didn't drink, but Big Bud and the other two guys would sample some. The next morning we'd get up to go uptown to have breakfast at the restaurant or the clubhouse, either one, before the Sunday baseball game. Sometimes it was a doubleheader, sometimes just a single game. Maudie would get the broom and whack Bud Williams. She called him some kind of a southern name that wasn't very complimentary. He'd grin and say, "Aw, Maudie," and grab the broom and hold it. She'd say, "Now, you turn it loose; I'm gonna whup your backside, and that goes for you too, Vernon."

Then she'd light into me, even though I was kind of her little pet. "Charles, I'm surprised at you," she'd scold me and whack us all on the backside. Bud would say, on the way out, "Don't worry. We'll have collard greens and ham hock and dumplings." We'd have all the milk we wanted to drink and apple pie too. Bud knew this, and he'd say, "Don't worry, leave it up to me. We'll have dinner."

On the way back from the ballpark, we'd stop at this one house over in the high-falutin' area, and Bud would say, "Watch this," and he'd break a bunch of beautiful roses off the rose bush. He'd take two and give us each one. So in we'd come, and Maudie would be sitting there. We came in the back door and went to go up the back stairs, and she'd be sitting there. "Well, how'd you boys do?" she'd inquire. The Colonel had already been there and told her that we'd had won the game or both games. Big Bud would go over to her and reach down and say, "Maudie, you're not mad at us." "Yes, I am," she'd say, "I'm mad, fit to kill," and all those southern terms I had never heard. Then Bud would say, "Well, all right, you can stay mad, but here," and he'd give her the two roses. She would just be like a little girl, although she and the Colonel were well up in age. Then Vern would give her another rose, and then I'd give her one, and Fritz the same. She would say, "Now you boys hurry up and get washed up. Now dinner will be ready. You're going to sit down and have Sunday dinner with us." And we had cornbread too.

One special person in Mayfield captured my heart. That spring of 1939, I was riding a bike and was almost run over by a young woman driving a car. I took one look at her, and I was interested. She was about five foot four and cute and bouncy. I asked, "What's your name?" and she asked, "Why?" I said, "Well, you almost ran over me on this bike." She said, "I didn't touch you." So I was introduced to her. Her name was Helen Deane Bullock. A bunch of the guys on the team always gathered at the drugstore, Stone's Drug Store, in Mayfield. It had an ice cream and soda fountain. Bud Williams was one of the older guys on the ball club. He was about twenty-eight and sort of a career minor leaguer. He told us these girls in Mayfield were nice. "These are southern girls. They're the nicest girls in the world," he said, "The way you want to do it is offer to buy them a cherry Coke." We ballplayers ran up a tab up at the fountain, buying a Coke for this guy or that guy. So I went in there, and there was Helen Deane Bullock with her friends. They were all happy about something or other. Sara was going with one of the ballplayers already. I took a look at Helen, and I asked, "You care for a cherry Coke?" She said, "Yes." Bud had told me what to do next. He said to buy one cherry Coke and ask for two straws. I asked why, and he said, "You just say one cherry Coke, two straws." I had Helen join me, and we sat on the stools. I bought a cherry Coke and said, "Two straws." The guy looked at me and put one straw in there and I put one straw, and I found out you can get pretty close that way. The next day the guy at the counter said, "That was a pretty neat trick." I don't mind telling you it sure worked, and it wasn't long before the love bug started nibbling.

We did have a little squabble over an episode concerning the movies in Mayfield. The theater showed movies on Saturday, in the morning and at night. Vern Stephens had a date with the shortstop on the local women's softball team, and he'd arranged for me to meet him for a double date, upstairs in the balcony. Actually it was a blind date. He'd fixed me up with the catcher, a pretty big girl who had kind of a broken nose but a very good personality. Stephens said, "We'll buy a bag of popcorn. You buy a bag, and I will too." Popcorn was a nickel a bag. So we were upstairs in the balcony, and all of a sudden I noticed down two rows there was Helen. She didn't talk to me for weeks. I'd ask, "Would you care for a Coke?" "No, thank you, no, thank you." Finally I broke her down. I was talking to her one time, while she was standing by a parking meter, and I had my back to the wall in front of the drugstore. I apologized to her. I said, "Vern, my roomie . . ." "Well, you didn't have to go with him," she cut in. I said, "Well, he says let's go and talked me into it." She answered, "Well, you picked a good one, didn't you?" I got all kinds of heck for that one. But we made up, and we celebrated our sixtieth anniversary this year. In fact, two other Mayfield Browns center fielders married Mayfield girls after I did—Ray Coleman, who later went up with the parent club, and Floyd Hundley. I don't know if there were others after them. I haven't kept track.

Actually I was bitten pretty hard, and one time it affected my play on the field. Helen Deane Bullock was up in the stands, and I couldn't keep my eyes off her. I had made a pretty catch the inning before out in the outfield, so I was kind of strutting around a little bit. In one particular part of the game, I was the hitter and I was looking down at our manager, Bennie Tate, coaching at third base. He was giving signs, but I didn't see him. My mind was on the girl in the stands. Finally he whistled at me, and I jerked around and looked at him. He motioned me over and said, "Uh, I guess if you'd keep your eyes off that pretty thing up in the grandstand, you'd start seeing the signs." I got embarrassed. He said, "Maybe you ought to bring her down here and coach third and then you'd see the signs." Then he walked back. I got the message.

Some crazy incidents happened that year while I was playing for Mayfield. I ran through an outfield fence at Paducah, Kentucky. All the ballparks in the league were old, but as long as we had a ballpark to play in, we played. In this game at Paducah, I was playing center and Joe Morjoseph was in left field. He was always saying he didn't want to move fielding, so I had to cover all the ground. A Paducah guy hit the ball out into left-center, and I tore out after it. I knew I was going to get it. Joe kept yelling to me, "Lot of room, lot of room." There was no warning track. I caught the ball and wham! through that fence I went. I broke the fence, about five boards, and I was outside the ballpark. My feet were inside the park, but the rest of me was outside. I still had the ball, and I was trying to show it to the umpire. Bennie Tate argued like heck. But the ump called it a home run, because the ball was out of the ballpark. We won the ball game anyway, and it was pretty funny. A cartoonist at Paducah drew up the scene, and somewhere in my garage there's a drawing of me going through the fence. That same year at Mayfield, I was the victim of a ball stuck on a nail in the fence. I went back to field a drive off the center-field fence, but the ball didn't ricochet off the wall. It hit a protruding nail and stuck a few inches above where I could jump. I jumped frantically trying to knock it loose, but the batter circled the bases for one of the stranger inside-the-park home runs in baseball history. I had a local photographer take a picture of that.

Another humorous play happened when we were playing night ball in Mayfield that year. We had lights strung along a wire from a light pole at third base to one by first base, right across the field. The other club was hitting, and a left-handed hitter hit a fly ball toward left field. It hit the wire, and our third baseman, Red Lanfersieck—somebody yelled at him—looked real quick. The ball hit the wire and started rolling, running down the wire, going foul. Red ran over and made a diving grab, one of the greatest catches you've ever seen. Nobody knew what the heck to rule it. Everybody gathered around mulling it over. The umpires, of course, were young rookies too, and they didn't know exactly what to call it. I believe they ruled the batter out, and he was just furious.

I would imagine most baseball fans have seen the movie *Bull Durham* by now and can remember the scene where the players turn on the irrigation hoses to avoid playing a game. What a wonderful episode, all of them sliding around on the tarp like maniacs! I took part in a similar incident at Bowling Green, Kentucky, back in 1939. We were scheduled to play a doubleheader one Sunday there, but we really wanted to go out to a river picnic and dance with some young women from a nearby summer school for girls. There was a place for swimming, with diving boards and floats out in the middle of the river. We were all young, and I don't think there was a married guy on the ball club. One of the veterans on the team, Bud Williams, knew a couple of the young women there and told us about the dance. Some of the girls had asked him to bring some of the ballplayers along. But how were we going to get to go? We had that darned doubleheader. Bud said, don't worry, fellas, he'd think of something. Saturday night, after we had played, Bud knocked on the door about 11:00 and said, "Let's go." I said, "Go where?" He said, "Come on. Never mind. Be quiet." He rounded up five of us, and we snuck out down the fire escape, violating curfew and a bunch of other restrictions. I didn't know where we were going, but one of the girls had the car. We all piled in, and out to the ballpark we went. We found a way in. We grabbed the big fire hose, put it on the pitcher's mound, turned that water on full force, and let it run all night.

The next day we dressed in our uniforms at the hotel and went out to the ball field. Word had already spread to a few of the other players that something was in the works. But nobody said anything. When we got there, the infield was totally soaked, with mud a foot deep all over, and the sun was shining bright. There was no way they could get the ground in shape. We stood around, moaning and groaning about who could've done such a thing, that we had really wanted to play the doubleheader. The manager dismissed us, and we started "consoling" ourselves that we would go to the movies. We said, "See you, Skip," as if we were innocently going off to the show. Instead Bud had a couple of cars lined up with the girls, and we scooted out to the river. There was a food place and some beer there, and they had fried chicken. They had a dance floor, a jukebox and all that, and we had a great time, swimming and dancing. To this day I'll bet the Bowling Green people have no idea that we engineered that stunt. We blamed it on the groundskeeper. So when I saw that scene in *Bull Durham*, my laughs were about Bowling Green and Bud Williams.

Another time Bud convinced us to go dancing over in Hopkinsville and got us fined. I was learning how to dance at that time. I didn't know how to dance. But we had a 12:30 curfew at night, and, boy, you couldn't stay out. You had to stick to the rules, and you had to be on time at the ballpark, and you had to do this and do that. They didn't fool around with you. But Bud knew a place out there in Hopkinsville where we could go dancing. We won our ball game, and out we went that Saturday night. They had a jukebox, dancing, and you could get beer or a Coke. There were a lot of girls, and we danced with them all. I learned a rugged two-step. I was no Fred Astaire, but I learned a little old two-step. And we stayed out. Heck, I was learning how to dance. All the guys were having a good time. There were six of us, Vern Stephens, Bud, Red Lanfersieck, Jim Russell, Fritz Klann, and me. So along about 2:00 A.M., I said, "Heck, I'm going to bed." They said, "Aw, go ahead." So I walked back to the hotel. It had an old iron-caged elevator, and I didn't want to go up because it made a lot of racket. We were on the second floor, so I walked up the stairs and tried to make no noise. Just as I hit the top of the stairs, the light was shining out of the door. I peeked around the door, and there was Bennie Tate, our manager, lying in bed, reading in his pajamas. He said, "Hi, Charlie, how are you?" I said, "Fine." He said, "Good night," and I kept going. The next guy came in at 2:30, and another guy came in at 3:00. Vern Stephens, the next-to-last guy, came in at 4:30, and Bud Williams, who'd arranged all this, never did come in that night.

The next day, we got together and found out the manager had caught us all coming in late. Big Bud, the ringleader, said, "Now, listen, you guys, every one of you has got to bust your neck. You've got to play like heck. We've got to win these games." It was a doubleheader. So we played the first game and we won, something like 13–2. I was the lead-off hitter. I was on base six times. Fritz Klann, the first baseman, who had been with us at the dance place, hit 2 home runs, the longest home runs ever hit in the Hopkinsville ballpark. He was a left-handed hitter, not a very big guy, but, boy, he hit those two a mile. Vern Stephens, another one out with us, had several hits. In the second game, Bud Williams pitched an 11–0 shutout. I was on base quite often again, I think eleven times in that doubleheader. Stephens had another great game, the darndest day you've ever seen a guy have. Jim Russell had a hell of a day too. I played that center field as if I my feet were on fire. And Bud pitched a masterful game.

Whenever we'd win a doubleheader, the traveling secretary would buy a case of Cokes. I think there were fifteen or sixteen guys on the club at that time. He bought a case, and we were sitting there. Everybody took their shoes off on the bus. Bennie Tate came off the field and onto the bus, where we were laughing and having a great time. We had won a doubleheader after all. He said, "You guys played a tremendous game. Oh, it was great. That doubleheader, we're on top, we've got a good ball club." "But," he said, "We're not going to let anything or anybody do anything to upset this ball club, I'm telling you." And he said, "The first guy that came in at 2:00, 2:30, I'm fining him twenty dollars, not mentioning any names. The second guy that came in at 3:00, I'm fining him twenty dollars. The third guy that came in at 4:00, I'm fining him twenty-five dollars. The next two guys are being fined thirty dollars. And that big son of a bitch that didn't come in at all, all night long, he's fined fifty dollars." Lanfersieck had gone home early, so he wasn't fined. You could've heard a pin drop in that place. After it was all over and we were dressed and getting ready to leave, one of the guys said, "Ah, don't worry, he'll never fine us." He was wrong. We paid that fine. Can you figure that? One third of my salary went for a good time after winning a doubleheader. Gosh darn it, I thought, that didn't seem right. But it was right, and he taught us a lesson. We played hard and went on to win the pennant. A few years later, when Stephens was with the Browns and I was with Detroit, I had breakfast with him. I asked, "Vern, did you ever get your money back?" "Hell, no," he said. I said, kidding him along, "I got mine back." He was furious that supposedly I got my money back and he didn't.

Bennie Tate never enforced a curfew in Mayfield, our hometown. There were only one or two places you could go. The Cardinal Inn, which was a dance place and sold beer, would close at 12:00 at night. They'd sneak beer in there. Graves County, where Mayfield was, was dry. Some guys would go over to Paducah, in McCracken County. They had a big bar right on the county line. People would go over there and bring a case of beer, a bottle of bourbon, and you could talk them into a drink at this place and dance. They'd have snacks. You could buy a sandwich, roast beef or baked ham, and chips. But the one over toward the line was outlawed. We weren't allowed to go there because there was a cathouse out there too.

We faced some fine players on the other Kitty League teams, guys who went up to the majors. Ellis Kinder was a tremendous pitcher for the Jackson, Tennessee, team. He finally went up with the Red Sox. He was an older guy. He had a curve like nothing you've ever seen, but I could hit him pretty well, because he was always throwing curves to the younger guys. George "Catfish" Metkovich was floating in the Kitty League that year. He was fishing down in Florida once and caught a catfish, which stung him. That's how he got his nickname. He was a good ballplayer, not a great ballplayer, but a good one. Danny Gardella also played in the league. He was a left-handed-hitting outfielder. Boy, talk about flighty guys, he was one. He'd be out there standing on his hands with his feet straight in the air, and he'd do a push-up standing straight up like that, or he'd chew the dandelions off the outfield grass between innings. Eventually he went up to the Giants, and he was one of the guys involved with the Mexican League. There was also a second baseman, Frank Filchock, who became more noted as a professional football player and coach. He became a fine football coach in the Canadian Football League and also coached the Denver Broncos their initial year. And Dave Koslo, who went up with the Giants for a few years, pitched for Hopkinsville. We couldn't be too friendly with them, because managers frowned on fraternization back then.

A couple of the managers were memorable. Hugh Wise, the manager at Owensboro, was an engineer, and he had built the ballpark. It was a beautiful stadium. We were friends till the day he died. Every time I saw him, he would say, I remember you doing this or doing that, and half the times I wouldn't remember what he was talking about. His stadium had a concrete fence, and once I shied away from the ball in deep right-center, which the right fielder, Jim Russell, should have caught. But I should have caught it, and, boy, I heard holy heck. Hugh Wise would remind me of that because he knew I was furious about it. Ben Tincup was the manager at Paducah. He was a Native American from Oklahoma who played and pitched in the big leagues a little while for the Phillies back in the 1910s.

There was a left-handed pitcher in the league, and I can't recall his name, who had trouble covering first base. The strange thing was he was a good athlete, an intercollegiate diver. He couldn't cover first base. We were over playing one night at Paducah, and afterward we snuck off to go to the pool. I took a look at this guy who couldn't cover first base, couldn't get his feet right, and couldn't get his body right to catch the ball. I looked up, and he was diving off the high board, doing triple somersaults and the jackknife and the swan dive and everything else. He had a body that was beautiful in flight, but ironically he couldn't run over to first base and cover the bag and catch the ball and step on the base.

My year at Mayfield was also my real introduction to segregation. The ballparks all had segregated seating, and there was a section of town where the black people lived. The black fans were absolutely great fans. I loved them. They lived and died for baseball. When I was in Mayfield and later down in Texas and Arkansas, the black fans had their own bleachers down either the left-field or right-field line. If you did something good, you were their hero. They were for you 100 percent. I loved that. They really enjoyed it. They knew baseball real well. If a guy loafed and dropped the ball or something, they'd boo him a little bit. I was glad to see that when segregation ended later, they could sit closer to the field. One of the black guys in Mayfield was good luck for us. Every time we saw him, we'd bring him over and ask him if he had his rabbit's foot. He'd let us rub that rabbit's foot. He got a kick out of that. We would cop a ball in practice and slip it to him through the fence, and he'd come in with that baseball. We loved him, and he loved it, because he lived and died with us. It must have worked, because we won the pennant.

In Mayfield there was a real good women's softball team. The Merit Clothing Company sponsored them. Vern Stephens, our shortstop, was dating the shortstop of the women's team. We played them one morning, just for fun. They were practicing, and a bunch of us guys on the ball club came out there. We challenged them, but, heck, we couldn't hit the ball. That girl was throwing that ball underhanded, and the ball was by us before we could swing. I think a couple of guys foul-tipped a couple of pitches, but they beat the heck out of us. The shortstop was a wiz. That girl could really play. My wife and I went back to a Mayfield High School reunion some years ago, and we saw her. She was a perky blonde then, and she's a perky grandmother now. She was one heck of a ballplayer. They had all the actions and motions, and their speed was fine—they could run like heck— but they didn't have much power, except the catcher, who was a bigger girl who could hit a softball out of the park. But I wouldn't recommend playing softball to anybody for any length of time. After swinging at that big ball, I had trouble hitting a baseball. They'd throw that little round ball at me, and I was missing it. I think I stood up there for five minutes before I even touched the ball. I was way out front.

When the season ended, I wanted to stay in Mayfield. I didn't want to go back to the coal mines, and besides that love bug was biting real hard. So I spent the fall and winter there. I also recall the World Series that fall real well. Right down on the court square on one of the buildings, they had the scoreboard up there, where they'd put up the scores. A guy would be listening to the radio, the play-by-play of the World Series. Cincinnati was in the Series against the Yankees, so there was a lot of interest in Kentucky. There were a lot of people, maybe 1,500, sitting on clay benches around the court square. They'd gathered around, waiting anxiously for the score to come up. If there was a zero, there'd be a groan, and if there was a run for the team they were pulling for, there'd be a big cheer coming up. It was a very good time.

Back then, however, players needed to get jobs in the off-season, but I wasn't sure what I was going to do that year. The Mayfield manager, Bennie Tate, was running a gas station there. When he found out I was staying for the winter, he offered me a job as a Santa Claus. I worked as a Santa Claus for the month of December. He said that a Santa Claus would bring a lot of business to his station. I had a great time. I wore longhandles underneath to keep warm, and I had a great big pillow under my jacket and a pair of big boots. I pumped gas. I washed windshields. I checked tires, and I hugged the girls. We were giving out some candy, some all-day suckers, as they called them. Nobody knew who I was. But there was old Santa Claus, going "Ho! Ho! Ho!" all the way around. I got three bucks a day for that. Some Mayfield people asked me if I would be a Santa Claus at the church. I was going with a cute little thing, I mean Helen, at that time, and I agreed. So when they had their big Christmas doings at the church, I was all dressed up in my Santa Claus suit. After I was through Ho!-Ho!-ing and asking them what they wanted and if they were all good, I walked off the stage and walked up the aisle, where this cute girl was sitting there with her friends. I asked her, "And what do you want, young lady, for Christmas?" She said, "I want *you*." She was the girl I was going with all the time, and I didn't know that she knew that I was Santa Claus.

As the spring of 1940 was approaching, I found myself in a dilemma. I didn't want to come back and play another year in the D league. I wanted to play up higher, but I didn't want to lose touch with Helen Deane Bullock. It turned out that she had a sister living in Austin, Texas. In our correspondence, she wrote that she was going to be down in Texas, so I found out the Browns had a club in Palestine, Texas, in the East Texas League. I thought, well, that's not too far. So I talked the Browns into assigning me to the Palestine Pals. The East Texas League was a Class C league, and it was considered a pretty good one. It was a good step up. If you made it there, then you could maybe jump a classification. Along about spring training time, I received my contract for $110 a month to play for Palestine. I thought, well, heck, I'll just go down and visit Helen Deane in Austin at her sister's place. I got on the bus and went down to Texas. The owner of the club had sent me a letter saying if I paid my way down, they'd reimburse me. I went on down to Austin, which is in the central part of Texas, and Palestine is up on the northeast side. When I got down there, we visited and I met Helen's sister and brother-in-law. Things were still pretty good. But $110 a month wasn't enough to get married on, and I didn't know if I was going to like it up in Palestine.

I went up to Palestine, and Dutch Funderburk, our second baseman from the previous year at Mayfield, was there. Dutch was a cowboy from San Saba, Texas, and he was always out looking for rodeos. He'd bet them five or ten bucks that he could ride this or that animal or rope a calf. He was great. He said, "Charlie, you're not going to like it here." I asked, "Why?" He said, "It's just not a nice town, and you're not going to like it here." I said, "Well, I signed." But I was worried about money. I had given Helen my high school ring. That was the clincher. I didn't have enough money to get married on. But one day in spring training at Palestine, after a workout, a guy came up to me and said, "You're Charlie Metro?" I said yes. He said, "Everybody says you're a pretty good ballplayer. You could play here, stay here." I said, "How did you know that? How did you know my name?" He'd seen my name and number on a sheet of paper they distributed to the spring training fans who'd come out to watch. He said, "By the way, I got something that's going to interest you." I said, "What's that?" He said, "Come on down to my hotel room." I said, "Well, OK."

I went down to the hotel room and found out that he was a Fuller Brush regional district guy. He said, "You know, you could make some money selling Fuller Brushes. You're a natural. You're a ballplayer here. You're popular." I said, "You're kidding, I never sold anything like that." Well, the wheels started turning. I needed some extra money. I thought, with $110 how am I going to buy a ring and so forth? That love bug sure had me. So I said, "OK, what do I do?" He said, "You just go out and you get these orders for these products. We don't have a guy in Palestine. Then you sign the orders and get the money and send it in to the office in Dallas." He told me that I'd get back 40 percent of what I sold, and I could go out and sell during the day and turn in the orders at night, or I could wait three or four days. I said, "Oh, fine, 40 percent. Let me try it here. How long are you going to be here?" He said, "I'm just going to be here today, so if you want to do this agreement . . ." He gave me the display kit that unfolded to show the samples, and he showed me this and showed me that and how to fill an order out.

The next day, after the workout, I went out and the first guys that I tried, all the ballplayers in this boardinghouse, placed orders for $20 worth of brushes, hair brushes, clothes brushes, toothbrushes, shoe brushes, and all that kind of stuff. I sold $20 worth right there, cash. Holy cow, I thought, 40 percent of that is not bad. So I headed for the town. I laid my map out, and I went to one house and I sold another $10 worth. At another house I sold $30 worth. I said to myself, man, this is a good deal, it won't be long until I have enough money for the ring. I turned those orders in. The season started, and I went out and I sold about $150 worth. I was almost going to make the amount of my salary pretty quickly. We went on the road for some games, and when I got back, I received the orders and delivered them. I was pretty enthused about this job.

So I went into the high-falutin' part of town where the big homes were. I saw this big white house. The guy who owned the ball club owned a plumbing company. He was a great big, gruff guy. He gave me heck because he thought that I overcharged him on the ticket to Austin, Texas, and argued that he was only supposed to pay my way to Palestine. That made me a little sore. I tried to get away with it but couldn't. It was just a couple of bucks' difference. I went up to the big white house and told them that I was their new Fuller Brush Man. I walked into the place and made a nice ten- or twenty-dollar sale. I asked the man's wife, "Who's your neighbor next door?" She told me, and I went over there. I didn't think anything about it. I knocked on the door, and a nice lady came out. I introduced myself as the new Fuller Brush Man, and she said, "Oh, come in." I went inside and spread the sample kit out, and she started ordering all sorts of stuff. Then her daughter came in, and she started saying she wanted this and she wanted that. The mother made something of a fuss over me. Her daughter apparently was marriageable and I was unmarried, and I guess she thought I was good-looking enough for her daughter. There I was, on my knees with the whole kit spread out, and they were ordering practically everything. I was writing the order up to their specifications.

All of a sudden the back door slammed, and the lady asked, "Is that you, honey?" He said, "Yeah." There I was, down on my knees, and in walked the owner of the ball club. I took one look at him, and he looked at me and said, "Don't I know you?" I didn't want to say anything. I just slowly took my display case and folded it back up. His wife had already written out the check for the whole sale and given it to me. He said, "I know you. You're that smart-aleck outfielder." I said, "No, sir, I'm not any smart-aleck outfielder." I said, "Thank you, ma'am," and I bowed out of there real quick. About two or three weeks later, he released me. He said that no son of a gun was going to make him look cheap by having another job while playing baseball on his team. So I wasn't around Palestine very long. I made enough money to buy a ring, though.

When the Browns found out that the Palestine owner had released me on his own, they were pretty angry because they thought I'd be a pretty good prospect, at least a Triple-A ballplayer. They turned me loose anyway. On the day of my release, we were playing the Longview team, and when the manager of Longview heard about it, he said to me, "Hey, why don't you come with me? I think we could use you. Are you ready to go?" I said, "Yeah, after the game." He said, "We're going to leave after this game." So I went to the boardinghouse, packed up my stuff, got on the bus, and went with them to Longview, Texas. The manager said, "Now here's what we do here. We got a dressing room, and we got a place where the ballplayers can sleep. We got a cot, a nice place, and it doesn't cost you a thing, in a situation like this. You go sleep here this night. I'll talk to you in the morning."

I was pretty down. It was about 2:00 or 3:00 in the morning. I was going to get up early that next morning. But while I was lying there in the Longview dressing room, I felt water dropping on my face. I was lying there on this cot. I looked up, and there was sky up there. I wondered what in the heck was going on. One guy nearby was white as a sheet. I said,

"What's the matter with you?" but he didn't say anything. I got my clothes on and walked outside. A tornado had hit the ballpark that night or early that morning and had torn part of the roof off the grandstand, torn the double fences all the way down, and torn the light poles, twisted them and turned the lights outside. And I had slept through it. Then the Longview manager told me that he couldn't use me, but that Texarkana could. He said they were going to head over to Texarkana and play them. They had to transfer the games there because of the tornado damage. He had called the Texarkana Liners and found that they needed another player. I said, "OK."

So over to Texarkana I went the next day, and, boy, I had a good time with that club. They were still in the East Texas League. I played center field in that ballpark, and I really enjoyed it. I loved Texas. Maybe I should have been a Texan. We had a manager by the name of Abe Miller, a veteran pitcher. I guess he was in his late thirties, maybe even forty. He was a wonderful manager. He'd wear me down in the outfield whenever he pitched, because he'd lost his best stuff, and I'd be chasing down a lot of hits. One day I think I made about seven or eight circus catches in center field. When I came in after the last one, Abe said, "Hey, kid, you're kind of playing a little shallow, aren't you?" I didn't know at first that he was kidding me. His nickname was "Payday" Miller because when he was with the Shreveport team in the Texas League, the owner would sell Abe to Minneapolis in the American Association and get enough money to meet the payroll of the Shreveport ball club. Abe would pitch up there for a month, and then they'd send him back down. This went on for two or three years, and that's why they called him "Payday" Miller. Abe liked me, and I liked playing there. He said, "Kid, you're going to do all right." One day he told me that the Detroit Tigers were going to have a working agreement with Texarkana the next year and I was one reason why. He urged me to play like heck when I came back the next year.

I had always wanted to catch a ball in foul territory *from center field*. In 1940 with Texarkana, I got my chance. In one game a high fly headed for the left-field foul line. There was a little breeze blowing toward left. I raced over there and called off our left fielder, Gordie Huston (who became a fighter pilot and was one of the first pro ballplayers to lose his life in World War II), and I made the running catch with both feet in foul ground. I prided myself on that, and I think I got into *Ripley's Believe It or Not* somewhere. Abe Miller chewed me out again. He said, "Kid, you're not supposed to play that position out there. You've got center field." But I was a rambunctious player. Every time we had a rundown, from the day I started playing professional baseball, I was always in the infield, backing up rundown plays. One game

I ended up covering home plate. We had a guy between second and third on a pick-off play. I came charging in toward second base. We failed to execute properly, and the runner headed for third base and got in there safely. I kept going and headed across the pitcher's mound to home plate. The guy at third decided to break for home while our guys were goofing around with poor throws. We got him on another rundown between third and home. I was standing on home plate, and the guy who had the ball at third overthrew the other guy in the rundown play. It came right to me. I just snagged it and tagged the guy out. When the inning was over, Abe Miller said, "Kid, I'm telling you something. I don't want my outfielders in on that rundown play." He had a great sense of humor. In another game, I came close to pulling off an unassisted triple play. I caught a dying quail to right-center and noticed the runner on second had broken for third and was stumbling trying to get back. I raced to second for the force out and then saw the runner from first was in between first and second. Our first baseman had come down to second to cover, so I chased the runner back toward first. He beat me back to the base, or else I would have had an unassisted triple play.

I saw a couple of crazy incidents that year in the East Texas League. When I was still playing for Palestine, I was playing center field one game in Tyler. On one of the fences, they had a big wire basket, probably four or five feet across. A local jeweler advertised, "Hit a ball in here and win a watch or a diamond ring." I saw a guy named George Kovach hit one in it, and he took the watch. The fans got a big kick out of that. But that particular game, we had had a big rainstorm during the day, and we were playing at night. There was kind of a swale, a little dip out there in right-center, and the water was flowing right down in there. We had a little pond, maybe thirty feet across with about a foot of water. A guy hit a ball out there, and I tramped over into the water and caught it. But the funniest part of that game was when their center fielder tried to field a drive in that water. One of our guys hit a line drive over the second baseman's head, and it rolled right into that pond. The center fielder saw it going over there, and he made a run and took a dive, a belly flopper, right into the water. He was swimming, and, of course, it was only about a foot deep. He finally got the ball and held it up in the air, triumphantly like he'd just made a great play. Our guy got a triple out of it. But it was the funniest thing I'd seen in an awful long time.

Speaking of water, what would you think of a bunch of players who ended up getting a bus stuck in a lake on a picnic outing? When I was playing for Texarkana in 1940, we had a game scheduled at Marshall. We were going to play a game Saturday and a Sunday afternoon game and then drive over to Longview or Tyler, wherever was the next stop on the road trip. Abe Miller would give us the Sunday evening off to do whatever we wanted. We heard about a picnic happening after the game out at a local lake, but we didn't have any transportation out to the lake. Claude "Bob" Williams, my roommate, said leave it to him. We knew the keys to the team bus were hanging above the hotel desk. Bob said he would distract the clerk so I could grab the keys. So we did and off we drove to the lake. I was the driver, even though I didn't even have a driver's license and had never driven a bus before. We had the directions, and I was in the driver's seat of the bus, and Bob was sitting right in the front seat. We managed to drive the four or five miles out to the lake. There were the girls and some other couples already having a great time. They had a diving board out in the middle of the lake. We had put our bathing suits on before we left the hotel. I said to Bob, the last guy out there is a so-and-so, and, boy, I just parked the bus and jumped out, off went my shoes and off went my shirt and pants, as I ran down the hill right into the lake. I swam out to the diving board platform. Actually Bob beat me, because he was a better swimmer.

We were all having a grand time at the picnic, laughing and carrying on the raft in the lake. Other ballplayers were there, including some from the Marshall team, but we were the only two from Texarkana. Suddenly we heard a strange set of noises. We looked over our shoulders, and there was that bus lurching down the slope toward the water. I had forgotten to set the emergency brake. The bus nosed into the lake, about halfway submerged, water right up over the hood, and then it stopped. Holy cow! What were we going to do? How were we going to get out of this mess? "Well," I said, "Heck, let's swim. We'll think of something later." Bob said, "Yeah, we're going to get in trouble." All the other couples and the kids that were around there were all laughing about it, and we were having a good time. We had chicken, and then some of the guys had beer and cokes. Finally it was time for us to think about getting back. It was kind of getting dark. Eventually we found a farmer who hitched his horses up to the bus and pulled it out. That little calamity cost us five bucks for the tow. We had to wait half an hour for the water to drain out, but luckily the engine started right up and we were able to drive it back to town.

We parked the bus behind the hotel and left all the windows down. The next morning, when we went to travel on to the next town, the bus was still sopping wet. Guys started complaining immediately about the wet seats. Abe Miller, who was last to sit down after checking the players onto the bus, felt the wet seat and started swearing at us. He said, "Gosh darn it, how many times do I need to tell you guys to put those windows up so the rain don't come in and ruin this? Dang it, this is the last time. I'll have you working out at 9:00 in the morning." By this time a couple of guys knew what happened and we were all snickering, but we never did tell him. But then again there had been no rain for days. We suspected that Abe knew what had happened.

Hanging around with minor leaguers could get risky at times. We were getting back to Texarkana from Marshall about 2:00 one morning after a night game. In that part of the country, they had a lot of watermelon patches. Being from Pennsylvania, I had never seen a watermelon patch. I said, "Why don't we get one of those watermelons?" The guys said, "Oh, heck, these farmers have shotguns. They'll get us pretty good." I was sitting in the back of the bus. Suddenly one guy said, "Oh, look at that watermelon patch!" Because I could run like heck, they nominated me to go in the watermelon patch. They told me how to "plug" a watermelon by making a triangle-shaped cut, pulling out the piece, holding it up to the moonlight to see if it was dark in color. Somebody gave me a little pocketknife, and we pulled over by the side of this field. There was a little farmhouse, with a porch light on, right over across the road, maybe fifty yards away. The guys told me to hurry. I asked, "How many should I get?" They said, "Well, get two of the biggest ones." I plugged one, and it was all right. Then I plugged another, and it wasn't any good, so I reached over and I got another one. Somebody started yelling, "Come on! Come on!" I grabbed both watermelons and put one under each arm. All of a sudden, I heard baboom! baboom! Shotgun pellets were raining on the bus. The bus started taking off, and I came running out of that field across that little gully on the side of the road. The guys were shouting out the window, "Come on, Charlie!" I was running like heck, and the bus was moving. I got over pretty close and handed one of the melons to a guy standing in the well on the front of the bus. I handed the other one through a window. I heard more shotgun blasts, but I was out of range by that time. I didn't know you could outrun shotgun pellets, but I did. The guys were all laughing at me as I was running down that darn road. Maybe about a quarter of a mile down the road, they stopped and let me back on. Heck, they had broken the watermelons up, and I only got a small bite. But I finally got a taste of watermelon from eastern Texas. I never did forgive the guys. I started to pull all kind of jokes on the guys after that, but they had the best of me. I'm still mad at them!

My roommate, as I said, was Bob Williams. Bob had been with us at

Mayfield in the Kitty League. He was a left-handed relief pitcher. One time while we were at Texarkana, he said to me, "Charlie, you're going to go somewhere in baseball. You ought to learn to speak in public." I said, "Heck, I don't know anything about public speaking." He was determined I'd learn. He'd buy a *Reader's Digest*, and after the ball game at night, we'd go up to the room after having a bite to eat, and he'd lie there in bed in his pajamas and say, "OK, read to me." So I'd read those funny stories and jokes and stuff out of *Reader's Digest*. Half the time I couldn't pronounce the words, and I never got the right meaning and the right "yuk" on the punchline of a joke, so he'd make me tell them all over again. I never did thank him for that, but later on in my baseball life I became a manager, and public speaking came in handy. I got where I could make an after-dinner speech without blushing. I sure did appreciate Bob Williams's making me learn that stuff.

In the East Texas League at that time was a guy by the name of Leo "Muscle" Schoals. Muscle played first base for the Marshall team, and, gosh, could he hit! He was one of the most feared left-handed hitters I'd ever seen in my life. I wondered what in the world was this guy doing down here, and I never did find out why he was still in the C league. To this day I still correspond with him. There were some other pretty good ballplayers in the league. Eddie Lopat pitched for Marshall for a little better than a half a year and then went up to Oklahoma City in the Texas League. He ended up being one hell of a pitcher for the Yankees. He had a change-up that was slow, another one that was slower still, and another one that was slower and slower. They said that he threw the alphabet pitch, one with twenty-six different speeds. Ted Williams said that he was one of the toughest pitchers he faced. I could hit Ed pretty well. I didn't hit very many guys, but I could hit left-handed pitching pretty well. I always kidded him in later years that if I'd hit him like that when I was with Detroit and Philadelphia, I would have been there still.

After the season that winter, I went out to California. Bob Williams lived there. I went out there with him, and I played some games in a winter league in San Diego. I played a few games against some of the big leaguers who lived out in that part of California. I got a job at San Diego with the Denstead Construction Company. We built homes. I was a carpenter. I really enjoyed that, but my arm stiffened up from all the hammering and sawing, and it took a month into spring training before it loosened up. I worked for Consolidated Aircraft. I inspected instrument panels on the B-24 bombers. While I was in San Diego, I registered for the draft. A pilot I met said I should join the American Eagle Squadron. I knew a little bit about that squadron, but he told me all about it and offered to give me flying lessons. So I took five flying lessons with him in one of those light planes. I didn't know too much about the instruments at all, and, boy, I had a dandy landing. I think I bounced a dozen times. I thought the plane was going to come apart. Amazingly, the instructor passed me, and I went up to March Field near Los Angeles and enlisted in the American Eagle Squadron. But when they did a security check on me, probably because my real name, Moreskonich, sounded kind of foreign, they found out that I'd been in that gas explosion back in Nanty-Glo. They said that I would have a cranial trauma. I didn't know what the heck that was, but that's why they discharged me.

Out in California I also took some jujitsu lessons from a Japanese instructor. He worked me over pretty good, but he also taught me quite a bit about self-defense and balance and mostly quickness of the eye. These things were a help to me because in baseball, especially hitting, you had to pick up the ball real quick. Then when the season started rolling around, I got itchy to play ball. But the aircraft company wouldn't let workers go easily. I talked the supervisor into letting me go back and play ball. He was a baseball man and managed to get me released. I got back to Texarkana a week or two before spring training started. Texarkana was an independent club in the Cotton States League that year.

In the meantime I had been corresponding with Helen Deane Bullock back in Mayfield. Just before Christmas, I had written her and said I'd like to send her a present. If she didn't like it, she wouldn't have to keep it. I had bought an engagement ring out in San Diego. I can't quite remember how much I paid for it. I believe it was ninety or ninety-five dollars, and I put thirty or thirty-five dollars down. I still owed quite a bit, and I was still paying five dollars a month on it. I sent it to her. I said, "If you don't want it, just send it back, and if you do, I want to know what finger you're going to wear it on." When she wrote back, she said it was on the third finger of her left hand, which I found out was the proper finger for an engagement ring. We set the wedding date for April 3. So I was feeling pretty good when spring training came around. But because I got away from San Diego so late, I didn't have time to go back to Mayfield before spring training. Helen had to come down to Texarkana. I sent her twenty-five dollars for the bus fare, but she didn't spend it. Her folks brought her down to Texarkana.

The day Helen arrived, April 3, we were due to play an exhibition game with the St. Louis Browns, who were barnstorming back toward St. Louis, from out in California or Texas. I went down to the field and talked with a couple of Browns players that I knew from the camp in Belleville, Illinois—

John Berardino, the second baseman, and Don Heffner, the shortstop. They knew that I had roomed with Vern Stephens at Mayfield. They told me the Browns had sent him to San Antonio, just before they came to Texarkana. So I was down on the field, and here came this bouncy thing in her white saddle shoes and her swirly skirt. I was standing out there by the third base line, talking to Berardino and Heffner, when she jumped me and grabbed me around the neck and hugged me, and we kissed. "Don't we have a date?" she asked. I said, "Yeah," and I was red as fire. Don Heffner said, "Boy, you young guys sure get around. You sure got the touch." I said, "Well, I'm going to get married." They asked, "When?" I said, "At 3:00." Berardino said, "Why the hell don't you get out of here?" Years later I saw John, who went on to become a fine actor, at a Dodgers game. He didn't recognize me at first, but he laughed when I reminded him of that wedding day. I also bumped into Heffner in the late 1970s or early 1980s, when he was a ticket seller at the mutuel betting window at Hollywood Park, but I forgot to bring it up with him. So off Helen and I went. I went back to my room and changed clothes. I had made arrangements with a local preacher. We were married at the chapel. I didn't have anybody stand up for me—I didn't tell any of the ballplayers—but she had her longtime friend Sara Hackney, from Mayfield, as her maid of honor. Helen's kid sister was there, as were her mom and dad. Jake Atz Jr., the manager of the team, raised my salary the next day to $120 a month and bought us two $7.50 meal tickets as a wedding present. We lived that year in Texarkana, in an apartment over a garage, and we darned near froze to death when it got cold.

Married life caught up with me a bit by midseason, I'm a little embarrassed to admit. I used an Ernie Lombardi bat, which was thirty-six inches long and weighed thirty-five ounces. I'd been used to the big-handled picks and shovels in the coal mine. They fit in my hands better than the thin-handled bats. So I had this big bat, and, boy, I was hitting like heck. By midseason I was hitting I think about .380, had 16 home runs, and about 85 runs batted in. I made the All-Star team. Then, for some unknown reason, my hitting fell off. I couldn't swing that bat very well. I could still run and field and everything else. But that bat got heavy. I'd gotten married, and it was hot down in that country, and the married life was good. But that bat was getting heavy, and I wound up hitting .287 and knocking only 3 more home runs and driving in only 6 more runs after the All-Star break. The players started kidding me about that, and one day after I'd been gone a week, I found some wise guy had sawn an inch off the fat end of my bat. I still continued to slump. I was having a heck of a time, shaking my head. I couldn't figure out what was going wrong. The next time I came out to the ballpark, a few days later, there was another inch cut off my bat. They kept sawing an inch off. By the time they got through with it, it was down to about thirty-two inches. Boy, I had a hard time living that one down. They'd all laugh at me and say, "Married life caught up with you."

As an outfielder, I always had speed and a pretty strong throwing arm. Once I won a contest by throwing the ball from the center-field fence to home, something like four hundred feet. I liked to show off these abilities whenever I could. I always wanted to throw a base runner out at first from center field. In a game in 1941, I pulled it off. J. P. Wood of Henderson, the Tigers farm club, was at bat. He was a little guy but tough as nails. He had played quarterback at Rice University. I had already robbed him of a hit to center field. I knew J. P. well enough that I would shade him toward right field and even cheat a step or two before his swing. Sure enough, he lined what should have been a single to right-center. I could hear him laughing, as if he were saying "Catch that one." I played it cleanly and rifled a throw to the first baseman, Charlie Bates. The peg caught J. P. nonchalanting it down to the base. He chased me all over the ballpark after that. He spent a lot of time cussing at me that day. That continued later, when we both got up to Detroit.

No matter where you go, you can't please everybody. That year I had one guy in Helena, Arkansas, that heckled me over and over. I made the All-Star team, and I played hard. I never gave anybody any chance to criticize me. But this guy would give me holy heck. He pronounced my name "Me-tro." He would say, "Me-tro, but me can't hit it." And that got to me. I could hear him. I'd be in the outfield, and here came, "Me-tro, but me can't hit it." Shortly after that, I needed a haircut. I went down to the barber shop—you could get a haircut for half a buck then—and sat down. I kept looking at the guy in the mirror who was cutting my hair, and I said to myself, "Yeah, I've seen this guy somewhere." Eventually the barber asked me, "Hey, by the way, what's your name? Are you new in town?" And I said, "Yeah, I play baseball." He said, "You do? What's your name?" I said, "Me-tro, but me can't hit it." He was scared and ran into the back room. I said, "Come on out and finish my haircut." But I was afraid to let him shave me. The funny thing is, we became friends. I used to hear from him. A couple years later when I went up to Detroit, I got a letter from him. He wrote, "I'm the guy that calls you Me-tro."

But it was a wonderful year. I loved playing there. Jake Atz Jr., our manager, was a young guy. His father had been a famous baseball minor league manager. He had changed his name to Atz, because his original name started with a Z. He'd heard that they used to pay the ballplayers alphabetically, so he changed his name to Atz so he'd be first in line for the pay. Young Jake was a wonderful guy. He was very thin and scrawny. He looked funny and he had a small head, so when he would wear the cap, he would pin the back of it. He looked funny as heck in that uniform. He knew the rules by heart. He'd have an argument with an umpire during the game, and he'd run out there, in that uniform that didn't fit, and he'd tear the page that covered the situation right out of the rule book. He was really sharp. I loved him, and I played like heck for him.

After the 1941 season, Helen and I stayed in Texarkana, and I worked on a construction crew building munitions plants, the Lone Star Ordnance Plant and the Red River Ordnance Plant. I got a job in the engineering outfit as a chainman, and then they moved me up to a transit man, which I learned real quickly. We stayed there half the winter. In December we went back to my wife's home, Mayfield, and we stayed the rest of the winter until I was ready to go to the Detroit Tigers' big league camp. I hadn't signed my contract with Beaumont, but they invited me down. I went down to Lakeland, Florida, and trained with the Tigers. Steve O'Neill, who was the manager with Beaumont, asked me, "Charlie, you think you can play in the Texas League?" I said, "Yeah, sure." There were quite a few ballplayers down there. I guess they had about fifty or sixty ballplayers with the Tigers at that time. I made a pretty good showing, so Steve O'Neill took me to Beaumont with him. I loved Steve as a manager. He was great with ballplayers. But he looked like he came from a family of prizefighters. He had a crooked nose and, boy, he'd look at you and you'd hustle. I was so fond of Steve O'Neill that we named our second son, Steve, after him. But in 1942, I was battling for the center-field position. I had had a better season the year before at Texarkana than the three guys who played in the outfield, but it was tough to break into a starting outfield that included Dick Wakefield, Hoot Evers, and Anse Moore.

When they formed the Beaumont club, the Beaumont Exporters, Steve O'Neill took me with them. Helen came down to Beaumont early, and we rented a small house for the season. We had to deal with a bunch of cockroaches in that house, but otherwise I was the happiest guy in the world. I was going to Texas, and I figured I was going to win my job. We had a lot of good ballplayers. Besides Wakefield, Evers, and Moore, we had my old friend J. P. Wood at third and John Lipon at short. John and I roomed together. He was a dead-end sort of kid from up in Michigan. He spoke Polish, and I spoke a little bit myself, being of Ukrainian descent, so we talked some in Polish, even in a game instead of using signs. That may have been the first time I also encountered that open mouth–closed mouth system middle infielders use with their gloves to say who will cover the base on a steal attempt. John loved to play pinball and figured out a way to drill a hole in the machine to ring up the score and win nickels. He was a good, steady ballplayer. He played for the Tigers and became a fine manager, managing until he was in his seventies in Florida. Joe Wessing was our second sacker, and Bill McLaren held down first. Our catchers were Joe Erautt and Harvey Riebe. Our pitching was good, if not great. Stubby Overmire became a good pitcher in his own right. Bob Gillespie was a big, long, lanky guy, the first I'd ever seen who threw from the side. Boy, he was devastating. But he never did reach any kind of success as a big leaguer. Most of those guys went up to the major leagues, and Earl Cook had been up with the Tigers the year before.

Without question, Dick Wakefield was one of the greatest talents that I'd ever seen. As I went along in later years, as a manager, scout, and coach, I'd compare prospects to Dick Wakefield. I recall one particular game with the Beaumont club that has to rank right up there as a player's greatest day. We were playing at Shreveport. The first time up, Wakefield hit a ball over the left-field fence, an opposite-field home run over a double fence. The next time up, he put one out right down the right-field line. The third at bat, he hit one over the center-field fence. Then he hit a ball toward left-center for a double, and he hit a ball into right-center for a double. The sixth time up, he drove a ball into deep right-center, but the center fielder for Shreveport made a heck of a catch, or Wakefield would have had 3 home runs and 3 doubles. I'll never forget it. He was big, six foot four or five. He was an outstanding runner. He had a great arm and could outthrow almost anybody. He could field the ball. And, man, could he hit. He always made contact. He could do everything. But there was a little quirk about him. He didn't have that real pride about all these things that he did. If he had been as intense with his all-around play as he was with his hitting, he would have been one of the greatest players ever.

Wakefield was one of the first "bonus baby" players. He got a lot of money from Detroit. He bought a car for himself and one for his mom. Dick was a nice, likable guy. But what an atrocious dresser! He'd wear a green shirt with purple pants, or orange pants with a red shirt. He loved cigars. In late summer that year in Beaumont, after our daughter, Elena, had been born, my wife and baby were at one of the games. We lived within walking distance of the ballpark. We had no car. We were walking by the clubhouse after the game, and Dick walked over and took a look at our daughter, who was a week or two weeks old. He said to my wife, "I wonder what they're thinking about at that age." My wife still talks about that. He was a good influence on the ball club. Every once in a while I was his caddie, so to speak. We'd be way out in front or something, and Steve O'Neill would send me out to play a couple of innings and spell Dick. But every now and then, we'd look up and the inning would be starting, late in the game, and there would be no Wakefield in right field. He'd taken his glove and gone in the clubhouse right outside the right-field bullpen. He knew I was going to be his caddie. He had a good sense of humor, and he'd say, "Aw, Steven Francis, don't get mad. You've got a guy who can field better than I can. Don't get mad." He'd talk Steve out of his irritation.

Wakefield led the league in hitting practically all year, back and forth with Hoot Evers in center, and Anse Moore was hitting fourth. How was I going to break into that lineup? I did play, mainly as a late-inning defensive replacement for Wakefield. Hoot Evers was a tremendous ballplayer, as he showed later with the Tigers and the Red Sox. And Anse Moore was good. I couldn't break in. Our daughter had been born that August in Beaumont, and I didn't want to leave there, so I played any place Steve O'Neill wanted me to play. I didn't want to be sent out, and Steve didn't send me down. So I played anywhere I could, second base, some shortstop. One game I got a split finger. The regular second baseman's wife was having a baby, and he was having pregnant signs. John Lipon threw a double play ball to me, and I took my eye off it. I had my bare hand close to the glove and bang! the ball split that darn little finger really bad. I hid the injury. I put tape on it and doused it with iodine. I had a chance to play some games, and I wouldn't let the manager know. I played with it hurt. It healed up all right.

I also caught some games. I almost got killed back there. My life was at stake every time, because I didn't know the signs. I was an outfielder. Earl Cook, a veteran pitcher, was pitching, and I asked, "What kind of signs are you going to use?" He said, "You just get back there and pick up the glove, and I'll throw it there." It was a good thing that he would almost hit my glove each time, because I'd have never caught his curve ball. He signaled where he wanted me to put my glove by placing his glove inside or outside his leg, and that was the way I'd move.

I even pitched in a game. At Beaumont, Stubby Overmire got spiked on the heel while covering first base the previous time he pitched. He told Steve that he could pitch and started the game against Shreveport. Stubby was pitching along pretty well, but all of a sudden he started getting hit. Steve O'Neill walked out to the mound to talk to him. Now every once in a while, I'd go down to the bullpen and sit with the guys and warm up the pitcher when they were warming up. Occasionally I'd get on the mound, and for an inning or two I'd crank up, as if I were a pitcher. I'd take my stretch and everything and throw a fastball. I didn't have a curve ball. This particular day when Steve walked out, I was warming up. He looked up, gave me the sign, and waved me in. I looked around and nobody else was warming up, and the catcher, Joe Erautt, said, "He wants you in there." I think I turned pale. I had never pitched in a game before, just in batting practice. The bases were loaded and there were two outs, and Steve brought me in and gave me the ball.

Harvey Riebe, our catcher, came out and said to me, "Now, Charlie, one is a fastball, two is a curve, and the wiggle is a change-up." I said, "What the heck is a wiggle?" I'd been playing center field. I didn't know what the heck the wiggle was. So he turned his back to the hitter and put his hands up, and he just wiggled his fingers. He said, "That's it." I said, "Well, we won't have to worry about that. I don't have a change-up, and I don't have a curve ball either." He said, "Well, that's all right. With your arm we'll throw the ball by this guy." I said, "OK." So he went back behind the plate. We were ahead, 7–4 or 8–5, something like that.

The guy at bat was Vernon George Washington. I might stand corrected on this, but I believe he had the highest lifetime batting average in professional baseball, something like .380 or .386 or somewhere in that outlandish atmosphere of batting. His only weakness was a weak top hand that caused him to throw the bat a lot. During games, while he was at bat, everybody would get down in the dugout, because if he took a hard swing and missed, the bat would come right out of his hands and twirl like a boomerang toward the stands. In Shreveport, during his at bats, the fans all along the first base side would reach over and pull up a four-foot screen to protect everybody.

So no less than Vernon George Washington was up at the plate for my pitching debut. He was a left-handed hitter, and in Beaumont there was always a little breeze coming in from right field. It was very difficult to hit a ball out of that ballpark. I knew that from playing the outfield, and the fences were a little bit deeper there too. So I said to myself, "Well, I'll just blow this ball by this guy." I got the sign from Harvey, one finger down for the fastball, and I took a look around. Then I got on the mound, took my wind up, and bang! I threw a fastball in there just a little bit below the letters. Washington took the pitch for strike one. Oh, boy, I thought, hey, this is pretty good. So I picked up the rosin bag and give it a little flip. The catcher crouched again and gave me the fastball sign again, and I cranked up and threw a pretty good smoker. I had a hell of an arm and I could really throw, but I wasn't a pitcher. This time the ball was a little bit lower, right down the middle, and he took it for strike two. Oh, boy, I thought, this is a snap. Everybody was giving me encouragement. John Lipon was telling me, "Great going." J. P. Wood called time and came over from third base and said, "Don't get careless, don't get cocky, and don't give this guy anything good to hit." I said, "OK." He went back to his position. I took a little time and walked back and got the rosin bag. I dusted off my fingers just like the big pitchers would do, and I tossed it over my shoulder. I thought, "Huh, this guy is going to be a snap. I might even have found a new career." So I cranked up and I threw as good a fastball as I've ever thrown right down the middle. The last thing I saw was that ball going to right field, and the right fielder didn't even turn around. Washington hit that ball as hard as I've seen a ball hit, into the wind. It cleared the fences and rattled around on top of some houses out there. Four runners crossed the plate, and I think I died, nearly fainted on the mound. We lost the lead and the ball game, and I lost the game for Stubby Overmire. He never let me forget it. He would say, "You're never going to relieve my ball game. I'm staying out there if I have to pitch on one leg." The story goes that Vernon George Washington told somebody on their ball club that no bush outfielder was ever going to get him out, and he was right. I somehow got the next guy out, but my ERA for my short-lived pitching career skyrocketed to 27.00.

Luckily my fielding was better than my pitching. One day in the Texas League, I made a combination of plays that the manager, Steve O'Neill, told about many times, even after he went up to the majors. Our center fielder, Hoot Evers, had pulled a groin muscle in this particular game. I replaced him in center. We were playing Tulsa at Beaumont. The center field fence was 405 feet dead center. Tulsa had a man on second base, and he was the winning run. There was one out. The next hitter hit a long fly ball out to center field, a little bit to left-center, toward the green fence background in center field. I turned tail, and I ran and ran and ran. Lord, I thought I was running for an hour. I finally got there, turned around, and caught the ball over my shoulder on the left side, two steps from the wall. I took the ball out of the glove as I was running, and I pushed off the wall. The runner at second base was a little bit off the bag toward third, thinking I wasn't going to catch the ball. He was just walking from there. When he saw I caught the ball, he came back and tagged up. I swung around, pushed off the fence, and threw the ball on the fly to third base. J. P. Wood just stood there at third as a great decoy, and when the guy slid in, he slapped the tag on him for a double play. I made a great catch and threw it on the fly. It saved the game as I recall, and I heard Steve O'Neill tell about it a dozen times. But nowadays you see guys going up over the top of the fence and catching balls nearly every game.

Travel conditions back in the minors were tough but fun at the same time. We traveled a lot by bus. They'd call it the Bus League. Some ball clubs had station wagons. Some had trucks. The buses were like school buses. They had low ceilings. You had to sit sideways and bend your neck to keep from bumping your head. The tall guys had a heck of a time! The guys that didn't do much in the game or had the fewest hits in the series had to fix the flat tires. And we had quite a few of them! But we had a lot of fun on the buses. Later we looked back on it and marveled how we traveled like that. We traveled at night right after a ball game. The clubs tried to save money on hotels. Right after the game, we'd pack our uniforms, put all our stuff in one pantleg and put rubber bands on the ends. We didn't have any duffel bags. You had to take care of your own uniform, hang your sweatshirts up, and wash your sweat socks.

Boy, were those uniforms hot down in those eastern Texas summers! In Texarkana in 1940, we got the hand-me-down uniforms from Beaumont. They were solid red, flannel uniforms with white lettering. One club, I can't recall which, had black uniforms. In 1941 and 1942, we had standard white home and gray road uniforms. Players would come close to fainting in all that wool. I did see one pitcher pass out from the heat. We were playing Oklahoma City in Beaumont one afternoon. Bill Voiselle, who later went up to the Giants, was walking off the mound about the sixth inning, after a long inning. He wobbled as if he were walking on air and passed out right at the foul line. They revived him right there. The uniforms were hot enough, but they always wanted you to wear a sweatshirt, usually made of wool, underneath.

Back to travel, when you got to the Texas League, you graduated to riding the trains. They called it the Train League. They'd tie us on the back end of a cattle train going from the northern cities, Dallas and Ft. Worth and Oklahoma City and Tulsa, down to Beaumont. Those cattle would moo and bawl the whole night or whole day long, and they didn't smell too good either. The city guys would complain. But it was enjoyable, and we'd get into Beaumont on schedule. Every once in a while, they couldn't get a Pullman, so we'd have to travel in a chair car and sit up in the seats. The manager would sit right up front. The coaches would sit up there. On a sleeper, the manager would get the private room on a Pullman. The coaches were like the ballplayers, low-class citizens. They'd make the coaches sit up or sleep in the upper berth. Because the distances were so great, sometimes we'd have to stay in hotels. At Shreveport we stayed in the Railroad Hotel. They put us on the second floor. They didn't have air conditioning in those days, and very few rooms had fans in that grade of a hotel. So we raised the windows, and sometime in the middle of the night the train would come rattling through. You could almost touch the train from the hotel, and you should have seen that smoke coming into the rooms. The track was between buildings. We'd have a heck of a time with that, but it was an experience, one more incentive to get to the big leagues in a hurry.

One time we had some real unusual transportation, U.S. Army tanks. We had a couple of exhibition games at an army base, Camp Polk, Louisiana. We were barnstorming back through there from Jacksonville. We played the Camp Polk team. They put two or three of us in the tanks and gave us a ride for a little maneuver. It was their idea. God, we got dusty and dirty, and those tank guys got a big kick out of it. There we were, dressed in our sport coats, sport shirts, pants, and fancy shoes, and they took us through the mud and dirt and everything. They gave us a good going-over.

About that time at Beaumont, I started thinking about managing. I would sit there and watch Steve O'Neill make all these moves. I started thinking, what would you do in this situation, how do you do this, how do you do that? I would coach first base too and he'd coach third, and then a couple of times he let me coach third. I enjoyed all aspects of that. It proved valuable to me in later years when I was managing. I could teach a few players some things. I always tried to pick a guy's brain, and I've had young managers do that to me too. I did the same thing, and I'd pass it on. And I was a fan all the time. I was an open-mouthed, wide-eyed fan. I recall seeing the great Paul Dean, Dizzy's brother, pitching for Houston for a while. I'd see a good ballplayer on a ball club, and I'd try to see why he was good and try to imitate him. This was especially the case at Beaumont and in the Texas League, where quite a few of the ballplayers went on to the big leagues. I watched Steve O'Neill and the other managers who had played in the majors.

I got to see the Hall of Famer Rogers Hornsby manage at Ft. Worth that year. He was a pretty good manager, but perhaps he was too good a ballplayer to manage the guys that you have to manage at that level. But what an exhibition he'd put on in batting practice! I'd come out early in Ft. Worth, and he'd have somebody out there throwing batting practice to him. He was in his forties, but he put on one of the darnedest exhibitions of hitting that I've ever seen. Hornsby would say, "Right field," and hit a ball to right field. He'd say, "Left-field line," and hit it there. Or he'd say, "In the alley, left-center-field alley," and he'd hit a line drive out there. Or "Here's a long one," and he'd jack one out of the ballpark. He never missed the ball. Of course, it was batting practice, but, heck, a lot of guys, including myself, would swing and miss the ball, or pop it up or nub it down in the dirt during batting practice. I got to ask him about why he wouldn't go to a movie or read a newspaper. He told me it was bad for the eyes. He didn't want to squint and put too much strain on his eyes. He would sit around in the lobby, and he'd talk baseball forever.

Our Beaumont club won the pennant. We had Shreveport down 3 games to 1 in the playoffs. We were expecting to be the Texas League champions and play the Southern League champions in a series. We had our bags packed. It looked like each player would get a hundred dollars, maybe two hundred dollars, in playoff money. But Shreveport shut us out 3 straight games. Gordon Maltzberger beat us twice. In later years I saw Gordie, when I was with the White Sox, and I said, "You son of a gun." He said, "What's the matter?" We had had a baby buggy picked out for our daughter with the playoff money. I said, "You cost us our baby buggy for my daughter." He laughed. He said, "Oh, no, you don't want to hit an old man." We were in our late forties or fifties. I said, "Well, I ought to." We laughed at that. So when we finished the season—and it had been a good year—Steve O'Neill said, "Charlie, you'll go to spring training with us next year." We went home to Mayfield, where I got a job as an inspector in a munitions plant, did a little hunting, and waited to see what the next spring would bring.

THREE

Up with Detroit and Philadelphia

After the Beaumont season in 1942, Helen and I and our baby daughter, Elena, went back to Mayfield to let the grandparents see their new grand-daughter. I had a job down in Beaumont for a month, but we wanted to go back up to Kentucky. About twelve miles away from Mayfield, in Viola, they were building a munitions plant and hiring a lot of people. I got a job as an inspector at the National Fireworks Plant. They made twenty-millimeter ammunition for anti-aircraft guns. I was the chief inspector. Nobody else seemed to know anything about it, but I had had experience working with explosives in the coal mines. I had about thirty people, a couple of crews, working under me, who were unloading components for the shells for the ammunition, which we could fill with powder and petrol and other explosives. I was also a quality-control inspector on the assembly line. I was working a lot of extra hours and making $150 to $200, sometimes even $300, a week.

Many of the guys on my crews were African-Americans. They still remembered me from the year I played at Mayfield. I was one of their favorites. When they found out that I was their boss, I was their hero. They called me "Mr. Charlie." The plant we worked at was on eight square miles of bottom land that was farmed. The government bought it and built the plant with the assembly lines and everything. They put a chain-link fence around the whole works. You couldn't have a fire or a garden in the plant. The rabbit population exploded inside this fence, without any hunting to control them. You couldn't shoot a gun on the plant grounds. This was farmland with a lot of corn, turnips, beans, and everything planted, and the animal population just zoomed. The black guys hunted them. They would get a hickory stick about twenty-five inches long, with a big railroad bolt on the end of it, and go down there rabbit hunting. They'd chase the rabbits out of the brush and take the stick and wham! throw it and bring them down. The stick would hit the rabbits on the legs, and the guys would run over there and catch them. They'd do this often at noon. One time they were about twenty minutes late getting back to work. I said, "What the heck were you guys doing?" I was the foreman. But a friend of mine there said, "Oh, Charlie, don't be too harsh on them. They'll bring fried rabbit the next day for you." I said, "You're kidding? They will?" I'd never had fried rabbit. So the next day I joined them. They ate their lunch real quick, and out they went into the cornfields and the briar brushes and down in the creek bottoms. They'd run around there, and those rabbits would come out of that brush and off they'd go. I said, "Hey, I want to do this." So they gave me a stick and off we went. They told me to wait until the rabbit zigs. You can't hit them when they're running away. So I waited and boom! I got one. I didn't want to take it home, so I gave it to one of the black guys. We would get fifty or a hundred rabbits at noon. The next day the black guys would bring fried rabbit that their wives had cooked up, and they all insisted I try it. That fried rabbit was great. I stayed in shape that spring by chasing rabbits. People didn't quite believe me when I told them that.

But I still had bigger plans than working in a munitions factory and chasing down rabbits. I was determined to play major league baseball. Steve O'Neill had told me at Beaumont that I would go to the Detroit Tigers' spring training camp. He liked my hustle and versatility. He'd give me a shot at going up to Detroit. Steve got the manager's job at Detroit in 1943, so I figured my chances were improving. I received my contract in January, but it was for only $1,800 a year. A lot of the ballplayers were leaving for the service, but I had a deferment because I was in that gas blast in the coal mine back in Pennsylvania. I felt that, heck, I wasn't going to go in the service right away, and I wanted a better contract. I was making quite a bit more money at the plant. I fired back a letter to the Tigers' general manager, Jack Zeller. It's worth quoting the original text of that letter:

January 31, 1943
Mr. Jack Zeller
Briggs Stadium
Detroit, Michigan
Dear Jack:
Received the contract and was rather surprised. I was always under the impression that Detroit was a Major League Club, so you can imagine the set back I received when I read the minor League Contract you offered me. I am returning it with the expectation of receiving one for $4,000 per season.

In your letter you pointed out the things I have not done well in the past, seems that you have overlooked an important fact, a fact that under the circumstances I did a dam [*sic*] good job and I know it. I don't have to exploit my last season's achievements because you already have that information, but keep in mind that I am a *ballplayer* first and last and not a *record* player, also that major league baseball is still major league baseball and provided that I am not of major league caliber and that I don't have the guts, determination, fighting spirit, and self confidence in my own ability as a ballplayer your organization or your future plans, then, Jack, just speak frankly.

I have a good job and don't intend leaving without some encouragement.

Very truly yours,

Charles Metro Moreskonich

Assistant Chief Inspector

Whoops! I waited and waited and waited. Maybe I wasn't going to get a raise. I had already come up against Jack Zeller the previous spring when I was with Beaumont. I had overheard him and Rip Radcliff arguing like hell over Rip's contract, calling each other names and stuff. Rip left in a huff, swearing at Zeller under his breath. Then Jack came out of his office and saw me sitting there. "What the hell do you want?" he shouted. I made my case that because I'd had a good year at Beaumont, I should get a raise to $300 a month. He countered with $200, but down at spring training, I got him to raise it to $250. So I didn't know what to expect. At last, near the end of February, I finally got a letter from Zeller. He wrote, "You cocky son-of-a-bitch, I hope you're as good as you think you are. Here's your contract." The contract was for $3,600. He doubled the $1,800 original offer. I thought, oh, boy, this was going to be all right, as I signed that contract and sent it back.

Spring training was at Evansville, Indiana, that year, because they had to train north of the Mason-Dixon Line. President Franklin Roosevelt had allowed baseball to continue, regardless who played, to boost the morale of the country, but there were still some wartime restrictions, such as where spring training could be. So in the spring I went up to Evansville. Gosh, it was cold and snowy there. We stayed at the McCurdy Hotel, which was right on the Ohio River. The river was at flood stage and washed stuff up on the lawn. We exercised in a big conference room up on the mezzanine floor. The whole ball club would get in that room and do calisthenics. We had to wear a coat and tie all the time, but we'd take the coat off and do push-ups, jumping up and down, hand sprats, and everything else. That was our spring training until the sun came out a bit and dried up the snow and some of the ice. Then we moved outside to the old Evansville ballpark. Evansville had a team in a B league. We dressed at the ballpark. It was a nice stadium, but in left field there was a little slope that went down to the fence and the water drained off there. Overnight it would freeze into a pond you could skate on. You should have seen the guys trying to catch a fly ball down the left-field line and running on that ice. And then we'd have snow flurries. But nobody seemed to complain about that. The weather wasn't good, but we got in shape. The weather didn't get much better by the start of the season. We opened in a sleet storm in Detroit in 1943. We played the game. There was almost an inch of sleet on the grass in the outfield. Somebody would get a hit, and the ball would roll out there like a snowball picking up wet snow.

Spring training with the Tigers was a thrill. I had a good spring. But I always was in good condition. I did an awful lot of running. I was excited about the players I met when I got to Evansville. Virgil Trucks, Dizzy Trout, Hal Newhouser, Tommy Bridges, John Gorsica, and Hal White were all on the pitching staff. Rudy York, Mike "Pinky" Higgins, Roger "Doc" Cramer, and Paul Richards all were there. Except for Hank Greenberg, who was in the military, these were most of the same guys who later took the Tigers to a World Series championship in 1945. There was a guy named Jimmy Outlaw, who was more or less my competition. And, of course, Steve O'Neill was giving a bunch of us guys from Beaumont a chance, namely Stubby Overmire, Hoot Evers, Dick Wakefield, and J. P. Wood. I met a lot of people I never thought I'd meet. The great Honus Wagner was coaching Pittsburgh at the time, when they trained at Terre Haute. I had a baseball for him to autograph, but I thought it would be an imposition, so I didn't ask him. I've regretted that ever since. Ted Lyons, of the White Sox, was right there at French Lick Springs, Indiana, or someplace like that. It was a joy and a delight. I was always a fan, impressed and excited about meeting all these legendary players. Best of all for me, I survived the cut and went north with the ball club.

I didn't play much in 1943, but I did everything again for Steve O'Neill except make the bats. My strong point was that I could play everywhere, and Steve brought me up for that reason. I took the place of two other guys. I threw batting practice, I worked out in the infield, and I worked out in the outfield. So I was kind of valuable to the ball club, and I could run like heck. I pinch-ran a lot. Rip Radcliff was on the ball club. He was a pretty good left-handed hitter. He had hit well for several years with the White Sox, but by 1943 he was about through. When you got to be thirty years old, you were supposedly through in the big leagues. Rip was well up there, at age thirty-seven, but he could sure hit. But he couldn't run, so I was his legs. Any time Rip would pinch-hit and get on base, Steve would boom out, "Charlie, you get down there and run." I scored a few runs that way.

Indeed I loved to run, and I loved to slide. In 1943 I was in a race with four of the fastest guys around the league. Leon Culberson of the Red Sox won the race. Eddie Lake, Dick Wakefield, and another guy I can't recall finished ahead of me. I'd tell everybody in that race it took four pretty good guys to beat me. And, boy, was I a sliding fool. *Baseball* magazine, August 1944, used a photograph of me sliding into third base at Fenway Park past third baseman Jim Tabor. And as the title of this book says, I was safe by a mile! *Baseball* also ran a picture of me sliding into home against the Yankees in 1945. Perhaps my best slide was against the White Sox in 1943. I was on second and came around third on a base hit and slid past the catcher, Mike Tresh, and reached back and touched the plate with the point of my finger. The umpire, whom I seem to remember was Bill McGowan, called me safe and said, "My, that was a dainty tag."

In the majors I had a lot to learn. Sometimes I could be pretty green. One afternoon some of the other Tigers persuaded me to try some chewing tobacco. Players chewed a lot and would try to spit on the back of one another's sanitary socks. That was supposed to be funny. I had never chewed before. I placed a wad in my cheek before the game and didn't think about it when O'Neill sent me in to run for Rip Radcliff. The next hitter slapped a liner to right field. I zoomed around second and slid safely into third. I stood up, dusting myself off. The next guy hit a fly ball. I tagged up and scored. I came in to the bench, and all of sudden I was feeling sick. Paul Richards came over to me and said that I did a great job going from first to third and then scoring on the fly ball, which wasn't very deep. He looked at me and asked, "What's the matter with you?" I said, "Nothing." I was feeling woozy. I was turning green, and Steve O'Neill came up to me and asked, "Charlie, what's the matter?" "I don't know, Steve. I was chewing tobacco, and I don't know what happened," I said. He said, "You better go in the clubhouse." I went in there and passed out on the trainer's table. They had to pop the tobacco out of me. During the slide, I had swallowed the tobacco wad! I had to leave the game, and the guys ribbed me quite a bit. I never touched the stuff again. That gave a new meaning to the phrase "green as a rookie."

Some guys gave me certain initiations as a rookie. Joe Kuhel was a first baseman at Washington at that time and a fine fielder. He taught me something about how you play. I was playing for Detroit, and I hit a ball to the infield in the hole. I came running down to first base and was bearing down fast on the bag. Joe had been a regular first baseman quite a few years, so he stuck his foot out over the bag, and I broke my stride. I missed the bag because I didn't want to step on his foot or his ankle. I was furious with him, and I said, "The next time I come down here you better not be close to the bag; I'm a smart-ass punk kid." And I would have if I'd had another chance. But I did have one occasion to throw a hip at him. I threw a hip at him one time, but he was smart enough and veteran enough to get out of the way. I remember him for doing that stuff. I broke my stride, I missed the bag, and I was out. I learned to play smarter. When you came up to the big leagues, heck, you were on your own. It was sink or swim. If you didn't know it, you'd better learn it by observing and watching a veteran ballplayer or else watching the opposition.

When I was with Detroit, I got a quick introduction to sunglasses. Heck, I'd never worn sunglasses. I'd never had a pair of sunglasses. I'd played in the minor leagues mostly at night, nearly all the time. There were no sunglasses. In day games, I learned to shade my eyes with my glove or turn away from the sun. Then, all of a sudden, I had to use sunglasses, and I didn't know how. I learned in a hurry. I misplayed a fly ball on a sunny day at Comiskey Park in right field with Hal Newhouser pitching. It dropped in. I picked up the ball, and luckily I threw out Thurman Tucker, who was a speedy outfielder for the White Sox, at second base. When the inning was over, I came in, and Newhouser said to me, "If he'd have been safe, I'd kill you." So I learned. You had to practice, putting them on the bill of your cap and flipping them down. If you didn't do it right, if you kept flipping them, by that time the ball went by you. It took a little bit of practice.

Along about this time, while sitting on the bench I'd get the scorecard and keep score. I would count the pitches the pitcher made, and I'd put it down each pitch as a fastball or a curve ball, and I'd put down what the batter hit. One time Dizzy Trout was pitching, and I was keeping score for him. Out on the end of the score line, I would put how many pitches were made. I'd total the pitches up as the innings went along. I got to where I could almost tell when a guy was getting tired. He'd be in the sixth inning and he'd have made 110 to 115 pitches, and I'd say "Uh-oh." On this particular day, Dizzy came off the mound after the inning was over and saw me writing stuff down. He said, "I want to see what you're writing after the game's over." I said, "Sure." We won the ball game, and after they congratulated Dizzy, he said, "Come over here, Charlie. Let me see what you're doing." I showed him. He said, "Hey, that's a pretty doggone good idea." I was counting the pitches, and I was learning what the guys were hitting. That wasn't going to help me too much playing the outfield, but I thought it'd help my hitting. He wanted me to do that for him every game, and soon the other pitchers wanted the same. So I sat there and did it all the time, for Newhouser, Overmire, Trucks, Trout, and Hal White. I was learning something about pitching. And I learned a heck of a lot about managing at that time. I'd watch Steve O'Neill. I knew the signs real well, and I'd wonder, why is he doing that? Why is he letting his guys hit? Pretty soon, I'd figure out the situation. Although I didn't play much, I didn't waste my time.

I might as well get this off my chest right now. When I played with the Tigers and later with the Athletics, people called us a wartime ball club. They called us "wartime ballplayers," "4-F'ers," "slackers," and everything else. I took offense at being labeled a "wartime ballplayer," and I still feel that way. We all played like heck. We played our hearts out. Major League Baseball didn't have to apologize for anything. If they could take our hustle and our determination to show the fans a good game and apply it to the players nowadays, you wouldn't have the booing that you hear today. We were all patriots. We had relatives in the military. Most of us tried to get into the military. Recall that I tried to enlist in the American Eagle Squadron and got rejected because of my injuries in the coal mine gas explosion. Or take the case of Hal Newhouser. He volunteered for the Army Air Corps, but the army doctors tuned him down because of a heart problem, which they called a leaky heart. Hal asked the doctors, "What can I do?" They told him he could be sitting in an easy chair, could be bending over to tie his shoes, or he could be in the bathroom, and he could keel over and that'd be it. He asked, "What if I play baseball?" They said, "Well, we don't know." He said, "Well, if I'm going to go, that's the way I'm going to go. I'm going to pitch and play baseball." And he did. He pitched all those seasons for the Tigers and almost won 30 games one year. He was a great competitor. He'd knock you down in batting practice. He is now deservedly in the Hall of Fame. I saw him shortly after his induction, and he hadn't put on a pound from his playing days. They said he was a "wartime" pitcher, but if you look at his record, after everybody came back, he was still winning big. He won 119 games, over half of his career wins, after 1945.

In addition to Newhouser, the Tigers had a pretty fair set of pitchers in those years. Dizzy Trout wasn't so dizzy, I'll tell you that. He was tough, and he was funny. He was a humorous sort of a guy. He won a lot of games, and he could hit. He was a real workhorse. I don't think I ever saw him with an ache. Years later, in 1957, he tried a comeback with Baltimore. He came out to Vancouver, and he tried to get himself in condition. He worked hard, but he'd lost the touch and just couldn't make it. But, boy, he was a good pitcher. Virgil Trucks was another guy who could fling it. They called him "Fire" Trucks for a good reason. He struck everybody out. Those guys would pitch every fourth day. Hal White was a good journeyman pitcher. He was a starter, and he pitched in and out of turn. He could do spot starts. Steve O'Neill was crazy about him. Later I gave him a job as a scout with the Royals, and he worked a bit with the pitchers. Stubby Overmire developed into a good pitcher in those years.

Tommy Bridges was in Detroit toward the end of his career. He had an absolutely great curve ball. Every once in a while, I would catch batting practice. Tommy would say, "Hey, Rook, get that glove." I'd get the glove, and we'd start warming up. Without telling me, he'd break off a curve that would drop down and hit me on the toes. Finally he would let me know. Then he'd say, "Now watch this. You haven't seen this." And he'd throw me the dangedest spitter you ever saw! That thing would hit me all over. I had a heck of a time catching it. I said, "When do you throw this?" He said, "You watch. You just keep watching me. You'll recognize it." Boy, if he'd get two strikes on a guy and maybe he had just one guy out or maybe this was the deciding hitter in the ball game, here would come that spitter. I never saw how he did it, and I watched him real close.

"Boom-Boom" Beck also pitched very briefly with the Tigers when I was there. He got his name when he pitched for the Phillies. The old ballpark in Philadelphia had a short right-field fence made of tin. They'd say when Walter Beck would pitch, it was Boom-Boom . . . Boom off the bat and Boom off the fence. He was a lovable guy, but he was on his way out. Rufe Gentry wasn't a bad pitcher, a real rugged, tough guy. He was always talking about his honey in the Carolinas. I think he always wanted to go home. Roy Henshaw was a left-handed pitcher, kind of a cute lefty. He didn't have very much stuff, but he wasn't bad. Jake Mooty was a little, short right-hander. He had the funniest motion I'd ever seen. When he would pitch, he'd bend his front leg way down, and it looked like he was throwing uphill, he was way down so low. He was pretty well on his way out at that time.

Johnny Gorsica was a fine relief pitcher. We roomed together. He kept a record of every game he was in. If somebody made an error behind him or something like that, he'd mark it down. I asked him one day, "John, what are you doing that for?" He said, "When I have contract negotiations, I don't want them saying something about my pitching, how many games I lost. I'm putting down what I've done, what's happened. If somebody made an error behind me and didn't get the job done, and we lost the game, I wanted it down." He negotiated a heck of a contract for himself, so I kind of kept doing that a little bit myself. What a good person he was. He was from Beckley, West Virginia. I was a bird hunter, and John was too. We'd get an autographed baseball and trade it for a box of shells. He was also a real snappy dresser, and he taught me how to trade baseballs for suits. Some people would do most anything for an autographed baseball from a big league club, especially if you had some big names on your club. We'd get a baseball and get it signed and trade it for suits and shoes. Chicago was a good place for that. A guy at Hart, Schaffner, and Marx was a great baseball fan. We'd go in there, and, boy, we'd get a suit almost for just a baseball. I was one of the best-dressed rookies you'd ever seen. All the ballplayers wore gabardine suits, light tan, dark brown, blue, green, and various shades of light brown. That was the rage at that time. Everybody wore a sport coat and a tie. It was the big league rule. I'd get an autographed baseball and trade it for a bottle of wine and a good dinner at the hotel. So I learned a little bit about trading, and we had a lot of fun.

On the Detroit Tigers in 1943 and 1944, Steve O'Neill used our two regular catchers quite effectively. Paul Richards, the veteran who was well up in age, caught Hal Newhouser, who was just learning the art of pitching. Bob Swift, who was also an established big league catcher, would catch Dizzy Trout. Steve had been a catcher, so he knew who was the best one and how to match them up. It worked out real well. Al Unser was one of our third-string catchers. He was a run-of-the mill catcher, just like I was a run-of-the-mill outfielder, but his son, Del, became a fine ballplayer. One of our other extra catchers, Hack Miller, was the happiest man in the world when he got his name in the big league record book. All he wanted to do was play at least one ball game. I've never seen a baseball player so delighted.

Paul Richards was a great teacher of pitchers. He became a successful minor league manager at Atlanta in the Southern League and later managed well in the big leagues. While we were together at Detroit, he tried to talk me into converting to catcher because of my arm. He said that I wouldn't have to hit much, because Paul himself wasn't a very good hitter. He batted only .227 lifetime. He said, "You don't have to hit, Charlie, with your arm and your intelligence and everything else." He directed me on how to throw. He'd say, "Get rid of it quick." And I would. Boy, I could really throw the ball down to second base. Later, when I was released, he tried to get me to go to Atlanta, but I took the Philadelphia offer instead. He said he'd have me back up in the big leagues. I didn't want to be a catcher, and I didn't want to go back down. I'd caught a little bit down in Beaumont and gotten beat up. But Paul was a shrewd baseball guy. I only saw him manage one game in Knoxville. I remember him making a brilliant switch. He was going to take a pitcher out, and he didn't want to use another pitcher, so he took the catcher out and put him on the mound. I had never seen that done, and I had never known that the catcher had been a pitcher. And what a job he did with Billy Pierce, who went on to pitch many years for the White Sox. Paul worked with him at Detroit and gave him a change-up on his curve ball. Gee whiz, Billy looked like a veteran after Paul got through with him.

A few other guys at Detroit in those years stick in my mind. Rudy York was great. Gosh, what a hitter! He could hit a curve ball almost out of the catcher's glove! If you look at his record, you'll see he led in a lot of categories. He led in home runs. He led in runs batted in. He was a big guy. He was only a fair first baseman. He couldn't move much around the base. He had come up as a catcher, but he couldn't catch. The Tigers tried him at third, but he almost got killed there. He couldn't play outfield very well either, so Hank Greenberg sacrificed and went to the outfield. He was lovable. They called him a big, dumb Indian, but he was a great player.

Don Ross was a third baseman who also played a little bit of outfield. He wasn't a bad ballplayer, but he had short arms for a big guy. Joe Hoover, our shortstop, was a hypochondriac. There was always something wrong with him. He had the sniffs and he had a headache, and his back would hurt, and his leg would hurt, and his arm would hurt. Every time we'd come home from a road trip, he'd go into the hospital for a checkup. Eddie Mayo was a pretty good regular second baseman. He was one of those guys who really played hard, but he didn't hit very much. Second basemen didn't have to be able to hit. Joe Orengo, who was a utility infielder, turned out to be a very, very fine executive with the San Francisco Seals for many years. He was in their front office; he did promotions, a little bit of everything. He would scout. He was one of my favorite guys. He was very considerate, always trying to help you. Chuck Hostetler had played semipro for many years and was well up in age when Detroit got him, but he could hit like heck. They kidded him quite a bit, called him "Grandpa" and "Grandfather" and everything else. Hank "Prince" Oana, a six-foot-two Hawaiian, was also with us. He pitched, played outfield, and also caught. He could do anything. He was a big, likable, rugged guy. Pinky Higgins was on the All-Star team in 1944. He was a good hitter, but he was one of those guys who hammered down the hitting part of the barrel of the bat to a flat surface.

You never saw such sinking line drives. I used to threaten him that I was going to tell on him if he didn't stop playing jokes on me. J. P. Wood was there, as a backup for Higgins. We roomed together a time or two, and I'd always kid him about my throwing him out from center field in the minors. I'd say, "You keep popping off about your hitting." I wasn't hitting very well, and he'd razz me. I said, "You don't stop bragging about your hitting, I'm going to tell the press and everybody how I threw you out from center field on a single." "Oh, no, don't do that," he'd beg me.

Roger "Doc" Cramer was a great player. He could be in the Hall of Fame. He hit .296 over twenty years. He lead the league in at bats, and he wouldn't walk much. He had this theory that "thou shall not pass," and they couldn't throw anything by him. He was a lead-off hitter and, boy, could he could get on base. A tall, lanky guy, he certainly could play center field. We practiced backing up each other and catching the ball if it bounced off the other guy's glove, a talent that I used and taught in the minor leagues. Doc was responsible for getting a warning track in the outfield at Briggs Stadium. They didn't have grass all the way down to the dugout, but they didn't have a track in the outfield. Doc had a hard time convincing Tigers officials to make the warning track twenty-four feet wide. They made it ten feet, which was not wide enough, because a guy going full blast toward the fence needs all the warning he can get. Cramer also tried to teach me to hit left-handed. He said, "With your speed, your arm, the way you can field center field, you ought to come out and hit left." Heck, I couldn't hit right-handed, let alone left-handed.

Dick Wakefield continued to hit well with the Tigers. I saw him hit a ball in Detroit that would have gone into the center-field bleachers but instead hit the flagpole and went down toward left field inside the ballpark. The flagpole was inside the park in deep center field. He was able to circle the bases before the fielders recovered the ball. The left fielder had gone over to back up the center fielder. If my memory is right, it was 440 feet to center field. Dick had a lot of speed. He could bounce the ball to the infield and beat it out. He said he was going to be better than Ted Williams, and I think if he'd had the desire, he might have done just that. But he never reached his potential.

Speaking of hitters, we got to see Harry Heilmann, the great Hall of Famer, take batting practice with the Tigers in 1943. Harry was broadcasting for Detroit. He'd come out, dressed up in his suit, and he'd take that bat and take a few swings. I don't know how old he was at that time, nearly fifty, I imagine. He'd hang out ropes, as we'd call them, clothesline ropes. He loved to hit, and we loved to watch. He could handle that bat. He wouldn't even take the suit off. One time, I recall, he swung at a pitch and hit it well, and rippp! went the back of his coat. Everybody laughed at him, and he thought it was funny.

I'll never forget my first major league hit. We were playing the St. Louis Browns at Sportsman's Park early in the season. Steve O'Neill put me in the outfield and gave me a chance to play. I was leading off, and I went up to the plate against Al Hollingsworth, who was a left-handed pitcher. He was almost through with his career. He threw me three so-called fastballs. I'd heard about the big leagues and how hard they threw and all that, and I was looking for something really fast. He was just goosing that fastball up there, so to speak. He threw me a fastball for strike one. Dang, I thought, that kind of fastball I can hit, I'll get him this time. He threw another fastball, and I took it for strike two. Then he came back with another one right down the middle, and I was scared to death. I couldn't pull the trigger. When I came back to the bench, Steve O'Neill said, "Charlie, you can swing. You can hit that ball. Swing that bat the next time." I said, "Yes, sir." He asked me if I was nervous. I said that I was, and he said, "Well, you won't be next time." So the next time I was up, Hollingsworth threw me a curve ball, and I ripped it down the left-field line for a double, my first big league hit. Of course, later I told my boys it was a stinging shot, but actually it went off the trademark of the bat, just into short left field down the line. But I did get a double out of it. We won the game. Boy, I thought, I'm going to be a great one. Whenever I'd see Al in later years, I'd tell him, "Boy, I really ripped you," or "I made a living off you," or "Every time I hit against you my contract went up." He claimed that he didn't remember, that he had pitched to lots of hitters. I said, "I remember. I'm going to refresh your memory." I'd tell him word for word about the pitch I hit for a double, but I didn't tell him he had struck me out the first time. But he'd come back at me with stuff like "We didn't spend any time on you in the clubhouse." He did recall striking me out. He kidded me about taking three strikes. He'd say, "I couldn't break a pane of glass, and that's about as slow as you could get." His wife, who was there at breakfast with us one time in Mesa, Arizona, while we were scouting, just laughed about these two old-timers going at each other. He's the guy who made the greatest quote I've ever heard about Reggie Jackson. He said, "There's not enough mustard in the world to cover that hot dog."

When you got up to the majors, you became instantaneously famous, even if you were a rookie. Kids wanted your autograph. When J. P. Wood and I joined the Tigers in 1943, somebody said, "Oh, you're famous now. You're going to have to have an autograph stamp to stamp your autograph requests." So we got them made. I had mine say "Charlie Metro." I still have it at home as a souvenir. J. P. Wood also had one. We had the little ink stamp box and the stamper. When we got into New York, we ran into some pretty knowledgeable kids. We'd stamp here and stamp there and stamp their paper and stamp their book and stamp everything. I even stamped my name on some foreheads of little kids. For the little girls who would be hanging around, I'd stamp their arms, and I'd say, "Now, don't wash that off." But some of the kids didn't like us stamping our autographs. They'd tear up the paper and throw it down. They wanted us to use that old-fashioned fountain pen. They'd splatter us if we used the stamper, so I quit using it. We had to dress in suits, and I had a real nice tan gabardine suit in New York. When I stamped an autograph for this boy, he let me have it with that ink pen, just whomp! When I got back to the hotel, I saw he'd got me all on the back and on my pantleg. That didn't go over very well, so I never stamped an autograph anymore.

At Chicago there was a photographer named George Brace who always took pictures of all the big league ball clubs that came into town. He was a photographer with one of the newspapers. When I was with Detroit, he took some pictures of me, and many years later, he sent me a postcard of my picture made into four different shots. He asked me for permission to use this card. I think I was scouting at the time, and I saw him again. He was retired, and retirement pensions weren't very good in those days, so I gave him permission. I said, "Heck, yes. Go ahead. Use them all you want." Every once in a while, even today, I would get the pictures of me in that uniform. Gosh, I didn't know I ever looked that young.

When I was with the Tigers, I became a poster boy of sorts for the Lady Marines. At games in Washington, there'd be a lot of military personnel sitting out in left field. I was in a game early one day, and the Lady Marines were out there. They were hooting and hollering, and the next day I happened to be out there playing again. Those were rare moments when I got out there a couple of games in a row. The Lady Marines had a sign that read "We love Charlie." I was their pinup boy. I was kind of embarrassed about it, but it was a lot of fun. Every time I caught a fly ball, they'd give me a rousing cheer. I thought to myself, That's not bad for a lifetime .193 hitter. They were taking pictures and everything, really having fun with me, and I went right along with it.

When I went up to the major leagues with Detroit, we traveled by train, on sleeper cars. That was the way to travel! The whole team was with you. The rookies had the upper berths. The guys who were regulars had the lower berths, and the next day's pitcher was treated like royalty! He got the best of all. He could take his choice of the berths. Of course, they played some tricks on us rookies. They didn't short-sheet us very much or do other similar practical jokes, but they'd always tell the rookie that in order to keep his arm right, he'd have to put his arm in the knitted sling that they had in the berths. Along about the next morning, he couldn't raise his arm! But it was a delightful way of traveling. You'd sit around in the chair cars and talk baseball all the time. Some guys would talk baseball all night long. The veterans liked to talk to the rookies. You got very close. If you played and did something that needed correcting, one of the veterans would take you aside and say, "Now, look, this is what you do, and this is what you shouldn't do." Of course, I was a wide-eyed rookie, and I listened to them. I wanted to learn everything I could. I'd never seen anything like this. I'd come out of the minors, where we traveled on buses and behind the cattle cars, so this was great. We also made a few trips from Detroit to Cleveland by boat, on Great Lake steamers. They'd give you a little room. We'd get on the boat at Detroit at 11:00 at night and be off the boat by 9:00 in the morning in Cleveland and go straight to the ballpark. We played mostly day games. In Detroit, we stayed at the Leland Hotel. Five or six of us guys stayed there. It cost us five dollars a day. We had a corner room. My family couldn't come up to Detroit very often, maybe only for a long home stand. When my wife and daughter did come up to Detroit, they would stay in the room, and the hotel would never charge extra. Gee, they even took care of the kids. The chef at the hotel was a great baseball fan. We'd get a baseball signed by the club and give it to him. He would send food galore, sandwiches and everything, up to our rooms. He treated us royally. Oh, he was a great baseball fan.

This is the first time that I recall starting pitchers going on the road ahead of the rest of the team to get a good night of sleep. Dizzy Trout was the one who talked Steve O'Neill into sending them ahead. I don't know whether it had been done before that. I wasn't on the major league scene prior to that. Every time we'd go from, say, Boston, or we'd come back to New York, we'd send the next day's starting pitcher on ahead. Of course, New York was a good town, full of entertainment, the shows and the nightclubs. I don't know that the custom worked very well, because I remember several times when a guy who went on ahead didn't last two innings. You can't know why, for sure. Maybe they got too much rest, maybe too little.

In the clubhouse, they put me next to the veterans, right next to Doc Cramer and Pinky Higgins in the corner. I enjoyed that because I learned a lot from them. Things would rub off. But, boy, would they play jokes on me. I'd get a pair of sweat socks, and I'd put them on and the toe would be cut out. You only got one pair, and there I was without toes in my socks. Then we had wooden shower shoes, what they called "clackers." They looked like a footprint and had a little strap right over the instep. They'd nail those to the wooden floor. There you'd stand like a comedian. And they'd open your bag and put it downward, so that when you picked it up, everything would come out. But I pulled a couple on Cramer. We weren't allowed to eat anything between games of doubleheaders. Every once in a while, you'd tell the clubhouse guy to go get you a Hershey bar. I didn't know about this rule that you weren't allowed to have anything. So there I was eating this Hershey bar with the peanuts in it, and one of the guys said, "You better put that away. Steve O'Neill sees you, he'll fine you twenty-five dollars." So I put it in my back pocket. Doc Cramer said to me, "Hey, Charlie, take my glove and set it out." That's when you could still throw your gloves on the field. I took his glove out to center field. When I was going out there, that Hershey bar was melting in my pocket, so I took it out and stuffed it in his glove. I turned it palm down, and in the next few minutes the sun melted that chocolate completely. I told one of the guys, "Watch Doc out there." He said, "Why, what'd you do?" I said, "Just watch him." Cramer put his hand in that glove, and all this chocolate came out. I could see him smelling it, wondering what it was. Another time I put a lit cigarette in Cramer's back pocket. I was getting back at them because they were always pulling something on me. They sawed my bat in half one time. I picked it up and the darn thing broke off. They'd sawed it almost through, and when I lifted it up, the weight of the barrel broke it down. I said, "I'll get back at them." I knew it was either Higgins or Cramer doing it. I said, "Watch him." Pretty soon you looked out, and Doc was looking up and smelling something burning. He was turning around and hitting himself on the back pocket. The cigarette burned a hole through his pocket and dropped down his pantleg. Higgins said, "What'd you do?" I said, "I didn't do anything, but look at him!" I wasn't about to admit that I'd pulled that. Doc came in, and he said, "You did that, didn't you?" I said, "Oh, no, I know who did though!" I never said I did it. He said, "Well, tell me." I said, "Oh, no, I can't tell you. I know who did it, Doc." He never did find out.

We had a couple of real characters on the Tigers. Dizzy Trout was definitely what we'd call a character. He had a very definite way of pitching to guys, but occasionally things backfired. In one game against the Browns in St. Louis, he took a 1-0 into the bottom of the ninth. He got two outs, but then he walked George McQuinn. Vern Stephens, my old roommate from Mayfield, was the next batter. Dizzy had said in the clubhouse that Stephens wasn't going to hit him. Dizzy thought there was no way Stephens could pull him, so he threw him a low inside fastball. Vern could hit anything thrown over the plate from the shoe tops to the shoulders. He jumped up off the ground and hit the ball right into the base of the scoreboard over the bleachers to win the game. Dizzy stormed into the clubhouse, cussing himself. He took a pair of scissors and chopped his hair off while he stood in front of the mirror. He cut off big chunks of his hair all over his head, so he looked like he was run over by a lawn mower. Oh, he was mad at himself for that pitch. Then he got himself a crew cut before they were popular. He caught heck from the other guys because he was the only guy with a crew cut on the club, but he persuaded Hal White to get one too. Dizzy Trout hated to come out of a game. When Steve O'Neill, who was a tough manager, walked out to talk to Dizzy, you could see Dizzy with his fist balled up as if to say, You're not going to take me out of this ball game.

Another time Dizzy entertained the fans at an exhibition game by sliding around in the mud. We were scheduled to play in the annual Hall of Fame game at Cooperstown, New York, in 1944 against the Giants, and we stopped in nearby Utica for a game the day before. The Eastern League franchise there was having some financial difficulties, so we agreed to hold a game to help out. Hal White and our first base coach, Art Mills, were from Utica. The day of the game it was raining like heck, but we went ahead and played anyway. We had a sold-out crowd, maybe five or six thousand people, in the stands with umbrellas, and we were saving the franchise. If we didn't play four and a half innings, they would have to refund the tickets. Dizzy pitched. Remember how in the movie *Bull Durham* the players slid around on the wet tarp during a rain delay? Dizzy did something similar forty years earlier. He got a base hit. You couldn't field the ball. You were in water in the outfield almost up to your ankles. I knew that because I played center field. Dizzy decided to steal second. He ran down to second base, where there was about two inches of water on the dirt part of the infield. About forty-five feet from the base, he went into a belly slide and slid all the way to second on the water and the mud. The umpires, who were big league umpires, got into the act and called him safe. Dizzy got up and took a big lead, and Utica got him in a rundown. He ran back and forth and then slid into third base the same way. The fans went crazy. And he went out there pitching with all this mud on his uniform. It was great. The fans really loved it and stayed right on through the rain. Utica eventually won, so they didn't have to play the last half of the fifth inning. We got the game in, and it was the most hilarious thing. Unfortunately, when we got over to Cooperstown, we didn't get to play the game. It wasn't raining there and we practiced, but they called the game off. I forget whether the Giants didn't even show up or just didn't get dressed. I was in the lineup, and it broke my heart. The plaque at the Hall of Fame just lists it as a cancellation.

Rudy York also gave us all some good laughs. In recent years there have been squawks about hitters getting an extra advantage by modifying their bats, often by corking them: drilling out the end, putting in cork, and replugging it to give the lumber an extra whip. Fans who think this is something new forget that players knew about this technique in my day. Doc Cramer would take an ice pick and run it right down the grain of the bat. This made some grooves on the hitting side, so the ball wouldn't slip off the bat. When I was with Detroit in 1944, one game I saw Rudy, our big slugger first baseman, drive 2 home runs out of Washington's Griffith Stadium and hit a double another time up. Rudy had some bourbon in a big Coke bottle, which he'd keep cool in the water fountain. In between innings, when he wasn't on base or fielding or going up to hit, Rudy would take a swig. I was messing around with the bottle during that game, and somebody almost hit me on the head with a glove. "Get away from that," someone warned me. Rudy kept taking swigs and hitting home runs. Griffith Stadium was a big field with distant fences. You really had to tag one to get it out of there. When Rudy hit the last blast, however, we heard a sound that resembled a rifle shot. The cork in his bat had shot out the end. After York circled the bases, the umpire, Bill McGowan, old "Number One," handed him the suspicious bat. "Mr. York, here is your bat," he said, shaking his head because there was no rule yet, and pointing to the ground, "and there is your cork." Rick Ferrell, who was the Senators' catcher, would tell that story for years.

One day the guys had a little fun with Rudy on the train. We had played a doubleheader at St. Louis. It was in the afternoon, and we were going to catch the train for the East. Every time Rudy hit a home run, a tailor in Detroit, who was a great fan of his and a Tigers fan, would make him a suit. Rudy would always get those big double-breasted suits. He looked like he was three feet wide across the back. These suits had pockets on the outside and in the inside lining. During this particular doubleheader, we had played a bad game, and Steve O'Neill was mad. I think Rudy was the culprit. I don't know whether he missed the sign or missed an easy play or forgot to do something, but anyway he was responsible for the loss. So we all got on the train. Rudy had a fifth of bourbon in his coat pocket. The Pullman car had a metal water cooler over in the corner. They'd put ice in there to cool the water, and they had those little Dixie cups with the pointed bottoms. Rudy had already had a drink or two, and somebody said, "Geez, Rudy, be careful. Steve is furious, and he'll be coming in pretty soon." You could hear Steve out there talking real loud and real agitated. Cramer told Rudy to get rid of the bottle. Somebody said, "Here comes Steve." Rudy didn't know what to do with it. He was standing there in the doorway of the men's lavatory, so he opened the top of the water cooler and dropped it in. No one could hear it, but when he dropped it in, the bottle broke. There was no ice or water in the cooler yet. Rudy went in the men's room, and Steve O'Neill came on the train and went back up to his berth at the other end. The porter came and poured some ice and water in the cooler. Cramer said, "God, I got to get a drink of water." He went over to the cooler and poured a cup. It was bourbon and water. Doc told all the guys there about this, and they all came over for some bourbon and water. Rudy came out of the men's room and found out what they're doing. He threatened the guys, "Get away from there." That was his bottle of bourbon, and he was trying to hold them off from the water cooler. The guys said, "We'll tell Steve. We'll tell Steve." Rudy was begging them to let him have it. I don't think Rudy got any more of his bourbon, but nobody got drunk. The porter had to come and pour more water in the cooler. I'll never forget it. Rudy was a delight.

During the off-seasons, I became quite a hunter. We were living in Mayfield, and I would hunt over in Illinois, across the river from Paducah, as well as in Graves County, Kentucky, and Union City, Tennessee. Boy, I loved that quail hunting. I stayed in condition all the time. I trained bird dogs, German shorthaireds. But I hunted with all kinds. I trained them. Everybody in town knew I had shells after a while, so they wanted me to take their dogs out and keep them fit. They would charge me a couple of quail for the use of their dogs. The country was full of quail. Years later Red Schoendienst and Stan Musial would come down to Graves County to hunt quail. I just missed meeting them. They knew some people down there. I also loved hunting duck and geese, but the recoil from the guns could ruin your shoulder. I got a sore shoulder one winter when I had shot a lot of ducks. I loved duck hunting. I would give them to the orphans' home because I had so many. Goose hunting was even tougher on the body because the shells were higher powered and the recoil from the higher shots came right down on your shoulder.

Getting enough shotgun shells was a problem during the war, until I made a friend with a boy's father who happened to be a purchasing agent for Montgomery Ward. While I was with Detroit, we were in Philadelphia, taking batting practice. We were about ready to get a new set of baseball caps, because they get sweaty and dirty. I was shagging balls down the left-field line. While I was standing there fielding a ball, a man and his son were nearby. The little boy said, "Hey, mister, can I have that baseball?" Now, you didn't dare give a baseball away at that time, but I looked at him and said, "Just a minute." So I rolled the ball down by the box seats right by the gate. I said, "Now, you slip your hand under there and you get that ball, OK?" So I kicked the ball down close to the gate, and he reached down and got it. "Hey, just wait a minute now. Don't go away yet," I told him, "Shhh, now, don't tell anybody." I took my cap off, because batting practice was about over, and I put it on his head and said, "Here, it's yours." His father saw me do that, and I made a lifelong friend. The next morning he called me at the Warwick Hotel, and we had breakfast together. We had long conversations about this, that, and everything else. He asked what I did in the wintertime. I said, "Well, I'm going to have to find a job, but before I find a job I'm going quail hunting." He asked, "What kind of a gun do you shoot?" I said, "Well, I've got all kinds, a twelve gauge, a sixteen gauge, a twenty gauge, a twenty-eight gauge, a .410, I have them all." He asked, "What do you do for shells?" Now mind you, this was during the war and you couldn't buy a box of shells. That fall, here came a note from the railroad depot that I had had some freight come in. I went over there, and I found twenty cases of shells. And a week or ten days later, here came the first Remington automatic made, sixteen gauge. I paid thirty dollars for it. It was brand-new, and I hunted all over that country with that gun and those shells.

While I was with the Tigers, I didn't get to see Hank Greenberg play because he was in the service. But one night in 1944, he joined us at the Grenadier Room in the Leland Hotel in Detroit and gave us some contract advice. Rudy York was there, and Greenberg came in in his military khakis. A rumor had started that Hank was going to ask for $100,000 when he came back. Rudy was arguing with him about it. Rudy said, "Ah, you're not worth that." I'll never forget what Hank said: "Rudy, you better listen, you big dumb Indian, you better listen. You don't know how much money you make till you see the numbers on that check. You don't know how to negotiate. You should be making $50,000 to $60,000 instead of that $35,000 you're making. I'm going to make $100,000. See these two guys here, Stubby Overmire and Charlie Metro? You see these two guys? They're not going to get paid $3,500 to $3,600. They're going to double and triple their salary, maybe get $10,000 or fifteen or twenty." Back then players didn't have much of a chance to negotiate. You took it or else. There were an awful lot of players in the minor leagues. Each major league club had fifteen or twenty minor league clubs, and some clubs like the Cardinals and Yankees had thirty-some clubs. They got the best ballplayers, and they would sell a ballplayer or trade for a better ballplayer along the way. But Hank was right. When he went over to Pittsburgh later, all the salaries began escalating. His salary was over $100,000 or close to it, depending on who you read and if you counted in the value of a horse he got from John Galbreath. Hank said that he was going to make $100,000 and that salaries would pick up for all the guys. The older ballplayers at times were very bitter about it. They had been regular ballplayers, and all of a sudden the salaries exploded, the per diem went up, and the hotels and travel were better.

Not many people remember this, but in the summer of 1943 there were full-scale race riots in Detroit. Gosh, that was terrible. It almost made me cry to see them happening. We didn't see anything happen up close, but we could see the fires. They were within walking distance. We had a whole bunch of military soldiers in full gear at the ballpark. We didn't have any games canceled, but you couldn't move around the city. We'd want to go downtown for a while, but the police and troops would discourage us, because they had cannons on Woodward Avenue at the cross streets, military squads patrolling the streets. Woodward Avenue was a battle zone, the dividing line, the way I understood it. I sent my family, who had been staying at the Leland Hotel, home to Kentucky. Oh, it was terrible. It was a dark, dark set of days.

The Tigers started out the year and played pretty well, but overall we finished fifth. The next year I thought I might have a pretty good chance, but then I was a little scared because in 1944 some of the ballplayers were coming out of the military. There were rumors that Hank Greenberg, Roy Cullenbine, and Dick Wakefield were returning from the service. I'd look at those outfielders and think to myself, "Uh, oh." But I worked like heck that spring, and I made the club again. I had a little trouble with the contract. The Tigers wanted to cut me back to $1,800, but I wouldn't take the cut. These negotiations were risky. They'd send you a contract, and you signed it or else you stayed home. I knew that the guys were coming back, but I finally talked Jack Zeller into paying me the same salary.

That spring I got involved with baseball union activities. I had been a union steward trainee in the coal mines, and I'd witnessed arguments between miners and sometimes between a boss and a miner. I had strong leadership capabilities. I had been captain of the football and basketball teams. The rumbling about the union started around 1943. I was a little bit active in that darn thing. I thought it was right. We were getting five bucks a day for meal money and no cab fare, nothing else, and there was no pension. I discussed it with Rip Sewell, the Pittsburgh "blooper ball" pitcher, down at Evansville. He was instrumental in stirring things up and today should receive a lot more credit for what he did. He never profited from it. He found out I was talking union with some of the ballplayers. (The Pirates almost went out on strike a couple of years later, in 1946). I contributed $250 to the union when they needed it. A while later we were over at Terre Haute, and I was picking up an infield ball for Honus Wagner. He asked me, "What do you play, kid?" I said, "Well, I'm an outfielder." He said, "Well, you better be careful. Now don't be talking too loud. It's a good thing, and it's going to help all the players, but be careful." So I talked it up quite a bit. I told Jim Russell, who was with Pittsburgh then, about how at the coal mines we went from eighty-five cents a ton to a more decent wage, how we got a dollar a day portal-to-portal pay, and how we stopped the company and the store from taking all your salary, how they had to give you at least $5 on your check.

Along about August, Jack Zeller called me up to the office and asked, "What are you doing talking about this stuff and that stuff?" Apparently he'd heard about me talking up the union around the clubhouse. That's the only reason I could think of, because I was doing everything the Tigers were asking, filling in and everything. Oh, boy, I started to back-pedal. I was worried. We had some disagreement going on anyway. The previous year he had not let me make the final road trip of the season, and I had missed the chance to get back to family and friends in Pennsylvania, and he was talking about the same thing this season. I was also a little grouchy about not getting enough playing time. Heck, I played defensively as well as any outfielder on the team. So he said, "Well, what do you want? Your release?" I said, "Yeah, give me the damn thing." He reached into his desk, brought out the release form, signed one, and handed it to me. He said, "Here, you want your release." I swallowed hard and said, "Where's my severance pay?" He said, "You don't get any severance pay." I said, "Yes, I do. I'll go to Commissioner Landis." He said, "Oh, is that so?" I said, "Yes, I will." He said, "All right." Zeller was a little cornered. Landis had freed ninety-one Tiger farmhands in 1940, and Zeller was probably skittish about crossing Landis. So I got him to give me my check for ten days' severance pay. He had the secretary in the outside office type up the release form, but as I was leaving, he started calling to me to come back, that he had made a mistake. I refused to go back and headed for the clubhouse to pack up my gear. But I didn't know what the heck I was going to do next.

While I was packing my stuff, Doc Cramer asked, "What's the matter? What are you doing?" I said, "Oh, I got my release." He said, "You what?"

I said, "Yes, I got my release, and I'm packing my bags." He said, "Let me see it." So I showed it to him and, and he said, "Oh, you lucky son of a gun." I didn't think I was very lucky. I didn't have a job. I was released. But Doc said, "You just wait here." It was early afternoon, before the game. He came back and said, "You call Mr. Mack. Here's the number. You call him tomorrow. Now, don't forget. You call him tomorrow. Leave your stuff here and call him tomorrow." First I tried Clark Griffith with the Washington Senators. He was interested but wanted me dirt-cheap, for $1,800. He had a lot of young guys, Cubans, and veterans, and he wasn't noted for having a generous pocketbook. So I called Mr. Mack in Philadelphia and never regretted it. He said, "Yes, yes, Roger has called me about you. We can use an outfielder, and he was very high on you. You're young, and you can do this and that, he said." Cramer had told me when Mr. Mack asked what my salary was not to tell him what I was getting. So I didn't tell him. Mr. Mack said, "This is what I'll do with you, Charles, I'll sign you to a $5,500 contract the rest of the year, and we'll do that next year too. If you're here with us, I will give you $7,500 for signing the contract with us." I stammered, "Uh . . . ," and he said, "You don't think that's right?" I was swallowing hard. I said, "Yes, sir, when do you want me to come?" Mr. Mack said, "Well, we're having a big day here at Shibe Park. Come on in, and I'll tell them down at the clubhouse that you're coming, but come on in and let me know that you're there. Get in here tomorrow. That's fine." Boy, I packed up my stuff lickety-split and told Doc Cramer. He said, "Oh, he ain't cheap, Mr. Mack." Everybody said he was cheap, but he was very generous, sometimes to a fault.

I left for Philadelphia and got there the next night. They were having a big Connie Mack Day at the stadium. I came into the stadium early. There was a transportation strike in Philadelphia, but they had at least thirty-five thousand people at the ballpark. How they got there, I don't know, because there were no subway trains or streetcars running. So I went up to the office and told Mr. Mack I was there. He said, "I'm very busy. You go on down to the clubhouse, and they will take care of you." So I went down to the clubhouse, and they said to come up after everything was over. I came back after the game, and they said, "Yeah, Charlie, here's your uniform, number 14." Mr. Mack had named and invited his all-time living American League All-Star team. They were going to be honored there. That was part of the program before the game. The clubhouse guy said, "Hey, take this baseball and go on and get yourself some autographs." Well, I knew about autographs a little bit. I said, "OK." So he gave me a pen, and I went over there and there was Babe Ruth. There was Jimmie Foxx. There was Al Simmons, and there was Lefty Grove, all from the Philadelphia club. There was Lefty Gomez, and there was Mickey Cochrane, and, oh heck, I can't remember all of them. But I got all their autographs on that baseball. Years later I found one of my sons bouncing that ball against the house on the driveway in Alabama. To this day, I still jokingly spank him every time I see him. Can you imagine what that ball would be worth today?

The next day I went up to the office, and Mr. Mack had my contract ready for the rest of the year. He gave me a check for $7,500, with taxes taken out. I said, "Mr. Mack, I'll do you a good job. I'll play like heck for you. I'll make the team. I can play center field. I can play left field. I've played everywhere." Playing for the great Mr. Mack was a special honor. Everybody had great respect for Mr. Mack. To this day I still call him Mr. Mack. What a baseball man he was! He would sit there on the bench, in his suit and starched collar. I don't ever remember him wearing a uniform. I saw him one time in an old-time baseball uniform with a square cap. His grandson, who became a senator in Florida, would be in uniform sitting cross-legged in front of his grandfather. Mr. Mack would direct us around with his scorecard. He'd point that scorecard out, high up for the outfield, low for the infield, and point it right at your position. You had to be alert. He was a great manager and an astute baseball man. He never would hold a meeting in a clubhouse. He suspected that they had spies in the clubhouse who would listen at the bench or through the stovepipes and vents. He was very suspicious of several clubs, especially Cleveland and St. Louis. He never missed anything. He called the plays. He had very simple signs. You did not talk back to Mr. Mack. You did what he said, no questions asked. Mr. Mack wouldn't let me go back to Mayfield for my father-in-law's funeral. He said, "No. You're a baseball player. You're right here."

On one occasion I had a little flare-up with Mr. Mack. I had a couple of hits and a walk in St. Louis, but later in the game, he called me back from the on-deck circle and put in a pinch hitter for me. I threw the bat down, and he said, "What's the matter, don't you like it?" I told him, "I got to like it, Mr. Mack. You're the boss. Besides, you own the club." He laughed. I got a twinkle and a chuckle out of him. I guess he figured I got my base hits for the day and I wasn't going to get another. Another time Mr. Mack called my name in the dugout and sent me in to pinch-hit. I saw him waving his scorecard to the outfield bleachers. "Hit one out of here, son," he said. "Which seat, Mr. Mack?" I asked, full of myself. Up at bat, I looked at three straight strikes. Back in the dugout, I saw Mr. Mack motion me over. He was dusting off the dugout bench next to him with his scorecard. "This seat, son," he said.

Mr. Mack was a pretty private person. He was a little more outgoing on the bench, but back at the hotel, he was very reserved. He didn't talk much about his great teams of the 1910s and 1920s and 1930s. I saw Mr. Mack get really angry only once. One game Pete Gray, the one-armed outfielder with the Browns, beat us with a double. Pete was a tremendous player, a great inspiration to the military guys who were wounded, even if his personality wasn't too great. He got a base hit and beat us in St. Louis. Mr. Mack was furious. I think that it was our fifteenth straight loss at that time. We weren't very good. I think we won one and went on to lose about six or seven more. But Mr. Mack called a team meeting at the hotel, and we all sat around the table. He started out with a pep talk. Then he got to Pete Gray, and he said, "By gosh, I can't understand this. A player with one arm can beat us." He took his fist and slammed it down on that table and said, "Goddamn it." Al Simmons, who was sitting next to him, said, "Mr. Mack." Mr. Mack said, "Aloysius, you be quiet." He said, "A one-armed guy beat us. Maybe we ought to amputate everybody's arm, if that's what it takes to win." I darn near died because I had never heard him say anything like that. And I think some of the other ballplayers couldn't believe it either.

One day Mr. Mack had me playing left field against the Tigers. I had played with them the previous season, so I figured I knew where they would all hit the ball. Doc Cramer came up to bat to lead off the game. He was a left-handed hitter. I looked into our dugout and saw Mr. Mack waving me *toward* the foul line. I took a couple of steps that way. Mr. Mack waved me over more. I took a couple of more steps. He started waving more vigorously. Geez, I thought, any more and I'll be playing in foul ground. I moved some more. He gave me the OK, waved the scorecard down. On the first pitch, Roger Cramer hit a scorching liner right at me. It would have hit me right in the chest if I hadn't caught it in my glove. I didn't have to move an inch. After that I listened to anything Mr. Mack said. He knew pitchers, and he knew hitters.

I had a great time playing for Mr. Mack. He liked a lot of what I did. I was a fair-haired boy. I wish I could have played longer, wish I could have done better for him. I didn't do too much hitting or playing with the Athletics. I was having a hard time at the plate, but I did have some real fine days. I became a pretty good utility player. I practiced at every position. I turned out to be pretty good, because I was forced to play different places because I couldn't break into my regular center-field position. So I'd go into left and go into right, and every once in a while I'd fool around and come into the infield. I'd play a little second base for Mr. Mack. He wanted to send me down to learn how to play second base, and I said, "Mr. Mack,

our club is not very good. I'll get a lot of opportunities to learn right here."
I don't know whether he liked that or not, but if he'd have played me more
there, I believe I would've become a good second baseman. Then I played
some third base. Later, when I started managing, I played quite a lot at
third base and some at second base. I even played a few games at first in the
Pacific Coast League with Seattle. Some guys are more natural at playing
several positions than others. I guess I had that type of physique that fit
right in with utility play.

I did some things for Mr. Mack real well. We were playing a game in
Yankee Stadium one day, and I got put in as a pinch runner. The next guy
walked, and I was at second base with one out. We were 1 run behind, if
I recall, or maybe the game was tied. Bobby Estalella was up to the plate,
and Bobby couldn't run very well. He was a good double play candidate.
So I was on second base, and there was one out. Bobby hit the ball toward
shortstop. I ran over there quickly and caught the ball on a hop. I dropped
it real quick, like I was trying to get away from the ball. Of course, the
umpire called me out, because a fair ball hit me. But at least Bobby got to
first base. When I came into the dugout, Al Simmons, who wasn't coaching
third that day but sitting in the dugout with Mr. Mack, said, "Oh, what a
bush damn play that is." I turned around and said, "I broke up the double
play, Al, I broke up the double play. That was a sure double play." Mr.
Mack said, "That's right, Al, he broke up the double play." The next guy
up, Hal Peck, hit a ball down the right-field line, driving in 2 runs, and we
won the ball game. Mr. Mack liked my play. He loved aggressive plays. He
asked, "Where did you learn that?" I said, "Well, Mr. Mack, I didn't learn
any plays. I just knew what I was going to do."

Another time we were playing a game in Boston, and the Red Sox had a
rally going. I was playing left field. I had a pretty good day that day. I had
had a couple of base hits and a couple of walks. Boston had a guy at third
base and another at second, with one out. The batter hit a fly ball out to
left, and I ran up that little incline that they had at that time. I saw the ball,
and I knew the guy was going to tag up, so I turned my back to the infield
and put my hands on the fence as if the ball were going over my head. The
guy left the bag at third, and so did the guy at second. I turned around and
caught the ball about three or four feet in front of the fence. I fired the ball
into third base and doubled the guy off. I thought Mr. Mack was going to
have a heart attack. He hadn't seen a play like that. He said, "That there
was wonderful. That was wonderful." We didn't win that ball game, but I
did some pretty good stuff like that.

Mr. Mack liked to play a guy against his previous club to see if he could rise to the occasion. We were playing in Detroit, and I was feeling pretty good. The bases were loaded. Stubby Overmire was pitching for the Tigers. I knew what Stubby was going to throw me. He was going to throw me that change-up of his. He had a dandy. It was kind of a little bit of a curve, like a change-up on a curve ball, and it was real slow. I was waiting for it, but I got just a little bit too much out in front of it, and the left fielder jumped against the fence in Briggs Stadium and caught the ball. I don't know whether I was happy or sad, because I loved Steve O'Neill, my former manager, and I had mixed feelings toward my old friend Stubby. But I wanted to do well, and I came close.

I've seen quite a few batting-out-of-order disputes in baseball, but the one that stands out in my mind happened when I was with the Athletics. We were playing in Philadelphia, and we were the ones who batted out of order. It seemed like George Kell had hit out of order. He was hitting in the third spot. Earl Mack would make out the lineup, and this particular day he got mixed up and put the previous day's lineup. He had Kell hitting second instead of third. Kell hit out of order, and the only guy who knew the rule was Mr. Mack. Kell hit into an inning-ending double play, and then he started off the next inning, promptly grounding out. He made three outs in two innings. I believe Charlie Berry, who played for the Athletics in the 1920s and 1930s, was the American League umpire in back of home plate. He came over and asked Mr. Mack what the ruling was, and Mr. Mack decided it for him. Mr. Mack was the only guy in the ballpark who had it right. And that's the way it wound up.

I can also remember when Mr. Mack said that baseball should take a week off right smack-dab in the middle of the summer, in July, and give everybody a rest to rejuvenate. He had in mind more than just the All-Star break, a week or ten days for players to rest, to go off and just forget about everything and rejuvenate, to rebuild their energies. But he said that baseball wouldn't accept that because July is a very profitable time, especially the Fourth of July, and the owners wouldn't want to lose the attendance. Mr. Mack had a lot of good ideas way back then.

When I went on to manage, there were many things I did that I learned from Mr. Mack. I was very consciously moving outfielders around. Having played center field, I was more geared to outfield play, so I would move outfielders around. Boy, when I'd see an outfielder completely out of position, I'd move him. The young guys didn't know any more about the ballplayers than anybody else, but because I played, I would always watch batting practice. I'd watch batting practice and get some hints. You'd see a guy come up there and swing four or five times and then bunt one.

Five swings was the practice at that time, and I'd watch the batters and see their tendencies. I got the practice of moving outfielders around from Mr. Mack. At the same time, I used to keep the scorecard of pitches. Mr. Mack asked me about that, and he told me, "Son, that's a fine, fine thing to do." I watched him on his pitcher moves too. He had Earle Brucker, a former catcher, as a bullpen coach. Earle would watch the pitchers too and sit right next to Mr. Mack. I'd hear them having conversations about pitchers. I tried to eavesdrop on their information, trying to learn. He was very astute on everything about baseball. Years later, when I was managing Montgomery in the Southeastern League, a Class B league, we played an exhibition game with the Athletics. Mr. Mack was there, and I came over to pay my respects. He said, "Hello, son, you're doing a fine job. I know all about you. You've had good success out there." I didn't know that he kind of followed his former players.

Going from the Detroit Tigers, who were a contender, to the Athletics, who weren't, was obviously a change. In the latter part of that season, I went up to Commissioner Landis's office in Chicago. I think it was in Chicago because it was centrally located. Phil Wrigley, at one time, thought that the commissioner's office should be in the central part of the United States, and he wanted it out by the airport, so the officials could fly in and go right there and stay overnight. But it never did go over well. I imagine if the major leagues ever get a true commissioner again and he's from the Midwest, they'll put the office in Chicago. Anyway, that day I wanted to ask Commissioner Landis if I would be eligible for a cut of the World Series shares if the Tigers got into the Series, because I'd started the season and played with them. Somebody had told me that if you were with the club the year they won the pennant, then you were eligible to share in the World Series money that they'd won, but it was up to the players. I didn't know the rules or anything. Landis threw me out of the office. He said, "You're no longer there." He sure told me where to go. In fact, Judge Landis would swear at you. He was a judge and everything, but, boy, if you came in there and he didn't like you, he'd let you know. But he was a fair man for the ballplayers too. He did a lot for baseball. I don't know that you could have a Landis in this day and age, but you certainly could have a guy who's stronger than what we have.

I guess my claim to fame is that I played and got a hit in a twenty-four-inning tie ball game, 1–1. We were playing my old team, the Tigers, in Philadelphia. But the game went twenty-four innings and ended up in a 1–1 tie. We were in the twenty-fourth inning, and they weren't going to turn on the lights. There was a rule there that you couldn't turn on the lights. Les Mueller pitched nineteen and two-thirds innings for Detroit, and Dizzy Trout came in to relieve him. Dizzy was tough. We got in the bottom of the twenty-fourth inning, and there were two outs at the time. If we made a third out, we'd have to play another inning. It was getting dark, and the umpires didn't want to play another inning. The umpire came over and said to Mr. Mack, "It is getting very dark. If this inning goes too quick, we're going to play another inning. But if it doesn't, we'll call the game." So with two outs Mr. Mack sent Joe Burns, a utility outfielder, up to pinch-hit for the pitcher. He said, "Take your time now, Joseph, take your time." So Joe took his time, getting a bat and exchanging that one for another, stalling for time because he might make the last out. Then Mr. Mack called time and pointed at me and told me to go up there for Burns. So I went up to pinch-hit for Joe Burns. He was furious about being taken out. My instructions were to not swing at the first pitch. I didn't, and it was a ball. I took my time. Dizzy Trout was out there just staring at me. I knew he was going to try to throw a fastball by me. He threw that fastball, and, dang, I hit a long line drive that went down the left-field line about ten feet foul. Doggone, that would have been something. I have relived that quite a few times. I got out just a little too far ahead on it. Then he threw me the curve, and I knew his curve. I singled very sharply through the hole into left field. The next guy went out, and the game was over. It probably lasted seven hours or so. It's in the books, twenty-four innings, tie ball game, 1–1. That was my claim to fame. So if you want a sports trivia question, name the player who pinch-hit for a pinch hitter in the bottom of the twenty-fourth inning, a 1–1 tie, and got a stinging single into left. My daughter was there, and they got a picture of her. I've got it somewhere in a scrapbook. She was just a little girl with pigtails about that time, and she was watching her daddy pinch-hit in the twenty-fourth inning.

The great Al Simmons was a coach with the Athletics in 1945. We roomed together in spring training on one road trip. Al was a tremendous hitter, and he would put on an exhibition in batting practice. He was a little heavy around the middle, but, oh, he'd hit that ball into those left-field stands. Then he'd rattle that ball over to right field, right-center. Then he'd hit one nine miles, clear out in that deep left-center-field stands. Once in a while, he'd hit one up there in the upper deck. I don't think I could even carry one that far. As I recall, I never saw great hitters like Al miss the ball in batting practice, never saw them pop up a pitch. If they hit a ball to the outfield, it was still a line drive, even one that maybe they didn't hit as well. But it'd be a line drive. I marveled at that. I watched that as I went along in my baseball career. I watched the good hitters in batting practice. That was the mark of a good hitter: when he'd take five swings, he hit the ball five times well. Al would come out early, and I would throw batting practice to him. He'd laugh like heck because we didn't have the pitching screens in those days to protect the pitcher. He'd rifle one up the middle and almost knock me off the mound and laugh like heck about it. So then I kept throwing outside, but he could hit a ball out of the ballpark in right-center as good as anybody I've ever seen. He'd rattle that right-field tin fence in Shibe Park like a shotgun.

But Al was frustrated. I believe he wanted to be a manager, but he never got the opportunity. I don't know if he would have been a good one or not, but he sure was a good hitter. Surprisingly, however, he couldn't teach hitting. He'd say, "Aw, anybody can hit that nickel curve." I asked him one day, "Al! How in the heck do you hit that outside pitch? I'm pulling it." "Well," he said, "I hit that damn thing over the right-field wall." That's a pretty good answer, but some things you couldn't accomplish. He used a real long bat, a thirty-eight- or forty-inch bat that had very little taper to it. It had that same roundness all the way out from way below the trademark, a big, thick-handled bat. I never did ask what the bat weighed, but when I picked it up, it was very heavy. I would imagine it weighed thirty-eight ounces. He used that bat to great success. Somewhere along the line, I had read that Babe Ruth used a fifty-four-ounce bat. Well, if you could get that around on the ball, it sure had to go a long way. But most of us guys couldn't do that. Al was a true Hall of Famer. Throughout his whole career, he never took a drink. Occasionally he would talk about the great Athletics clubs of the late 1920s and 1930s, about Jimmie Foxx and Mickey Cochrane and Mule Haas and Jimmy Dykes and those guys. He said they had one heck of a club. He thought those A's clubs were just as good as the Yankees and even had better pitching.

Of the pitchers on the Philadelphia club, Bobo Newsom was the biggest character. Bobo wanted the youngest, most inexperienced catcher because he wanted to pitch and call his own game. He'd get racked up pretty good. He was a workhorse of a pitcher, and I loved him. But he would shake off and shake off and shake off until finally he'd throw what he wanted, and BANG! there'd go the ball. He always wanted to pitch against the good ball clubs. He pestered Mr. Mack to death. He persuaded Mr. Mack to let him pitch against the Yankees one particular day in Yankee Stadium. I was playing center field, and I think I chased down thirty-five balls. He talked Mr. Mack into disrupting the rotation, and I guess Mr. Mack decided to teach Bobo a lesson. It was hot. By the sixth inning, my tongue was hanging out from chasing all those balls, left-center, right-center, holy cow. Bobo came in and said, "Mr. Mack, I think I've done enough." Mr. Mack said, "No, I'll tell you when you've had enough," and he sent him back out there. I don't think Bobo disrupted the rotation any more after that. But he was always wanting to pitch against a good ball club. He never had a sore arm. He didn't have muscular weightlifter's arms; he had round, fat arms. He always called himself "Bobo," as in "Bobo will tell you this" or "Bobo will do this." He was a delight, and it was a pleasure being on the club with him.

Bobo was a very superstitious guy. When I was still with Detroit, I was playing center field against him one game. He was just a pitcher on another ball club then. One of the Detroit ballplayers, perhaps Doc Cramer, said, "Hey, Charlie, take these pieces of paper out there, and when you go over the mound, throw them on the mound." Bobo was pitching, and, boy, he went crazy when somebody tore paper up and put it on the mound. He made them stop the game, made the groundskeepers come out and pick up all the papers. He wouldn't do any of his own gardening, as they called it. When I got over to the Athletics, Bobo accused me of thinking up that trick on my own.

Sometimes the other guys on the Athletics played tricks on Bobo. Mr. Mack would allow us to play a little cards on occasion. We were playing cards with Bobo one time, I don't recall who all was there, Bill McGhee, Dick Siebert maybe. I was sort of an onlooker, just learning how to play. There was a bunch of guys who played poker. Now Bobo was a self-proclaimed expert on everything. McGhee said, "Well, how are you on the horse races?" Bobo said, "Oh, I'm pretty good." So they had the form out of the newspaper, and Bobo would pick a horse out and McGhee would cover the bet. Or McGhee would bet and Bobo would cover the bet. The trick was, every once in a while we had the radio on and you could get the results from one of the eastern tracks. McGhee would say, "Well, I've got to make a phone call," or "I got to do this," and he would leave and be back in a couple of minutes. What he was doing was getting the race results immediately, the live race results, a couple of minutes before the radio reported them. So Bill would take a look at the entries and say, "Well, I think I'll take this horse," and Bobo would cover the bet. McGhee already had the results, and he'd bet ten dollars and get odds of three to one. Bobo had to make a payout. McGhee was a sharpie. He took Bobo for $150, and Bobo never did catch on. Bobo would say, "What, you got bladder trouble or something?" He never did figure it out.

Another character on the Athletics was "Jittery Joe" Berry. I had played against him in the Texas League. He was a delightful guy. He had the right nickname, "Jittery Joe." He'd move around the mound all the time, pick up dirt, kick the dust out of his spikes, look around, and everything else. He had a play that would really frighten the heck out of you. Every once in a while, when we had a runner on second base, "Jittery Joe" would be moving around a lot and he'd be sneaking over toward second base, and all of a sudden he'd make a mad dash at the runner who was leading off and almost get him! I asked around if he'd ever gotten anybody, and they say he had gotten a couple of guys in the minor leagues. Can you imagine the pitcher running off the mound and tagging the guy out at second unassisted? He had a good arm. He wasn't a big guy, but he had a good arm. But what a joy to watch! You knew he was going to do that trick every time. He'd try it once a game. Every time he was pitching he'd try one time, so you'd always be watching for him. You'd say, "There he goes. He's going to get ready. He's going to go get him!" And Joe would dash for second. He almost got Hal Newhouser one game.

Russ Christopher, a big, tall, right-handed sidethrower, was also on the club. He had a terrible heart condition. He died at an early age. His skin was blue. But he pitched, and he was a good pitcher. In 4 games in which he was pitching and I was also playing, I got a base hit. The hits drove in either the tying or winning run, and Russ won those 4 ball games. He'd take me out to dinner. That was great. He kidded me about that all the time. I saw Russ's brother, Lloyd, years later, and Russ must have told him about my hitting, because Lloyd and I became very good friends when he was out in the Pacific Coast League, where I played against him. Lloyd was a big outfielder.

Don Black was a story in himself. He was a good pitcher. But Don had a weakness for John Barleycorn. At spring training in Frederick, Maryland, in 1945, Mr. Mack asked me if I'd room with Black, because I wasn't much of a drinker. I thought, "Uh, oh!" But I couldn't turn the manager down. I said, "OK." He said, "Now, I want you to take care of him. I want you to watch him. I want you to steer him away from any bar. I don't want him to have a drink." Don was an immaculate dresser. You'd never know he was snockered from his appearance. Other guys would be all a mess, but Don was always dressed snappily, sober or drunk. I followed Don around everywhere. I'd go with him to a restaurant, when I didn't want to eat. I'd go to a theater, when I didn't want to see a film. I just followed him around like a little puppy dog and kept him straight the whole spring training until we went over to Curtis Bay, Maryland, and played two games with the Coast Guard club. Curtis Bay had quite a few big league ballplayers in the Coast Guard at that time. The Coast Guard quartered us in the barracks. I was in the upper bunk after the game was over, just resting. I nodded off and fell asleep real soundly. When I awoke, I looked down and there was a bunch of guys sitting around. There was Don right in the middle. Somebody had broken out a bottle or two, and they were having a great time. I looked and said, "Oh God! Mr. Mack will kill me." I went down there, and when Don saw me coming, he took off. We didn't see him again for a week! I caught heck from Mr. Mack for letting him slip away.

One time we had just ridden the train all night into Boston from Philadelphia. At breakfast, I was sitting with Al Simmons, Dick Siebert, and Don. Don was bombed. He ordered split-pea soup, and when he went to get a spoonful, he passed out and fell face down into the soup. He was blowing bubbles. Mr. Mack was seated a couple of tables away. Al Simmons got up right away and went over to Mr. Mack to distract him, while we tried to do something for Don. Mr. Mack told Al, "Aloysius, you don't have to protect the boy. I see him." Another time my roommate, Larry Rosenthal, talked me into going and having a beer with him at a place in Cleveland. We didn't notice there were a couple of other ballplayers in the club. But then all of a sudden the spotlight went on them, and the emcee called for a drum roll and announced the presence of a couple of Philadelphia Athletics in the crowd. One was Don Black, and as usual he was inebriated. The emcee told him to take a bow. Every time I'd see Don after that, I'd imitate the emcee, and Don would get furious with me. But for all his drinking, Don was a good pitcher. Later Don pitched a no-hitter for Cleveland. But while pitching in September 1948, he had a cerebral hemorrhage and eventually died in 1959. Don Black could have been a fine pitcher, but those things go along with the game.

Jesse Flores also pitched for us. He was a real good guy. I loved Jesse Flores. He didn't have a lot of stuff, but he had a lot of determination. I bought a couple of sport coats that Jesse liked so much that I gave one to him. Every time he'd see me, in later years, he'd keep telling me he still had it. His son became a fine scout and judge of talent in California. Charlie Gassaway was on the Philadelphia club and went out to Oakland with me. When he was through playing baseball, he became a sheriff down in Tennessee. Steve Gerkin was a one-shot guy at Philadelphia. Every time he pitched, he lost. He never won a game. He was quite an Alibi Ike, always had an excuse why he lost the game. But he was very sincere. When he was going to pitch, he'd go up and down the bench and plead with all the ballplayers to help him win one ball game. He never did. He finished 0-12. Carl Sheib was a big, young, likable guy who had come up as a seventeen-year-old and stayed up with Philadelphia for ten years. He never became what you might call an outstanding regular, but he had great potential.

Dick Siebert was a solid ballplayer with the Athletics. He was a first baseman. But we also had Bill McGhee, who was a first baseman and couldn't play anywhere else. Mr. Mack experimented with Siebert in left field at Shibe Park. We were playing the Red Sox one game, and they had the bases loaded when a guy hit a fly ball out to Dick. He came running in and camped under the ball, but all of a sudden, he ducked and threw his hands over his head. He'd lost the ball in the sun. Three runs scored. He couldn't find the ball. He was blinded. We called time out, and somebody ran sunglasses out to him. When he came in, Mr. Mack asked, "Richard, what happened?" He said, "I didn't have my glasses." "Oh, you'll wear them now, won't you?" "Yes." So about two innings later, the Red Sox loaded the bases again. Siebert had the glasses on out there, when another guy hit another fly ball to left. Darn, you couldn't have planned it better. Dick camped under the ball, and again he ducked his head and everything else. The ball hit him on the back of the head and bounced. Three more runs came in. He came in, and Mr. Mack asked again, "Richard, what happened?" He said, "I forgot to flip the glasses down." Dick became a fine college baseball coach in Minnesota. I've never run into him again, and I've often wondered what he told his ballplayers about sunglasses.

Many of the other position players stick in my mind. George Kell would have his best Hall of Fame caliber years after he left the Athletics, but one thing I remember about him was that he batted with his hands split about three inches apart. The club brought him up from a Class B team, where he hit .390 or something like that. Irv Hall was a second baseman when I was there. He was a frail type of a guy. I think he was teaching school back in the Philadelphia area. Ed Busch, our shortstop, seemed to be always wanting to go home. When he was traded to Oakland, he didn't report out there. Frankie Hayes was one of our catchers, kind of a journeyman. He was around quite a few years. Buddy Rosar was our other catcher. He was from Buffalo. He was always threatening to go home and be a fireman. Finally somebody said, "Well, why don't you go home and be a fireman?" I guess he did eventually. He was a fine catcher and made some All-Star teams. But he was always dissatisfied, always wanting to be a fireman.

In the outfield we had Ford Garrison, a good, young prospect, and Joe Cicero, an older guy right off the local sandlots. Larry Rosenthal was one of my roommates at Philadelphia. He had played for the Yankees, the Indians, and the White Sox. We were playing at Yankee Stadium, and Rosenthal hit a game-winning home run, pinch-hit, if I recall right. The next day, Joe McCarthy, the Yankees manager, made this statement in the paper: "Rosenthal, Rosenthal. I can't spell it, and I can't even find him in the averages, Rosenthal. The only way you'll find him in the averages is if you turn the standings upside down. And that's the only way he's leading." We cut it out of the paper, and I kidded him unmercifully about that. He won the ball game, and he got great satisfaction. He was from Milwaukee, and he was one of the few Jewish ballplayers in the game. He was a good guy. He couldn't run worth a darn. I ran for him. It was a terrible insult to have another guy run for you. It meant you were too old, decrepit. I had a lot of fun with Larry when I did. I mentioned that to him on many occasions. One guy who could run like the dickens was Hal Peck. They called him "Old Three Toes." He was in a hunting accident, and he shot some toes off one of his feet. I don't know which foot it was, left or right. But he was climbing a fence with a shotgun bird hunting, was the way I got the story, and he pointed the gun down and the weight got on the trigger, and he had the safety off and, bang, it blew his toes off. But he could run, and he could bunt a ball on a dime. He'd just put a little marker out there, and he'd say I'm going to drop it on that. He was a left-handed hitter.

The other regular outfielder was Bobby Estalella. He was a Cuban and very dark-skinned. A lot of people thought that he was black, even though this was before Jackie Robinson. We'd heard a little bit that a black ballplayer might play in the major leagues, when I was at Philadelphia. There was some conversation about it, not an awful lot because it seemed like it was a taboo subject. But I would hear some southern guys talking about it in very crude and rude language. To me, Bobby's color didn't matter. I marveled at his abilities. He was some kind of a ballplayer. He spoke Spanish. He was a lovable guy, most always had a big smile. Every once in a while, he'd get hot, and they'd back away from him. He could hit pretty well. He led the team in hitting in 1945.

Dave Keefe was a coach of the Athletics. They called him "Three-Finger Dave." He had lost some fingers in some manner, I never did know how. He'd throw batting practice. He threw that durned three-finger slider, as he called it. He was tough. He was well up in age and had pitched in the big leagues. But you couldn't hit him. He'd let you know that slider was coming. And he'd throw it and, boy, it would get by you before you knew it. I don't know how he would do it with that stubby finger on his hand, but he had that uncanny pitch. Mr. Mack, one time, said that he ought to cut everybody's fingers off!

At the close of the 1944 season, I was wondering how I was going to get back to Mayfield. I bought a car from a friend of mine, Joe Nacchio, who worked down in Panama, in the Canal Zone. He lived in Philadelphia and was quite a baseball fan. Indeed, he tried to arrange to have the Athletics come to Panama for spring training. Mr. Mack, however, had already made other plans. Joe and I happened to be talking about it at Yankee Stadium during a game, and Larry MacPhail came by and got interested. I think one of those springs the Yankees took Joe up on his suggestion. In any case, he had bought a Buick from the Baldwin Locomotive Company, which was in Philadelphia. This was an executive car that they hadn't even licensed. I bought the car from Joe, but this was during the war and you needed gas rationing stamps. How was I going to get enough stamps to drive back home to Mayfield? I asked Yitz Crompton, a wonderful clubhouse guy that the Athletics had at that time, if he had any stamps. He didn't have any, but he told me how to get home. He gave me a dozen baseballs. I paid him a dollar apiece, so that he wouldn't get into trouble. He said, "This is what you do. Get these autographed by all the players and Mr. Mack." I said, "OK." When Mr. Mack saw these baseballs, he asked me how I got them. I said, "I bought them." He said, "Well, that's fine." So I had all the guys autograph them. Yitz told me, "Now, when you need gas, I'll get you a tank of gas with one of those baseballs. Put those baseballs, in that box, on the front seat. When you pull in the garage, at a filling station, the attendant is going to stick his head through the window and say, 'Yes,' and before you answer him, let him see those baseballs." It worked. The guy would say, "Wow, what are those?" I'd say, "Well, those are Philadelphia Athletics autographed baseballs." "Oh, oh, how do I get one?" he'd ask. I'd say, "Well, I need a little gas." "Oh, that's no problem," he'd answer. So he'd fill up my tank with gas, and I'd pay for the gas and give him a baseball. I got all the way back to Mayfield with about six or seven of those baseballs, trading for the right to buy some gas at filling stations during the war.

During the war, we played a bunch of exhibition games with military teams. We played at Bainbridge, Curtis Bay, and Annapolis in Maryland; Norfolk, Virginia; Great Lakes Naval Base near Chicago; Camp Leonard Wood, Missouri; Camp Polk, Louisiana; heck, we were all over. We did our part to build up the soldiers' and sailors' morale, and the military guys loved it. They let the servicemen in for free at one time, and they had a section of the stands for them at the major league ballparks. Later they charged them half price, or a quarter or a dollar or something like that, at ballparks. I thought that was a great thing to do. The military guys were great. They were wonderful fans. We were a link to their hometowns. They would find out where you were from and, oh boy, they'd give you a big cheer. Somebody would be from Georgia, and there'd be a Georgia guy there playing, and they'd root for that guy. We'd play those games and we *loved* it! At the time, good food was tough to get. You couldn't buy steaks and such. When we played at those places, they'd always feed us right before the game, and, boy, we scarfed up those steaks and those desserts. Then we'd go out there, and the base team would beat the heck out of us.

At Norfolk, Virginia, when we played the navy club there, they put up a canvas fence, which was three feet high, and they shortened the distances so the sailors could see a lot of home runs. I was playing center field, and one of their guys hit a high fly ball to left-center. I went back there and jumped the fence, ran back about five or six steps, and caught the ball. The umpire called it a home run, which it was, but in disgust I put my hands on my hips and held my glove up to show the baseball. The navy guys cheered like heck. I was their hero because I'd caught the ball. But they allowed the home run. Another time I caught a ball off of Hank Majeski, a Boston player who was in the Coast Guard, and ran up the stairs in left field. As I passed him in the outfield, he said, "I'll kill you if you catch a ball like that again." When we stayed in the barracks that night, he made me sleep in the upper bunk. He said, "That'll teach you to rob me of a home run."

At Great Lakes Naval Base, there was a real good team, mostly made up of major leaguers. Mickey Cochrane was the manager there. Pinky Higgins, the third baseman for Detroit, was in the navy and stationed there. Major league umpires would come and umpire the games. They had a young outfielder there, Johnny Groth, who everybody raved about. Higgins talked about him to Mr. Mack. He said, "Take a look at that kid out there." Boy, he did everything. He played center field. He could run. He was an eighteen- or nineteen year-old kid in the navy who had played maybe one year of professional baseball. But he was fantastic. As it turned out, the Tigers signed him. Some years later Johnny came out to Denver when I was the manager, and I reminded him of that game.

In the game at Great Lakes Naval Training Base, I got to hit against "Rapid Robert" Feller, who was in the navy. Bob wouldn't throw the curve ball too much when he was pitching there. I guess he didn't want to hurt his arm, although he had a good curve. Feller wouldn't try to get you out with cute stuff. He came right at you. So Bob threw me nine straight fastballs, and I fouled off six of them. Three or four of the fouls hit Bill McGowan, the umpire, in the mask or pads. He was mad at me. I just kept throwing that bat at the ball. After the sixth foul, McGowan said, "You better swing at this next one." The next pitch was about a foot over my head, and I swung at it. I got out of there, because McGowan was going to call it a strike anyhow. But I hit against Feller and fouled off six of them. I was so proud I thought of asking for a raise!

On another occasion during the war, we were up at one of the bases in Massachusetts. I think it was a Coast Guard base. They had simulated machine gun target practice. The plane would flash on a screen, you had the machine gun, and you were supposed to shoot it down. You were strapped in there and just shooting. George Kell tried it and got the highest score that anybody had ever gotten who ever went through there. The sergeant said he didn't know how many thousands of guys they had tested that way. Then he made a statement to Kell that I'll never forget. He said, "You'll be a batting champion." Later, when the Athletics traded him to the Tigers, George became a batting champion and went on to have a Hall of Fame career. I mentioned that to George one time.

I saw some funny things during my time with the Tigers and the Athletics. I saw Nick Altrock in 1943, when he was with the "Clown Prince of Baseball." He and Al Schacht were a team. He was funny. He'd come out there and turn that bill of the cap backward and sideways and would mimic an argument with an umpire, kicking dirt over in the dugout and everything. We'd laugh like heck. But I also witnessed some terrible things. I saw a line drive break the leg of Al Benton, a big, right-handed pitcher for Detroit. He was pitching against Philadelphia. Bobby Estalella hit a ball right back through the box, and it hit Al right on the shin and broke his leg. He had all of his weight on his front leg. He was out for the year. But it healed, and he came back. He was a pretty good pitcher, real competitive. Another time, in New York, when we were staying at the New Yorker Hotel, I got up one morning, looked out the window, and saw the Empire State Building on fire. An army bomber had flown right into it. I called my roommate, Ed Busch, over, but he didn't believe me until he saw it for himself. We had to evacuate the hotel. Another day I saw a kid fall out of the upper deck at Shibe Park. I was with Detroit. It was on the third base side. I looked up and I saw this kid running down, out of control, on the steps. I turned to one of the players and said, "That kid's going to fall out!" And, boy, he hit the railing and tumbled down and landed on a bunch of people who looked up. He walked away unhurt. If he'd landed on those seats, oh, my gosh! And another odd occurrence was when I bumped into Moe Berg in the street in Washington. Moe was a CIA man. He could speak about a dozen languages. He looked like a cloak-and-dagger guy. He had a raincoat on. He recognized me. He knew me. He knew everybody. We chatted for a while. I inquired, "What the heck are you doing here?" He said, "Oh, nothing."

My family, of course, followed my adventures in the big leagues. My father sure could read a box score, and he especially kept track when I played with Detroit and Philadelphia. He could figure out all the statistics, even though there were a lot of zeros behind my name in too many of those games. He talked about Mr. Mack quite a bit. He loved Steve O'Neill. My sister would write me letters and ask what happened and so forth in those days. She came to see me in some games in New York. One time the usher wouldn't let her come down to talk to me. They were pretty strict. Finally she said, "That's my brother, and I'm going to stand here and you're not going to stop me!" Finally the guy looked at me and asked, "Is this right?" I said, "Yes." I thought she was going to hit him with her purse!

Hank Greenberg of the Tigers came out of the service in 1945. He was a hard worker, a dedicated player. He made himself into a fine first baseman. I was playing for Philadelphia when we went into Detroit to play a doubleheader. I got to see Hank trying to recover his hitting abilities. He practiced hitting until his hands were bleeding. He had his fingers all taped up. In the first game, he hit fly balls to right-center. Usually Hank was a pull hitter to left. In the second game, he did the same thing. He hit some balls pretty well, hit a couple of fly balls, and I caught one or two of them. Then, in his last time at bat, he got hold of one and hit the ball into the upper deck in left field. The fans in the stands just erupted. I thought those fans were going to come down and carry him off. It was a great moment for him, a great moment for everybody and especially pleasing to me. In fact, I was rather happy that he hit it. We didn't have a very good ball club, and if anything, I happy for him. Oh, he was a fine player. Many years later, when I managed in Triple-A, I was on the plane going to a minor league meeting and Hank was on the flight. I sat beside him. That son of a gun told me everything about my career. He was an official with the Cleveland team. An extremely fine person, he should have been the commissioner of baseball.

We had some great umpires back in those years. Red Jones was a delight. He was funny, and he worked real hard. He was kind of a jolly umpire. You couldn't get mad at him, even if he missed a play. Old "Number One," Bill McGowan, was great. He was a class umpire. He had real demonstrative movements. We all had great respect for him. You never argued with Bill McGowan. You talked, two gentlemen talking. You never cussed or anything. If you did, you were gone. In his day he had been an amateur boxer and gotten laid low with one punch. Boy, if you mentioned that to him, you were a goner. So I went up there once, not knowing about that, and mentioned his boxing. He said, "Who put you up to that, Bush?"

I said, "Uh, I think it was Roger Cramer." McGowan went over and ran Doc out of the ball game. George Pipgras was an old Yankees pitcher. He was great on balls and strikes. I started kidding him a little bit: "Hey, you're favoring the pitcher, aren't you?" These guys were competitors too. You didn't dare say that too loud or too long, or you weren't around long. We called Bill Sommers "Old Apple Head." I was kind of a bench jockey with Detroit. Some of the veterans told me to call him "Apple Head." I yelled out there, "Apple Head." He came running over there and chewed out the wrong guy. But he was a fine umpire.

I guess I should say something about the stadiums where I played in the majors. Fenway Park in Boston was great. We stayed at the Kenmore Hotel in Kenmore Square. You'd roll out of bed, and you were right there at the ballpark. You could meet the fans. It was a very comfortable ballpark. Of course, the Green Monster was there in left field, but also the field slanted upward to the wall. I asked Ted Williams about that once. He wasn't sure why it was like that. It looked like it might have been fourteen feet higher than ground level. Once, a minor leaguer, Nick Cullop, who was up for a short time and couldn't field very well, made three errors on one ball. He came charging in to field the ball; it went through his legs, bounced off the wall, and went through his legs again; and then he threw the ball away at third base. I saw balls hit the scoreboard, but I never saw a ball go in one of the inning holes. That was Fenway Park, one of the most delightful ballparks. I was involved in a crazy incident there when I played for Philadelphia. I hadn't hit a home run in the big leagues yet. I had come close a few times. But in Boston I got hold of a pitch. Unfortunately I hit it too much on a line. It hit one of the loudspeaker horns above the wall. If I'd put it two feet to one side or the other, it'd have gone into the net above the left-field wall. I got a double out of it. Left field was short down the line, but it angled out fast. I played left field there, but it was tough. The ball would come off of that monster and hit that slope and give you a difficult bounce. Ted Williams played it like an expert. Right field was short down the line, but it curved out real fast. I saw home runs that kind of curved around the foul pole. When I was with the Tigers, I saw a Tiger pitcher almost get hit on the head by a home run while he was in the bullpen beyond the right-field wall. That woke him up in a hurry. I also saw a ball hit a pigeon in midair at Fenway while I was with the Athletics. Somebody hit a ball out to right field. It hit the bird, and both of them dropped right straight down. The ball was in play.

Fans can cause some problems for outfielders by reaching over the fence. I saw it in Boston, down the left-field line, where the stands were only about three feet away from the line. I saw fans just reach over when an outfielder was camped under it and catch the ball. In fact, I was playing left field with Philadelphia when a fan tried that on a ball hit down the line. But the funny thing was, he didn't catch it. It hit his hands and came down, and I caught the ball. The ball hit alongside his palm and dropped down. The umpires couldn't see it. There may have been only two umpires, instead of three, at that game. Ordinarily the batter would have gotten a two-base hit because of fan interference. But I caught the ball. I was watching it all the way. I threw the ball in, and they called him out. Nobody said a word, because you couldn't see the play real well.

Yankee Stadium was wonderful, but it had a huge outfield. There was a strange thing about Yankee Stadium. The wind was very tricky. It would be blowing in the Stadium. It'd be blowing up high, and you could see the flag waving in toward home plate. When the wind hit the grandstand, it would come down to field level and swoop back up. On a low line drive, you'd better look out. You had to back-pedal in a hurry. I was playing center field for the Athletics, and we had one of those days. One of those low line drives whipped me. I thought I had it all the way, and it just kept going. It just caught a little wind current, just enough to whip me. But a high fly ball would hang up for you. It was a snap. You could just come walking in. It was very deceiving. If I'd ever had an opportunity to talk to Joe DiMaggio at any length, I would've asked how he played that center field. Left field could be tricky too. There was a little curve in the stands. If you weren't careful, the ball would get down that line and get by you. Yankee Stadium had a short right field. What would Ted Williams have hit in Yankee Stadium? What would Joe DiMaggio have hit in Fenway Park? Seven hundred home runs? Eight hundred? At one time there was a lot of conversation about trading each to the other.

New York was fascinating. Every once in a while, we'd see a Broadway show. Somebody would get tickets. We played a lot of day games. There were an awful lot of celebrities who'd come out to the ball game in the afternoon, and they'd sit close, in box seats close to the visitors' dugout. You'd get to know them, and you'd find out that they were in a stage show or something, and you'd say, "Hey, how about a ticket?" They'd get us tickets just for an autographed ball. It was very enjoyable.

Briggs Stadium in Detroit, when I came up, was also wonderful. It had a lot of personality. I think that ballpark and Fenway Park and Wrigley Field are my three favorites, but they've since replaced the Detroit one. In Briggs Stadium, you were very close to the fans. The box seats, the upper deck, all the seats were close. The flagpole was directly in center field, a hundred feet above where everybody could see it, but where the outfielders could see it to judge the wind. Briggs Stadium had a 4-foot or so wire fence on top of a 4-foot concrete one below, which went all the way around the ballpark. Right field was kind of interesting. It had an overhang. I think it was 325 feet to the foul line at the bottom of the fence. But the upper deck was a 10-foot overhang. Every once in a while, you'd see a fan reach over from the upper deck in right field and catch a fly ball that the outfielder was going to catch. I don't know how the umpires ruled on that. I'd never seen it myself, but they just told me about it.

League Park in Cleveland also had a long left field and a short right field. They had a tall screen out there. I didn't like the stadium in Cleveland. It seemed like it was always raining there. The conditions were always rain and fog. The stadium was close to Lake Erie and was not comfortable looking. It was a very old ballpark. Players didn't like to play there because it was very dull, and the wind was always blowing off the lake. Sportsman's Park in St. Louis had a screen in front of the seats out there in right field. And they had a screen on top of the grandstand, or extended grandstand, so that balls hit out of the stadium wouldn't land on Dodier Avenue. It had the worst infield in baseball, because both the Browns and the Cardinals played on it. The grass never got a chance to grow back. Shibe Park had a concrete left-field fence, which was probably eight or ten feet high and had a little wire fence on top, so the fans couldn't interfere with the ball. In right field was the tin fence. Old Comiskey Park had a very big outfield with a brick fence. I saw the women of the All-American Girls' Professional Baseball League practicing there in 1943. Griffith Stadium also had a gigantic outfield, especially left field.

Clubhouses varied throughout the league. Detroit had a beautiful one, one of the better clubhouses in the American League. At Philadelphia the home clubhouse was pretty good, but the visitors' clubhouse was always downgraded. You didn't have anything. Sportsman's Park had the worst clubhouse I'd ever seen. The lockers, those metal ones, were maybe twelve inches wide. The mirror would be cracked. In the spring they had a big potbelly stove, where they'd have a fire to keep it a little bit warm. Comiskey Park was kind of the same way. They had a room upstairs where you'd dress. League Park didn't have much either. If a clubhouse had a whirlpool, it was just big enough for one guy sitting down, or maybe two guys standing. There was nothing like the magnificent clubhouses the players have today.

I've mentioned several times that I just couldn't hit the curve ball. Not until I became a playing manager in the minor leagues did I get some mastery over the curve, and then I became pretty good at teaching younger players how to hit it. But in the spring of 1945, it was the knuckle ball that did me in. A day or two before the season opened, we played the Triple-A International League club in Baltimore. I hit a home run each game. I had the center-field job won. I had had a real fine spring training with the Athletics, and I thought center field was all mine. But we opened against the Washington Senators, who that year had four knuckleballers—Roger Wolff, Dutch Leonard, Mickey Haefner, and Johnny Niggeling—and Rick Ferrell, a catcher who could catch a butterfly in midair. Oh, gosh, I hate to even bring those guys up. I wake up at night in fright about those knuckle ball pitchers. How would you like to have your career ended by four guys who could throw the knuckle ball? I was batting leadoff. I went 0 for 16 or 0 for 20 or 1 for 21 or something like that. I didn't crack the lineup again until June. If I ever run across any of their kinfolk, I'm going to tell them, in a nice sort of way, about how those four guys destroyed my career.

In what turned out to be my last stretch of games with the Athletics, I hit 3 home runs, all to help Philadelphia win ball games in 1945. My clouts helped beat Boston once and the Yankees twice. The one against the Red Sox was a 3-run homer off Jim Wilson, right down the left-field line at Shibe Park. Years later Jim became the director of the Scouting Bureau and hired me right away. I would kid him about that homer every chance I got. Then I hit a curve ball off Jim Turner of New York, with the score tied 3–3, and beat him in the ball game in Yankee Stadium. I hit the ball down the left-field line about six feet over the fence, and the outfielder couldn't quite reach it. You never forget those good ones, those good base hits. Jim Turner became a pretty good pitching coach for many years with a few ball clubs. But the one I hit the day before, in New York off of Hank Borowy, went the farthest. I hit it right next to the bullpen in the lower grandstand, which is out there by the gate in Yankee Stadium. I guess it went four-hundred-plus feet. We were behind a run, 6–5, and had a man on base. I hit Borowy's curve ball into the seats, and I hit it pretty well. I gave it that big home run trot around the bases. The next time I came up, I was flat on my back. He knocked me down. This home run actually helped Hank, because I think the very next day he was traded to the Cubs, and then he helped win the pennant for them. I never saw Hank after that, but I was going to tell him that he owed me a dinner. I never got those home run balls back. To my knowledge I never saw a fan bring a ball back to somebody to get it autographed or give it back to a guy. Those 3 home runs were my peak in the majors. I hit quite a few in the minor leagues, especially when I became a playing manager.

But that wasn't enough to save me in 1945. The Athletics needed a shortstop, so they traded Charlie Gassaway, Ed Busch, and me to Oakland for Jake Caulfield, all the way across the continent in the Pacific Coast League. After I had hit 3 home runs! I pleaded with Mr. Mack, "My gosh, Mr. Mack, you couldn't have sent me any farther." I was on my way west. Every time I'd see Jake Caulfield, who later retired from the San Francisco police force, at spring training at Phoenix, I'd tell him, "I'm going to punch you right now." He lasted only one year with the Athletics. I said, "If you'd quit one year sooner, I'd still have been in the big leagues." And we'd have a laugh over that.

FOUR

Go West, Young Man

After my release from Philadelphia and my trade to Oakland in the Pacific Coast League in the summer of 1945, I headed west to join my new club. I traveled on the train that was taking troops to the West Coast for the Pacific Theater, where the war was still going on. I drove my family down from Philadelphia to Mayfield and then went west. The train was completely packed. You couldn't get anything to eat. A couple of civilians who were on the train at the station in St. Louis told me I'd better get something to eat before I got on, because there wouldn't be any food on the train. So I bought myself a whole bunch of crackers and stuff in bags. And for some reason, I had a bottle in my bag. I don't know why I ever had it, but I guessed it was going to be a long trip, so I bought a bottle of bourbon and put it in. I paid something like fifteen dollars for it, at wartime black market prices. I put it in my bag and didn't think anything of it.

I got on the train, and we traveled into Missouri. I went into the men's lounge, and there was a Catholic priest having himself a nip out of a little half-pint bottle. Boy, he was down, oh gosh, was he depressed. We struck up a conversation. He said that he was going out to Nevada somewhere, being punished. He was from Boston and had a Boston Irish accent. I think his name was O'Brien. He was drowning his sorrows a little bit. He told me his story. I told him who I was, how I'd played at Fenway Park and so forth. We had a good chat. The train kept going on, across Missouri and into Kansas. We sat up all the time. There were no sleeper berths. The next morning, I offered him some of those extra cheese and crackers I had at the time. He said, "Oh, Charlie, you wouldn't by any chance have a pint of whiskey with you, would you?" I said, "No, Father, I don't. I'm not much of a drinker." I never thought about the darn bottle in my bag. Now Kansas was a dry state. And Kansas is a big state. It took a little while to get across. About halfway across later that day, I remembered the bottle in my duffel bag. I brought it in there and opened it up. He gave me the dirtiest look you've ever seen. He said I made him suffer for half a day across Kansas. I said, "Father, I swear, I forgot I had it." He said, "Never mind, cousin, let's just open the bottle." So we got one of those little paper cone cups, and he filled it up and had himself a drink. He insisted I have a little spot with him, and I did. Then I said, "Well, I've got to go take a nap, see if I can't find a seat or sit on those duffel bags of the soldiers and take a little nap." I hadn't slept very much. I left the bottle with him. He said, "Bless you, my boy, bless you." By that evening, I guess we'd crossed the Kansas line into Colorado. I came back and noticed the bottle was almost empty. I said, "You keep it, Father." He got off in Nevada somewhere. He had a small church out there.

As for myself, I was on my way to Oakland. I got there on a Sunday. I had been on the train four days. It would stop places, or we'd have to let another train coming the other way go by. I went to the ballpark. They had a doubleheader that day. I reported up to the front office, and they were surprised that I'd come that quickly. Usually guys from the big leagues didn't show up for two or three weeks. Vic Devincenzi, the owner and general manager of the Oakland club, gave me my contract and asked me if I was ready to play. I said, "Yeah, I think so." They gave me a uniform. I pinch-hit in the first game and played center field in the second. I hadn't slept in nearly two days. In my conversation with Devincenzi, I told him that Mr. Mack had paid me for the full year. He said, "Well, I don't care about that. We'll pay you from the time you arrived. I appreciate you coming." Mr. Mack had also told me that if I got out there real quick to join the club, he'd give me a two-thousand-dollar bonus. When I got out there, I asked Devincenzi to wire Mr. Mack and let him know I had made it. I didn't tell him why. So Devincenzi wired him, and I received a check for two thousand dollars. Vic Devincenzi said, "Well, we'll give you the same thing that you were being paid back there." So he gave me the salary that I had had with Philadelphia, and not only that, but he paid my Pullman fare all the way back to Kentucky after the season was over. I said that he didn't have to do that, but he insisted. I started off on the right foot, at least financially, in Oakland.

Out there my manager was none other than Casey Stengel, before he went up with the Yankees, before he became great. Casey was one heck of a manager. He was one of the those guys with a sixth sense. He was an innovator in every sense. He knew what to do. They used to call him a clown sometimes. There was that story of when he was a player with the Giants, and the Dodger fans were on him pretty heavy, and he tipped his hat and a sparrow flew off his head. He'd found a sparrow out in the outfield and put it under his cap. He was giving the fans the bird. I think they loved him for it forever. And they made fun of his speaking patterns, his so-called "Stengelese," especially in front of Congress. They questioned him, and I think he had them in an uproar. He was an absolute delight as a person. But he wasn't a clown. Good, gosh, Casey had it all. He knew how to handle pitchers too. I was surprised and pleased. He had been an outfielder when he played, but he had learned how to manage pitchers. Usually an outfielder was not supposed to know how to handle pitchers, but his example helped me do a pretty good job myself handling pitchers later. I'm extremely fond of Casey Stengel. He played me at all the positions with Oakland. I played third base, short, a little second, some outfield. He treated me very well. Once, just as Mr. Mack had, he called me back after I had gotten 2 or 3 hits and said, "You've got all you're going to get." But otherwise he was real good to me. He stuck up for his players.

It was truly a marvel to watch he and Lefty O'Doul manage against each other. It was like nothing I'd ever seen. These were two masters, exact opposites. Lefty was a tremendous, classy manager. He had been a pitcher at one time, until he became an outfielder and hit .390 or something in the big leagues. He was a great teacher of hitting. He took players like Gene Woodling and turned them around. He gave Gene a new stance. Woodling was one of those guys who crouched way down low, and, boy, could he hit after Lefty got through with him. O'Doul had been over to Japan. Lefty O'Doul's name in Japan, as far as baseball went, was the same as Babe Ruth's was here. They called him "the man in the green suit." He wore green suits. They loved him over there. He didn't want to go manage in the big leagues, because the owner of the San Francisco Seals paid him more money than he could have made in the majors. We played 7-game series in the Coast League to cut down on travel. You would always try win at least 5 against the club you played. But it seemed every time Casey and Lefty O'Doul managed against each other, the series would wind up 4 games to 3. One team would win 4, only to have the other club come out and win a third game. I don't recall it ever going 6-1 or 5-2. Lefty and I became good friends. He coached third, and I played third base for quite a while, a week to ten days or something like that.

One Sunday evening after a game, we stopped off at Casey's home in Pasadena, and he was telling us about one of his deals that he had made back in the early part of the war. He had a friend who owed him a lot of money and who planned to get rich raising turkeys. Casey had loaned him quite a bit of money. This went on and on for a year, then another year, and the guy couldn't pay him back. Finally the guy came to Casey and said he wanted to settle up. But, he said, the only way he could pay Casey was to give him the ten thousand turkeys he had stored in some freezers. Casey agreed to that. When they shook hands, according to Casey, the guy said, "Casey, they're your turkeys, you turkey." Casey stayed friends with the guy. Then the war came on and, with food shortages all around, Casey sold them at quite a profit. Those turkeys weighed anywhere from eighteen to thirty pounds. He sold them and made a little fortune, at a dollar something a pound, perhaps even more, to the military. He had ten thousand turkeys in the freezer, and he sold them all. Casey said, I had him right where I wanted him. Casey was shrewd.

Much like Mr. Mack, Casey liked some of my heads-up playing. One game against San Francisco, I was playing third base because Bill Hart got sick and couldn't play. I came up when the bases were loaded, with two out, and we were ahead 5–1. Ted Jennings was the Seals' third baseman. I looked down at third base and saw he was way back on the grass. So I laid down a perfect bunt with the bases loaded and drove in a run. Then they got us out. When I came into the dugout, somebody said to me, "Boy, that was a bush play if I've ever seen one." I said, "What was?" "Bunting with the bases loaded!" I said, "I got us a run, didn't I?" And Casey said, "Yeah, yeah, kid, yeah." He said, "Don't be criticizing the guy who drives in a run." When I went back out to third base, Lefty O'Doul said to me, "Hey, Met, that's probably going to be the winning run." And darned if it wasn't. They scored 4 more runs, and we held on to beat them 6–5. Years later, when I was managing Denver, I ran into Casey on a plane to Minneapolis. Casey had a sister or niece or someone who lived in Denver. He said, "Hey, kid, how are you?" We got into a conversation. He'd always talk to me in a whisper, so you'd have to get lower so you could hear. He said, "You know, they kind of gave you a little hell that time back there." I said, "When, Casey?" He said, "Well, in San Francisco when you dragged a bunt, you got us a run." I said, "Well, I'll be darned, Casey, you remember that?" He answered, "Yeah, you did right, you got us a run. Don't let them kid you. That was a hell of a play. You got the guys a run. That run was probably going to beat them."

Casey knew how to motivate his players. He would make a statement, "Okay, fellas, if we win this series . . ."—it was maybe 3 games to 2 and we had a doubleheader coming up—"if we win five games to two, the dinner will be on me." We'd get out there and hustle like a son of a gun and beat them both games, and win five games in a seven-game series in the Coast League. He'd walk around afterward and pass out money, sometimes five dollars, sometimes ten dollars, all out of his own funds. He'd reward us. He loved that. We loved that. We got meal money, but this was a bonus. Ten dollars, you could have a fine dinner on that.

To give a further idea of Casey Stengel's brilliance, I'd like to tell about his spring training camp. I went through one of his camps with Oakland. He had a system that I thought was the most fabulous thing that I'd ever seen. Later on I copied it. He'd take the whole ball club, and he'd start you from the hitter's circle. He'd say, "All right, each one of you is an individual now, and you're the next hitter. What are you thinking out here? What's the score? What run is that guy in front of you? What run do you represent? How many are out? Then when you go up to the plate, you know how many are out. You see if it's the first out, if there's one out, nobody on or whatever it is. Now you're in the ball game. What do you do when you walk up there? You look down for the sign when the situation demands it." He gave this lecture right at the on-deck circle. He'd say, "Now you're the hitter. You're not a run. You're nothing until you swing that bat. You got to know how many are out. What's the score? What run am I?" Then he'd say, "And then when you answer yourself all of those things, you look down and see the sign. Now we got a guy on first base, and you're the hitter, and he's the tying runner or the winning runner, or maybe you're four runs behind, or maybe you're three runs ahead, now you look for the sign. See whether the manager wants you to bunt, hit and run, steal, all the things that enter into the situation of the game."

Then he'd walk us all down to first base, where he'd say, "When you're walking down to first base, when you get a base hit, or running down to first base with a base hit or walking down on a base on balls, you keep your head up and start looking at the coach right away. He may be giving you a sign. Be alert. When you get to first base, now you're one quarter of a run. Now you got to ask the same questions that you asked yourself back there at the on-deck circle. Now the coach is going to tell you. Don't be looking at your shoes or figuring out your batting average if you got a base hit. Be looking at the coach at third base, or looking at the coach and listening. You can listen and look at the same time." He was remarkable for his instruction. Then he'd say, "When you lead off a base, you got to know everything. When you get to second base, you're one-half a run. Now, if you paid attention to the outfielders, you know the right fielder's got what kind of arm, center fielder, left fielder, you know that when you're on first base. Now you know it again when you're on second base. Now you know it again when you're on third base. Now, if the ball's hit in front of you, and you're a runner at second base, you know what to do. If it's hit back of you,

you know what to do. So now, if the hitter is a poor right-handed hitter, you got to be careful about the ground ball in the hole, because usually the only play the shortstop can make is the play at third. Then when you get to third base, you cannot be doubled off on a line drive to the infield. It's a cardinal sin. To be doubled off at third base on a line drive. If I have a gun, I'm going to shoot you! I'm going to drop you right there."

Casey would go over all sorts of things about baseball. He'd say, "Now take a look at those outfielders, every pitch. See if they moved around. Get in the game. Someday you're going to be a manager." Casey would take a look at me, because I was very aggressive. I wanted to learn, darn it. Some of my instructors in baseball would just say, "Get up there and hit the ball." They wouldn't tell you the ins and outs like Casey could. Later, when I went on to manage, I used a lot of Casey's techniques. I made all my ballplayers watch the outfielders throw from the outfield, before they could go in and change their shirts and have a Coke or whatever. I copied a lot of Casey's terminology from 1945 and 1946. One of his favorite phrases, one that I repeated, was when he'd hear somebody say, "Well, I tried." He'd say, "Hell, a mule can try! Do it." He was from Missouri, and I guess that's where he got it.

The Pacific Coast League was a great league. A lot of the players would never want to go up to the majors. They played out there simply because they'd get a salary for the month out there, and they played six months, sometimes 180 to 200 games. Then they'd have a couple of weeks for the playoffs, so you got yourself maybe a month's extra pay if you were in the playoffs. If you made $1,000 a month or $1,500, you made more than you did at the minimum in the majors. There was no minimum starting salary starting in the big leagues, so if they wanted to give you $5,000, you had to take it. The seven-day schedules in the Coast League were great. We'd take two-week road trips. We'd play Wednesday, Thursday, Friday, Saturday, and a doubleheader Sunday, or some configuration like that. We'd get Sunday evening, Monday, and Tuesday off. We wouldn't have to show up at the ballpark until Wednesday. Oh, the players loved it! I don't recall whether we played a nine-inning and a seven-inning game, or two nines, probably two nine-inning ones.

The train trips in the Coast League were wonderful. When I was with the Oakland Oaks, we'd leave Oakland on a Sunday evening after a doubleheader, about 7:00, by train. We'd get on board and play cards. They'd allow us to play limited poker, quarter limits, so nobody would lose too much money. It was very enjoyable. We'd get into Seattle Tuesday morning, making a couple of stops along the way. Somewhere up in Oregon, maybe Redford, the fans knew that the ballplayers would come in there, and they'd bring out fried chicken and sandwiches, food of all kinds. We had a couple-hour layover, and gee, you got to know all these people, and they were a lot of fun. We'd autograph stuff, and every once in a while we'd sneak a baseball or two and give it to some little guy out there. We'd get to Seattle about 9:00 in the morning, go straight to the hotel, and then we'd play that night.

The Coast League parks were delightful, great places to play. I'd like to tell about the Portland ballpark. In left field, right down the left-field line, you could look up and see a canyon. This was high country in Portland, with a lot of forest really close by. When I was with Oakland in 1945, we were playing a Sunday doubleheader there. We got the first game in. I looked over, and everyone was going to the clubhouse and getting undressed. I said, "Aren't we playing a doubleheader?" The manager said, "Yes, we're playing a doubleheader, but we're not going to play." I said, "What do you mean?" He said, "Go out and take a look." I went out, and one of the guys said, "Look, it's dark up the canyon." I didn't know what he meant, but I looked up and here came the rain down through that canyon. You could see a sheet of rain coming down. We had to run way inside. It was one of the dogdarnedest downpours you ever saw. They didn't even have time to put the tarp on the pitcher's mound. The second game was called.

Out in the old Hollywood ballpark in the Coast League in left center field was a sign with Jane Russell advertising the movie *The Outlaw*. It was a very provocative sign. She was wearing a low-cut dress. It was a big, wide, high sign. If you hit the ball over the top of the Jane Russell sign, you got two free tickets to her movie. Out at the old Oakland Emeryville park, there was a similar arrangement. They had a sign exactly where the left fielder would play. The outfield fence was a double-decked one. They had a target there that read "Hit me for a thousand dollars." It looked like there was no way you could hit that target with the left fielder right there. But we were playing the Los Angeles Angels there the last day of the season in 1945, and they had a big outfielder, Glen Russell, who, on the last swing he had, hit that darn thing right in the middle and won the thousand dollars. I found out later this was rigged. Both clubs were out of the playoff picture, so the batter told the pitcher that if he'd groove the ball, throw nothing but fastballs, so he could hit the target, he'd give him half the prize money. I guess our pitcher got half of it.

When I got to spring training in 1946, at Boyes Hot Springs, there were a lot of young players, many just coming out of the service. I think we had eighty or ninety players on one field that spring. I looked around and saw all these young guys, and there I was, just hanging on, so to speak. I thought I'd better do all I could to make the club. During the exhibition games, I noticed we had no batboy, so I just jumped out there. I wasn't playing that game. I was sitting on the bench, and Stengel was there. He had no coach, except for Billy Raimondi, his catcher and fill-in manager the year before, who was going to be Casey's coach, his right-hand man. So like a batboy I'd run out there and get a bat. I'd get the balls, the foul balls, give them to the umpire, and everything else. Casey called me and said, "Hey, kid, what are you trying to do? Get my job?" I said, "Yep, Casey, if you turn your back, I'll get it." I was doing anything to stay with the ball club. I was bound and determined to go back to the big leagues. I would run and run to the outfield. I played center field. I'd run to the outfield and run in. In fact I'd even beat the first baseman from his position on the third out. The fans got a big kick out of that.

We had some good players on that Oakland team, but Jackie Price was by far the biggest jokester. He played infield for Casey. Jackie was always pulling something. One of his best ones was where a guy would be reading a newspaper on the train in the chair car, and he'd come along and light the newspaper. The guy would have it spread out, reading it, and the flames would start coming up, and the guy would drop it fast. You'd laugh like heck, and all the people would laugh like heck. Of course, you'd get up and stomp it out. I think Stengel found out about that, and he said, "We'll have no more burning of the papers."

Jackie would put on shows on Sunday. He had a sling, the type that David had when he slew Goliath. He would put a baseball in it, whirl it around, and throw the living daylights out of it. He'd throw it five hundred to six hundred feet. He would just twirl that darn thing and throw it. At Oakland there was a two- or three-story factory over the deep left-center-field fence. Jackie hit some of those factory windows a couple of times. He also had a trapeze type of thing, and he'd hang upside down and hit batting practice upside down on one leg. He'd throw a baseball or warm up with a pitcher that way too. He would throw to third base, second, first. He'd warm up with three baseballs at one time, throw to three guys at one time. He'd leave his fly open on his uniform and catch the ball in his fly or in his shirt. He'd pull his uniform up over his head and throw a ball, and he'd catch it. He was just marvelous. I wish they had somebody like him now. He was tremendous. Bill Veeck eventually took him up to Cleveland.

While he was at Oakland, Jackie had some snakes as a hobby. Some of us were having lunch, and he came in and sat down with us. He ordered a sandwich. The waitress brought his order. He took one bite and let out a big yell. He reached and pulled a little green snake out of his mouth. The waitress ran off screaming. He also had a great big black snake. Once we were on the train going from Oakland to Portland or Seattle, and it was a long trip, two days. So we did a lot of sitting in the parlor car. Jackie Price was in there one day, and there were half a dozen or so people, including two very nice, elderly ladies, sitting there. Jackie had the newspaper way up in front of him. We didn't know what was going on, but we knew he had a snake somewhere. So he was sitting there, with the newspaper in front of his face, and all of a sudden his pants unzipped, and he had this snake around his waist under his shirt, and that darn snake came out through the fly of his pants. Those two very proper ladies screamed. That snake came out there about a foot and a half. Jackie was just nonchalant, not paying attention to it. All of a sudden, they started laughing hysterically. One of the ladies said, "That's the funniest thing I've ever seen. I've laughed so much I've wet myself." But when Casey found about it, there was no more of that snake in the parlor. And I understand Bill Veeck at Cleveland fired Jackie because he pulled a similar stunt on a train full of women bowlers.

But the most amazing thing Jackie did, I thought, was his bazooka gun stunts. He put a baseball in that bazooka gun, and he'd set his jeep at a certain speed, and he'd shoot the bazooka up in the air. Then he'd hop in the jeep and go out and catch it as it came down. Every once in a while, he would set the wheel on the jeep at a certain speed in a circle, shoot the bazooka up in the air, then get over there and catch the ball just like an outfielder as it was coming down, but he'd fall off the jeep. The jeep would go around and come back. He'd whistle, and it'd come back to him. He'd always take a little batboy and put him on this jeep. Once he put my son Steve on and told him, "Now, don't you dare touch that wheel." Steve didn't know what he was going to do, so when Jackie fell off the jeep and it started going around, Steve jumped back at the wheel and held it steady while it was going around. Fans loved it. He'd also take that bazooka and aim it out over the center-field fence. He did it at Vancouver, when I was managing there. He was quite an attraction at the minor league ballparks. He shot a ball with that bazooka gun, and it must have gone a thousand feet.

Les Scarsella was my roommate at Oakland. Les was a great hitter. He had great years in the Pacific Coast League. He could have played more in the big leagues, but he could make more in the Coast League. At the time, he was making $1,500 a month and playing six months, making $9,000 a year in the Coast League, plus a chance at more money in the playoffs. He told me Cincinnati had offered him a contract for $5,000, but he wouldn't take it. He didn't want to take a cut to go to the big leagues. But he was a good Triple-A player.

We had two guys named Martin on the Oakland team. Babe Martin came to us out from St. Louis. He was in the Browns organization at one time, and I knew him from that. He was a catcher. We were playing in Portland one day when some leather-lunged fan was giving him a good roasting. Portland had a dugout that sloped down kind of like a sunken shed. Babe had taken just about all that he could take from this heckler who was sitting right up there, and he took a running start and jumped up on the roof of the dugout, scrambling up, crawling up, wanting to get the guy, shin guards, mask, and all. He was going to get him, but he couldn't make it. He kept sliding down. Finally somebody grabbed him by his shoes and pulled him back down. He later became a councilperson or something in St. Louis. The other Martin was Hershel. He came out to Oakland when I was there. He's the guy who ended my career with Oakland. He was a better ballplayer than I was. He was a switch hitter, and he hit a ball once over the roof in left field, and I thought, my God, who can hit a ball that far? When I found out he was coming out to Oakland, I thought, uh-oh, good-bye, because I remembered that home run he hit. Hershel went on to become a scout, and every time he would see me, he'd say, "You got me to thank for your managerial career."

We had some characters on the pitching staff. Mitch Chetkovich was a real nervous sort of guy. He was always doing crazy things on the mound with the rosin bag. Ralph Buxton was another good pitcher. He was a pine tar guy. He had a screwball, and he used that pine tar all the time. He'd get it on the baseball. He also used a little bit of spit on his "out" pitch. When he threw it, it was like throwing through rain. He could get away with it in the Coast League, but I don't know whether he did in the big leagues. Gene Bearden went up to the big leagues with Cleveland, and he pitched down in Mexico the winter I was there. He pitched the ball game that clinched the pennant for the Indians in 1948. Tom Hafey had been in the Browns organization. He was a knuckleballer and a nice guy. I liked him very much. And Johnny Babich, who had pitched for the Athletics and the Dodgers, was a coach. I had a chance to talk to him about the slider or the "nickel curve." Supposedly he was the first big league pitcher to throw that pitch. They told me that he had a good one. He didn't last a long time, only five years, in the majors. But he taught that slider to a lot of pitchers. A couple of years later, I managed against him when he managed Idaho Falls in the Pioneer League.

My year at Oakland started my long friendship with Billy Martin. I go back to 1945 with Billy. He was just a kid at Oakland and Berkeley, hanging around the ballpark with another young guy, J. W. Porter, who was signed out of that area, as were quite a few guys. Red Adams was the clubhouse guy and trainer for the Oakland Oaks. I guess he spent about every dime he made buying kids gloves, a pair of shoes, or maybe a pair of pants. Red was truly a wonderful human being, a great benefactor. He didn't like to see the kids get into trouble. Billy was one of the those guys who could get in trouble even at that time. He probably weighed about 130 pounds. Skinny, at one time he looked like he was going to add a little height to him, but he never really did get big. Billy was a brash kid. I loved him because he was a fighter from the start. He was cocky, he was sure of himself, and he was very knowledgeable about baseball right from the beginning. We became very fast friends. He used to come out to the ballpark early, and I'd go out early too. He always called me "Big Leaguer." He'd say, "Hey, Big Leaguer, how about throwing me some batting practice?" I'd say, "I'll throw you some, if you throw me some." And he'd say, "OK." So I'd get out there and throw him batting practice. He loved to try to hit the ball back through the box. We didn't have screens at that time and, boy, he'd hit one through there and laugh like heck. He never would throw batting practice to me. All of a sudden, after he was done hitting, he'd say he had to do chores in the clubhouse. He would say, "Oh, I got to go. Red is calling me. He wants me to do something." He pulled this on me, but finally I got to where I enjoyed the little games with him. You had to like this little, fresh, cocky kid. He said, "I'm going to be a big league ballplayer; I'm going to play for Oakland." I'm going to do this, I'm going to do that, he'd say and, by gosh, he did.

Back in the 1880s, I understand, guys like King Kelly used to run from first to third when the umpire's back was turned. I saw that happen occasionally in my playing days. I can't recall whether I was with Oakland or Seattle at the time, but we were playing a series with the Angels in Los Angeles. I was playing in the outfield when a ball was hit to right field. Bill Schuster, a shortstop for the Angels, was on first base. I looked at him and, zoom, he cut across the infield, right about twenty feet in front of second base, and headed for third. I looked up and blinked. Everybody was watching the ball hit out there in the outfield, kind of in between the fielders. I couldn't believe it. I shook my head. I said, "No, this can't be." I'd never seen anything like it. They told me Schuster used to do it all the time, whenever a guy hit the ball like that.

Bill Schuster was the best guy at the hidden ball trick that I'd ever seen. He played only a bit in the big leagues but in quite a few Pacific Coast League games. One game, when I was with Oakland, I was standing triumphantly on second base. I can't remember whether I had stolen second or hit a double. Bill started a conversation: "Hey, Big Leaguer, hey, Big Leaguer." I said, "Yeah." He said, "Geez, you big leaguers are pretty good ballplayers. You hit that ball pretty good. You run good. I watched you throwing in infield practice. You've got a heck of an arm." He was just pouring these compliments on me. I thought about calling timeout, but the umpires wouldn't call timeout for just anything back then like they do now. Now they call timeout if you blink. Somebody had told me, "You want to be careful of that guy, that Schuster, now. He'll pull a hidden ball trick on you." I said, "Not on me, he won't." I wandered off second base, and Schuster was giving me all this conversation about coming in the deal for Jake Caulfield. About then, I said, "Yeah." He said, "Jake's not going to play, I guess. He wants to be a policeman or something." I said, "Oh, really?" I turned around, and I'd wandered about ten feet off second base, and the first thing I know he was between me and the base. He said, "Hey, Big Leaguer, look what I've got." He had the baseball. I don't know where he had it, whether he had it inside his glove or under his armpit. Most of them would have it under their armpit so that they could wave their hand and the glove and show you there was nothing there. He just dropped the ball in his glove. I said, "You touch me with that ball, and I'll hit you right between the eyes." "Oh, no, you wouldn't, you're a big leaguer." He danced around, and finally he said, "You may as well give up." He was really clever with it. I said, "You'll never get me again." He tried to get me other times, but he couldn't. He'd do it to anybody and surprise the heck out of them. The fans would look for it. I watched him get somebody else on our ball club, but the guy just ran all around the infield and then the outfield, with Bill Schuster chasing him. It happened to me, and I had to be able to laugh about it.

When I was playing for Oakland, we'd go down to Hollywood to play the Stars, the baseball team. The players loved it. We'd go to the Farmers Market that was out by Gilmore Field. The variety of food was tremendous. The Hollywood Stars that season wore shorts. We gave them a good roasting about that. Chuck Stevens, who I had seen back at Johnstown, was their first baseman. The other stars, the movie stars, also would come out to the ballpark. They'd come down and kid you, and they'd give you a blast, especially if you turned around and said something to the umpire. Toward the end of that year, we were winding up a series in Hollywood, and they were having a big farewell dinner program. They brought in a bunch of big Hollywood stars. Phil Silvers, who was just an up-and-coming guy, was there. George Jessel, Danny Thomas, Jimmy Durante, and the Marx Brothers were there too. I sat with Zeppo and Chico, and they were as funny as they could be. Groucho was one of the featured speakers. This was a stag gathering, and it was great. The brothers booed him, and they got as big a kick out of me sitting there with them. They asked me all about Casey Stengel and the big leagues and Mr. Mack. They were really, truly great baseball fans. I wasn't into autographs then; I wish I had been. We would also go out to the studio. Bing Crosby and Bob Hope were doing their "road pictures" at that time with Dorothy Lamour. Crosby and Hope were a riot. In one scene, Bob Hope was being chased by a husband, and he jumped into bed. The guy's wife was in bed, and he jumped into bed and pulled the covers up, but there was a whole bucket of green frogs jumping all over him, and Hope came flying out of there. The cuss words that were used! I guess they used to do that to each other. We got a big kick out of it. Bing owned an interest in the Pittsburgh Pirates, and Hope owned part of the Cleveland Indians.

In the middle of the 1946 season, the Oakland club released me. Casey had to release me. He had a chance to win and needed a little more help, another outfielder. He called me in and said, "My dandy little road apple, I've got a chance to get this guy and I've got to turn you loose." Casey made a phone call to the Seattle Rainiers. He told them, "I've got a kid here, pretty good ballplayer, do you real good in Seattle." He told the owner what they were doing. In fact, Casey said, "I want to do something for this guy. This dandy little road apple played his heart out for me." I did a pretty good job, but then I wasn't in the right place. Casey negotiated and got me $2,000. He said, "I want $2,000 for him, and if you're not satisfied, I'll give you the money back." Seattle paid the Oakland club $2,000 for me, and Vic Devincenzi gave me that. He had dropped my salary in half, from $1,600 a month in 1945 to $750 in 1946, so this $2,000 helped out. Casey gave me the check and wished me luck. It kind of nearly broke my heart when later that season I hit a sacrifice fly that beat Casey in a game. I loved the guy.

So we drove up to Seattle from Oakland, where we had been living. My family was with me there. We drove up with my daughter and my oldest son, Bud, who was just a little guy then. I was still having a hard time hitting back then. I just hadn't played enough. I'd take batting practice whenever I could. I still could manage to throw. Then I started coming around. Earl Sheely, who'd played for the White Sox in the 1920s, was the general manager up there, and Jo-Jo White was the manager. I played six positions. I even played some first base at Seattle. We also survived a little earthquake in Seattle that threw all the cornerstones of the buildings way up high.

Jo-Jo White and I were friends from when we had played at Philadelphia. When I was with Oakland, however, I got in his way once while he was coming around third base. He stumbled toward the dugout out of the baseline, but he got thrown out at the plate. That cost them the game. He remembered that when I came to Seattle and chewed me out. But I won some games for him, so he forgave me. The story I should tell about Jo-Jo involves a poker game. We were playing low-stakes poker on the train going north one time. We were down to the last hand. I had a pair of threes in the hole, and it turned out he had an ace. We raised each other quite a few times, and finally he called. I folded. He bluffed me and won about a hundred dollars. Years later, when Jo-Jo was a coach for Joe Gordon with the Kansas City Royals in 1969, he would kid me about that game.

In Seattle in 1946, I played center field between Lou Novikoff, the "Mad Russian," and Bob Johnson, the underrated American Indian outfielder who had a fine career with the Athletics. Neither of them could move much. In fact, Novikoff was what we called a "postage stamp" fielder, covering just a little bit of territory. He called over to me at the start of a game and drew an imaginary line with his foot right next to him. "Hey, Meeeetro," he shouted, "you cover everything up to this line." Johnson did the same in right field. I had my work cut out for me. Lou had been up and down with the big leagues, and he was a terrific Triple-A hitter. Lou was a case in himself. He thought he was just the greatest ballplayer who had ever lived. His idea of hitting was "thou shall not pass," and nothing came toward the plate that he didn't swing at. But he couldn't run. There was always a bet as to who would win, he or the ball, when a fly ball came his way. I don't think he ever went after a ball. Today he would make a good designated hitter. He went up there for a purpose, and that was to slash and swing and hit that ball. He kept calling me a "Polack." He knew I was Ukrainian, but since he was a Russian, he didn't want anybody to think that anybody else was Russian or Ukrainian or whatever. I kept telling him I wasn't Polish.

Earl Torgeson played first base for Seattle when I was there. He went up to the big leagues and was an outstanding ballplayer. He and I roomed together for a couple of road trips. He was a fun-loving guy. Once he said, "Hey, when we get back, if we get an off day, we'll go out and play golf." I said, "OK." I had a set of clubs, and he had a set of clubs of his own. I was playing a little bit of golf, not much. So we went out on the golf course, going down this front fairway, about the fourth hole, which was a long hole running along a slow, meandering creek that looked like it was about four feet deep, when Earl, hitting left-handed, drove one right in the middle of the creek. I laid one up there, just about as far, but on the fairway. We walked up there, and there was his ball lying in the creek. He started cussing—he was very competitive—about his golf drive. I said, "What are you going to do about it?" He continued cussing. Finally he got so mad that he threw his bag of clubs right into the creek. I said, "What'd you do that for?" He said, "Never mind." He was furious. He said, "I'm going back." I sat on the bank of the creek, taking my shoes off and rolling up my pant legs, and he said, "What're you going to do?" I said, "Well, I'm going in and get those clubs." He said, "No you're not." He took a running dive and dove right in the creek after his clubs. He didn't want me to get his clubs. He brought them out and dumped the water out of the bag. He said, "Let's go. Let's play." I said, "You're lying. You're on three now." We had a good day.

Tony York played shortstop for Seattle when I was there playing some second base for them. He came from Irene, Texas. He was a good Triple-A ballplayer, and everybody called him Irene. One day I called him Irene, and he threw the ball at me at second base, on the double play, and almost killed me. He said, "Irene, am I?" I said, "Hey!" In self-defense I caught the ball. We didn't get the double play. We got the force out at second, but we should have had a double play. He said, "Take that. Irene, huh?" So I didn't call him Irene anymore.

Seattle was very enjoyable, and I thought that the next year I had a good chance to make the club again. We went back to Mayfield, and I got ready for spring training. I really thought I had a good chance to make the majors again. Seattle was an independent club. They could have sold me to anyone. My family and I drove out to Bakersfield for spring training. At Kingman, Arizona, we ran into a sandstorm. We checked into a little old hotel there. That sandstorm kept us locked in there for half a day, and we stayed there that night. The sand came under the door, under the window sills, through the ventilators. It was half an inch deep in the room. It was dusty all over, in our bags and in our clothes. And we had all kinds of trouble with the car. We couldn't get parts or anything, and the muffler and the tailpipe went out and everything else. It darn near used up all our money. We had a cocker spaniel that barked at everybody. We lived in a little efficiency motel on the edge of town where the married guys were staying. But I hustled like heck throughout spring training. I was doing everything they wanted. I thought I had the club made. In fact, Jo-Jo White, the manager, told me I did. But then the day before we were due to go to San Diego to open up the season, he called me and they released me. I said to Earl Sheely, "I did everything that you ever asked. I played whenever you asked me to." But they had a situation where they just had to make a move, and I was the low man on the ladder. It was one of the darkest days of my life. We were down to our last $3.75. I went to a bar and sat there wondering what I was going to do, how I had gotten myself and my family into this mess. I drank a bunch of beers, drank up $3.50 worth, and tipped the bartender a quarter. I was as blue as I had ever been in my life.

But in baseball you have your ups and your downs. I guess during my lifetime I had as many downs as ups, and there was always somebody to lend a strong helping hand. The next day my career veered off in another direction. Earl Sheely, the guy who released me from Seattle, recommended me to the Yankees as a manager. Joe Devine, the famous Yankees scout out on the West Coast, contacted me through the Seattle office and offered me a position as a playing manager. I had befriended him many years earlier. Of course, I jumped at the opportunity. I didn't have much choice. I didn't want to be out of baseball. It had been only two and a half years since I had been up in the majors. That offer started me out as a baseball manager in the Yankees organization in 1947 at Bisbee, Arizona. From then on I was hooked on managing. I was going to make that my career, if I didn't make it back to the big leagues.

I have fond memories of that Bisbee team. Maybe it's like your first child—you always remember that baby the most. We had a couple of fun-loving guys on the Bisbee club, but the biggest character was Clint Courtney. Clint was very feisty. They called him "Scrap Iron." Paul Richards gave him that nickname. Now, as I look back, I can see why. He was what we called a hardhead. He was aggressive. He'd keep the ball club on its toes. They also called him a billy goat, because I don't think he ever took a shower. He was one of the first catchers to wear glasses. Man, was he unpredictable! Once we were staying in a resort hotel at Mesa, Arizona. The owner had just bought it, and he made us a deal to stay there. It was very nice. There was nobody in it except him and his cleanup crew. When we had come in after a night game, one or two of the guys, I don't know which ones, had taken a smoke bomb and attached it underneath Courtney's bed, to the bedsprings. Then they had plugged it into the light socket. When the day's game was over, they came in, turned the lights on, and, whew, the smoke bomb went off. Boy, it was blowing smoke all over. Now this blew the lights out, blew the fuse out for the whole wing where we were staying. We had to shower or bathe and dress in the dark. So Courtney took a shower, and then his roommate took a bath. Courtney was out there trying to find his clothes because we were leaving that night. He lit some newspaper, and it started burning. He threw it over on the dresser and, boy, that burned the varnish, and everything else darn near went up in flames. So Courtney and his roommate grabbed the mat and the towels. Courtney grabbed the paper and threw it in the toilet. Then that stuff caught on fire, so they grabbed all these mats and towels and soaked them in the tub and threw it over the fire here and there.

Once we were in the bus, here came the innkeeper, all agitated. He said, "Mr. Metro, I want you to come in here and see." I said, "What's the matter?" So he took me upstairs to the second floor and showed me the damage. Man, it looked like a war with all that smoke, and things singed and everything, and towels blackened and burnt. I took out my list and saw that it was Courtney's room. So I accosted Clint, and he was man enough to say he did it, but he started coming up with all kinds of excuses. I said, "Clint, you're going to pay for all of this." I asked the man, "What do you estimate the damage is?" He told me something like eighty or ninety dollars. I said, "Get your money out, Clint." He had just gotten out of the service and had his discharge money. He still wore his olive drab underclothes from the service. So he had the money, but he said, "Aw, Charlie, I don't want to pay that." I said, "You're going to pay it, or else I'll fine you. When I get through, the Yankees will know all about it." He said, "Oh, no, no, no," and he paid it. We didn't have too much trouble with hotel rooms after that. "Chahlie," he called me. "Chahlie, you ought to find out who did that." They were pretty good at sticking together—nobody told me. Everybody kept quiet about it.

That episode taught me a lesson. Whenever I would make my speech on conduct with the players, about the Yankees' way of conduct, the Cardinals' way of conduct, the Tigers' way of conduct, I made it a point to bring that episode up. I'd tell them that if they destroyed anything in the hotel, if they were out of line in the coffee shop or the dining room of the hotel or any café in town, I would fine them and notify the parent club. So I never had too much trouble with guys breaking stuff. Oh, I had guys who would break the curfew, and I'd threaten them. When I'd catch them, I'd threaten them that I was going to tell their wives about them coming in at 2:00 or 3:00 in the morning. I had them right where I wanted them.

One time Courtney used some pieces of cheese as padding in his catcher's mitt. Rather than buy a sponge, he would use a couple pieces of cheese to soften the blow there. I don't what kind of cheese it was, but there were two slabs of it. He wouldn't buy a sponge. Boy, when that was over, you could smell it for weeks. The umpire would say, "What the heck do I smell here?

What the heck's that?" Of course, I'd say that Courtney messed his pants. Now how this came about was sort of crazy. Courtney had a great arm, and when he was catching, he'd fire the ball back to the pitcher, time after time, after twenty-five, thirty-five, fifty, sixty, seventy-five pitches. Finally all the pitchers came up with fat hands. Then he started throwing them down to me, after we got the third strike, and I was getting a fat hand. I told him to stop, and he kind of laughed. So when I got him in the dugout, I backed him up and said, "You throw one more at me, and I'm going to bust you." I didn't know that it was against the rules for the manager to hit one of his ballplayers. I was going to bust him good. So he quit doing that. Finally he came up with a little bit of a fat hand himself. I told him, "Why don't you get a sponge?" And I heard that some catchers put a piece of beefsteak in their gloves. But he went to the store and got a piece of cheese, cut it off the end of a square block of cheese, some white cheese that they had. It was about half an inch thick. He cut the square edge off of it, put that in his catcher's mitt, and caught the ball. It protected his hand. I'd never seen that, but after several games, it got to smelling pretty bad, and he quit using it. There are some things the ballplayers would do that you wouldn't believe.

Jim Wert was my first baseman. Years later, at the All-Star Game in Seattle in 1979, at the Kingdome, he was the custodian of the press room and press box. He ran things in those two areas. I hadn't seen him since 1947. We were both a little grayer, both a little older but, boy, it was quite a reunion. He was a fine young man and a fine ballplayer. Wert's father used to draw cartoons about our team on the letters to his son. One time he drew me holding a big heavy bat with .389 on it and me saying, "Boy, this is getting heavy!"

Lynn Stone was a good, young third baseman, but he got beaned and played shy after that. He didn't have a career on the field, but he went into the front office, eventually with Louisville. He also became general manager of Churchill Downs and later helped me get into a Kentucky Derby. Frank Lucchesi was a utility infielder who also drove the bus a lot. Warren Howe was my left fielder. He had arthritis in his elbows and couldn't straighten his arms. Jim Bynon, my right fielder, had a consecutive-game hitting streak. Frank Finnegan was my big center fielder. He never met a high fastball he didn't like. Wayne Peterson, my shortstop, could hit fine—he hit .360—but he had a lot of trouble in the field. He made seventy-three errors! Hillman Lyons was a backup catcher. He had been a Marine at Guadalcanal and had grabbed a bayonet with his left hand in the attack. He was from Murray in western Kentucky and had worked for me at the munitions plant in Viola. He was a fine guy and eventually became general manager at Charleston, West Virginia, for the Milwaukee Braves organization.

Joe Valenzuela, one of my pitchers, no kin to Fernando, was a local hero. He was Mexican in heritage and wanted to pitch against Juarez. He pestered me to let him start. So I did, one day game. Juarez got to him for 11 runs in the first inning. Nobody hit him hard, just a bunch of dinky bloops and seeing-eye singles. He settled down and didn't allow them a run after the first inning. We still lost, 11–0. Jim Propst was another one of my pitchers. He was a left-hander. He'd been in the service and was one of the most nervous guys I'd ever seen. It was like he had St. Vitus's dance. We decided to release him. But he hung around and asked to pitch batting practice. I let him, and he struck out all our guys! I called Eddie Leishman or Joe Devine and said that we had to re-sign him. Propst turned out to be my best pitcher.

My next association with Billy Martin was when he played for Phoenix in the Arizona-Texas League in 1947. Casey Stengel kind of liked him and signed him. I don't know whether Oakland or the Yankees owned him. Anyway he came to Phoenix. He was somehow property of the Yankees, which was kind of bending the rules a little. You weren't allowed to option or have a working agreement with two clubs in the same league. They had players on option, and the rules were kind of sketchy. But anyway, Billy was there. He had 250 base hits in 130 games. He hit .392 and batted in 190 runs. I was hitting only about .339 in that altitude and the light air down there, and he'd let me know it. "Have your fun, Big Leaguer," he'd say, "You'll be down there where you belong, and I'll lead the league in hitting." Later, every time he'd see me, if there was somebody around, he'd want me to tell how well he hit at Phoenix. He would say to me, "You didn't hit nothing. I saw your batting average. Which was not much on the major league level."

Billy Martin and Clint Courtney started their feud when Billy played for Phoenix and Clint was my catcher for the Bisbee farm club. One game Clint barreled into the Phoenix second baseman and manager, Arky Biggs. At that time, you had one pair of spikes, and if you wore them down, you kept playing with them. Clint had a pair of spikes that were half worn down. He hit the ball to right field, and he never did stop. He just kept going. I thought he was the hardest-headed ballplayer I ever saw. He slid into second base and knocked the ball out of the second baseman's hands. While Courtney was lying there, Biggs hauled off and hit him alongside the head and broke his own hand. Courtney jumped up. Next thing, everybody came out. Billy squared off with Courtney. Billy would fight anybody anytime. The strange thing is that the Yankees owned both ballplayers. Here were two guys in the same organization fighting. Later the Yanks traded Courtney away, to the St. Louis Browns, because, as I understand, they had quite a few scraps. Billy would fight at the drop of a hat. Courtney was not quite as aggressive. If he had the advantage, he would. He wasn't a match for Martin. Billy got the best of him all the time. But Billy would take on anybody. He was a fierce competitor. He was on everybody all the time. If his own players didn't hustle, he would get on them. You could hear him shout, "Run that ball out!" Even if a guy was a big home run hitter, such as the first baseman at Phoenix, I could hear Billy getting on his case.

Billy and I used to go to the movies together. The man who owned the Phoenix club owned a chain of movie theaters in the area. I can't recall his name. I would see him many years later. He was great with the kids and would give them passes for the theaters. It was a little warm in Phoenix. We would play night baseball because it was warm in the afternoon. The kids would all go to the theater in the afternoon. Billy would say, "Hey, Big Leaguer, come on. I've got a couple of tickets." So we would go. He would take me to the theater. He got in free and I had to pay, but I thought this was great. Billy was always picking your brain. "What are the big leagues like? What's Triple-A like? Did you play Triple-A?" he'd ask. Now I went from an A league to the big leagues during the war. He liked to needle me.

But Billy also was interested in my batting tee. We would go out early to the park, set up the batting tee, and hit a bunch of balls. We would hit them inside the cage so we didn't have to chase them. He would ask, "What am I doing wrong?" There he was, hitting nearly .400 in the league! He wanted to learn all about hitting. I had been studying hitting a lot, because I had to teach. I found out that the first thing you have to do is get a bat that you like. He had a bat that he liked, kind of a thin-handled bat. I don't know what the model was. I said the next thing you have to have is plate coverage. You have to get a comfortable stance where you can cover the plate. If they throw you outside, you step right in and hit the ball. Billy was very good at that. He could hit the ball anyplace. Every once in a while, he would make a mistake: he would hit the ball out of the ballpark. The ballpark, a double-decked deal, wasn't very big, but a home run is a home run. I taught him to bring the force of the ball right at the impact, kind of like chopping a tree. I said, "Billy, did you ever chop a log or a tree?" He said, "Yeah, a couple of times." I said, "You know how you swing that ax, that's how you have to hit a ball." I also told him, "You've got to hold on to that bat so that you don't get in the habit of turning the top hand loose. That will turn your head and your head will go." He liked that. I didn't see him too much after he went into the big leagues, with the Yankees. But he was a pretty good hitter.

Billy holds the dubious record of hitting into four double plays in a seven-inning game, and I'm partly responsible. We were playing a doubleheader at Bisbee. I was playing third base. He hit two shots, one down the line, one down to my left. I made what they call an "unconscious play" on them both, turned them into a double play both times, second to first. He hit the ball so hard, we had him easily. He hit another one to our shortstop, who had seventy-some errors that year, but even he made a great play and turned it into a twin killing, short to second. Then Billy hit another one to second, for a second-to-short double play. We made four double plays, just bang, bang, bang, bang. Four double plays in a seven-inning ball game. I guess that's the world record. I don't think you can hit into more than four double plays in seven innings.

Billy was always bragging. Many times when I was scouting, he would invite me to get on the bus and come to the hotel at the ballpark. I'd be catching a plane with him, and he was always bragging about his hitting. Finally he had a guy with him who actually saw him hit .390 and have 250-some hits. I had to tell him, "Yeah, that's right. Ah, the fences were 270 feet down the left field and 300 to left center." Years later I was together with him and Mickey Mantle in Dallas. I went out with Billy because he would let me drive. He wouldn't let a lot of people drive, but he'd let me. The conversation was all about how much he hit at Phoenix. He was teasing Mickey, "What did you hit at Joplin when you were down there?" Billy had to go to the bathroom, and Mickey said to me, "Charlie, I'd give anything if you could give me something on him and shut him up." I said, "Listen, you want to stop Old Pinocchio?" (They used to call Billy "Pinocchio" at one time.) Mickey said, "Yeah." "Tell him that he holds a world record that nobody could ever beat, hitting into four double plays in a seven-inning ball game." Billy came back in a few minutes, and they started bantering back and forth, and finally Mickey said to him, "Hey, don't you hold a world record of some sort?" Billy said, "Yeah, yeah. I drove in 190 runs." "No, no, didn't you hit into four double plays in a seven-inning ball game?" Mickey asked. Billy looked at me, and I turned my palms up as if to say, "Not me. I don't know anything." That's the only time I ever saw Billy really shut up.

One game against Phoenix, Billy Martin nearly got the best of me. I was on third base, and Billy was playing third. Our batter hit a slow ground ball to Billy. He fielded it and made a big motion to throw the ball over to first, but he didn't throw the ball. I broke for the plate, and I was hung out to dry. Billy said, "Hey, Big Leaguer, look what I've got." I said, "You touch me with that, I'll deck you. You're not going to get me." He said, "Big Leaguer, I think I've got you." So I got into a rundown. Billy threw the ball to the catcher, who threw it back, and then I was a little closer to home. I barreled right over the top of that catcher. The ball was there, but I took it right out of his glove, ripped it out while he was covering home. Billy said, "Why, you dirty, rotten rat."

I have to tell a story about Billy Martin and a big piece of turquoise in Bisbee. The Phoenix club stayed at the Copper Queen Hotel. Billy was with Phoenix, and I was managing the Bisbee Yanks. We were having a luncheon at the Copper Queen, and I was the speaker. It was one of the first speeches I ever made as a manager. I don't know whether I went over real well or not, but anyway they all seemed to enjoy it. Billy saw me when I was coming out of the luncheon, and the conversation got around to a great big rock, about a foot and a half high and two or three feet long, that was holding the door open. The hotel manager came out, and he was talking to Billy. Billy asked what that rock was, and the hotel guy said, "That's turquoise." It was a great big hunk of turquoise. There was a lot of turquoise in the rock. Billy asked him, "Is that valuable?" "Oh, is it valuable! Yeah. They use it for everything. Men are making bolo ties and this and that, and women are making jewelry out of it, and everything else." Billy asked him how much it was worth, and the guy said, "Oh, a lot of money. Why?" Billy said, "Well, somebody will steal it." The hotel guy said, "You want it? You can have it." Billy said, "You really mean it?" He went over and tried to pick it up. He couldn't even budge it! This great big hunk of turquoise! I wonder where it wound up, maybe as a lot of jewelry.

We had our share of crazy happenings in 1947, when I was with the Bisbee club. We rolled into El Paso one day and beat Sid Cohen's club by something like a 35–10 score. I put a pitcher by the name of Charlie Pickett in my place, and he hit a home run and a double. I never saw so many line drives. I was the only guy who didn't have a big game. Sid Cohen complained that we ruined their crowd draw for the year. The next day's game, with a big crowd, turned out to be a pitchers' duel. Somewhere about the middle of the game, we scratched out a run on a couple of walks and a hit. But there were no signs of power for either club. In fact, the outfielders were coming in on hard-hit balls. Along about the fourth inning, our catcher, Clint Courtney, came up to me with a worried look on his face. "Skip," he said, "there's something wrong with these balls." "What do you mean?" I replied. "Well, they're real cold." I grabbed the ball out of his hand. You bet they were real cold! They were frozen! Sid Cohen, probably out of embarrassment, had ordered the balls frozen to "cool off" our hitting. I told Courtney to keep quiet. Cohen's team couldn't hit those "rocks" any better than we could. We ended up winning, 1–0. On later occasions when I'd see Sid Cohen, I'd say, "Hey, Sidney, it backfired on you, didn't it?" He'd say, "Yeah."

Another time we had the distinction of hitting a mirage in the desert. We were traveling overnight by bus to make a game in El Paso the next day. Frank Lucchesi, who we were trying to make into a utility player and who later went on to manage the Philadelphia Phillies and Texas Rangers, was driving the bus. He was one of the guys who could drive it, and he really enjoyed it. He would sit up there and imitate Vaughn Monroe, crooning "Racing with the Moon" and other tunes over the hours. We would use our uniforms as pillows and try to get what sleep we could. He had his leg propped up going across those deserts. Every once in a while, he'd say, "Dip." Out in that country, the road would dip down. I finally asked one of the guys who was from Arizona, "What the heck's these dips?" He said, "Oh, that's for the water." I said, "Water? Out in this desert?" You couldn't see a drop of water anywhere, sun shining and all. He said, "We'll know if we ever hit one." Those dips were for flash floods.

This particular morning we were tooling along on schedule to make El Paso. Lucchesi was singing away. It was a bright, hot day about 10:00, not a cloud in sight. Then one of the guys shouted, "Hey, Luke, there's water up ahead." Somebody said, "Aw, go back to sleep." The guy said, "No, it's water." "G'wan," replied Lucchesi, "it's just a mirage." We hit that "mirage" going about fifty or sixty miles per hour. There had been a rainstorm, and a flash flood up in the mountains just came barreling down like out of a hose. We plowed into all that rushing water. We stalled right in the bottom of that thing, and it was about five feet deep. The whole bus got flooded. Mud poured in on top of the water. Our uniforms got soaked and dirty all at once. The sun was shining, probably ninety degrees at the time. Guys poured out of the bus and waded through the water and started rolling their pant legs up. We had to sit there until the water receded, but it went down pretty quick. We must have looked like drowned rats when we got off the bus at El Paso, the most ragtag sorry excuse for a team possibly ever. The Arizona guys gave us a pretty good time about that. And to this day, Frank Lucchesi is the only guy I ever knew to hit a mirage while driving.

As I say, Frank Lucchesi fancied himself quite the singer. He was always imitating somebody. One game, unbeknownst to me, some of the guys arranged for a little delay. All of a sudden the lights went out and a microphone appeared on the mound with a spotlight shining down on somebody singing. I didn't know who it was at first. But there in black face with a pair of white gloves on was Lucchesi singing Al Jolson's "Swanee." He was going through all the motions, and he got a rising ovation from the fans. They took up a collection, and he got enough to buy Cokes for all the ballplayers. They wouldn't allow beer in the clubhouse. He bought Cokes and milkshakes and everything. I think he got about eighty or ninety dollars, which was pretty good; I think some of the ballplayers weren't even making that much a month. He put that on pretty good, and the response surprised him. I thought he was real good, and we tried to get him to do it again.

Good gosh, it got hot in Phoenix, when we played in the old ballpark back in the C league. It would get to 120 degrees easily during some of the day games. One real scorching Sunday, one of my Bisbee players, Jim Bynon, who was from Arizona, brought a couple of eggs to the park and broke them on top of the metal dugout roof. "You guys ever see something really hot?" he asked. Within two innings they were fried as hard as rubber. We had ammoniated ice water in buckets. Somewhere along the line I had read that if you kept your ankles cold, the rest of your body would cool off. So we had buckets where you'd slosh your feet, spiked shoes and all, around for half an inning and keep cool. We had another bucket that you could use to douse your face, with your eyes closed, and towel off.

We had a flash flood one morning at Bisbee, up the canyon, if you want to call it that. Right-center field was a creek. That water came down and seeped through, flowed under the fence, all over the field into the dugout. I was busy at the office with the business manager. I came out there right after the water stopped flowing, and I asked the groundskeeper, "Well, will we be able to play in a couple of days?" He said, "Oh, yes, we will, skipper. We're going to play tonight." He was right. By 5:00 that night, he was scraping the infield. The water drained off and the field dried out quickly, and we played that evening. The water doesn't stay very long in that desert country.

The times with the young guys in the lower leagues were a lot of fun. A couple of years ago, Gil McDougald told me, "The big leagues are not fun. They're not fun." We had a lot of fun in the minors. We had a big bus down in Bisbee, Arizona, one of those Tanner Bus Lines buses, where you roll back the top, a touring bus for sightseers. That was our traveling bus. It had staves over top of it, and they pulled the canvas over top when it was raining or if a dust storm came up. When it was really nice, they'd roll back

the canvas. It was very enjoyable. Every once in a while, we'd get caught in
a real quick shower like they have down in those deserts, and we'd get wet
before we could get the canvas top up.

Joe Valenzuela was from that area and was quite a local favorite. He was
the only guy who had a car there. So the guys always told me, "Skipper,
hey, Skip, don't forget, fill up the bus, fill up the bus, when you get home."
I'd fill up the bus before they got there. Then we'd be ready to go on the
next trip, and the dang tank would be empty. The guys had been siphoning
gas out for Joe's car. Dutch Deutsch, the business manager from back in
the East, in New Jersey or New York, kept asking me, "Charlie, what's the
matter with that bus? You just put gas in it again." I said, "Darn if I know,
Dutch." To this day he doesn't know, but if he happens to read this, he's
going to find out what happened to that gas.

Once we had a pretty good fight at Phoenix. I ran in there to be a
peacemaker or some darned thing, and I got blindsided. Somebody broke
my nose. Nobody would tell me who did it, but I finally found out. A
friend, a fan in Phoenix, told me who it was, so the next time, I got the
guy back. He was a catcher. I blindsided him too. The kids would fight
and knock you down. They'd turn to me, and I'd say, "Well, go get them."
And the rumble would start. We also had battles with the St. Louis Browns
farm club at Globe-Miami. At Bisbee we had a kid, a guy who pitched. He
wasn't a very good pitcher, but he was a good bus driver. So we let him drive
the bus sometimes. We played at Globe-Miami, Arizona, which is way up
in the mountain country, where they had copper mines. They took all the
tailings from the copper mines and spread them out on the field where we
played. There was no grass on the infield, no grass on the outfield. When
we'd win a ball game, this driver would say, "Let's go," and he'd go round
and round and round and round and buzz the field after the game was over.
And he wanted to do it before the game, but I said, "No, we'll start a fight
if we do that." So we didn't do that. Boy, we played them tooth and nail,
because every once in a while they'd beat us and there'd be a real going-over
about the "great Yankees." We finished third that year, and I think they
finished fifth the first half and fourth the second half, so I guess we got the
best of them.

But I did see one of the most unusual plays I've ever seen on that all-dirt
field at Globe-Miami. Frank Finnegan, a big outfielder I had, hit a ground
ball real hard to the shortstop. Now, mind you, this was an all-dirt field,
and there were tailings and pebbles and everything else. You were taking
your life in your hands sometimes on a ground ball. The shortstop took a
couple of steps over to his right to field the ball, and it went through his legs

on a bad hop. The left fielder came over to field the ball, and it bounced over his arm. The center fielder was backing him up, and he let the ball go through his legs. They should have given three errors on the play, on the one ball. Finnegan got an inside-the-park home run because nobody, not the shortstop, the left fielder, or the center fielder, touched it. It was a very unusual play.

Ballplayers are a superstitious bunch. I had quite a few superstitions myself when I was a playing manager. One time in my managing career in a C league, I had cantaloupe for breakfast fifteen days straight because we were winning. When we ran out of cantaloupe, we lost. Boy, I blamed everybody for that. It was the cantaloupe that did it. Then Hillman Lyons, our backup catcher, had a real wild T-shirt, a multicolored, bright T-shirt. He wore that shirt and we won a ball game. He wore it again and we won another ball game. For three or four days in a row, he wore it, and we continued to win. Well, the fifth day came around, and Hillman came out, and he didn't have the shirt on. All the ballplayers chased him back up to his hotel room to put the lucky shirt on. He wore it for nine straight days. Now we were down in Arizona, where it was mighty hot, and that shirt got mighty ripe. Guys would walk five paces behind Hillman. Finally he washed the shirt and we lost.

The team in Juarez, Mexico, lasted only a half a year. I don't know if that was the first time a Mexican team was in a professional league in the states or not, but Juarez was in the league. The ballpark wasn't much over in Juarez. You went from one world to another when you crossed that border. But the Juarez fans were wonderful. They were great fans. They kind of reminded me of the Canadian fans when I was in Vancouver. It got a little rough when the team wasn't winning, but I guess all fans react that way a little. I loved El Paso and Juarez. We stayed at El Paso and went by bus over to Juarez. We had our own bus. Later I loved to go there and scout. El Paso fans loved their players. If one of their guys hit a home run or got a big hit in the ball game, he would take his cap off, start in the dugout on the third base side, and run around and scream all the way to the first base side with his cap off. Fans would drop in dollar bills and coins, and the guy would make thirty or forty dollars and maybe not even win the ball game!

One day we were playing at Juarez. They had a team in the league the first half of the season. I made about twenty bad decisions in the game, and we lost, something like fourteen or fifteen to one or nothing. Boy, I thought to myself, how did I make all those decisions? Every darn one of them turned out wrong. We played in the afternoon, and that evening I went out and had a bite to eat and came back to the hotel in El Paso.

We were up on the eleventh story. The window was open. There was no air conditioning or anything. I sat there, trying to read a magazine, but I couldn't focus. I threw it aside and tried to go to bed, but I just rolled and tossed. I got up and went over to the window. It was probably 5:00 in the morning. I was standing at the window, on the eleventh floor, looking down, and I said to myself, "Oh, my gosh, I'm not going to jump, am I?" I was talking to myself, going over every decision I had made, wishing I'd kind of second-guessed. I went over to the dresser and looked in the mirror, and I was talking to myself. I startled myself and said, "Well, this is the last time I'll do this." I made a vow at that time that I would never, ever bring the game home or second-guess myself. I'd give myself ten or fifteen minutes to talk it over with my wife or with the newspaper guys, although they didn't interview me much at that time, and that was all. I think that was one of the best decisions I ever made as a baseball manager, and I carried that all through my baseball career. If you look back, you could second-guess yourself on thousands of things.

Joe Vosmik, who'd played with the Indians and some other American League clubs, managed Tucson in the Arizona-Texas League in my first year managing. I was learning how to manage. I was cocky, doing this and doing that. I was a playing manager, and I thought I knew all the answers. The next time we came around to play him at Tucson, Joe said at home plate, "After the game, Metro, come on out, I'll buy you a sandwich, and we'll have a beer." I said, "OK." I wasn't real sociable. I didn't know that people would do that. So he took me out, and like a father, he said, "You got a good chance. You're aggressive. You're young. You've got a good chance. Don't ruin your chances by being a smart-aleck and everything." He kind of read me the riot act, and I took that to heart and I kind of changed around. I was still aggressive and very daring in my managing, but I've always valued what Joe Vosmik told me.

I've already mentioned inventing the batting tee when I was a kid in Pennsylvania. I used it professionally with Bisbee, when I managed them in 1947. I had great success with it, and I had an awful lot of ballplayers use it. It's a great instrument in teaching. With the batting tee, you can actually see the ball hit off the tee. No matter what the pitch is—fastball, curve ball, whatever—that pitch has to pass over home plate. The batting tee helps you learn to swing in those zones. You know right when you're making contact. The bat meets the ball, and you feel it in your hands. Even I finally learned how to hit using that batting tee. I went on to hit over .300 three or four times as a playing manager. I wish I'd patented it. I had a patent pending, but I ran out of money and I couldn't complete the patent process. It's the forerunner of the T-ball game kids play now. I sold the tees for twenty-five bucks. I'd be a millionaire today.

In Bisbee we had some great fans. Bisbee was a little bit of a rough town because of the union and the copper mines. One of the fans said, "Hey, Charlie, ever go rattlesnake hunting?" I said, "Heck, no." He said, "You ever see a rattlesnake?" I said, "Oh, yeah, we had them up in Pennsylvania. Kind of like timber rattlers, you'd see one occasionally." He said, "Well, I want to take you rattlesnake hunting." I said, "OK. When do we go?" He said, "What about day after tomorrow? I'll come out and pick you up at 6:00 in the morning, and we'll go out here. I know where there's a lot of rattlers." "How are we going to catch these things?" I asked. He said, "I'll show you." So he picked me up that morning in his pickup truck, and we went out there. He had two long poles about twelve feet long, and they were rigged up like a fishing pole, except they had loops on the end at the last eyelet. You'd see a snake, and you'd put that loop over its head and jerk the line and you'd pick it up. I asked, "How far can these rattlesnakes jump or strike?" He said, "Oh, don't worry about that." But before we went out, he wrapped my legs and ankles up in some real thick canvas strips, and he got me a pair of boots. I asked, "What's that for?" He said, "Oh, in case one of them strikes you." Well, boy, we got a bunch of them. He showed me how to catch them, and after that I think I woke up a dozen times a night with those snakes striking at me. A few days after that, he came out to the ballpark and he had this little package. He said, "I brought you a real tasty food." I said, "What is it?" He said, "I got some barbecue, some fried stuff for you." I asked again what it was, and he said, "Well, taste it." So he gave me a taste, and it tasted good. I thought it tasted somewhat like chicken or salmon or something. I asked again what it was, and he said, "Rattlesnake." I was sick for a week.

That fall, a big Mexican player, Manulo Fortes, who managed the Juarez club, invited me down to play in the Mexican winter league. I said, "Can I bring my family?" He said, "Oh, yeah, sure." I said, "Well, I'll go down and see." I told my wife I'd go down ahead of time and find an apartment, see what it was like, and then call her to come down. She said, "Fine." So I finally got eight hundred dollars a month to go down there and play for Mazatlan in the Mexican winter league. As the time went by, the conditions were rougher, and I kept telling my wife I didn't know whether she should come down there, the food was not like we had, the kids were young and everything. She said, "Well, come on home." I struggled between making a salary playing there and going back to Kentucky. I enjoyed playing in the league, but I lost 45 pounds. I went down there weighing 188 pounds, and

when I told them I was going home on the 20th of December, right before
Christmas, I weighed 145. I was playing shortstop, and I couldn't eat. I just
couldn't eat. I couldn't get used to the food. I played for about three months.
We played in Culiacan, Hermosillo, Guaymas, and Los Mochis. Mazatlan
was a very beautiful place. I really enjoyed that. We played three games a
week, Friday, Saturday, and Sunday. We'd go out toward the beach during
the week and swim around in the water and have a good time. Incidentally,
one thing that brought me back from Mazatlan was that my wife traded
the house we had for another one and bought a new car. That brought me
home in a hurry.

This was right about that time that Jorge Pasquel tried to organize the
Mexican League into a major league and recruit major leaguers from the
United States to come down and play. They raided Vern Stephens, Danny
Gardella, Max Lanier, Sal Maglie, Mickey Owens, and other guys. They
all tried it, and a couple of guys got punished later by the majors. I saw
Pasquel at a restaurant one time. He was with three bodyguards. They
had the automatics that looked like cannons strapped to their waists. He
found out that we were baseball players in there having dinner that night.
We played all day games down there. So he invited us over, and we had a
long chat with him. He asked me about Vern Stephens, my old Mayfield
roommate, and I told him that the Browns didn't pay him much, that he'd
probably get some of those players. He did, but the league collapsed. Vern
escaped punishment.

The Mazatlan team wanted a catcher, so I told them to get Clint
Courtney. Courtney came there and caught. I played shortstop. As his
manager at Bisbee, I had been a little tough on Clint. He was a little
hardheaded, and I was trying to teach him stuff. But now in Mexico, we
were equals. He was the catcher, and I was the shortstop. In Bisbee, every
time he threw the ball down to third base, he'd throw it on a short hop.
Here in Mexico he said, "Charlie, practice the hops"—"Charlie" with a
Louisiana accent—"Charlie, you got to practice." I'd been telling him all
summer long he had to practice the hops on throws and bad pitches. Now
he said, "Anybody can catch a ball in the air. You got to field the hops,
Charlie." I heard my own words coming back to me. I got mad as heck at
him. He marked my shins with that ball something fierce. Oh, he was an
asset to me. But he taught me something that I used throughout my whole
baseball career: practice those things that you can't do well. If you're a good
hitter, don't just hang around the batting cage; improve the other parts of
your game. If you're a great fielder, don't just show off your skills in the
field; learn other skills. Clint Courtney taught me that.

We rode the train between ballparks, and one of the things that the Mexican players loved to do was pull tricks on us American guys. We were getting ready for the first train trip, which they said was leaving on a Monday. I knew we were just going to play Friday, Saturday, and Sunday, so I wondered what the heck we were doing leaving Monday. We played all day games, no night games. So I got packed up, my bags and my uniform, and went down to the station Monday. I waited and waited, but there was no train. So I waited all day for the dang train and the people around there were cooking and selling their vegetables out by the train station, and I was waiting. Finally I came storming back into the hotel, and Clint Courtney started laughing at me. I was "taking care of him." He said, "Charlie, you got to take care of me." He didn't need taking care of; he was fine. I came back and said, "Kid, did you know what time that train was supposed to leave? They told me the train was leaving at noon, and I was going to be early." He said, "Noon. Thursday."

I had the great privilege of spending time in a Mexican jail for my hitting abilities. We were playing at Hermosillo. We were there for a Friday, Saturday, Sunday series. I was playing shortstop. I wore uniform number 6. In the Friday game, I got 3 base hits, and I scored the winning run or one of the big runs. The next day, Saturday, I hit a home run, with one man on, in the top of the ninth inning, and we beat them by 1 run. After the game, we rode these old buses on which you stood on the side of the running board. That was our transportation to the hotel. We got on this truck or bus, and the police stopped us as we were going out of the parking lot. They wanted number 6. They said it in Spanish, and I didn't know what the heck the number was. Well, I had number 6, and they took me off the bus. Boy, the police just hauled me off in this car and threw my ass in jail. I had hit the home run to win the ball game, and they threw me in jail. I stayed in jail all night long, in my uniform, fuming, back of bars in that jail. Finally, on Sunday morning, the manager came and got me out, just in time to take a shower, re-dress, and go back out to the ballpark. I was fuming. I hadn't had anything to eat that night and no breakfast. So they had bananas. They had a lot of bananas down there, those big oversized bananas. I ate about three of those bananas for breakfast.

So we went out there to play Sunday, and I was still fuming. I was as mad as a son of a gun. I hit another home run. And wouldn't you know it, I won the ball game again with that home run. The Mexican players who could speak a little English started telling me, about the seventh inning, "Oh, boy, they're going to throw you in jail again, Charlie. They're going to throw you in jail." I said, "They won't this time." When the game was over and we got on the bus, I made every guy in the ball club take off his uniform shirt and throw it in a pile in the middle of the bus. The police came again looking for me, but everybody pointed different ways. I had said I would kill any guy who pointed at me. The police started laughing and let us get away. I was afraid I was going to spend another night in jail there. Everybody else got a big kick out of it.

When Clint Courtney and I went down to Mazatlan in the winter league, after the 1947 season, we got involved in some interesting gambling. I had heard some rumors that Clint was a pretty good Ping-Pong player. One time in Mazatlan, we were at this club in town. There was a hotshot there playing Ping-Pong. He was pretty good, but Courtney said, "Hey, Charlie, I can beat that guy. Let's set him up. How much money you got?" I said, "I got a hundred dollars, and I'm going to send it home." He said, "Naw, don't send it home. We'll run that up. All I want is 10 percent of your winnings." I said, "OK, but what about the losses?" He said, "Oh, no, you've got to stand the loss." I had never seen him really play Ping-Pong. So he started in and said, "Bet him five dollars." They took my five dollars, and Courtney lost. Clint said, "Well, Charlie, get some odds." Through sign language and one of the Mexican boys, who spoke a little English, I said, "I've got to have some odds." They gave me five-to-one odds that their man could beat Clint. He said, "Bet ten dollars." I said, "Ten dollars, we lose." I was starting to lose my confidence in Clint Courtney as a Ping-Pong player. He said, "No, Charlie. Get some odds. Bet twenty-five dollars." "Clint," I said, "I've already lost fifteen." He said, "Bet twenty-five dollars and get odds." So I talked to them and got ten-to-one odds. I put up twenty-five dollars, and Clint lost again. I looked at him, and he said, "Charlie, we got them. Bet fifty dollars. Try to recoup. They'll go for it." So I went over to them and said, "I want to bet fifty dollars." They gave me ten-to-one odds. Courtney started in, and the guy didn't even get a point. We cleaned up. We did it twice, and we cleaned up. We won five hundred dollars on the darn thing. Courtney said, "Charlie, give me my fifty dollars." I said, "Heck, I'm giving you a hundred dollars for that!"

We also got in a Hollywood movie down there in Mexico. They were filming one of those South Sea island movies, with Dorothy Lamour, I think. Mazatlan is way down near the Tropic of Cancer; it was real tropical down there, palm trees and everything. The film company hired us as extras. The director was a baseball fan. We got thirty bucks a day for that. Clint Courtney, Earl Perry, Danny O'Toole, and I were there. We were having a great time. We put on those grass skirts. We were "natives." We were all dressed up with the leis and grass skirts down to our ankles. We were supposed to be attacked, some sort of attack or something, so we were whooping it up, with imitation spears and stuff. We lasted, I think, about five seconds in the picture, in the background. We all looked pretty goofy in those outfits, but it was a lot of fun. O'Toole was a pitcher from Cincinnati, a great big, red-headed, freckle-faced, Irish kid. He pitched at El Paso, and he was on our Mazatlan club. But they wouldn't let him be in the movie, because he didn't look "native" enough.

But there was another side to Mazatlan. One thing I couldn't get over down there was how poor the young kids were. They had no shoes. When I got my paychecks, I'd go down and take half a dozen of the kids over to the markets and buy them those little harachi shoes. I guess I bought about fifty pairs. They cost a dollar or fifty cents, I think, American money. Many years later, when I was scouting for the Dodgers in the late 1970s, I took my son Geoff down to Mazatlan. We took a trip down there, and I showed him where I had lived and played and all that. And I took him over to the little store where I used to buy those harachi shoes. The man back of the counter said, "Señor, I know you." I said, "No, you don't know me." He was an elderly man, and this was thirty years later. He said, "Yes, Señor, I know you." I said, "Where do you know me from? I haven't been down here in thirty years. Well, tell me about me. My son is listening." "I know now," he said. "You're Carlos Metro. You used to bring all those friends of mine in here and buy harachis from my father." My son said, "Gee, Dad, I didn't know you did things like that." "Oh, yeah, I did some of those things," I told him.

When I was in Mexico, I got into a throwing contest with a center fielder who had one of the greatest arms I've ever seen. His name was Mala Torres, and he was the size of Stan Musial and hit just like him. He was a heck of a good hitter. He was strong, and he probably weighed about 170, 175 pounds. But the thing that really struck me as outstanding was his arm. He made some fantastic plays in center field. I was down there in Mexico as a shortstop. I'd played third base one year in the C league at Bisbee, and they put me at shortstop. I could throw. I had a good arm, an outstanding arm. So I thought I'd challenge him. He couldn't speak English very well, and I couldn't speak Spanish, so Manulo Fortes, who could speak English well, translated. I said, "Tell Mala Torres I want a throwing contest with him." So he told Mala, and he was pointing at me, Carlos, and motioning about throwing. I told him accuracy and distance. And he agreed. I knew what he was saying. Mala Torres asked how much, and I said, "One hundred pesos." The exchange rate then was about twenty to one, so about five bucks. He told Mala Torres, but Mala said, "No, no, no." I could see him shaking his head. He said, "Five hundred pesos." I said, "OK." We went out to the field Sunday morning before the game. The sun was nice and warm. I was feeling great. I was strong. We went back to the center-field fence, which was 385 feet away from home plate. I drew a line and stepped off about 10 feet from the fence, making it about 375 feet. But he said, "Oh, no, no. From back here at the fence, one foot on the fence and take your steps and throw." I said, "OK." He said, "*Por favor*, please," for me to go first, I guess. I was warmed up real good, so I took the baseball and I threw it right over the pitcher's mound, about 10 feet in front of the pitcher's mound. That was a pretty good toss. He said, "Three." So I threw another just about the same. And then I threw the third one, and it landed on the pitcher's mound. I thought that was pretty darn good, and I threw them right in line with the plate. I gave him a baseball. He took that baseball and threw it against the backstop. I looked at him, and he kind of grinned a little bit and said, "Carlos, Mala champion." I could understand that. I said, "No, no, right on home plate. He took the next ball and threw it within 4 feet of home plate, right at the batter's box. I said, "Five hundred pesos, Mala, you." He laughed like heck and kidded me all the time about that. Sometime later, he got a tryout with San Antonio and made the club. Everybody ranted and raved about him. But he wouldn't play, because he was homesick. If they're ever going to put a Mexican ballplayer in the Hall of Fame to represent Mexico, they ought to dig up his record.

In the spring of 1948, we were going to spring training at Boyes Hot Springs in California, and we ran into a heck of a snowstorm at Donner Pass. In 1947 I had finished third in the Arizona-Texas League with Bisbee, and the Yankees gave me their Twin Falls, Idaho, Yankees farm club job. They moved me up into a faster C league. The people out there in Idaho wanted me to come out for a get-together, an introduction to the new manager, a luncheon and so forth, so we went out. I took my wife and my daughter, Elena, and my son Bud. We had the car, a Nash, all packed up, and we went up to Idaho. This was in March. Joe Devine and Eddie Leishman were there. I made the speech, and we stayed a day, but I had to go to spring training. When you go from Twin Falls, Idaho, to Boyes Hot Springs, you go down through Sacramento. You go down through Nevada and over Donner Pass. We tried to get a report on the pass, and they said it was snowing a little bit. We didn't think much about that snow, so we started up Donner Pass. Holy smokes! I looked out on the side, and the snow was stacked up on those homes along the road. The snow was clear up to the second-story windows. Along came a bus, and we just got right in back of it. We took off and crossed Donner Pass. We were the last car to get through. When we finally got down, there was a check station. They said, "How did you get through here? Don't you know that we're closing this pass, the road, for two weeks?" I don't know what would have happened to my managerial career then if I'd been two or three weeks late. But as it was, we got through. Safe by a mile!

We had a very exciting year at Twin Falls in 1948. They hadn't won in some time up there. I think the Yankees had been there one or two years prior to this, and they didn't have a good team there. I came up there, and, boy, they'd already labeled me as a fiery playing manager and everything else. They built that up like something you've never seen. I had a pretty good club. We were allowed three veterans. I was a veteran, the first baseman was a veteran, and another guy was too. If I have a favorite ball club of all time, of all the clubs I managed, the 1948 and 1949 Twin Falls, Idaho, Cowboys in the Pioneer League would be it. We would take infield practice and never make an error. They'd never make a bad play in the field. They never missed a sign. They were just about perfect. I had Bruce Schroeder, a left-handed pitcher who I thought was a can't-miss prospect. He got married, and I think his wife didn't want him to play baseball or something like that. We also had Bob Maruca, a big right-handed pitcher. He was big and strong, but he couldn't master the curve ball. Jim Eskenberry was definitely a big-league prospect. He was about six foot one and weighed about 180 pounds. Joe Devine had a rule that if you bumped your head going through the doorway, they'd sign you; if you could walk through the door, they wouldn't sign you. We laughed about it because all these kids I had at Twin Falls were big and tall. Eskenberry couldn't throw the ball to the second baseman on a double play, on a ball hit back at him, or field a bunt with two men on. He'd try to throw the ball to third base and throw it away into left field. Eskenberry hated being lifted from a game. I could tell when he wasn't right. He won eleven in a row for us that year, but I'd go out there and I'd say, "Give me the ball." He'd hand me the ball, and I'd put the ball down by my side, and I'd turn around and he'd follow that ball around. He wouldn't take his eyes off the ball. I knew that I'd better get him out of there. But when he just nonchalantly wouldn't care, when he wouldn't look at the ball, I'd let him stay, because he was right. He wasn't worried. It worked pretty good. I did it a couple of times. I didn't want to undercut his confidence. He was a good pitcher. He had good stuff and should have gotten to the big leagues, but he hurt his arm. Those things happen. Incidentally, Jim and I have become real good friends. He lives here in Colorado, and we've gone to some Rockies games.

Charlie Noah was on our Twin Falls club. He was a right-handed pitcher from USC or UCLA, I can't recall which, one of those colleges. We got quite a few ballplayers from there. We'd get them from the schools out there because we were the farm club. I never could satisfy Charlie. He was pretty sharp with a comeback, and no matter what I'd say or anything, he'd make a little remark about it. Finally I got tired of it. He started in a ball game, and in the first inning he got shelled a little bit, got racked up pretty good. In the second inning, he got racked up pretty good again. By the third or fourth inning, I think they had us down eleven or twelve to nothing. Then we get a couple of runs, and he was out there on the mound, and I just let him stay. I let him stay, and he got the message. I said, "You pop off anymore? The next time you pitch, you'll stay." He wasn't a very good pitcher, but he was a joy to have on the team, because he kept everybody loose.

I call some of the players every once in a while. I get to thinking about them, and I give them a call. I called Tom Kelly when he became an executive with Weyerhauser lumber company, out there in the Northwest. I asked him if I had been tough. He said, "No, you were the fairest man I've ever seen." So that was quite a compliment. Bill Renna was a big football player at Santa Clara who the Yankees signed and sent to Twin Falls his first year. He hit like heck up there, and they called him "Bull," because he was a big guy. He was a delight to have on the team. He'd been a successful football player. I believe he was a fullback, but I'm not sure. He had a short major league career. He was fighting a tough, uphill battle with the Yankees. They had some pretty good ballplayers at that time. Hal Smith came out to my club. We had a regular catcher who was going to catch, so we sent him out. Eventually he wound up with the Pirates in the 1960 World Series. He hit the home run that tied the score and allowed Mazeroski to win the game.

I had Gus Triandos, who later went on to the big leagues, mainly with Baltimore. We converted him into a catcher. He was a first baseman and did a little catching. He was a big, gangly, tall kid, eighteen years old or so, six foot something, and around two hundred pounds. He was so tall he had trouble squatting and blocking the low pitches. So I put all the equipment on him, grabbed a bucket of balls, stood about twenty-five feet or so from him, and kept throwing balls at his feet and in front of him. He became somewhat quicker getting those balls. He wasn't the fastest runner, sort of an Ernie Lombardi type of catcher. But I had him steal one time in the Class C league. He had a good sense of humor. Gus was a wonderful person and a good ballplayer. He loved to hit on 3-0. I'd give him the sign to hit 3-0, and every once in a while he'd hit one nine miles. He couldn't catch the knuckle ball when he went up with Baltimore. Hoyt Wilhelm shortened his career.

At the end of one of the seasons in Twin Falls, four or five of the players bought an old car, I think for fifty bucks. This was 1948 or 1949. They were all from the Bay area, Jim Eskenberry and the others. They bought an old car, and they chipped in to drive it home. It was one of those touring cars, but I don't remember what model it was. It had the canvas top and canvas on the sides and everything. You could put the roof down. If they'd kept it, they would have made a fortune now. They got home with it, and Gus Triandos was the one who put "California or Bust" on the side of it as they left Twin Falls after the season was over.

Joe Polich was our shortstop. The Yanks were grooming him as a replacement for Phil Rizzuto. Joe was the most natural ballplayer I've ever seen at shortstop. He didn't know what a bad hop was. He had a tremendous arm. He could throw off balance from in the hole. He could run, and he could hit the ball into the alley. But he had this terrible quirk about him. He didn't want anybody else to be better than he was, and he pouted whenever somebody got more base hits than he did. He pouted and resented it. He got down on himself about it. The Yankees gave him a bonus at that time, and I understand that he turned down a thirty-five-thousand-dollar bonus with the Pittsburgh Pirates. Bing Crosby had tried to talk him into going with the Pirates.

One of my all-time favorite guys, Gil McDougald, played second. We needed a second baseman, and one of the guys told me that there was a kid down in San Francisco who was pretty good. I had a lot of San Francisco and California kids. They'd keep telling me about this kid down in San Francisco. Red Strader, who was a football coach and a bird dog, a part-time summer scout, for the Yankees, told me that Gil had the strongest, most determined face you've ever seen on an athlete. That came from an established football coach and stuck in my mind. So I talked to Joe Devine at the spring camp. I looked around and didn't see any other second basemen. I said, "Hey, Joe, I need a second baseman." He said, "Oh, you can play." I said, "No, Joe, I can't play second. I tried it, and I can't play." He said, "Oh, yeah, you can play second base," and then he relented. "Well, we'll get you a second baseman," he promised. I said, "Well, what about this kid down there that they're all talking about?" He said, "Oh, he can't play. I don't know if he can play. He wants to play. Maybe we ought to just . . ." I said, "Well, bring him up. If he wants to play, maybe we can get by with him until we get a second baseman." He said, "OK." So here came this kid, kind of tall, skinny, and gangly, kind of Ichabod Crane–looking. We started working him out, and he turned out to be a bumblebee. He ran like a girl, with his feet pointed out. He fielded the ball way back under him, and he threw it funny. And he had the worst-looking stance I'd ever seen. He held the bat parallel, way back as far as he could put it. He looked like a bird dog on point. But altogether, when somebody hit him a ball, he'd field it and throw the guy out. When we had a difficult play to make, he made the play and caught the guy at first base. And when he ran, he could beat out ground balls. When he got to bat, if they threw it inside, he'd hit the ball down the left-field line, and if they'd throw it outside, he'd hit to right field. If they'd throw him a curve ball, he'd bust the heck out of it. About a month later, Joe Devine asked me how Gil was doing. I told him to come out and see for himself. Joe saw his batting stance and said, "He'll never hit like that." I said, "Joe, he doesn't know he can't hit." Gil, of course, went up to the Yankees, became Rookie of the Year in 1951, and played in eight World Series. Years later in Chicago, when I got to talk with Rogers Hornsby, he told me about McDougald, and I said, "Rog, did you try to change his stance?" Hornsby had managed Gil at Beaumont, in the Texas League. He said, "Heck, no. That kid could hit it any way you threw him."

For some reason, during spring training at Boyes Hot Springs in 1948, Gil McDougald's room assignment got fouled up. He didn't have a room or something. He came up to me and said "Charlie, I want a couple of days off." I said, "Well, heck, Mac, you haven't made this club yet." He said, "Well, I'll make this club." I said, "What is it you want to do?" He said, "I want to go down to San Francisco." I said, "Why?" He said, "I want to get married." The Yankees had a rule you couldn't get married during spring training or the season. I said, "Well, you better talk to Eddie Leishman and Joe Devine." He talked to them, and they asked me what I thought. I said, "Let him go." So he went home, and he got married. He stayed three days and got married. He came back and brought his wife with him and took her to Twin Falls and had a heck of a year. When I met his wife a few years ago, I told her that I had been planning to release him because he went home to get married, and she said, "Glad you didn't." They raised a big family, and he became a highly successful businessman in New York.

A few years ago, the Rockies put out a poster of Dante Bichette hitting a ball off the top of a mountain, but we did something like that thirty-five or so years earlier. The team was going from Twin Falls, Idaho, to Billings, Montana, and we went through Yellowstone National Park. We came to Yellowstone Falls, right in the middle of the park, and stopped there. One

Charlie at age two with his father, Metro Moreskonich, about 1920.

Third grade friends: *left to right*, Charlie, Billy Locke, and Adam Soha.

(*Left*) High school seniors: *left to right*, Danny Krawetz, Charlie, and Nick Witychak.

(*Below left*) Charlie after his release from Easton, 1937. The Brooklyn cap was a gift from Dodgers pitcher Van Lingle Mungo.

(*Right*) *Middle row, right*, Charlie with the Pennington Gap team, 1938.

(*Below right*) Back home in Nanty-Glo, Pennsylvania: *Left to right*, Charlie with the mayor and a friend, 1938. Charlie is being given an inscribed bat to celebrate his first year as a professional baseball player.

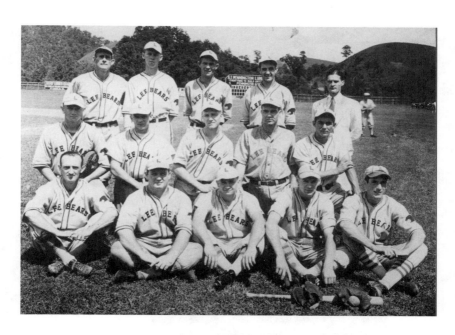

(*Left*) Charlie and Helen Deane Bullock courting, 1939.

(*Below*) The Mayfield Browns of Kentucky, 1939. *Back row, third from right*, Charlie; *front row, right*, Vern Stephens, and *back row, third from left*, Jim Russell—both future major leaguers; *front row, left,* manager Benny Tate.

(*Right*) Helen and Charlie visiting Charlie's mother, Pauline Moreskonich, in Nanty-Glo, Pennsylvania, January 1942.

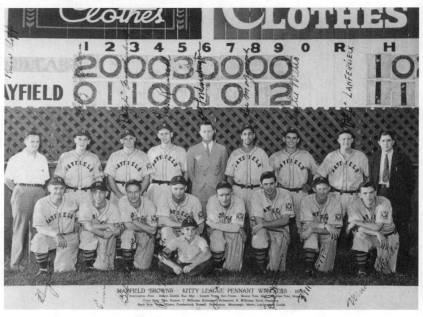

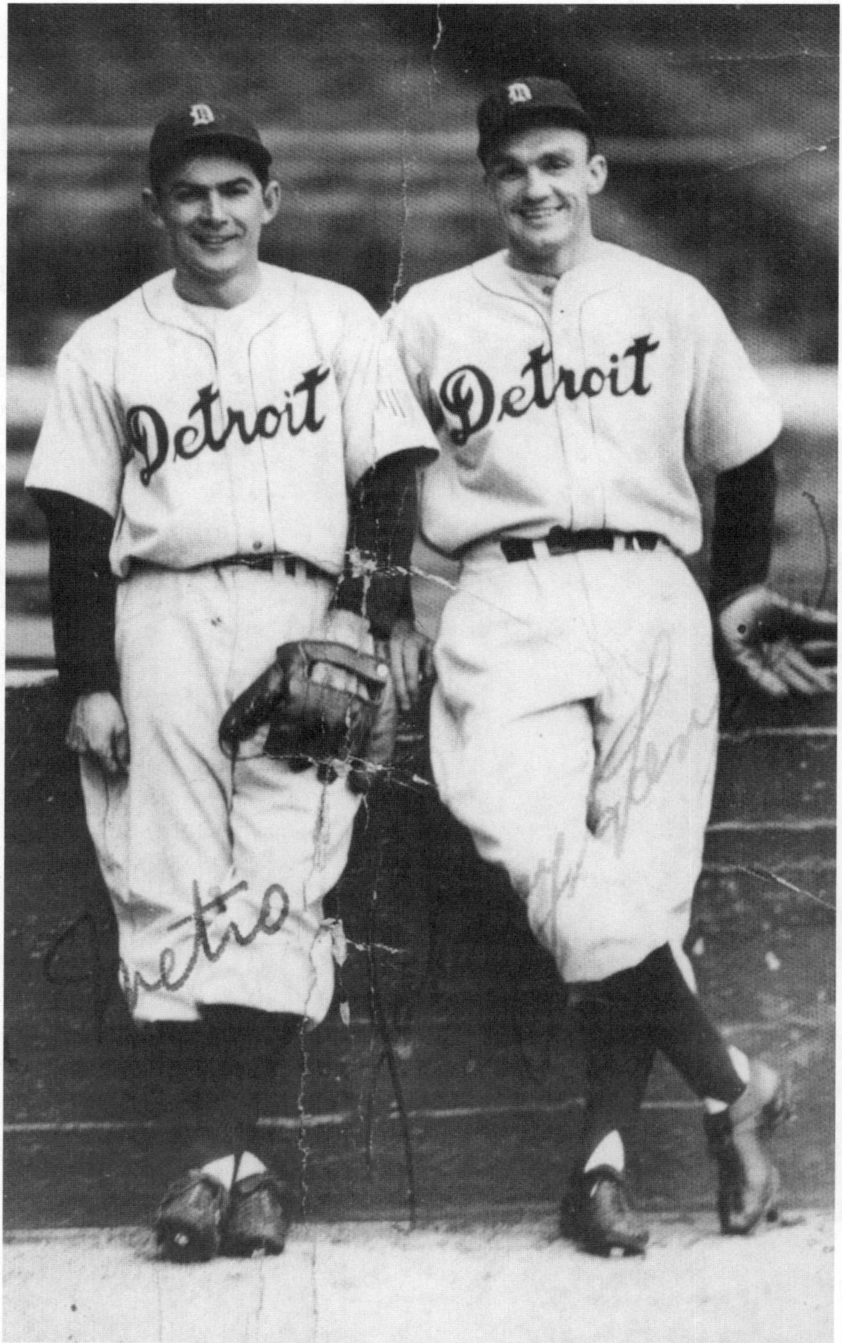
Detroit
Detroit

(*Left*) Charlie (*left*) and John
Gorsica, playing ball in
Philadelphia, 1943 or 1944.

(*Above*) *Left to right*, Al Simmons,
Charlie, and Mr. Mack, gathered
when Charlie was playing for
Philadelphia in 1944.

(*Left*) Charlie at the batting tee in Twin Falls, Idaho, 1948.

(*Below*) At Yankees spring training in Boyes Hot Springs, California, 1948. *From left*, Syl Johnson, the right-handed pitching instructor; Charlie; and Lefty Gomez, the left-handed pitching instructor.

(*Right*) Charlie (*at left*) with Ty Cobb in Twin Falls, Idaho, 1948. Cobb's advice to Charlie: don't change; be aggressive; be tough.

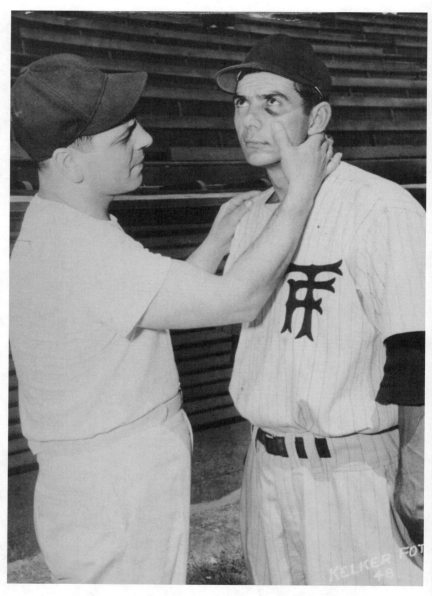

Charlie with a shiner after a fight in Twin Falls, Idaho, 1948. Joe Soares is the trainer.

of the guys said, "Wow! Look how deep that is!" I got the brilliant idea of hitting a fungo into the Yellowstone River canyon right by the falls. There's a ledge there. So I broke out the batting practice balls, and Gus Triandos says, "Let me hit one." I said, "OK." We drew a line that you hit from behind. So Gus hit one way out there. Then it was Gil McDougald's turn to hit one. He really got off a good fungo shot, and we all hit. We hit the whole bag of practice balls into the canyon. I said, "Now, we won't be able to take hitting practice." "Aw, we don't care," they said. We gave McDougald the world record. I might stand corrected on this, but I think it was 1,570 feet, right down into the Yellowstone River, right to the falls way down. We gave him the championship because he was 2 feet back of the line. Triandos was on the line. A few years ago, Gil was out in Denver for a golf tournament. I hadn't seen him since 1948. I don't think he'd gained an ounce. I told him that he had the world record for hitting fungoes. He said, "Did it really go that far?" I said, "Yes, it went that far."

We opened the 1948 season in Pocatello, Idaho. They had a business manager named Marvin Milks, who later became the general manager of the Seattle Pilots in the American League expansion of 1969. We were very good friends. Back in 1948, he knew me from somewhere, I can't remember where or when, but he said, "Charlie, it's cold in Pocatello. We'll be lucky to have 1,000, maybe 1,200, people Opening Day. If we're real lucky, we'll have 2,000. If the game gets out of hand, you're beating us or we're beating you, do something. Stir something up. I heard about you down at Bisbee." I said, "What do you want me to do?" He said, "Ah, do anything, but just get them stirred up. So next time we'll have a little better showing." I said, "OK." Milks said, "I'll buy you the best gabardine shirt money can buy if you do something." I said, "OK, you got a deal."

So I was the playing manager, and as luck would have it, they were beating the heck out of us. I think the score was 12–2 or 12–1. It was no contest. We weren't doing any good. So in the seventh inning, I came up to bat. I took the first pitch, and it was right down the middle. I turned around and gave the umpire hell. Another pitch came right down the middle, and I took that one too, and the ump, of course, called it a strike. I took my cap off and was getting ready to throw it down, and he said, "You throw that down, and you're out of here." I put the cap back on. I said, "That wasn't a strike. What, you can't see?" I said all those things that you tell an umpire, short of getting thrown out. The next pitch was way outside, and I said, "You going to call that a strike?" "No, that's a ball," he said. But the next pitch was right down the middle, and I took it for strike three. I went kind of berserk. There it was, in the seventh inning, not much chance to win the ball game, and I started stomping around. I kicked dirt on the plate and on his shoes and everything, and I threw the bat down. He threw me out of the ball game, but I refused to go. Finally I went over to the dugout, and I grabbed the ball bag, and I threw it out onto the field. All the balls rolled out. Every time the ump would go out there and throw the balls back, I'd throw the balls back at him. I don't know how long I delayed the game.

The Pocatello fans were going a little nuts about it. They were getting a little riled. So the umpire called the police. Here came two great big cops. They had their clubs. I was back of home plate arguing with the ump, and they picked me up off the ground by my arms. I said, "Now, wait a minute. I'm just putting this on for Marvin." They said, "Is that right?" I said, "Yeah." So I said, "I'll go, I'll go, but let me run away from you." They said, "OK." So I broke loose from one and then the other, and they chased me around a bit. The next day Pocatello had 3,800 people. Fans wanted to see this. Years later, when I saw Marvin Milks with Seattle, I said, "Hey, Marv, where's my shirt?" I never did get that gabardine shirt. As a manager you tried to do things, within reason, to stir up the fans. You always had to kick dirt or throw your cap down or throw a towel or two, the shin guards, when they threw you out of the ball game.

While I was in the Pioneer League, we had an awful lot of scouts come into Twin Falls. It was a great place. They loved to go fishing. Joe Devine loved to come up there because he loved to fish. We took him down to the fish hatchery. He caught a fish out of the hatchery, and he loved that.

We played all night baseball and we had a nice ballpark, and the scouts would all come in. Longtime big leaguers such as Syl Johnson, Harlond Clift, and Glenn Wright came by. I held workouts in the morning. It was kind of compulsory. I didn't tell anybody it was compulsory, but they wanted to work out. The players loved it. They came out there in their shorts and spiked shoes, just to get a little bit of sun. I'd bring all the scouts out, and I would pick their brains. I'd get Syl Johnson, a right-handed pitcher, to show the pitchers how to throw a curve and everything. I'd utilize them. I'd get down there, and I'd wake them up. Harlond Clift, who played third base for the Browns for many years, came into Twin Falls to scout my club. Harlond was an advocate of pulling the ball. He said, "Pull the ball, pull the ball. Maybe on occasion hit a ball the opposite way." When he saw my ball club pulling the ball so much, he was just like a kid with a new toy. He said, "I haven't seen anything like this in a long time. Have those guys keep pulling that ball."

Out there in the Pioneer League, I had the privilege of meeting up with two of the greatest ballplayers ever, Ty Cobb and Mickey Cochrane. Cobb's son, Herschel, ran a Coca-Cola plant in Twin Falls. He spent a lot of time up there. I think he was grooming Herschel to take over his investments in Coca-Cola. Ty would come out and watch our games. He kind of adopted our ball club. He'd come out to the ball games, and he'd sit there in the press box with the announcer and yell instructions and everything at me. Boy, if I did something wrong, you could hear him all over the ballpark. You dumb son of a blank blank, he'd shout. I thought sometimes he was going to swear at me. He wanted you to play for 1 run all the time. Get 1 run, he'd say, it takes 2 to beat them, and if you're playing at home you need 1 run first. He was always urging me to use the sacrifice. Well, Twin Falls was a Yankees farm club, and although it wasn't a dyed-in-the-wool rule for the Yanks, they wanted their guys to hit, to swing the bat. They didn't want them up there taking pitches and getting walks. So I had a little rule, of my own, that I wouldn't give any bunt signs or anything, no take signs, for the first half of the game. I'd let them hit for the first four or five innings, to see how they'd do. Boy, we'd jump out and get a lot of runs. This drove Ty Cobb crazy.

One time I called a squeeze play, and I thought Cobb was going to die. I was coaching at third. Gus Triandos was the hitter. The pitcher was due next, and I called time and talked to Gus. I said "Hey, Gus, don't let these guys walk you now, because I don't want to take the pitcher out." He asked, "What do you want me to do?" I said, "Squeeze, no matter where the ball is." They threw the ball up over his head, and he jumped up and put down a squeeze bunt. Ty Cobb told me later on that was the greatest play he'd ever seen. He loved that execution. He also loved the double steal. Once in a while, you'd see you had a perfect situation for a double steal. I always wanted to start the guy at first base, because nine times out of ten they'd throw and the guy at third would come in, and I taught that.

Of course, Ty had the reputation of being really nasty, but I didn't see that side of him. I did see the aggressive side. If he was talking to you and you weren't paying attention, he'd smack you around by the collar and turn you around to get your attention. But he was a very gracious man. He had an apartment, where Herschel lived, in a building he owned. We had a little old plywood house that we were renting, weeds were growing up in the back. Ty would come up the alley, and we'd sit on the back stoop. He had his brown-and-white shoes on and was dressed up in cream-colored pants and everything. He'd come there and sit down. He talked baseball constantly. He'd say, now, Charlie, you got to do this and you got to do that. He'd say, don't be afraid to steal. I did have Ray Jacobs, who stole a whole bunch of bases, who led the league in steals. Ty loved that. He'd tell me how to take leads and everything. He'd say, now when you get 1 run, get 2. When you get 2, get 5. He said, "The best offensive weapon in baseball is not going to beat you. They can't even tie you, even a home run with the bases loaded can't even beat you." So he would preach that, and I learned quite a bit. He came over three or four times, every time we'd come into town. One time he got down on his knees and told my wife how to plant nasturtiums, how to weed them and everything else. Here's a man who's supposed to be terrible over there telling her how to prune and nurse nasturtiums, and I didn't even know what the heck they were. Ty Cobb was something else.

I hunted ducks with his son, Herschel, on the Snake River. I worked for the Chrysler-Plymouth dealer at Twin Falls in the wintertime. Bing Crosby was a friend of the dealer, and he came up and we all went down on the Snake River to an old lodge. There was also a guy from Elko, Nevada, a dentist, who was a trapshooting champ. And we sat down there, and it was cold! Oh, Lord, it was cold on the Snake River. Herschel was kind of a wild guy. It'd be below zero and he'd be going up and down that Snake River in a boat, scaring up the ducks. He'd shoot them, and then he'd go down with a net and put them in the boat, with his shirt off, and it was below zero. This particular time we were playing poker and shooting ducks. We had all the shells we wanted. We'd sit under a bush and ducks would come in, and we'd take the plug out of our automatic and shoot, shoot, shoot, bringing three or four of them down. I could shoot pretty well, and I put my hands on the barrel to keep them warm. Then the game warden came down, and of course, two or three of the big guys there told the game warden that we'd shot something out of season and that I didn't even have a license. I didn't have a duck or waterfowl license. They had me right where they wanted me. They said, "Take him. Take him to jail. If he didn't have a license, take him to jail." That made me sweat. I said, "Is there anything I can do?" The warden said, "Yeah. You put those ducks in those bags and put them in my truck." I put about five or six bags of ducks in his truck. He took them right down to the orphanage. I got off the hook. It was tough living that down, because he was a great baseball fan.

Mickey Cochrane was the other Hall of Famer I encountered during my years at Twin Falls. I met Mickey at Billings, Montana. Mickey was associated with the big automotive people in Detroit. One of the big company officials had a big ranch up near Red Lodge, Montana, if my memory serves me correctly. Mickey was in Billings. He was a little bit on the sauce at that time. We stayed at the Rainbow Hotel, the finest one in Billings. I would go in and maybe have a beer. The rule was that players couldn't have a beer in the bar. They had to stay out of the bar, and even some of the big league managers had that rule, so I had to carry that out. No ballplayers could be seen in the bar having a beer or drink or whatever. So I'd go in there, and one time Mickey was there. He recognized me, and we started up a conversation. I talked him into coming out to the ballpark, but he didn't want to come out in the mornings. But he'd come out to the ballpark and watch me, and at night I'd see him again. He told me all about catching. He told me how to handle Gus Triandos. He said, "You ought to put the shin guards on that big boy. He's got a pretty good arm. He don't know how to throw good. Tell him to shorten up on the back, come straight up and throw instead of winding up." I said, "Well, he played a little first base." Mickey said, "Oh, that's what I thought." He said, "Put all the stuff on him. Put his shin guards on, his chest protector, and his mask, and get a bag of those practice balls and get out there about twenty-five feet in front of him, and put him by the backstop. Try to hit him on the shins and try to hit him on the knees and make him squat down and fall in front. Just keep that ball in front of you all the time. Don't angle your body." I absorbed all this stuff. Any time an ex–big league player or a scout was in town, I would always corral him and pick his brains. That's the way I learned how to do my managing at this time, and I passed this information on to my other catchers later. He also taught me something about criticizing players. He said, "When they're winning, you can really give them all kinds of heck. You can correct them. Something that a player did three days ago, or a week ago, if you're winning the games and you're on a streak, you can go over there and give him heck and chew him out for that play way back there. But when you're losing, don't criticize a ballplayer." He had some property or some family or something up there, near the Red Lodge area. My kid sister, Ann, lived and ranched out there in that area too. She knew Mickey Cochrane's daughter. I think my sister and she had the hots for the same cowboy out there at one time. I'd kid Mickey about it, and he'd kid me about it. He'd say, "I hope your sister gets him." And I say, "Well, I hope you're daughter gets him." We'd heard about the cowboy.

I've had catchers who couldn't throw the ball back to the pitcher. At spring training at Boyes Hot Springs, the first or second year I was managing in the Yankees organization, we had a catcher like that. He was a fine looking specimen of an athlete, about six foot one, but he had the worst footwork. He didn't know how to shift back of the plate. He'd throw the ball into center field past second base. I worked with him over and over. We tried all sorts of things to teach him how to shift, but he couldn't get the hang of it. Finally, one Saturday night, I went to this dance at the Sonoma Mission

Inn. The players didn't have an early curfew on Saturdays. They could stay out until midnight, and then they had to get up in the morning and go to the church of their choice. So I went to this dance that night. I went to see how they were getting along, and everything was fine. I looked up, and there was this catcher doing the damnedest jitterbug you've ever seen. The footwork was amazing. I told Joe Devine, the West Coast scout in charge of the camp, and Eddie Leishman, the Yankees farm director, and they looked at me as if I were crazy. So I told the catcher, "Next time you do the jitterbug back there!" He learned a little bit better footwork from that. He got the idea from his jitterbugging. I can't remember the catcher's name.

We had a contest called the potato race. You'd get three guys from your club and three guys from the visiting club, and you'd line them up. You'd give each guy five baseballs, practice balls, and they'd walk out there ten yards and put a ball down. Then they'd walk out another ten yards and put down another ball, and so on until they got out there about sixty yards with the last ball. Then you'd get the guys all back in, take their caps off, and put the caps on the line. You'd line them up like they were in race, 1–2–3 Go! They'd run out, get the first ball, bring it back, put it in the cap, and go after the next one. By the time they got out to the one sixty yards away, half of them would stagger and fall on the way back. The fans loved it. There was usually some small cash prize or free tickets or something. The managers would pick the guys, and they'd often pick some burly guy. Once we talked Gus Triandos into doing it. He was almost on his knees by the end of the race.

As a manager, I had my share of fun with the men in blue. We were in Billings in 1949 for a game when I got into a dandy of an argument with an umpire. We were getting the heck beat out of us in one game, so I put myself in at third base. I'd broken a bone in my neck in batting practice by swinging at a curve ball that I thought would be a fastball. I was wearing a brace. So finally I thought it was time to take this thing off and try and see if I could be of help. I was a playing manager. I was having a hard time not playing. So I went and played third base. We had a play there real soon after I went in the game. I caught a throw and tagged out a guy who was trying to stretch a double into a triple. He was out by ten feet. But the umpire was out of position over by second base and called him safe.

I thought, oh, boy, this is my chance. I didn't want to play. I was hurt. So I started in on the ump. I called him various names and said stuff like "How can you be an umpire when you can't see a guy twenty feet away?" I was ranting and raving, waving my hands, but the fans were kind of ignoring it. I took my cap off, and he said, "Throw that cap off, and you're out of this game." I put it back on. I still had the ball in my hand while I was arguing with him. He said, "Let's get going. Give me that ball." I said, "You want this ball?" He said, "Yeah." I threw it down and said, "Here, pick it up, you . . ." Well, that got me tossed out of the game. He said, "Before you go, you pick that ball up and give it to me." I said, "You want this ball, you want this ball, here get it." I threw it clear up over the grandstand. The Billings fans went crazy.

Morey Enright, who was the business manager of the Billings Mustangs, went berserk with joy. We got the heck beat out of us. He came in the clubhouse and said, "Charlie, that's the greatest thing I've ever seen. Can I play this up?" I said, "Do anything you want." I was still mad. He said, "Sure you had him by about ten feet." That made me madder. So he called me up after I got back to the hotel and asked if he could quote me on an early-morning broadcast. I said, "You can quote me any way." He said, "How about, 'That's the blindest so and so I've ever seen. I had him out by ten feet, no, fifteen feet.' Can I quote you on that?" I said, "Absolutely." Then the newspaper, I think it was called the *Billings Gazette*, ran a story that Charlie Metro was furious and going to take revenge and everything else.

About 8:00 the next morning, they woke me up and I had to go speak to an early-morning breakfast club of the civic leaders. I got there, and they asked me what I was going to do. I said, "Well, I'm not going to pay the fine, I'll tell you that." Somebody said, "Well, the umpire is quoted saying you're going to have to replace that baseball." I said, "I'll replace it." So we went out to the ballpark later. We could hardly get in. Fans, maybe five or six thousand, were standing outside, milling around, trying to get into the ballpark. Before the game, I took the lineup up to the plate. I wasn't in the ball game. The umpire asked, "Where's the baseball?" I said "What baseball?" He said, "Well, you've got to replace that baseball you threw." I had anticipated that, so I had put the oldest ball in the ball bag in my pocket, and I handed it to him. He said, "I want a new ball. You threw a new ball out, that game ball." I said, "Well, I'm not getting you another." He rolled it over to the dugout. I went over and got it and rolled it back. He said, "One more time and you're going to be out of here." Oh, the fans went crazy. So I went back and got a new ball out of the bag. I took it out of the box, and I made a big presentation of giving it to him and he bowed. And I did some pantomime stuff.

So the game started, and I went to coach third base. Morey Enright got on the public address system and said, "Folks, our esteemed opponent, Charlie

Metro. Let him know how you feel." Out of the crowd came hundreds of balls: old baseballs, footballs, golf balls, soccer balls, kickballs, gumballs, every kind of ball concocted, you name it. You never saw anything like it. I was standing at third base, watching all these things go over my head and land on the field. I took it pretty well. Oh, geez, the players laughed like heck. The umpire kicked the balls over to me, and I'd throw them back at the fans, then they'd throw them back, and it took about fifteen minutes before we got them all. But it was a tremendous thing, and I really enjoyed it. I kicked the balls off the field finally. They were throwing them at me, but I went through all the motions. The next day they had the biggest crowd in the history of the ballpark, Cobb Field. Some years later I ran into Bob Cobb, the guy they named the field after and who owned the Brown Derby restaurant. He reminded me of this show I put on in 1949 at Billings. I said, "You know, I never did have to pay for that baseball," and he laughed like heck. But you did some of those things to kind of stir things up. The leading clubs were always the ones that were hated, so you'd stage a rumble or create a fracas, and that was always good for attendance.

I loved to play in Montana at Billings and Great Falls. Billings was one of my favorite cities for visiting. I knew a lot of people up there. It was a great place to play. The Great Falls club had a working agreement with Seattle of the Coast League. They were called Great Falls Electrics because they had a big powerhouse plant on the river there. But the thing that stands out in my mind was that Great Falls had a business manager named Nick Mariana. In the fall of 1948, he was at the ballpark and he heard this terrible sound. He grabbed his camera and went out, and he took pictures of a flying saucer right back of second base. From the grandstand, he took pictures of this object, a whole bunch of pictures with his camera as quickly as he could. He said it took off and left. The story came up in the newspaper. Well, there was a big air force base outside of Great Falls, kind of a jumping-off place to Alaska during World War II. Before that ink dried on the newspaper, here came all these government officials, the colonel and everybody else. They took his camera. They developed the film, and he never heard any more about it, but he did get one picture of it, which showed a little speck over the center-field fence. That's the first and only time I ever came in close contact with an unidentified flying object. And I met a great friend in Great Falls, Eddie Newman. He owned one of the finest dining places in the whole western part of the United States. In fact, many motion picture people and radio and TV people would come up there just to have dinner at his place. He was a great host. Eddie and I were friends for over thirty-some years. He came down to spring training with me and traveled with me when I ran the club at Chicago in 1962.

Billings had a black outfielder named Eddie Moore. We played against him. Everybody on some other clubs just gave him a going-over. They'd knock him down, and he'd get up. This was 1949. That was the period in baseball when Jackie Robinson had just broken the color line. Pittsburgh sent Moore out there because they thought there'd be less hostility in the West for a black player. They put him to the test. He played pretty well. He hit .312 with 14 home runs and 90 runs batted in. His Billings teammates accepted him. My guys, who were mostly from California and the Mountain West, didn't have any problem with him. But he couldn't stand the treatment from the other clubs.

Even if the umps were on your side and you were playing well, baseball contained so many unexpected events you just had to grin and bear them. I have seen plays so crazy and unpredictable that I still disbelieve them. I've seen the ball field itself cause some of the strangest occurrences ever. When we were at Twin Falls, I saw a play that gave a different meaning to the term "gopher ball": an inside-the-park home run due to a gopher hole. There were a lot of gopher holes in the outfield, which the groundskeepers would try to fill. But one game against Salt Lake City, one of our sluggers, Charlie Buck, a left-handed hitter, whammed a ball off the left-field fence. Instead of bouncing back in, it hit the wall and dropped straight down into a gopher hole, one the groundskeepers had missed, at the bottom of the fence. Out there on that prairie, the gophers were in the habit of tunneling back and forth under the fences. The opposition outfielder chose not to grab it. He threw up his hands as if the ball were in an obstruction. He expected the umpire would rule it a ground-rule double. Charlie circled the bases. We all went running out there, and there was the ball lodged right under the fence. It was not all the way out and it was not all the way in! Soon both teams were in an uproar. We demanded that it be called a home run, and Tommy Thompson, the Salt Lake manager, wanted the ground-rule double. So the umpire went out to the fence and looked at where the ball was. Then he took out his pen and drew a line across the ball. He picked it up and examined it majestically. "Gentlemen," he spoke, "this is my ruling. One third of the ball outside the park and two-thirds inside—the majority has it. Home run." That was, I think, one of the greatest decisions I've ever heard an umpire make. Thank you, Mr. or Mrs. Gopher!

Two of the funniest things I ever saw as a manager involved jack rabbits. At Twin Falls, we had all these young guys from San Francisco and Los

Angeles, all city kids. They were up there in Idaho in sagebrush country. The guys all lived in this boardinghouse. The landlady had these rooms for the guys. She would cook for them, and they would pay her a little bit. One day some local guy said they ought to go rabbit hunting. So these city kids got some shotguns and rifles and went out in the desert and shot these rabbits. But they were jack rabbits. They shot jack rabbits. They brought them back. The guys were going to take a nap, so they stacked the rabbits on the kitchen table with a note: "Could we have these for dinner tonight?" They took a picture of that. These guys didn't understand they didn't cook jack rabbits. At least, I've never heard of fried jack rabbit. The city guys never heard the end of it.

A lot of strange things can happen on road trips. In the Pioneer League in 1948, Joe Soares was our bus driver and trainer. He eventually went up to the Yankees and was a trainer for twenty-seven years. We were going across the desert from Salt Lake City to Twin Falls, Idaho, in the middle of the summer. I had a big outfielder who was a Mormon guy, a kid by the name of Ray Jacobs. He knew all about the area. As we traveled along, these big jack rabbits would get up on the road, where it was nice and warm. The desert would cool off at night. This particular night, I was sitting up front, and Joe Soares was driving the bus, and all of a sudden I saw a jack rabbit jump and fly up and fly off. This was right in front of the bus as we were driving along across the desert. And this was about 2:00 or 3:00 in the morning. I looked again, and there went another one, zoom, jumping, as if something hit him or something. This went on for quite a while. These jack rabbits were jumping off, and all of a sudden we realized what it was. One of my ballplayers was up on the roof of the bus, on the luggage rack, and he had a .22 rifle. He was shooting those jack rabbits with that gun. I thought the jack rabbits had gone crazy or something.

We had a dandy fight, when I was with Twin Falls, against the Salt Lake City club. Salt Lake City was a farm club of the San Francisco Seals. We had a big rivalry with them. One of my outfielders, Ray Jacobs, who had a bit of a mean streak in him, slid into their second baseman, who was a little guy. All heck broke loose. There was bad blood between us anyway. Boy, we had a dandy. I ran out, and I got hit. When I got up from there, I had dirt on the back of my cap, my shoulders, my butt, my heels, and so forth. The guy that got me was John Bilbrey, who had been a light heavyweight boxer in college. He got me good. He hit me from the side, broke my nose, blacked both of my eyes. I was bleeding as if I were going to die. One of my pitchers, Bob Webster, went after him. I looked up, and Bob was knocking him across the diamond. The next time we played, we had a sellout house, and there were police and sheriffs everywhere, standing around to prevent the fans from getting into it. Somebody took a photograph of me with my black eyes, with Joe Soares, the trainer, looking at them. Both of them were black. That picture became quite popular around town. It appeared in a souvenir booklet, for which players sold ads to get some money to add to their salaries. It took a whole page. And a bank in Twin Falls made a big blow-up of the photograph—with the words "We are proud to sponsor 'One-Punch' Charlie Metro"—and put it in the window. I had a devil of a time living down that fight.

I'd like to tell three quick stories about managers in the Pioneer League. Dick Gyselman played in the Coast League for Seattle. He was another one of those guys who played a long time in the Coast League. He became the manager of Great Falls in the Pioneer League, and he played third base in the league over the hill. We had a play against him one day for which I thought he was going to whip me. I was playing center field, and he was on second base, with a man on first base. I came running in for a fly ball. I kept hollering, "I've got it, I've got it." I could see nobody was going to catch it. So he tagged up at second base. The ball dropped in, and I fielded on the first hop. The second baseman, Gil McDougald, went back to second. I caught it on the first hop and flipped the ball to him for a double play. I thought Gyselman was going to whip me. Charlie Root managed Billings in the Pioneer League in 1948. Early in the season, we were exchanging lineup cards at home plate, when the umpire asked him if Babe Ruth had really pointed to center field before hitting a home run off him in the 1932 World Series. I thought he was going to hit the ump. I have to tone down what he said, but in effect he said if Ruth had done that he would have knocked him on his rump on that pitch. Bobby Mattick managed the Cincinnati Reds Ogden club in the Pioneer League in 1948. He had a left-handed pitcher by the name of Cliff Ross, who could throw like nothing I'd ever seen before. I was a little leery of this guy. He was wild inside, all over the place. We scored 13 runs against him in the first inning of one game. I think he walked all the guys, over thirteen in a row. Bobby let Cliff stay in. Years later, when Bobby was managing the Toronto Blue Jays, I had the occasion to remind him of that game. He didn't like that. He didn't have much of a sense of humor.

When I managed on the lower level in the minors, managers drove the bus, did the groundskeeping, served as the traveling secretary, and often became the father-confessor. They played if they were playing managers. They did everything. They made the hotel arrangements and distributed the meal money. They just did everything. If they applied for a job, they could say they were well-rounded. When we'd travel in the C league, some of the guys would be out of money on the way home. We'd have to stop at a diner or someplace to eat, and I'd ask, "Who all's going to be hungry?" Everybody was hungry. They had no money. I'd say, "Well, I've got so much money. . . . I'm going to tell you what you can order." "Well, you go ahead, order for us." Everybody loved hamburgers and stuff like that, or ham and eggs, whatever time it was, and all the meals. So I'd order once in a while. It was not unusual.

Fortunately I was never booed very much either as a player or as a manager. The one time that did happen was when I was with Twin Falls, Idaho, in the Pioneer League, playing Idaho Falls. I slid into second base, and the fielder had his leg stiff, and I slid right in and broke his leg. Years later, when I wound up back in Idaho managing again, the fans at Idaho Falls remembered that. They booed me when they made the announcement. I could hear them: "There's that guy who broke that guy's leg!" They gave me a pretty good going-over. Then I won them over. That's what you have to do. You have to win the fans over.

At one point in 1949, my Twin Falls team was in fifth place, 15 games out, but we made quite a stretch run, taking something like 40 or 42 games out of 48. Bob Clements, who was a scouting director with the Pirates, made a comment down in the Bay area, bragging about Billings leading us in the Pioneer League. We were in fifth place. Joe Devine heard about that comment and got furious. You never saw such a flood of players as we had transferred up to Twin Falls. I had to release three outfielders who were hitting over .340 to make room for the new guys! We caught Billings and won the pennant. We were playing Billings a doubleheader on the last day. We went into the last day with a 1-game lead, so that meant we had to win 1, and they had to win 2. We won the first game real easily. They fell apart, and we beat them very handily. In the second game, I told the players, "Go soft. Do anything you want." Well, that was really quite a show. We won that game also. That was one of the most fun games I've ever managed. And I did it on other occasions later, with different ball clubs, and it was really a lot of fun to watch that. I told them, "No signs. Do whatever you want."

Johnny Temple was the shortstop for the Cincinnati Reds farm at Ogden in the Pioneer League. He was an outstanding ballplayer. He lead the league in hitting that year. He eventually went up to the majors and played a long time. But while we were playing there, it rained like heck before the game, and we didn't take any practice. All I heard from my guys was, "Ahhhh, it's wet," and this and that. During the game, Temple got 4 base hits. We lost the game, and, oh, all the alibis about the mud and everything else started. So after the game was over, I just sat everybody down, and we had a good heart-to-heart talk. I told them, "If you'll watch those guys, they're standing on a dry spot now. You just watch the opposition. You watch that Temple. He got 4 base hits against you. You watch him. There was no mud out there where he was playing, but there was mud where we were playing." I said, "Are you going to lead the league in crying?" I got the message over. They didn't complain or give alibis anymore.

At Twin Falls, Idaho, slot machines were legal. Heck, they had slot machines even in the bank lobbies, restaurant lobbies, clothing lobbies, gas stations, restaurants, everywhere. The players hung out at a place called Bo's Burgers. Bo was one of the first guys to have those big hamburgers, and he gave a free hamburger to every ballplayer on the team every time we won. You could accumulate those free tickets and buy breakfast there. And they had slot machines. The Yankees had a rule that the players couldn't play the slot machines. If I saw them doing that, I was supposed to fine them. So I called a meeting and said, "No slot machine playing." Well, the guys sat on the stools at the bar and at the tables and watched people playing the machines. They watched one guy put in probably $100 and never hit. So three of them got together and put up $5, and on the last dollar they hit the jackpot, with bells and everything else. It paid off $1,200. The next day, word got around that some of the ballplayers were playing the slot machines. So I called a meeting and said, "All right, you guys, who played the slot machines? It's a $25 fine." As I walked out, I said, "I want that money in my locker." I had a little locker in the corner. Everybody was laughing and kidding. I went out and came back in, and there was a stack of twenty-five silver dollars in my locker. Nobody would tell me who it was. To this day, I don't know who did it. But they gave me the $25.

In 1949, the All-Star Game that July was at Great Falls. We had snow! I think I had three ballplayers on the All-Star team, and I was managing the one team. We went up there and it was *cold!* A cold front or something blew in and brought snow flurries. It was cold, but we played the game. That same year at Twin Falls, we won the pennant, and snow affected the playoffs. The 1949 season was over in early September, and we were finishing up our playoff series with Pocatello. Rain and snow interrupted the series, so we listened to two World Series games. That was the year that Joe DiMaggio had a bone spur on his heel and was out half the year and then came back to carry the Yankees. I can remember that vividly. Joe Clements, the radio announcer in Twin Falls, had me doing the play-by-play with him in the studio. We got the account in by ticker tape. But at one point we had a gap in the tape. Joe turned the microphone over to me. Now I had no experience with broadcasting. What was I supposed to do? So I made something up to explain the delay. I had dogs running all round the field! What a way to end the season!

FIVE

Points South

After the 1949 season, the Yankees decided to retrench on their farm system. They offered me a position with the Fond du Lac, Wisconsin, club, which was in a Class D league. They had other guys in mind for the jobs higher up in Binghamton, New York, and elsewhere. I didn't want to get demoted to a D league, so I refused to take the Fond du Lac job. Luckily Bill Walsingham, who was with the Cardinals farm system, found out about the retrenchment. He called me up and offered me the playing manager position at Montgomery, Alabama, in the Southeastern League. This was about two weeks before spring training. I accepted, because this meant a step up to a Class B league. I had befriended one of their ballplayers somewhere along the way and showed him my batting tee. He was fascinated with it, and the Cardinals loved it. They ordered twenty-five from me. The Cardinals batting coach, Harry "The Hat" Walker, who was a pretty fair hitter in his days in the majors, put a batting tee in every one of their farm system clubs. He was a great student of hitting. The only thing they criticized Harry for was that he hit everything to left field. He never pulled the ball. But that's no crime either. He had some pretty good batting averages. So I started out on a career with the Cardinals, and we headed south.

As usual, we had an adventure when we moved to Alabama. We left Twin Falls and headed to Mayfield. We were coming into the Cairo, Illinois, area, where the Mississippi River is, and the lowlands were flooded. We were pulling a little luggage trailer with our Plymouth coupe, with the kids and our cocker spaniel. We were going through this water in the low country. We looked down, and there was water seeping through the bottom of the car. We were the last car to get through. There was a police car in back of us. Nobody else could come through. How we got through that, I don't know, because the water was swirling all over the road and everything else. It was frightening, but we made it. Safe by a mile again!

It was a delightful year. I loved working with the Cardinals. We trained over at Albany, Georgia. The Cardinals had a four-diamond complex over there. They brought all the ballplayers there to evaluate them. Walter Shannon, the farm director of the Cardinals, would hold a meeting every evening. They had a blackboard with all the players and the clubs listed. They had a club at Lynchburg and one in the Western League, my club in Montgomery, and one in Houston in the Texas League, and then they had their Class D clubs. They had ten or twelve clubs listed there. We would talk over where the players should go. They'd ask me what I thought of a particular player. I'd say something like, "He can play Double-A. He's a pretty good ballplayer, Double-A," and they'd assign him to Double-A. They went on dividing up the players. Everybody was getting three or four ballplayers. But after a while, I noticed we didn't have anybody on my club. So finally I said, "Hey, when am I going to get a ballplayer?" They gave me a ballplayer to pacify me, but eventually I got a pretty good team together. I got all of what they called the troublemakers, the tough guys, to handle. They'd send them down to me. Oh, boy, I had a Foreign Legion down there. Nobody wanted them. I'd say, "Don't you want this guy?" They'd say, "No, give him to Charlie." So I got guys who wanted to go home and guys who were hurt and everything else. They gave me all these doggone ballplayers, and I surprised the Cardinals officials. I molded them into a pretty good ball club. We finished third. We were called the Montgomery Rebels that year, and the Montgomery Grays the next three years I was there. We bought a home there. We loved the South. My wife was a southern girl, from Kentucky, and the kids loved it.

When I had the pleasure of working with the Cardinals in 1950, I saw "Vinegar Bend" Mizell pitch at Albany. He was a local hero and what a likable young man! A real joy. He was from down in Mississippi, and the kids followed him around like he was the Pied Piper. He had the perfect name, "Vinegar Bend" Mizell. It was always a joy when your paths crossed and you became acquainted with a guy like that. I saw him at spring training and tried like heck to get him on my ball club, but I couldn't get him. I knew that when I saw him warming up. I also met Ken Penner when he was a scout and a minor league pitching instructor for the Cardinals. I remember him teaching the stiff-wrist change-up. I tried to teach it and never could master it.

Not too many of the players from that 1950 team stand out in my mind. We did have Bernie Gerl, who had survived a bus accident, in Minnesota I think. He wore very thick glasses. He was one of the most courageous players I've ever seen. We had a first baseman named Ed Mickelson, a great big guy, six foot four or so, a beautifully built ballplayer. But he had a quirk. He always thought he was going to get hurt. Here was this guy, 210, 215 pounds, just a magnificent athlete. Not only that, but he was the best hitter I'd seen in an awful long time. He was hitting .500 after 60 games. He was always saying he was going to get hurt. He didn't want to slide, because he was afraid he was going to break his leg. But he would hit home runs. I recommended him, and the Cardinals took him up at the end of the year. He had a good spring the next year, as I recall, but they didn't keep him. He had short stints with the Browns and the Cubs, but he never caught on in the big leagues. It was a great disappointment to me, because I thought he was a definite major league ballplayer. Years later Ed visited me when I was in St. Louis scouting the Cardinals.

Playing managers had to have a lot of talents, but once I got a guy called out from outside the ballpark. One game at Jackson, Mississippi, in the Southeastern League, I got into a hassle with an umpire and got ejected. The rules said you couldn't stay in the ballpark or get up in the stands in uniform. In some leagues you could, but down there you couldn't. Once you were out of the ball game, you couldn't run your ball club. I walked down the left-field line and back of the left-field stands, and I climbed up on the post. There was a foul pole on the foul line and an anchor pole, and I climbed up the fence and stood there giving the signs. I was outside the ballpark. I was flagging hand signals from there. One of their players hit the ball down the left-field line right at me. It could have knocked me off that post. I caught the ball, in foul territory barehanded, and I took it and threw it down real quick to the left fielder. He was pretty surprised, but he made like he caught it. The lights weren't very good in those minor league ballparks. The umpire called it a fair ball and ruled the batter out. Willis Hudlin, the Jackson manager, went wild. He was laughing and pointing at me out there on the post. He and the ump had quite a discussion. The umpire came out and was going to tell me to get off the pole. Finally I relented, because they were going to get the police.

But there were always other mysteries and uncontrollables. One day in the early 1950s, we were whomping Hudlin's Jackson team something like 15–2. I was playing right field. Near the end of the game, I looked into the dugout and saw the batboy and the rest of the guys packing up the bats and other equipment. I couldn't believe it. They were violating one of the sacred rules of baseball: never pack up the equipment until the game is over! I was out there yelling, "Unload the bags" and everything else, but nobody knew why I was going crazy. The black fans were in the bleachers down the right-field line out there, and they were giving me all kinds of heck. They had a lot of fun with me, and I was answering them back. "We're going to get you, Charlie," they said, "We're going to get you. We're going to beat you." One black guy had a rabbit's foot, and he kept teasing me with it. Can you guess what happened? You're right. In the bottom of the ninth, Jackson put together a rally, and we helped them out with some bonehead defensive mistakes. Their hits fell just beyond our fielders. Our second baseman thought there were two outs and put the ball in his pocket instead of relaying it to first for what would have been a game-ending double play. When the commotion settled, the final score was 16–15, Jackson. If you go down to that Jackson ballpark today, you'll probably find them still hitting! We never did get them out. Every time I saw Willis Hudlin after that, he would point his finger at me and laugh. And I'd say, "Willis, we're both old guys now. Look out." That day, however, I was so mad at everybody that I walked home in my uniform. I wouldn't even ride the bus. I walked all the way back to the hotel in Jackson.

You can always count on players to do some crazy things. That first year at Montgomery, I had a pitcher named Dick Loeser and a Latino catcher named Arnie Riesgo. We were playing in Vicksburg one day when they got into a fracas. I was playing in right field. I had a bad back, and I was having a hard time. On top of that, my pitcher was having a rough time. I made one trip to the mound and went back to right field. I told Loeser he was going to be the reliever, so he and Riesgo went to the bullpen to warm up. I was watching them. Loeser threw his first pitch without much control, and it hit Riesgo on the shins. Arnie picked up the ball, threw it back at Dick, and hit him on the shins. This went on for a few pitches. They kept throwing at each other's shins. Before I knew it, they were slugging each other. The umpires called time, and I had to come in to talk with the umps. One said he was going to throw them out of the game. I said, "You can't throw them out." He said, "The heck I can't." I said, "That's the way we warm up our pitchers." The ump threw them out anyway. They had to leave, but I looked up there and they were pushing each other around again. They had to get them in the bus finally. Dick went on to become an executive with Rawlings, the sporting goods company. I don't know what ever happened to Arnie.

In 1950, when I was managing Montgomery, I went back on the mound for part of a game. We had a series against Pensacola. I'd used quite a few pitchers in a doubleheader the previous day. Then we had a single game and another doubleheader scheduled the day after that. So my pitching staff was pretty much depleted. We were getting racked up pretty good in the single game. So I, the playing manager, went in to pitch. I gave up 9 runs in the ball game. We lost twenty-two to something. I really caught heck from the management, and the league president said I made a farce out of it. He was going to fine me until I explained it. When I told him that I had used up all these pitchers and had a doubleheader the next day, he let me off. As it turned out, we won the doubleheader the following day. But my pitching days weren't long.

I never had many serious injuries, but I did have a back problem when I was a playing manager in the B League in 1950. That was a terrible time for me. I couldn't bend over and everything else. It almost got to a point of consensus among three surgeons that I would have to have it operated on, but I refused. A neighbor who was a country doctor kind of guy asked me if I had a pair of cowboy boots. I said, "Yes," and he said, "Put them on." I did, and that straightened up my back. I haven't been bothered by it since.

One of the guys who impressed me in the Southeastern League was Jim Rivera. He played at Pensacola. If ever there was a ballplayer in perpetual motion, it was Rivera. He never stood still. What a wonderful ballplayer he was. Talk about hustle, he was the last word in hustle. He never sat still for one second in the ball game. If he wasn't on deck, he was walking up and down the dugout. You knew he was going to be a big league ballplayer. He just hustled his way right into the big leagues. He became a very good ballplayer for the White Sox. Jim had been in prison for some very small infraction at that time. Earl Mann, the Atlanta manager, went to bat for him and got Jim out and gave him a job as a ballplayer. I made a good report to the Cardinals on him.

Bert Niehoff was a manager in the minor leagues. I managed against him in 1950. He was a veteran manager and a veteran player. I don't know much about his playing days, but if you watched him, you learned a lot. He was one of those guys who I used to watch very carefully. If I saw somebody do something well, I would copy it and try to improve on it. I'm very fond of Bert. He always made it a note to warn me when we were at the plate exchanging lineups. He said, "If you go to sleep, young man, I'll beat you. Don't go to sleep. I want you at your best when I beat you." He didn't have much of a club; I had a better club than he did. But he always had a word of wisdom for you, and I loved the guy for that.

I knew Whitey Kurowski when we were minor league managers together. I had the Montgomery club in the Southeastern League, and he had Allentown in a Class B league in Pennsylvania. He had a very strange thing in his right arm. He didn't have a complete bone in his right arm.

They took x-rays and found this out. I asked him one time how he threw, and he said, "I just picked up the ball and threw it." The muscles just held everything together.

When I was at Montgomery, as usual I had to get a job in the off-season. We didn't get paid for a full year back then. The most popular line of work was being a car salesman. It was kind of seasonal and there was a lot of turnover, and not only that, but my boss, Joe Hedrick, the president of the ball club, owned a Plymouth and Dodge truck dealership. Joe hired me as a salesman, but one day he said to me, "Charlie, I've got an idea and I want you to consider it. And I'd like for you to do it." I said, "What's that, boss?" He said, "I want you to do a fifteen-minute sports show for me. I'll sponsor it. And we'll include that in your salary draw." I said, "Well, fine. Do you think I can do it?" He said, "Yes." So I did a fifteen-minute sports show. I covered the football season, the Alabama Crimson Tide and the Auburn Tigers, the great Southeast Conference teams. I kind of predicted who was going to win and so forth. I had a great time. I also followed a man named Frank McGee, who later became quite a nationally known figure in broadcasting the news on a national network. But I had a lot of fun with that. Every once in a while, I'd get twisted up and reverse the scores or something like that. That show led to a question-and-answer sports show where fans would write in questions to the moderator, and he'd ask us guys on the panel. I covered baseball, and we had a football and basketball man and another guy who had general sports knowledge. I did pretty well on baseball, and, by gosh, I was very seldom stumped. The narrator would give us points on the answer's quickness. I barely beat out Willie Finkelstein, the proprietor of Willie's Sports Palace. He was pretty good on basketball and football, but I nosed him out. It was very interesting and entertaining, and that almost led to a television show. In those years I also did some off-season football and basketball refereeing, both for the money and to keep in shape.

I made Vince Lombardi famous. I might as well take credit for it now. This goes back to my managerial days in Montgomery. I was asked to go out to take a look at a shortstop, a high school boy at Lanier High School. I knew his dad very well, and he asked me to look at him too. This student was playing baseball there and also was an outstanding quarterback. I went out there and watched him. This was in 1950, 1951, or thereabouts. I observed this boy. He had a very peculiar way of throwing. He kind of brought the ball up by his ear and made just real short, snappy throws. So when I got through watching him, I had a chance to talk to his father. I said, "Ben, I don't believe your son will ever make a living throwing a ball like that. I don't think he'll ever do it well." I suggested that his son go to college. He had a scholarship for football at the University of Alabama. After college, the Green Bay Packers drafted him. His name was Bart Starr. If I had signed that boy to a Class B baseball contract, you'd have never heard of Vince Lombardi. I met Lombardi once in Chicago, but I never got the opportunity to tell him that.

I was always on the lookout for ways to strengthen my wrists, make them quicker, and improve my hand–eye coordination, so I took some fencing instruction at Montgomery. There was an instructor at the girls' college there, and I took some lessons from him. He was very slight and wiry, but he was a little sadistic. I taped the foil to my wrist, but before I got it taped, he gave his own foil that twist, and BOOM! like you see in the movies, there went my foil. As I stooped down to pick it up, he cracked me across the back. He was making me angry. I got up and started at him, but he just whipped the bejesus out of me. Obviously I wasn't going to win a gold medal in fencing. Overall I didn't care, because all I wanted was quicker hands. It worked. But I want it on the record that I had no intention of stabbing any umpires!

Another delightful opportunity to play Santa Claus came again in Montgomery in the early 1950s. The school asked me if I'd be their Santa Claus for the kids. The kids were little crew-cutted guys. So I got all dressed up and got the beard and everything on, and my wife gave me a ride up to the school. She parked way out of the way, so nobody would see her bringing Santa Claus. I went in the school and entertained the little guys. I walked up to the front row where the kids were sitting and just patted the head of this one little guy, and I said, "Now all you children be good." When I got home and changed out of the Santa outfit, school was over and my little guy, who I had patted on the head, said, "Dad, Dad, Santa Claus patted me on the head and said he's going to come see me."

When the Montgomery franchise moved over into the Sally League in 1951, we were an independent club. The owners liked me so they kept me on as playing manager. This was a Class A league, so I took another step up right there. I had guys from Triple-A and guys from Double-A, and guys on their way out playing their last gasp. We opened spring training with eleven ballplayers, and we had fourteen for the season opener. That's all we had. Management was trying to get us players. Ben Goldsman, one of the finest people I'd ever met in my life, was the major owner. He controlled all the beer and liquor in the state of Alabama. He was a big distributor. He had a professional basketball team in Montgomery, and he'd bought them a beautiful bus. There were individual speakers for radios and, oh, it had everything in it. He's the guy who had all the connections. He knew everybody in the Southern League and the Texas League. We'd get a guy from Shreveport, and we'd get a guy from Atlanta, and we'd get a guy from here and from there. We went out and won the darned pennant. Boy, we just ran over everybody. The people in Montgomery presented me with a new Dodge car after the season.

Kirby Higbe was a character and a delight. I got him at Montgomery in an A league after he was on his way down from Atlanta. He didn't know what a dollar meant; he just squandered his money. He was living in the past, as if he still had a major league salary. I had to bail him out of quite a few situations. With our ball club, he was on his last legs. But what a joy he was! Not a negative word in his body. He thought he was the best, and he was good. He was a pretty good pitcher. He'd say, "Give me the ball." He was a knuckle ball pitcher. The catcher couldn't catch him. Jack Parks hated like heck when I brought Kirby in to relieve, but I kept Parks in. In one game Kirby walked a guy, and then there were three straight passed balls. Jack couldn't hang on to the knuckle balls. The guy scored a run without benefit of a hit, but we won.

I'd run my pitchers quite a bit. One day Kirby Higbe was complaining about the running. He said, "You run me right out of my shoes." Kirby was well up in years, and he wasn't taking good care of himself, but he was a heck of a pitcher. I said, "No, Kirby, you just go on out there and run." It was hot. You had to build up stamina because of the heat. In fact, we had one July that was 100 degrees every day for thirty days, or something like that. You wanted your pitchers in condition. I knew that because I'd been there the year before. So the next day Kirby came up to me while I was running the pitchers, and he said, "I told you you were going to run me out of my shoes." He showed me the soles of his shoes. They looked like tongues that were hanging out and flapping. I'd run him so much his bare feet were hitting the ground. So we didn't run as much anymore. I eased up on them, even though Kirby might have been playing a trick on me.

In 1951 I had a pitcher, Charlie Samaklis, who was a sinkerballer. One day I came in the clubhouse and he had an assortment of game balls, all rubbed up by the umpires and ready to go, laid out on a table in front of him. Oddly enough, he was swinging a hammer down on them. I went up and noticed that he was tapping phonograph needles into each one. Those needles were enough to help his pitches sink even more wickedly. The opposing pitchers, however, didn't know about the needles and they couldn't control their pitches, which would sail or shoot outside the zone. We put a stop to that pretty quickly, because after all it was *illegal*, but that says something about the inventiveness of our pitchers. Pitchers all wanted to get an advantage. Some would be gardeners and cover over the rubber with dirt. Then they would sneak ahead three feet or so. I'd look up amazed to see a pitcher I knew couldn't throw that hard who was mowing them down with fastballs. Sure enough, he had gardened that mound. It's been done many times in many places. But I still say they got to catch you, and all's fair in love and war when it comes to "bending" the rules.

Spencer Davis was a left-handed pitcher. "Onion" was his nickname. I don't know why they called him that. He became a principal at a high school down there in Georgia or Alabama. Carl Lindquist was another one of our pitchers. If they didn't catch him, he used to cover up the rubber on the mound with dirt and pitch from three feet in front of it. We also had Al LaMacchia. We had been young guys in the Browns organization. He was with San Antonio when I went over to Beaumont. Our paths crossed again in Montgomery. Al was married then. My wife would invite the girls over, when we were on the road. Al was a little heavy. I worked the living daylights out of him. I was two years younger than he was, but I was his manager. He thought that because we'd been Brownies together, I should go easy on him. I ran him a little harder. And it turned out he had a good year. I got his weight down to where he was another one of those guys who'd say, "Look at this waistline. I've got to go get a pair of pants that fit." His wife appreciated me working him so much. She says, "You got him down to his schoolboy figure he had when we were first married." So she thought I was great, but he didn't. We're great friends. He became an executive official with the Toronto football club and a good scout.

Jack Parks was one of our catchers, and "Puddin'head" Jones's brother, J. W., was our other one. Grady Wilson played third. Angel Fleitas was at short. He became a barber in Miami, and I bumped into him one time there later. Bill Johnson was our second baseman. I had Banks McDowell in center field and Lennie Morrison in left. They were veteran players, and, boy, I had a tough time with those guys because they were almost all older than I was. And big Dick Greco was my right fielder. We ran away from most of the league that year.

One of my claims to fame is that I played in a game in which we made double plays in seven consecutive innings. While managing Montgomery in the Sally League, I was playing third base in place of our regular third baseman, Grady Wilson, who was injured. I started a couple of double plays, but we made seven straight double plays in this nine-inning game. Second to short, short to second, third to second, we made them every which way. Later I went in at second base, and I was involved in one at second as the pivot man. And we just missed another one in the eighth inning. I was also involved in that. The runner gave me a pretty good nudge at second base, and I was just a shade late with the throw to first. I've got to believe that this is some sort of a record for consecutive double plays in a baseball game.

Signals can cause the darnedest turnabouts. As you probably know, minor league managers often double as third base coaches, so they dispense the signals to hitters and base runners. Signals may look confusing—well, they're supposed to confuse the opposition to begin with—but there is a method to the madness. Usually there's an indicator sign that changes from game to game or sometimes even in different innings. Say, if the steal sign is a tug on the hat or skin to skin, what alerts the runner is the indicator, such as pointing at the belt buckle. Otherwise the twitches and jerks and wipes across the letters don't mean anything. We managers and coaches would get quite adept and flashy with our body language. It spices up the game. But things can go wrong—or more right than you could ever expect.

My Montgomery team was playing in Savannah one steamy evening in 1951, when the mosquitoes were pretty thick and angry. They were like dive bombers, and there were so many of them that occasionally the groundskeepers had to smoke the field. We were losing, down by 5 runs, and I was standing in the coach's box wondering how I'd gotten us into this mess. It was the top of the ninth, and we were down to our last out. Dick Greco, our big right fielder and quite a home run hitter, was the batter. He drew a walk, but that didn't seem promising, because Dick wasn't much of a runner. Well, at that time my steal sign was skin on skin. As I was coaching over there at third, a mosquito nailed me and instinctively I slapped at it. Dick Greco's eyes must have gone full wide, because the next thing I knew, he took off for second base on the next pitch. Even more surprisingly, he made it! Now I was getting quite irritated. Even the greenest rookie knew that you didn't steal a base with your club down by 5 runs in the top of the ninth. While I was fuming, another mosquito attacked me and again I swatted my arm. Again the next thing I realized was that big Dick Greco was rumbling into third base with another steal. I muttered to him, "Wait till I get you in the clubhouse after the game," as he lay there after his slide with a slaphappy grin on his face. I turned back to watch the pitcher work to our batter, but somehow I slapped my arm again at another mosquito. Greco, probably as bewildered as the opposing team at this point, nevertheless took off for home and slid in safely! As if that wasn't astonishing enough, our next few batters connected and put up 4 more runs on the board to tie it up. Then in the tenth, we pushed across another one and won the game. The newspaper the next day proclaimed me an absolute genius for such daring base coaching. I didn't have the heart to tell them that it was just the dang mosquitoes.

Sometimes as a minor league manager you have to make some unexpected moves. We were playing in Savannah, and the third baseman and first baseman got hurt, and the center fielder's wife was having a baby, so he left the club, and the second baseman split his finger. So I wound up with Kirby Higbe, a pitcher, in center field. I wasn't playing at that time; I had that bad back. I put a pitcher at third base, a pitcher at first base, two pitchers in the outfield, and a catcher at shortstop. We played with that arrangement and won three straight games. Kirby would run Dick Greco, my right fielder, off the ball. Onion Davis, one of my left-handed pitchers, played first base. Then when our pitcher got in trouble, I brought Onion in to pitch and put the other pitcher on first base. They tell me that Paul Richards used those moves in the big leagues. Well, heck, I used them down there in Montgomery in 1951. This was the darnedest thing you'd ever seen. We won all three ball games. Higbe was sensational. He was all over that outfield. He wanted to hit a home run, but I can't remember whether he did or not. I know he got a couple of big hits. I got into the spirit of things. I said, "So you don't have to have me manage this club? You can handle it, huh?" They said, "We're not going to have any signs." I said, "Yes, you are." But they wouldn't obey my signs. They'd get up there and swing and hit. You never saw the likes of it. I didn't fine them, not with them winning three ball games, of course. The next day the guy whose wife had a baby came back. We restructured the club and so forth, and I did have to play a couple of guys longer, a couple of pitchers, but that stretch of games was a delight.

One time with Montgomery I shuffled my lineup by picking numbers out of a hat. Just once, and I wound up with my big hitter, my home run hitter, Dick Greco, hitting ninth in the pitcher's spot. I had to go through with it, because that's the way it came out. Oh, he was furious. I thought he was going to pinch my head off. But I had to stick with it. I think I had the pitcher hitting second, but Dick was mad at me. He took it out on the ball. He drove in 7 runs. He hit a home run with the bases loaded and drove in 3 runs with a double or a triple. He was having a rough time, taking the third strike with men on and everything else, and it was my job to shake him out of that because we didn't have extra players. After he hit the home run, he wasn't mad at me anymore.

The groundskeeper we had at Montgomery was Sarge Carakar. He worked for the city, and he was a groundskeeper. He was a great big, blustery guy. He had a group of black workers. He'd been a major or a colonel in the army, had twenty years in, and then he retired. But then he went back in and became a staff sergeant. Boy, he just lived and died with my ball club. He loved baseball, and he'd fix the field any way you liked. He'd cut the mound down for the pitchers, if they wanted it down. The mound was supposed to be fifteen inches high, standard height everywhere, and he'd shave it down to twelve for the sinkerball pitchers. Once, when we played the Cardinals farm club from Columbus, Georgia, he gave us a boost by repositioning first base. The Columbus guys were big and fast. The Cardinals had all fast guys. Sarge came out there one day and said to me, "I'll fix those guys." He had a grudge against Columbus. They beat us pretty good once in a while. I said, "What are you going to do?" He said, "Well, I won't tell you." Midway through the game, it dawned on me that our infielders were throwing out Columbus's speedsters. From my coaching spot at third base, I peered over at first base and sensed that something was a little bit different. I got to wondering, "What in the heck is coming off here?" Sure enough, Sarge had put first base at *ninety-three* feet, so that you could throw those fast guys out by half a step. We were getting those guys on double plays, and when they'd hit a slow roller, we'd get them. We won the game. There are a lot of ways that groundskeepers help you win ball games.

Umpires don't reverse decisions very often, but I had a reversal when we were playing a game at Columbia, South Carolina, in 1952. Ernie White was managing the Columbia club. I protested a game in favor of the other club. To reconstruct the play, they had a man on first base and the hitter, a left-handed hitter, hit a ground ball, kind of into right-center. The base runner came around third. Our right fielder picked up the ball and threw it between second base and the mound, and it bounced into the dugout. The guy who had hit the ball was rounding second. He should have been awarded home, two bases on an outfield wild throw. But the umpire just bulled his neck and said, "No." So Ernie White protested the game. I had a pitcher named Roger Higgins, who was in umpire school. He walked up to me and said, "Charlie, Ernie's right." I said "Yes, I know. It's two bases on a wild throw from the outfield." Ernie protested and wanted the run, but the umpire wouldn't give it to him. Dick Butler, who was the league president and lived and had his headquarters in Columbia, was sitting up on top of the roof with the writers. I thought he was going to fall off the roof when he saw me coming. I walked up and protested. Dick said, "What are you protesting?" I said, "I want you to give him that run." He said, "What?" I said, "You're going to give him the run. The rule says he's got to." He said, "There's no way I'm going to give him a run. I don't care." I protested, and I won the protest. We won the game, so it didn't make any difference. That run didn't do much. But it could have turned out to be the winning run. I won the protest, and Dick Butler bought me lunches for a year and a half after that. We were going to play the game over, which is what you had to do regarding a protested game. But it didn't amount to anything—it wouldn't have affected us or them. Columbia won the pennant. They had a good ball club. So we just let it slide. There was no need to replay it.

I thought managers who were pitchers or former pitchers were the easier ones to manage against until I ran against Ernie White down at Columbia. Boy, he was tough, and he was a pitcher. He was a real tough manager. He did everything right. He was on clubs that hit like heck and clubs like the Cardinals that had great pitchers. We had some great battles. I loved managing against Ernie White, because he was sharp and he knew how to handle pitchers. He had some pretty good pitchers down there.

Man, could it get hot in the South! I came close to getting dehydrated at Columbus, Georgia, one time. Like a fool, I put a rubber jacket on. Down there in the South, the humidity was something. I liked the hot weather. I was just one of those guys who liked to sweat. It was a great workout really. But I put a rubber jacket on, and I darned near passed out. I couldn't get any air. But I got to the point where I wouldn't let anybody say anything about the heat when we were playing in the South. It was hot in Savannah; it was hot in Macon, Georgia; it was hot in the Carolinas and Augusta, Georgia, and Columbus, Georgia; it was hot everywhere. But I wanted my guys to ignore the heat and concentrate on winning. I'd say, "The next guy that says it's hot, it's too hot, it's going to cost him twenty-five dollars." One time it was really boiling hot in Savannah. They'd had a summer shower, and it was steaming. The guys were sitting there, and all of a sudden, without thinking, one of them said, "God durn, it's hot here." I snapped, "What did you say?" He said, "But that's the way I like it."

We experienced quite a weather event at Macon, Georgia. I had the Montgomery club, and we came to the Macon ballpark, a concrete and steel ballpark, not very big. The players were taking batting practice, and all of a sudden everything got quiet and here came a heck of a hailstorm. The hailstones were as big as baseballs. The guys all came running in. We were in the grandstand. Somebody shouted, "Tornado!" I said, "Well, let's get down." We went downstairs, and the tornado ripped through there, ripped through a nearby military base, and sheared off the ends of the barracks where the married sergeants lived with their families. It looked just like a dollhouse. It ripped the whole side of the barracks right off. It was one of the doggonest things I had ever seen.

In 1951 and 1952, we won the Shaughnessy Playoffs. Frank Shaughnessy was the president of the International League at that time, and they named the playoffs for him. The first four teams would play. The first- and fourth-place, and the second- and third-place, teams would play, and the winners of those games would play for the championship. In the 1952 playoffs, Columbus had us beat by two games. It was 3 out of 5, and they were up 2 games. Then we played them back in Montgomery. They got cocky, talking about checking out of their hotel after the first game in Montgomery. We beat them the next 2 games, and we told them they could check out of the hotel this time. In the last game, Dick Greco hit the winning home run, and we beat them 3 out of 5. Greco took his uniform shirt off, and holding it like an apron in front of him, went through the stands, collecting money from the fans. They were throwing dollars, coins, and everything at him.

I saw an interesting fan promotion stunt at Montgomery. They had a whole wheelbarrow full of coins—nickels, dimes, quarters, halves—and they'd take the coins out and scatter them all over the infield on the grass, mostly right around the mound. I don't know how much money was in those wheelbarrows. At the word "Go!" the winning fan would run out and pick up as many coins as he or she could in a certain time. I can't recall how much time the person got. I saw it several times. One time this girl was putting coins down her blouse.

I became friends with Hank Williams down in Montgomery before he died. They used to have something called the Hadacol Caravan in the South. Hadacol was a patent medicine, one of those cure-all things. It had 15 or 20 percent alcohol in it. Hank would perform with the caravan. When we traveled around in the Sally League from Macon to Columbus, and from Augusta to the Carolinas, to Columbia and Charleston, South Carolina, and to Jacksonville, we would either follow or precede the Hadacol Caravan. They'd postpone the game we'd play, so the groups could perform. So I got to know Hank Williams real well. A couple of years after he passed away, they built a statue for him in Montgomery. It was made out of concrete, about six feet high, and featured him and his guitar and his bird dog.

While I was managing Montgomery, we were going to play Jacksonville, Florida, right after the All-Star Game, which was also being held in Jacksonville. We had three players on the All-Star team, and I was the All-Star manager. So I gave all the players permission to bring their wives or their girlfriends down to Jacksonville. They could stay the three days of the All-Star break and three days of the regular season. That made everybody happy.

Ben Geraghty managed down there at Jacksonville in 1951. Ben was one of the guys who survived the Spokane bus crash that killed so many young ballplayers. Ben was very serious, so I'd agitate him when we played him at Jacksonville. He was a chain smoker, and he'd get down in the dugout trying to sneak a smoke. You weren't allowed to smoke there. When I'd coach third base, I'd see him smoking and I'd tell the umpire. He'd go over and warn Ben. He would get mad as heck at me. We had a friendly feud. Then one day he got thrown out of the ball game in Jacksonville. He was standing down the runway. I made the umpire chase him out of there. A few years later, when we both managing in the American Association, Ben at Louisville and me at Denver, Ben said, "If you say one word . . ." I said, "You still smoking?" There was no place to smoke in Mile High Stadium, so Ben would get a towel and hold it up in front of his face, so you couldn't see the smoke. But he had great rapport with his guys. He was a fine manager.

Both my old major league managers, Steve O'Neill and Mr. Mack, visited me while I was managing games at Montgomery. Steve came through Montgomery, and we put our son in uniform and my wife was holding him sitting in the stands. I said, "Steve, come over here. I want to show you something." So my wife handed me our boy, and I said, "Look at him. Guess what his name is?" He said, "What?" I said, "Steve. After you." Mr. Mack came down for an exhibition game with the Athletics. Bobby Shantz was pitching, and I doubled off him with the bases loaded. I was a big hero in Montgomery. Mr. Mack stayed around after the game and said, "Son, why didn't you hit like that for me?" I said, "I'm older and wiser, Mr. Mack."

I witnessed the breaking of the color line in the South in the early 1950s. The Sally League had some good black ballplayers. Jacksonville had Hank Aaron, who, of course, became one of the best players ever, and Felix Mantilla, who turned out to be a pretty good ballplayer too. Earl Wilson was a fine-looking pitcher with the Red Sox farm club when he pitched at Montgomery in the 1950s. He was one of the first black ballplayers to play in the city of Montgomery. Gosh, he was a good-looking athlete. He could throw hard, and he had a lot of endurance, a lot of stamina. He was a good pitcher for years in the majors. Later Columbia, South Carolina, had Frank Robinson. Frank played there two years. Here were the black ballplayers breaking into minor league baseball in the South. Montgomery was the "Cradle of the Confederacy." This was real tough for them. Those guys took a hell of a beating from the fans. They wouldn't let them eat or stay in the white hotels. They'd have to stay out in a boardinghouse for blacks, I guess, all that kind of stuff. Then the black fans were confined to their own bleachers down the left-field line or the right-field line, wherever it was. They weren't allowed to mingle in the crowds, and it was terrible. I had seen the race riots in Detroit in 1943. I had played with Bobby Estalella, who was a black Cuban, at Philadelphia. And I had seen what happened to Eddie Moore at Billings. As players and managers, I think we were more accepting of black players sooner than was the average fan. We marveled at the playing abilities of many of the black players and respected them. We knew just how hard it was to hit or throw or pitch or run or field as well as many of the black ballplayers did. I can't say enough on their behalf, how they overcame the pressures and everything else down there and the treatment they received.

I could relate to some of that racial stuff because I was of Ukrainian descent, the oldest son of immigrant parents. All this to me was a crime because I was brought up to believe that it was your ability that counted, not what race or ethnicity you were. As far as I was concerned, the great equalizer was that round baseball. That made everybody equal. As a first-generation American Ukrainian, I went through a lot of that stuff. People looked down on us. I had many a fight as a kid growing up because I was called a "hunky." I fought and I fought. I'd win some and I'd lose some. I got tired of fighting. So I knew what was going on. My ballplayers were my ballplayers, and I protected them. But I didn't have any black ballplayers on a club I managed until I got to Vancouver.

In 1951, my first year in the Sally League, the team's board of directors called me in one day. There were twelve directors: bankers, automobile dealers, equipment dealers, pillars of the community, fine, upstanding people. I thought, Oh, boy, I'll probably get a raise. That's what I was thinking: I'm going to get a raise. The board said, "We want you to do something for us tomorrow, Charlie." I said, "What is it?" They said, "We want you work out a ballplayer for us. We want you to give him a good workout, a fair workout, and tell us exactly what you think." I said, "OK." We set it up for noon. That was fine, because we played at night. So come noon here came all these directors. And three black men showed up too. One was the president of Tuskegee Institute, another was the president of Alabama State, and the other guy was a minister. The young guy they wanted me to work out was also black. I can't recall if he was in or out of college. He was a fine football athlete, and I think he had played some baseball. So I gave him a workout. I had a couple of kids who hung around there chase balls for us. I said, "Gentlemen, this is what we're going to do.

I'm going to let him swing a bat and run to first base and we'll time him. Then I'll time him around the bases." He turned out to have average or even slow speed, five seconds down the base path to first, fifteen or sixteen seconds around the bases. That was pretty slow. He was all musclebound from football. Next we tried him out at shortstop. I hit him some ground balls to test his arm, and, gee whiz, he was bouncing the ball over to first base. After about ten minutes, I said, "Well, let's go to the outfield." I put him in right field, which was a little slanted up in the ballpark. I hit fly balls and ground balls to him, and I had him throw home. He was bouncing the ball on four or five hops, and then the throws would roll. Then we did some batting practice. He couldn't even hit the ball out of the infield. After we finished, the three black men asked me what I thought. I said, "Gentlemen, this is not the young man you want, this is not the athlete you want to represent your race here in Montgomery or in the South. You've got to get a better ballplayer. He's got to be good. You can't subject a young man like this to what he's going to get. You have to get an outstanding ballplayer, the best athlete you can find." They thanked me for the fair tryout and my evaluation. The minister turned out to be Dr. Martin Luther King Jr. He wrote me a letter again thanking me for the tryout and telling me they took my advice on the young man. I hope I still have that letter somewhere. It may have burned up in a house fire we had at Montgomery in 1959, but I'm still hoping one day to find a copy of that letter.

In the games, I didn't want my pitchers knocking any of the black players down. These were outstanding ballplayers. They did well. Their records speak for themselves. I didn't want any kind of an incident there. Once in a while, a guy would do it on purpose, against my orders, and knock a guy down. They'd brush Hank Aaron back, not knock him down but brush him back. Then they'd throw a strike, and Hank would hit that ball nine miles. If I ever see Hank Aaron again, I'm going to ask him if he remembers the time I said, "Let your bat do your talking," as I walked by him. I don't know if he'll ever remember that, but he sure let his bat do his talking. You could tell Hank Aaron was going to be great. He was a second baseman for Jacksonville. I made a report to John McHale, in our Detroit organization, that I'd just seen the best ballplayer I'd ever seen. I remarked that he couldn't play second base, that they'd better put him in the outfield or at third base, even though he didn't have the so-called build of a third baseman, but not at second. He was a little bit shy of the runners coming in. Some guys get that way. But he could hit that ball. He had the quickest wrists you'd ever seen. He had a kind of a nonchalant attitude when he walked up to the plate. They didn't have helmets at that time. He'd walk up and stand in the box with just kind of a lazy, sleepy attitude, until he swung the bat. Look out! We were playing Jacksonville in Montgomery, and in back of the left-field fence was a street and then a graveyard next to a church. Aaron came up and hit the ball to left field. He got all of it, as we used to say, every bit of it. Over in the graveyard was the statue of Hank Williams. Aaron hit it clear over the top of that. It's been a long time since I've seen a ball crushed like that. He led the league in hitting. Hank was liked. He wasn't disliked. You disliked him because he was the enemy, not because he was a black ballplayer. He was disliked because he was beating the heck out of you. When I saw a ballplayer was good, I had great respect for him.

When I was at Augusta in 1955, Frank Robinson was with the Columbia, South Carolina, ball club. He looked like one of the greatest hitters I'd ever seen. I made some wonderful reports on him. They didn't know yet what position he was going to play. He had something wrong with his shoulder where the blood would bleed through his skin. He couldn't throw very well even when he went up to the big leagues. He faked it for a long time. He was very quick releasing the ball. I don't know if he ever threw a guy out. He finally wound up at first base. One game against Columbia, I told our pitcher, Bob Cruze, a left-hander, "Now don't wake this guy up. You understand?" I also said to my catcher, Gabby Wytucki, "After I leave here, you go back to your position and come back out and remind him. OK?" He said, "Yeah." The fence in left center was 395 feet away, the scoreboard was way up high on a telephone pole, and there were trees, a schoolyard, and a school back of left field. Cruze didn't obey my orders. He knocked him down three times. The second pitch, I went back out to the mound and chewed Cruze out again. When Frank had three balls and no strikes, Cruze threw a fastball down the middle. Robinson hit that ball over top of the scoreboard, over top of the trees, on top of the two-story schoolhouse. I guess it was the longest-hit ball I'd ever seen. I think he took out all of his frustrations of being in the South on that one ball. I gave Cruze quite a talking-to, and he just kind of laughed it off. Frank thought that when I went out there to Cruze after the second time, I told Cruze to knock him down. Frank reminded me of that quite a few years later, when I was managing the Royals. He said, "Did you tell that guy to throw at me?" I said, "Heck, no!" I think he still thinks I had him knocked down, but I didn't.

Chris Sidaris played second base for me in the Sally League in 1952. I'll never forget him. He couldn't throw the ball to first base. He couldn't throw the ball to second base, to the shortstop on the double play, but he could field like heck, and he was a good hitter. In fact, when we released him, he was hitting .367. But he couldn't play anywhere. You didn't have the designated hitter back then. He couldn't play the outfield. He did the same thing when I worked him out in the outfield. He couldn't throw the ball. He'd take the ball and throw it, and it'd wind up over there twenty or thirty feet away or over somebody's head. I worked with him, and he improved a little bit, but not enough.

In addition to Tony Venzon and Augie Donatelli, I knew another umpire from my hometown area, my younger brother John. He had played a little baseball, gone in the service, come out, and played at Harrisburg in the Class B league. He'd hurt his back in the service, and it held him back, so he went into umpiring. He was training to be an umpire, so one spring training I got him some work doing games in Montgomery. I asked him one day, "John, how do you like umpiring?" He said, "I love it, with the exception of managers." I said, "What's the matter with managers?" He said, "We have to start out perfect, and then we have to improve. I have two hundred decisions to make back of the plate on balls and strikes. All you have to do is make one little decision and go out and either take your pitcher out or leave him in." But just because he was my brother, I couldn't go easy on him. I instructed my players to give him heck, which they proceeded to do. They gave him a pretty good going-over and jumped on him about every call. His neck and ears were red all game. He'd come over and warn them two or three times. Finally, the third time, he said, "One more word out of you to those guys"—he pointed his finger at me—"and you're out of this game. I don't care if you are my brother, you're out." So I didn't say any more to him.

The next morning I was in the kitchen eating breakfast when he walked in. He was staying with us. I greeted him brightly, but he was real silent. "Would you like some breakfast?" I asked. He grabbed a notepad and scribbled, "Yes." "Eggs?" "Yes," he jotted. "How do you want them fixed?" I asked. "Scrambled," he wrote. "Toast?" "Yeah. Not too brown." Helen came in and she said, "What are you two doing?" I said, "Well, he's mad at me, I guess. I said he was a lousy umpire yesterday and the guys got on him and he thinks I told them to do it." She said, "Well, you probably did." John wrote down, "Where's the paper?" So I had to go out and get the morning paper for him. He sat there reading the sports pages. He was so mad at me that no amount of feigned innocence could get him to speak to me the rest of the day. We made up pretty good later. He never got mad at me again. I wouldn't have made him breakfast. He had a sense of humor, but he was serious about his work. He umpired three or four years in the minors. His back was bothering him, but he was a good umpire, and I hired him as a scout, and he became a very good scout for the Royals. Then he went into the Scouting Bureau and had a very nice career in baseball.

In 1953 the Detroit Tigers entered into a working agreement with Montgomery. That year was a complete disaster. We finished last. I had never managed lower than a third-place club. I never had anything but pennant-winning clubs and playoff teams and champions. But Detroit sent me a ball club of a lot of young guys. I think I had eight of nine guys who were "bonus baby" ballplayers. They came down with their big cars from Detroit and everything else. We just had a country-club type of attitude, and that's the way we played. We were lousy. I wasn't used to ballplayers not winning. I was trying to get these guys to win, but they were just having a good time, with their money and everything else. I don't think any of them went higher than Triple-A, if that far. They were good ballplayers, but they were spoiled rotten. We finished a very good last. Even though we didn't have the most talented players, we still played tough. For five or six innings, boy, we would give them heck, and then talent would take over. It just crushed us. They'd bring a pitcher in and stop us. If I brought in a pitcher, they'd clobber us. We were a very good last, a glorious last, as I used to say. I had never heard that phrase yet, but we qualified. Strange as it might seem to a lot of my friends and people, I was never booed very much as a manager, not even when I finished last. I'd get a ragging from the visiting ball club while I was coaching third base. They'd call me, "Hey, genius," "Boy Wonder," and everything else. But I was never booed.

One incident stands out in my mind concerning these 1953 players. I caught a lot of flak for it. I lived in Montgomery, and I was well-respected. I had had a good ball club there for three years. There was a nightclub in town my players went to occasionally. I had a policeman friend on the force, and I knew the chief of police, Captain Powers. I said, "Don't let my boys get in trouble, OK?" They assigned this policeman to the night beat and told him that if he saw my players misbehaving to let me know. One morning at 3:00, he called me and said, "Charlie, your boys have been whooping it up." I said, "Where?" He said downtown at this club. He said, "They're raising hell. You better get down here." So I dressed and went downtown. I walked into the place, and they were upstairs, whooping it up, having a great time. We were stuck in last place, so I was furious. I really didn't know how to handle it. So I said, "All you guys are fined." There were eight of them. I stood out on the street—the officer was with me—and I recorded the time the guys left. At 4:30 the last single guy came out, and another guy, who was with his wife, came out at 5:00. So the next day I had a meeting, and I fined them all a hundred dollars apiece. Now this was a Class A league. A hundred-dollar fine was unheard of. All hell broke loose. It hit the newspaper, and even *The Sporting News*, that I fined eight guys one hundred dollars apiece in an A league. Oh gosh, you should have seen the editorials that I got. Detroit sent a scout down to tell me that I was going to have to relent, or it would cost me my job. I told him, "You get back up there and don't come down here. They broke the rules. They knew the rules." My rule was that if a guy wanted to stay out, he should let me know. I didn't want people waking me up at home or on the road. After he went back to Detroit, the Tigers sent the farm system director, and, whew, he really gave me a going-over. Finally Muddy Ruel, the assistant general manager at Detroit, came down. He was the only guy who backed me. In fact, he said, "Kid, don't change. Don't let the ballplayers rule you. You've got to manage the ball club." I've always had a great deal of respect for him.

The eight players didn't like it one bit. We were getting ready for a road trip, and all eight of them didn't want to go. Our roster was seventeen, maybe eighteen, players. I counted all the players on the bus. I asked them, "You want to play?" They said, "Yup." We had nine guys. I told them that I'd come off the retired list if necessary and put myself in. So finally I said, "Ten o'clock. We're leaving. Let's go." I closed the bus door, and we started out. Then one of the eight guys came running after us and stopped the bus. He said, "Can you wait a minute, Skip?" I said, "Yeah, what are you doing?" He said, "We're having a meeting." I said, "OK, I'll give you five minutes." He went back, and pretty soon here they came, all eight of them. But we didn't have a good ball game. It was a terrible club.

John Baumgartner played third base for me at Montgomery in 1953. He was a fine physical specimen. But he was like some ballplayers who just had a quirk, and I never knew how to overcome it. They just couldn't meet the big league challenge, but he was a big league prospect. He had power, good speed, a good arm, everything, but every time he'd get a chance, he'd flub up. I'd give him a chance at spring training or whenever I could, but he wouldn't grasp it. He was one of those terrible disappointments to me. I tried to drive him. I used every tactic I could. I'd pat him on the back. I'd insult him. I'd needle him. I'd praise him, overpraise him. I did everything. I just couldn't reach the guy. Sometimes you just can't. He dropped out of the picture, and I don't know how far he went after that year.

I must have held the record for getting tossed out of games for four years running in the Sally League in the early 1950s. One time, an ump tossed me as I was handing in the lineup card at the plate. During the previous night's game, I had questioned his eyesight, judgment, ancestry, and assorted other subjects real thoroughly, and he had ejected me. The next day I handed him the card quietly, but he thumbed me out. "What did I do? What did I say?" I pleaded. "Nothing," he replied, "but I know what you are thinking." Bill Terry, the Hall of Famer first baseman and former manager of the New York Giants, was the league president. He hauled me into his office in Jacksonville and gave me a good dressing-down. He told me that I was out of line, that I was a good manager, and that I was of more help to my club when I stayed in the game. He praised me for being a family man and a good role model in the community, but then he turned right around and chewed me out but good. "You don't straighten out, you SOB. You think you're going to run this club your way? You're not going to swear at my umpires," he raved at me. After I recovered, I said, "Bill, I understand you swore at some umpires too." By coincidence, I had come across a magazine article that showed Terry, himself jaw to jaw with an umpire, on his way to getting ejected. I showed it to him that day. I thought he was going to throw me out of his office, but he did have a good laugh.

One of the joys of coming back into the Tigers organization was Tiger Town in Lakeland, Florida. Tiger Town was the spring training complex for the Tigers. It had been a training base for the Royal Canadian Air Force. It had four fields, right next to one of the runways. It was very nice. We stayed in the barracks. We enforced a curfew at Tiger Town, especially in a camp where the players were all in the barracks. We all slept in the barracks and ate in the mess hall and all that. The players would have a curfew, usually at 11:30. All lights went out at 11:30, because you had to get up early.

We had some great instructors at Tiger Town. One of the best was George Moriarty. He had been a player, a manager, and an umpire. They tell me he was an excellent umpire. He played in Ty Cobb's time, and the story goes that George Moriarty was the only guy that Cobb feared. I guess the stories get bigger and longer, but supposedly Moriarty threatened to break Cobb's back or his neck if they ever got into a fight. He was a bull, a gorilla-type man with long arms. He knew a lot about base stealing. He taught me how to take leads off first base. Rather than walking off at an angle from the base, as you see the modern players do, a runner should, George said, "get in a straight line." He said, "A half a step a foot is the difference between being safe and out at second base. Why give them that extra half a step or two feet?" He taught the ten-foot leadoff, although a faster, quicker guy could take an extra step, an extra three feet. He taught about diving back into first base, but he didn't recommend diving into second base. He made you take a direct line between first and second, second and third. The best thing, I believe, that I ever learned from him was helpful when I was coaching third base. He said that the runner at third base should put his right foot almost on the chalk line and take as much lead as you think is proper. His left foot would be back, kind of angled like that, so that the catcher couldn't see how far the runner was off the base. When the catcher's squatting back there, he can't see the bag. If you had a right-handed hitter at the plate and the runner was doing that at third base, you could steal an extra three, four, or even five feet. Pitchers can see you, but they don't have many pick-offs at third base. George said, "You can get a real good jump." I taught that for many years. Down at Tiger Town, I used to get him aside, and I found out that things I thought were new, the older guys had done fifteen or twenty years before. I'd look at this man and say to myself, "How could this big, strong guy who looks like a lumberjack steal bases?" But he did. I learned a lot from George Moriarty.

Marv Owen was another instructor at Tiger Town. He had been a fine third baseman with the Tigers and had been involved with Joe Medwick in that sliding incident in the 1935 World Series. I had played against him in the Pacific Coast League, when he was with Portland. Down at Lakeland, he came up with what he called a "trap wall." It was a concrete block wall, probably fifteen to twenty feet high, similar to a handball court wall. On one side of it, you had all dirt for the infielders to work on, and the other side was grass. You worked out on both sides. You'd take a baseball, put a mark on the wall, and throw the ball and hit that mark to improve throwing accuracy. Then you'd take the hop off the wall and practice trapping short hops.

Bernie DeViveiros was a longtime friend of mine. I spoke highly of him when I was working for Detroit. I told them they should bring him to Tiger Town to teach sliding. He was the Doctor of Sliding. He taught the bent-leg slide and the fadeaway slide. He would teach sliding on the grass at the drop of a hat. He was tremendous. What a positive influence he was. He could also teach bunting real well. But on sliding he was the expert. Schoolboy Rowe was a pitching instructor at Tiger Town. He was a big, long, lanky guy, but he had been a good pitcher in his heyday in the majors. I never saw him pitch, but he was a good instructor. He was the guy who started the phrase, "How am I doing, Edna?" He was pitching in the World Series and went by the stands and asked his wife that question. The reporters played it up. Hitters would come up to the plate, and bench jockeys would say, "How am I doing?" He loved to play golf. He would try to hide it, and then we'd kid him. He was a big country boy.

When I started managing in the Detroit organization, after I left the Yankees and the Cardinals, I couldn't understand why Detroit wouldn't hire their outstanding former ballplayers to be instructors. I finally talked them, either Jim Campbell or John McHale, into hiring Mickey Cochrane. He came down to spring training and was a great help. He wasn't interested too much, but he did come to spring training. Mickey was great. Gee whiz, I'd sit there and talk to him, and he'd tell me all about the catching. He said, "Never let your catchers have their right arm bare, because when they give a sign for a curve, they flap the arm and it jumps. When there's no flap, no arm, it's a fastball, and when it wiggles, it's a change-up. You can read the catcher's bare arm." Another former Tiger was Tommy Bridges. He had that great curve ball, and I thought he could teach the young guys the curve, but he never did. He wouldn't teach it. He was a roving pitching instructor, but he never did much. He wouldn't give up his secret. It was very disappointing to me that he didn't pass it on. And at one time I recommended that Dizzy Trout and Hal Newhouser should be instructors in the organization. These were famous ballplayers, and I couldn't understand why the parent club didn't take advantage of their knowledge. Heck, all that knowledge was going to waste. I fault John McHale on that. For some reason he just didn't think that the older ballplayers knew anything. He kind of looked at them as dinosaurs.

The managers at Tiger Town were some great guys too. Bill Norman called everybody "Laddie Buck." Everybody called him the same thing. He was a manager in the Tiger system and got a shot at managing the parent club. He was just a fun-loving, beer-drinking good guy. Billy Hitchcock was another manager in the Tiger organization. He had played with several American League clubs. He was from Auburn, Alabama, and had gone to Auburn University. I knew him way back then because I lived in Montgomery. Chuck Dressen I misunderstood for many years until I became associated with him when he managed the Tigers. He was astute, very sharp, and cocky. He had played professional football too, with the Canton Bulldogs, I believe. He was like a banty rooster. He'd fight anybody. I misunderstood him because I kept reading about him being feisty and everything else. But he was direct. And he knew baseball. Jack Tighe is one of my favorite guys. He managed the Tigers in 1957 and 1958. He was a good developer of young ballplayers, a very astute, sharp baseball guy. He'd been around a long time. He had a good sense of humor. I loved to work with the guy.

Tony Lupien was another manager in the Detroit organization. He had been a first baseman for the Red Sox back in the 1940s. He and I roomed together at Tiger Town in the barracks. He told me that I was too soft-hearted. That was sort of funny, because many of my ballplayers would say I was the meanest, roughest, toughest, most demanding guy who's ever lived. But Tony said I was soft-hearted. We'd sit there and talk. Tony had the bad habit of liking his bourbon a little too much. He had this little sack with two little shot glasses and a bottle of booze. We'd sit there, and he'd pick my brain on managing. Gee whiz, he'd diagnose everything. He had a reason for every move he made. I never ran across him again. I wish I had. I was going to point to some books that told how rough and tough I was as a manager.

Danny Litwhiler was a good ballplayer with the Cubs. I never saw him play, but he became a manager in the Tigers organization. Later he became a real good college coach. We roomed together, and he'd pick my brain night after night. I can't even recall what years they were, but it was with the Detroit organization. I was kind of an innovative type of guy. I had worked for the Cardinals the one year, and the Cardinals had a trick play that George Kissel would teach. George was a lifelong employee of the St. Louis Cardinals. I believe he was a schoolteacher. George would figure out plays, and Dan Litwhiler wanted to know all the trick plays. Usually I didn't like trick plays, but this was a good play. We'd sit there, and we'd talk it over and over. He was a tremendous college baseball coach.

We had a lot of fun down at Tiger Town. Somebody was always doing something to break the monotony. Bernie DeViveiros and Pat Mullen would put on a skit called "The Great Raker." Somewhere along the line we had a microphone and loudspeakers on the tower, and Bernie and Pat would get up there, and Pat would interview Bernie. Bernie played "The Great Raker," a minor league raker who had come up and was about through in the big leagues. Then they would bring up these young rookie rakers, and Pat would interview them. Pat would ask, "Raker? What kind of a grip did you use on the rake?" Bernie, who was Portuguese, I believe, talked with an accent and would say, "I holded it this way. I putta my right hand on the bottom, and I putta my other hand on the top and I rake it dis way. . . . I take a bigga rake. . . . I move it away out and then I move ita close. The kids of today . . . they don't know how to rake." Pat would say, "Were you a raker from way out, or in, or were you a side raker?" Bernie'd say, "Well, I mixed 'em up." Pat would ask, "Raker, what's the length of your favorite rake?" Bernie would answer, "Well, I like it a sixty-inch rake, young kids they come up they don't have a good rake. Young kids have a shorter rake, and they rake too fast. Me, I like a sixty-inch rake, I like to reach out and I like to come back. I like to rake around the mounds; I like to rake around the home plate. Young kids, they don't do that. I think I'm gonna stick around a little longer; I'm not gonna retire. You took a look at that young raker. He should be in a Class D, but he's up here trying to be a big league raker. He can't be like me." They'd use baseball terms, and it was quite hilarious. I was very fond of both of them. I didn't get a chance to play with Pat Mullen when he was a Tiger and I was there. He always had a good sense of humor and was a joy to be around.

One time at Tiger Town, we found a water moccasin down in the outfield. The field was right close to a swampy lake. One of the groundskeepers killed it with a shovel and brought it in. There was a game that afternoon with the Yankees over at Henley Field. One of the Detroit guys—I think it was Pat Mullen—took this snake over there, cut its head off, and put it in the Yankees dugout. The dugout was real low, and it had a little shelf on the back where you'd sit down and you'd put your arms. He took this snake and rolled it up into a little round coil. Yogi Berra went in there, I guess, and he sat down in the shade and put his hands over where the snake was. When he touched that snake and didn't see the head, he took out of that dugout, and they say he's still running.

At Tiger Town, guys were always pulling tricks on you in the barracks. Wayne Blackburn was such a guy. He was from Cincinnati. His brother was the famous Blackburn who coached the Cincinnati basketball team. Wayne was a little outfielder and a nice person. By God, he was great. Wayne was always asking me different things, about this and about that, and I was always trying to pull jokes on him, because he'd laugh like heck at everything I did. So after the workout, before dinnertime at Tiger Town, I'd take a little nap, and Wayne would always come by and say, "Metro! You asleep? You asleep?" He'd come in, shake me, and wake me up. I'd say, "Goddamn it, Wayne! Get out of here." We had a room, called the Bamboo Room, where Jim Campbell and all the scouts and the managers and everybody would come in and sit and talk about the players. We had two or three hundred players down there, I guess. One guy couldn't see them all, so we'd talk about them. And we'd have a beer or two. By the end of a long evening, we'd have a big wastebasket full of cans. I took those cans into my room one time, and I stacked them on top of the door. Old "Blackey"—we called Wayne "Blackey"—opened that door and those cans came tumbling down. You could hear them all over the place. He took off! I pretended I was still asleep and hadn't heard a thing. He asked me, "Say, Metro! What happened down there?" I said, "I don't know." The next time he came through the window. He wouldn't go through the door again to wake me up. Wayne was a delightful guy.

While I was at Tiger Town, I experimented with the pitching machine.

They wouldn't let the kids use it. One of the young pitchers got his arm busted or something by putting it in there. It had to be run by one of the managers or scouts or somebody like that. I was always on it, helping the kid hitters. They couldn't pick up the ball out of that steel arm. So I cut the shirtsleeve off of an old sweatshirt and taped it on the machine, and the ball would come right out. Then I got to fooling with it. It was throwing only fastballs. I wanted the ball to do something. So I took a piece of tape and rolled the tape in a little roll about the size of a cigarette. I cut that in half and taped that on the edge of the extended arm. When that ball came sliding off that, it did a lot of tricks. I had a lot of fun with that. When the ball came off there, it would go this way and that way. I would put the tape on the end in different ways. When I put it across the end of that thing, the ball would take off and jump. I was always trying to improve the equipment.

Casey Stengel had a technique of building a club very closely that I copied at spring training, when I became a manager. After announcing all the rules and so forth, he would line up five or six guys at home plate, and they'd run down together, run down in a row, down to right field to the foul pole. Next they'd walk to center field, then run to the left-field foul line, and finally walk back in to home plate. After two or three of those trips around, he'd say, "Speed it up." And then you'd stretch. I'd put three guys on the right-field line and six on the left-field line, and they'd run across the outfield, line to line, straight across. We always had plenty of fields down at Tiger Town and different places. I'd run them foul line to foul line. After they did that, they could talk and kid around a bit. Then I'd give them a baseball, give the one in the middle a baseball, and he'd toss it in the air to the guy to his right and the guy on his right would toss it to the one in the center. I always put the fat guy, the guy you want to lose a little weight, in the middle. They'd run all the way down, tossing the ball back and forth, and they'd do the same thing coming back. You'd run them. They'd have a chance to catch their breath, and then you'd run them again, for half an hour, twenty minutes. Then after you broke them in to that routine, the next time you'd have the guy in the center roll the ball to the guy on the left, and he'd roll it back to you in the center, while you're running, just like in a game, just like when a pitcher has to come in and field a bunt. I did this with outfielders, infielders, everybody. When you had a big squad in spring training, you had to create methods to teach skills to a lot of guys at once. We did this in Tiger Town, teaching base running. We'd line up four guys at first base, and they'd take the same lead and watch the pitcher.

As soon as he'd make his motion, you'd teach them how to get the good jump and then you'd find out real quick who was real alert in getting the jump on the pitcher and who wasn't.

At Tiger Town, we dressed in the minor league uniforms or the Tiger uniforms. Usually it was the Tiger colors. A lot of the players would have the numbers on the back, and you would identify them that way. We had different socks for the different classifications. One would have green, one would have dark blue and orange striped, one would have solid blue, and somebody would have the half-and-half dark blue and orange socks. I instituted a way of identifying a player who was hurt. I had him wear one regular sock and one white one, a sanitary sock. You'd know that he had a sore arm or had a bad back or his legs were injured or he had blisters. I thought it was a good idea, but it didn't go over very well.

At Tiger Town, we had an early camp where guys paid ninety-five dollars to come down for two weeks. They came from all over the country. I noticed this one guy on my club sitting back there. He was hiding. He had a pencil, and he was writing down notes. I took a look at him. He had a crew cut, but he looked a little older than most guys that we had down there. They were mostly kids trying out and having some fun and everything. Finally I asked him, "What are you doing?" He said, "Well, I'm making notes." He was a high school baseball coach, but he had come down to camp. He was a lot better ballplayer than all the other kids. So I made him my coach. I made a fan forever.

We had a couple of unusual ground rules at Montgomery. The outfield fence was about 365, 370 feet to left-center. We had a sign saying that it was so many feet, and the sign was like those "Don't Walk on the Grass" signs on a stake. It was nailed on top of the fence. When I made the ground rules for the ballpark, that sign was part of the fence. So, when I was no longer there and was over at Augusta in 1955, we were playing at Montgomery. By then they were a Red Sox farm team, and Cedric Tallis, who had been the general manager for a couple of years while I was there, was still general manager. They had the bases loaded, and their guy hit the ball out toward the fence. It was going to go over the fence, but it hit the sign. Well, I knew the ball was in play, that the sign was part of the fence. I made my players read the ground rules. So we recovered the ball and threw it back in. We got two outs on the play, and they didn't win the ball game. Cedric was furious with me. We looked up the rules, and they'd never changed the ground rules. He didn't even know his own ground rules. The next day I went out and took the sign off the fence, sharpened the stake, and pounded it in his front lawn. He accused me of doing it, and I very innocently said, "Not me! There are a lot of fans here that maybe don't like your ball club." He was very angry with me but apparently not too angry, because he hired me to manage Vancouver in the Pacific Coast League. After the third year out there in Vancouver, I admitted that I had put the sign on his lawn.

There was another quirky ground rule at Montgomery on the first base side. There was no fencing in front of the bleachers, so an overthrow at first base, or a wild throw from the third baseman to shortstop, would go in there. The rule was just one base if it went under the bleachers. That was a pretty good rule because you couldn't scramble under there, and usually there were some kids who would crawl under and one would get the ball and run off with it, which was all right. I was always in favor of the kids getting those baseballs.

I was demoted to Durham, the Durham Bulls, in the Class B Carolina League for the 1954 season. Let me get this straight right away. I'm sure most baseball fans have seen the movie *Bull Durham*. Well, I want it known that I did not allow any of that hanky-panky in the clubhouse. I had a couple of pretty good ballplayers there. I had Bo Osborne, who went up to the big leagues. Bo came to me in Montgomery in 1953 in the Sally League. He was a seventeen-year-old kid, right out of high school. He was an outstanding football player. Several universities in Georgia and Alabama were disappointed when he chose baseball. Right field was very deep in the Durham ballpark. In fact, nobody on our ball club had ever hit one out over there. But Bo Osborne hit quite a few home runs there on top of the building in right field.

Bob Shaw was an absolute delight. He pitched for me at Durham and Augusta. He was kind of a happy-go-lucky, nutty guy. He was funny, one of my favorite guys. He drove me crazy. He was always kidding me about the panic button. He had this little plaque with a button on it in the dugout, and he called it the panic button. You were supposed to push it when things were going tough. When he'd warm up or go in the game, he'd say, "Charlie, disconnect the panic button." I said, "I'll get you one of these days." But he was fun. He got back at me. One time we had an off day and went up to the big lake, where some of the big fans had motorboats and water skis. Bob knew how to drive a boat very well, and he got me on those skis and kept me out there for half an hour. I couldn't get out of bed the next day. I was so bound up from trying to stay up on those water skis. I didn't know how to ski. Shaw was one of the finest conditioned pitchers that I've ever seen in my life. I remember one time, he was leading everybody during a run, like the lead horse on a team of horses. He ran them all into the ground but made them keep up with him. He'd egg them on and ridicule them, shouting to come on, don't do this, don't do that. He was a good pitcher. He was with the White Sox with Al Lopez later.

Ernie Neville was one of my left-handed pitchers at Durham. He was sort of a local hero, but he was a Class B ballplayer and he wouldn't do anything. He had been one of the candidates to be manager, so I guess he resented me a bit. He wasn't a bad pitcher, but in truth, he was done. He couldn't compete with those young kids. But we kept him on the club for the local fans. He just wouldn't do anything but stand around. He was waiting for me to falter, so he could take over as manager. I knew it, but that didn't faze me. He wouldn't do this, he wouldn't pitch this, and if I'd say to walk the guy, he wouldn't walk him and all that stuff. He'd fight me at every turn. I was getting tired of it. So I decided to teach him a lesson somewhere along the line. He didn't have much one game, so I brought everybody down from the bullpen and put them on the bench. I let the other team clobber him. If you ever see Ernie Neville's book, you'll see he doesn't say very many complimentary things about me.

Some other Durham players trigger memories. I had a catcher, Jim Sady, who was from California. He and his girlfriend got married there. Or they were married and didn't tell anybody. Toward the end of the season, with six weeks or so to go, we were flirting with third, fourth, fifth place. Jim came down with a big case of homesickness. Every day for five weeks, he kept pestering me to let him go home. Well, I couldn't send him home. You had to have two catchers. Dolph Camilli's son, Dick, played for me at Durham. He had asthma. I'd see him in the dugout between innings, with his inhaler, trying to get some air. He went on to work for the State of California, in Sacramento. Steve Demeter played third base for me at Durham. He was a pretty good, hard-knocking type of ballplayer but never quite had enough. Harry Durkin, our shortstop, went on to become a lawyer. He was quite a student of baseball. He later convinced the Giants' heiress to donate money to the Minor League Professional Baseball Association.

At the Durham ballpark in the Carolina League, right field was a really wicked sun field! We were playing Burlington, a doubleheader on a Sunday, and I asked our business manager if we had any sunglasses. He said, "Yes." We got them and outfitted our guys. So the other manager wanted to use glasses in right field. They didn't have any. I wouldn't give them to him. I told him to go to hell, they weren't going to use our sunglasses. The owner of the Burlington ball club, a big lumber baron, was upset with me. There I was, a new guy, a Yankee carpetbagger, whatever, in the South, and I wouldn't let them use my sunglasses. And I didn't. We beat them, because the ball dropped in on their right fielder. In the second game, the manager stole home on us with the bases loaded. My pitcher didn't think the runner was going to go, and they beat us that one. Then later in the season, we went back to Burlington, and they got back at me. I went to the mound, then to the home plate to exchange lineup cards, and finally to coach third base. On the count of "one, two, three" the fans threw every kind of sunglasses at me. The ground was covered was them, like they'd shaken an apple tree. They had a heck of a crowd. I saw in the paper that they had a surprise cooked up for the visiting manager, and I guess the word got around. The owner of the club got a big kick out of that. I said, "You did that to me, didn't you?" He said, "Yes. How do you like that?" But it was all right. I took it in stride.

At Durham, I did a couple of things that I had always wanted to do to see if I could get away with them. We were playing at Fayetteville, and they had a big left fielder named Jack Hussey and a first baseman named James Pokel, who hit 38 home runs to lead the league. Fayetteville could hit. In this particular game, we got two outs on them in the last inning, we were ahead by 1 run, and Pokel was coming up. They had a man on third base. So what did I do? I walked Pokel. I put the winning run on base. The next guy was a right-handed hitter, Hussey, and I had a right-handed pitcher on the mound. So what did I do? I walked him. I put the winning run on second base. The next guy was a right-handed hitter. He hit a line shot in between the outfielders in left-center, but our center fielder, George Bullard, ran over there and made a sliding, diving catch to save the game. I wanted to do that in the big leagues, but I didn't have guts enough to do it. We put the winning run on base, put the winning run on second and another run on first. The game would have been over if Bullard hadn't made that great catch. The next day the papers called me a "genius."

Eddie Popowski was the manager at Greensboro in the Carolina League. He was a fine manager. My father thought he was a better manager than I was. Every time I'd see him, I'd say, "You son of a gun. You're the only man that my father thought was a better manager than me and would tell me so." He'd laugh like heck. My father used to come down, visit us, and watch some of our games in Montgomery and Durham and Augusta, partly, I think, so he could get away from the vow he made to my mother and my sisters not to drink in the state of Pennsylvania.

In spite of all that, we went into the last twelve games of the season battling for a playoff spot. We were in fifth place. We played Danville, the fourth-place club; Greensboro, the third-place club; Burlington, the second-place club; and Fayetteville, the first-place club; all in a row, 3 games each. At Danville, which was a Giants farm club, some Hollywood outfit was making a movie of some sort, and they had the cameras and reflectors and actors and everything. They'd stop the game a little while and take shots of the dugout and the players. I can't recall what the movie was about. The Danville team got carried away with their importance, so we beat them 3 in a row. That brought us to 3 games behind Danville. Then we beat Greensboro 2 out of 3, and Danville won only 1, so we kept picking up games on them. We went to the last game of the season. We had to win our ball game, because the Danville score was already on the board. We were down by 1 run and had a man on second base with two outs in the bottom of the ninth. Our batter, Jim Sady, my backup catcher, fought their pitcher in one of the finest at bats I've ever seen. Finally he got a hit to center field and took second, when their fielder tried to get our runner at the plate. The next guy, Bob Taylor, another left-handed hitter, hit another single, and we won the ball game. We finished fourth and got in the playoffs, but Fayetteville beat us in the first round. Years later, when I was in Sacramento, Sady invited me out to his house for dinner. He was working for one of those big corporations like General Dynamics. He made me tell his family the story, and I told his kids that that was the finest thing their dad had ever done, that he played like a big leaguer that day.

Dusty Rhodes lived in Montgomery when I was there. Dusty eventually played with Phoenix in the Pacific Coast League, when I managed Vancouver. Dusty had that fabulous World Series in 1954, in which everything he did was right. They gave him a Mercury down in Montgomery at a banquet in his honor. He took it out, and in twenty minutes it was totaled. This brings back a memory of this guy who had his wife call me up at Montgomery and ask me who was going to win the 1954 World Series between the Giants and Cleveland. Being an American League guy at the time, and looking at the Cleveland Indians, who won 111 ball games and had four guys who won 20 games, I thought they were unbeatable. When this lady called, I said, "Well, I don't give out information of that kind. I'm not any better than you. A housewife can pick it better than me." I was trying to get out of it. I asked, "What are you going to bet?" She said, "Well, we're betting quite a bit." I said, "Don't bet the grocery money." She said, "Oh, quite a bit." I hedged and hedged and finally my wife said, "The Giants are going to win; the Giants are going to win in four straight," in the background while I was talking on the phone. I was telling her to hush, telling my wife, Helen, to be quiet. But she kept saying, "The Giants are going to win it in 4 games." Finally I told the lady that there was no way I could tell. She hung up and called me back again. She said, "My husband insists that you tell us." I said, "Well, if I was going to bet, I'd bet on Cleveland." The Giants, of course, won it in 4 games, and to this day, I haven't heard the last of that. I was supposed to be the expert on baseball. I'm lucky to still be married.

In 1955 Detroit sent me to Augusta, Georgia, back to the Sally League. This was a promotion for doing well at Durham. I had a pretty fair ball club at Augusta. We finished third. Keith Jones was another guy I had had back in Montgomery. He had the most uncanny talent. He would tell me what moves the Detroit organization was going to make, and he'd always be right! It turned out his girlfriend was the telephone operator, and she had eavesdropped on a few conversations.

Tom Yewcic was a great talent. He was a catcher in the Tigers organization. I had him at Augusta. But he had this quirk. He couldn't throw the ball back to the pitcher. He could hit. He had power. He hit 10 home runs before the Tigers took him up to Buffalo. Nine of the 10 home runs figured in victories for us. He could receive pretty well, but he couldn't throw the ball back to the pitcher. He'd throw the ball back to the pitcher, with a runner on base, and the ball would go into center field. I worked with him a lot. I threatened to fine him and everything else. I had the shortstop and the second baseman backing up the pitcher almost all the time. Bob Shaw was pitching the game at Augusta for us and Yewcic was catching. I told Shaw, "Now, Bob, you be careful out there if he throws that with a guy stealing." He said, "OK." So the first time Bob made a pitch, somebody hollered, "There he goes." Bob ran off the mound. Yewcic still almost got him. So the next time I said, "Bob, why don't you just duck down." Tom's throw was still wild, and it hit him right in the butt. Shaw ducked down and hid his head. He didn't want to get up. He looked around and said, "Oh, you missed me. Hey, Tom, you missed me." Yewcic never did conquer that tendency. But he played college football, quarterback, at Michigan State, went up to the American Football League, and became an outstanding punter for the Boston Patriots. He was a Pennsylvania guy, from Conemaugh, about eight miles from Nanty-Glo, where I grew up. We played them in football. They beat the living daylights out of us.

When I had the Augusta club, my third baseman, Tom Sarna, once hit a ball into the alley in right-center for three bases. It'd been raining, and the field was all wet. We were still playing. He came sliding into third base while the throw was coming in from the outfield relay man, but he twisted and sprained his ankle. Tom lay there groaning. I shouted, "Get up, get up." I was laughing; I wasn't mad at him. He was about three or four feet away from the base. The home plate umpire came up the baseline, and a field umpire went out there to see that the ball was in play and everything was in order. The plate umpire slipped and fell, and three baseballs fell out of the umpire's sack and rolled over near the slider. There were four baseballs right by my guy. He was still groaning there, three, four feet from the bag. I was still shouting, "Get up and get to the bag. Get up." The third baseman grabbed a ball and tagged him. The umpire said, "That's not it." The baseman picked up another and tagged my player again, but the ump said, "That's not it, either." So the fielder threw it aside and picked up another. I said, "That's not it" before he tagged him. Then very triumphantly he picked up the last ball and tagged the guy, who was still groaning. The umpire said, "Out!" One out of four, the baseman finally got the right ball.

When I was at Augusta in 1955, Pepper Martin, the "Wild Horse of the Osage," was managing the Macon club. During an exchange of lineups one game, Pepper came up and gave the umpires a Holy Roller Christian fellowship talk. He was giving them all this born-again Christian talk about how we're going to do this and we're going to be nice and we're not going to swear and cuss out here. I was watching and listening to all this, and I didn't know whether it was an act or the truth. I remembered Pepper Martin from his wild days with the St. Louis Cardinals "Gas House Gang." In the game, there was an argument, and their shortstop was arguing with the umpire. Pepper came out there, and he began choking his own ballplayer to get him out of there. I thought Pepper was going to hit the umpire. It was one of the darnedest thing I'd ever seen. I said to myself, "This is Pepper Martin. He was so nice and so polite and so Christian, and now he's ready to choke his own ballplayer and kill the umpire."

When I was with Montgomery, I ended up with one of Pepper Martin's uniform shirts. We trained at Albany, Georgia. They gave me a uniform, and I can't remember the number of it but stitched inside were the words "P. Martin." These were hand-me-down uniforms, and good Lord, this was 1950, six or so years after Pepper last played. That shows you how far down they sent those uniforms. Years later my sons Bud and Steve were trying to break into the construction business back in Buckingham County, Virginia. The county building inspector was tough. Here were two young guys who weren't from that part of the country, and he gave them some harsh inspections. Then they found out he was a Cardinals fan. One of my sons called me up and asked, "Dad, do you by any chance have that Cardinals uniform that you had, and whose uniform was it?" I said, "Oh, it's out there in one of those boxes." He said, "Why don't you get it out?" I did and saw "P. Martin" was stitched on it. He said, "I want it." So I got it dry-cleaned and sent it to my boys. They gave it to the inspector. This man, I understand, would sit in front of his television and watch the St. Louis Cardinals, while wearing that Pepper Martin shirt. My sons gave it to him. Nowadays I scold them. I say, "Do you know what I could get for that shirt right now?" They say, "No, Dad, it was a good thing. It made him happy, and we're doing all right."

One game at Augusta, I couldn't do anything right. Just about everything I called backfired. In the first inning, I had two men on and the batter hit a short fly to the outfield. I started waving the runners on. There was nobody out. I waved them around and they kept going, but their guy caught the ball, relayed the ball to second base and then over to first for a triple play. In the next inning, I coached them into a double play, and in the third inning, the same thing. After that I went into the dugout, and I said, "You guys play this game any way you want to. I'm leaving. Do whatever you want." One of my ballplayers asked, "Well, if we win the game, will you buy the beer." I said, "I'll buy you two cases of beer." This was on a Sunday, and you couldn't buy beer in the stands at that time. I turned the club over to them, and I went in and got dressed. This was a way of kind of relieving tension, giving the guys a chance to play a fun game and do whatever they wanted. So I sat up in the stands and watched them. All heck broke loose on that ball club. We were losing by about 6 or 7 runs by the time I left. But, boy, we scored runs, this way and that way. I think I had Kirby Higbe managing, and he was making some of the darnedest decisions I'd ever seen. But we ran away from them by a big score. And, of course, I had the two cases of beer on ice. We were an older ball club. They really enjoyed that. They wanted to do this often, but I said, "No, no, you know, I'm the manager, and if you start doing this, you're not going to need me. So let's forget this from now on." So we finished out 1955, and I had no idea what was in store for me the next year.

SIX

The Road Back to Triple-A

When the next year, 1956, started, I couldn't begin to guess that it would be one of the stranger years of my career. The year started for me in the South and ended in the West with a stop in the Midwest in between. You can almost hear Casey Stengel saying, "Who woulda thunk it?" This was one of those years that try men's souls. It was a year I'll never forget, although I wish I could in some ways.

After I had a pretty good year at Augusta in 1955, the Tigers organization assigned me to the Charleston, West Virginia, franchise in the American Association. This was yet another step up, this time to Triple-A. But Charleston was a disaster for me. I ended up managing there only three weeks, 22 games. I wanted to take up all the young ballplayers that I'd had at Montgomery and Durham and Augusta. But they wouldn't give me young ballplayers. Charleston had sold out two years in a row, and the Tigers wanted to put a winning ball club there. I knew I could win with those young guys. I could handle young guys, I could convince them, and I could pep them up and everything. They stuck me with a bunch of older guys and some very young ones. A lot of the older guys were unhappy and dejected and disgruntled. This made it tough for me as a manager. A lot of them were through. They couldn't play. They were trying to play themselves in shape, and that wasn't the way I did it. I had some guys like Hal Woodeshick, one of those big, heavyset guys, lazy as hell, who wouldn't do anything you wanted him to do, who thought he had all the answers. The pitchers who complained the most never did much. I got these guys late, just before we were breaking camp in Florida. Oh, it was a mess. But I took their club, and I lasted about the first month of the season. We were 5-17. So I was released about the second week of May. When you get fired from a managing job, they blame you for everything, including the pregnant wives. Everything.

But before I was released, I got a guy who would go on to the Hall of

Fame. His name was Jim Bunning. He came down from Detroit, and he brought all of these problems down to me. Like the older guys who were disgruntled, Jim was no different. So finally I said, "You're going to pitch the opening game." We were still practicing a couple of days at Charleston. "You're pitching the opening day. In two days you're pitching. You're going to go nine innings. Have you been running?" I ran him that day. He said, "Yeah." I said, "Are you in shape to pitch?" He said, "Yes." So he pitched, and in the bottom of the ninth, I walked out to take him out. He had been leading 9–1, but they scored 7 runs off him before we got the last guy out. He said, "I came down here to pitch, and damn, I'm going to pitch." So I said, "OK." Ron Sanford, our second baseman, made one of the most sensational, game-saving, diving plays I've ever seen in my life. And we beat them 9–8, I believe, that day Jim pitched. He was a terrific competitor, very tough to hit. But after that opening game, he just kept moaning and groaning. I told him, "Jim, there are sixteen clubs in the big leagues. Just think that other clubs will like you, if the Tigers don't like you, so why don't you just forget all that and bear down? Have yourself a good year. And if they don't keep you, why you might end up at Philadelphia or somewhere else." He looked at me as if I had holes in my head. I said, "That's right, I don't want your problems. I'm here to help you and not listen to your crying." I touched a nerve. He turned out to be a pretty darn good pitcher. He pitched real well for the next two or three times, before I was released. He went on to win 100 games in the American League and 100 games in the National League, one of the few pitchers who've done that in baseball history. Years later he was managing Oklahoma City in the American Association, and I said, "Hey, Jim, how do you handle those guys that they send down to you?" He looked at me and laughed. Later he became a congressperson and a senator from Kentucky.

One thing I remember about Charleston was how hard it was to fly in and out of there sometimes. The clouds and storms could roll into that valley real quick. Opening Day in 1956, we held up the game about an hour and a half until Spike Briggs, the owner of the Detroit club, flew down in his plane, the "Gray Goose." We won the ball game. Afterward in the clubhouse, my coach and old friend Stubby Overmire said to me, "Gee, Charlie, we got it." I said, "Yeah. It's in the books, Stubby." But then in came Spike Briggs and John McHale and their entourage, a couple of other guys who'd come down for the opening. I think Spike had been drinking up there in the press area. He didn't say, "Nice going" or anything like that for winning the game. Spike came in and said, "Well, you almost blew the damn thing!" We won the game. It was a win in the books. Sort of without

thinking, I said, "Ah, 'blew' your ass. . . . We won the game!" To the owner
of the Detroit Tigers! No wonder I lasted only a month!

After the Tigers released me at Charleston, I was dejected and disap-
pointed. I asked if they could send me back to Augusta, but they said they
wanted me to go to Terre Haute, Indiana, to manage their team in the
Three-I League. They were going to shuffle the Terre Haute manager to
Augusta and the Augusta manager to Charleston. So I went to Terre Haute.
My wife had been in a car wreck. The mayor's son had run into her and
wrecked our car, so she had to stay in Charleston about two or three weeks.
I went ahead and joined the club. I was going to find a place for us to live.
But when she and the kids arrived, I told her not to unpack the boxes,
because the situation looked shaky in Terre Haute. I had a fairly decent ball
club. In my opening speech to the players, I said, "I'm unhappy. I don't
like it. I'm down here. I need a job. I want a job. I want to manage, and
I'm going to do it." I won the ballplayers over, because I was really crushed.
I whipped them into pretty good shape, and, heck, we were fighting for
the league lead against Evansville, the Milwaukee farm club. I took over a
sixth-place ball club, and it looked like we were going to catch Evansville
just before July, but the Terre Haute club folded financially.

The owner, Paul Fritz, was a great baseball fan. He owned a little hotel,
sort of a third-rate hotel, but still a fine hotel. He catered to the railroad
people who would stay there. But he couldn't meet the payroll and had to
disband the franchise. I walked into his office one time, and he said, "I got
to meet the payroll." He was taking some bonds out of a safe. I said, "You
mean to tell me you're cashing in your bonds to meet your payroll." He said,
"Yes." I said, "Well, this club is going to fold then." He said, "Well, I don't
believe I can make it any further." This was still the Detroit organization,
so I called John McHale. I told him, "John, this man is cashing his savings
bonds and he'll lose his hotel if he can't make the payroll." John said, "Well,
I guess we'll just go ahead and fold the club." I said, "OK."

During my brief stay with Terre Haute, I did have the delightful opportunity to talk with the great Hall of Famer Paul Waner. He was scouting
for the Braves, I believe it was, at Evansville, Indiana. He was staying at
the McCurdy Hotel. After one night game, probably about midnight, I
went into the dining room to get a sandwich. Waner was there. He saw me,
recognized me, and called me over. We sat there—he was drinking beer and
I had a sandwich—until about 5:00 in the morning. All he talked about
was hitting. This was one of the most interesting conversations I've ever
had with any baseball person. I imagine only talking with Ted Williams
for five hours about hitting would equal or surpass that talk with Paul. He

talked about everything, and he even told me some of the things that he would do if he were a player again. He said that he'd put the bat on his shoulder, parallel to the ground, and that's where he'd hit from. He always said he'd hit with his belly button, which meant coming around real quick and bringing the bat around. I really enjoyed my long talk with Paul Waner.

Mentioning Waner, of course, brings up a story about his ability to hit while he was a little less than sober. We all heard the story of how one spring the Pirates barnstormed from the West Coast with the White Sox. The Pirates were at San Bernardino, I think, and the White Sox were out there somewhere, maybe Pasadena. The two clubs were barnstorming through Texas. Paul Waner went on the wagon, and as the story goes, he couldn't get a base hit. Now Paul was a magician with the bat. I'd seen an exhibition that he put on. He'd say, "left field," and he hit it down left field, right field, through the middle, through shortstop, and so forth. They barnstormed all through Southern California and Arizona, and they were over somewhere in New Mexico or Amarillo when "Big Poison" decided he'd had enough milkshakes. So he and Ted Lyons, the great White Sox pitcher, went out and they tied one on pretty good. The next day Paul went on a rampage. He got five base hits! They say he couldn't hit unless he had had a drink. That doesn't downgrade him in my estimation. Some guys just got drunk, but they played every day and they played hard and tough. And they were winning ballplayers.

When we disbanded the Terre Haute club, I asked John McHale, "Where do you want these ballplayers? I'll handle all this down here." He asked me who could play, and I told him a couple of guys could play in an A league, so we sent some to Augusta. Then we sent some players to another B league, and some players to a D league, and then some out to Idaho Falls in the C league. Then came the question of where I would go. John wanted me to go to Georgia, but I wouldn't go there. I said, "John, you can't ask me to go down there." Finally he asked, "Where do you want to go?" I said, "I'll go to Idaho Falls." Stan Wasiack was managing Idaho Falls, and he was from Georgia. So we arranged that switch. Stan was happy to go to Georgia, and I was familiar with Idaho Falls from my days in the Pioneer League. In early July, about July 3, when we were in second place, the Terre Haute club folded. I got everybody going, all the players packed up, and got it all settled.

We packed our car and headed out toward Idaho. We drove all night, and we slept in the car or up on top of the luggage trailer. We couldn't get a motel or anything. I had to be there on July 7 because the directors were meeting and they were making all these rules. And they were going to introduce me as a manager. We traveled on the Fourth of July, and we had car trouble again. But we got out to Idaho Falls the morning of the seventh. We hadn't contacted anybody to find out where we were going to stay. They gave us the name of the motel, but I needed a haircut and a shave. I hadn't shaved in four days, and we all needed to freshen up. My wife, Helen—Babe I call her—decided she'd go to the beauty shop and get her hair fixed and everything. So I said, "Babe, you go ahead and take the kids to the café and let them order something to eat and go ahead to the beauty parlor, and I'll go ahead and get a haircut and a shave."

I went into the barbershop about 8:00 in the morning and got an Idaho Falls newspaper. A kid would come around and hang the sports page in barber shops and beauty shops and hotel lobbies and restaurants and such places. I was sitting there while the barber cut my hair, and I told him I wanted a shave. So I leaned back, and he lathered up my face. A kid came in and pinned the sports page on the bulletin board. The barber, who I later found out was a rabid fan, said, "Charlie Metro, I remember him. He's that son of a bitch who broke thirteen guys' legs. He broke every guy's leg, and, gosh, he's mean. He's now a manager. But they say he's a good manager. I think he was good; I saw him manage, boy, oh, gosh, but he's mean, he's rough. Oh, gee, he'll break everybody's legs." I had broken a kid's leg sliding in a game at Idaho Falls back when I was with Twin Falls, and I thought, uh-oh, they'll never forget me for that. This guy was shaving me, and I was listening to him. The other barber was sitting over in the other chair, and the one shaving me was telling him all these stories. I thought, when he was shaving me, cutting around my neck, holy cow, I better not say anything to him. He got through and put some aftershave on my face, and I asked him how much. He was still calling that mean "Metro" all sorts of names. I paid him, and he gave me my change. He asked, "Oh, by the way, what do you do?" He hadn't asked me. I told him I was that mean son of a bitch who broke those thirteen legs, and I'd go on doing it! He turned white. I got out of there in a hurry. Later I talked to him, and he found out that I was a pretty good guy.

We had a delightful time at Idaho Falls. That's where I first got my love of horses. We fell in love with the area, living on a ranch, riding horses, and becoming true westerners. We lived out on a ranch with Bish and Lucille Jenkins. We became great friends, and we lived out there with them. They never charged us any rent for the place. They kind of adopted us. The kids had a great time, riding, fishing, horses, ponies, and everything. Oh, it was a dream. After the season, we stayed out there for a while before we went back to Montgomery. Bish was a horse trader and a cattle feeder, and we're lifelong friends to this day. He was like a father to me. Right when I needed a lift, he helped me straighten out my thinking and get back to the positive way of doing things. I'm indebted to him forever. And he also started us in the horse business, which I'm also very thankful for, because it gave my wife and me an off-season interest. They were wonderful people. Dwight Evans, who went on to play all those years for the Red Sox and was the Rockies' hitting coach for a year, was their grandson. A few years later, I had Dwight and his mom and dad as my guests when I was managing the Cubs at a game at Dodgers Stadium. And twenty years after that, when Dwight was playing for Boston and I was coaching for Oakland, I had him pose side by side with me with our bats in our hands for an eight-by-ten photograph. I sent it to Lucille, who was a great fan. It said, "Charlie Metro and friend." She got it framed, and it was just wonderful.

That year I was at Idaho Falls, Lucille had a bad accident on the highway right by the place. Her face was cut up and everything. She was very despondent. But she was an avid fan, so I thought I'd do something for her. She wanted to know my signs, so I said, "OK, I'll give you my signs." I showed her my hit sign, my squeeze sign, all my signs. They had seats right back of home plate at the edge of the screen. I said, "Now, if you want me to do something during the ball game, give me these signs. I'll look over there at you. When I touch my nose, I'll ask you for the sign, see?" She said, "OK." She'd sit up there in the stands right back of the screen, and I'd flash the sign to her and ask yes or no, and she'd say yes. I'd maneuver her a little bit into certain calls. Then every once in a while, she'd jump the traces and give me a sign. For example, she'd call a bunt. Well, I wanted a bunt too, but I wouldn't tell her this. This gave her quite a boost. She recovered her good humor and was rejuvenated. If we'd lose, we'd go to the house after the game and I'd say, "Bish, I got to fire my assistant manager. She called all the wrong plays." She would laugh. Bish and I would give Lucille a good going-over, and it was wonderful.

Every once in a while, you misjudge a player who you think can't miss. One summer at Twin Falls, I saw a guy who had great talent. One afternoon I saw a bunch of kids, a high school team, and I saw this big, strong, 195-pound kid. Boy, I was just elated, wild about him. I told our scout about him, and I kept pestering and pestering. We signed him. It was my first recommendation. He had the finest physique I'd ever seen. He was a left-handed hitter, and he could run like heck. In batting practice, he'd hit the ball over all the outfield fences. I never saw anything like it. I just drooled. I said to myself, boy, I found another Mickey Mantle, another Joe DiMaggio. But when they put him in the game, all he did was freeze at the plate. Never took his bat off his shoulder. Somebody had recognized that in him early. That's why he was available.

A manager's got a lot of things to do, and sometimes you have to do things that you don't want to. I had a young ballplayer on the Idaho Falls club. He had a date. Young guys would meet their girlfriends. He was nineteen, and I think his girlfriend was eighteen. The girl's mother came out to the ballpark and said, "You're the manager, Mr. Metro, you're the manager?" I said, "Yes, ma'am, I am." She said, "I just want to tell you one of your ballplayers is going out with my daughter." I said, "That's not unusual." "I'm worried," she said. I asked, "Why?" She said, "Well, they're going all the way. I want you to talk to him." I said, "All right, I will." So I called him aside and said, "Hey, the mother of your girlfriend says you guys are going all the way." He said, "That's right. We're practicing the rhythm system." That was a new one. I'd never heard of that. So I said, "OK." When the mother came out again the next day, I said "Yes, ma'am, I talked to him, but they both talked it over and both agreed that they'd practice the rhythm system." She said, "Oh, really?" I said, "Yes." "Well, that's all right." Off she went, and everything was fine. So I solved that one pretty well. I don't know whether they married or not. If they did, I never heard.

During the winter of 1956–57, when I was back at our home in Montgomery, Cedric Tallis came through Montgomery—we both had homes there—and asked me how would I like to manage Vancouver in the Pacific Coast League. He had given up his own vacation to come to Montgomery to make me this offer. We were going to put the house up for sale. I had known Cedric since he was the business manager in Montgomery when I had that terrible club in 1953. Now he was out in Vancouver. He asked me, "How'd you like to manage in a higher league?" I said, "Well, I could manage in Charleston, but they didn't give me much of an opportunity." I didn't say anything bad about it. He asked, "How would you like to manage Vancouver in the Pacific Coast League?" They were an independent club, and they had finished last the previous season. I said, "Are you serious?" He said, "Yes." So I said, "OK, what are you going to pay me?" He gave me a figure of $14,000 a year. I had been making $5,500 the year before. Cedric liked the way I handled a ball club. So I jumped at the chance, and everything seemed to be falling into place. The Coast League paid pretty good salaries. Sure, you'd play 188 games, 200 games, or so in a season, compared to 154 games in the big leagues, but the money was still good. By 1959, I was making $15,000 a year in the middle of a two-year contract with Vancouver. Mayo Smith was managing Cincinnati and offered me a job as a coach for $9,000. I couldn't make the financial sacrifice. It was a tough situation, but if you wanted to manage in the majors you might have to take a cut.

But the toughest part was that I had to tell the Idaho Falls people that I was taking the job in Vancouver. The only people who were on my side at first were Bish and Lucille Jenkins. They knew that I wanted to manage higher up and this was my big chance. I had re-signed to go back to Idaho. The people there had made me a very interesting proposal, giving me a building lot there if I'd come back to the Pioneer League. Well, I cleared it with the people I had signed with in Idaho Falls. They eventually understood that I needed to go from Class C back up to Triple-A, and we started out on what turned out to be the most wonderful experience of our lives: three years in the Pacific Coast League, with good ball clubs and a lot of good players, in a wonderful city. Gee whiz, we had a great time there. At that time, the Vancouver Hotel was the tallest building in town, and now it's a big modern city. Queen Elizabeth Park, out by the ballpark, was just gorgeous. Flowers were blooming, and everything was green. Things were greener in Vancouver than any place I'd ever seen.

I can never say enough good things about baseball wives, especially mine, Helen. She's really something to admire. She really came through like a trooper. For example, when I got hired at Vancouver, we lived in Montgomery. We still had our home there from when I managed in the Sally League. When I got the job with Vancouver, I had to go out in advance and set up spring training and everything. Helen and the kids, our daughter, Elena, and our sons Bud and Steve stayed back in Alabama so they could finish out the school year. When school was out, they prepared to move out to Vancouver. When Helen asked how she was going to do that, I said, "Oh, heck, our forefathers and foremothers, when they crossed the country, when the back wheel fell off, the lady would get back there and hold that axle all the way across. I think if they could do that so could you." That didn't go over too well. "I'll tell you when I get there," she said, among other words. So Helen loaded up the car, bought a two-wheel trailer, and loaded it with everything that she could take. She hitched it up to the Buick, and off she went from Montgomery, Alabama, to Vancouver, British Columbia, with three kids, two pet dogs, and a litter of pups. She dropped off the pups, one in Kentucky, one in Nebraska, one in Idaho, and one in Washington State. My son Steve won a battery-powered car in a television contest. A Montgomery station had a contest to name this singing pig who sang a jingle in a commercial for a meat-packing outfit. Steve named him "Caruso" and won. Helen pulled that thing in the trailer all the way into Canada. When she got to the border and the customs guy asked if she had anything to declare, my wife said, "Oh, we've got a little car here. It's not worth much, about a hundred dollars." My son Steve said, "No, it isn't! Mother, you know it's worth nine hundred dollars." The guys at the border said, "OK, you can go." When she got to Vancouver, I asked, "How'd the trip go?" "Oh, wonderful. Nothing but problems," Helen said. But she and the kids and the dogs and the trailer made it.

At Vancouver, I was bound and determined this club was not going to be run like the Charleston club. Here Cedric Tallis and I started our working relationship. I had first met him in Montgomery in 1954 or 1955. He was starting out with the Red Sox organization. Cedric was from New England, and, although I thought at times that he wasn't thinking very sharp, he was a real thinker. He was really one of the finest people I was associated with. Cedric and I worked great together. We disagreed at times, but we disagreed for one purpose, and that was to better the club at all times. Most of the time when a general manager or business manager disagrees, he wants to run it this way, and you, the manager, want to run it that way. But we never had a serious conflict. Cedric would argue about the caliber of a ballplayer. Maybe I'd say this guy couldn't play, and he'd say, yes, he could. So we'd say, "Let's find out. Let's check him out." We had a great rapport. Cedric was wonderful.

We started out 1957 at spring training at Riverside, California. We were an independent club, but we had a little bit of an agreement with Baltimore. Cedric had met Paul Richards, the Orioles manager, and I knew Paul from my days with Detroit. Paul sent us a bunch of ballplayers. The Orioles had withdrawn their farm team from San Antonio, and I had to train those guys at Riverside. We had one diamond. We had a clubhouse that wasn't very big, two guys to a locker. They sent me a whole ball club out there, mainly the Double-A ball club from San Antonio. We had a lot of different ballplayers from the White Sox, the Orioles, the Yankees, and the Red Sox. We had ballplayers from everybody. Cedric had gotten acquainted with all of the teams the previous year at the meetings. John "Spider" Jorgensen was my playing coach. He had played with the Dodgers and in the Coast League quite a while. I made him a coach. He was a wonderful guy, a great coach, and a good ballplayer, even at that time. On the lighter side I got to meet Joe E. Brown at Riverside. They had a big banquet, and Joe E. was there. He put on that act of his, "Elmer the Great," and, oh, what a riot. I've seen that done at the baseball meetings. He was a joy. He was that pitcher who made the bad pitch and followed miming cussing out the guy, without ever saying a word. It was a delight.

We had too doggone many guys there at Riverside. I wanted to concentrate on some of the guys who weren't going to make my club. I knew that if the ballplayers were lower on the list, they were on the San Antonio roster, but not yet. So I told Spider, "Well, John, we better take a look at them. We're going to take a look at these guys." We had a lot of black guys at the camp. There were no problems with this in Vancouver. Vancouver was the first club on which I had black ballplayers. I eventually had Joe Taylor, Joe Durham, Charlie White, Charlie Beamon, Lenny Green, and Connie Johnson. They stayed in our hotel. Wherever we went—Sacramento, San Diego, Phoenix—they stayed right with us. They were my ball club, and that's where they stayed. I insisted, and so did Cedric Tallis. One exhibition game, I made up the lineup with eight black ballplayers. That might have been a first, eight black players starting a ball game, outside of the old Negro League days. The only white ballplayer was Buddy Peterson, our shortstop. The other team, Hollywood, had a catcher and a first baseman who were black, and the umpire was black. When the first baseman hit, we had a black umpire, a black catcher, a black pitcher, and a black batter. I turned to Spider and said, "John, these guys can play ball. You're going to see them go up." They were good ballplayers.

In Vancouver, there was a guy named Frank Welters, who owned gold mines, oil wells, real estate, and everything else. He was a real promoter. He bet somebody a thousand to one that we'd be in first place when we opened at home in 1957. I had told him we had a good ball club, that we were going to win. He took me at my word and bet a thousand dollars at a thousand to one with some other big guys that we'd be in first place when we opened the season at Vancouver. We had 12 or 13 road games before we came home. After the last game of the road trip, we were tied for first. It looked like we were going home in first place. We were 12-1, if my memory serves me right, but we played one fewer game than the other club, so they were percentage points ahead of us. Frank Welters lost the bet, but he had them sweating. They would have had to come up with one hundred thousand dollars.

In 1957 the weather in Vancouver went our way. I don't know that we even had a game rained out. Every time we were at home, the weather was beautiful, the sun was shining, and the flowers were blooming all the time. And then we'd go on the road, and it would rain like heck in Vancouver. We'd come back home, and the sun would shine again. We'd go on the road again, and it would rain again. This went on the whole year. The baseball gods were with us.

The next year, 1958, the pattern was just the opposite. After we trained in Yuma, Arizona, we played games at Riverside and Sacramento and Bakersfield, but every place we'd play it would rain. We got up to Vancouver, and it was raining there. We didn't get on the field for seven or eight days. We finally opened up the season, and it was still muddy and raining. The club had been fine-tuned, but we lost our edge with all the rain. I trained the guys under a viaduct going over the river to the airport. It was the only dry place we could find in British Columbia. I tried to train them in a mushroom factory, and I tried to get us a lumberyard. We couldn't find a place to train the ballplayers. I had them running around the columns underneath the viaduct, bouncing the ball off the concrete columns, just to loosen up. That weather did a number on us in 1958. Cedric and I were pushing for a new domed stadium way back then, in 1957, 1958, and 1959, when you never heard of those things. I was invited back to Vancouver several years ago when they opened up the new domed stadium. They kept calling on me for my input, but they built it a little too much for football. Right field is very short. It wouldn't take much to move right field back, maybe move some seats to the longer part of the park.

In 1959 we got a bunch of players from the Baltimore Orioles. They were young guys, but some of them were good. They all believed in me. Paul Richards believed in me, and he knew that I wouldn't hurt a guy. He sent us his best ballplayers, the best he had. Ron Hansen, Marv Breeding, and Lenny Green all went up to the majors. Hansen stayed up for fifteen years, and I was instrumental in his coming over to the White Sox when I coached for Al Lopez in the 1960s. Ron turned out to be a pretty good infield coach in the major leagues. He certainly could field the shortstop position. The best, however, was Brooks Robinson, who went on to a Hall of Fame career. When we took infield practice, I'd try to get a ball by Brooks and Hansen. I'd try to finesse them. I'd try to throw the ball way out there and then cut it back in, and then I'd try to cut it the other way, but I never could hit a ball through. I saw some great third basemen play. I saw Graig Nettles make great plays, but Brooks was the best I've ever seen. I'll never forget one play he made in Vancouver. If I could have a darn tape of any play I'd seen in baseball, that's the one. The ball was hit to his left, and he went over and stretched his arms up way in the hole, almost back on the grass, angling back. He had his glove down near the ground because, as he always told me, he could bring the glove up more quickly than he could get it down. So the ball took a wicked hop, but he took the glove and put it back of his head, caught the ball, took a spin, and threw the guy out at first base. He was great. Later on, when I was coaching for Oakland, I had a lot of arguments with Clete Boyer, who'd been a great third baseman himself on the Yankees, about who was the best. He said, "What about me?" I told him, "Well, the only reason I don't have you there is because Brooks played for me, and I've seen him more than I've seen you, but you were pretty close, I tell you." That satisfied him. But back in Vancouver, I tried to hit a ball through the left side of the infield and couldn't do it. Jimmy Adair was scouting for Baltimore and came into San Diego prior to the All-Star Game. He said, "Uh, are these guys that good?" I said, "Absolutely, Jimmy." He said, "Well, why don't you tell the writers that?" So I told the writers that I had the best left infield in baseball, including the major leagues. Up at Baltimore, Paul Richards heard about it and called me up. He said, "Charlie, are you sure?" I said, "Paul, you better take them up. I don't know what they'll hit up there, but they're pretty good. They will win you hundreds of ball games."

One game I saved Brooks Robinson's career. He was playing third base, and the field was wet from rain, slick near the dugout, which was pretty close to the field. During this one game, Brooks came over toward the dugout for a foul pop fly. I had taken the screen off the top part of the dugout because you couldn't see through that big screen. So I had that taken off, but the crew forgot to take off these blunt hooks where you hooked the wire screen. The hooks were as blunt as your finger, but Brooks slipped and caught the hook right at the elbow. I caught his elbow. The tendons were hanging over that hook. He was on his heels, almost sitting down. We lifted his elbow and slipped it up over that hook. He had to get twenty-one stitches on the inside of his elbow, and he was out for quite a while. If he had fallen and torn anything more, I don't know whether he'd have been able to play baseball again. But he came back and regained his form, and the Orioles called him up.

I've stayed in touch with Brooks over the years. When I was inducted into the Cambria County Sports Hall of Fame, Brooks was the guy who introduced me. There's not much more I can say about Brooks Robinson, except that he might have become my son-in-law. I still catch heck about it from my daughter. She was sixteen or so when Brooks was at Vancouver. He asked her if he could take her to the show or have a date. When my daughter asked me, I said, "Absolutely not. You're not old enough to go with him." Brooks at that time was twenty or twenty-one, maybe not even that. By the time she was over eighteen, he was gone to the majors, and she went to college. To this day, however, she tells me that I could have had a Hall of Famer for a son-in-law. She keeps reminding me of that. I don't know if I ever told Brooks that. Maybe someday he'll know about it.

We had some pretty good pitchers at Vancouver in those years. George Bamberger was on my ball club at Vancouver in 1957. He had a bad arm, and he was downcast and everything. I started putting him through my program of conditioning pitchers. Somewhere along the line, he made a remark that he didn't start pitching till June. I said, "That's OK, because we won't start paying you till June, George, so get out there and run." I said, "If you do what I'm telling you, I'll send you to the big leagues." I got him in wonderful shape. About June, he came up to me and said, "Hey, Charlie, lookie here!" He could take quite a tuck in his pants. I said, "Gee, George, you better get a pair of pants that fit you!" He lost considerable fat weight, and he went on to be one of the best pitchers I had for three years. He had winning years. In fact, he pitched both games of a doubleheader and lasted all but one inning, and he won both games. He held the Pacific Coast League record, for many years, for innings without issuing a walk. When he was adding to the record, the umpire called a ball on a pitch that was really a strike. It was a close pitch. He called it a ball, on a 3-2 pitch. It was definitely good enough to be a strike. You don't take that kind of a pitch when you're a hitter. We were furious at the hitter because he didn't swing at the pitch and thought it was a ball. Pitchers had to learn everything the hard way. George went up to Baltimore for a short time at the end of one year. But he didn't have enough to pitch in the big leagues, wasn't quite fast enough. They laid off the curve. He had a good curve ball, and a good spitter too, which he could get away with down in Triple-A but not in the majors.

The Orioles liked him and made him a minor league pitching coach. George was well up in years at that time. When Hank Bauer got the Orioles manager job, he asked me about Bamberger. I asked him, "What do you want him for?" He said, "As a pitching coach." I said, "Get him. Don't consider anybody else. This guy will do you the best job that you'll ever see on the major league level." And he did. Eventually he had four guys who won 20 games one year. Ray Miller succeeded George when he left Baltimore to manage Milwaukee, and Miller would run his pitchers like I ran George and all the pitchers. In fact, a couple of the guys told me that I was running them until they were sterile. I told them, "Well, your wife'll appreciate that." George was a pretty good manager too. Pitchers as a rule don't make good managers. But George knew when to take a guy out. He had known when to take himself out. When he knew he was done, he'd give you a sign. I tested him one time, and he was right. Almost lost us the game, but he was right.

Chuck Estrada was another fine young talent who went up and won 18 games for the Orioles in 1960. He got a sore arm a couple of years later, and they accused me of ruining his arm. It was rumbled around, and I had to straighten everybody out. I said, "Chuck had two great years after I had him at Vancouver. How could I have ruined his arm?" With Estrada, I had orders that he wasn't supposed to make more than seventy-five pitches in a seven-inning ball game. He was one of those guys you'd clock at ninety miles plus. He was a young guy, and he had a fine year. The next year he went up to Baltimore and had a good year. He should have gotten the Rookie of the Year Award. One game at Salt Lake City, Chuck was very eager to pitch. He went down to the bullpen, and the bullpen catcher soft-talked to him that he was going to pitch in a couple of days. My pitcher got into trouble in the game. I went out there to talk to him, and here came Estrada. The umpire had motioned him in the game, and there was nothing I could do about it. I had to let him pitch. Oh, boy, did I catch heck for that. I was pitching him too much. Another time he was pitching a one-hitter, and he'd pitched his allotted seventy-five pitches. I was going to take him out. He talked me out of it. I didn't want to tell him I had orders up above. I said, "This is your last inning. You'd better get him out. You need three pitches to get him out." I had to do a little fudging on saying how many pitches he made. He made seventy-eight. Paul Richards was very strict on that with young arms, just so many pitches and that was it, regardless. I often wondered what I would do if a guy was pitching a no-hitter and going into the bottom of the seventh inning. He'd already reach his seventy-five pitches, whether I took him out or left him in. I never had to face that one.

Erv Palica came out to Vancouver from Baltimore. He was a good pitcher, and he had been a good one with the Dodgers. He had one quirk, and it usually cost him dearly in the ball game. I had a heck of a time with him. He would hang a curve ball, and doggone it, it seemed like he never got away with it and it would always hurt him. Boy, you'd hear me screaming about that curve ball. "Don't hang the curve ball!" But otherwise he was a good pitcher. He'd pitch anytime you wanted him to, but every so often he would ease up. Erv would go along and have five or six wins and maybe one defeat. Then he'd want to call it quits. He wasn't a quitter, but he thought, boy, I've got a good year already, so I'm just going to take it easy. I didn't like that. It was a long season. He'd get mad as heck at me. But he was a good competitor, and he was a winning pitcher for us. He was also a pretty good hitter. Sometimes I'd use him as a pinch hitter.

Wes Stock, who pitched for us at Vancouver, was also a Baltimore prospect. He had come out of the service, and he had bad teeth. I talked the Orioles front office into spending the money on his dental bill. I understand they did, and he turned out to be a good pitcher and an excellent pitching coach in the majors. I like to think he learned to condition his pitchers from me. Art Ceccarelli was a pretty good left-handed pitcher, but he didn't have the desire, I guess, to go up to the big leagues. But then he also lacked a little bit. There were an awful lot of good ballplayers at that time, and you had to be a little extraordinary, which Art wasn't. Sandy Consuegra was a fine relief pitcher in the big leagues. He had a very good motion, very smooth, like he wasn't even trying. Don Ferrarese was a good left-hander. He won quite a few games. He had the quirk of having a bad inning during the game. I'd turn my head when he was having a bad inning. But he always felt he was going to have a bad inning. I got him over that, and he did a real good job. Mel Held was much the same way. He pitched well for us. He was always in the game, always keeping it close. But all of a sudden, we'd be leading 2–0 or some such score, and he'd walk a couple of guys or give up a couple of hits and maybe a home run. This was a manager's dilemma. This all would happen real quickly, so quickly that you didn't have time to raise your hand to get somebody up. So finally I got to where he'd get into this sixth, seventh, or eighth inning, I'd have a guy warming up, and, boy, the minute that first guy got on, I had Mel out of there. He'd get a little disturbed at that. I'd answer him this way, "Mel, you won the ball game, didn't you?" We had Sandy Consuegra, who could save games with the best of them. I'd tell Mel he won the game. But he wasn't satisfied. I was questioned many a time by the press on why I'd take my pitchers out. So finally one day I just said to myself, I'm going to leave Held in. I let him go, and, dang it, he blew the lead in the sixth inning. I should have had him out of there, and I knew I should have. Luckily we came back and won the ball game.

I also had Art Houtteman for a brief stretch. I had known him when he was a young kid, when I was with Detroit, working out with the team. He and I used to take infield practice together, because even though he was a pitcher, he was an all-around athlete. But he was involved in a nasty car accident that set him back in his career. When I got him at Vancouver, he was on his last legs. Paul Richards was trying to reconstruct him because Paul was there at Detroit at the time when Art showed such promise. Dick Marlowe was another pitcher who came down to us from the big leagues. As a manager, you want your pitchers to do the job, to make a great effort. One game, I brought Dick in with the bases loaded and no outs and the game on the line. He looked at me with a funny look on his face, and I said, "Strike them all out." Damned if he didn't. What a masterful job.

Charlie Beamon was another pitcher for us out at Vancouver. He was Baltimore's property. He had to be, in my assessment, one of the finest pitching athletes I've had. I've had quite a few that I could put in that category. Charlie Beamon could do everything. He was strong as an ox. He could run, and he could swing a bat. Charlie was black, and I don't know whether he thought that somebody was always against him. Sometimes you'd get a player, black, white, Latino, it didn't matter, he'd think the whole world was against him and had dealt him a bad hand. Beamon was a tremendous athlete and should have been a good big league pitcher. He won for us out there. It's a mystery why he didn't do better in the majors. Sometimes a manager just can't do it all for a player. Sometimes he has to help himself.

Connie Johnson, who had pitched in the Negro Leagues, wound up at Vancouver after his career was about over. He was with Baltimore. Richards sent him out there to us. He hated to run. He was a big, long, lanky guy. He could pitch a little. I don't know if he ever had a sore arm, and I don't know how old he was when he was out there, but it was about the end of the line for him. Years later, I saw him at the opening of the Negro Leagues Museum in Kansas City. He looked at me, and we both started running opposite directions from each other, in a kidding fashion. I didn't know if he was still mad at me. He hated to run.

The 1957 Vancouver pitching staff was moaning because they weren't pitching often enough. I didn't have a standard four- or five-man rotation. I had seven good pitchers—George Bamberger, Mel Held, Morrie Martin, Charlie Beamon, Eddie Erautt, Erv Palica, and Don Ferrarese. So to be fair to each of them, I called them into the outfield for a meeting. I said, "You guys tell me what you want to do. We can't go on with this seven-man rotation. I said you're unhappy and so am I. We've got to be fair about this. What do you want to do?" So they said they would stick with the seven-man rotation, which would take six days, because we had a doubleheader on Sunday, and if a pitcher didn't go nine innings, I could drop him out. I said, "Is that what you guys want?" They said, "Yeah." So I let them pitch nine innings. We had twelve straight nine-inning games. And the strange or beautiful thing about this is that I had very few sore arms or injuries on my baseball teams. I attribute that to conditioning the pitchers. I didn't have to use Sandy Consuegra for 14 games. Finally I called him aside and said, "Sandy, we're going to cut your salary. You're not working." He couldn't understand that. I was trying to be a little bit humorous, but he took it the other way.

For catchers I had Charlie White, Jim Pagliaroni, and Jerry Zimmerman. All of them were big leaguers. Charlie had played a brief time with Milwaukee. He was a good catcher. Because he was black, sometimes the pitchers couldn't make out his signs during night games, so he would put some white tape on his fingers. We got Zimmermann and Pagliaroni from the Red Sox. Zimmerman turned out to be a fine coach at the major league level. He coached for many years for several clubs. He was a good, quiet, unassuming guy. Jim Pagliaroni was a real good-looking ballplayer. To this day I guess he's still mad at me. Charlie White had gotten hit on the fingers one game. When you get hit on the throwing hand on the fingernails, that splits them wide open, and you can't throw and you can't catch. The only thing you can do is just wait it out, three or four days usually, before you can begin to catch again. So Jim Pagliaroni was catching, with Charlie out, and he got hit on the hand. He wanted to get out of the game, but I had nobody else. I said, "Jim, you got to catch." He said, "I can't catch." I said, "You've got to catch" He said, "Why don't you get Charlie White to catch?" I said, "Jim, this is the way I look at it. Charlie White has split fingers and can't catch, and you've got your fingers hit and you have sore knuckles. Put it in ice water. You're hurt the least, so you've got to catch." We had only two catchers at that time. He was ticked, but he was a pretty good ballplayer for us.

We also had Toby Atwell. In 1957, we needed a catcher real bad, so Cedric got Toby from Pittsburgh. It took him three weeks to get out there, and when he came out, boy, he was tough. This was a problem you had as a manager in Triple-A. When you got a ballplayer down from the big leagues, he brought his problems with him. Apparently Toby was never used to taking signs, because he never would look down at me for the signs. Finally one day he looked down at me for a sign, and I gave him the squeeze bunt sign. I thought he was going to have a fit right there at the plate. He didn't like the idea of Toby Atwell, the big leaguer, squeeze bunting. He stepped out, and I gave it to him again. He stepped out again, and I flashed it three times. The next time he stepped out, I put down five fingers, which meant a fine of fifty dollars if he didn't execute it. He laid down a perfect bunt and squeezed the guy in. The players, of course, knew what I was doing. They saw me give him the sign and him back out. When he executed the bunt, the guys grabbed a whole bunch of towels, jumped out of the dugout, and laid down a path of towels to the bench. He finally broke down and enjoyed it. Toby did a pretty good job for us.

Ray Barker also played for me at Vancouver. He had some of the finest abilities I had seen in a long time. He was a left-handed hitter and a right-handed first baseman and right fielder with a good arm. He had a beautiful home run stroke. He had what I call "loft power." But he had a personal problem at home that just destroyed him. I didn't know until the late part of the season. The trainer, who was a confidante of the players, told me that Ray's mother and dad were not getting along. He'd get these letters from home and would just almost stop playing. He would loaf and get mad and everything. This happened almost every time he'd get a letter. Finally I tried to ask him about it, but he never would tell me. He should have been a fine big league ballplayer.

Kal Segrist came out to Vancouver from the Yankees organization. He played third base. He had a lot of good tools, but he had kind of a lazy, laid-back attitude that, I guess, didn't fit in with the Yankees organization. I think Kal was with the Orioles for a short time, and he became a fine baseball coach down somewhere in Texas, West Texas State or Texas Tech. Barry Shetrone was a center fielder, a long, lanky kid, a left-handed hitter and a right-handed thrower. He played in Triple-A for us. He wasn't supposed to play there, but he did. He was one of the finest-looking prospects I'd ever seen. He could hit a ball on two hard hops to shortstop and beat it out. He could run. He just had everything going for him, but somewhere along the line he went wrong and never did reach his potential. It was a sad thing that Shetrone didn't play a lot of years in the big leagues.

Players do all sorts of things when they get angry. At Vancouver I had a player named Jim Brideweser. He was the son of a minister, I think, and he came down to me from Baltimore. Jim was an angry guy. When he didn't get a base hit, he had the habit of taking his helmet, banging it on the concrete dugout step, and busting it. I saw him do that a time or two, and I said to myself, "Well, I'm going to break him of that habit." So the next time he made an out and busted a helmet, I went over and put my hand on him and said, "Whoa, whoa, now wait a minute." I handed him one of our oldest helmets, and bang, he broke that. I took another old one and, bang, he shattered that. He did that to four or five helmets. When he was through, I said, "Jim, you're fined for a new helmet for all the ones you broke." He never broke another helmet. But he brought all these problems down, and I had to counter that. He couldn't play for me. One time when he didn't get a base hit, he stood out there with his arms folded, the ball was hit to right field on the ground, and he didn't even make an attempt at it. I think I put a hole in the dugout roof. I really had a shouting match with him, and I didn't want to. He said, "Ah, you don't like me." I said, "No, I don't like the way you're playing. I don't like the way you're acting." He started criticizing me some more, and I said, "Well, now, Jim, you played for Paul Richards with the White Sox, and you played with the Yankees for Stengel. You couldn't play for those guys, and now you can't play for me. Well, I'm in pretty good company. I think I'm flattered with that compliment."

Willie Tasby came out for a little while. Willie was all mixed up. He didn't want to come down from the majors. He thought he was a good big league ballplayer. He was disillusioned, and this was a tough job for a manager, especially in Triple-A, because you get these guys directly from the big leagues and they bring all their troubles right down to you. Willie was that way. I had a pretty good ball club, and you don't want a guy who's dissatisfied on the club like that. He'll contaminate your club. He'll bring them all down and make them disgruntled. He's like the measles. So I didn't want him. I just said, "I don't want him. Send him somewhere else."

Jim Marshall also played for us out at Vancouver. He went to the big leagues for a while and later became a manager. The thing I remember about Jim was that when he came to us, I had him in the lineup against San Diego, who had a couple of good left-handers, Bill Werle and Vic Lombardi. Jim walked up to me after I had the lineup made up, getting ready for the game to start, and he said, "Skip, I want you to know something." I said, "What's that, Jim?" He said, "You know, I can't hit left-handed pitchers." I said, "You can't?" He said, "No." I said, "Well, you've got thirty seconds to learn." He went up to bat and turned out to be a fine hitter. He hit 30 home runs and drove in a lot of runs for us.

Buddy Peterson is my favorite all-time bumblebee. He loved to play. He was the first guy I'd ever seen run full speed to first base on a walk, long before Pete Rose came on the scene. Buddy played shortstop. One particular day at Vancouver, it was raining and there was no way the game could be played. But Cedric Tallis wouldn't call off the game. Cedric wouldn't call off the game if there was two feet of water on the field. That's all right. General managers should try to find a way to play the game if at all possible. But this time it was impossible to play. The players were all downtown. They had a card game going, not too much gambling, and somebody said, "Well, let's have a beer." So they had a beer, and they had another, and they called up the office. The game was not called off yet, but it was raining like heck and there was no way to play. So they had a drink or two too many, and they didn't come out to the park. But Cedric said we were going to play. We actually ended up playing the game, so everyone came out. Buddy was one of them, but there was no way he could play. I came into the clubhouse, and he had his sweat socks on and his stockings on, that was it, and he was not in any condition to play. I finally talked him into getting in the whirlpool. When he got in the whirlpool, I dunked his head under briefly to sober him up, and I told the trainer, Hal Younker, I'd fire him if he let Buddy out. If you had nine players like Buddy Peterson, who played as hard as he did, all the other managers could fight for second place, because the first place would be yours. He was a good ballplayer, played a long time. He played in Japan, everywhere. Later I hired him as a scout with the Kansas City Royals.

Speaking of players performing under the influence of too many spirits, I recall another episode at Vancouver. Joe Taylor showed up one game having had a bit too much. Late in the game, a close one, I needed a pinch hitter. Joe volunteered. I had my doubts, but he kept at me until I let him go up to the plate. "I can do it, Charlie. I can do it," he kept saying. Well, he went up to the plate and took three quick strikes. Never even lifted his bat off his shoulder. After the game, he came up to me and chewed me out. "Charlie, you shouldn't have sent me out there. You knew how drunk I was," he said.

We had some fine umpires in the Pacific Coast League. Emmett Ashford was an umpire in the Coast League when I was at Vancouver. He later was the first black umpire to become a major league umpire. Emmett was another one of my all-time favorites. I recommended him to Joe Cronin, the president of the American League. Emmett was flamboyant, but he hustled all the time. He was always in the game. He looked like he was playing, making every play, playing every pitch and everything else. Now the umps just stand around, and even the dead lice would fall off them, I guess. I'd like to see them be a little more aggressive, whether they are or not. Emmett was the hustlingest darned guy I'd ever seen. He really tried. When he'd call a guy out, he'd really throw that arm like he was throwing a big haymaker, and his uniform coat tail would fly in the air and everything. There was no doubt about it when he made the call. Finally, one day I had a dispute at first base with him. I thought the guy was safe. I said, "Emmett, why don't you go home tonight after this game is over and practice that in front of the mirror, some fancy safe call like you do this out call?" He said, "OK." The next day when he was umpiring, he made a call, and he threw his arms up and got up on his tiptoes like a swan and waved his hands out like a bird flapping. I went out again to argue the call. He said, "How do you like that?" I said, "Emmett, you don't need any more practice."

Emmett Ashford had a great sense of humor, and occasionally we'd have some fun with him. At Vancouver the umpires came through a tunnel right in the middle of the dugout. The umpires would come and stand there and get ready to go out. One game George Bamberger got a couple of "Root for the Mounties" stickers they were handing out at the ballpark and slapped them on Emmett's back. These stickers were about four or five inches square. George would hit him on the back of his blue suit and say, "Now, Emmett, do a good job today." Emmett would say, "OK," and George would hit him again. Emmett would go out on the field, at home plate with his back to the fans, and the fans would roar. He thought they were rooting and hollering for him. This went on for about three or four innings, and when he turned around to brush off home plate, the base umpire came in and took the stickers off and showed them to him. Emmett went right along with it. I thought that was one of the most comical things I'd ever seen.

Another time we were having a big Hawaiian day in Vancouver. An awful lot of Canadian people would go to Hawaii from there. They were giving away two all-expenses-paid tickets to Hawaii. They asked Emmett Ashford if he would put on a hula skirt. So Emmett put on his swimming trunks and this hula skirt and flower things around his neck and ankles and wrists. He went out there, and while they played the Hawaiian music, he put on a pretty good show. He stood out there at second base, fooling around the bases. I thought it was great.

In another game at Vancouver, they had only two umpires, and Emmett was umpiring the bases. We had a close play at second base, and I went out there to argue. The meeting got out of hand a little bit, and when he turned around, I said, "You don't know the rule." Emmett strode right into the dugout into the umpires' locker room and came back with the rule book. He pointed right to the rule and said, "Here it is. Here's the rule. Here it is. There." I said, "Let me see that." I grabbed the rule book and I turned around and ripped one side and ripped the other and threw it up over my shoulder. And I started off, just waiting, cringing, to hear "You're out of here." I snuck a peek back. Emmett was picking up the torn rule book and just shaking his finger at me, giving me a tongue-lashing. The fans loved it. I thought, oh, man, I'm going to get fined and suspended for that little episode. The kicker was that Emmett was right about the rule.

A few years later, I had the nice opportunity to recommend Emmett for the major leagues. Joe Cronin, whom I had known for many years, called me and said, "Charlie, what kind of an umpire is Emmett Ashford?" I said, "Joe, he's a very good umpire. He'll bring hustle to your big league umpires. On occasion he might get a little exuberant about throwing guys out, but I don't think that is offensive or anything. He puts it on a little bit, which is all right. He's a great fan favorite, and he's one of my favorite umpires too." Joe said, "Can you send me a letter on him?" I'm sure that there's a letter in an American League file somewhere where I recommended Emmett Ashford, and he went to the big leagues. He was a good umpire. I had the reputation of being tough on umpires, but I wasn't. I demanded the same hustling and focus from an umpire as I did from my ballplayers. I believe that I personally recommended more umpires to the major leagues than any other manager in baseball. I recommended Bill Haller and Stan

Landes and a whole bunch of guys, Cal Drummond and Mel Steiner and Chris Pelekoudas from the Coast League. One day Steiner and I had an argument in Salt Lake City. Mel said, "What the hell are you doing here? Get your ass out of here before . . ." "Well, you better be careful," I said, "because my sister's up there in the stands, and she's a lip reader." He said, "Well, I'll turn my back. Now you better get out of here." He was a good umpire. I recommended an awful lot of umpires, and they were all good.

I always wanted my players to know the rules. I would always try to get a supply of official rule books and pass them out to the players. I did that in Triple-A as well as in the low minor leagues. I put them in their lockers in the Coast League. For pitchers I went through the book and everything pertaining to the pitchers I marked off with a piece of clear tape, taped those pages together, and put them in the pitchers' lockers. For the batters, I did the same with the hitting rules. Along about the middle of the season, I would go through the lockers and see if they'd broken the tape, to see if they read the rules. Not too many had, so I grabbed one of the taped books and stood before them in the clubhouse and ran my thumb through the tape to break open the pages. Many of the players quickly turned around in embarrassment. I insisted that players know their rules.

Speaking of rules, occasionally I'd catch an opposing manager napping. Connie Ryan was a manager out in the Coast League when I managed Vancouver. I don't know whether Ryan was one of those guys who was living in the past or not, but he didn't take good care of himself. I think Connie was nipping at the bottle. And he didn't know the rules real well. He'd go out the second time to the pitcher's mound and forget that the pitcher had to come out. You'd have to go out to get the rule enforced, if the umpire missed it. And he'd raise holy heck. One Sunday game, I had to explain the rule. He thought I'd misread it. I said, "Connie, you've got to take the guy out. Either that or you're out." He said, "Well, he's not going to throw me out." So I turned around and left. I didn't care what they did with him. But he was a pretty good ballplayer in his day.

I ran into George "Catfish" Metkovich again when he managed San Diego in the Pacific Coast League and I had the Vancouver club. The third base coaching box at San Diego was all dirt. It had no grass growing over there. I don't know why, but there was no grass. I had the habit of rubbing out the coaching box lines. I'd take my spikes and just rub them all out. We were playing San Diego, and I started doing that in the first inning. Metkovich got furious, and I didn't know why. So, between innings, they put the lines back on. When I came out again, I left the lines there, but in the third inning, I came out and I rubbed them out again. And he was furious again. Then I figured out that his signs were connected with the coaching line. When he stood with one foot inside the line and the other foot outside, the hitter could see that was the "take" sign. When Catfish was inside the box, that was the "hit away" sign. If he had both feet on the line on one side, it was a bunt, and if he had a foot on that side and this side, it was a squeeze. I figured those things out, so I'd rub out the lines. Oh, he was furious with me.

One game at Portland, I caught their pitcher throwing an illegal pitch. He was putting a little oil of some kind on the ball, and the ball was cut. I knew he was doing it, but I couldn't find out how. We were getting beat, but I had a good club and they had a terrible one. Finally, toward the end of the ball game, I looked at his white uniform and there was a dark spot right on the right-hand side where he was wiping his hand. I said, "Uh-oh . . . that's where he's getting it." So I had our clubhouse guy swipe his uniform. I took it down to the cleaners and had it cleaned. This was when we played the same team for a week at a time, so that when it was his turn to pitch again, the uniform was clean and there was no more of that grease on it.

Sometimes we would work the angles ourselves. I was part of a dandy scheme at Vancouver in 1957. On Sunday we'd often have a sellout crowd. When we played San Francisco, we had this big Sunday crowd, and we put them out in the right field. They put up a rope probably twenty-five feet from the fences, and the overflow fans would sit down on the ground or stand and watch the game. I told Joe Gordon, the Seals manager, that a ball hit into that area where the fans were would be a home run. I went out there just to check that everything was all right before the umpires came out to see it. I told the fans, "Now, look, if we hit a fly ball out here, you guys grab that rope and move it in as far as you can. When one of the San Francisco Seals hits a ball out here, you move back and give plenty of room." We had 2 home runs hit in there. Owen Friend and Joe Frazier hit one each. But when Marty Keough of San Francisco hit one out there, the fans just kept moving back, squishing everybody against the fence. We made the out. So I thought that was all right. It was ethical, seeing that it was the home field and I made the rule and told the umpires, but I didn't tell them that the fans could be part of the game.

Usually when you can read the opposite pitcher, you've got him where you want him. When I was managing Vancouver, I had a little left-hander, Don Ferrarese, who could really read the opposing pitcher. He was very good. He said to me, "Charlie, I can give you every one of these pitches this guy's making." So I said, "All right, tell me." He would say, "Fastball," and it would be a fastball. He'd say, "Curve ball," and it was a curve ball.

But sometimes it didn't help. We were playing the Seattle club there in Vancouver in 1959. They had a pitcher named Mark Freeman, and we had all his signs. We were able to tell our hitters what to look for. When Freeman threw a fastball, the palm of his hand was facing you. When he threw the curve ball, you could see the side of his wrist, the inside of the wrist. We called every pitch. Mark Freeman pitched a no-hitter against us that game. And we knew every pitch that was coming!

We had a young visitor clubhouse boy named Al at Vancouver. He was a tall, spindly kid, about fifteen years old. He kept pestering me to take him to spring training. I said, "You can't go." One day, however, he said, "Skip, I can get you the signs!" I said, "What signs?" He said, "They have their meetings, and they don't tell me to get out." I said, "Al, do you mean to tell me that they let you stay in the clubhouse while they're having their meetings . . . on their signs and everything?" He said, "Yes!" I said, "Well, if you can get me the signs, Al, you'll go to spring training next year." So he'd slip into the clubhouse just before the game, and he'd tell me all the signs that they were using. This worked pretty well, except with Joe Gordon, who managed the San Francisco Seals. We'd know his signs, and they still beat us. The pennant race went down to the last week, and they beat us. But Al gave me the signs of all the ball clubs, and we used them and knocked the heck out of a lot of clubs. We finished second. I took Al to spring training the next year at Yuma, Arizona, and gave him meal money.

And we got a lot of help from our groundskeeper. I'm sure you've heard the saying "Baseball is a timeless game." As Yogi said, "It ain't over till it's over." Well, once up in Vancouver we were able to use time to our definite advantage. Like many ballparks, the Mounties' stadium had a big clock in center field. But this clock took on some extra importance because the city of Vancouver had a restriction against playing baseball after 6:00 on Sunday evenings. No exceptions. They'd stop the game in mid-inning, midpitch even, to follow that rule. You couldn't even buy tickets on Sunday. You had to plan ahead and buy them during the week.

We had a groundskeeper there in Vancouver, Gene Edlund, who lived and breathed baseball. He manicured that stadium to perfection, a pretty stadium in a gorgeous city. He knew every square inch of that park by heart. So I shouldn't have been surprised when one day he came up to me with a plan concerning the clock. "Skip," he asked, "you know that clock in center field?" "Yeah, what about it?" I answered. "Well, I know how to control it," he said. "What does that mean?" I asked. "I mean I can make it run faster or slower," he said. "So what?" I wondered, but I had a pretty good idea what he had in mind. "I can slow it up if we're having a rally on Sunday or speed it up if the other team is about to score and tie or win," he smirked. I was always on the lookout for new strategies to toss another game or two into the win column, but I wasn't sure about this one. Managers often stalled during rain delays or coming up on curfews, or on the reverse side, hustled their players out to get a run before the storm or deadline hit. In the old days before lights, oncoming darkness brought on many a shenanigan. So I thought why not, but let's be cautious. "If you can do that, Gene, go ahead," I said, smiling, "but I don't want to know anything about it. If you connect me with it, I'll mutilate you." I didn't want to be guilty by association.

As luck would have it, a couple of Sundays later we were playing Tommy Heath's Sacramento club in a doubleheader. During the second game, we were down by a few runs as the time wound up toward 6:00. But right as were coming to bat about quarter to six, I looked up at the clock and it seemed to stop. We put together a bunch of hits and a bunch of runs—8, I think—and took the lead. I looked up at the clock again, and it had hardly moved a minute. I couldn't believe it. Gene was right. He *could* slow down time. But I couldn't let on. Sacramento finally got us out, and we took the field. Now I really began to sweat. What if the clock is broken? What if they catch on? What if Sacramento gets some runs and beats us? Sure enough, the first couple of Sacramento batters got on, and our lead looked in jeopardy. Our pitcher looked shaky, hanging on for the game's end. But when I peered up at the clock again, this time I saw that old minute hand zoom straight up to 6:00. Never had I been so glad to see a clock move so fast. The umpires called the game, and we held the lead. In the press room after the game, Tommy Heath, who was a veteran manager, came up to me and said, "Hey, Charlie, you got a pretty good ball club, but you better do something about that damned clock. There's something wrong with that clock." I never had the nerve to tell him the truth.

Gene Edlund helped out another way by tinkering with the third base line. Recall that future Hall of Famer Brooks Robinson was on that Vancouver squad. We knew he could field just about any bunt down the line, so Gene cut the grass short, and then when he was running the lime down the line, he tilted the liner to the infield side. This created an artificial trench of sorts that would keep the ball fair. We instructed Brooks to grab anything headed that way, because it wouldn't roll foul. But our guys would bunt down that line, the other team's third baseman would come in and let it roll, expecting it to go foul, only to see it gently dribble down that hardly noticeable trench. Groundskeepers still do such things today.

Gene Edlund also helped us with sun glare. In Vancouver we played night games, but the sun would stay late. Summer days were long, and the sun would come right over third base and sometimes blind the first baseman. So Gene put up two posts like a goal post right back of third base and constructed a shade. When the visiting team was hitting, he would raise the shade to eliminate the glare in our first baseman's eyes. But when we were hitting, he would lower the shade to let the glare hit their first baseman. He did this for a while until somebody made him stop. But if we'd have won the pennant and had been dividing up the money, Gene Edlund would have been cut a full winner's share.

Vancouver was wonderful. The Canadian fans were really great. There were a lot of kids out there in Vancouver who hung around the ballpark. It was like a neighborhood, a little residential park. They'd swipe our balls, every darn foul ball that was hit out. Cedric was pulling out his hair. He said, "What are we going to do?" We'd run out of baseballs in practice. It was getting expensive. I said, "I'll tell you what, Cedric, let's bring these kids in here and let them shag in the outfield. We've got insurance, don't we?" He said, "Yes." I said, "Well, let's bring them in here. I'll control them." He agreed to it, so we brought the kids in. We had seven- and eight-year-old kids, ten, twelve and everything else. We had Chinese, Japanese, French, Indians, Hindus, and Anglo-Canadians, everything you could think of. They were all bright-eyed and wanted to be ballplayers. They'd borrow the gloves, and I'd set the rules. No stealing of baseballs. I'm going to give out two baseballs. We'd take turns. They could borrow the gloves, but no stealing. Every once in a while I had to shake a boy down and say, "You give me that ball." There'd be a bulge in his pocket or his shirt. I laid the law down. But mostly they were great. All these kids had long hair. So I lined them up, and I said, "From now on, men, you're going to have to have crew cuts." My son Steve was on the club as a batboy, running around in a uniform. I brought him down to show these kids. He had a burr cut. I said, "This is the way I want it." So the next day they came out, and some of them didn't have it cut enough, so I separated them out and said, "I'm going to give you time to come back and have it cut." So they did. But there was his one little guy who was crying. I said, "Well, if you want to be on my team, you got to." So the next day, here he came, and here came his mother. He was a little *girl*, and she had a crew cut. I said, "Now, Ma'am, I didn't know that she was a little girl." I apologized and said, "Well, let her stay here. She's all right. Let her stay." And she was part of the team.

They were my crew, Charlie Metro's crew. Gang, I called them. Years later, at an anniversary celebration for a horse racing friend of mine in Denver, a younger guy in his thirties told me he knew me from some place.

I played a little cat and mouse with him, but when I told him my name, he almost fell over. He said, "I'm from Vancouver, and I'm one of your gang." There he was, six foot three or four. I said, "You ever swipe one of my baseballs?" "No," he said, "you gave me one, and I think I still have it." He was a highly successful patent attorney for a large company. I told him he'd better get a crew cut. Then he turned around to this woman who was his wife and said, "And this is the girl who had a crew cut!" They grew up and got married. She remembered me and said, "My mother gave me holy heck because I wanted my hair cut in a crew cut. I loved it!" I said, "Are you a tomboy now?" She said, "Oh, yes." We had a great reunion.

Cedric Tallis was a very intense guy where baseball was concerned. Everything he took up, he did with intensity. One day at Vancouver, one of my ballplayers said, "Skip, come on out and take a look at this right field." So I went out there, and there were a lot of holes and the grass was chewed up. I said, "What in the world is that?" We decided they were golf divots. So I went in and told Cedric, "We've got a terrible problem out there in right field." He said, "What is it?" I said, "There's divots out there. Some dumb nut is out there, when we're not here, practicing golf." He said, "Charlie, that's me!" I said, "Well, let's go out there. Hell, we don't want to lose the ball game on account of this, have a ball bounce the wrong way or something." Cedric had put a flag near the right-field line almost against the fence, and he was practicing his approach shots with his irons. He didn't think it'd have any effect on the game or anything. Because he was the general manager, he kept this up throughout the season. He turned out to be a heck of a golfer. At the start, I played even with him. I wasn't very good, but I played even with him. Then he got really good at it. One day we were playing at one of the country clubs there in Vancouver, and we were approaching the final hole. Cedric got off a real good second shot that landed up on the green probably in pretty good shape. After hacking a couple of times, I got up there too. Then we noticed that the greenskeeper had replaced the hole. Cedric's approach shot was a hell of a shot, about two feet from the flag, but mine was within six inches. Boy, he was furious. He was going to get that greenskeeper fired. I said, "Cedric, how can you? The hole is still par two. Heck, the guy's got his job to do." But he was still mad.

When I started out at Vancouver, you couldn't play Sundays. You had to buy tickets previously. The ballpark was in kind of a residential neighborhood. It was a big park. Right over center field was Queen Elizabeth Park, with a lot of flowers and trees. There was an inclined hill behind center field and left field, and on a Sunday, that hill would be covered with spectators. The stands would be packed, and they'd be up there. Cedric would get furious at all those people seeing the ball game for nothing. But I told him, "Cedric, don't get mad at them. Why don't you get your concession guys up there and get some money out of them?" So the next Sunday that we played there like that, he said, "Watch this." Here went a bunch of the vendors, kids with their cokes, peanuts, and popcorn and French fries too. They came back, and I think Cedric made two thousand dollars out of that crowd. There must have been a thousand people up there. He said, "Boy, that was a great idea." I said, "Well, where's my commission on that?"

As usual I had to do some discipline with the players. One matter was shaving in the clubhouse. A few years ago, when the Ted Williams Museum had its grand opening, I was sitting with Hall of Famer Jim Palmer. Jim asked, "Hey, Charlie, did you really take shaving out of the clubhouse?" "I sure did," I said and told him about what had happened at Vancouver. I expected and demanded my ballplayers to be alert. I had the pitchers keeping record of pitches, and I wanted my pinch hitters, my extra men, ready too. We were playing a home game, Erv Palica was pitching, and we were behind 1–0. Finally we got a guy on third base with two outs in the seventh or eighth inning. I wanted to use a pinch hitter. I didn't want to take Erv out. He was pitching a fine ball game. I didn't want to take him out, but this was the last chance to get a base hit. I had an outfielder named Carl Powis, who was an extra outfielder, so I was going to use him as the pinch hitter. I was coaching third, and our dugout was close by. I said, "Where's Powis?" I called time, holding up the game. Erv was in the on-deck circle, wanting to hit and get a last chance at winning the game. If I took him out, he had no chance. So I was looking for Powis. I couldn't find him. He wasn't anywhere I could see, not in the bullpen, no place. So I let Erv hit, and he hit a nice fly ball to left field for the third out. I went storming in the clubhouse to find Powis, and there he was, stripped at the waist and shaving while the game was on. He was my last chance to win the ball game with a pinch hitter, and there he was, shaving. This made me furious. I tried to do that trick where they pull a tablecloth on a table or a towel on a shelf out from underneath the stuff on it and everything stays there. Well, the stuff didn't stay on there. I tore everything up. I paid the clubhouse guy fifty bucks to replace everything. But I wouldn't let guys shave in the clubhouse. I said, "Wait till you go home! What the heck, you're going back to the hotel or you're going home. Go shave then. And if you don't want to shave then, shave before you come to the ballpark." We didn't shave in the clubhouse anymore.

Usually we didn't have any problems with customs at the U.S.-Canadian border, but at first I had to give the guys a warning. "Now listen, you guys, no smart-aleck shots, nothing. You just open your bags if they want them. Tell them what you've got. You tell them, and don't get smart." But I had a wise guy, Owen Friend, on the club. I guess they'd had a few beers or something before we got on the bus from Seattle. When we got to the border, he said, "Aaaah, this is a bunch of crap . . . stopping us." The customs guy said, "Thank you, sir." They kept us there until 5:00 in the morning. Boy, the ballplayers were ready to castrate old Owen Friend for that. We never had any more problems after that. I told them, "Now, look. You're in Canada. When you're in Rome, you do as the Romans do." Owen Friend was a real wise guy. You couldn't buy beer in the ballpark, but since I had an older ball club, and they liked to have a beer after a game, I'd order two cases of beer for them. But I said, "You cannot walk out of the clubhouse with a beer in your hand." Who walks out of there with a beer in his hand? Owen Friend! Man, they had him against the wall in no time at all.

When I got to Vancouver, my father came out to visit. He had made an oath that he wouldn't take a drink. But he came to Vancouver, and we won 12 of the 13 games when he was there. Cedric would take my father into the dressing room and give him a beer. You couldn't sell beer in the stadium that year. My father would have a couple too many, and he'd come into the clubhouse. I'd say, "You been having beer?" He said, "Oh, yeah." I said, "What about the oath?" He said, "Oh, no, only in the United States." Cedric kept him there because we had had that winning streak. Finally we sent him back home to Pennsylvania, where he kept his word.

When I was managing the northern division team in the All-Star Game in the Coast League at Vancouver, I switched my outfielders during the game to keep everybody happy. Vada Pinson, from Seattle, and Barry Shetrone, from my Vancouver club, were on the team. They were both outstanding center fielders. So I started one in center and the other one in right field. The next inning I switched them, and so forth, alternating throughout the game. I didn't favor either one of them because they were both outstanding. I'd never seen it done before, so who knows? I might have been the first to shuttle outfielders in an All-Star Game. Many years later, Pinson, who went on to have a fine career mainly with Cincinnati, told me how much he appreciated that.

Back of the first base dugout in Vancouver, there would be some of the most beautiful gals of all descriptions there, a covey of gorgeous women. These were wives or girlfriends of the visiting club, or women they'd put on the pass list. If the women were there, my coaches and I knew it would be a fast game. "We've got it tonight. This'll be a fast game," Spider Jorgensen would say. Sure enough, we'd play the game in a hour and forty-five minutes or an hour and forty minutes or so, and off they'd go. Everybody on the visiting team was in a hurry to hit the nightclubs and the good eating places after the games. And we'd win.

Paul Richards invited me down to Scottsdale for spring training. He'd been sort of following my career. He ran a real good camp. He wanted his players all to be moving, nobody sitting around, nobody standing around. Paul was a genius as a manager. He did so many things way ahead of everybody. He ran a good organization, and he knew ballplayers. He was excellent with pitchers, probably one of the best pitching coaches I've ever seen. He could smooth a guy out in ten minutes. I learned a lot from him. When I was managing in spring training, I wouldn't let the guys stand around and talk to each other in the outfield. You had to have ten yards of space around you. Everybody thought that I was a real SOB for doing that. Richards was much the same way. He said, "I don't want two guys together. Heck, they'll be talking about women, talking about where they're going to go drink and everything. I don't want them to talk. Let them do that on their own time. This time is mine." I used that philosophy all the years that I managed.

One day at camp, Richards told me to hit fly balls to a group of outfielders, Dave Nicholson, Bob Nieman, and Floyd Robinson. They had a bunch of outfielders. And they had some guys from the lower leagues. I asked, "Well, for how long?" That was the wrong thing to say, and he just gave me that stare like only Paul Richards could give you. Lum Harris, one of Richards's coaches, came and gave me some advice: "You don't ever ask Paul Richards how long you want him to do something. Don't ever ask him how long. He'll keep us here till dark." So I started hitting fly balls. I kept hitting them and hitting them, and this went on for three or four, maybe five, hours. I had blisters on both hands. This was early in the spring, and I wasn't used to the roughness of the bat yet. Bob Nieman came in after a while, and I said, "Where are you going?" He said, "I quit." I said, "If all you guys quit first, then I can quit too." They said, "So why don't you quit?" I said, "Hell, no, I ain't going to quit." Bob said, "You go tell number 12, that long-legged SOB, that I've had enough." I said, "Oh, no, Bob, you go tell him. I'm not your messenger boy." Every time he'd see me later on, I'd say, "I'm not your messenger boy." We carried that on. He was a fine ballplayer. He could hit. He wasn't very speedy and didn't run very well, but when he got to the ball he would catch it. But I won over Paul Richards that day. I was one of his fair-haired boys then.

One spring training with Vancouver, I had Pat Gillick on the squad. He was a pitcher trying to make the team. I would have our pitchers run in the outfield during the game, setting the stints according to when the pitchers pitched in the games. Usually I told the pitchers to run until I told them to stop. Because my coach, Spider Jorgensen, was a player-coach and was trying to get in shape for the team, I was often running the whole practice myself. One day I forgot Pat was running in the outfield. I went into the clubhouse after the workout, showered, and shaved. Only then did I have the nagging sense that I had forgotten something. Sure enough, Gillick was still running. His father, a sheriff, had told him always to obey his manager. I waved him in. Later on Pat became a fine general manager in the big leagues.

One game we were playing in Seattle, and Lefty O'Doul was their manager. I had always been a great admirer of Lefty. I thought he was one of the greatest managers I'd ever seen. This game there were a couple of young guys, seventeen, eighteen years old, giving me heck from the third base area, which was real close to the coaching area. Lefty was laughing. He looked up and told the boys to give me a good going-over. After one of the innings, I walked over there, and they were still giving it to me pretty good. I said, "You two guys be careful who you're talking to because I played here seventeen years ago, so I may be your daddy." They didn't know what to say to that. I got the biggest roar out of the fans, women and everybody. Those two young guys slipped away. Lefty O'Doul told me that was the greatest comeback he'd ever heard. Whenever he'd see me again that summer and later, he make me tell it again.

One day in Vancouver, I had the occasion of a lady walking into the clubhouse. The door opened right under the grandstand. It wasn't a big ballpark, so our clubhouse was closer to the big part of the grandstand. I had dressed real early one Sunday afternoon and was standing outside the clubhouse, when she walked by. This lady, who was in her mid-twenties and probably had had a beer or two, asked me where was the ladies restroom. I said right there, and I pointed to our clubhouse door, which had nothing on it. She opened the door and went busting in there. I grabbed the door and went in a ways to watch her, as she walked around the clubhouse with all these guys in the nude. She came out with the damnedest shocked look on her face that I had ever seen. I kind of slid away from her, because I didn't want her to get me. I tell you she was just in a state of shock. I don't think she had ever walked in a locker room before. I'm sure she had opportunities to tell that story at the ladies circle club a time or two. The players just laughed and kidded me about relaxing the clubhouse rules.

I saw a cricket match in Vancouver one time at the ballpark, and I was amazed at the abilities required by that game. I had thought it was just a bunch of dandies playing in white pants and white shoes and a polo shirt. But it took quite a bit of skill. I tried it, and I was amazed. Hey, I thought, this is not as easy as it looks. André Rodgers, who was with Phoenix then, and later was my shortstop with the Cubs, was from the Bahamas, and he knew how to play cricket. He was in that match. But you can see why Americans like baseball better. They were looking for action, and baseball was giving the action, the pitcher throwing a fastball, the catcher catching a fastball, the runner running the bases, the batter trying to hit the ball, and then hitting the ball and running to first base. Everything was action, action, action, and people like that.

Of course, I saw some great fielding plays, but probably none better than one by Marion Fricano. Marion was pitching for Seattle in the Coast League, and we had the bases loaded against him one game. George Bamberger, our pitcher, was at the plate, and I put on the safety squeeze. Fricano made the greatest fielding play by a pitcher I have ever witnessed in my baseball days. George laid a perfect bunt down the first base side, about three feet inside the line. Marion fielded the ball before George could pass by the ball, tagged George as he was going to first base, came in and dove toward home plate at the runner, and tagged him out too. It was the greatest combination of fielding plays I'd ever seen. I'd like to see it again sometime, but I don't think I ever will.

And there were some crazy moments with the Vancouver club, such as when Bob DiPietro tried to catch a ball in Portland. DiPietro was kind of a funny, lighthearted guy, but he was a pretty good ballplayer. We were playing up at Oregon, on the way back to Vancouver, and he was in right field. One of my guys hit the ball out there to right field. The fences were about twenty-five feet high, old wooden plank fences. It was lumber country up there. DiPietro went back and jumped up to catch the ball, but he got his hands in between the boards and his fingers got stuck there. There he was, up on his tiptoes, and the ball was lying there, and the runners were circling the bases. You could hear him hollering all the way to the dugout, "Help me! Help me! Help me!" He was mad at the umpire. He thought that the hitter should have gotten only a base hit, instead of a home run, because of the injury.

The Vancouver years marked my first experience with plane travel. It was great and quick. But it took away the camaraderie of your ball club. The planes changed the mode of travel and changed the chemistry of a baseball club. There was no closeness. You didn't talk baseball very much. You didn't get to know your players well. You didn't get to know them personally. You weren't a family, as such, on the plane, because you sat with one guy and you couldn't get up and wander around. It was quick, but as soon as the plane landed, the players would scatter. They'd either have a bus to pick you up, or else you'd take cabs to the hotel. Then you wouldn't see the guys until you went to the ballpark. When a game was over, they'd scatter again.

When I was with the Vancouver club, we played quite a few games with college teams, which were getting good by then. We played the University of Southern California and UCLA, and we played Pasadena Junior College too, or somebody like that. The college guys coming up brought some changes to the game. Some of the college guys had been taught by coaches who weren't professional coaches. A lot of college and high school coaches had played professional baseball, but many were amateurs. You had to teach these college players the fundamentals of professional baseball. I always tried to teach the major league way. Joe McCarthy said it best, I think: "There's only one way, and that's the major league way. You make one mistake, maybe two, you're gone. There are no maybes." I had been up there long enough. I had kept my eyes and ears open, and I listened to them, so I pretty well knew what it took. I had difficulty with the college players. They had their minds set on the way they wanted to play. Not all of them were problems though. Bill Renna, from Santa Clara College, was great, one of the finest players I had enjoyed handling. But something changed. The college athlete would come out mostly thinking he knew it all already. It was tough on some of those guys. They didn't want to run, and, boy, I was a Simon Legree on running. Occasionally you got a college guy who wanted to learn. He was smart enough now to realize that perhaps his coach wasn't a professional and wasn't teaching professional techniques.

Down the trails of baseball—I can laugh at this now—every baseball guy was going to get rich somehow, real quickly. Sometimes you stepped out of your element. You were better off just sticking to what you knew best: baseball. While I was in Vancouver, a guy came around the ballpark with a timber deal he was promoting. There's a great amount of timber in that part of the country. He came by, and he got my ear and started in about this timber deal. He had half a section of timber available. All I had to do was go up there and just start timbering it out. He said there were a lot of lumbermen up there, guys that you could hire on a percentage basis. Boy, he made this look good, so I asked him, "Well, what's it take to get in?" That was the wrong question to ask. He said, "Well, usually I like to get one man at $1,000." I says, "Well, I'm kind of interested," and he brought it down to $750, seeing as I was the manager of the Vancouver ball club. So

I gave him the $750, and he wrote out an official agreement and everything else. I went home and told my wife. A couple days later, we drove up to see the claim. I found out where it was, about sixty miles from Vancouver up along the coast. We got in the car and drove up there through God's country. We stopped at the ranger's station for directions. I walked in there and introduced myself. They knew me as the Mounties' manager, because they'd listened to the games. The ranger asked, "What are you up here for, Charlie?" "Well, I'm in a little timber deal." He said, "Oh, no." Then the other ranger there said, "Charlie, you know, that the timber deal . . ." I said, "Well, while I'm here, show it to me." He took a pair of binoculars, and we walked up on a little rise, and over there was the timber. God put that timber there, and only God was going to get it out. It was the darndest thing. I asked, "How many guys have fallen?" The ranger said, "He makes a thousand dollars just every once in a while on this thing. Did he get you?" I said, "Yes." So I'm no longer a big timber baron. I had to swallow the loss. I tried to sell the claims, but there were no takers. Once, later, I saw the guy who sold it to me, but he ran the other way when he saw me coming after him.

One winter in Vancouver, in the off-season, I sold investments for Investors Syndicate of Canada, an investment company that was based in Calgary, somewhere up there in Canada, but they also had an office in Minneapolis. I had had the good fortune to have good clubs, and I was well-known. You kind of take advantage of it in the sense that you use your popularity. I sold a one-hundred-thousand-dollar savings certificate, which was based on a twenty-year term. I received cash for it. That was unheard of. The buyer had sold his importing-exporting business and he was retiring. He wanted to do something for his trusted employee, so he bought this certificate for him. The president of Investors Syndicate of Canada flew out to Vancouver to find out who was this salesman that sold it. It had never been done before. But I did very well at that. I kind of wish I'd stayed with it, but we left Vancouver, coming back to the States.

I had three marvelous years in Vancouver. My family loved it. We had three good ball clubs. The Mounties finished second in 1957, third in 1958, and second in 1959. We drew nearly eight hundred thousand people over those three years with only an eight-thousand-seat stadium. It was just wonderful. But then Cedric decided to leave. His wife, who was British, was about to lose her landed immigrant status in Canada. I didn't want to stay with Cedric gone. Cedric took a position over with Seattle. He decided to change managers at Seattle and contacted me about taking the job. But I had already gone to the baseball winter meetings in St. Petersburg and had agreed to take the Denver position. He got to me too late, just by a day, if I recall right. This was too bad, because Cedric and I worked well together. For a guy who never played baseball, he was probably one of the best judges of baseball talent around. Eight years later we reunited to put the Kansas City Royals together. For now, though, it was off to Denver.

SEVEN

Mile High, Here We Come

When we left Vancouver after the 1959 season, we decided to move back to Montgomery. We still had our house there, which we had rented out to some nice people. I wasn't sure where I'd be the next year, but I would go to the winter meetings and try to get another managerial job. We waited for the kids to have a break in their school year, and in the latter part of November we left Vancouver. We stopped first at Idaho Falls and then went on to Nebraska. My wife's sister was married and living there. The plan was that I would go down to St. Petersburg for the winter meetings, then fly back to Nebraska and drive us the rest of the way to Montgomery.

While I was at St. Petersburg, I found out that the Detroit Tigers knew all about me and that they had set up a working agreement in Denver. Of course, I knew all the Tigers officials, Rick Ferrell and Jim Campbell, and they said, "Charlie, there's an opening in Denver. Why don't you see Bob Howsam?" I went to Bob and convinced him that I was the man for the job. He asked me, "What are your standards?" I told him I was very demanding. I said, "Bob, my standards are higher than yours. If my standards ever get lower than yours, you can fire me." He said, "Well, all right, you've got the job." I told him about my family and everything, where they were, and that we had a home in Montgomery. He said, "Well, what are you going to do with that?" I said, "Well, I'll probably sell it, or rent it. We've got it rented out now."

I called up my wife in Nebraska, and I said, "Hey, Babe, I got a job, guess where." She said, "You better wait until I tell you that part of the house burned up bad last night." The house in Montgomery had caught on fire, and our neighbors traced us to Nebraska and called to let us know the bad news. She said, "You better go to Montgomery and take a look." I said, "OK." So I went to Montgomery, and, oh gosh, what a sight! This had been a real nice ranch house we had rented for a while and then bought.

It had cork floors and all this magnificent paneling. It was a nice home. We were crazy about it. But anyway, when I went back to take a look, I saw some pictures of the fire on television. The firemen were chopping holes through the roof and actually tried to save it and all of our stuff. The kids in the family we rented the house to had lit some papers in a fireplace, which really wasn't for burning anything, and the woodwork and mahogany venetian blinds had caught on fire. The house was fully furnished with our furniture. Everything was there. We even left clothes. A lot of my baseball memorabilia burned up. I had gloves, autographed balls, caps from all the clubs I'd been with, a couple of uniform shirts. Also a lot of my hunting stuff burned up. I picked up the phone and called my wife. I said, "Babe, there's no need of us coming back." She said, "How bad?" I said. "All that stuff you had in that closet is gone, burned, the floors were warped up, and oh, gosh. What do you want to do?" She said, "Well, where are we going?" I hadn't told her yet about Denver. I was going to surprise her. Finally I said, "We're going to Denver." "Denver?" she said. "Well, that's right out here where we are." I said, "Yeah, stay there and I'll come." So I went right out to Nebraska, and we stayed there a couple more days. Then we headed for Denver. There had been some talk in the late 1940s, right after my year at Bisbee, about my getting the job at Denver, when they were in the Western League. Now I was finally heading for Colorado.

In Denver I received one of the worst introductions you could imagine. It was like Charlie "Who's He?" Metro. They gave my playing record with Detroit, never mentioned Philadelphia, nor one thing about my record as a manager. I had just come off of three successful years in the Pacific Coast League. Instead they dwelled on my major league batting average, .193. Chet Nelson, who worked for the *Rocky Mountain News*, was the one who wrote that. When we became acquainted later on, Chet couldn't stop apologizing. If we were in a bar together, he'd always buy me a drink. But I didn't get a very good reception at first in Denver because of him.

But when I got to spring training at Tiger Town, it was a different story. I left for there a boy and came back a man, if I can use that terminology. I initiated and did some things that they had never seen. I had run my spring trainings for the three years with the Vancouver club. I had run everything. I was the boss, and I had a playing coach, Spider Jorgensen, who was great. I had the respect of all the ballplayers. I treated them like men. In fact, I should never say this, but I helped the ballplayers get better contracts when we were out there.

At spring training, I told quite a few ballplayers they were going to be in the big leagues. They were in my camp at Tiger Town. I told that to Jim

Northrup and to Mickey Stanley, who played for the Tigers for many years in center field and then played shortstop in the World Series against the Cardinals in 1968. I told Mickey Lolich, "You'll be in the big leagues, if I can ever get you in shape." He was kind of roly-poly, but he was great. I loved the guy and wished I'd had him. I never had him on my club. He would imitate me. I used to wear my cap way down low on my forehead in spring training. I wore my pant legs right below my knees. I thought I had big, strong-looking legs in those black socks. At the morning workout, every one of my guys had his cap pulled down, way down over his ears, and his pants rolled way up. A whole bunch of them had a black shoelace through a loop in the pants into the back pocket. I went along with it. I had to. I acted like I was mad, but I wasn't. I had a watch tied with a black shoestring to my belt. I'd say, "All right, you guys, get out there and run for fifteen or twenty minutes." Quite often I'd forget them. One day Lolich came out, and he had a watch on a string, and he was cranking it up, his cap was down, mimicking me. Finally, one day, one of the guys—I think it was Lolich—said, "Haven't we run enough?" I said, "Five more minutes." They went out and ran five more minutes, and I put the watch back in my pocket and forgot about them. Eventually he came up and said, "Let me see that watch." I didn't have any hands on the watch. The next day they all had those black shoestrings on their belt, and when I told them to get out there and run, they looked at their "watches" and held up their fingers like for five minutes. But in that way I got them to do their running. We had a good club, and the running helped us get off to a fast start. When we opened the season up with Dallas and I started running those guys, the pitchers before the game and a lot of hit and run in the game, they'd never seen anything like it. We just shocked them, and we beat them.

When I managed at Triple-A, out in the Coast League and in the American Association, I always had at least three pitchers go nine innings at least three times in spring training, getting ready. I had a five-man rotation. The other two, for various reasons, would go seven innings two or three times. So the pitchers were ready to go, and we'd always get off to a good start. And everybody else would have to play catch-up. That's why maybe I was so successful. At the start of spring training, we'd have intersquad games, and I'd pitch everybody and give everybody a chance. I'd pitch three guys three innings apiece. But I also had a system that a lot of my pitchers liked. I would name three guys to pitch in a ball game, and the first guy would pitch three innings. When he was through, he'd go down to the bullpen with the catcher, and the catcher would call signs as near as he could see the next pitcher pitching three innings. This first pitcher would pitch three innings in the bullpen like a simulated game. Then the second guy would go out and pitch three, and then go down to the bullpen. The last guy would pitch three innings before he went in. So I would get eighteen innings out of three pitchers in a nine-inning ball game. The catcher would face toward the pitcher's mound and toward home plate, and he could pretty much tell if it was a curve ball or a fastball, and he'd give a sign and the pitcher would throw the same thing. The next guy coming in, for his three innings—the fourth, fifth, and sixth—would just warm up. Sometimes the guy out on the mound would have a heck of a time and make sixty pitches, and the guy warming up would do the same. He'd make sixty pitches too. I was getting endurance and arm strength from all the pitching staff. I don't know that anybody's ever done that. At least I've never seen it.

When I was at Tiger Town, back with Denver in the early 1960s, Jim Campbell was the Detroit general manager. He was a fine guy. He would have been a good commissioner of baseball. He was a great baseball man. But he had a rule there at spring training that everybody had to do duty. We had two-story barracks. We had the mess hall left over from the training base days. We had an indoor hangar where we took the ballplayers when it rained, and we'd set up a batting cage in there. But I had to do duty. Now I thought this was almost beneath me then. I'd been a Triple-A manager! "Oh, no," Jim said, "You are no better than Joe Gordon." Everybody had to do duty, so I did.

The food was great at Tiger Town. Mel Murdock, who was a chef up in one of the big hotels in Detroit, would come down to spring training and do the cooking. He was a master chef, and he was a baseball fan. The food was terrific. We had about five or six or seven clubs, Triple-A clubs, Single-A clubs, B, C, D, quite a bunch of ballplayers. This mess hall was on the military model. We'd stand in line. The guy who did the duty had to see that players couldn't have seconds until everybody went through. Then you could have all you wanted. The food was desserts and pies and Jell-O and puddings. And plenty of milk. One time I decided to have a little fun, so I spread a rumor quietly that there was saltpeter in the Jell-O. Nobody would take the Jell-O. Mel came out and said, "What's the matter with the Jell-O?" "I don't know, Mel," I said. He tasted it, and it was OK. I tasted it and said, "I don't see anything wrong." He just scratched his head. So the next time he made a pudding with vanilla wafers, which was superb, I did the same thing. The next time I said the beans had the saltpeter. They must have caught onto me, because they wouldn't let me stand duty anymore after that.

The players still had a curfew at Tiger Town. But every once in a while, when I had Triple-A clubs, my rule was that if you're going to stay out a little late Saturday night or something, just leave a message on my bed that you're going to stay out. This was so they didn't catch the guy out way late and fine the heck out of him. Because the guy on duty at night would report, and if it was my ballplayer on the Triple-A club, then I had to take action. Some Saturday nights, I'd have about fifteen notes on my bunk bed. I'd say, "Oh, oh, I can't keep tab of these guys." I'd carry the notes around in my pocket, and then the next day, I'd put those guys through a pretty good workout. You tried to respect the players' needs and wishes and treat them as adults. You didn't want spring training to be like a compound or some darn thing. At Tiger Town, I thought we handled it pretty well.

When I was on duty, I had to wake the guys up in the morning and close things down at night. I'd put the music on over the loudspeaker in the morning and wake them up at 7:00 A.M.. At night I'd have to stay up till 11:00 P.M.. Everybody did that. You had to check rooms and everything. You had to announce the time every thirty minutes. In the evening you'd take the messages at the office for the ballplayers, long distance calls and everything. You played the music all evening. I was a Country and Western guy, so I'd put on Ferlin Husky's "On the Wings of a Snow White Dove." I liked that song, so I played it all night. It went out over the loudspeaker in the barracks and everything. Oh, they got tired of "Snow White Dove." You could hear them throwing things and cussing. The guys would get mad at me, and somebody swiped the record. I went out and bought six more copies and hid them. Sometimes I had to do duty twice a week, if somebody finagled me into it, and I'd play that record. If they'd break it, I'd grab another and keep playing it. Finally all the records disappeared, and I talked to Jim Campbell about it. I said, "Jim, you know those kids are breaking those records and that's company property. You ought to do something about it." He said, "Yeah, yeah, I will." But I think maybe Jim was the guy who stole all the records.

Down at Tiger Town, these kids would come down to spring training and get blisters on their feet, athlete's foot, and, oh, gosh, bunions, just the worst-looking things. Now your legs and feet had to be good, so in the clubhouse we had these three-foot-square trays that the army cooked with, full of foot powder and benzoin, three or four inches deep. The kids would come out of the shower and put their feet in the benzoin and then the powder. I thought, aw, heck, I'll have some fun with this. So I bought a big can of molasses, which was the color of the benzoin. I went out to the clubhouse early and poured it in the benzoin tray. They came out of the showers later and put their feet right in the molasses and then in the foot powder. Oh, were they mad, but laughing at the same time! Nobody accused me of that because our dressing room was right there close. I wish I could have gotten them all. We had a lot of fun.

In spring training, you always played like heck until it was cut-down day. You always carried some extra players, and then you'd cut some. As soon as you cut those, you had let-down with the guys who made your club. I don't know why, but every club that I ever had, and everybody else had the same problem. You cut down, you had let-down. Then you had to work them back up, and sometimes you'd have a hard job doing that. Other times they'd come around quick. We had that with Denver. You had to coax some guys along. One guy, Phil Regan, wanted to drive his family to Dallas for the season opener. I agreed but told him he better be there. He was, and then he wanted to drive to Denver. I said, "You better be there." I converted Phil Regan into a relief pitcher. He didn't want to be a relief pitcher; he wanted to be a starter. I said, "Phil, if you relieve in one month ten times, you will learn more in those ten relief appearances than you will in all your pitching, because I'm bringing you in with the bases loaded and nobody out." I guess I convinced him. He went twenty-one and a third or two-thirds innings without allowing a run, when he came in. He was phenomenal. He proved me right. He was called "The Vulture" in the big leagues, where he did a tremendous job. He'd go in there and just scarf up that win or save. I brought him in in every conceivable type of situation. I like to think that I had a great hand in making him a relief pitcher.

I had a reputation as a real tough and demanding manager. I don't think I was tough, but I was demanding. I never wanted a ballplayer to ever leave me and say I didn't try to help him, so the players had to do the things I wanted them to do, and I wasn't teaching wrong things. I was a great conditioner. A pitcher with the Denver Bears one year was interviewed, and one of the writers asked him about me, "Is Charlie Metro as tough as they say he is? Is he as mean as they say he is?" The pitcher said, "I don't know about that. He sure has one redeeming feature." The writer asked, "What is that?" My guy said, "I don't know. He must have one redeeming feature."

At Denver I had a ballplayer who was a little on the hard-headed side. He rebelled at most everything I wanted a ballplayer to do. One day he said something, and it flared up. He challenged me to a fight, and I accepted it. I said, "I'll meet you in the clubhouse tomorrow at 3:00." The next afternoon at 3:00, he showed up. I was sitting in my office, and he came in and said, "I'm ready." He had a pair of leather gloves on, with the fingers cut off. I said, "What do you have there?" He said, "Well, I don't want to hurt my hands." I said, "Well, what do you have under there?" He had wrapped tin foil around his hands. Boy, that was a lethal weapon. It'd be like getting hit with a brick. I said, "Are you going to use that?" He said, "You're darn right!" So I reached over and got a fungo bat. He said, "What are you doing?" I said, "You got that and I got the fungo. You go ahead and make your first move. I'm going to use this." He said, "Would you hit me with that?" I said, "Would you punch me with those gloves like that?" He said, "Yeah." I said, "Well, I'll hit you with this, right across the face." He said, "You would?" I said, "You're darn right!" So he sat there and said, "Well, let's talk about this." So we talked, and I explained to him that I couldn't have one guy always refusing to do what I wanted. He came around to my way of thinking. We shook hands, and the guy turned out to be one hell of a ballplayer for me. Later he became a teacher in Philadelphia, and he looked me up years later when I came in with a ball club. We went out to dinner, and he kept me out till 3:00 in the morning, reminiscing, telling me what a fine thing I had done to straighten him out. He was a very successful high school teacher. I felt real good about that, thinking how close I came to perhaps getting whipped myself and maybe ruining a young man.

I wouldn't let my catcher stand in the on-deck circle with his shin guards on with two outs. I made him take them off. Joe Cronin happened to be in the stands in Denver one game when I made Mike Roarke take his shin guards *off.* After the game, Joe said, "Charlie, why make that catcher stand up there with his shin guards off? He ought to have his shin guards on to speed up the game." I said, "I don't want the negative appearance. If he's got his shin guards off, he's more interested in getting a hit rather than being ready to catch the next inning. He's really giving the impression that we're not going to make the third out." Joe hadn't thought about that. I always had the second catcher, as soon as we made the third out, go out and warm up the pitcher. By that time, the catcher was ready to go. It wasn't a time-consuming thing.

Every once in a while, you get to be a genius when you're a manager. We were playing Louisville in Denver, and a banker friend of mine came down from Montana to see us. I left him some tickets. The banker didn't want to see the game, because it wasn't too good, but my friend Eddie Newman said, "Well, Charlie will show you something in this ball game." Louisville got 3 runs in the first inning. Before our turn at bat, I looked down the grandstand and saw Eddie coming with this friend. They sat down, and he threw his palms up as if to say, "What's this? Three to nothing, and it's just the first inning?" I just gave him a big hello salute. Our first two guys made out, but the third guy, Steve Boros, hit the ball out of the park. I shook hands with him as he came past third, and I turned around to look at the crowd. The next batter, Jim McDaniel, also hit the ball out of the ballpark, making the score 3–2. I strutted around a little more. Then the next guy, Bo Osborne, hit one out too. Boy, you should have seen me putting it on! But would you believe it, the next guy came up—it was Ozzie Virgil—and he hit one out! Now we were leading them, 4–3 in the first inning. Finally, Coot Veal, our shortstop, who didn't hit a home run all year, hit one up against the wall, but the Louisville guy caught it. That would have been something! Five in a row. We won the ball game in the bottom of the ninth inning, 11–10. We had the bases loaded with one out, the score tied at 10 each. The batter hit a little dribbler back to the pitcher. He threw to first base with the winning run going across the plate. What a smart manager I was! I got us into position to win the ball game on a mental mistake. We had really good clubs the two years I was at Denver. I had managed against Ralph Houk when he was at Denver and I was at Charleston. Ralph was a pretty good manager. He had a tough reputation. He had been a major in the Battle of the Bulge. He wouldn't take anything from anybody. Later I would always kid Ralph, when he was always talking about the Yankee ballplayers and the Yankees ball club here in Denver, about who won the first Triple-A pennant in Denver. It wasn't Ralph Houk. It was me, with the 1960 Bears club. Louisville beat us in the playoffs. Then in 1961, we finished third, and again the Louisville club knocked us off in the playoffs.

On those clubs we had Bo Osborne. He had been with me in Montgomery in 1953, when I had that terrible team. He had just been signed by the Tigers and had joined the club as a seventeen-year-old. He was so green that he didn't know that he had to chase the ball if somebody threw it over his head. Bo would have been a good football player. In Denver, when the Broncos were a new franchise, Bo outpunted their punter, kicking in baseball spikes, just goofing around! But they wouldn't let you play two sports then, or else he would have made a good punter. He had a fine year for us in 1960. In fact he darn near won the Triple Crown. He won the batting championship and the home run title, and he tied for the RBI lead with Steve Boros, our third baseman. Bo was an excellent first baseman and a tremendous base runner. He never made a mistake all year. But people got down on him because he was a big, heavyset guy. Here he was, winning the batting title and the home run title and tying for the RBI title in Triple-A, an excellent fielder and an excellent base runner, and a wonderful guy. But he weighed about 230 pounds. Everybody said he was too fat. Eddie Stanky, who wasn't one of my favorite guys, came through town scouting for somebody and said, "Who's that water buffalo out on first base?" I said,

"That 'water buffalo' is going to win the Triple Crown." Stanky said, "Aw, he's too fat. What are you paying him?" I said, "We're not paying him by the pound." When Bo moved up to Detroit, unfortunately, the guy that he was going to try to beat out was Norm Cash. Cash won the American League batting title in 1961. Detroit tried to make an outfielder out of Bo, so they wanted him to lose weight. He went down to a 195 pounds , and that's what he hit, .195. I thought if he'd gone with a different club—he couldn't make Detroit, unfortunately—he would've been a fine big league ballplayer. He struck out occasionally, not overly much, but he could hit, could put the ball in play. He would have been a great asset. Later I hired Bo as a scout for the Royals.

I'd like to tell the story about this little third baseman we had in 1961. During spring training, I'd always hit infield to test the guys out. I wanted to see how good they were. At Tiger Town, we had nice dirt on the clay base, but the wind would blow a lot of the dirt off. So then the infielders were fielding ground balls on clay, and that's tough. I had four third basemen, three Triple-A guys and this other kid, a new kid from a B league. So I started hitting to these guys. The first guy complained that it was too rough, that it was beneath him to have to field in such conditions. I went to the next guy, and as I was hitting ground balls to him, the ball hit him above the eye, gave him a shiner, and split his eyebrow a little bit. Seeing that, the next guy wasn't going to field on this ground either. So I asked this other kid from the B league to step in there, and pretty soon he was stopping everything I hit at him. The balls were bouncing off his chest, and he'd field this way and that way. He got my attention. I said, "Hey, do you think you can make my club in Denver?" He said, "Sure." I said, "You want this job?" He said, "Yes, sir." I said, "Why don't you take it, run these guys off?" He ran them off. Don Wert made the club and won the batting championship on his last swing of the bat, a base hit to right field. When Don was fighting for the batting championship toward the end of the season, the official scorer, Frank Haraway, called an error on a ball Don hit. Everybody on the bench thought it was a base hit, and they gave Frank holy heck, waving at him and everything else. But Frank stood his ground. Don won anyway. He was neck and neck with a guy playing for Louisville, and Don could have sat down and waited to hear how that guy did. But he wouldn't sit out. He said, "Heck, no, I don't want to sit out. Ted Williams didn't sit out when he hit .406." Years later I told that story to Ted, and he just beamed. Wert went up with Detroit the next year and spent ten years in the big leagues. He was a superb fielder. Don had a gadget to warm up the hitter before he went up to hit. It was like a propeller with a baseball on either side and was mounted on a stand. You'd stand there and hit that propeller, and it'd go round and round. You'd try to hit the baseball as it was moving. I had to get permission from the umpire to use the contraption, because a visiting manager figured that this gave an advantage to my club. I said, "Well, we'll move it over there for them, when they're hitting, if they want it." They refused it. But Don Wert won the batting championship with that thing.

The previous year, I had asked Jake Wood, the second baseman, the same question. I said, "Do you think you can make my club?" He said, "Yes, sir," and he ran somebody right off of the club. They criticized us quite badly about Jake because he was a very slow starter, but then he would catch fire. For the first month of the season, oh, gosh, he looked like he ought to have been playing with the girls instead of the big leagues, or on the sandlots somewhere. But I could see he was a diamond in the rough. Every time I got a call from the front office at Detroit, they would ask, "What about Jake Wood?" They wanted to move him elsewhere and send me somebody else. Finally I had to say, "Forget Jake Wood. He's going to stay on the ball club. Leave him alone. He's going to be all right." I fought the Tigers organization not to give up on him. Then he started hitting, and he carried the ball club. He was a fine ballplayer. He could run like heck. He stole quite a few bases for us at Denver. I'd give him the steal sign. I loved to steal and hit, instead of hit and run. He did it seven times that year, and nobody made much note about it. If a guy hit a ground ball through the middle and Jake was rounding second and heading for third, I never stopped him. I didn't wave or windmill my arms. I'd just stop a guy. When Jake saw that there was no stop sign—I had my hands in my pockets or in my belt loop, just nonchalant—he'd head for home. He scored from first base seven times on a cleanly handled base hit to the outfield. I loved that about Jake.

Jake Wood had one problem, though. He wouldn't eat. I don't know what kind of a background he came from, if he was saving his money for something or if it was anorexia, but he wouldn't eat. He'd take meal money and everything, but he just wasn't eating. I understand he did that up in the big leagues too. Because Jake was black, he ran into some segregation problems. We had a confrontation with a hotel over breakfast one day. I was sitting in the coffee shop, having breakfast and reading the paper. Jake came in, and the hostess wouldn't serve him. I motioned him over to my table and told him to sit down. The waitress wasn't going to serve him. I said, "What do you want, Jake?" He told me what he wanted, and I ordered two orders of bacon and eggs and milk and toast and jelly. I made them serve him. It was tough, what Jake and the other blacks had to go through. I got in trouble a time or two, but I insisted on equal treatment.

I was also crazy about Bubba Morton. I had him for a while down at Terre Haute and Idaho Falls. Then he joined us at Denver while I was the manager. I was in his corner. He was a good ballplayer. He was one of the finest all-around base runners I'd ever seen. He could steal a base. He never made a mistake. He took the fullest advantage of any little mistake an outfielder or infielder made on a ground ball or a base hit. Bubba would take the biggest lead I've ever seen. Several times with Denver, Bubba would be on third base and I'd say, "Bubba, let's see how far down the line you can go and get back safely." His eyes would get big, and I'd say, "That's about right." At one time, I thought he was shaking hands with the hitter, he was so far, and then he came back with no play on him. But he, too, had a little quirk. He thought everybody in the world was against him, but that wasn't the case. He could have been a pretty good outfielder, but he let this resentment stuff get in the way. I was fond of him. The only reason I took him out was because he had the lowest batting average among our outfielders. Bubba got furious with me one day. Here he was hitting .340 or .345 and playing regularly, and I took him out. I just thought I'd give him a rest, but he didn't want a rest. It almost became a shouting match. Finally he said, "Ah, you don't like us Negroes. You don't like us Negro ballplayers." I said, "Just a minute. Sit down, Bubba. Calm down and sit down. This is why I'm doing this. I looked in the paper this morning, and I see where Ozzie Virgil is hitting .400, and George Alusik is hitting .380, and Jim McDaniel is hitting .375, and you're hitting .345. You're the low man, so I'm giving you a day of rest." He accepted that. When the Tigers took up Ozzie, Bubba got to play every day. He was an everyday sort of ballplayer. I understand now he's up in the Pacific Northwest somewhere. Whatever he's doing, I'm sure he's highly successful.

Ozzie Virgil Sr. was from the Dominican Republic. He came to my ball club at Denver, and then Detroit picked him up. He had a fantastic record for us. Ozzie was hitting about .400, and in a part-time role. I played him everywhere—third, second, outfield. He had 77 hits and 55 runs batted in, and was batting .381, when they took him up to the big leagues. I was crazy about him. He did everything well. Later, when I was putting together the Kansas City Royals, I was going to draft him as a player-coach out of the Giants organization, where he was with their Triple-A club, but I spoke up out loud. Tom Sheehan, a scout and front office guy for the Giants, overheard me, so they put him on the big league club and protected him.

Mike Roarke was my right-hand man at Denver. He had played at Boston College, and somehow he knew John F. Kennedy. Mike was an absolutely great handler of pitchers. He could bring a pitcher through a tough jam.

He could nurse a guy through when a guy didn't have too much stuff. He was fabulous with that. We had a sign to let me know the pitcher was losing his stuff—the catcher would toss a handful of dirt toward me, and I'd pick up a handful of dirt and toss it to let him know that I knew and would watch him. Sometimes I'd give a guy an extra pitch or two to see if he was having a short lapse. Other times I'd walk out there and make the change. Mike Roarke was the pitcher's friend, and he turned out to be one heck of a good pitching coach for many years on the major league level. He managed once or twice, and I don't know why he didn't pursue it more or whether he didn't get opportunities. Mike was a fine person. I can't understand why he couldn't hit. Every time I looked at him, I saw myself reflected in him. He could catch, receive, throw. For a big man, he could run. He had occasional power. He was kind of like I was. I could do everything but hit for the average. Mike was the same way. I couldn't understand why, because he had been a tremendous athlete in college.

Coot Veal was a shortstop, out of Macon, Georgia, with the Detroit Tigers organization. He was a skinny guy. He rated with the best fielders I'd ever seen. He wasn't much of a hitter, but he turned out to be a good baseball player. He'd get the most out of a time at bat. He could advance the runner, squeeze a bunt, sacrifice the guy over, hit and run. He did all those things. He fancied himself a home run hitter, but his best shot was a deep fly ball to short left field. I had him when he was a freshman out of college. He was also a fine basketball player. He should have been up in the big leagues for many years.

I had Bob "Buck" Rodgers—at Denver as a catcher in 1960—up early to let him see what it was all about, and then we sent him down to Birmingham to catch regularly. He was a great prospect, but the organization felt they were pushing him too much, and because we had Mike Roarke, Bob wasn't going to catch as much as he should, so we sent him down. He was catching a game for me one day at Denver, and he was chewing gum. I could see him chewing gum and that mask jumping up and down and getting in his way. I said, "How in the hell can you concentrate on the hitter, the pitcher, and work these hitters chewing gum? Spit it out!" So, many years later, while I was scouting in Arizona and Buck Rodgers was the manager of the California Angels, I walked out early before a spring training game, and he saw me and came over. He put out his hand to shake hands, and he said, "Don't chew gum. You can't chew gum and catch at the same time." He remembered it. I wonder if he passed that on to any of his own catchers.

George Alusik was a fine minor league ballplayer. He had a real good year with our club at Denver in 1960. He played right field. He had a major league arm and good power and did well for us at Denver. Although he was a good guy in the clutch, he had only one gait and he could never get out of that speed. Everybody thought he was lazy, but he wasn't. He never made mistakes throwing to wrong bases from the outfield. He wasn't a fast runner, but he was steady. I believe this mannerism, the fact that he looked like he was never putting out full tilt, was what kept him back in the minors. Ossie Alvarez finished up the season with us at Denver. He was a nice little ballplayer. He loved everything I did. He built up my confidence and my ego. I'll tell you, if you have a ballplayer like that on your ball club once in a while, it's great. I loved the guy. I said, "Ossie Alvarez, what are you trying to do, get a job or something?" And he laughed like heck. He was always jacking me up when I needed a little pat on the back.

Tony Bartirome was an absolute delight. I had Bo Osborne as a first baseman, and Tony had been there the year before. Tony was a good-fielding, little first baseman, not a very big guy. He was a left-handed hitter and thrower and was one of the most positive guys I've ever seen. I kept him on the ball club because he was great for the club. I regret one thing—I wanted to play him at shortstop or second base, because he was a left-hander, and I wanted to shake up things. I was hoping one of my infielders would catch a cold sometime so I could put him in there. I'd come in from the coaching box line when we were behind, and Tony would say, "Don't worry, Skip. A couple of hits, a couple of bases on balls and a choke-up play, and we got 4 runs. We'll get them." That was his idea of a rally! He became a fine trainer with the Pittsburgh Pirates for many years. If I could pattern a ball club with guys as positive as he was, I think I'd send a wire to the other managers: "Forget first place." What a guy to have on a club!

Jim Baumer was one of the big bonus kids from out in California. He played for us in Denver in 1961 and was a fine second baseman. One time at spring training at Tiger Town, I had an episode with Jim about curfew. They locked the barracks where the players slept. The night watchman would take names and get the numbers, where they were and what rooms they went in. This one night, they saw me in the office and snuck around. The night watchman came up and said, "They're out there sneaking around." I said, "Who?" He said, "Your ballplayers. I know they're your ballplayers on the Denver club." I didn't pay much attention to him, but I understand that Jim Baumer was one of them, along with a couple of others, and that they all climbed in a couple of the old planes and slept there all night long. Jim went up to the majors with Cincinnati, and then he went into the front office with the Phillies. He was a scouting director of minor leagues, or something like that. He was a good baseball man. I'd see him quite often.

Jerry Casale has given me many a sleepless night. I rarely second-guessed myself in baseball, but I did on him. He was pitching the final game of the playoffs for us against Louisville in 1961. We were losing 1–0 going into the bottom of the ninth. If we won this ball game, I had a chance to be a big league manager. Jerry was a pretty good hitter. He was a real wild swinger, and he loved to hit! He'd love to hit a ball a long way. We got the bases loaded with two outs, and he was the hitter. He had the bat in his hands, and he was anxious to hit. I can still see him today, eager to hit. Instead I put in Sandy Amoros. I thought to myself, "Well, here's an established big league hitter, left-handed hitter, right-handed pitcher." I took Casale out. I regret that to this day. I should have gone ahead with the guy, and died with him, because he pitched a hell of a ball game. If admitting this is an apology, I hope somebody tells him about it. If I could ever do it again, I would have let him hit. I wouldn't care what anybody else would have said.

Although we were more of a hitting team, we had some good pitching. I told my guys not to worry about the altitude. You pitch, and we will get you a lot of runs. In 1960 the staff had the second-highest ERA in the league, but we won. Ed Donnelly won 17 games, Al Pehanick won 12, and Gordy Seyfried also won 12. Phil Regan won 9 as a reliever. Fred Gladding came up to Denver, and I made a reliever out of him. Later on he became a fine pitching coach. He was a workhorse pitcher, an easygoing, great big, lumbering guy. He would come in and always give you a good effort. He was one you liked to have on the ball club. Harry Perkowski was on the Denver roster when I took over as the manager. Bob Howsam had him as Denver property. Perkowski was a left-handed pitcher, but he was about at the end of the line. He had been in the big leagues, but they sent him down. He was too heavy, but I got him in shape in spring training. He didn't want to run. Oh, gosh, he ran hard as he could for as big as he was, but he turned out to be a pretty good pitcher for us. Joe Grzenda gave me fits. He had tremendous talent, but his head was not on straight. Ron Nischwitz was a pretty good pitcher in 1961. He won 11 games. He went up to Detroit for four years.

Some of the guys who later won the World Series for Detroit in 1968 went through my camp. They were just young guys down there, on the Triple-A rosters, so they went through my camp. Mickey Stanley was one of the finest fielders I had ever seen. I would hit fly balls to Mickey. There were no fences there. I'd hit them on the right-field line, and I'd hit one on the left-field line, and dang if he wouldn't catch the ball! I would have had to hit the ball out of the county for him not to be able to get it. He was a tremendous outfielder, and in the World Series, he played a heck of a shortstop, which didn't surprise me at all because he was a terrific young kid. In fact I drooled when I had him because I wanted to bring him up to Denver. I would have put him in center field and said to heck with everybody else. Dick McAuliffe played for me at Denver. He could hit, but he had that real open stance, and everybody wanted to change him. I said, "What do you want to change him for? He's hitting 300. Leave him alone." Willie Horton was there too. You could see that he was going to be a tremendous hitter. He had a short stroke, as we call it. He was powerful, and he got bigger and stronger as time went on. Surprisingly, at the start he was pretty good outfielder, but I believe weight kind of caught up with him a little bit. Jim Northrup also went through my camp. He was a tremendous ballplayer and turned out to be a pretty good broadcaster with the Tigers. He was one of those guys you looked at and said he was one of those can't-miss guys. He played real well, but I think later on in his career he got a little lazy or something. He should've played longer, maybe fifteen years or so.

During these years in Denver, I got to know some great baseball guys. Harvey Kuenn was a lovable guy. In Tiger Town, I had many occasions to watch him. Harvey was a fine hitter. He was an easygoing sort of guy, and he later managed the Brewers pretty well. He eventually lost a leg. Vern Rapp was my coach at Denver. He was a good baseball man, but his downfall, if you want to call it that, was that he just couldn't handle the press. I think his personality was such that he couldn't make the adjustment. I recommended him to Bob Howsam one time. We were sitting together in the stands in Denver. I said, "There's the best manager in the league." Bob Scheffing was a personal friend and a good manager. He was a pretty good ballplayer when he played. He was a better manager than he was a ballplayer, but you could say that about me too. I admired Bob. I was very disappointed that when he got the Detroit manager's job, and even though I had had those good years at Denver, he didn't ask me to coach, because I think I could have been an asset to the parent club.

Johnny Pesky and I crossed paths and became acquainted when he managed in the Tigers organization. Johnny wound up in Detroit as a player. We were together down in spring training all the time. He managed Victoria in the Texas League. He was in line for a promotion, the Denver job, but I got it instead. Pesky was a fine guy, and he managed and coached for the Red Sox for many years. We didn't dare ask him about the controversial play in the 1946 World Series in which he might have delayed throwing the ball to the plate to get Enos Slaughter. I'm sure he's been asked about that a thousand times. They made a lot of stories and poetry about Pesky:

"Pesky, throw the ball." "Johnny, Johnny, why don't you throw the ball?" I've heard all sorts of versions of that. And I'm sure John has heard enough of it.

Bill Haller was an umpire in spring training in Tiger Town, and I was impressed with his hustle and his willingness to learn. I watched him work, and he was good. Ed Dougherty was president of the American Association at the time, and I told Ed that he ought to try and get this guy for Triple-A. He was a real up-and-coming umpire. Ed called Dewey Soriano when he found out that Bill was scheduled for a B league. They took him from that B league right to Triple-A. Very shortly after that, he went to the big leagues. Bill remembered that I had recommended him, and every time he'd see me, he'd thank me. His brother, Tom, who was a big league catcher, also knew about it and was nice to me.

When we first got to Denver, we rented a house on Cody Court in Lakewood. We liked the city so much that we bought a home on West Eighth, not far from the Lakewood Country Club. We loved the size of the city at that time. There was so much to do in the area. It was convenient for flying anyplace in the country. Sometimes I would have a three- or four-hour layover at Stapleton Airport, and my wife would come get me and I'd go home and check up on things, do some "honey-do's" while I was home. Then we would hustle back to the airport. The kids, of course, went to school in Denver, and our daughter, Elena, graduated from high school at Lakewood. The kids enjoyed Denver thoroughly, and the boys all got into sports. The area had one of the best school sports programs we'd seen. Bud graduated from Lakewood, and Steve and Geoff from Arvada West. Geoff wasn't into sports as much but was a motorcycle enthusiast. He is quite mechanically minded. When I got jobs elsewhere, we decided to keep Denver our home. In February 1963, we put down some firm roots. We bought a little ranch, fifteen acres, outside the city. We loved looking at the mountains, and sometimes when I'd be somewhere else I'd look for the mountains to get my bearings.

When we came to Denver, we made some good friends. I met a man by the name of Merlyn Williams, who worked for the Jefferson County Bank at the time. Merlyn eventually went downtown to Colorado State Bank and became president of the bank. He was very influential in a financial way. He financed our home and a lot of things that I was doing. He was a tremendous baseball fan. One year, I took him to spring training, and I showed him all around the place. He was like a boy with a new toy. I had him as my guest when we were in the World Series with the Dodgers. I had a field pass for him, which allowed him to watch the hitting and everything.

He told me that money couldn't have bought that. They were great friends to us, he and his wife, Margo.

I never pushed my sons into baseball. If they wanted to play, OK. If not, that was OK, too. In fact all three of my sons played a little. But my son Bud was a track star at Lakewood High School near Denver. He was on the relay team and also on the pole vaulting squad with his good friend Nick Kerner. They were two top pole vaulters. One afternoon, Bud came home from school all excited. He said, "Dad, do you know about the new pole they have for pole vaulting?" I said, "No, I don't." He said, "Well, they got a fiberglass pole." I said, "What the heck is that?" I used to do a little pole vaulting when I was a kid in grade school, and the bamboo pole was in vogue then. He said, "This is a fiberglass pole. It's light, and you can get two or three feet higher with it." I kind of brushed it off a little bit, but the next day I went down to the Wilson sporting goods store, which Cliff Buck, who later became an Olympics official, ran. I talked to him about this pole. He didn't have it, but he gave me a brochure about a company in Southern California that did. I went back to the house, picked up the phone, and called. A man answered, and we got to talking, and I said, "Well, do you have these poles?" He said, "Yes." I said, "I'd like to have one for my son, Bud, and his friend in high school." "What does your son weigh?" he asked. I said, "About 145 pounds, and his friend about 148 or 149." He said, "Well, you need this kind of a pole, this length." I think it was fourteen and a half feet or something of that nature. So I ordered one. He said, "By the way, who are you?" I told him my name. He said, "Metro?" I said, "Yes." He said, "Who was your roommate at Texarkana in the East Texas League?" I said, "A guy by the name of Bob Claude Williams." He said, "You're talking to him." We reminisced quite a bit and he said, "Charlie, I'll have that pole freighted to you right quick." It cost me $50. When it finally came, I had it leaning up against the house. Bud came home from school and said, "Dad, what in the world is that tube out there?" I said, "I don't know." He went out, looked, and came in, just yelling as happy as could be. It was a fiberglass pole. He and Nick just out—pole vaulted everybody. They went up to thirteen feet and then to fourteen feet. Nick was a little bit better of the two. He was a year older than my Bud. They broke that one, and I bought them another one for $55, and then they broke that one, so I bought another one for $60. They used those poles in their sophomore, junior, and senior years and parlayed those three poles into full scholarships, Nick Kerner at the University of Colorado and Bud at the University of Wyoming. That was a pretty doggone good investment, a little better than $180 for two full-time athletic scholarships. But it almost got me injured. One day I was at an indoor arena in Golden, and I saw the pole vaulting stuff. I had my suit on, but I grabbed that pole and ran down that runway and cleared eight feet with my shirt and my coat tails flying and everything. I impressed my son, but, boy, I almost killed myself. I landed on both feet wrong, crossed and everything else. It's a good thing they had the sawdust in there, or I'd have been done. You never lose that urge to compete physically.

The black ballplayers had a tough time in the South, when we went to Louisville. In 1960, when I managed the Denver Bears, I was the first Triple-A manager in the American Association to have his black ballplayers stay in the same hotel with the white guys. It was at the Sheraton Seelbach Hotel in Louisville. I had three black players—Ozzie Virgil, Jake Wood, and Bubba Morton—who I had managed briefly at Terre Haute in 1956. When we got to Louisville, I didn't know what arrangements the traveling secretary had made. We got to the hotel, and the three black players started to leave. I said, "Where are you guys going?" They said, "We have to get out of here." I said, "You're staying here." We started to check everybody in, and I said, "Check these guys in." But the clerk refused to let them stay in the room they were registered for. By this time, about everybody was gone. The clerk started giving me some lip. He said, "We don't let Negroes in here." I said, "The hell you don't." He started to say something, and I reached over and grabbed him by the collar and his necktie and jerked him toward me. But he must have pushed some button because a security guard and the police came and hustled me off to jail. To this day, Bob Howsam probably doesn't know that his manager spent that night in jail. But my black players stayed in that hotel. Near this same hotel, I witnessed a protest by blacks against discrimination in the hotel's restaurant. The law enforcement guys broke it up with high-pressure hoses.

Heck, I had black ballplayers out in Vancouver, and they all stayed and flew and ate with the rest of the team. I wasn't going to let it be any different in Louisville. I had seen what Hank Aaron and Frank Robinson and other black ballplayers had gone through when I was managing in the South. I didn't have any negative feelings about the black ballplayers. When I managed, they were my ballplayers and I treated all my players the same way. To me a ballplayer was a ballplayer. If he was good, he was good. I had some black players who didn't play worth a darn, had a lot of ability and wouldn't play worth a darn, and I didn't want them. Then I had ballplayers who had great ability and played great.

As the manager, I got to tell guys when they were called up to the parent club. Sometimes you'd walk in and use a little psychology, put a real distressed look on your face, and say, "I've got some news for you." Sometimes the blood would all drain out of their faces when I told them that. I did that to Ozzie Virgil when I had him at Denver. He was having that excellent season. I called him up and said, "Ozzie, I've got some news for you," with a sour and distressed look on my face. He recoiled and started saying, "Nah, nah, nah." I said, "Now, Ozzie, wait a minute. Just take your time. You're being recalled to Detroit." Man, you could see the relief on his face. It was a joy to tell a ballplayer that he was going up.

Every once in a while, a sportscaster would ask me what I said out on the mound to a pitcher when I would make a visit and the infielders would come in for a conference. I offered to wear a microphone and let them do a live broadcast of what we talked about. I promised we would keep it clean. With some pitchers, we would have had to have one of those bleep buttons. I made that suggestion right here in Denver, but one of the broadcasters thought that it was bush league. Now sometimes they mike the coaches and manager.

I was always trying to get an edge here and there on the opposition. George Freese was playing third base for Houston in 1961, and he would hit us pretty hard. I had a defense planned against him, and I've always had regrets that I never got the perfect situation to spring it on him, when they were beating the heck out of us or we were beating the heck out of them. I was going to move my right fielder and center fielder all the way over to the left field and have all three guys about twenty yards apart. I was going to take the second baseman and put him on the left side of the infield and put the first baseman right over second. In fact, every ballplayer except the pitcher and catcher would be left of second base. I was going to call that my "Deep Freese" defense. I've always regretted not doing it, because I believe I had read about Lou Boudreau and the "Williams Shift." I was always afraid that Freese would bunt, although I really didn't think so, because he was such a fierce competitor. This would have given him a challenge: either he could bunt to first base and make everybody a laughingstock, himself included, or he could try to hit against my "Deep Freese." But I never did it. They might have called me a "revolutionary." The one time I tried it partway, the umpire said I was taking too much time, stalling in the game.

I had quite an experience with a fan at St. Paul, when I was managing the Denver ball club. This guy was sitting back of our dugout, and he was giving me holy heck. He stayed on my case the whole ball game, called me "genius" and "boy wonder" and "handsome." When he said, "You look like Clark Gable," and I'd say something, he'd say, "Yeah, he's dead!" He gave me a roasting like nobody's business. So I said to myself, "I'll fix this guy." Before we played St. Paul again, I went down to the five-and-dime, the Woolworth store, and bought a water pistol. Then I went over to the cosmetics counter and bought some ten-cent perfume. I said, "I'll get this guy." Sure enough, the game started and while I was coaching third base, he started in on me. I took it for an inning or two, but I was laying for him. Then he stood up to shout even louder, because I was not answering him. He was not getting a rise out of me. He was giving me everything he had! He called me "bow-legged" and this and that, and said, "Your belly's hanging out." Finally I went over during the game while he was still standing, waving and shouting at me. I picked up that water pistol filled with all that cheap perfume, and I let him have it all over! You could smell it all the way to the coach's box! The ballplayers all got up to see what I was doing, and he was hiding his face. I let him have it. He had a suit on and everything. The next day, he called me up to apologize. I said, "I don't want your apology." He said, "Yes, I'm going to apologize to you. Would you have lunch with me?" I said, "Well, I haven't had breakfast yet." He said, "Well, I'll buy you breakfast." He was a car salesman, and I think the St. Paul ball club hired him to get on the opposition ballplayers and managers. We became friends, and every time we came in there, he'd invite me out for breakfast. I didn't have to squirt him anymore. One time was enough.

At Denver, Bob Howsam had his own DC-3 plane. It would carry only twenty guys, so if we had a couple of extra players, they would fly commercial. The rest of them would fly the DC-3. That was an experience in itself. When the season was over, Bob leased his DC-3 to Frontier Airlines. It was a real good, safe plane. Once we were flying into Denver, circling, and somebody said, "Hey, look at those fire trucks down below." They were putting that foam on the runway. All of a sudden, we started to land. One of the landing gears was stuck, and they were preparing for us. We made it OK. And that same year, we had an adventure at Charleston, West Virginia. I had managed there briefly, so I knew all about the fog. On our first trip out of Charleston, Vern Rapp, my coach, said, "Hey, Skip, we got to fly out of here. You'd better hurry." I said, "What the heck's the matter? Hurry? I'm in no hurry." "Yeah, you better hurry. Now come on, get showered and get dressed." I started hurrying up, and we bounced out of there. Everybody grabbed their bags, and we got on the bus and took off. We got to the plane, our DC-3, and everybody was loading the gear and box chicken dinners. I said, "What in the heck is the hurry?" Vern said, "You'll find out when we get on the plane." The fog was coming in. The pilot says, "Everybody buckle up your seatbelt." We took off, and dang, if we didn't get off the end of that runway and you couldn't see Charleston. We just beat the fog. Otherwise, we'd have been fogged in until probably the next morning.

One of those years with Denver, we were playing at Louisville, and there was a big Country and Western music show in the big coliseum at the fairgrounds, right next to the ballpark. Now I was a Country and Western buff. The actor who played Perry Mason, Raymond Burr, was there and he had all kinds of Country and Western guys on the program. Our game started at 7:30 P.M. and the show started at 8:30, and I was wondering how the heck I could get to see the show. I was really depressed, because it was going to be a good show. But the day before, I'd been talking to the umpire. We were talking about different things, and I mentioned the fact that I loved Country and Western music. So the night of the show, in the first inning we scored four or five runs. This umpire was back of home plate. In the second inning, we had a close play at the plate, and I ran up there to dispute the call. He said, "What are you doing here?" I said, "Well, I'm up here to question the call." He said, "Did you say something?" I said, "Say what?" He said, "You're out of here. Now get out of here." I said, "I didn't say anything. All I said was 'Say what?'" He ejected me from the game, and as he turned away, he said "Hey, Charlie, enjoy the show." So I went over to the fairgrounds and saw the whole show. I left my coach, Vern Rapp, in charge of the club. We knocked the heck out of them. Nobody knew about it, and I saw a pretty good show.

Every once in a while, you needed some relaxers, some pranks in the clubhouse, to let off some tension. The ballplayers were kind of fun-loving, and every once in a while they'd get themselves an unsuspecting pigeon. During a rain delay, it would often take thirty or forty minutes to get the field ready for play again. So one time the ballplayers got together and started an argument about how strong this guy was, how he could lift three guys off the floor. They would do this just enough to trick the pigeon into lying down on the floor. So the bets started going around, and I got in on it too. I was betting that it couldn't be done. I bet twenty-five dollars. We put these bets in a hat, but they were all phony bets. They had the pigeon all lined up. I'd never seen this, but they told me how to be making the bets. Two guys lay down on their backs right on the clubhouse floor, side by side, with space in between, and they put the unsuspecting pigeon, who said it couldn't be done, in the middle. They wrapped their arms around his neck so he couldn't move. He was immobile. Then the little guy who was going to pick all three of them went over to the guy in the center. They unbuckled his belt and pulled off his sweatshirt and took his pants down. There he was in his athletic supporter. The other guys broke out the merthiolate and the benzoin and the blue ointments. Then some guy brought out a jar of honey, and they poured that all over him. They took foot powder and sprinkled it all over his privates. He was squirming and fighting. Somebody painted a target with merthiolate around his navel and even his nipples. Everybody got in on the act. Once they did this to one of the players who had just been married a couple weeks before and joined the club. They painted him one side red and the other side green. Finally the guy just gave up, quit fighting, and didn't move. I think it was a great relaxer, a fun-loving thing. No harm was done, and the money went back to everybody who had bet.

Other times, if it was a guy's birthday, they'd wheel in this great big, round cake, as big as a kitchen table. It was like a big birthday cake, a cardboard birthday cake with candles on it and everything else. They'd bring it in when the guys were undressing in the clubhouse. Then the lid would start to come up and there would be a nude stripper. The guys would all get together and chip in and pay her for this engagement. One of the guys would have a boom box playing the music, and she would dance like a cobra weaving back and forth, right in front of the birthday guy's locker while he was undressing. These things helped a club relax. But we could get serious when we had to. One evening, we were playing at Dallas. The ballplayers were allowed to leave two passes for friends. I looked back of our dugout at the ballpark that evening, and, whoa, there was a covey of some of the best-looking females I'd ever seen. I asked one of the guys who they were. They said they were from the strip joint, the burlesque house run by Jack Ruby, the guy who a couple of years later shot Lee Harvey Oswald after President Kennedy's assassination. I said, "Well, what are their names?" One of the guys said, "Well, there's Bubbles LaRue and Heather and Tootsie." I asked, referring to one they hadn't named, "Well, what's that one's name?" They wouldn't tell me her name. She was pretty well-endowed. But I made a statement that we'd better win this ball game. That's all I said. We won the ball game.

Geez, I hated rainouts and rain delays. I think they wait too long to call a game. I recall managing the Denver club and going into Houston. It was the last game of the season for them there, and then they would go on the road. We had the top club, we had the pennant won already, but it started raining, and the umpires kept us there till 3:00 in the morning. I finally went out there in the rain, standing there with an umbrella. I was getting soaking wet. I took a big running jump and landed on the baseline and splattered mud all over the umpire. They called it finally at 3:00 in the morning. Judge Roy Hofheinz was there, and he said, "That's the greatest act I've ever seen, Charlie." It was a farce. I don't know if there were twenty fans still there, maybe just the players' wives.

Bob Uecker, one of the funniest guys in baseball, was in the Braves organization with Louisville. Even back then, he was a wild guy, real funny. He really enjoyed playing the game. Uecker was a better player than people imagine. But that danged Uecker cost me a chance at becoming a major league coach or manager. I had about six people looking at me for such a position. It helped if you won the pennant and the playoffs. In 1961 we were playing Louisville, and at one point they were leading, 3 games to 1. But we came back to tie and force a seventh game in Denver. They were beating us 1–0 in the bottom of the ninth in the seventh game. Bob Uecker was the catcher. The first guy up for us, young Jim Hughes, an infielder, hit a triple. The next guy hit the ball between short and third, and their third baseman came up with the ball and spun and threw to home on one hop to Uecker. He caught it up by his ear. It darn near got away from him. Then Louisville loaded the bases with two walks, still with no outs. The next batter hit the ball in the hole, and the shortstop, Amado Samuel, didn't go for a double play but threw the ball home. Uecker came up with the ball, fell on home plate, and the guy was out on a force play. So then we had the bases loaded with one out. The next hitter also hit the ball to the shortstop, and again he threw home. Uecker caught the hop again up by his ear and fell on home plate again for another force out. Then I brought Sandy Amoros up. He had made that great catch on Berra for the Brooklyn Dodgers in the 1955 World Series. But now he hit a weak fly ball to the outfield. Louisville shut us out, and we lost the series, 4–3. Every time I see Bob Uecker, I want to punch him. I say, "You could've dropped one ball." But the next year, Uecker or no Uecker, I would get my first taste of major league managing.

EIGHT

A Car Missing a Wheel

In 1962 I got my first opportunity to manage in the major leagues when the Chicago Cubs hired me as one of their rotating coaches. I had had a string of good seasons managing in Triple-A. I'd managed in All-Star Games in the Pacific Coast League and the American Association. I had sent a bunch of ballplayers up to the big leagues. In Denver, in 1960, we won the pennant, and we got into the playoffs again in 1961. I thought I was going to go up with Detroit the next year, but the Tigers had other plans. They gave the manager's job to Bob Scheffing. I know I was considered for the Kansas City job in 1960, when Bob Elliott got the job. I was asking for twenty thousand dollars. I had been making fifteen thousand. I understand that Bob took it for thirteen thousand dollars. He must have needed a job, which is fine. Then I was also interviewed by Bill DeWitt for the Cincinnati job when Mayo Smith was a lame duck manager and they were going to replace him. Both times they told me that they wanted a more experienced team manager type of guy, which could be a brush-off or a gentle way of saying they wanted somebody else. So when the Cubs came calling, I was ready for a big league job.

Rube Wilson, who was a top scout for the Cubs, contacted me and followed my Denver club around in 1961. He watched me manage quite a few games in the American Association and asked me if I'd be interested in joining the Cubs in the rotating coach system that they used that year. I asked him to give me a little time to think about it. I called Harry Craft, who had been in that system in 1961 and who would manage the new Houston expansion franchise in 1962, and he said, "Yeah, Charlie, take it because you have to be exposed on a major league level. You'll get some exposure, and people will know who you are. Down there in the minor leagues they know you, but they aren't familiar with you in the majors." So I called Rube later on and told him I would be interested. I met with John Holland, the general manager, during the World Series that year, and he offered the job. It wasn't exactly a good-paying one, but it was an opportunity. He explained to me that I would be third in line in the rotating coaches sequence. After your turn, you rotated down to the Cubs' Class C farm club. Elvin Tappe would be the first guy, Lou Klein would be the second guy, and I'd be the third guy. The Cubs had used the same system in 1961. But when it came to my turn, I went to Mr. Wrigley and talked with him. He asked me whether I would go down to Class C, and I said, "I'll go, but I sure as hell won't like it." Mr. Wrigley let me manage the Cubs the rest of the season. He said, "Well, then you don't have to go."

Players and managers look for good luck wherever they can find it. Helen and I had had four children. When our daughter, Elena, was born in 1942, that year we won the pennant at Beaumont. Our oldest son, Bud, came along in 1946 in Mayfield, where we had won the pennant in 1939. When Steve was born in Montgomery in 1950, we won the pennant right around then. When Geoff was born in Denver in 1961, we had just won the pennant there. It seemed every time we had a child, the town we were living in won the flag. So in 1962, when the Cubs called me up to coach and eventually manage in the majors, I turned to Helen and asked, "Well, what about it, Babe? Should we keep the streak alive?" We were both in our forties then. "Oh, no, you're on your own on this one," she said. The 1962 Cubs finished in ninth place, just ahead of the Mets. What does that tell you? So you Cubs fans, don't blame me, blame her!

The Cubs had a rough season that year. We had some great players on the team, future Hall of Famers Ernie Banks, Lou Brock, and Billy Williams. Ron Santo, who should be in the Hall, was at third. Kenny Hubbs, our second baseman, who died tragically after the 1963 season, was Rookie of the Year. André Rodgers, our shortstop, was good but would have been better at third base. We had Buck O'Neil, the great first baseman from the Kansas City Monarchs, as a coach, the first African-American coach in the major leagues. We were a little thin at catching, and our pitching staff had a combined ERA of about 4.5. The ball seemed to find the weakest guy we had somewhere on defense all the time. It was like driving a car with only three good tires and one bald one—we were going to go only as fast as the bald one would let us. Or sometimes I say we were like a three-legged racehorse, three sound legs and one bad one. That horse is going to run just as fast as that crippled leg will go. I've always wondered, if we'd had the pitching and catching talent to match up with the other clubs, how close we could have gotten to the top and how long I would have managed the Cubs.

This was my first job as a manager in the big leagues. I had managed Triple-A clubs in spring training against major league clubs, but that didn't seem the same. So when I managed my first game in the National League in 1962, I found out that these guys weren't any greater than how I had pictured them. The good ballplayer was good, the great ballplayer was great, and the bad ballplayer was bad. They all had problems, strengths, and weaknesses. I was really surprised at the lack of teaching some of the players had had, major leaguers on your team and players that you managed against. I expected that the ballplayers would play to the best of their abilities. I would not ask for more than what they could do. But I walked into that Cubs situation and, gee whiz, it was like a country club. They pretty much were doing things like they wanted to. I didn't think they applied the intensity that I expected of a big league club. Not all of them. Unfortunately, there were enough to drag down the club. We had some real professionals—Santo, Williams, Banks, Hubbs, George Altman, Brock, and some of the pitchers too. They were all fine. They were professionals. But then we had those guys who liked to play golf. We played games at 1:00 in the afternoon. Some of the guys would get up and play nine holes before they'd come to the ballpark, and then I had to use them in the game. I didn't like that, so I told them to get their clubs out of the clubhouse, to take them home. That didn't go over very well.

In my minor league managing days, I was just absolutely positive about everything. I just figured that we're going to win, and we did. I didn't like to surround myself with negative people. But we had a lot of negative people with the Cubs. It was a very tiresome thing. I wanted players with a positive attitude. I wanted to hear a guy say, "Yeah, I'm good, yeah, I'm good, yeah, I covered the plate, yeah I'm good," rather than cry about it, say this guy did this, and find the reasons why it didn't go his way. I've seen a lot of negative attitudes, excuses on ball clubs, and those guys were the losers.

We got off to a bad start in 1962. The Cubs opened in Houston, against the new expansion club. As part of the coaching system, I was coaching third at the time, and Elvin Tappe was running the club. Houston was playing at the Colt .45 stadium, a temporary stadium, while they were waiting for the Astrodome to be built. They had temporary bleachers all the way around. It would seat maybe twenty or twenty-five thousand. Paul Richards was the general manager of Houston. He let the grass grow so it was about four or five inches high in the infield. I noticed when I was hitting infield, I'd hit the ball real hard and this grass would slow it down. All we did was complain about the grass. Along about the fifth inning of the ball game, I ran across the infield, and there was a practice ball still there. That's how deep the grass was. There was nothing we could do about it, because the home team was in control of the field. Some clubs do that to their advantage. Sparky Anderson did that in Detroit because he had guys who couldn't run. Houston beat us three in a row, and, oh, everybody cried about it. We couldn't hit; we couldn't get a guy on base. Santo would hit a ball as hard as he could, and it looked like it was going through the hole between short and third, but the grass slowed it enough for the Colt .45's third baseman to pick the ball up and throw him out. It was the same way over on the first base side. We didn't have much luck with that field.

But we had some great players on that team, three of them in the Hall of Fame. Ernie Banks was a great guy and a delight in every respect. He came out with his famous slogan, "Great day. Let's play two!" He was always exuberant and positive. I don't know why he never got an opportunity to manage, because he was a real student of the game in a quiet sort of way. He was a great wrist hitter. Once he was in a slump, and he asked me to throw batting practice to him. I was the head coach, and I said, "Hey, that'd be great." He said, "Yeah, you've got a good arm. You can throw." I asked him one day what pitcher gave him the most trouble and what his theory of hitting was. He said, "Well, I look for the ball over the plate. I don't care who's throwing, what it is, if it's where I'm looking for the ball, the zone, I hit it. If it's not in that zone, I take it." He had a fine year when I managed there in 1962. He hit .269, with 37 home runs. Ernie had already switched from shortstop to first base. He had good hands, but he had slowed down at shortstop.

There's one episode concerning Ernie that almost got me in trouble. He was having trouble with his eyes, so he had his eyes dilated on a Saturday. When they dilate your eyes, your pupils are real big and you can't see. People from all over the Midwest had come to Chicago that Sunday to see the Cubs play the doubleheader, and I had to keep him out of the lineup. I didn't want the opposition to know that he was not available. I let them think maybe he got a cold or the sniffles or something, but I didn't want to tell them that he had his eyes dilated. We'd probably need him as a pinch hitter. But, man, did I catch heat from the writers! Holy smokes! I wouldn't tell them. So finally, the second game of the doubleheader, I put him up in the ninth inning as a pinch hitter, and he singled sharply to left. His eyes had come back to normal, I guess. Jim Enright, a sportswriter for a Chicago paper, came up to me and he said, "I'm going to crucify you." I said, "Well, go ahead, Jim. Do whatever you want." I don't know whether we lost the doubleheader or won the first game for a split. We had had a good crowd, because doubleheaders were a great attraction for the Cubs. I said, "Well, go ahead. Before you do that, I want you to go over and talk to Ernie." Enright went over, talked to Ernie, came back, and said, "Well, you could have used him." I says, "No. If I could have used him, Jim, I would have used him earlier. But he had his eyes dilated. Did he tell you?" He said, "Yeah." I said, "Well, you owe me an apology." From that day on, Enright and I were good friends.

I was involved in some controversy about a proposed trade for Ernie. I came out to the ballpark early one day on the road, and I was talking to the Cardinals. Bing Devine wanted to make a trade to get Ernie. So we had a meeting in Chicago, up in the white tower, the Wrigley Building. We were going over the ball club, and I was running the club at that time. They asked me about this or that and a trade for Ernie. I said, "Well, we can trade Ernie Banks to St. Louis and get a handful of pretty good ballplayers." Mr. Wrigley got up and said, "Mr. Banks will not be traded, ever, from the Cubs." I said, "I didn't mean I wanted to trade him." I was back-pedaling in a hurry. But they tried to test me as a rookie manager, and I didn't fall for it, but I said we could get some pretty good ballplayers from them. But the trade was squashed. Mr. Wrigley said, "He's going to live and die right here." He was very fond of Banks.

I was very fond of Billy Williams. He was a Hall of Famer from the start. Billy had the sweetest swing I guess I've ever seen by a ballplayer. He always swung the same way and hit line drives, left-center, right, wherever, and when he hit one well, he'd hit a home run. Billy would get up there, and he'd just start laying out those ropes, hanging those ropes out there, hitting those clothesline drives. All those doubles. And he knew he was going to do it. He had that arrogance I love so much. He could do it all, and he was an excellent fielder on top of his great offensive abilities. He was a durable player, and he held the National League record for most consecutive games played.

Every once in a while, I learned something from a ballplayer. In Wrigley Field, down the left-field line, the fans were not very far off of the line, as I recall. Down the side on the ground was a little gutter where the water rolled off. If you hit a ball down that left-field line and it hit the side of the stand, it would roll down that gutter. I kept telling Billy Williams, "Bill, get over there and hustle after that ball. Get it into second base because it may not be a double." He said, "It's a double, if it's in the gutter." I said, "No, it's not a ground-rule double, but it's a double, if the guy can make it." He said, "There's no way you can throw a guy out at second if it's down the left-field line. It's a long throw. Now if I go over there and hustle after that ball like you're mentioning and one of them gets by me, it's a triple and maybe a home run." I said, "All right, OK." So we were playing Milwaukee, and Wes Covington was in left field for the Braves. Wes wasn't a very good fielder. As luck would have it, one of our guys, who was pretty much of a pull hitter, hit a ball down the left-field line. Covington ran over there to field the ball and throw him out at second base, but the ball didn't come up like he wanted. It was in that gutter, and it went by him and hit the wall. Our guy chugged into third base. If I'd known that sooner, I would have sent him home, even though it might have been close. I learned that lesson from Billy Williams.

After I fined Ron Santo a hundred dollars one time for not running out a ball, he remarked, "You never fine those black guys!" I said, "Listen, Ron, you're fined for not running that ball out, and I'll run the ball club." So Billy Williams hit the ball out to right-center. We had a man on first base with two outs, so he was running. He was rounding third and heading for home. The center fielder lost the ball, and it dropped in. Billy was kind of loafing going into second base. They threw him out, and we didn't get the run. So I stuck him with a fine too. Many years later, when I was in Arizona, Billy and his wife were in this eating place. We were there at the bar, and I bought them a couple of rounds. Then we had something to eat. They had me pick up the check. He said, "What is it?" I said, "Well, never mind." He said, "You still owe me ten or twenty dollars." The check was about forty dollars, and he figured I still owed him the rest of that hundred-dollar fine.

Lou Brock was a young outfielder who the Cubs kept wanting to send down. But I wouldn't let them. I spoke up for Lou and said, "Don't ever trade this guy. He's going to be a hell of a ballplayer." I told him I was going to make a star out of him, which is what happened. He was a tremendous athlete. I worked him pretty hard. In fact I told him in the workout, "If you do everything I tell you, Lou, I'll send you to the Hall of Fame." He reminds me of that now and then. I'd get him out at 8:00 in the morning when we were playing an afternoon game and wouldn't let him quit. Once in practice, Lou sidestepped a wicked line drive I hit at him. He jumped away from it. I said, "Are you going to jump away from a line drive that was hit to you? Aren't you supposed to catch the ball? Stop it? Throw it back in?" He said he wanted to be alive for the game, or something like that. I said, "If you don't stop the ball, you won't be allowed to play!" He also had a lot of problems with the flip-down sunglasses. He'd never used sunglasses. So I told him, "The sun shone yesterday and is shining today and is going to shine tomorrow. So you better learn how to use the sunglasses." He did. He became a fine outfielder with the Cardinals. If the ball was hit in the air, in the outfield, no matter where it was, he'd catch it. Lou's a fine person, one of my favorites. He's a great speaker. He was at a banquet in Denver right before the All-Star Game in 1998, and he gave me some pretty good zingers.

Lou Brock is one of only three players to hit a home run over the center-field fence at the Polo Grounds. Hank Aaron and Joe Adcock, who both played for the Milwaukee Braves, are the other two. Brock hit his one Sunday against the Mets, when I was managing the Cubs. It was a beautiful day, no wind blowing, just a gorgeous day. Lou hit a ball to the right of the opening where the steps were that led up to the clubhouse, about thirty or forty rows up into the bleacher seats. It was the longest ball ever hit in the Polo Grounds. His went farther than those other two. And Lou wasn't as big as Joe Adcock, but I guess he was as big as Hank Aaron. That was quite a thrill for me to see a young guy like that hit a ball that far. He justified my faith in him.

I would ask the player, "Let me see you take your leadoff." In batting practice, I'd make the pitcher take his stretch and let the base runner get off first base and take his lead. I'd look at him moving, and I would refine it. I was one of these guys who hated to change a guy, but sometimes I'd refine his technique. Lou Brock was probably the finest example of that. Lou was kind of a nonchalant. He'd just stand there, then boom! he was off like a shot. I tried to get him to take a longer lead. I said, "Why don't you take a nine-foot lead or a ten-foot lead?" "No," he said, "I'm not comfortable that way." So I said, "OK, do it any way you want to." You don't want to change a guy like him. You can only refine him a little bit.

Ron Santo should be in the Hall of Fame. He's got the stats to be there. He was a good, hardnosed ballplayer. Of all the ballplayers that I've had, if I wanted one guy to have up at the plate to fight a pitcher for a base hit, I think I'd take Ron Santo. He would *battle* that pitcher. He had power, and he was a pretty good fielder. One game in Chicago, Ron was up there hitting. The wind was blowing out, as it does sometimes at Wrigley Field. He fouled a fly ball, straight up in the air. I was coaching third, and I could see the wind was grabbing that ball. Santo was standing at the home plate, and I was yelling at him to run. "Run your ass," Ron yelled back. The ball came down fair. The catcher didn't catch it, and it was ten feet or so on the grass right in front of home plate. But Ron was still standing there. The catcher picked up the ball and tagged him out. I fined him a hundred dollars. Oh, gosh, he was furious. I said, "You'll run the next time when you foul pop a ball. You'll run the damn ball out. That's what I expect now that you're going to do." He was fuming. But he paid the hundred dollars. I don't know whether they gave it back to him or not. The next day we were playing, and Santo hit a foul ball that went straight back up on the screen in Wrigley Field. He tore like a shot down the first base line, hauling as fast as he could. He kept on going around the bases. When he got to third, I was laughing like heck inside and trying to keep from laughing out loud. He said, "How do you like that one?" I thought it was great. I did him a disservice one time. I didn't know this, but he was diabetic. He would eat candy on the bench, and that was taboo. You didn't eat anything on the bench, peanuts or anything. Now you can eat all the sunflower seeds you want.

We had some other good players on that 1962 club. George Altman was a big, tall, lanky outfielder. He had good abilities. He made the All-Star team in 1961 and 1962, the year that I was there. He was a good solid ballplayer but a little short on power. From a big guy like that you were looking for massive power in the range of 30 or 40 home runs. He played left field, and some right field too, but he didn't have the arm for right field. André Rodgers was our shortstop at Chicago. He was a tremendous prospect when I saw him at Phoenix in the Pacific Coast League. He was long, tall, lanky. He could do everything, had some power and everything, but he couldn't run all that fast. He appeared to have a lazy way about him. But he wasn't lazy. He just appeared that way. There used to be a standard that you had to hustle and run to the water cooler and everything. If you shuffled out there, they thought you were lazy. But he was a good ballplayer. I was pleased with him. I played him all the time with the Cubs. He and Kenny Hubbs made a pretty good double play combination. Hubbs was killed in a plane crash in 1964. In his great rookie season with us, he set the mark for consecutive errorless games for a second baseman. He was learning how to fly. I told him he was a darn fool and he would kill himself. But he said he wasn't going to be bored. He had a great future.

Don Landrum came over to the Cubs from the Cardinals when I was managing. He barely had put his uniform on when I put him in to pinch-hit. We had the bases loaded, Don got a walk, and we won the game. One day he said, "Skip, if you need a base runner or pinch runner with Warren Spahn pitching, I can steal on him anytime. I can steal on him. I can read him like a book." So I said, "All right." One game we had a situation against Spahn, and we needed a base runner. I called on Don and said, "Get in and run." He said, "Can I steal?" I said, "Anytime you want." Don stole the base on Spahn just like that. Later on, when I talked to Warren Spahn, he said, "That son of a gun, I don't know why he could steal on me. He stole on me all the time." I wouldn't tell Warren what I knew. Warren had some habit, which I can't remember now, that tipped Landrum off when he was going home.

We had a bunch of catchers on the Cubs that year. Sammy Taylor was a left-handed-hitting catcher. We didn't have him long, only 7 games. We had four catchers, and the other three were apparently a little bit better. Moe Thacker was a journeyman catcher. He lived in Louisville and owned a chicken franchise there. I was always going to go through there and stop at Colonel Sanders and have a dinner on him. I was going to just sign the tab and give it over to him and walk out, see if I could get away with it. Dick Bertell was a good young prospect, but he was in the service part of the week. This wasn't fair to him, because he didn't get to swing a bat while he was marching or drilling or whatever he did in the service. Cuno Barragan was yet another one of our several catchers. I knew him from out in the Pacific Coast League. Every time we'd have him catch, we'd win the ball game. He was a winning catcher. Some guys have that gift. I made a statement about it, and I got the other catchers mad at me. One of the writers said, "Why are you catching Barragan?" And I said, "Every time he catches, we win." He was a pretty good receiver. Billy Conners was a young guy, a catcher, with the Cubs at spring training. He was a little bit short on catching, so I suggested that he become a pitcher. He went on to be a pitching coach for many years. I guess I was the guy who converted him from one position to the other.

Our pitching staff had its ups and downs. Bob Buhl was my favorite. Bob came to the Cubs after an illustrious career with the Braves. He was a tough pitcher, a tough competitor. I wish I could have seen him and had him when he was in his prime, because he would show flashes of that tenacity with the Cubs. Two incidents stand out in my mind about Bob. One game he talked me out of walking a guy when there were men on second and third and two outs. Wes Covington for the Phillies was the hitter, a left-handed hitter. I walked out, and Bob said, "Get back in there, Skip. I'm going to get this guy out." I said, "I want to walk this guy. Pick the next guy." "No," he said, "I want to get this guy." He didn't want to be put down. He thought he could get him. Covington hit one off the tin fence in right field for a two-base hit. When Bob came in after that inning was over, he said, "Well, I owe you one." I said, "OK." But, gosh, I loved him as a pitcher. The other thing about him was he couldn't hit to save his life. He was right down there with Hank Aguirre as the worst-hitting pitcher. His best shot was a two-hopper to the pitcher. I thought to myself, "One of these days, when he hits the ball back to the pitcher, the pitcher is going to drop his glove and catch it barehanded." I would have loved to have seen that. One day we had men on first and second. Bob was batting. I gave him the take sign with two strikes, and the look he gave me! He was furious with me. I would make him take, take, take, hoping that he'd walk, but nobody would want to walk Bob Buhl. He was furious with me, but I explained it to him, "Bob, if you hit a ball back to the pitcher, they'd get a double play and take us out of the inning." He calmed down and agreed with me. He said, "If I were in your situation with me up to bat, I'd have me take four strikes!" But, boy, I'll take his pitching anytime. No wonder he won those championships with the Braves.

Our other pitchers were more erratic. Cal Koonce had a fine year. He didn't stay long. He was a little too short, but he was a clever pitcher. He'd battle back on you sometimes. He just wouldn't give in. He didn't have overpowering stuff many times. But he had it around the belt; boy, he was a gutsy pitcher. Dick Ellsworth turned out to be a good pitcher. He was the only left-hander we had on the ball club besides Jim Brewer, who joined us real late in the year. I thought Brewer could make a pretty good reliever. Then after I was gone, a year or so later, the Cubs traded him to the Dodgers, and he justified my belief in him. He turned out to be, truly, one of the top relievers in baseball. He had a good screwball, and he mastered it and it got even better. Don Elston wasn't too bad a pitcher. He stayed up there three years, but he was getting toward the end of his career. Don Cardwell was a big, strong pitcher with a good arm. He was strong as a bull! He could throw like heck. But he was one of those guys that they labeled as a million-dollar arm and ten-cent head! Not that he was dumb, but he was hardheaded. He thought he could get everybody out, which was a good trait. But when you can't get everybody out, you've got to resort to something else. I thought he was a waste of great talent.

Glen Hobbie was not a bad pitcher for the Cubs. He came down with a sore shoulder. I asked why he had a sore shoulder, and I got to quizzing him about what he would do in the off-season. He was a bird hunter. Now I had been a good bird hunter, a quail hunter myself. But I used a double pad on my shotgun and a low brass shell so you didn't get as much recoil. Glen said he loved to hunt birds and ducks too. I don't know where he was from. I said, "Well, you'd better stop using that shotgun, and use low brass shells so it doesn't kick." That's what was causing his sore shoulder, that constant recoil of the gun. I think it shortened his career.

Barney Schultz was a fine knuckle ball pitcher, a reliever. But we had a stretch of games where I had really had no occasions to bring him in. I had a long reliever, a middle reliever. Finally he came up to me, and he was very stiff. He said, "You know, I got to have some work!" I said, "Well, Barney, maybe I can throw you in batting practice." He said, "No, no. I've got to get some work in a game." I said, "Well, be patient and we'll see." That afternoon I used him. And the next day, I used him again. And the next day after that, I used him again. I used him for five straight days. He finally came up to me and complained about his arm. I said, "You're in the bullpen. You wanted some work. Get down there in the bullpen." He pitched 9 straight games, which I believe was a record at that time. A few years later, Barney pitched for me and was a pitching coach at Tulsa.

The great Kansas City Monarchs first baseman Buck O'Neil was one of my coaches on the 1962 Cubs. If you've seen Ken Burns's PBS *Baseball* series, you know who I'm talking about. Buck was already in the Cubs organization as a scout. He's the guy who signed Lou Brock. I never did take full advantage of Buck's knowledge, but I did tell him that he was the guy to watch Ernie Banks. Buck was a first baseman and who better to teach a guy to smooth out Ernie, who had already made the transition from shortstop to first base? Buck was a knowledgeable baseball man. He managed a lot of great ballplayers. Indeed he'd let you know, even get carried away praising the abilities of Satchel Paige and Josh Gibson and "Double Duty" Radcliffe and "Cool Papa" Bell, who was so fast that he'd turn off the lights and jump in bed before the lights went out. Those stories were wonderful. He was as excited as I was to be up there in the big leagues. But he was also very reserved. The only regret I have is that I did not put Buck in coaching at first base in some games, when I could have. I've told this to Buck. I said, "Buck, doggone it. I was going to put you on first base as coach. Who knows the quickest moves to first base better than a guy who spent his lifetime playing first like you did?" He said, "You know, Skip, I wanted that, but you gave me the responsibility of coaching Ernie Banks." One March a few years ago, Buck was in Denver for a banquet. When we greeted each other again, we both had tears in our eyes. Now I don't know if was that because we are old friends or because we remembered the 1962 Cubs! That would make anyone cry! If you look back at the record, it's one that you don't like to recall.

Rube Walker was another one of the coaches with the Cubs when I was there. They tell a story about his romancing that cured him of it for the rest of his life. Rube was a bachelor. He was courting a divorcée at spring training. I don't know whether they were serious or not, but anyway they were staying at the motel during spring training down at Mesa, Arizona, where the Cubs trained. One day Rube Walker was entertaining his girlfriend in his room when there was a knock on the door. Rube said,

"Come on in." This guy came in. It was the woman's ex-husband, and he had a gun. Rube was stuttering. The guy pulled out the gun, pointed it at Rube, and said, "I ought to shoot you, you son of a bitch!" Rube Walker, thinking fast, said, "I sure would appreciate it if you wouldn't." That's the way the story went.

Elvin Tappe was one of the college of coaches with the Cubs. He was the first guy, and then he talked his way out of being rotated down to the minors. I don't blame him. I didn't want to go down either when it was my turn. He did some catching and playing. El was in the Pacific Coast League when I was out there, and I told him many times later on that we never even mentioned his name in the meetings. We just bypassed him. That's as bad an insult as you can ever give a ballplayer. I told him that a couple of times. One Cubs game he was hitting, and we had men on first and third. He called time and walked up to the coaching box at third base and said, "Charlie, listen. This is a tough situation, but if you want to put in a pinch hitter for me, you go ahead." And I looked at him and said, "Elvin, you go up there and get yourself the best swing you can and hit a good 'Tapparinni' back to the pitcher for a double play." And damned if he didn't. That was the sum total of his base hit, hitting a two-hopper to the pitcher for a double play. And I'll never forget it. I haven't forgiven him, but it was funny. He didn't want to be in that situation. But he was a good guy. He didn't know how to manage. He had never managed before, I don't believe.

I enjoyed my season with the Cubs very much. I learned a lot about people. I didn't care all that much for the rotating coaches system, especially switching pitching coaches. John Holland, the general manager, once asked me, "What do you find wrong with the coaching system?" I said, "Well, there are a lot of good things." He said, "I want to hear the bad things." I said, "The worst thing is rotating the pitching coaches. You shouldn't rotate the pitching coach, because you've got ten pitchers that are half of your ball club. They're delicate. They're just like a watch. You can't drop a darn watch on the floor and expect it to work well. You can't throw it against a wall. Pitchers are just like that. They get in a groove, and you shouldn't change them. With the rotation system, each guy's going to have his idea on how a guy should pitch, and now all you have is complete confusion with your pitching. That I don't like." John said, "Well, who do you like?" I said, "I like Freddie Martin, because about all our pitchers are all three-quarter sinkerballers, and Freddie knows how to work with that style. He's the ideal guy to be the pitching coach." I also told that if I had my way completely, I would have my pitchers run more, because I was a great believer in conditioning. I also told him that we should keep the base coaches the same, so the players got used to them. That's why I had been coaching third base from the start. I also said I would have picked Buck O'Neil for my first base coach, because he had been a first baseman all his career. That's where he belonged, not a second baseman, not a catcher, not a pitcher, not a guy who's never coached out there. And last I told John that we ought to work a little harder. You could always back off, but if you start out slow, you can't start tightening the strings up without getting a lot of flack.

Mr. Wrigley asked what I did like about the system. I said, "Well, I tell you, Mr. Wrigley, the best thing is when you rotate these guys down in the minor leagues. You're putting big league coaches in all your organizations, especially when you have your pitching coaches work with the pitchers, or a catcher who works with the pitcher and the catchers. You can teach them faster. Infielders can go down and work with the ball clubs' infielders. You can send a Bobby Adams, who was a major league infielder, down there and work with your double play combinations. You can speed them up and smooth them out. From the standpoint of developing players for the major league club, teaching them the big league way is important. You better get a lot of positive people down there who don't like to lose, who can cheer up a clubhouse because they don't like to lose." I also told Mr. Wrigley that I didn't think our spring training facility was too good, because there was no extra field there.

We sure faced some excellent players that year. The great Sandy Koufax, of the Dodgers, threw a no-hitter against us when I was running the club. In another game, he was pitching against the Cubs at Wrigley Field, and he had 15 strikeouts on us. The next guy came up, 3 strikes, 3 fastballs, 16 strikeouts. Next guy, 3 fastballs, 17 strikeouts. I put in Jim McKnight as a pinch hitter. One of the players said, "Jim, go up and get a hit off this guy." He said, "Oh, well, this guy's not going to strike me out on three pitches, I tell you that." Koufax threw 3 fastballs in a row. McKnight foul-tipped the third one. The next one, strike three, for 18 strikeouts. At the end of the game, Jim said, "I told you he wouldn't strike me out on three pitches." Koufax set the National League record, I guess, for the most strikeouts in a game. Sandy started out terrible in his career. He couldn't control that ball. All that ability, all that talent, but couldn't find his control. The Dodgers stayed with him, and, boy, did he come around. He retired early, at the top of his game. But he had a problem a lot of people didn't know about. He wore the flesh off his pitching finger completely, if I remember right. It took a little off his pitches. He would doctor up his finger with tape and paint the tape so you couldn't see it, because the umpires wouldn't allow that. His finger would take a little while to recover, and every time he'd pitch, the problem would come back. That's why he retired early. I guess he couldn't pitch with it as often as he wanted. Koufax had a fierce pride about him.

Lew Burdette was pitching for Milwaukee at that time. He was pretty tough too. Of course, Lew had a reputation for wetting down the ball. One game, when I was coaching and running the club and he was pitching against us, my hitter topped the ball down the third base side toward the coach's box. I picked it up and wiped it like there was something on it. I could read his lips what he called me. "Give me that ball back!" he said. I said, "Oh, no." I rolled it back, and the umpire got mad at me. The umpire's supposed to throw it out. But I kept wiping my hands on my shirt and pant leg, as if there was an awful lot of spit on that ball. I never caught him though. He hid it real well.

Roberto Clemente played right field like nobody I'd every seen play it. He was truly an all-around ballplayer. He could do everything. He was probably one of the three or four finest right fielders of all time. He had the best arm I'd ever seen. He was absolutely superb at taking the ball off the wall or near the line and then turning around and firing it into second base. We learned this the hard way one game at Forbes Field. André Rodgers was on first base. A left-handed hitter hit a ball real well right down the right-field line. Rodgers was coming around second. I was waving him around from my third base coaching box. Even though Rodgers couldn't run too well, I thought it was a sure double, because I had looked over that area before the game. But Clemente took the ball on the angle, spun around, and threw it to third base. I got that sinking feeling. Oh, God, I just hid my face. He threw a perfect strike to third base. Don Hoak, the Pirates' third basemen, just stood there and decoyed. I waved frantically at Rodgers to slide, but he was out by fifteen feet. Clemente was the master of that play, over and over.

Stan Musial gave us fits. We were playing the Cardinals in St. Louis, at Sportsman's Park. They had men on first and second, in the bottom of the eighth inning, with two outs. We were ahead of them by 2 runs. The guy at the plate was a left-handed hitter by the name of Musial. I called time and walked out. I called the catcher, Dick Bertell, over and stood on the mound. I said, "Bertell, can you take orders?" He said, "Oh, yes, sir!" I said, "Cardwell, can you take orders?" He gave me a stare. I said, "Now this is what I want you to do. Don't throw this guy a fastball. Do you understand? Don't throw him a fastball strike. You get that?" "Oh, yes." Stan Musial could hit a fastball at night, blindfolded, with the lights out. I said, "If he gets a base hit, we're still out front." No sooner did I get back to the dugout and turn around, and here came the pitch. Cardwell tried to throw a fastball to Musial, and he hit it on top of the roof in right field. Now we were behind 1 run, and I was furious. I said to Cardwell, "Now why did you throw the fastball?" He said, "I was going sneak it by him." Years later I went into Musial's restaurant, "Stan and Biggies," in St. Louis. It was a fine restaurant, with superb food. As I walked in there, Gene Kirby, who was the program director for Dizzy Dean and *The Game of the Week,* saw me and motioned me over to join them. He said, "Stan will be over in a minute." Stan came over and said, "Hi, Gene, hi, Diz. Heh, Charlie, how are you? Don't throw me a fastball." He must have read my mind and knew that Cardwell was going to throw him a fastball.

We had a rumble with the Braves one day when I was managing the Cubs. I ran out, and I was going to get right in the middle of things, when all of a sudden my feet were off the ground. Joe Adcock got me from behind and pinned my arms at my side to lift me up. He was a really big guy. He just picked up me up off my feet, and I was running on air. He said, "Charlie, you don't want to get in on this." I said, "Turn me loose." "No, Granddad, you're liable to get hurt!" Then I looked at who it was, and I said, "Maybe you better hold onto me, Joe. Don't let me out there, no matter how much I beg you." I loved him for it. He saved me. I'd have probably gotten a broken nose again. Those young guys were just swinging and taking shots at everybody. Joe was a thoroughbred horse man from down in Coushatta, Louisiana, where, incidentally, Clint Courtney also came from. Joe became a fine thoroughbred breeder. I saw him years later at one of the Keeneland yearling sales in Lexington. He had a friend with him, and we started chatting. I said, "Joe, you were giving signs to Aaron." He said, "No, not me." I said, "Aaron was giving signs to you, wasn't he?" He said, "No, no." I said, "You're lying to me." There we were, two older baseball guys. I said, "I ought to hit you right between the eyes. You were stealing those signs and giving them to Aaron, that's how." "No," he said, "it was Aaron giving the signs to me." I said, "I knew it was some way you were getting . . ." His friend thought we were going to start slugging each other. But it turned out to be a good joke, and we laughed and kidded about it. Joe was pretty good at giving signs, and he was pretty good at taking them.

Speaking of great players, they played the second All-Star Game of 1962 in Wrigley Field. Usually the host city would provide a manager or coach for the game. I was the head coach or manager at the time, but Freddie

Hutchinson of the Reds, who was the National League manager, didn't name me to the team. I felt bad about that. I was very disappointed. Heck, I would have pitched batting practice, anything, just to be on that team. I did get a game ball signed by all the National League players. There were seven or eight Hall of Famers on that baseball, but I don't have it anymore. A friend of mine kept after me to price the ball. Finally, to get rid of him, I priced the ball at $350, and he bought it. He's got a fine collection of memorabilia, and that ball is one of his prize pieces.

We also faced some players who weren't very good, namely, the New York Mets. In the last game of the season, against the Mets, the Cubs pulled off a triple play. The Mets were the only team we finished ahead of that year. And they were awful. As Casey Stengel asked a couple of times, "Does anybody here know how to play this game?" One of the more colorful Mets was Marv Throneberry. "Marvelous Marv" was a fan favorite when he played in Denver. He was a lovable guy, and he was terrific on those Miller beer commercials for many years. He had a pretty good, doggone good year and was a good ballplayer despite those errors everybody remembers. He had had a tremendous year at the Triple-A farm club in Denver previously, in the late 1950s. One game against the Cubs, he came up and hit a ball a long way into right field. It was a sure triple. Marv couldn't run too well, but he made it to third base, standing up, before we got the ball back in. But I looked up, and the shortstop was waving his hands, and the second baseman was waving his hands at second base, and Ernie Banks was waving his hands over at first base. Marv had missed both bases. If he'd kept going, I think he would've missed third. He stood at third base with his hands on his hips, a bewildered look on his face as he was called out. He had an expression like, "What, me? I did that?" I think it was one of the most comical things that I'd seen in an awful long time.

All my managerial career, I had been an innovator, looking for a new way to improve my players' abilities. When I came on with the Cubs, I had them install a trap wall down the left-field line in foul territory during spring training. I'd seen Marv Owen use one at Tiger Town. The wall was probably fifteen feet high, made out of concrete blocks. On one side of it you had dirt, so that an infielder could practice fielding hops off the wall, just like kids did with a rubber ball. The other side had the grass so that the outfielders could field short hops on the grass. I had my outfielders George Altman, Billy Williams, and especially Lou Brock work on trapping the ball off that wall. It's some of the greatest practice you can do to improve outfield fielding. I think it's a tremendous teaching tool. An hour with that trap wall would be more than you'd get in a month of infield practice.

I haven't seen a doggone trap wall in any minor league system or spring training site, except the Diamondbacks, since then. I don't know why. I guess it's not glamorous enough.

But my most interesting attempts at innovation were trying to become a ventriloquist and using graphology to analyze the personalities of the opposing managers. You've all heard time and again fielders during a game. A pop fly goes up, and someone yells, "I've got it!" The relay heads for the base: "Cut second!" or "Let it go!" A base stealer takes off: "There he goes!" Common enough shouts in a game, right? But what if the command is coming from an opposing player? Or manager? Or coach? Just a little bench jockeying, huh? Part of the game. But what if the base coach is a ventriloquist, and there's a phantom voice coming out of nowhere? What is this, baseball or vaudeville? In 1962, when I was at the head of the Chicago Cubs, I tried to use ventriloquism and graphology to snatch whatever wins I could for the club.

Here I was, a rookie major league manager who had to learn a lot of things quickly. I first got the idea of learning ventriloquism probably as early as 1946. Sacramento's third baseman, Steve Mesner, had a high-pitched voice. He could disrupt plays occasionally. If I could only throw my voice on the field, I could manipulate plays our way. I thought of this as being alert to the possibilities within the rules. There was a husband-and-wife ventriloquism act playing on State Street in Chicago. She would sit on his lap and talk in the man's voice, and he would sit on her lap and talk in a woman's voice. It was a clever act. One evening I attended their performance. They heard I was there that show and had me introduced. Afterward I asked them if they could teach me to throw my voice. I became friends with them, and they agreed to teach me. They were great Cubs fans. They had a long apartment where they practiced. I went there a few times, but I just couldn't get the hang of it. I just didn't have the right voice box or something. One time, however, when I was coaching first base against the Giants, I succeeded in distracting their first baseman, Orlando Cepeda, from catching a foul pop. I thought he was angry enough to pinch my head off! Another time I had Eddie Mathews of the Braves furious at me when he misplayed a pop up. I just stood there with my hands in my pocket not saying a word. I wish I could have really mastered that. There's nothing in the rules that says you can't throw your voice.

And can a manager rest easy knowing his opposition is studying up on handwriting analyses in the other dugout? Yet another mystery of the game, or an invasion of weirdness? Voice throwing didn't work out, but graphology did. Somewhere I had read that during World War II, General

Dwight Eisenhower had selected his officers partly on the basis of their handwriting. I wanted to get a bead on each of the other managers. I had played for Casey Stengel at Oakland in 1946 and had managed against Freddie Hutchinson in the Coast League, but I didn't know much about the others. Their handwriting would be some sort of a giveaway about their styles and personalities. I mentioned this to a friend, who had a friend who knew of a famous handwriting expert in California. On opening day, they had this scorecard with each of the National League teams represented in color by a player with a squarish face with the team cap on. I got each of the managers to sign this scorecard, and I signed it myself. With the help of a go-between, I had the graphologist analyze the autographs. It cost me about $250. We didn't even tell him who or what it was for, and the expert may not even have been much of a fan.

I often wondered how many games those graphology studies might have helped win. I even thought of getting the players' signatures too. I learned a lot from the analyses. It would've taken me months and months to learn this stuff about these guys. They were very revealing. I found out who were the toughest managers, who were gambling managers, who were sound managers who played by the book, and who would do unorthodox things. It was very helpful. I got so I could read some of the managers pretty well. In most cases, the profile was right on target. Here are those graphological profiles, misspellings and all. Judge for yourself how closely each profile came to describing your favorite manager or managers of the era.

Fred Hutchinson of the Cincinnati Reds:

> Considerable vanity and egocentricity. Too eager to win. Pretended amicability—calculated friendliness. Critical in a superfluous manner—wastes time on unessentials [sic]. Excellent rythm [sic]; good agility. Persevering, industrious and power of will, schemes up plays that are over complicated but confusing results not justifying the energy expended. Susceptible to flattery. Cannot see the forest for the trees. Judgement defective because he is too much obsessed by details. Introvert but talkative not effective because he emphasizes everything. Works uneconomically—takes too much time weighing and considering all sides of a problem. Does not adapt quickly to new circumstances. Defensive attitude.

I knew Freddie Hutchinson from my Detroit days, when he was a pitcher, and I was a young guy down in Tiger Town in the organization. I had managed against Freddie when he was the manager of Seattle. What a competitor! Boy, he managed tough. And he played tough. They tell stories about him in Detroit, about how after losing a ball game he'd punch out the lights as he went back through the tunnel from the dugout to the clubhouse. All those lights went out, pow, pow, pow. He was a delight. I loved the guy. You couldn't help but like him. He was a good manager, for a pitcher. They say pitchers don't make good managers, but he was. Sometimes he let his pitchers go a little longer than they should have, sometimes one pitch too many. When he'd lose a ball game real tough, he'd sit on the bench and send in a message that said, "I want the clubhouse cleared out in thirty minutes, I'm coming in." Everybody would clear out. Somebody bought one of those big punching bags that would roll over and pop back up and put it in his office. When he lost the game, you could hear him punching the heck out of it, so the story goes.

Walt Alston of the Los Angeles Dodgers:

> Friendly obliging and good nature. Appeals to the players sportsman-ship, fun, gamesmanship. Not critical or carping. Warm, genuine reassurance emphasizes courage and unselfishness. Good strategist. Plans far ahead, figures the whole season. Impulsive and instinctive, responds with intuition and repetition. Not very profound or scien-tific often inaccurate. Look for errors in judgement due to too casual an attitude. Be opportunistic with this man. When emotional not so reliable. Thinks with continuous associations—not very original however. Will repeat often. Favors long hitting and throwing. Over optimistic. Loves the game. A generous, obliging soul not concerned about money.

I found that "laid back" was just about a perfect description of him. He would lay back and run a good ball club. He would just let his ballplayers play, and their superior talent would get you toward the end of a game. Walt was shrewd. He let all of his talent do all the work. He didn't overmanage or undermanage, either one. Alston never played in the major leagues, but he made it to the Hall of Fame as a great manager. I can relate to that, because I wasn't a great player either. I had to pay attention. I had to learn everything. I became a pretty good manager in the minor leagues. I kept my eyes and ears open. Walt was a knowledgeable baseball man. He was very strong in his judgment. He didn't look like it, but he was very strong. His pitching rotation would be almost set all the time. I thought that was great. I always liked my rotation to be perfect. Of course, in the minor leagues you didn't always have a lot of choices. I'd set up my minor league pitching rotation and keep it that way. If one guy faltered, then I'd bring the other guy in there. But Walt Alston had his rotation all set up. He also liked the running game too, with Maury Wills breaking the stolen base record at the time. I often wondered how I would have done if I had had the talent he had on that club. They pushed the Giants right down to the wire that season.

I found out one time just how shrewd Walt was when I tried to fake him into believing I was going to use my left-handed pitcher in a game. We had only one left-hander with the Cubs in 1962, Dick Ellsworth. Jim Brewer came up later. We were going right down to the end of a game with the Dodgers, and it looked like I was going to need a left-hander. I didn't have anyone, but I sent Dick Ellsworth down to the bullpen. I said, "Dick, go down there and just soft-toss." Then I looked at Walt Alston, and he was waving and laughing. He knew darn well I didn't have a left-hander to bring in there. And he had five or six switch hitters on his ball club at that time. He'd just bring them in and turn them right around. I thought I'd try to scare them to death, but I didn't do much scaring! He'd run those left-handed batters or switch hitters in against us, and I didn't have a left-hander to throw at them. Walt called my bluff and just laughed.

Birdie Tebbetts of the Milwaukee Braves:

> Power of conception—producing ideas; persuasive use of words. Appeals to player's hopes, wishes, desires. Has illusions—fantasies. Projects frequently discernment and discrimination [sic] poor. Likes things complete—not one-sided. Reacts on common sense basis. No abstract ability. Interprets everything generally. Urge for action. Ambitious. Fatherly towards team. Good at fienting [sic], that is, making one play seem like another. Does not utilize individual abilities of the players for concerted movements. Dislikes newness and improvisations. Old-fashioned, batchelor [sic] type at heart but good father. He needs sagacity and spiritual intensity. Tight cogent, organized strategy will succeed against this man. Move in hard when he is moody and drifting. That is when he seems inconsistent.

I thought that Birdie Tebbetts overmanaged quite a bit. I found out that he had a set of signs for every hitter, and three different sets of signs. We tried to break his code, but we figured that he might be confusing his ballplayers more than he was confusing the opposition. But he was very sharp. He had been an extremely intelligent ballplayer, a catcher. He was a good manager. But I don't believe he realized that all the ballplayers didn't have his knowledge and intelligence. That's a tough thing to face, when you think your ballplayers should know what you know about the game and they don't. He would call on players to try to execute, and they didn't do it. I always said that you can't expect a guy who's hitting .230, batting eighth, but who's a good fielder or a good player to have on the club, to come up in the bottom of the ninth with the bases loaded and hit one out when he's never hit a home run before. Birdie expected his ballplayers to be as sharp and intelligent about the game as he was.

One time when I managed against Birdie and he had the Milwaukee club, I called for a squeeze bunt three times in a row and got 3 runs. Eddie Mathews was playing third base. Birdie made some sort of a statement in the press that what I did was kind of bush league play, showing his ball club up. But we only beat them 4–1. I didn't see anything bush about it.

Gene Mauch of the Philadelphia Phillies:

> Conducts his team like an orchestra leader. Coordinates, harmomizes [sic]. Thinks quickly, reacts smartly with certainty of aim. Diagnoses situations like a doctor. Competent, matter-of-fact, helpfull [sic]. Always sets up objects and events for some spectacular play. Intimate understanding of each player. Prescribes ease and dexterity, practice body hygene [sic]. Good at personnel selection. Slave to timing and orderly proceedure [sic]. Does not take advantage of breaks. Self-esteem but no self-interest. Adapts himself too much. Poor in resistance not demanding. Appeals to the mechanical side of his player's [sic] neglects their personal and psychological motivations. Never secretive. Signals ovious [sic]. Very fair.

Gene Mauch didn't always have the greatest talent. The rap on him was that he overmanaged. Heck, when you don't have great ballplayers, you do overmanage. When you have great ballplayers, you sit back and push buttons. They used to call those guys "push-button managers." But Gene never had all that great talent when he managed. When he did get pretty good talent, he would finish up there pretty high. He was great with the press. They gave him the title "Boy Wonder," and he was. He managed a long time. I don't know whether he'll ever go into the Hall of Fame or not. But he was great for the owners and the team and the players and the city that he represented. He was a pretty good innovator. Gene wasn't afraid to try things. In Shibe Park in Philadelphia, they built a great big metal fence in right field. It was still there when we played the Phillies there in 1962. Gene changed his bullpen from left field to the right-field line. If one of his players would hit a ball out that way with runners on base, one of his guys in the bullpen would wave a white towel if the ball was going to hit the fence. He'd just wave it and wave it and wave it to signal keep going, it's hitting the fence. I think Gene won a few ball games with that darn trick on that right-field fence. Gene was always figuring out things. But in 1964, I watched as a scout in Philadelphia when his club died, blowing an 8-game lead. I believe his big pitchers let him down. Unfortunately, he never won the big games.

Danny Murtaugh of the Pittsburgh Pirates:

A good and dangerous manager of baseball. Executive, direct, persistant [sic] and brilliant. Reliable sense of duty but not conventional. Explores the heights and depths of the game. Never satisfied. Likes change, imaginative variety. Touchy, precise, sarcastic. Pushes, drives misses nothing. Appeals to the abstract, the psycological [sic] values as well as the facts. Strong roots in the ground. Great scope and range but always practical. Has too many irons in the fire—scatters. Needs concentrated effort. Goes beyond his powers and limitations. Imparts nervousness to players. Slightly fussy and petty may have inferiority complex. A modest man of threatening intellectual force. Is no doubt going places. Curiosity is his weakness. Get him to go to [sic] far out, be extravagant. Will lose because he does not use the energies of his players economically.

Danny Murtaugh was the toughest guy I managed against. Danny was very difficult. Good gosh, you never knew what he was going to do. He had good talent, and he got the most out of it. I loved to manage against him because you really matched wits with him. It wasn't talent against talent— it was matching wits against him. He got us sometimes, and we got him sometimes. I think he had us a little more than we beat him. He was a tremendous manager, and he was a great guy. He had a way of getting your attention. He'd start talking to you and start whispering. He'd go away, and you'd say, "What? What did you say?" He'd just keep talking and turn his head. You never did hear what he was saying. Then he'd start laughing. Danny had a sense of humor, which I didn't know till later on. He was always trying to find out something. He'd talk to you at home plate, ask things like, "Why isn't that guy playing? He's a good ballplayer. Why isn't he playing? Is he hurt or something?"

Alvin Dark of the San Francisco Giants:

He has initiative, daring and the imagination to deploy his forces in diverse ways. He, however, neglects details, does not take difficulties sufficiently into account—may fail because of his overconfident attitude. He likes pleasure and is not disciplinary enough to be a leader. Atheletes [sic] will like him for his great sportsmanlike manner, his tolerance, and his ingenuity. He will gamble and lose often because, because he analyses [*sic*] the obvious and omitts [*sic*] in his calculations obscure but important factors. He is often aloof because he is easily influenced—thus players on the bench can distract him from his original intentions. In this case, someone else is the real manager of the game, the players or someone above. Remember he dislikes to make decisions—or they are made too quickly. He is a better friend than a boss.

Alvin Dark had been a fine ballplayer on the major league level, a leader type. I understand he had also been a good football player at Louisiana State University. He was a good manager. I admired him. A lot of the ballplayers didn't seem to like him. I don't know why, but I liked the guy. He was a tough manager. He played a good nine innings and threw everything at you. The players had to respond to situations, and some players, if you throw them in a tough spot, will have all kinds of excuses. Sometimes I thought he overmanaged, but he was a good manager. Al was tough in the clutch. I thought he was very fair with his players, but he wouldn't put up with a guy loafing. He had respect as a manager. I've always felt that great managers were the ones who had the respect of the players—not fear, but respect.

Johnny Keane of the St. Louis Cardinals:

Here is a leader—not a diplomat or strategist. He is demanding, exact, persistent, insistent and resistant. He compells [*sic*] others to adapt themselves to him. He trys [*sic*] to influence others but resists others influencing him. He is forceful and untiring. His weakness is his compulsion, obstinacy and one-sidedness. In new situations he will respond with stereotyped patterns. No illusions here, this matter-of-fact and systematic man will win where efficiency and organization is called for but not resourcefulness and strategy. Here is complete honesty but no pussyfooting. His ideal is beauty esthetic precision—his taste is Renaissance the unity of the Greek Gymnasium—mental and physical symmetry. He is relentless to himself and others. No weakness. When irritated he is clumsy and awkward. He does not finish with the same self-consciousness with which he begins.

Johnny Keane had been a longtime minor league manager. I could relate to that, because I had been a minor league manager for quite a few years too. You become stubborn in what you want and how you want it. Johnny was a good, solid baseball manager, and he was tough to manage against.

He had a pretty good ball club. He wanted everything programmed, which is something that you learned in the minor leagues because you were alone. Managers were alone. You didn't have a pitching coach or other coaches, like they do now. Johnny had picked up his views because of his minor league days.

Casey Stengel of the New York Mets:

A pioneer, explorer, discoverer type. Goes into things with great verve and enthusiasm. Assumes responsibility in a paternal manner. Outspoken and unambiguous. Mentally objective, emotionally subjective. Rational, ethical, spiritually sincere. A real sales manager—wins through conviction not persuasion. He is modest in ego, noble and grand in conception, demanding more and expecting more from his men after he shows them how to do it, using his great originality which always appears at the end of the game. His script shows that he has really studied the history of the game. He acts like a psychiatrist to his boys—open, receptive, giving standards that are capable of flexiblity only when necessary. He loves to excell [sic], loves to surprise you at the finish, loves the new. His handwriting seems to prove that the pennant seems to hang on the personality of the manager—at least when all other things are equal.

What can you say about Casey Stengel that hasn't been said before? About the only thing that I could say about him that maybe hasn't been said is he was an absolute genius when handling ballplayers. He knew everything that a ballplayer could possibly do. I can recall quite a few stories about how Mantle would test him, because Mantle was the type of guy who would irritate him, but Casey would go along with it because Mickey was a great ballplayer. Casey knew how far you could go with a guy who was playing a position for the first time, and he was great at knowing when to send up a pinch hitter, even for a guy who was hitting well. He knew more about baseball than anybody I've ever seen. He was tough to manage against even when he had the Mets, who didn't have a chance in the world.

One day that season, I found out just how tough he was. We were down by 1 run to the Mets going into the later innings. We got a guy on first base, and hopes of at least a game-tying rally rose. I was coaching at first base, right near the Mets' dugout. I heard some snoring and turned around to see Casey asleep on the bench. "Gotchya, this time," I thought to myself. Then I heard him start mumbling groggily, "My glove, where's my glove?" Surely he's gone off his rocker this time, I assumed. But shortly here came Gil Hodges out to play first base. Hodges, then on the downside of his brilliant career after his Dodger years, was probably the best right-handed-fielding first baseman in the game. And wouldn't you know it he would choose that inning to display his greatness? George Altman, our next batter, rocketed a shot toward the hole between first and second. Hodges moved over and smoothly scooped it up and shoveled the ball to second for a force out. Our next hitter, Billy Williams, hit an even harder ball right in the same place. Again Hodges snatched it up and got another force at second. End of another rally. The Mets held on to win by one. All with Stengel asleep on the bench!

Harry Craft of the Houston Colt .45's:

Dignity, love of elegance, and craftmanship [*sic*] of the building variety is here shown. He will apply the traditional rules of the game and methods. He will waste time, effort and money. He will be self-assured but very cautious. He will be too slow in explaining or making decisions. A reserved, conservative individual but some artful showmanship and much color and ornament. Pride is one weakness, slowness to adjust another, clinging to mothbitten ideas another. However, his boys will play as one team, undivided just as you were playing another country or blueblooded fraternaty [*sic*] club. If a club's success depend upon politics this man's influence with higher-ups must not be discounted. He appeals to teamwork, patriotism and to making a name for yourself. Only with good men can he succeed. This man is very productive, watch him always.

Harry Craft's and my paths have crossed many times. I'm still mad at him. Way back when I had the Twin Falls club, the Yankees wanted me to take the Fond du Lac club. That was a demotion from Class C to Class D, and I refused to go. The cutoff line was at Harry. There were three of us below. I was right underneath Harry. If they'd cut it underneath me, I'd have gotten the Binghamton job in the Eastern League, an A league. I was in line for it, but they gave it to somebody else, and they moved Harry into another slot I could have had. So I'm still mad at him, because I'd have still been with the Yankees. Harry was a good manager. He was very reserved. When he walked out there, he was usually pretty calm. He didn't adjust to situations at all like I thought he would. He had been a good ballplayer, a tremendous outfielder. I had never seen him play, but I read enough about him. He was tough to manage against. He played you right to the hilt.

And Charlie Metro of the Cubs? Here's how the graphologist characterized me:

Objective, matter-of-fact and efficient. Knows and likes his material, and is master of it. Purposive—pursues goal without interuption [*sic*]. Steady, quiet. Strong effective personality. No showmanship. Not decorative except order and arrangement. Inclined to be serious. Conservative. Is exact. Likes symplicity [*sic*]. Needs enthusiasm and persuasiveness. Appeals too much to the player's reason should appeal more to their values (personal) and ideals. Very observative [*sic*]. Conservative—dislikes change. Possibly narrowminded but very good insight. A good leader in times of peace but not in times of war. He is sane and soberminded. Best balance of all the managers.

I thought the evaluation was very accurate, because I could look in the mirror and just assess myself. I disagreed only a bit. I thought I was a better manager in the clutch—"in times of war"—but I took some of the criticism to heart and worked to improve myself as a manager. I did always take my players' personal values into account. I didn't have much showmanship at that time, but I became quite a bit of a showman when I managed later on. I always felt that I was tough in the clutch, that I could outmaneuver another manager, when things were really tough. I was pretty tough but fair. I certainly liked simplicity, but I wasn't very simple about my spring trainings. Most of my practices and signals were pretty simple and direct, not very complicated. I made them simple and to the point. My signals were very direct too, not overly complicated like Birdie Tebbetts's.

One game Ron Santo hit the ball down the left-field line, and the umpire called it foul. Santo was furious. I went out to argue that the ball was fair. I was standing on third, and I could see that it was a fair ball, but the umpire called it foul. I got in a little heated argument, and I was ejected from the game. So I told one of the coaches to take over. I went down to the clubhouse, and there was my bullpen catcher, stripped to the waist, shaving, during the ball game. I was furious. I had just been thrown out. Santo had lost a double. So I said there'd be no shaving in the clubhouse. I wanted my ballplayers in the ball game. We went on the road to play New York. We won 3 games, and then we went to Philadelphia and won 2 games against the Phillies. We won 5 in a row, I was so mad about shaving in the clubhouse. Finally one of the coaches talked me into allowing shaving again, and we lost the next game. Ernie Banks said, "Skip, that was a bad move." I said, "What was?" He said, "We win five in a row." The Cubs hadn't won five in a row in years. He said, "That's the only thing that got them motivated, and you give them back the shaving." We wound up ninth. I think they were more interested in shaving than winning ball games.

I never saw food in the clubhouse until 1962. We were playing Houston, a doubleheader, and we got the heck beat out of us in the first game. We played a sloppy game. We had twenty or twenty-five minutes after the first game was over, before we were going to play the second game. I came into the clubhouse, and the Cubs were just scarfing that food down. There was this luau all set up, just gorgeous. They had half watermelons full of fruit and everything else, fried chicken and gravy, oh, gosh, everything. One guy had a pretty nice spread out there. They were laughing and eating, fighting with the food. And here we had lost the ball game. I lost my temper. I grabbed the edge of the tablecloth and again tried to do that trick of pulling it out from underneath everthing. But it didn't work! The tablecloth was tied on one end. Everything went all over the place. I sure did make my point. Somehow you had to try to instill some determination to win. Only later on did food in the clubhouse become more acceptable.

The 1962 season had its share of crazy or quirky happenings. Wrigley Field, of course, had those vines on the fence. If a ball lodged in the vines, it was a two-base hit, a ground-rule double. If it fell out onto the ground, it was a live ball. One game one of our guys hit a ball out there that bounced and lodged in the vines. The umps ruled it a ground-rule double. But when our players went out there, they shook the vines and the ball dropped. We wanted an inside-the-park homer out of it. But the umps wouldn't allow it. By agreement, there is no time limit on how long it had to stay in the vines. Anyway, they ruled it as a ground-rule double.

Chicago had two airports, O'Hare and Midway, and occasionally a guy would get confused about where a flight was taking off. I was with the Cubs, and they didn't tell me which airport. Apparently they thought I knew. So I went to Midway, which was the closer one, but the club was flying out of O'Hare. I just barely made it. Another time I was informed that evening after the game that there'd be a meeting at 10:00 the next morning. I assumed that it was at the ballpark. I hopped into a cab and went out to the ballpark, but nobody was there. Everything was locked up. The meeting was at Mr. Wrigley's office. I was half an hour late. There I was, running the club, and I hadn't even asked where the meeting would be. That was a little bit embarrassing, so I had to apologize. Those things happened in baseball.

Nuns are some of the best baseball fans. The best event I saw with the nuns at the ballpark was at Forbes Field. They sat way up in the upper deck, a little beyond first base. They were dressed in their nun habits and everything. One game with the Pirates, one of our hitters hit a foul ball that was headed for all these nuns. There must have been two or three hundred up there. I don't know how many, just the whole section was full of them, with their white-and-black black habits. One nun stood up and caught the foul ball. She was like a queen bee being surrounded by all the honey bees. They were just milling around and yelling, and I said, "That's proper. They've got those nuns sitting up there as close to heaven as you can get them. I know that that one who caught that ball is going to be famous forever." That was a beautiful sight.

In 1962 I suspected the Pittsburgh Pirates of using an electrical signaling system to steal our signs at Forbes Field. While the Pirates were batting, the third base coach, Frank Oceak, stood with one foot on a platform that covered the motorized, sunken tarpaulin. We thought that there were one or two guys in the scoreboard area or bleachers with binoculars spotting our catcher's signs. Then it seemed that they would relay some sort of buzz down to Oceak, who would then whistle to the batter what was coming. But we couldn't prove that some funny business was happening. We tried to do a little signal wizardry ourselves. Before I came to the Cubs, they had a traveling secretary who had been a catcher in the organization. His name was Don Biebel. Up in the center-field scoreboard, there was a hollow, open space. Don would sit there and get the signs with a pair of binoculars. He'd put his foot up against the side to signal our batters. One foot was a fastball. Two feet up in the corner was a curve ball. Not that this did much good. When I was with the club, we also had a television camera in center field, and we were getting the signs from there. The guy would whistle, one for the fastball, two for the curve. I didn't even know about that darned thing until Bob Shaw, who was with the Milwaukee Braves and who had played for me in the minor leagues at Durham, came over and said, "Charlie . . . I know what you're doing!" I didn't know a darned thing about it. It didn't help. Heck, we got beat in both games of that doubleheader.

Jocko Conlan was one of my favorite umpires. You could talk to him, and you could argue with him. For an umpire, he was not a big guy. When I was with the Cubs, I read in the paper that Jocko was an honorary sheriff in Arizona. Somebody told me that I could kid with him. I said, "How?" They said, "Well, remember Matt Dillon, and Chester or Festus was dragging his leg kind of . . . ?" I went up there to argue with him, dragging my leg. He said, "What're you doing?" I said, "Well, Mr. Dillon?" He said, "What are you talking about?" I said, "Mr. Dillon, I kind of think that perhaps you weren't exactly right on that pitch." He said, "Get out of here!" I kidded him from then on. After he retired and I'd see him down in Arizona, I kept calling him "Mr. Dillon." He'd say, "I wish you'd forget that." He wasn't a very big man, but he was a fine umpire. He was a good choice for the Hall of Fame.

The 1962 season brought a reunion with an old friend or two. Augie Donatelli, the great National League umpire, and I went back a long way, back to our hometown of Nanty-Glo, Pennsylvania, and the St. Louis Browns tryout camp in 1937. But along the way, Gus had decided to trade in the player's uniform and become a man in blue. He had been a prisoner of war in some of those German stalag camps. He should be in the Hall of Fame, because he was a great umpire. But when I got to manage the Chicago Cubs in 1962, I couldn't wait for the first game when Donatelli would ump. I would have to pull something. I got an opportunity when we went into Pittsburgh for a series, and there was Augie assigned to ump second base. Now I knew from the occasional visit in the off-season that many of our old friends went to a bar called Hank and Mike's in Nanty-Glo. Augie worked as a liquor salesman in the off-season, and the bar was one of his clients. That afternoon I reckoned that they'd be watching the game on television. Nothing much controversial came up in the game, so I tried to start a squabble at second base. On one particular force out, our runner slid in and was clearly out. But I couldn't waste the chance. I jumped up and sprinted out toward Donatelli, waving my arms in the air. "Met," he asked, when he saw me coming, "what are you doing out here? The guy was out by a mile." "I know, Gus," I said, still continuing to fling my arms around, pointing at the runner and everything, and pretending to shout at him. "You know that, and I know that, but there's probably a whole bunch of guys at Hank and Mike's back in Nanty-Glo right now, and half of them are saying that you're right, and half are saying that I am. What do you think of that? I'll bet you a dinner most of them are favoring me." Some time later, when I was back in Nanty-Glo, I found out I was right. Most of the guys had favored the manager over the umpire. But Gus and I had a chuckle about that one for years.

When I was running the Cubs, I had two friends, Bill Wickert and Bill Cousins, who worked for the Illinois Institute of Technology. Wickert had been a business manager in 1947 at Ventura, California, when I was at Twin Falls, Idaho, and they were both Yankees clubs. He was a real die-hard fan. They had been paying attention to some experiments done on a couple who did long-distance swimming on Lake Michigan. The woman won her race because, according to Bill Wickert and Bill Cousins, she was at her thirty-day peak. Mr. Wrigley was kind of fascinated about that. He was a brilliant man. One day I was in his office, and he asked, "Why is a pitcher so superior one day, and the next day too, and also the next day, but then you bring him in with two or three days' rest or something and he just can't get anybody out?" He said, "We're going to get some scientists and we're going to measure our pitchers in spring training. We'll wire the guys and take and make a graph of their physical energies and find out if at any given time in a month their superior energies are really up there high. We'll chart this scientifically." The Illinois Institute of Technology was going to donate some money, and he would donate the rest. They were going to wire the pitchers with biosensors. Mr. Wrigley said, "Charlie, wouldn't you like to have this information as a manager?" I said, "Would I? I'd love to have that information, why to bring this guy in and not that guy." I thought it was a great idea, a breakthrough. Nothing ever came of it with the Cubs, although it was on the table to try the next season. Perhaps somebody's doing it on the major league level now. It would be a tremendous advantage.

The great Hall of Famer Rogers Hornsby came into Chicago and out to the ballpark. He called me over before batting practice, and we chatted. I had gotten to know Rogers just a little bit back in 1942 in the Texas League. Now, in 1962, Hornsby gave me some good advice when I was managing the Cubs. Rogers was a tough guy too. He said, "Charlie, don't change. Don't let those guys change you. You run the club good, but, boy, they've got a lousy club. They need a good director of scouting to get some better ballplayers. They're living on these guys too long." He was an astute baseball guy. I told him I remembered his hitting exhibitions, and he recalled seeing me play back in 1942.

Charlie Grimm was with the Cubs when I was there, and he was one of my benefactors. I didn't listen to him one time when I should have. He said, "Mr. Wrigley would like to talk to you. Why don't you go up and see him?" John Holland was the general manager, and I never did like to do those kinds of things without the general manager knowing, so I refused. To this day I regret not going up to see Mr. Wrigley. Later on, when I was with the White Sox, Charlie said to me, "Charlie, if you'd gone up there to see Mr. Wrigley, you might still be running the club. He liked you, I liked you, and we liked you, but you were too distant." So I regret that. Charlie Grimm had been a good manager and player.

The Cubs let me go in November. I thought I had a chance of being rehired. Eddie Newman, my longtime friend from Great Falls, had had a conversation with Colonel Robert Whitlow at the restaurant. Whitlow was going to become the Cubs' next general manager. Eddie pumped me up to Whitlow and told me to call him about the managerial job. I didn't call Whitlow because I really didn't believe that he was going to be the general manager. How wrong I was!

I think I did a good job with the Cubs. If I had been a little bit more diplomatic, I might have been there another year, maybe five or so. I spoke too honestly and too point-blank, which was my way of doing things. Yet I thought I was an excellent manager. But I didn't get the chance. The Cubs didn't renew my contract. After 1962 there was a chance that I might have gone on to manage the Indians or the Red Sox. I wasn't paid very well with the Cubs. We had ten coaches, and the club must have divided up the salary structure so everybody was paid equally. I didn't have much of a contract. It ended in October, at the end of the season. Sometimes I would have my contract cover the whole year, from January through December. But the Cubs contract ended with the season.

Some of the Cubs coaches and players may have complained to Mr. Wrigley that I was too strict. Right at that time, I was offered $4,500 by a magazine to tell my side of the story. I refused because I didn't want to say anything negative about the Cubs. I threatened that if they kept on criticizing me that I would really blow the lid off one of these days. I told them that I had been keeping a diary for every game, like a report. Everything quieted down.

I was just then negotiating for another home out in Denver. I was strapped, and I needed a job quick. Ed Short of the White Sox called me and offered me the chief advance scouting job, the first full-time advance scout in baseball, I believe. So I took it. In the meantime, after I'd agreed with the White Sox but they hadn't announced it yet, I had an offer from Cincinnati, and Birdie Tebbetts offered me a coaching job with the Braves too. Later on, after I wasn't rehired by the Cubs and I'd signed up with the White Sox as a special assignment scout, Birdie saw me and said, "Charlie, you made a move too soon. You were a hell of a manager." I said, "Now why are you bringing this up now? I thought you were still mad at me for those three consecutive squeeze bunts I called against you." In the other league, Cleveland and Boston expressed some interest. Sometimes I regret not taking one of those positions, but I don't look back.

NINE

Scouting, the Toughest Job in Baseball

I had very many enjoyable days at Comiskey Park as a special assignment scout and coach for Al Lopez. I was crazy about him. I'm indebted to him forever for giving me an opportunity to coach for him. He rewarded me with a job when I needed some time toward my pension. In 1965 I was more or less an outfield coach, but his ballplayers knew how to play, so it was almost as if I were along for the ride. Al is one of the finest people I've ever known. You talk about class in the big leagues, Al Lopez originated the word. I wish I had done a better job for him. I always regret that. I wish I could have stayed and been a coach for him for more years, because he was totally knowledgeable about baseball. I'd sit there and watch him and try to pick the time he was going to make moves. He was a superb handler of pitchers, as good as anybody's ever seen. He just knew everything there is to know about pitchers. He and Ray Berres, the pitching coach, were quite a team. Ray would be in the bullpen and would get a pitcher up to warm up. He could read Al's mind. They just worked like the left and right hand on the same guy. I would sit there in the dugout and try to figure out when the pitcher was weak or when he was going to go bad, but I could almost never get it exactly right. I thought I was pretty good at judging pitchers, but Al was always way ahead. There are a lot of fine managers, but I would have to say that Al Lopez was in a class by himself.

On occasion he'd get really loud. One day I remember there was a terrible call on a base runner. Al jumped up and said, "I got to go on this one." What he meant was he was going to be thrown out of the game. Because the call was against us, Al went out there, and the ump threw him out. But Al was right. The television sportscaster said that he was right, that the umpire had made a wrong call. Al was great with his ballplayers. He did tell me a time or two when we'd sit around—Al loved to have a beer, which is not a crime or anything—and he would say to me, "Now, Charlie, just

remember this. Don't ever have a lazy ballplayer around your ball club."
He disliked a lazy ballplayer. I'd say, "Why, Al? Some lazy ballplayers are
pretty good." He'd say, "Yes, but they pull everybody down to their level,
lazy ballplayers do." I won't mention names, but I saw him get rid of a
couple of ballplayers who were lazy. The other thing he didn't like was what
he called a clubhouse lawyer, a guy who was always dissatisfied. The road
trip was too long, or it was raining, or the field was muddy, and on and
on. The clubhouse lawyer always complained, and he made everybody else
complain. It would bring the team down. Al said, "Get rid of him. You're
better off without him." And he was right.

We didn't have much of a club in those years, but the White Sox finished
second all three years I was there, twice behind the Yankees and once behind
the Twins. Everybody hustled. Everybody tried. We had Jim Landis in
center field, and then Ken Berry came up. We had Ron Hansen, Early
Wynn, Tommy John, Gary Peters, Pete Ward, Moose Skowron, Nellie Fox,
Hoyt Wilhelm, Juan Pizarro, and Eddie Fisher, all guys who liked to play
hard and tough. Al did a remarkable job motivating the players. I had seen
him manage the White Sox in 1959, when they won the pennant and played
the Dodgers in the World Series. I thought, there's a guy who can really
manage. When I got to see him up close, I was even more impressed.

Al had some good coaches. Tony Cuccinello was at third. Tony coached
for Al Lopez for many years. Everywhere Al went, I think Tony coached
for him, at Cleveland and for the White Sox. Tony was one of my all-time
favorite people. Our lockers were close together. He was always pulling my
leg, kidding me. He almost won the batting championship in 1945. He lost
it to Snuffy Sternweiss of the Yankees by a point. Tony loved to kid you
with a very straight face. And I'd kid him. I'd say, "Hey, what do you think
of Babe Ruth?" Tony was with the Boston Braves when Babe was there. A
while back, I saw an ad in a collectibles magazine about Tony having a Babe
Ruth autographed bat, which he sold for nine thousand dollars. When I was
down in Florida getting Al Lopez's hands for the Hitters' Hands project, I
called Tony and kidded him. I said, "How'd you get that Babe Ruth bat?" He
laughed like heck. He said, "Can you imagine that, getting nine thousand
dollars?" Babe Ruth had given Tony that bat when he was on the club. Babe
probably said, "Here, kid." He gave him the bat, and Tony had kept it all
these years and sold it. Don Gutteridge coached at first. He was truly a
fine person, a good guy. He had played for the Browns and Cardinals way
back. He was bowlegged as heck. He laughed a lot because they'd always
kid him about his bowlegs. Don was a very astute first base coach. Johnny
Cooney had been there too but had retired due to age. When he retired, I

replaced him. He was a left-handed thrower, but he batted right-handed. He would get really incensed when you started talking about guys who were left-handed throwers and right-handed hitters. He'd say, "Well, what's wrong with it?" We'd give him a pretty good going-over.

Ray Berres, who'd been a longtime catcher, was the bullpen coach, the catcher and pitching coach. When I was with the White Sox, I asked Ray once, "Do you ever wonder why a pitcher comes in and throws one ball, two balls, and maybe walks the guy or gets in trouble?" He said, "Aww, yeah." So I told him about a guy who had called me up one night at a hotel when I was managing the Cubs. This guy said, "Charlie, I know why the pitchers are wild when they come in and walk a guy or two." I said, "Well, all right. Why?" I could tell he was an elderly guy. I said, "How old are you?" He said seventy-five or something. I was being polite, even though he had woken me up. He said, "The reason the pitchers are wild when they come in is the umpire gives them a new ball. A lot of times in late innings they don't have the balls rubbed up, and they give them a new ball. That ball is slick, and the pitcher can't control that ball." I said, "Well, I'll be darned." Here was a man telling me something that had bothered me and probably a lot of managers in baseball, and I never could figure it out. So with the Cubs a couple of time, I made them take a bag of new balls and rub them up down in the bullpen just before they came in. Ray's first reaction was that I got even with the Cubs. He says, "Well, we can't use that many new baseballs." I said, "Ray, what do you do with that bag of balls after you use them in the bullpen. Don't you use them for batting practice?" He said, "Yeah." I said, "What's the difference?" Ray did a little bit of that rub-up stuff, and it did work. I did that many times as a manager at Tulsa and later at Kansas City.

As a special assignment scout, I was instrumental in bringing some players to the White Sox. I did a pretty good job for the White Sox. For some of the trades, I gave a lot of good input, due to a lot of good scouting of Baltimore. We got Ron Hansen and Pete Ward and Hoyt Wilhelm from the Orioles. Then I had a little bit to do with the Tommy John trade from Cleveland. I helped bring in Smoky Burgess as a left-handed pinch hitter. Ed Short, the general manager, gave me that assignment, and I went into Pittsburgh and saw Smoky. I was very much impressed. Here's a guy who had been a regular catcher, who could hit, but the Pirates weren't playing him very much. So we made the trade for him. Smoky came over to the White Sox and pinch-hit for quite a while. But Smoky was pretty big around the waist, and I watched him. They all tried to pitch him, as the saying goes, "under the boiler." That was the terminology for a guy who had a little bit of a protrusion of the stomach. They'd try to pitch him in, inside, fastballs inside, and he'd just hit screamers to the outfield anyway.

One day at Comiskey Park, Al Lopez sent Smoky up to pinch-hit, and he got a base hit. Then, when the inning was over, Al said, "Charlie, go tell Smoky he's in to catch." I went and told Smoky that he was going to catch. I thought he was going to faint. He hadn't caught in what must've been a couple of years. All he had done was pinch-hit. So very reluctantly, he got his shin guards, taking his time. The umpire came over and said, "Al, what's your changes?" Al said, "Burgess is catching." Smoky put the other shin guard on very slowly, put the chest protector on, got the mask, and went out and caught an inning or two. Al laughed like heck. He didn't laugh too often. He kind of grinned. When Smoky was going up to the plate and kept looking back, Al would hang his head down so that Burgess couldn't see him laughing. But it was a great thing. I thought it was wonderful, because it kind of relaxed the ball club. Al liked that. He was always doing a little something that would relax a ball club. While Smoky was catching, the other guys went into the clubhouse and decorated his locker. Smoky was mad as heck. But then he cooled off and joined in the fun. But he said, "I told you guys that I was a great catcher." Everybody would applaud. But that's the one time I saw a ballplayer almost pass out because he was told to go in and play. Smoky Burgess, I loved the guy.

Bill Skowron was another one of my favorite guys. I loved this guy too. I was scouting for the White Sox, and every time Moose would see me, he'd say, "Get me back with the White Sox." He was a Chicago guy. Finally I had some input in that, and we got him back with the White Sox. As a scout, I was in his corner. They'd listen, and I had pretty good judgment on players. He was a good guy and a good ballplayer. I had managed against him when he was with the Yankees organization. Kansas City came through Montgomery, and, boy, what a club. What a hitter he was! Every time he swung the bat, the ball would rattle the fences. He was a very aggressive clutch hitter. He could rise to the occasion. That's an intangible talent that everybody would like to have, but few do. Moose was a very good fielder. He played hard and alert.

I insisted on Pete Ward coming over to the White Sox in a deal with Baltimore, because I had worked with Pete out in Vancouver. He was a pretty good hitter. His father was a hockey player. Pete played a little hockey too. We signed him for the Orioles, and I carried him on the ball club for twenty-five days or so. I got him a little bonus to sign. I liked him. He was very aggressive. He loved to play, quite a cocky kid. When the White Sox had a chance to make the trade, I said, "Make them throw Pete Ward in the deal. He can play. He can hit." Al Lopez said, "Well, what kind of a fielder is he?" I said, "Well, he's not too good a fielder, but if you hit him a thousand ground balls at third base, he'll do pretty fair. But he can hit, and he can drive in runs and has some power. Don't make the deal unless you get Pete Ward." The Orioles threw Pete Ward in the deal along with Ron Hansen and Hoyt Wilhelm. So the next spring, when I was coaching for Al Lopez, I hit thousands of ground balls to Pete Ward. I'd never hit so many ground balls in my life, but he'd battle them all. I hit him ten thousand ground balls if I hit him a hundred during the two hours of batting practice. He'd get out there, and I'd just keep hitting ground balls until I couldn't move. He became a passable third baseman.

I was instrumental in getting Danny Cater for the White Sox in a trade for the 1965 season. I was sitting up in the booth with Ed Short, and he said, "Well, we got this guy and tell me about him." I was giving him a scouting report after he'd made the trade for him, kind of on my say-so. I said, "The only thing at fault I can find is he has no power." And I think he hit a bunch of home runs with the White Sox, 14 that year. I said, "He can't reach the fences." I'd no sooner said that then he swung the bat and hit it into the left-field seats, which in the White Sox park was a pretty good poke. Then he hit a couple to left-center. Every time I was around Ed Short after that, he'd say, "I thought you said this guy doesn't have any power." I'd say, "Well, he doesn't." But every time I'd say he didn't, he'd hit a home run.

The White Sox traded Luis Aparicio to Baltimore when I was there. I was somewhat involved in the trade. When Luis found out that I was, he kind of got mad at me. I said, "Hey, Louie, it's part of the game." I was telling the White Sox to get Ron Hansen, and they made the trade. But Luis was a fine ballplayer. He helped bring the stolen base back. Aparicio and Nellie Fox were the defense guys with the White Sox. Luis was a great shortstop. He was equal to any other one in the league. Gosh, he was a winning ballplayer, that son of a gun. He'd drive you crazy on the bases. He'd get on base, and you knew he was going. He'd upset the pitcher. It was a good offensive weapon. Here was a guy who would get on base on a walk, or a little dinky hit, or an error, or a clean base hit, and, man, he was a threat right away to get in scoring position.

I scouted Rick Reichart for the White Sox. He was up at the University of Wisconsin. He was supposed to be a very impressive ballplayer. I talked to him, and the White Sox asked me about him. I wasn't that high on him, although he was a fairly decent ballplayer. But he broke some barriers there with that two-hundred-thousand-dollar bonus. I think the bonus was bantered around, and his father or his coach or somebody let it out, and I think it kind of scared us off a little bit too. At that time it was unheard of to give two hundred thousand dollars to a free agent college guy.

We had some other pretty good players on those White Sox teams. Jim Landis was as fine a defensive center fielder as I'd ever seen, and I'd seen most of them. Landis was superb. He wasn't much of a hitter, but he made up for it fielding. Landis could catch any fly ball in the ballpark if it was fair. Al Lopez had me hit to the outfielders when I was an on-field coach. I had a little routine with those outfielders. I'd get them out in left field and I'd hit a ball, a high fly ball down the right-field line, and they'd go from left field to right. I could just about drop a fly ball within a twelve-foot square. Landis loved it. I never could get one past him. I don't know whether he cheated on me at the start, but he would come up with the ball. I saw how good an outfielder he was. They traded him, I guess, because Ken Berry was coming up at that time. I saw Berry make a play at Indianapolis when I was scouting down there about which I thought there's no way a human being could catch that ball. It was 440 feet or something close to that to the center-field fence. Then there was a flagpole in center field. Ken Berry ran around that flagpole and made a spectacular catch. I don't know what he was doing out there, but he sure did make a hell of a play.

Tommy Agee was an outfielder with the White Sox when I was there in 1965. He was a pretty good outfielder. He was what some people called a "stargazer." Every once in a while, you'd be talking to him, and he'd never hear you. You'd be talking to him, and he'd be gazing off, looking by you or something. It's no bad habit, but he could play. He could do a lot of things. He was a pretty good ballplayer. Floyd Robinson was also there. Floyd was a good, regular, everyday ballplayer. He was all right. A little short on a lot of power, but he was all right. Tommy McCraw was a journeyman outfielder and first baseman for the White Sox. I don't mean that disrespectfully. I mean that he was a good journeyman outfielder, the type of guy you want on a ball club, a nice guy, a good hustler, who did everything you wanted him to do.

Dave Nicholson had probably the greatest ability for a young man that I had ever seen, and I had seen some good ones. He was big, strong, very powerfully built. He could put a charge in a baseball like nothing I'd ever seen. He could hit the ball out of left field, right field, center field. It didn't matter to him. When he swung the bat, the ball would whistle. I saw Dave hit a ball, when he was with the White Sox, right over the top of the left-field stand in Comiskey Park. What a tremendous shot! How he got fouled up I don't know. I don't know where it happened or how it happened. He got to where he was taking too many pitches. He'd hit well enough in batting practice, but he just never could carry it through to the game. He'd freeze for no apparent reason and take the strike right down the middle. He led the league in strikeouts in 1963, with 175. Later I did buy his contract for the Kansas City Royals, as a safety-valve type of player, hoping perhaps he'd wake up. Some ballplayers wake up late in life. We invested fifty thousand dollars in his purchase, and he gave us his time. He did a good job at Omaha, and then we brought him up for a little while. But Dave just never quite could do it on the major league level.

The White Sox pitching staff was pretty fair. Eddie Fisher threw a mean knuckle ball. He was a good person to have on the club, what we used to call a real pro. Eddie was great. Joe Horlen was a good pitcher. Al Lopez liked him. He was always a good reliever. He never put on an ounce of fat. He was also a tremendous golfer. Boy, he was a pretty tough guy. He gave you a good day's work. Gary Peters was a good left-hander. He was a real fine athlete. Gary was a fun-loving guy. He and Joe Horlen worked together pretty good, a good left-hander and a good right-hander. Juan Pizarro not only could pitch well, but he could hit. He was one of the better hitting pitchers I'd seen. I mentioned that to Al one time. I said, "Why not use this guy as a pinch hitter?" Al did, and Juan got a hit, and Al let him hit for himself. Bruce Howard was kind of a regular pitcher, an in-and-outer, not too bad. Bob Locker was another pretty good pitcher. Ray Herbert was another solid pitcher, another in-and-outer. Dave DeBusschere was also on the squad. I'd seen him and scouted him at Indianapolis. He should have been a pretty good pitcher, but I think he was sort of leaning toward basketball even then. He was a little bit disgruntled about being sent to Triple-A. He turned out to be a good basketball player for the New York Knicks.

Hoyt Wilhelm, the great knuckleballer, was with the White Sox when I was there. He and his catcher, J. C. Martin, were a team. When Al would bring in Hoyt, he would bring in J. C. He was the only guy who could catch Hoyt's knuckle ball. That's the first or maybe second time I'd seen a double switch in baseball, bringing two guys in, putting the pitcher in the place of one guy and the other guy in place of the pitcher who would come up to hit. Ted Williams said Wilhelm was a tough one to hit. He was a great choice for the Hall of Fame. He pitched many games. I guess he was pretty close to fifty years old when he quit as a pitcher. I think Hoyt's mad at me because we picked him in the expansion draft for the Kansas City Royals and traded him off real quickly before he even pitched for us.

Tommy John came over from Cleveland when I was with the White

Sox. I had some input there. He was the type of left-handed pitcher who didn't have an awful lot, but, man, he was sharp. Later in his career, they reconstructed his arm. They called him the "Bionic Man." Tommy John ought to sit down and write out his exact rehab program. All of these guys who have arm problems should take a lesson from him. Tommy fought his way back through sheer determination and conditioning. He ought to put that down on paper and just say, "Here's the way it should be done to recover, to rebuild from an arm operation." He also should be in the Hall of Fame. He had a pretty good record, 288 wins. If I were on that committee, I'd vote him in the first time. Not only did he have a great career record, but he was very consistent. I don't recall him ever missing a turn. He pitched in turn all the time. But if I ever see him again, at another card show, I'm going to mention to him to write up that conditioning program that he did.

There's not much else you can say about Early Wynn, except he was probably the toughest competitor who ever lived. They always said he'd knock his mother down, even his grandmother. I don't know if his grandmother ever heard that, but I'm sure she would have put him over her knee and paddled him pretty good. I liked him. He got his three hundredth win the first year I was with the White Sox. It was tough coming. It broke my heart to see him struggling for that last win, that magic number for a pitcher. He tried and he tried and finally he got it, but if he hadn't ever gotten it, it wouldn't have made any difference to me or a lot of other people. He was a true Hall of Famer.

My main role with the White Sox was scouting, so I'd like to cover that subject in some detail. I had the opportunity to become one of the better scouts. Bill Veeck said that I was one of the top three scouts in baseball, and, with all modesty, I had to agree with him. I figured I was a pretty good scout. I was always at the ballpark early. Ed Short, of the White Sox, once asked me, "When do you get to the ballpark?" I said, "Ed, I'm always there early." I was in Philadelphia, scouting the Phillies in the National League, and I was sitting and talking down by the backstop. I was talking with Gene Mauch. There was a phone there. I was talking to Gene, and the phone rang, and he said, "Answer it." I answered. Somebody said, "Charlie?" I said, "Yeah." He said, "This is Ed Short." I said, "Well, what is it, Ed?" "You told me you were always out at the ballpark early. Where are you?" I said, "I'm right down by the dugout . . . talking to Gene Mauch." He said, "Let me talk to Gene." So I handed Gene the phone. I could hear him saying, "Yeah . . . yeah . . . we're talking. . . . We're going over some ballplayers." Gene gave me back the phone. Ed never called me again, because I was always at the ballpark early.

When I came to the ballpark, I immediately counted players. I'm a player counter. I wanted to see who was there. I wanted to see if somebody couldn't run. I wanted to see the players. I know the starting pitcher sometimes stays in the clubhouse until it's time to take some batting practice. But I would watch everybody else. The extra guys or the pitchers all hit early. I would watch them. I watched every guy on the ball club. I knew what they looked like, their size, whether they were left-handed or right-handed. I always watched the infield and the outfield. I watched to see who was running, which pitchers, how each manager conditioned his ballplayers. Then, when the practice would start, I'd watch the throwing arms from the outfield, the infield, the catcher. I watched to see which guys had good hands, who was trying to catch balls in between hops. It told you a lot. You'd see what kind of range a guy had. You could tell real quickly whether or not a guy had good hands, especially a catcher. Later on I started timing the pitcher and the catcher and their releases. I had the times for how fast the guy could go from first base to second, and how long it took for a pitcher from the time he started his motion until the catcher caught the ball and then threw to second. Because I had been a center fielder, I always looked to see how well the outfielders were making their throws. It still disturbs me today to see some clubs taking outfield practice lightly, guys not making good throws or hitting a base. Usually they're the last-place clubs.

We were always back of home plate. For a long time, I had scouted from the dugout as a manager. You made scouting reports on all your opposition. I could scout a pitcher better from the dugout than I could from back of the plate. It was a new experience scouting back of home plate. You could see the ball moving, but I knew the ball was moving by the way the hitter or the catcher was moving back there. When a game would start, I always sat in the back row, as a scout. I never sat in front of other scouts because they would be talking to you, and all you did was keep turning your head. A scout has two assets, his eyes and his mind. You didn't care about hearing anything. You always wanted to see everything, because if you turned your head, you missed something. That's the same way in a baseball game. You always sat in the back. I'd get to talking to the guy up front and pump him and pick his brain, and all the while I was still watching. I learned this from a couple of old scouts. Hollis Thurston told me, "Charlie, learn to talk without looking at somebody. Talk out of the corner of your mouth, without turning around. Always talk straight ahead. Never turn your head."

Good scouts never turn their heads. Now, with the radar gun they have, everybody's looking down at the gun, and something happens on the field, but they don't see it. I would zero in on a player if I had an assignment to go see a particular ballplayer. I would watch that ballplayer and never take my eyes off him all the time that he was practicing.

We had to make reports on every ballplayer that we saw while scouting. When you really didn't like him or a guy didn't have what it took, you just put down "K.P.," which stood for "can't play," and you wouldn't waste your time writing more. It got to be quite a joke, "K.P.—can't play." But if somebody was a real good player, you wrote "C.M.," which meant "can't miss." I liked that one because they were my initials too. I was one of the first guys, I guess, in the first organization that eliminated the "Race" column on the scouting sheets. I would just rank a ballplayer on his skills. Later on Bill White told me how much he appreciated that.

Scouting is probably the most important thing about a baseball organization—and the least appreciated. Scouting is a science. Without good scouts, an organization is mediocre. I'm talking about good scouts who can evaluate a ballplayer. Anybody can look at a Johnny Bench after he's an established ballplayer and just take one glance at him and know he's a superstar. But a good scout sees a diamond in the rough. I've made some pretty strong statements on behalf of some players. Some you missed, because sometimes you'd see them when they were off. The pitchers were tough to scout. We always saw them early in the spring, high school kids, college kids. You had to be real careful. You didn't see them all at the best of their ability. Hitters were much easier. I could scout hitters real easily.

There are some things that the outstanding scouts recognize in a ballplayer that managers don't necessarily see. Your appraisals of a ballplayer as a manager and as a scout were a little different. When you could combine the two, as I could because I had been a manager and a scout, you get a pretty doggone good picture painted in front of you. I prided myself on that, because I looked at a ballplayer from the eyes of a manager first and then as a scout. It's surprising sometimes. A guy who was a pitcher might become a real good scout of other position ballplayers. And a former position ballplayer might become a good scout of pitchers. I could pick regular ballplayers pretty well. Picking pitchers was a little bit more difficult, but having handled all those pitchers in my time, I was able to assess them pretty well too. You don't have to have been a player or manager to be a good scout, but I would see things as a manager that the guys who hadn't played wouldn't see.

Advance scouting was tough. Ed Short offered me the special assignment super scout job. I guess I was probably the first full-time super scout, advance scout, whatever you want to call it. I scouted the American League, and it was very interesting. I got another perspective, another view of the players. Advance scouting had its own challenges. You had to be there early, and you had to know their pitcher and what he threw, when he threw it, what he threw when he was behind in the count, what he threw when he was ahead in the count, whether he'd go with his best pitch against the best hitter, or whether he'd fool around and not throw it. That was tough. Then you always had to know who was their hot hitter too, who was trouble, and how to get a certain guy out. You had to pick that up, and you had to be accurate with it. You couldn't be guessing, because ball games depended on it. There's always a situation in the ball game where the game is on the line. It's going to be just one pitch, one hitter, one situation. You may have only one situation where it will bust the game wide open, when you'll either win it or lose it. So you had to be pretty careful about that as an advance scout. You had to stay ahead, a couple of series ahead. You had to know the hot hitters and who was injured and who wasn't, how many players they had ready, who was mad at the manager and who wasn't. You had to get everything you could. It was espionage. That's what it was. The better the job you did, the better for the team. Later I got three World Series rings with the Dodgers for my work.

You have to see the whole ballplayer. You want to try to read him. You want to see what he does out there, if he strikes out or if he hits the ball well, whether he hangs his head down or holds it up. You have to try to read his professional attitude. Sometimes you can't get a read on a guy, but then, otherwise, a lot of times you'll see him moping around and, if he's an infielder, they'll throw the ground ball from first base to him on the ground, and he'll nonchalantly pick it up and just throw with no zip. He's down on himself, and it'll carry over. If he shows too much of that, you say, "Heck, I don't know that we want to fool with this guy." You have to read everything you see. Sometimes a guy will kick the dirt and get out there and grab that glove and then they throw the ball to him and boom! . . . he'll fire it over there and sting the first baseman's hand. You'll read that this guy's aggressive. He didn't like to fail, or he wished he had that pitch back, and so forth. These are all the things that add up whether a ballplayer is good or not. Then you want to see what he'll do in the tough situations, when the game's on the line, whether he advances the guy, whether he drives in a run, or whether he gives a weak effort. It's all right there, and it's deeper than a lot of people think, but you have to read it.

When you were scouting either a college player or a high school player, you had to project him into the future. You had to visualize whether or not he was going to grow, fill out. You dug into his background. You tried to talk to his teachers, his family, his friends, any kids watching him play, and his girlfriend. You'd ask, "What kind of a boy is he? What kind of a student is he?" If he was a tremendous raw talent but had come from a real rough family or maybe had done drugs or something, you had to ask him some pretty tough questions. You asked about his habits. Usually a young athlete in high school or college would be straight, clean, maybe not have very many bad habits. You'd like him to be a fairly decent student too. But now you have to ask if he smokes, if he drinks, if he's a beer drinker, if he's drinking the hard stuff, if he's on the drugs. If he answered yes on those questions, I wouldn't touch him. I wouldn't touch him, because you were going to be embarrassed. When you would needed him the most, he would let you down. I have bent over backward many a time for ballplayers. Sometimes I regretted doing that; other times it turned out well. But I did stand in their corner, was behind them, especially if they wanted to be helped. But there were some young guys who just wouldn't be helped. They had a mind of their own. With them, all you're going to get is a lot of trouble.

Good talent evaluators are the success of a baseball club. The rules of the draft now, where clubs pick according to the order they finished, weakest clubs first, sort of get in the way of good scouting. Maybe it would be fine to bring some competition back. Heck, I can recall when a bunch of guys would be sitting in the stands watching the game, and I'd say, "Well, I've got to get going, got to go home. I've got to get my reports done and see this or that free agent." "Where are you going?" they'd ask. Then two or three or four of them, of maybe half a dozen scouts, would get up and leave. They'd all wind up at the game right there in the same town and wouldn't tell anybody. It was very competitive. They'd try to pick your brains on everything. On one occasion, this one guy, who was a know-it-all, was bugging me, trying to be real clever and everything else. I turned to this scout friend of mine and said in a low voice, "Hey, have you seen that kid out there in Boise, Idaho? He's going to be number one, he's going to be outstanding, that son of a gun. He's a pitcher, but he can play all the positions. I forget the name of the team, but he's on a high school team there." This clever scout heard everything I said. Three weeks later, I found out that he had made a trip to Boise. He was scouting scouts. Now it's another welfare type of thing where an inefficient organization that doesn't have the direction gets rewarded. They ought to throw it wide open. If I see a ballplayer and I'm working for the Colorado Rockies, I will live with that ballplayer and then I will sell him and sell him and finally go ahead and sign him. I don't know if that will ever come back. But it was successful. Now they say that the Yankees built a dynasty. They did, but it wasn't only because of money. There are other clubs that have a lot of money in baseball. Clubs are owned by very wealthy men and women. Money is not the complete answer. Good scouting is the backbone of a good organization.

Once, while I was sitting there back of home plate in Boston, scouting, there was a young guy in a wheelchair. I think he'd had polio or something and couldn't walk. They sat him right back of home plate where I was, and he'd cut his eyes over to what I was doing. I'd write on top of my scouting reports, "Stop looking at my reports!" He'd laugh like heck. Then I taught him how to time a runner from home to first base, which I could do pretty well without a watch, after seeing so many runners for so many years. I could just about tell you within a tick what their speed was. I'd say, "Now don't tell me." This guy in the wheelchair finally got really good at timing the runners. I saw him for two years there, and then I didn't go back there anymore. I hope his life has been good, and that I helped make it a little better.

I worked with Hollis Thurston when we both did advance scouting for the White Sox. Hollis had been with the White Sox for many years and was a great friend of Al Lopez. I don't know why they called him "Sloppy" Thurston, because he was the most meticulous and well-dressed man I've ever met. I never saw his tie out of whack. He was perfectly dressed. He was a dude, if I could call him that, but he was a sharp baseball guy. I cherish the fact that I was friends with him and we traveled together. Hollis had a great sense of humor. He'd always come up with some joke. Hollis Thurston was one fine person.

We were scouting the Phillies together in 1964 on the off chance that the White Sox might play them in the World Series. That was the year the Phillies blew an enormous lead. We sat there and watched that ball club die in the final ten or twelve days of the season. They had a chance to get in the World Series. But they kept asking us every day, "So who's going to win?" I said, "Cincinnati." Hollis Thurston said, "No, Cincinnati won't win. The Phillies are going to win one." The Cardinals snuck in front of them both. The Phillies put a lot of pressure on Jim Bunning. He was the guy who would lead them out of the wilderness. He had to win the game no matter what. He was asked to do his job, and he should have done it. I thought Gene Mauch panicked a little bit. His pitching kind of collapsed on him. The team pressed too hard. I said to him, "Gene, you've got your ball club this far. Don't let anybody tell you what to do. You do it yourself."

Hollis said, "Charlie, that's the greatest I've ever heard." He knew Gene, all the way back to California.

When you were traveling with the club or a scout, there was always something to look forward to in certain cities. I always thought Boston was great. When I was coaching for the White Sox, Brent Musburger, the sportscaster, and I used to go on those history tours of Bunker Hill and the old lighthouse, and the tall ships, and everything. I loved to go to Boston. The ballpark was great. I wish I'd played for the Red Sox. New York was fascinating, all the stores and stage shows and restaurants. It was a very enjoyable. Baltimore was great with the seafood. Oh, boy, it was great. Philadelphia had some wonderful places to dine, some fine seafood places. The South was great. You always had southern food. Atlanta was great. Texas was too. You'd have a lot of barbecue. San Francisco was a great, great town, just to go there. It was tremendous. Even Cleveland had its pleasures. We'd go to Gallagher's in Cleveland later on in years. It was Bill Veeck's hangout. I walked in there one day, when I was scouting. I looked at the bartender, and I said, "I know you." He said, "I know you." It was my boyhood friend from Jenners, Pennsylvania, Frank Harnicher. His brother Shorty was the manager of a little ball club back there. Frank was the bartender. We went over a lot of old times in that session. On one occasion, I let the hospitality get the better of me. Don Beck, who was an official with Continental Airlines, saw me one day in Kansas City when I was about to catch a flight to Chicago. He insisted we go over to this wine tasting that Continental was putting on at the hotel. I was only going to have one glass of wine, but I had a few more than one. When I went to get on the plane for Chicago, I somehow got on the plane for Denver. We landed, and I called my wife. She said, "What the heck are you doing here?" I mumbled an answer, but she's still mad at me. Luckily it was an off day, so I got to Chicago the next day.

Comiskey Park was a pitcher's ballpark. The outfield was quite expansive. The walls were bricked solid with no padding. Later there were these screened-in areas for picnics and the bullpens. They used to wet down the infield a lot, because we had a bunch of older guys whose legs were shot. I saw the World Series there in 1959. It was quite a deal. I remember Bill Veeck saying that the fans would be wondering who would get the best seats. I was sitting in the far upper deck, down the left-field line on the foul side of it. I was late getting a seat, so that was the best I could do. All the Hollywood people were there. They weren't given choice seats down in the box seats by home plate. The regular baseball fans got those. Veeck did something for the lady fans that I'd never seen done. The ushers came around in their blue uniforms—the head usher wore a pair of white gloves—and the other usher had a great big, long box that contain long-stemmed roses. Every lady in that section got a long-stemmed rose. That was a real big way of thanking the people.

I've seen fans in the stands really get clobbered. Oh, golly, that foul ball! I was sitting in the stands at Cleveland, scouting for the White Sox, on Opening Day. The White Sox were going to play Cleveland there pretty soon. I was sitting there, half-asleep, and there were a couple of people next to me and a couple of people back of me where the scouts would sit. Then a batter just foul-tipped a fly ball that came zooming back up over the top of the screen. It clobbered this guy, hit him right between the eyes. You could hear a thump. But that son of a gun got up and said, "Where's the baseball? I want the baseball." Another fan had it. The crowd started chanting, "Give him the ball." One of the funniest episodes I've ever seen happened when I was sitting in Cleveland, scouting a game early for the White Sox before we played them. A foul ball came right back up over the stands, real high, just drifted back, and a guy was shouting, "I got it. I got it." He had a beer in his hand, and the ball landed right in the beer! Down it went and splattered up over the edge of the stands. He had a distressed look on his face. He lost his beer, but he got a ball.

The old White Sox shortstop Luke Appling was a delight. I've heard quite a few stories about Luke, but the one that always pleases me the most is about watching Luke take batting practice. As extra guys with the Tigers, we wouldn't get too many swings in batting practice, if any, but we liked to go out to the ballpark early and watch them take batting practice. Luke was a star of the ball club, a good hitter, a good fielder, good at driving in runs, good everything, just a good, good ballplayer. The White Sox then were noted for their stinginess. You couldn't get a baseball out of them. Luke was popular, and everybody wanted an autographed baseball from a big league club, and especially from a guy like Luke. So he'd ask for the baseballs, and the White Sox management would send a message down, "No!" He couldn't get any baseballs for autographs. So Luke would take batting practice early. I don't know whether he hit third, fourth, or fifth, I forget, but he'd lead off the batting practice. He could foul off every pitch. He was noted for fouling off pitches. He'd foul the balls into the grandstand, and the kids would grab the balls. Luke would flip the bat and look up at the press box as if to say, "Take that!" I saw him do it once, and they talked about him doing that all the time. I understand he got baseballs pretty much whenever he wanted. It was either that, or he'd lose them all in batting practice.

Luke was a scout for the White Sox when I was there. He was a fine man and well deserving of the Hall of Fame induction. Luke was bald. One time the White Sox were in Washington, and I was scouting there. Luke was in the lobby, and I came over, and there were couple of White Sox guys he might have been scouting, because they were in the farm system. They came and chatted with him. I kept looking at Luke, and they were all laughing. The three of them were laughing and kidding, kidding me and everything else. I was kidding them back. I was very fond of the White Sox people. I kept looking at Luke and wondering what was so funny. Then it hit me. He had on a hairpiece. But when I turned around at the desk where I was registering, he had taken it off. I began to wonder again. Finally he took it out of his pocket and put it back on his head, and I started laughing like heck. He was funny. He worked with the Tigers at one time as a scout. He came down to Tiger Town, and we had a lot of fun. He was always pulling something on somebody.

In the early 1980s, Luke hit a home run off Warren Spahn in an old-timers' game. He was seventy-some years old when he hit it. I guess Warren hung a curve or a screwball or something. Whenever I'd see Luke after that, he'd brag about that home run. I'd say, "Hey, Luke, how far did you really hit that?" He'd say, "Oooh, Charlie, I hit that 370 feet." I said, "370 feet!" I'd seen somewhere in the paper that they'd brought the fences way in. I said, "You probably hit it about 270, didn't you?" "No!" he said. He wouldn't admit he'd hit it 270 feet. I don't know what the distance was, but it wasn't 370 feet. Appling was an absolute delight.

Bob Allison of the Twins was a big, strong football player type. I think he had played football in college. We faced him when I was with the White Sox. I called his hand on one thing when I saw him out scouting. He wore his pant legs way up high and showed off those massive legs of his, those "oak-tree" legs, as I called them. I said, "Bob, I know why you wear those pant legs that high." He said, "Why?" I said, "You're a low-ball hitter, and they try to pitch them below your knees where you've got those pant legs up there high, and you can kill that ball." He said, "Don't you tell anybody about this." I said, "I won't." He was a pretty sound ballplayer, very impressive, and a wonderful guy.

Dick Stuart had been in the Pacific Coast League when I was there, and he had hit balls at Salt Lake that were just clear out of sight. But he wasn't the world's greatest fielder. "Dr. Strangeglove," they called him. I happened to be in the stands scouting Pittsburgh when he was playing for the Pirates. There was a breeze blowing. Dick had a good sense of humor. The wind blew a hot dog wrapper over toward first base from the stands.

It was just tumbling like a little tumbleweed. Dick reached down to pick it up, made the catch, and then he dropped it. The fans were going to give him a standing ovation, but then they booed the heck out of him for missing a catch.

One of those spring trainings when I was with the White Sox, I was scouting down in Florida. We were staying at the Yankee Clipper Hotel. Eddie Mathews, the great Braves third baseman, saw me and said, "Hey, Charlie!" This was after I was manager of the Cubs, and he knew me. He was a fine guy. I was crazy about him. He said, "Have you got a car?" I said, "Yeah." He said, "How long are you going to be here?" I said, "We're going to leave in four days. I got to go home." I'd been down there about a month. He says, "Well, how about me borrowing your car?" I said, "What're you going to do with it?" He said, "Well, I just want to borrow your car. I'll bring it right back." It was four days later before he brought it back. I was wondering where the car was. It was a rental car, and I thought, "Oh, my gosh, what if I leave and he turns in that automobile in a month or two?"

Another spring training I was in Phoenix, and I was driving my pickup truck down there. I was in the quarter horse business, and every once in a while, I'd run across a horse or a trailer or something that I needed, so I'd buy it and tow it home. I was getting nine cents a mile, incidentally, for use of my vehicle, so I thought I'd make some expenses. That spring there was a man down there I was trying to do some business with on buying a mare. As I was driving down a street where there was a lot of construction going on, I saw they were cutting down a lot of trees. I walked over and looked at the trees, and they were cutting down pecan trees to widen the road. So I walked up to the man and said, "Who's the foreman on this job?" He said he was. I said, "What are you going to do with those pecan logs, those trees?" He said, "Why, you want them?" I said, "Yeah, I'd like to have one. By the way, are you a drinking man?" He said, "Yeah." I said, "Bourbon?" He said, "Yes." So I walked across the street to a liquor store and bought him a bottle of Canadian Club, brought it back, and gave it to him. They sawed up those pecan trees in four-foot lengths and loaded up my pickup truck. Everybody down there who saw the logs in my truck would say, "Things that tough, Charlie?" I'd say, "Well, no, not exactly." Oh, they gave me a good going-over. So I drove the truck home with that load of pecan logs. I took a good look at that wood. I split a couple of them, and it was beautiful wood. So I ran an ad in the paper in the want ads, "Genuine Pecan Logs for Sale." I put a sign, seventy-five dollars for this log, seventy-five dollars for that log, fifty dollars for that, eighty dollars for this one, sixty-six dollars for this one, and so forth. I had them stacked out there with those tags on the end. Then here they came, gunsmiths, people who worked with hardwoods. They were ecstatic. I sold the whole lot. I had enough money out of that to rework my truck engine and buy a new set of tires. All for taking a little heat from my buddies in Phoenix.

In 1965 the Houston Astros opened the Astrodome. It was the Eighth Wonder of the World. Judge Roy Hofheinz, the owner, should be in the Hall of Fame. He brought the twentieth century to baseball. He installed many innovative things. He had the moving scoreboard and everything. He had the first Astroturf field there. The stadium was absolutely magnificent. The parking was fine. There were some difficulties at the start, though. Outfielders and fans would lose a fly ball in the ceiling panels. Then they painted the panels dark green, and after that you could find the ball pretty good. But the ball wouldn't carry. There was kind of a vacuum in there. It was difficult to hit for distance. I was kind of in on the ground floor, when Judge Roy started building it. When I saw the dugout he put in the Astrodome, I said, "Gee whiz, Judge, that's an awful long dugout." It was about three times the length of an ordinary one. He said, "Charlie, everybody, every baseball fan wants to sit right back of the dugout in those box seats, and this way we've got plenty for everybody. Besides, we make more money on those box seats than we do on the regular seats." Along with Bill Veeck, Judge Hofheinz was the Barnum and Bailey of baseball.

I got to know Judge Roy Hofheinz better later, and I consider him a very good friend. I spent a lot of time with him and marveled at all the things that he'd done for the Astrodome. One day he said, "Charlie, after the game, come on up." He had an apartment in right field in the Astrodome. I went up to the apartment, and we chatted and had snacks and everything. He told me the biggest problem he had at the Astrodome was rats. They came into the stadium to get all the food that was dropped. They couldn't get rid of them at first. They had a heck of a time. Then pigeons also came into the Astrodome. You couldn't shoot a pigeon. The only thing you could do was poison them. But the pigeons were smart. They wouldn't eat any of that stuff. They'd eat all the popcorn and the peanuts and all the stuff that was dropped. But the rats were a big problem. I guess they finally got rid of them somehow.

During the All-Star Game celebrations at the Astrodome, all of the New York and big eastern sportswriters came out there. I was attending the game and sat down with Dick Young, of the *New York Daily News*. The food was fabulous. There were islands of seafood and cheeses and grapes and a champagne fountain. All you did was put a glass under it and get yourself a drink of fine champagne. There was everything, chicken, big stacks of ribs, stacked up like cordwood. Everybody was dressed very neat, the waiters and everybody. If you ordered a scotch and water or something, you almost had a personal waiter. As soon as he saw that glass was about empty, he'd pick it up and start refilling it. Dick Young wanted to see what the cowboys did, what the West was like and everything. So he ordered a steak. I ordered the small steak, and he ordered a big one. He wanted it done a certain way. But when the waiter brought it, Dick said, "Oh, this is not the way I wanted it." "Well, how would you like it, Mr. Young?" He told the waiter, who brought out a whole loin of the slab of steak. It was a great big slab, a foot and a half long. Young was flabbergasted. "Mr. Young, if you care for more, here it is," they told him. He asked for a certain wine, and he got it. When this feast was all over, Judge Roy had all the remaining food taken to an orphanage and children's hospital in Houston.

In the winter of 1965–66, I went down to Puerto Rico to manage San Juan in winter ball. There was a chance I might manage again in the majors, maybe even with the White Sox, so Ed Short sent me down there to brush up my managerial skills. I didn't stay down there long, about two months. My son Steve was on the wrestling team and wanted to play football, so we left in good faith, and I was back in time for the winter meetings. While I was in San Juan, the White Sox replaced me. That winter there was a big hurricane. Geoff's teacher back in Denver wouldn't believe his story. But the thing I remember most about Puerto Rico was all the fraternization between players. When I was coming up, fraternizing got you in trouble. We were instructed: no fraternization. You could get fined. Umpires would sit in the stands before the games and take down numbers of guys fraternizing, and you'd get a letter from the league office and a twenty-five- or fifty-dollar fine. But in Puerto Rico, I'd look up and all the American guys were fraternizing with the other team. There'd be two or three American guys on every club, and you'd see them gathered around by the cage, talking by the grandstand and everything else. When the Latino players came up to the United States, they'd fraternize. There'd be a Latino player on the other club, one or two, and they'd fraternize. The black ballplayers would do the same thing. I didn't pay much attention. I just said if you're going to fraternize, find out who's the manager, who's in a slump, who's wife is mad at him.

Down in Puerto Rico, I saw Joe Hoerner pitch. I take pride in the Joe Hoerner situation. The tag on Joe was that he had a bad heart or something and he couldn't throw overhand. He was kind of a sidearm, left-handed sinkerballer, almost an underhand pitcher. They said he couldn't pitch, but he showed me he had everything that it took. In one game, Joe got in a ruckus with the other team, and just like that he knocked three guys out flat. Bob Howsam was the general manager of the Cardinals. When I came back to the winter meetings, Bob asked me, "Who did you see down there, Charlie?" I'd worked for Bob in Denver. I said, "I saw a pretty doggone good left-handed reliever, Joe Hoerner. If you ask me, they're going to release him." That's the way I talked, and the way you could talk to Bob. If you're going to ask me, you're going to listen. He said, "Well, I want to know." So I told him that if he could get him, get him. I gave Hoerner one of the finest recommendations. Boy, he had a lot of guts, a lot of heart. He didn't back away from anybody. If he threw at a guy and the guy came out there, I think it was all over in a minute. Joe was tough. I loved him. He wanted to pitch, and he did a good job. Bob Howsam drafted Hoerner. They made a deal. Joe went on to spend fourteen years in the big leagues, with a 2.99 career ERA.

Bob Howsam offered me the manager's job at Tulsa in the Pacific Coast League for 1966. Even though it was a trip back to the minors, still it was Triple-A. I had some very good ballplayers with the Tulsa club who went up to the big leagues, and one guy went on to the Hall of Fame. We had Bobby Tolan, Ted Savage, Walt Williams, George Kernek, Alex Johnson, Coco Laboy, Tracy Stallard, Dave Ricketts, and Steve Carlton. Savage, Tolan, Williams, Johnson, Ricketts, and a pitcher named Harold Gilson were black. I had a whole bunch of black ballplayers. By 1966 they were able to stay in the same hotels with the rest of the team. Even though the Cardinals took up some of my best players, we still won the division. We patchworked a little bit, and we got some nice surprises too along the way, from some of the players that we added from a lower league. But losing players in the middle of a pennant race came with the territory. You hated to see it, but your prime job was to develop players for the parent club. I like to say I had a good reputation as a developer. I had sent a whole bunch of guys up to Baltimore from Vancouver, and to Detroit from Montgomery and Denver. I prided myself on that. We won our division, and we played a little World Series of sorts with Seattle, who won the Pacific division. Bob Lemon was managing there. We played a 7-game series. The series went the full 7 games, and we lost in the last inning of the final game. It was a tremendous series, one of the finest ever played.

I have fond memories of that Tulsa team. Walt Williams was one of my best players. They were starting to call him "No-Neck," but I wouldn't let anybody call him that. I called him Walter. He liked that, and I liked that too. Walt had been with the Cardinals' Double-A club at Little Rock. He was a fine little ballplayer. I was crazy about him, but he was stealing at

Charlie with his umpire brother, John, at spring training in Montgomery, Alabama, in the Sally League, 1952. Montgomery went on to win the pennant.

(*Above Left*) The Metro family in December 1956, the day Charlie learned he would be managing the Vancouver Mounties the next season. *From left*, Helen, Charlie, Steve, Elena, and Charles Jr. (Bud).

(*Below left*) Three speakers at a luncheon during Vancouver Mounties spring training in Riverside, California, 1957. *From left*, Spider Jorgensen, comedian Joe E. Brown, and Charlie.

(*Above*) Charlie with sons Steve (*left*) and Bud in the Vancouver dugout, 1957. Bud and Steve were batboys and worked out with Charlie.

(*Left*) Charlie with the Denver Bears, managing the team to its first Triple-A pennant, 1960.

(*Below*) Rival managers Casey Stengel and Charlie, 1962.

(*Right*) At the White Sox father-son game: Charlie with his youngest son, Geoff, 1965.

(*Left*) Charlie in the Tulsa Oilers dugout, 1966. So many new players were on the field that pitcher Steve Carlton had just called from the mound, "Is this my ball club?"

(*Below*) Ted Williams and Charlie, who said, "I lost that smile later when the Senators beat us," 1970.

(*Right*) Charlie coaching with the Oakland A's, 1982.

(*Above*) Charlie and Billy Williams with a Hitters' Hands sculpture in Raelee Frazier's Denver studio, 1993.

(*Left*) Helen and Charlie at the Metro Bar CM quarter horse ranch in Arvada, Colorado, 1999.

the wrong times. He'd steal a base when the situation didn't dictate a stolen base, or even an attempt. So I told him, "You can't steal anymore unless I tell you." Every time he got on base, he'd look over there and give me the steal sign, and I'd either say "yes" or "no." I had no steal sign. I'd just say "yes" or "no." If I said "no," he wouldn't go, but he'd argue with me a bit on my sign.

Bobby Tolan was one fine ballplayer. He should have been an outstanding ballplayer. He had the tools. He could run like heck, was a left-handed hitter, had a good arm, could field like heck, and was a pretty doggone good hitter, with some power. He was an ideal center fielder. He should have been a great lead-off man, but he never reached his full potential. He could do everything, steal bases, bunt, drag bunt, dump the ball down, hit in the clutch. But it just seemed like he never really reached the top in all of his departments. He was one of the first players to play without a contract, in 1974 in those labor wars that led to free agency. I think he got mixed up on that. Maybe people shied away from him after that.

Alex Johnson had big league written all over him from the start. I don't understand why people thought so poorly of him when he went up. I would've had him anytime, anywhere. All you had to do was tell him what to do, and he'd do it. I told him, "Alex, a big guy like you ought to be hitting more home runs." He said, "Well, OK." I said, "I'll tell you when. The sign is four fingers straight down." I'd put down four fingers, and he'd hit one out. The first time I saw the "high five" was in Tulsa, in 1966. But Alex refused to give you the high five, so I would put my hand down, with the finger pointed down when he came by. He would touch me that finger. Everybody got a kick out of that. He didn't want to give you the high five.

Ted Savage was a fine ballplayer, but he had one little quirk, and we corrected that. He'd be going real well, but he'd want to get out of the lineup. When a guy's going real well, you want him to play. Finally I told him, "Ted, you do what I tell you." He was an all-around ballplayer, an excellent base stealer, alert and everything else. I said, "If you do what I tell you, you'll go back to the big leagues and get some more time. Pension time, and you'll be a ballplayer. You're an intelligent guy. Heck, you might want to coach. You might want to manage someday. You don't know. You might be a college coach." Then he had an operation that would have kept an ordinary ballplayer out of the lineup for three or four weeks. Three days later, he was back in the lineup. I guess he took our conversation to heart. He had a good year. I loved the guy. He's still working with the Cardinals in some capacity, public relations, I believe, and I'm sure that he is doing an excellent job.

Dave Ricketts was a fine person, a good coach, and a good catcher. But he got the heck beat out of me one time against the Iowa Cubs. He was going back and forth with a hitter, and I came running up to intervene. I jumped on the batter, and all hell broke loose. By the time I realized I was overmatched, I was flying on my back. A lady sitting in the box seats right there said, "Charlie, what are you doing down there?" I looked up at the guy above me and said, "You'd better get out of here before I hurt you." He was ready to hurt me bad. Dave Ricketts was the guy who started it all that night. I recommended him as a coach, and he spent the rest of his career as a coach for the Cardinals. He was a good baseball man. He should have been a manager. He would have made a fine one.

Other Tulsa players stick in my memory. George Kernek got his opportunity with the Cardinals, but sometimes a guy just doesn't have enough. He was very down. I told him that there was nothing wrong with being a good high school coach, that he could be the best in the business if he wanted to. He became a coach, and many years later, his mother wrote me a very nice note thanking me for helping him. I haven't seen George since Tulsa, but I'm sure he's been very successful. Coco Laboy, my second baseman, was a good ballplayer. He went up with the Montreal Expos and had a fine year. I had him swing at a tire on a rope. He hit almost 20 home runs their first year. Elio Chacon was my shortstop at Tulsa. I don't know where they acquired him from, but he was a pretty good, steady ballplayer. But he probably cost me another shot at a big league manager job. In the playoffs against Seattle, we had the tying run on third base, and Elio bunted, without any sign from me, into a game-ending and series-ending double play. I could have gotten my picture in *The Sporting News Guide* and gotten noticed again.

The pitching staff was composed of a few good guys and a bunch of characters. Ron Piché was a Canadian, born in Québec. He was a nice guy and a good pitcher. He became highly successful in the organization up there in Canada, with Montreal. He was a good guy to have on the ball club. We've remained friends for a long time. Jim Cosman was a big right-handed pitcher. He never did reach his potential with the Cardinals. He pitched for us down in Tulsa. I understand he went on to become some district executive for Rawlings Sporting Goods. Tracy Stallard was a joy. Gosh, he'd keep you loose. When I found out I had him in spring training and recalled that he was the guy who threw Roger Maris the home run ball that broke Babe Ruth's record in 1961, we wouldn't let him forget it. Tracy was good to have on the ball club. He was loosey-goosey and fun-loving. He'd been a good pitcher. Tracy could do anything you wanted. Dick

LeMay pitched for me in Tulsa. He wasn't too bad a pitcher, but I had him when he was kind of on his way out. You'd get a guy from the big leagues who had exhausted his ability. But he was still a good pitcher. There are spots for those guys now. He became a fine scout. Larry Jaster was also with us, finishing up his career.

Art Mahaffey was in a similar situation. He had a sore arm, and it took a little while to get him in shape. I told him I had had pretty good success with pitchers who had sore arms getting their arms back. I said, "You do what I tell you, Art. You run the way I tell you. You condition yourself the way I tell you to. Here's the schedule. You pick out the days you want to pitch. You pick out your different schedule." So he said, "I'll do it." I got him in good shape, and even though his arm had been bad, I got him to work fairly decently for us. I thought that he'd get excited about it when he pitched a pretty good ball game. But he decided he had had enough. He thanked me for doing everything I could. I really appreciated his thanking me. Shortly after that, he retired. But he was coming around. I think if I'd have had him all year, had gone through spring training with him, I might have rehabilitated him. I had done it with George Bamberger back at Vancouver.

Bob Radovich was a pitcher on the club at Tulsa, and he was very much out of line. He wasn't taking care of himself or anything, and I just got angry with him. I just didn't want him anymore. We were leading the league. I called a meeting, and I said, "All right, you guys decide. You've got five minutes." And I walked out. They put Radovich through the mill. I think he was already a little bit drunk. He'd had a few beers before he came to the ballpark. They stripped him to the waist and put him in the shower and everything else. They said if he ever did it again, they'd shove him out the door in his shorts. That happened in Denver when the Tulsa club came in for a series. We decided to keep him. One time he got really drunk and started jumping up and down on his bed like it was a trampoline. I poked my head in and saw his roommate, Tracy Stallard, trying to calm him down. Radovich finished out the year. I heard that recently he got religion and turned his life around. But he was a trial for me.

Fritz Ackley was another one of my pitchers at Tulsa. He was really a workhorse type of guy. He'd pitch anytime that you wanted him. He'd start. He'd relieve long and short. He was a happy-go-lucky type of guy. I understand that he's somewhere up in the North Woods working as a guide. But Fritz could give me fits. I had a rule that you weren't supposed to miss the plane. I had a fifty-dollar fine on any guy who missed the plane. One day Fritz, one of my favorite guys, missed the plane to San Diego. All the players knew about it. But when we got to San Diego and had a meeting outside the clubhouse, there was Fritz, in uniform. I said, "Hey, where you been?" He said, "Where have I been? I'm here, aren't I?" I said, "Yes, but you missed the plane." He said, "But I'm here! I'm on time. So what if I missed the plane?" He had me stumped. He had taken a commercial flight and beaten us there. I said, "Well, Fritz, you know that if you miss a plane I've got a rule that says it's a fifty-dollar fine." He said, "But Charlie, I'm here." All the guys started laughing, and somebody said, "That's right, he's here." I said, "Well, I'll tell you what I'll do. I think I'm a fair-minded guy. You can have a choice. You can either pay the fifty-dollar fine for missing the plane—there's a little gray area there . . . you can argue that point—or else, I'll fine you two cases of beer." The whole ball club in unison said, "Take the beer, Fritz. Take the beer." So we fined him two cases of beer. I thought I settled that very diplomatically, and everybody was happy. We won the game. As it turned out, Fritz relieved in the game and had a save. When the game was over, we walked in the clubhouse, and couple of the writers were there from the San Diego club. I said, "Just a minute. You can come in in a minute." I went in and said, "Hey, Fritz." He already had a beer ready for me. He said, "You're the first guy to get a beer."

The most delightful pitcher, however, was future Hall of Fame pitcher Steve Carlton. I didn't have him a long time, but he was superb. He was the first guy to strengthen his arm by plunging it into a barrel of rice like Roger Clemens and others did later. Carlton was a fidgety sort of guy on the bench. We were always having to try to keep him calm. But he was a wonderful person, and you could already see the makings of his superstar career. One game he seemed especially nervous. He was pacing up and down the dugout in uniform. I finally said, "Why don't you just sit right before the game gets started, before I go up with the lineup card?" I said, "What the heck's the matter with him?" One of the ballplayers said Steve's wife was at the hospital and was going to have a baby. He was expecting. I said, "Gee, I didn't know that." I told him to get out of there. He jumped out of the dugout, and I think he dashed to the hospital in his Tulsa Oilers uniform.

That summer St. Louis was scheduled to play the annual exhibition game at Doubleday Field in Cooperstown as part of the induction ceremonies. As is often the case with those exhibitions, the major league clubs call up a Triple-A pitcher to handle the pitching duties. The Cards called for Carlton. They wanted to know what my schedule was for Steve. I said, "Well, he is scheduled to pitch the day after tomorrow." They said, "Well, don't pitch him. We want you to have him come with us, and we're going to have him pitch at Cooperstown." They called in the afternoon, but I forgot about it. Right before that evening's game, I suddenly remembered and called Steve over. "Pack your bags, Steve," I told him when he came into the dugout. "Why?" he asked. "You're going to Cooperstown," I said. "Already?" he said.

At the annual organizational meeting that year in St. Louis—Gussie Busch, Bob Howsam, Stan Musial, and Red Schoendienst were all there—I gave them a glowing report on Steve Carlton. I said, "This guy is the finest left-hander I've ever met. He's got a tremendous arm. This guy is going to win 20 or 25 games each year. He's going to be a star. He's going to be outstanding. He's got the right mentality." Stan Musial, who was a left-hander, said, kind of kidding, "What about left-handers?" I said, "Well, he's delightful. You know how they say left-handers are in a world of their own, and he is. But he can pitch." Then I told them about a game he pitched in when we had a makeshift lineup after the Cardinals took up five or six of my best ballplayers in the middle of our pennant race. I walked out to the mound before the game, when Steve was about to make his warmup pitches. But he seemed a bit hesitant. I said, "What's the matter with you? You got something wrong?" He said, "No, nothing wrong." Then he looked around and said, "Is this my ball club?" I said, "Yep." He said, "Wow! What do you want me to do?" I said, "Strike them all out." He said, "OK," and turned around. He won his ball game. Steve was tremendous. I loved this guy as a pitcher in every respect. He was fine on the ball club. He was a good, dedicated worker. Why the Cardinals traded him to Philadelphia, I don't know. I think he was asking for more money and wasn't very diplomatic. It turned out to be another of the bad trades in baseball. He went on to have that Hall of Fame career. Steve is a great guy at the autograph sessions. Whenever I've run across him, he'll come over and say, "Skip, how are you? How's your family?"

A. Ray Smith, the Tulsa Oilers owner, was a tremendous baseball guy. His type of baseball man should be in the Hall of Fame. They shouldn't always have only big leaguers in the Hall of Fame. They should have a Hall of Fame, too, for these outstanding baseball men who were in the minor leagues. I can name many of them. A. Ray was good with the fans. He had what he called a "Foul Ball Club," up on the roof of the grandstand, for visiting dignitaries and season ticket holders. A selected box seat holder would come up and have a drink or a beer or something or snacks. Now they have stadium clubs. He loved to have a manager come up and meet the fans, get in touch with the fans, talk baseball with them. That wasn't always easy if we'd lost or were playing badly. But I would go up to the Foul Ball Club and visit with A. Ray, and the writers would come up too.

Once we were talking about the club, and A. Ray said, "Why, hell, anybody can manage this club." I said, "Is that so?" John Ferguson, a sportswriter for the Tulsa newspaper, was listening. A. Ray gave me a wink, so I went along with it. He was going to kid me about it, and I was going to kid him back. I said, "Well, if you're so smart, if you think anybody can manage this club, then you do it." He said, "Well, I will manage the club." I said, "When do you want to manage?" He said, "Well, I'll manage Saturday night." I said, "All right, you can manage them." John Ferguson was writing all this down, this big incident. I said, "You'll manage the club. I'll be in uniform, but I'll go upstairs and I'll sit in the broadcasting booth and help broadcast. You put a uniform on. I'll give you the signs and everything." He said, "OK." Ferguson took that bait, hook, line, and sinker. We set a date, and Ferguson publicized it, and darned if A. Ray didn't manage the team. We pulled it off. The game went into extra innings. Tracy Stallard was pitching a tie game. A. Ray was down on the field coaching, and he kept looking up at me in the booth. I kept throwing my hands up to indicate to him he was on his own. The announcer doing the play-by-play, Max Krieger, was asking me, "Is that right?" whenever A. Ray made a move. I was second-guessing him. I said, "I wouldn't do that." But A. Ray would do the other thing, and it turned out right. We went into the thirteenth inning, and the other team beat us. Tracy lost the game, 2–1. I would have given a month's salary if we could have won that game for A. Ray, because to this day it's still a topic of conversation. He would have had a 1.000 percentage in the record books. They asked me about the contract A. Ray signed, and I said, "Well, he signed a dollar contract. That's all he's worth." We played that up also. It was a delightful year there in Tulsa.

In 1966, with the Tulsa team, even though we had a superb bunch of players, we hit a losing streak that seemed to drag on and on. The parent club, the Cardinals, had taken a few of the good players up for the pennant stretch. Nothing I did could shake us out of our slump. Les Moss's Indianapolis club was chasing us, and I could see that pennant starting to fade. To make matters worse, I was scheduled to talk at a breakfast of the combined civic clubs in Tulsa. The losing streak was at 9. How was I supposed to be funny? What cheer could I bring to those glum faces? As I waited my introduction, however, the morning paper came to my rescue. The sports section headline read "Oilers Lose Nine in a Row, Pad Lead." As luck would have it, the Indianapolis club trailing us had lost 10 in a row.

We had dropped 9 but gained a half a game! I grabbed the paper and held it aloft, threw my chest out, and flashed a giant grin. "I'll bet you didn't know what a genius of a manager you had hired!" I said. That broke them up at the breakfast tables. For the rest of the morning, I had the crowd eating out of my hand. When we won the pennant later that summer, we got the last laugh. I had all the players sign the newspaper. And Les Moss would cuss me out every time he saw me.

In Denver in 1966, an ump threw me out of a game over some dispute about his parental ancestry. I had managed in Denver five years earlier, and I wanted to show the city I hadn't lost anything. But the Bears beat us bad in the first two games of the series. I was embarrassed. I wanted to beat them. In the third game, we had a close play at the plate. Bobby Tolan got called out. My next hitter, George Kernek, was stomping around and giving the umpire heck. I ran in to question the play. Before I could say anything, George said, "Skip, he was safe, he was safe." So I gave the umpire more than a little argument, and I was thrown out of the ball game. Well, this was really embarrassing now. Finally I went into the dugout and said, "Hey, Bobby, were you out or safe?" He said, "No Skip, I was out." That made me a little furious. I was getting thrown out, and the umpire made the right call. The clubhouse in Bears Stadium was out in right field. As I was walking toward the exit, I passed by second base and yanked out the bag. I put it under my arm and kept walking. I kept right on walking with it despite the protests of the blue crew. I got in the clubhouse and locked the door. I wouldn't give them the base back. It took them twenty minutes to get another base. I was fined $150 and suspended three days. A. Ray Smith, the general manager and the owner of the Tulsa club, paid my fine. Then he called Dewey Soriano, the president of the league, and gave him the saddest story that I've ever heard. He told him my wife was going to leave me and everything else. "His wife is mad at him, and he's got to straighten up," he said, "Besides, I'm not paying him that much." He was paying me very well, in fact. But A. Ray said, "I'm not paying that much, and he can't afford it." So Dewey reduced the fine, but I never did pay it, because the club was paying my fines at that time. And I became the oldest guy in the league to steal second base. Brent Musburger sent me a telegram: "Congratulations. Now you're only 101 behind Maury Wills."

When I was managing Tulsa, we had an exhibition game scheduled with the parent club. The Cards were a top club, and we had a lot of good ballplayers there at Tulsa. The Cardinals came in with their regular club. Red Schoendienst was the manager, and Stan Musial also flew down. The game was at Skelly Field, which was shaped for football. It had a right-field line of 248 feet, and even a temporary screen to cut down cheap home runs. A. Ray Smith was afraid the game would turn into a farce, and the Cardinals didn't want a farce either. So we moved first base back 3 feet. It was almost comical to watch great base runners, such as Lou Brock, who could run 90 feet precisely in their sleep, get a puzzled look on their faces when the base proved to be one step more than usual. A. Ray Smith, our owner, may have known, but he never let on. Let this be a lesson to young managers and players: measure those base paths! The game wound up 6–5, St. Louis won, and everybody, including the nineteen thousand spectators, had a good time. It was a big payday for the owner and for the club. I never have told Lou Brock. One of these days I will tell him the reason he was so puzzled.

One game at Tulsa, we were getting the heck beat out of us early in the game. I walked over to the bench, and Tyler, the groundskeeper, was there. He said, "Charlie, you're getting beat pretty bad." I said, "Yeah. Why in the hell doesn't somebody turn the lights off?" He said, "OK." So he turned the lights off! They took a while to come back on. A. Ray Smith came down and said, "What's the matter?" I said, "I don't know. The lights are off." He went and got Tyler. While the lights were out, the concessions boomed. I was exonerated. I wasn't blamed for anything. The other manager cooled off, and we came back strong and won the ball game. I said to A. Ray Smith, "We got a way of increasing the concession revenue." He said, "Oh, no. We're not going to have any more games delayed by the lights going out."

Hawaii was in the Pacific Coast League then. You talk about some traveling! We'd go over there for a week and play a doubleheader on Sunday, a night game, and then catch the 12:50 flight, the last flight out of Hawaii for the mainland, to Los Angeles, and fly all night long. A. Ray Smith had a DC-3 plane of his own. We flew on that plane, and the guys I wasn't going to use would fly the commercial flight. We'd get in about 5:00 or 6:00 that evening and have to play a ball game. We'd flown all night and day, thousands of miles. We'd get the heck beat out of us that night. Heck, nobody slept. We'd been on planes all night and all day. I wouldn't even let the ballplayers kiss their wives when we got back. We had to go straight to the ballpark and play.

The Cardinals started a program of pregame exercises, and I carried it on with their Triple-A club. We'd do exercises before we started practice. We'd do stretching, which now everybody does. We'd sit on the ground and stretch our legs. We'd jump up and down and flap our arms. It was good. I didn't think much of it at the start, but, boy, was I was won over. We had very few guys hurt. But I had one pitcher at Tulsa, Harold Gilson, who didn't want to do any of that. I would always run my own pitchers, so I could see that they weren't hurt and could get close to them and encourage them. But Gilson wouldn't do that either. I finally got fed up with it. He was a great prospect, a tall, lanky left-hander with a good arm. He lacked a lot of experience, in pitching and everything else, but he was a definite big league prospect. But he wouldn't do anything. I couldn't let him disrupt the whole ball club, so I told him, "Here's the phone number. Call up the Cardinals and tell them you can't play for me." Gilson never made it back up. I understand he ended up selling automobiles. It was a terrible waste of fine talent.

The first day of spring training, you welcome everybody. You have a meeting and welcome everybody. That takes maybe thirty minutes or an hour, depending on the manager. He lays down the rules that he wants and what he expects. My rules were pretty simple. I wanted the players always on time. I didn't want to wait for anybody. I would excuse a player during spring training, or even during the season, if he was late because of a situation with the children or his wife or something. But I never accepted any inexcusable lateness. I was pretty tough, harsh on that. I would give a choice. When I took over the Tulsa club, I had that one rule that you had to be on time. Two of the ballplayers who had been on the team the previous year, Bobby Pfeil and Dave Pavlesic, decided they were going to test me. They were late for our little pregame players' get-together and calisthenics. These two guys were not injured, and they stayed away. They were testing me, kind of like testing the old gunfighter to see if he's still the boss. So they tested me and were late, and we waited and waited and waited. They were about twenty minutes late. When they both came in, I said, "Why are you late?" Before they answered, I said, "Was your wife sick?" They were both married, I believe. "No," they said. "Did you have a flat tire or something?" "No." "Did you forget about the game that was today?" "No." "Why are you late?" "Well, we just didn't feel like it," they said. So I said, "Well, I'll tell you what I'm going to do. I think I'm a pretty fair guy. We'll do this in a diplomatic way. You're late, and you know what my rule is. You can either take a fifty-dollar fine for being late, or you can come out tomorrow morning at 9:00 and run till I tell you to stop. Take your pick." These two guys were rebels. They were really testing me. I said, "Well, make up your mind. We got to go to work here, and the guys are all waiting in uniform. You guys are in civilian clothes." One of them, the tough one I guess, said, "Well, I don't know." I said, "I'll tell you what I'll do. I'd like to give you another chance, another option. You can either come out here 9:00 tomorrow and run till I tell you to stop. I'll be here.

Or pay a fifty-dollar fine. Or you can get your asses in the clubhouse right now, leave your uniforms, go in to the office, and tell them you can't play for me and tell them why." That was the end of that. They came out in the morning and ran until I told them to stop. I sat up there, having a coffee and a couple of doughnuts and chatting with A. Ray Smith. Everything was fine. That's the way I handled it, and that's the way I wanted it. We had no problems after that. Later I hired Pavlesic as a minor league manager when I was with the Royals.

Once at Tulsa, Bill Cooper, the trainer, got a couple of cases of Coors beer. We always had some for the groundskeepers. I finally said, "Why are you getting Coors?" He said, "I get a good deal on this." Bob Howsam, the general manager of the Cardinals, came down to visit our ball club. He walked into the clubhouse after the game to say hello to the players, and he saw us drinking Coors beer. Bob said, "Oh, my gosh, I better get the heck out of here, Charlie. We'll all get fired. What if one of the officials of the Anheuser Busch brewery, Budweiser, would come in here?" Bill Cooper said, "Aw, Mr. Howsam, I get a good deal on Coors." Bob said, "Heck, I'll get the beer in here." So he called the distributorship, and we had Budweiser in the clubhouse after that.

Beer is all right in the clubhouse. I see nothing wrong with it. Now they have everything in the clubhouse. Gee whiz, they have luaus and barbecues and everything else. They have everything. They're generous with the clubhouse. Visiting clubhouses do that quite a bit. The home clubhouses don't offer as much, because the guys have got their families and they're going home. But when you go on the road, they put out a pretty good spread. They have everything but hard liquor. I have never seen hard liquor in the clubhouse. Beer is all right. I advocate it. It's a relaxing thing. You can sit there and go over things with a guy when he has had a rough time. You can console him. If he's had a good day, you can sit and talk about that. You were always talking baseball, which doesn't happen very often except in the clubhouse. Because of the travel, and because everybody has a single room in the hotels, players and managers really don't have time to sit around and really talk baseball as much as we used to.

Les Moss was in the White Sox organization when I was there, and then when I was managing Tulsa, he managed Indianapolis. One time Les said to me, "Charlie, I got some sandwiches in my apartment. We'll have a beer or two. Come on over." I said, "OK." After the game at Indianapolis, we started to head to his place, but before we went, we stopped at the concession stand, where Less wrote out a check for five hundred dollars and the concession manager gave him five hundred dollars' worth of coins wrapped in wrappers. I thought, "What in the heck is he doing with that?" He had all kinds of coins, half dollars, quarters, dimes and nickels, even some pennies. He said, "I'll bring them back tomorrow, or I'll bring them to the bank." The concession guy said, "Fine." So we went to his apartment, and he made a sandwich or two and a beer. Then he said, "Let's look at these." He had a book about old coins, and he was looking for old ones. He said he was making more money off these old coins than his salary was for the summer. I thought that was pretty sharp of him.

When I had the Tulsa club in the Pacific Coast League, I did the scouts a big favor one day in spring training. I'd been a scout for three years, and I knew many of the other scouts. They were all down there in Arizona, watching the major teams and the minor leagues plus the college clubs that would come down and play the University of Arizona and Arizona State. We were about ready to open up the season in Phoenix. I looked up, and there were about fifteen or twenty scouts. They called me over and said, "Charlie, now remember, you're a manager now, and you've been a scout all these years. You know that we have to see as many ballplayers as we can. We've been down here for six weeks, and we want to get home. We want to see as many ballplayers as we can. Show us your ball club." I said, "OK." As it turned out, I threw nine pitchers in that ball game, and we won it by a big score, 14–12 or something. And it was one of those games. I had one guy left, and he pitched the next day. The scouts saw my whole pitching staff. I made all kinds of changes in the ball game, so they saw all the players. They gave me the thumbs-up sign when they left the next day.

At the end of the 1966 season, I planned to come back to manage the Oilers again. At least that's what A. Ray Smith and I thought. I signed a contract for the next year, for a raise, and sent it in to the St. Louis office. In December, A. Ray had a banquet, the Diamond Dinner, in Tulsa. Mickey Mantle and Billy Martin and a bunch of other baseball guys were there. I still assumed I was coming back to Tulsa. But I hadn't gotten my copy of the contract back yet. I called St. Louis and talked to Stan Musial about it. He didn't know what the situation was and told me to hold on about heading to spring training with the Cardinals. Over the Christmas holidays, I went to Bob Howsam's house for a cocktail party. By then I heard rumors that he had left the Cardinals and gone over to Cincinnati. I asked Bob, "Which side of Tampa Bay am I going to be on this spring?" The Reds trained in Tampa and the Cardinals in St. Petersburg. Bob just grinned at me and said, "Don't worry." He hired me as a scout for the Reds and sent me to Arizona to scout the clubs there that spring. I regretted leaving A. Ray Smith, who wasn't too happy about it, but we remained friends.

Bob Howsam should be in the Hall of Fame without question. At Cincinnati he built a dynasty that they compare with the greatest dynasties of all, with the 1927 Yankees and clubs like that. He built that Big Red Machine that ruled baseball in the 1970s. When I was there, in 1967, we rewrote the play book. I had quite a hand in that, using my managerial experience. Later I noticed Sparky Anderson used that playbook quite a bit when he became the Reds manager. I like to think that I had something to do with putting together that dynasty. I did scout Johnny Bench.

Bob Howsam sent me to watch Buffalo, which was a Reds farm club in the International League. He said to go down and take a look at this catcher that they had down there. His name was Johnny Bench. So I went to Columbus, Ohio, where the Bisons were playing, and took a look at him. Holy smokes! I tell you I'd seen some young ballplayers, but Bench was really something. John was maybe eighteen, nineteen years old, six foot one, powerful-looking, about 200 or 198 pounds. He could throw like heck, and he could hit a ball a long way. While I was there, he was in kind of a slump. He'd hit a ball real well, but it wouldn't go out of the ballpark.

I had been a pretty good student and teacher of hitters in my managerial years, so I spotted right quick that he wasn't bending over at the waist. I never liked to change a guy, anything about him. I just liked to refine his strong points or gradually eliminate a weakness. John wouldn't bend over, so when he'd swing the bat at the ball, he'd hit it a little bit out on the end and the ball would go 380 feet and wouldn't clear the fence. Lou Fitzgerald, his manager, was an old friend of mine from the Sally League days at Montgomery. I had him send John over to me. I said to him, "John, bend over. Don't change anything else. Just bend over a little bit at the waist. That's all." I was sitting in the stands, and he was standing right there near the backstop. I said, "Take a swing at this wire here on the backstop the way you're standing regular." He'd swing and barely hit the wire. I said, "Now stand in the same place and bend over and swing." He'd hit the wire. He was just about two inches too far away on his swing. Well, Bench put on a pretty good show. He hit 4 home runs the rest of that series.

Years later, I was scouting for another club and sitting in the Houston ballpark. The Reds' trainer, Bill Cooper, who had been my trainer at Tulsa, came up to me and said, "Johnny Bench is having a little trouble." I said, "Yes. I can see that. He's standing straight up again. Tell him to come on over, and I'll chat with him." So Bench came over, and I said, "John, you're standing up again." He said, "No! I can't be." I said, "Yes, you are. You're straight up. Everything else is fine." He said, "All right. I'll do it." He went up to the plate the first time at bat, in the Astrodome, and hit a ball clear into the upper deck for a home run. As he came around home plate, he gave me the thumbs-up sign that he was off and running.

When I got back to Cincinnati, I gave Bob a report on Johnny Bench. I said, "I've seen the finest young ballplayer I've seen in an awful long time. Bring him up. Don't waste him down below. Bring him up. He'll never go back to the minors. He'll hit 30 home runs. He'll drive in 100 runs a year. He'll be the best catcher in baseball. He's got the greatest arm I've ever seen. I believe he can play anyplace on the ball club, first base, second, short, third, outfield, anyplace. He'll be an All-Star for ten years, and it wouldn't surprise me if he goes in the Hall of Fame." I wish I had kept a copy of that letter.

Cincinnati was playing the Dodgers at that time, and Vin Scully, the Dodgers announcer, came up to the press room after the game. A Cincinnati field announcer was bragging about Bench. He said to me, "Hey, Charlie, tell Vince about our prospect." So I told him. I said, "I saw the greatest catcher that I've ever seen." I told him exactly what I wrote. Vin said, "And what is the name of this phenom?" I said, "His name is Johnny Bench, and he belongs to us. Keep that name in mind." Every time Vin Scully sees me, he reminds me of the Johnny Bench report. When I was scouting for the Dodgers later, he'd say, "Why don't you find us a Johnny Bench?"

Tony Robello was the scout who found Bench in Oklahoma. He went to a game and saw this kid playing third base. The kid was rocky and a little bit on the clumsy side. Everybody saw him as a third baseman. Then Tony happened to come back and see him catching. Tony saw him as a catcher and signed him. The rest, as they say, is history. Later I asked Tony if he would have signed Bench on the strength of his third base play. He said, "Yes, but I would have put him in the outfield. We were going to draft him regardless if I'd only seen him as a third baseman. Because he could run, he could throw, good arm and everything. But when I saw him as a catcher, that was it."

When I worked for Cincinnati, Ray Shore was a batting practice pitcher and a coach. One day one of the writers came to me and said, "Why don't you do something for Ray Shore?" I said, "What's that?" He said, "Well, he's not getting paid that much." I think he was getting something like three or four thousand dollars. Bob Howsam had inherited that salary structure from the previous general manager, Bill DeWitt, who wasn't known for letting loose of a buck very easily. So I went to Bob and said, "Why don't you give this guy a decent salary? He's pitching batting practice for us and coaching and everything. You're going to get the blame for it if the story comes out, and somebody will probably break the story." So Bob gave Ray a nice raise, and he turned out to be a pretty good coach. I also recommended him as a scout. He turned out to be a fine baseball man. I also helped Dave Bristol get a two-year contract. And I told Bob not to lose Larry Shepard, that he was too good a pitching coach. I had managed against Larry when he managed Billings in the Pioneer League.

As a scout, you would go off for a week or more to cover teams and scout possible trades. Sometimes it became a burden to get your laundry done on these trips. You didn't always have time to send your laundry out. In Cincinnati, they had the Palm Beach Clothing Company. I went there, and I bought myself three striped seersucker jackets. They were very comfortable and light. One was blue, another was brown, and the third was red. Then I bought trousers to match. I also bought shirts that you could wash and wear, so you could do them in the hotel room. So one time I was going to go out to dinner with one of the scouts, a friend of mine in Cincinnati, and he knocked on the door. I hollered, "Just a minute." What I was doing? I had put a coat and trousers on and stepped in the shower and washed the coat, inside first. Then I would reverse it and wash it the other way. I also reversed the trousers to wash them. Then I'd hang the coat and trousers up and they'd be dry by the time I came back from the ballpark or dinner. So I opened the door with these pants on backward, inside out, and the coat inside out. I told my friend never to tell anybody about this. But he never let me off the hook. He said, "Have you lost your mind?" I said, "No, I'm just saving on my laundry and valet, and not only that, it's light and it's washable, and I'm enjoying it." But the word got around. He said many times, "I wish I had a picture of you coming out of there soaking wet with that seersucker coat on and with those washable pants."

Once, when I was scouting Baltimore in the American League, I looked at the top of the outfield fence at their stadium. It had a jaggedy edge, those sharp pointed spikes common on mesh fencing. I said to one of the guys I was sitting with, Lee MacPhail, "Why the heck don't you have padding? Put the padding on that fence on there?" He said, "Oh, why, nah, why? That's just expensive." I said, "Well, what if Mickey Mantle came into town and made a jump out there and threw his arm up over top of that fence? Those points would stick in his arm and go two inches deep." MacPhail said, "Well, that'd be tough." I said, "Yes, it would be tough. You'd lose one of your best fan attractions in baseball. And while you're doing that, why don't you put something on the bottom of that so a guy can't get his foot stuck underneath, as he's going over toward the fence?" I believe, and I may stand corrected on this, but I believe Al Kaline got his arm caught on that fence and was out for a little while. The next time I came into Baltimore, they had put padding on the fence and boarded up the bottom spaces.

I got to see the great World Series of 1968. I was already linked up with the new Kansas City Royals expansion franchise. Ewing Kaufman, the owner, sent only three of us—Joe Gordon, Cedric Tallis, and me—to the Series. The traveling secretary had some more tickets, so he gave them to me. He said, "Take them in there and sell them, and just return the money for them." My sister Kay lived in Detroit, and my sister Ann was coming in from Montana, and they wanted to see the World Series. Kay called me and said, "Brother, I got to have tickets." I says, "I can't get tickets." Then I got this whole bunch of tickets from the Royals. She said, "Well, I need this many." She was working for Timken, who made roller bearings, and everybody in the place wanted tickets. They didn't believe she could get tickets. She sent her son down to where we were staying, and I gave him a sheet of tickets for the game. She took them and scalped them, and she became a VIP in the office. So now, right before the first game, she called me up and said, "I got to have four! I got to have four of the best seats!" I said, "I can't get four!" But I had them. I just wasn't paying much attention to it. I said, "For whom?" She said, "For the big union guy and the guy that's the president of the company." So I got them box seats right in back of the Tigers dugout. She said I made her a big person at the plant. I saw the game in the upper deck, right close to the right-field line, the three of us from the Kansas City Royals. I was a Tigers fan, of course, although I had worked for the Cardinals too. But I was kind of rooting for the Tigers. Mickey Lolich did a superb job, winning 3 ball games. I got quite a bit of satisfaction out of seeing one of my old pitchers I had trained in spring training be a hero. But then it was off to Kansas City and the new expansion club.

TEN

Putting All the King's Men Together

In 1968 the American League awarded expansion franchises to the Kansas City Royals and the Seattle Pilots for the 1969 season. Cedric Tallis, whom I had managed for at Montgomery and Vancouver, signed on as general manager of the Royals. He knew all about me and was after me to join his staff. I was working for Bob Howsam as a scout for Cincinnati. I had signed a contract to go back with them. But Cedric came after me. He stopped off at our house here in Denver and asked me if I'd stop by Kansas City on my way home. I said, "Yeah, I'll stop by." So I did. Cedric took me down to the office, and we had a meeting with Ewing Kauffman, the owner of the ball club at that time. Charlie Truitt, the financial man, was also there. Ewing Kauffman was a fine man. I didn't say too much. I listened to them selling me on the idea and everything, because Cedric had done a pretty good job of selling me to Kauffman. As we talked, I finally said, "Could I ask you a couple of questions?" Kauffman said, "Sure." I said, "What are you interested in the most on this ball club? Are you interested in winning or making money?" He said, "Both." I said, "If you make money and we lose, are you going to be happy?" He said, "Heck, no." I said, "Well, then don't you think that if you win, you're going to make money?" He said, "Yes." Then he said, "All right, what do you think, Charlie?" I said, "Well, Mr. Kauffman, I'm a great believer in winning. I don't think there's anything else but winning." He said, "Fine." So he gave me a little time to think this over. He said, "Where are you going?" I said, "Going home to be with my family, and then I'm going back on the road for Cincinnati." Then, after Charlie Truitt and Kauffman left, Cedric and I went out for lunch. He said, "Do you want to come on board?" I said, "Yeah, it's interesting, but, Cedric, I want to manage again." He said, "Well, that's something that I want to talk to you about." So we agreed, on a handshake, that I would manage the club after we had selected the players. I said, "Well, that's fine."

Cedric and I got along great, and he was a fine baseball man. In fact, he hadn't played baseball, and he had just a little bit of a background as a business manager. He wasn't a uniform guy. But he had an uncanny way of making trades. He proved that at Vancouver when I was his manager for three years in the Coast League. He could get ballplayers I never thought he could. He knew ballplayers real well. With that combination, we got along great. We didn't always agree. If you agree about everything, you don't need one or the other. That's kind of the way I looked at it. So he said, "Well, Charlie, this is what I'll do. I'll give you a three-year contract to do this, and anytime when we get this thing started and the time is right, I'll give you the manager job." I said, "OK." We shook hands on it. He wrote out the agreement for me to be the Director of Player Procurement, a three-year contract at $22,500, I believe, with a major league per diem when I would cover the club. Kauffman said, "When do you want to get started?" I said, "Well, you better clear this with Cincinnati, so they don't accuse you of tampering." So he called Bob Howsam, and I think Bob let me go very reluctantly, because I had worked well for him.

When we started in Kansas City, we had a yellow pad, pencils, and a borrowed telephone. With that we started out forming an organization. I was in charge of player procurement. Then Cedric hired Lou Gorman from Baltimore, who had applied for my job. There had been a lot of applications for the job. We got ready for the upcoming expansion draft at a hotel in Boston, if I recall correctly. I had a great backlog of major league players, especially American League ones, from which the Royals could draft. Each expansion club could select thirty players. Each existing American League club could protect fifteen players. Then, if one of the clubs lost a player to the draft, it could protect three more. Each expansion club was supposed to select three players from each of the ten American League clubs. We were going to get thirty players. I had seen practically all the players that we selected and that Seattle, the other expansion club, chose. I had seen them in all sorts of leagues. We took some fine ballplayers—Dick Drago, Jim Rooker, Bob Oliver, Joe Foy, and some others.

When we did our selecting for the Kansas City Royals, we went a little bit to the younger ballplayer at the start. Seattle went for the older ballplayers. When they did that, I was really happy about it. So was Cedric. Along about the twentieth pick or so, we decided we'd go after a couple of older guys and trade them. By this time, the clubs were getting smarter than we were, and they were protecting their younger players. We found ourselves without a shortstop. There weren't very many good, unprotected shortstops available. We had to take Jackie Hernandez from Minnesota. He turned out to be a fine infielder for us. But it wasn't another year or two years before we traded him for Freddie Patek. So we took a couple of older guys. We selected Hoyt Wilhelm and traded him to the California Angels for Ed Kirkpatrick and another catcher, a young guy, and an infielder. That was the plan. We went for the younger guys.

But in the regular draft, they wouldn't let us select from the minor leagues until the Triple-A, Double-A, and Single-A clubs had made their choices. Then we selected after that, eighty or ninety players. Only two or three of them made it to the majors. We didn't have much of a choice. So I started aggressively building a farm system. I hired a lot of good baseball people. I worked in an adaptation of the Cubs' rotating coach system. I didn't like rotating pitching coaches down to the minors, but I made sure each club had major league coaches to teach the big league ways. We tried to match the coaches to the strength of the teams. If we were developing pitchers at one club, we'd send our best pitching coach there. If it was infielders, there went our best infielder coach. We also tried to balance things out. If the manager had been a pitcher, we sent that team a guy who'd been an infielder or outfielder, and vice versa. I set the standards. I told them they had to be firm, but they had to be fair. I didn't want any fooling around.

A lot of interesting things happened putting the expansion club together. One thing that I did, and got criticized violently for, was send a form letter out to every minor league manager in baseball at that time, B, C, and Single-A , Double-A, and Triple-A. I asked them to list their All-Star team prospects, their big league prospects in their leagues. Gosh, from some of the managers, I got back some of the dandiest letters you ever saw. Boy, they ripped me from one end to the other. They called me everything in the book. They said I was unethical and everything else. But I knew a lot of them, and I told them not to put their own players on a list. So I got a lot of lists, and I selected quite a few players from those. But, boy, I got heck from everybody for that. I got the idea from Bobby Bragan. When he was managing in the Dodgers organization, he sent me a letter asking me about my team's prospects, and I stored that idea away for future use.

The other thing that happened was I got accused of tampering. I'd seen seven applications from Yankees people for jobs in the organization. I caught heck from that. Lee MacPhail, who was a major executive with the Yankees, called me up and told me I was tampering. I said, "No, I was not tampering, because I didn't seek those guys out. They wrote seeking a job on Yankees stationery, so I wasn't tampering. I would get permission from your ball club, and I'd talk to you." General William Eckert was the commissioner at that time, and he gave me all kinds of heck too. Finally

I said, "Quiet down," and I told him the whole story. I said, "If you guys don't get off my back, I'm going to publicize these names of the people that are writing on the Yankees ball club stationery asking for jobs, and you'll find out what kind of boys the Yankees people have." I never heard another word from him. He wasn't a very good commissioner.

During the expansion draft, there was a rule about players in military service. If the player was in the service and was coming out before the season would begin, he would be eligible for the draft. A club would have to protect him. There were two ballplayers I'd seen in the Yankees organization but couldn't find on any lists. I had good reports on them and had seen one of the guys play, but I couldn't find them. They weren't on the forty-man major league roster. They weren't on the minor league Triple-A roster. So they had to be in the service. I had a heck of a time finding out. I paid a newspaper clippings service, $75 per name and $1.50 or $2 per clipping. They'd send the clipping to me if the name appeared somewhere. This was how I located Bobby Murcer. He was at Ft. Huachuca, Arizona, playing for the base team. The other guy was Jerry Kinney, an infielder, who was in the Navy in Hawaii. I got his name also. So the Yankees were really protecting seventeen ballplayers, not just fifteen. Murcer and Kinney were not on any roster. So I found them, and I kind of raised heck. I didn't get very far, but I got some satisfaction causing a little flack for the Yankees, after they'd accused me of tampering. The league changed the rule at the last minute. We didn't get a chance at Murcer or Kinney. Later on I could have shot Bobby Murcer. He broke up a no-hitter that Jim Rooker was throwing against the Yankees when I had the Royals. We lost the game, 2–1.

I don't think a lot of people know this, but the Yankees didn't protect Mickey Mantle in 1968. I told Kauffman that I didn't think they would protect Mantle, because Mickey was talking about quitting. I said, "Let's select Mantle number one. When we do select him, let me talk to him before. I can't tamper, but let me talk to him. Will you pay him $250,000 a year for three years?" That would have been quite a salary at that time. He said, "Why?" I said, "He can do everything for us. Even if he can't play, he'll be our PR guy. He can coach for us on the field, if he wants to. He can do color commentary on television. He'd be our ambassador to the public. We'll get the whole states of Missouri, Oklahoma, and Texas. He's from Oklahoma, and he played at Joplin as a kid and at Kansas City. We'll tie him up with a good contract." Kauffman bought the idea, but then just before the draft, we got a telegram saying that Mickey wouldn't report, that he was retiring. But to this day, I think that was a phony telegram. I think the Yankees did that because they didn't protect him. That way, with

Kinney, Murcer, and Mantle, they actually got to protect eighteen guys in the first round.

Muriel Kauffman was involved in getting the name *Royals* and handling the design of the uniforms. I think she was Canadian and loved the Canadian people. But when the new Montreal club wanted to use the name Royals, she somehow got the name for Kansas City. I guess the Montreal people were furious, but they had had the name only on the minor league level. Everything for the Royals was royal blue, including the covers of the player instruction manuals. Everything in the stadium, the stadium club and boxes and everything, were all royal blue. The uniforms were royal blue, even the road ones, which had a tinge of that color. They were very nice. I don't know that she actually designed them, but I'm sure she made the final decision. She was a very neat lady, and everything was very classy.

Besides Cedric, the general manager, and Charlie Truitt, the financial guy, we had Lou Gorman and John Schuerholz in the front office. Gorman always had some young guy already installed in the Hall of Fame. He'd brag about some young guy down in the farm system, "Oh, this kid's going to be in the Hall of Fame." And the kid hadn't swung the bat even one time yet for the Royals. Sure, he looked great, but he had to do it on the field. Writers would do that too, making those early judgment calls on guys. I call them "fiction writers" when they do that. Schuerholz, who became the Braves general manager, was an assistant to Gorman in the farm system. He was a sharp young guy, willing to learn. I came down hard on him one time. He was calling one of the other clubs to compare drafts. I said, "Get as much information as you can, but don't give them anything." We were occasionally losing out on getting good prospects, such as when the Giants beat us to Dave Kingman.

Joe Gordon became the manager of the Royals that first year. I had a handshake agreement to be manager sometime later. But Joe wasn't the first choice. One side, the Kansas City sportswriters, wanted Hank Bauer, who had managed the Orioles. Hank, the tough Yankees outfielder, had also played for the Kansas City Athletics. The other group wanted Bob Lemon to manage. My first choice was Billy Martin. But for some reason, somebody there didn't like him. I had seen Billy managing at Denver, and I thought he'd be fantastic. So instead of settling for me, which I thought would happen because of the handshake agreement, they picked Joe Gordon. That was all right. I didn't mind that at all, because I knew Joe pretty well and respected his abilities. He was kind of a happy-go-lucky type of guy, but when the chips were down, he was devastating. I'd learned that by managing against him in the Coast League, when he was with San

Francisco and I was at Vancouver. I had also worked with Joe in the Tigers organization, so I knew all about him. Joe did a great job for Kansas City. The Royals finished fourth in the West division. We wanted him to stay on, but Joe didn't like managing. He'd get nervous as heck. He had been a great ballplayer, but the managing didn't appeal to him. Toward the end of the first year, 1969, Joe asked me to go down on the field and give him an evaluation of the players that we were playing against. So I went down on the field, and Joe said he wasn't going to come back. I said, "You're crazy. I'll get you a two-year contract. You're good at managing." But I couldn't talk him out of it. He felt he was tied down too much. He couldn't express himself.

One of the biggest things we had to deal with while starting the new club was that the thirty players we selected felt that they weren't wanted. A lot of the guys were really crushed. The Yankees didn't want me, the Tigers didn't want me, and so forth, they'd moan. We had to undo that. So when we gathered for spring training in Ft. Myers, Florida, we started to reverse those attitudes. I also talked to those ballplayers. It was tough. I got them all together and said, "Now, I don't care whether the Yankees wanted you or not, we wanted you." I repeated that often. "We wanted you. That's why we got you. Here's the opportunity. You're in the big leagues. We could have signed another ballplayer, but we wanted you." I kept harping on that, and finally we got some good chemistry going with the players. Then I left them in the hands of Joe Gordon.

Joe asked me to come down and set up the conditioning program. We were very good friends, and we discussed conditioning quite often. Joe had been a gymnast in college. He was very agile. He was a heck of a guy and a great ballplayer. He should be in the Hall of Fame. He asked me to do the conditioning program. I conditioned pitchers by running them, and I also controlled their throwing the ball. I'd give them ten to fifteen minutes to warm up their arms, and they would throw little curve balls and throw fastballs and work on their control, and I controlled the time. We did this every day for ten days. They ran all the time. I also made pitchers get in pepper games. They don't even know what a pepper game is today. One hitter, one fielder, one ball, one bat. Every movement that you make playing pepper is used in a baseball game. I wasn't thrilled with a lot of these exercises like lying on your back and pumping your legs up. I never saw a play in baseball where you were lying on your back. My pitchers never had sore arms, so Joe was very pleased with that. The players rebelled a little bit. They'd gripe, but I never saw a good, healthy ballplayer complain. Baseball players that are hurt complain quite a bit.

I had a little exercise about concentration I ran in spring training with the Royals. It didn't go over very well, unfortunately. I lined up the players and had them do warmup throws. Two guys threw the ball back and forth. Second basemen and shortstops, double play combinations, threw to each other. Outfielders threw with another outfielder, catchers with another catcher. Third basemen tossed the long throw with first basemen. Every time a guy made a bad throw, he had to run around the ballpark. Every time a guy dropped the ball, the guy who was careless had to run around the ballpark. During the first two or three days, there was a lot of grumbling. Finally I got the message over to them: when the ball is thrown to you, you've got to catch it. If the ball drops, there's no play. You have a heck of a time executing a play if you drop the ball or throw it badly. After about the fifth day, we only had one guy still grumbling, my good friend Lou Piniella. I understand that now, as a manager, he doesn't take any grumbling. I saw him getting on a couple of guys who were careless while he was managing. And this year, his Seattle Mariners are having a tremendous season. So maybe Lou has learned something from me. That got the message over, and that's the way you teach.

We had some guys who couldn't run very well, so we brought in some Olympic track coaches, including Wes Santee, to help our guys run better. We paid them one thousand dollars and expenses. They were great. They helped some of our slower runners drop their times running to first base. They taught the guys how to pump their arms sideways going around first base to speed up their turns. Also they taught guys racing toward first base to bend at the waist and go across the base like a sprinter to get the call from the umpire. The guys liked this type of coaching, but the organization didn't pursue it any further.

The players we drafted or traded for the first couple of versions of the Kansas City Royals were an interesting lot. We selected Roger Nelson first in the expansion draft, but that was over my objection. I didn't want to take a pitcher first. I wanted to take position ballplayers first, because I'd always felt that a pitcher can come along faster than anybody. But I was shot down on that decision, and we selected Roger Nelson first from Baltimore. Lou Gorman talked Kauffman into picking him first. I had seen Roger Nelson when I was with the White Sox, and I didn't think much of him. He didn't turn out worth a darn. He had a concave chest, and I was told many times by a lot of knowledgeable baseball men that those guys will always get hurt. Those guys always come up with sore arms and sore shoulders. He didn't have a long career with us.

We selected Joe Foy as our number two pick. We got him from the Red

Sox. Cedric had worked for the Red Sox organization years before, and he took some pleasure in getting Foy away from them. Joe was a fine ballplayer. He had his best year in 1969. But he wasn't taking good care of himself. He was smoking marijuana, and he was just losing control. He was a hell of a ballplayer, but we didn't know about his habits. There must have been only two clubs in all of baseball, the Royals and the Mets, who didn't know. My scout was watching, but he didn't give me that information. We traded Joe to the Mets.

I scouted Lou Piniella when he was with the Portland club. I liked a lot of things about him. I liked him especially at the bat. He was a tough out. But he had a quirk. If he hit a ball hard to an infielder, say on two hops, he'd run a few steps down the line and quit. If he hit a ball hard, a long way, and a guy made a great play, he'd drag himself out there and mope in the outfield. We were going to select him next in the expansion draft, but Seattle beat us to it. But we made a trade for him. I took Steve Whitaker, an outfielder, from the Yankees. He had had a good year, but the Yankees exposed him to the draft. We took him, and we found out why. He was all messed up in his private life. So we traded Whitaker to Seattle for Lou Piniella. We finally got Lou.

When I managed the Royals in 1970, Lou had won the Rookie of the Year Award the previous year. But he continued to loaf. After he hit a ball real hard and a guy caught it, Lou loafed on a fly ball, and it got away from him. The batter made a double on what should have been a single, and I got mad at Lou. I thought, "Well, somebody's going to have to teach this guy to play, to be a player for nine innings and not do all that stuff." He could play better than he was. I knew it, and he knew it too. I forgot about his Rookie of the Year Award, and I took him out of the lineup. He never forgave me for that. Here he was being honored, and then he didn't play. But I believe that I woke him up at that time. In fact I know I did. He was a better ballplayer after that. Years later, when I was scouting the Yankees for the Dodgers in the World Series, I made a strong report on him. I never let a personal thing stand in the way of being honest and truthful on a scouting report. I said that he was the toughest out on the ball club, and he was. He was the toughest out for us. He was very selective at the plate. Later, as a manager, he started out weakly, but then he turned out to be a real good one. That didn't surprise me, because he was very dedicated in his approach to hitting.

Lou has always had a terrible temper and disposition. Lou would put it on; he'd throw a tantrum. I claimed it was due to his Latin temperament. He took quite a shot at me when he wrote his book *Sweet Lou*. It was uncalled for, but I took it. I came back at him with a newspaper quote. I said, "Lou wouldn't play, wouldn't hustle. He could, but he just wouldn't. He was terrible that way." Years later, he apologized to me down in spring training, and we've been good friends ever since.

I like to brag about getting Amos Otis for the Royals. My first year there, while I was watching the Mets play the Cardinals at St. Petersburg, I saw this kid playing third base, but it didn't look like he wanted to play there. So I found out about him and talked to him. I said, "Why don't you want to play third?" He said, "I'm a center fielder." Well, I put that down in my book. He was Amos Otis, and we traded for him later. I remembered him, and when we got the chance, I said, "Let's get Amos Otis." Jimmy Adair, one of our scouts in Texas, who I knew from my days in the Cotton States League and with the Baltimore organization at Vancouver, was high on a big Mets farm system pitcher named Bob Johnson. Bob was just a big, fun-loving guy. He used to ride motorcycles and everything. He was a little bit on the nutty side. They called him flaky. But he was a good competitor. Jimmy Adair also praised a left-handed pitcher named Jon Matlack. He told us to get either one or both in the trade. So we made a trade with the Mets, Joe Foy for Amos Otis and Bob Johnson. We couldn't quite get Matlack. We worried we were pushing our luck, and it would kill the deal. Otis turned out to be a fine outfielder, a perennial All-Star. He played center field regular for fourteen or fifteen years. One year he was the Colorado Rockies' hitting coach. I don't know how well he did at that, but he'd make a good outfield coach. Geez, he knew how to play that outfield.

When Amos played center field for the Royals, he would catch the ball one-handed. He made it look so natural. It was unusual at that time to catch a ball one-handed. Most everybody was catching two-handed. I came up trained to use both hands. You had to use two hands. I did get away from that when I was at Texarkana. If I was chasing a ball down up against the wall, I couldn't always get both hands up, so I starting using just one hand. But one day I told Otis, "Amos, if you ever drop a ball one-handed, I'll shoot you." He said, "Well, if I ever do, you can, Skipper." I never saw him drop one. He was a remarkable outfielder.

The trade with Pittsburgh for Freddie Patek turned out very well for the Royals. I was very much instrumental in that trade. I was still associated with the club. I wanted to take Patek in a minute. I talked to Joe Brown of the Pirates and asked him if either one of his shortstops, Gene Alley or Patek, was available. I think Freddie was a little dissatisfied with sharing the job. Joe said, "Alley won't be traded." I said, "What about Patek?" He said, "Yeah, we'd invite a trade conversation on that." I brought all that information back to Cedric. I said, "We can get Patek." He said, "You can?" I said, "Yeah, get him. That'll cement our ball club, a shortstop." Cedric said he'd heard something negative about him. I said, "Don't pay any attention to all that stuff. He's unhappy because he's not playing regularly. He's a regular ballplayer. He can steal a base, he's got some power, and he's a good take-charge guy. He can do some things for you. He's better than anybody we've got in our organization. Get him." So both clubs started putting together packages. They liked Bob Johnson, the guy that we got in the trade from the Mets. We traded Bob Johnson, Jackie Hernandez, and Jim Campanis for Patek, Bruce Dal Canton, and a catcher. It turned out to be a tremendous trade. We got a ten-year shortstop, in my mind an All-Star shortstop. He was a good base stealer. He had good baseball sense. Freddie knew the situation of the ball game, when to steal, when not to steal. He wasn't out for the glory of stealing a base. He was a team player. I recognized that in him.

I was also involved in the opportunity to get John Mayberry from Houston in 1971. I was scouting that year. The Royals asked me about him, and I said, "Get him. We don't have a real good first baseman. This guy is much better than who we have." We traded them Lance Clemmons, a left-handed pitcher, who they wanted in the worst way. We got Mayberry, and John did a good job for Kansas City for quite a few years. He made the All-Star team six times.

Buck Martinez turned out to be a pretty good little catcher for quite a few years. Bob Quinn, who had worked for the Phillies, knew about him. We drafted him from the Philadelphia system in the regular draft and paid twenty-five thousand dollars for him. He turned out to be one of the finest draft choices we ever made. We had regular catchers, but the Royals wanted to advance him real quickly. He wasn't quite ready. So we sent him to Omaha for some experience. When he came back up, he was a real good catcher. Later, when he was with the Brewers or Blue Jays, he tagged out two guys at home plate on the same play, even though he broke his leg in the collision. That would have been a good one to see. Buck went on to become a fine broadcaster, a telecaster, for one of the big league clubs, and now he's the manager for the Blue Jays.

Al Fitzmorris was in the White Sox organization, and I selected him on the basis of what I'd seen of him when I was with the White Sox. They kind of criticized me for selecting these kids out of the B leagues. I don't know what roster he was on, but we selected him. For four or five years, Al had the best record of any pitcher in major league baseball. They all complained and worried that he was a motorcycle, black-studded-jacket guy. I didn't care about that. All I knew was he had a good arm and could pitch. He had a pretty good voice, and he loved to sing. He'd appear as a guest singer in nightclubs. I heard him one time. He was pretty good. Back then baseball people frowned on those things. Now players can do anything they want, it seems. They don't say a word about it. But heck, there's nothing wrong with a ballplayer being a singer.

We selected Mike Hedlund in the expansion draft from Cleveland, and it just goes to show how things happen in scouting. I was coming into Cleveland to scout the club for the Reds. The Indians had an off day on the schedule, but as it turned out, they had an exhibition game going with the Pirates. As I was flying in, I noticed the lights were on at the stadium. When we landed I grabbed my bag, got a cab, and said, "Take me to the ballpark." The driver said, "There's no game there." I said, "Yes, there is. The lights are on." So out we went to the ballpark, and sure enough there was a game. Cleveland had Mike Hedlund pitching. I was very much impressed, and I remembered that the next year during the expansion draft. He did a pretty good job for the Royals, but unfortunately he had a terrible tragedy in his family. His wife's sister and mother, I believe, were killed in an accident, and it just kind of tore him up. He never did reach his potential pitching ability, but he was a pretty good pitcher overall.

The rest of the pitchers were a bunch of mixed results. Dick Drago was a very fine choice of ours in the expansion draft. He was a hard-working guy, tough on the mound. He was one of those rugged guys. He pitched well. We selected him from Detroit. Bill Butler was another guy we selected from Detroit. He was a left-handed pitcher. He never did really reach his potential, but he was a good, strong, hard-throwing left-hander with a good curve. He was an in-and-outer. I thought he'd be a good ballplayer. I personally scouted him, but I guess I misread him. He didn't have as much intestinal fortitude as I thought. That's something that you've got to read about a player and see if he has it. Wally Bunker came over from Baltimore in the expansion draft. He had a pretty good year, but he had a bad arm and was pitching on nerve, or, as they say, "pitching on guts." Today they'd operate on his arm, and maybe he could've come back. He was a good pitcher in his day with the Orioles. Tracy Stallard, who had pitched for me at Tulsa, tried out for the Royals. He was one of my favorites, but he was on his way down and out careerwise. He was still a joker. He would wear chains around his legs like he was a prisoner or something, jokingly protesting about my tough conditioning program.

Jim Rooker came from Detroit in the expansion draft. He was an outfielder. I had seen him when he was with Buffalo. We selected him as a pitcher, and he turned out very well. I insisted we get him, and he did a good job for the Royals and later for the Pirates. Later he became a terrific announcer with Pittsburgh. Jack Tighe and Stubby Overmire, my old friends in the Detroit organization, took me out to dinner and tried to confuse me about the players. They ran up quite a tab on me. But I could tell Rooker was a fine prospect. Tom Burgmeier also pitched for us. He had one other great asset besides the fact that he was a pitcher. He was a good hitter. Gosh, he was a good hitter, and he'd put on an exhibition of hitting at the old Municipal Stadium with the Royals. We selected him in the expansion draft. He would hit that ball as far as any ballplayer on our club could in batting practice. I thought he might have made a pretty good outfielder, because he had a good arm. But maybe it was a little too late to convert him. I think I even used him as a pinch hitter one time. He went on to pitch for seventeen years in the majors. Dave Morehead came over from the Red Sox. He should have been a pretty good pitcher, but he came down with a sore arm, as did Jon Warden.

Jon Warden was the first guy we selected from the Detroit organization in expansion. We didn't have a full scouting department. I was probably the only guy for a long time. I had a backlog of all the ballplayers I had seen in the American League and minor leagues and everyplace else. One day I went into Detroit, and the Tigers started Jon Warden. He pitched real well this one day. He didn't pitch long, but he was well-built and looked kind of like Eddie Lopat or Whitey Ford, maybe a little heavier. We selected him, but the big danger of not seeing him again bit us on the behind. The next time he pitched, he hurt his arm, and I understand he never pitched again. We didn't know that. The Tigers were laughing at us when we chose him.

Then there was Moe Drabowsky. I had heard about Moe while I was at Vancouver when he was with the Cubs. He was a fun-loving guy. You couldn't take him too seriously. One game, when I was managing the Royals, Frank Robinson came up to the plate with a man on third at Memorial Stadium. Moe was pitching. I went out to the mound and said, "We've got first base open. There's a man on third. I think maybe we'd better walk this guy." I had managed against Frank and remembered the home runs he hit in Columbia, South Carolina. Moe said, "No, I can get him out." I walked back to the dugout. Moe got him out all right. Frank hit it clear up into the left-center-field stands, the closest a ball ever came to being hit out of Memorial Stadium there. I never took a pitcher's word after that.

We lost out on getting some pretty fair pitchers. Not selecting Jim Palmer was one of our great mistakes. When Lou Gorman came over to the Royals, I asked him about this young guy Palmer. Some of my friends had told me he had a great arm. Lou said, "Oh, he's got a sore arm." I said, "Well, we ought to draft this guy. I know about him. A friend of mine in Baltimore told me all about him, and he's a heck of a pitcher." Lou said, "Oh, no, he can't pitch." I have always wondered how good Jim would have been if he'd been with the Royals, how he could have improved on what he did in his Hall of Fame career. Maybe it was best that Jim wasn't selected by an expansion club.

I made a mistake with Orlando Peña, and I guess I better admit it. I was managing the Royals, and I hired two guys to pitch batting practice. Peña was one of them. He had a little bit of a palm problem of some sort, and when you're hired as a batting practice pitcher, you pitch every day. He pitched every day for Kansas City. He traveled with the club, and we paid him a salary of ten thousand dollars. Then his arm came around, and I considered putting him on the roster. But Cedric said it wouldn't look good for a batting practice pitcher to be put on the big league roster. I said, "He's got a pretty successful career ahead." But we didn't put him on the roster. Then Joe Brown of the Pirates heard about him through Howie Haak, who had scouted him and watched him throwing batting practice. We released him, and he signed with Pittsburgh. I told Orlando, "You're going to go over to the Pittsburgh Pirates. Sign with them." He got a tremendous salary out of them. He turned out to be a pretty good pitcher.

Another guy we missed out on was Mike Marshall. I regret this a lot. We intended to grab him out of the Detroit organization. But the Seattle Pilots snatched him up right before we could. I had him down as the next pick. I knew all about him, that he was a workhorse, that he had that great arm. He wanted to pitch every day. And he could. I may stand corrected, but I guess he pitched the most relief games of anybody in one season. He was the type of guy you wanted, and, doggone it, we missed him.

The rest of our position players were a motley crew. We bought Luis Alcaraz from the Dodgers. He started for us at second base. He was a journeyman ballplayer, just a little bit too short of talent to be even a utility man. Hawk Taylor was a catcher, and he played a little bit of outfield and other places too. He wasn't a bad ballplayer. He was my long ball pinch hitter, a guy who could maybe bang one off the fence. He turned out to be a pretty good college baseball coach. Paul Schaal played third for us sometimes. He was a fine young man. He wasn't great, by any means, but he was a pretty good ballplayer. He became a doctor or optometrist or something. We made a trade with California for Ed Kirkpatrick, and he turned out to be a very fine day-by-day ballplayer. He was real versatile. He filled in here and there, caught a little bit. He played five years for the

Royals. Scott Northey, Ron Northey's son, was a disappointment. I selected him in the expansion draft from the White Sox organization. I knew him, and I knew his father real well. His father was a pretty good hitter. Scott had all the tools to be a good ballplayer, but he never put them together and just faded away. Mike Fiore was another disappointment. Frank Skaff scouted and recommended him. He had seen him in Baltimore. And Joe Keough, Marty's son and Matt's brother, didn't catch on either. We drafted Bob Oliver from Minnesota. He was a pretty good journeyman ballplayer. He could play first base or the outfield. He was a nice, lovable kind of guy. Later he became a policeman, I believe, an officer out somewhere in California. Every once in a while, I hear from him. It was a pleasure to have him on the team.

Pat Kelly started his career with us. When he was with Kansas City, Pat kept throwing the ball over the relay guy's head. I told him to throw the ball down, make that relay, get that ball shoulder high. In one ball game, he overthrew the relay man twice. After the second time, I took him out right in the middle of the ball game. I caught heck about that. They said that you can't show up a ballplayer. I said, "Yes, I can. If he doesn't learn from that, he won't learn from anything." He learned and turned out to be a pretty good ballplayer.

Dennis Paepke came over in the trade with us from the Angels with Kirkpatrick. He didn't play very often, but we needed some insurance and backup guys, especially to stock the Triple-A Omaha club in case we had an emergency. Kauffman also wanted a good team in Omaha for business reasons. We spent good money to bring in some good players to place at Omaha. We brought Jack McKeon up from the Carolina League to manage that club. We were under the gun in trades, because we didn't have much, and the other clubs could set the price at whatever they wanted. We'd have to pay it. So we had to have reserves, and Paepke was one of our reserves.

In addition to Buck Martinez, we had Ellie Rodriguez and Fran Healy as catchers. Ellie was our Opening Day catcher. We selected him from the Yankees. He was a journeyman catcher. Buck Martinez took over the job. Ellie should have been a good one. I don't know why he didn't develop into a real first-string catcher. I had three catchers and was rotating them and trying to find the right combination in Kansas City, and it just never did work out. Ellie did better over with the Angels, even made the All-Star team, but that may have been because you had to have a guy from each club. Fran Healy was probably as fine a physical prospect as you'd ever want to see for a catcher. We got him and Mike Hedlund from the Cleveland organization, out of the Eastern League. He was big, and he could throw like heck. But he had a terrible quirk. He couldn't throw the ball back to the pitcher. I happened to have three of those guys in my time. I never could correct any of them, but I tried. He also couldn't run worth a darn, but the Olympic track coaches helped him drop his running time to first base from 4.5 to 4.1. Fran eventually became a pretty fine announcer. But he couldn't or wouldn't play. He played nine years, but he wasn't worth a darn to us at the Royals. He's still mad at me.

We also lost out on a couple of good ones. One was Bobby Grich. He was with the Baltimore Orioles organization. I asked Lou Gorman, "What about this guy Grich, this kid Grich, down there somewhere in the lower leagues?" He says, "Aw, he can't play shortstop. He's too fat, too big." So we didn't draft Grich when we had the chance. I regret that one. And because Syd Thrift did a terrible job covering the Washington Senators organization, we blew a chance to get Toby Harrah.

I did a favor for Eddie Sawyer, who had managed the Phillies in the 1940s and 1950s. He was our scout in the East on the major league level. We were involved in the regular draft, but we were way down in the order. We picked after the Single-A leagues. We were drafting to fill out a rookie league roster. By that time, the talent was thin. They'd picked it pretty clean. Eddie came up to me and said, "Charlie, I'd like you to do me a favor if you will." I asked him what, and he said, "I got a nephew who could get a scholarship, if you draft him. Draft him way down there, anyplace." If the college coaches saw you draft a guy, even if he was way down in the order, they'd go after him. They figured we were doing the scouting for them. They would offer him a scholarship. So we did. We drafted the young man somewhere about fiftieth or sixtieth. He got a scholarship. Eddie was forever indebted to us for that.

I gave my son Bud a contract with our Corning, New York, D league farm club when I was Director of Player Procurement. We needed players. He was a fine college athlete, a track man. He was on the relay team. He was faster than I had been at his age. He was also a pole vaulter and held the Skyline Championship at Wyoming. Bud could run, but he couldn't play baseball. He had one official plate appearance in professional baseball. He has one run batted in. He walked with the bases loaded. I had to release him. Can you imagine that? Releasing your own son. He said, "Why, Dad?" I said, "You can't play, son. You can't play." He wasn't too disappointed. I made him what he called a "general all-around flunkey." He sold tickets and concessions, was the clubhouse guy, washed sweatshirts and sweat socks, and swept the stands. And I didn't cut his salary.

We had to start our farm system out from scratch. We began with D league, or rookie league, clubs in Kingsport, Tennessee, and Corning, New York. My old Denver Bears star Bo Osborne was the manager at Corning. I set up playbooks, instruction manuals, for use throughout the system. I had done all these manuals for many years, all the way back to my major league playing days. I would draw an outline of a baseball field, the infield and the outfield, and I would diagram various plays, cutoffs and relays, backup plays, and so forth. I would outline the play as the game progressed, and then the next day I'd get the ballplayer aside and go over the correct way to handle it. Years later, Al Campanis, who was working for the Dodgers, saw my diagrams and asked to borrow them. He put them together into a book. When I heard about that, I asked him for some copies. I got his permission to use it, and I had over two hundred copies of those made. For the Royals, we revised the book and printed it up in great numbers with royal blue covers. In the diagrams, we colored the base runners in royal blue and the fielders in red. Then college and high school coaches in the surrounding states heard about the manuals and kept sending in requests. We flooded Missouri, Kansas, and other areas with the manuals. They became kind of recruiting tools for the Royals. For us they were an important part of the program of developing these ballplayers.

Another thing that I did at that time for the farm system was put a batting cage with a pitching machine in all of our minor league ballparks. I assigned Lou Gorman this task, but Lou, who had never swung a bat in a batting cage, built the cages only about ten feet wide. The players would swing and hit the side of the cage. We had to remake them. I also had them set up a batting cage for the catchers, fill the machines with balls, put all the gear on the catcher, and aim the pitching machine into the dirt. The catcher would practice for half an hour or an hour in the dirt, blocking bad pitches, backhand and everything. We'd also put a base in there and have the machine throw the ball to an infielder to practice stepping on the bag. I used those cages and machines for everything I could think of. I was the innovator on that. I don't know if somebody else had ever done it, but I was the first one, I guess, to use those techniques on the minor league level.

In the late 1960s, I had the idea of setting up a baseball complex down in Florida. I had arranged for the purchase of a site near Sarasota. A Sarasota mover and shaker who owned a department store and was a big White Sox fan alerted us about a place five or six miles out of town, right where the interstate was coming. We paid $128,000 for the acreage. After spring training, the fields would go basically unused. I approached Ewing Kauffman about it, but he wanted his idea of the Baseball Academy. What I had in mind was a four-diamond setup, sort of a cloverleaf pattern with fields on different levels, in which Royals farm prospects would play three 90-game seasons a year, 270 games in all. That way everybody could get in enough at bats or innings pitched to give us a real good look. I would have former big leaguers teaching specific skills in the game. I wanted to hire Tommy Henrich, Billy Herman, and Billy Jurges as instructors. I hoped that the plan might catch on and attract a few other franchises, so we could get a league of sorts going. But Kauffman had his own ideas and wanted Syd Thrift to run it. Thrift and maybe Lou Gorman shot down my plans. Years later, as the Rockies were forming, I approached Don Hinchey with this same idea, but I don't think anyone considered it seriously enough.

The academy was something of a disaster. Thrift got a bunch of high school coaches to instruct at the Royals Academy. I never saw such crazy instruction. One guy had the batters holding the bat straight up and down for bunting. I thought, "The first time a guy foul-tips a bunt attempt inside and it hits him between the eyes, that'll be the end of that." They destroyed the topography of the site. Instead of my cloverleaf pattern, they just bulldozed wherever they wanted. They goofed up the irrigation system, didn't get the joints right, and it ruptured. Then they had to tear up the fields again. I recommended that they put natural turf in the infield, because the infielders were used to the turf and they would be playing some clubs on the road who had grass. Big league clubs had grass in their parks. But I also wanted one of the infields to be artificial turf, because the Royals were constructing a new stadium in Kansas City with artificial turf. There were some good features. They had two beautiful homes on the premises, one for Syd Thrift and the other for his assistant director. The players' quarters were better than any motel. They had a dining room with a chef. The guys could take college classes at a nearby community college. And I arranged for batting cages with tarps on top so they could hit in rainy weather. But overall the experience should have been better.

Steve Korcheck was one of the instructors and Thrift's assistant director. Steve was truly a fine person. He had played with the Washington Senators in the 1950s. He was a good baseball guy. Syd Thrift left something to be desired as a person, and he tried to downgrade Steve. It didn't work, but Steve left anyway. Later he became the president of a college. Several years ago, I saw him at the junior college baseball tournament in Grand Junction, Colorado, and he looked just about the same as he had in 1970, only he was a little grayer.

Tommy Henrich, "Old Reliable," was a delight. I hired him as a scout for the Royals and wanted him as an instructor at the Baseball Academy. Tommy made a statement about hitting that I've never forgotten. I said,

"Tommy, what pitch gave you the most trouble?" He said, "Off-speed pitches. But that fastball, I made my living off the fastball. I knew I was going to get a pitch one time during a ball game, that fastball. Sometimes I'd hit it more if the pitcher wasn't too sharp. But the good pitchers, I knew I was going to get a fastball. I had to get all of it." I said, "Is that when you hit that home run off Don Newcombe, in the World Series in 1949?" He said, "He got me three times, but I got him, one swing. That was the difference in the ball game, 1–0, I believe, wasn't it?" Billy Herman was another one of the guys that I was going to hire as one of the instructors at the Baseball Academy. Tommy Henrich was going to be my left-handed-hitting coach, and Herman was going to be the infield coach. It would have turned out real well if we had put those guys, instructing, in personal one-on-one instruction.

I handled the scouting department also, as well as the development of our minor league clubs. I hired Rosie Gilhousen, Tom Ferrick, and Dale McReynolds as scouts, and some guys in the East. I hired Ferrick as a specialist, a pitching scout. He was an excellent one. I guess he's still with them. I was crazy about Tom. My biggest mistake, though, was hiring Syd Thrift. He was a pusher, never satisfied. We signed him to a contract, and three days later he was dissatisfied, and we had to give him another contract. He cried—not my type of guy. But anyway I signed him from a big league club. He didn't do a good job for us.

Dale McReynolds worked with us at Cincinnati at one time. He was also a schoolteacher, I believe. He was an excellent teacher of scouting. I made him the Central Division supervisor. We had a West Coast Division, a Central Division, and an East Coast Division. Regarding salary, I always found out what a guy was making with his previous club. Dale was making, I think, eight thousand dollars with the Reds. I set the low standard at ten thousand dollars. I sent him a contract for that amount, but then I realized that he was going to be a supervisor. So before the contract came back, I sent him a contract for twelve thousand dollars. Then I thought, "Well, gee whiz, he's going to be teaching all these guys." So I raised him again, this time to fifteen thousand, even before he got the first contract. He called me up and asked, "Charlie, have you been drinking?" I assured him I wasn't. He said he'd never been treated so well in his career. I told him he was now. I also hired my brother John as a scout. He had umpired for three or four years in the minors, but his back was always bothering him from all the bending over. He was living in Arkansas and would cover Oklahoma and parts of Texas and Louisiana. Somebody else would cover Missouri. He had his own area, and I got him a good contract. I sent him a contract for ten thousand dollars for three years, but Dale McReynolds raised him to twelve thousand. He was a very good scout. He did a tremendous job of teaching the Royals way of scouting. Then he went into the Scouting Bureau and had a very nice career in baseball. Buddy Peterson, my old shortstop at Vancouver, was another one of the scouts I hired. In fact, later on I recommended that we hire him with the Scouting Bureau too. When they changed things in Kansas City, I went to bat for him with the Scouting Bureau. He was a good scout, very conscientious. Don Motley and Frank Evans were Negro League players who I hired as scouts with the Royals. Don went on to become the director of the Negro League Museum in Kansas City. I saw him at the opening in 1995 and again at a banquet before the All-Star Game in Denver in 1998. Don made some joking comments about me.

Jay Hankins was the scout for another organization. He lived in the Kansas City area, and he wanted to come on board with the Royals. I said, "What's your territory?" I was very strong on having a scout in the local area. We didn't want anybody to get away, to let somebody else scout a local ballplayer and get him. You'd catch all kinds of heck if you lost a ballplayer in your own state or own area that you should have known about. I asked Jay, "Would you like to scout for us?" He said, "Yes." I said, "I was thinking I was going to ask you." I don't know who he was with. I said, "Well, I can't interfere. I can't tamper with you, but if you think you can get out of your present commitment, I'll give you a job." He got free, and I gave him a job. The first guy he recommended to us was Paul Splittorff. In the course of the conversation, he recommended a ballplayer, a left-handed pitcher from Morningside College. Jay said the clubs weren't too high on him, but he recommended Paul Splittorff strongly. We drafted him. Boy, did he come along quick! Paul got a little bit perturbed with me because I didn't keep him on the Royals, but I didn't want to ruin him. I didn't want to bring him up too fast. We had an opportunity to send him down, and he went. When he came up, he stayed for good. He became an all-time favorite in Kansas City. He went on to become an announcer for the Royals, and he does a fine job. Paul's a knowledgeable baseball guy. Jay Hankins earned his salary for ten years by recommending Paul Splittorff.

I didn't get some guys I wanted for our scouting system, but we had a good one. If you look back at the history of the Kansas City Royals, they were in the first division for twenty years, and it was mostly due to the groundwork of good scouting and good instruction. I feel good about that, because I was kind of a top guy in that development. Mickey McDermott, the old Red Sox pitcher, became a pretty good scout for us. I gave Max

Lanier, the old Cardinals pitcher, a job with Kansas City scouting and doing some work for us. Max was one of the major leaguers who played in the Mexican League in the late 1940s. After his death a few years ago, I received a very fine letter of thanks from his wife. We put all those people on the insurance policy, and lot of them hadn't have anything like that before. We talked Ewing Kauffman into making the policy a blanket one. I feel good about that, because it helped Max's family after he died.

I offered Cal McLish a job as a scout for Oklahoma and parts of Texas for the Royals. He said, "Charlie, I'll take the job, but I think I want to coach." I said, "Well, Cal, we'll sign you." I made him an offer and everything, and I said, "If you don't get the coaching job, you're with us." He called me a week or two later and told me he got a coaching position. Tony Robello was another one I missed out on. Tony worked with the Cincinnati Reds for many years. When I was the head of scouting at the Kansas City Royals, they tried to hire Tony. He said, "I can't leave Cincinnati." I said, "Tell them somebody's asking for you, Tony, and maybe you'll get a raise. Tell them somebody's made an offer. Don't tell them who!" He said, "You know, I'm friendly with Bob Howsam." Tony called me and said, "I can't." I said, "Well, fine, then get yourself a little better salary." I guess he did.

Bird dogs are very loyal to the organization. But they are often forgotten. When I was with Kansas City, I ordered ten gross of Royals baseball caps, and I'd call a scout up and ask him how many bird dogs he had. We distributed those caps. When a scout would go in and talk to a young boy, or the parents, he'd take a couple of baseball caps and give them to him. It was a good selling point for the organization. I also got them Royals windbreakers. This was a real coup, if I can call it that, because we had loyalty like no other team had in the scouting department. I also talked Kauffman into buying big Samsonite traveling bags with the logo of the Kansas City Royals for the scouts. That went over real well. Then, because most scouts had only one car and their wives needed one while they were away scouting, I convinced Kauffman to supply company cars. I tried to get them Cadillacs with the Royals logo on them. Kauffman was wild about that idea, but somebody in the front office said, "Oh, we can't spoil them." I said, "Have you ever ridden five hundred miles in an old jalopy across some of those country roads trying to look at some kids for the organization?" So we finally got big Pontiacs for the scouts. Kauffman insisted that they keep the cars washed, but they would have to pay for that out of their per diem. I got the scouts' per diem raised to twelve dollars a day. I got them gas cards. I also got them some seats behind home plate at Municipal Stadium. I recommended to Cedric that we save a dozen box seats back of home plate for the scouts, and another thirty or so reserved seats higher up, so if a guy wanted to sit a little higher, he could. I maintained that to do their jobs the scouts needed to be able to sit right there without being bothered. The Royals began to treat their scouts better than many other teams did. It was a great organization in that respect.

Bird dogs were a necessity in a good scouting system. At Kansas City, when I hired Rosie Gilhousen, he had his network of bird dogs and scouts out in Southern California. He was a fine scout. Rosie knew good ballplayers when he saw them. I gave him a three-year contract and five thousand dollars more than he'd been paid before. He had an agreement with his bird dogs and associate scouts that if one of them recommended a ballplayer that he signed to a professional contract, that bird dog or associate scout would get a certain amount of money. If the player got to the big leagues, the guy would get a nice bonus. He'd treat them real well. So we had a club at Phoenix in the wintertime, and Rosie called me and said, "Hey, Charlie, I want to bring my bird dogs down there." I said, "How many are there?" He said, "Oh, I guess about twenty or twenty-five." I said, "Well, gee whiz, that might be a little expensive." He said, "Oh, no! We'll drive there in a bunch of cars. We got a lot of friends down there we can stay with. I just want them to see the players." We had a bunch of players who were there in college. He said, "This will be great for them." I said, "All right, go ahead."

So down to Phoenix they came. I guess he had twenty or twenty-five bird dogs, and I met them all. I didn't know a lot of them. Rosie was pretty good. He said, "You know, you're the boss. You ought to have this outfit. You should be director of scouting." I said, "OK. That's enough said." I was having second thoughts about being scouting director. We met at one of the fine steakhouses there in Phoenix, right down by the river. I said, "We'll meet at 6:00." He said, "Oh, heck, cocktail hour is about 4:30." I said, "All right. Just run up the tab, and I'll be down there." I had some calls I had to make, and about 6:30 I came down there, and, boy, they were having a great time. There was the whole bunch of them, and they had a big room. I said, "Set the thing up, Rosie." And he did. They had a great big table in one of the side rooms, waitresses and all. He said, "What can we have?" I said, "Heck, whatever you want." So they started in. When I finally got the bill, it was $1,800. They made me tip the waitresses 25 percent. That brought the bill to something like $2,400. I said, "They're going to have a new Director of Players when I get back and this bill goes in." When I got back, Charlie Truitt, the financial guy for the Royals, called me and said, "I got to have an explanation on this. I'm going to take it to Kauffman." I explained Rosie's system of bird dogs to him, that they were basically working free of charge, and that I thought we should reward their loyalty somewhat. I said, "Heck, Charlie, we have a doctor and a dentist and a president of a bank working for us through Rosie." He said, "You do?" I said, "Yes! These are men who are just delighted to be associated with a big league club, and we've got Royals guys out there." He still hemmed and hawed, but I said, "If there are any problems, I'll pay it out of my salary. And I'll go to Ewing." Charlie Truitt back-pedaled real quickly. He didn't want any embarrassment for the club. The bill was covered. I thought this all paid off real well. Rosie's group had eleven players on the Royals' forty-man major league roster by the second or third year. And Rosie was the guy who eventually signed George Brett. He and his bird dogs got a lot of ballplayers for Kansas City.

When I was running the Kansas City Royals spring camp, I made some scouting notes on the ballplayers coming in to play us. We were playing the Cardinals, and Bill White came over and said, "What are you doing?" I said, "I'm just marking down some things here on the scouting report." He said, "Let me see that." He looked at it and got a big grin and said, "You're the only one." I didn't know what he was talking about. He said, "Charlie, you're the only one." I said, "What is it?" He said, "You don't have the 'race' on there. Why?" I said, "I don't care what color he is, or whether he shaves or he doesn't shave, or what he is. I just want to see if he can play baseball. If he can play, I don't care who he is." Bill White and I became fast friends from that moment on. I saw him a couple of years ago, and he reminded me of that day.

When Joe Gordon decided not to return as manager for the 1970 season, the Royals offered me the job. When I took the manager position, I had been troubled with a bleeding ulcer for a couple of years. I wouldn't tell anybody, not even Cedric. I just suffered with it. I had it operated on on February 1. When they cut into it, the blood spurted to the ceiling. I even registered at the hospital under Moreskonich because if the Royals knew, they might have made a change. On February 15, I was in Ft. Myers for spring training. To the extent that I did a lousy job for Kansas City, I blame it on the ulcer. I wouldn't stay away from the scotch and water. I had lost thirty pounds during that time, from 195 down to 165. I wasn't physically strong. When I took the job as manager, I began to have second thoughts about it. I'd always wanted to manage again, and this was an ideal situation. I'd been in on the ground floor of the organization from the start. I made all these contributions to the ball club, setting up a farm system, hiring all the scouts, and putting out player manuals. I did a fair job as manager for the Royals, but I was released. I was crushed. I don't think I was treated well when things got a little tough. Cedric got into a shouting match with Mrs. Kauffman, who was very active in the ball club and a very gracious lady. Kauffman asked me if I wanted to be the general manager, but I wasn't a desk guy. I didn't even like all that desk work that I was doing as the Director of Player Procurement. I told him no, and he didn't like that.

Before I became the manager, Cedric had hired two coaches, and he was trying to get a third, Bob Lemon, to be the pitching coach. Harry Dunlap would coach first base, and Joe Schultz, the former Seattle Pilots manager, would coach third base. Joe was a fun-loving guy. He had a pretty good sense of humor. Sometimes they'd think he was very serious. I don't know what kind of a catcher he was. He had been in the Browns organization way back there, but our paths never crossed. Then I hired Danny Carnavale to be my bench coach. Danny was a longtime former scout and manager. We knew each other in the Tigers organization. I had to inherit a couple of them. I wanted to pick my own men, but it was all right. I wanted Galen Cisco to be my pitching coach in 1970, but he turned it down. We had drafted him from the Red Sox. He must have known something, because I didn't last very long as manager.

Prior to my stint as a manager, we were out to Kauffman's house. He invited us out, something he did quite often. While we were there, we had dinner and so forth, a very sociable type of thing. Joe Cronin and his wife were there. It was a very nice affair. Ewing called me over to the side and said, "Charlie, I just want you to know that I really appreciate the job that everybody tells me you've done. I know you've done a fantastic job assembling this ball club and everything. I'm giving you a thousand shares of Marion Laboratory stock." I wasn't too much of a stock market guy at that time, and I said, "Oh, gee, that's great." He said, "I've got it down. You've got the certificates." I said, "Why don't you just keep that, Mr. Kauffman, and as we go along, I'd like to buy some more or earn some more of this stock. And I'd like to even take part of my salary and buy stock." He said, "Fine." I gave him a form that would allow him to sell my shares. But he also gave me fifty shares of voting stock. I kept the letter about that. But when I was fired, he got a little bit angry at me. I said some things I shouldn't have said, and he said some things he shouldn't have said. About two weeks later, Charlie Truitt came by, and he wanted the stock back. They took the stock back from me. Boy, that really turned me off. That Marion Laboratory stock was worth about thirty-three thousand dollars, about thirty-three dollars a share. It split three ways, and then two ways, and then three ways again. I would have been an extremely wealthy man. I tried to get the fifty shares of voting stock, but the current corporation had no record of my owning them. I tried showing them the copy of the letter I'd kept, but they never got back to me. I kind of wished I had kept my mouth shut. But at least Kauffman and I parted friends.

The first thing that I did at Kansas City's Municipal Stadium was put a batting cage down the left-field line. I might stand corrected on this, but I think I was the first one in the major leagues to do that. We installed a cage and pitching machine. I set them up on what they used to call the picnic area. I changed the bullpens from right field to our left field, so I could see the catcher and the pitcher warming up. I would warm up my pinch hitters. As the game would unwind and come to a point where I needed a guy to get a base hit, I would use the pinch hitter who could get on base. I'd tell him to get down there and take his cuts with the pitching machine. If I wanted an extra-base hit or a long ball, I would have a long ball guy warm up. It wasn't very well lit down in that corner, but they got to swing at live fastballs, at eighty-five miles an hour, eighty-six or whatever it was, instead of waving at three pitches when they went to bat. Anyway I had great success with that, had an awful lot of pinch hits, consecutive base hits, eleven straight, I think, including some game winners.

But I got in trouble with the American League. Bill Rigney of the Angels complained. He wanted to warm up his pinch hitters. I said, "Go to hell, Bill. This is my cage, my ballpark." Rigney raised heck. Joe Cronin, the president of the league, sent Charlie Berry, the chief of umpires, down to Kansas City to see about this. Their biggest complaint about the cage was that it was distracting to the game, taking the play away from the action on the field. Can you imagine that? As if the fireworks and all that music blaring on the loudspeaker weren't distracting? I argued this with Charlie Berry, who had been a fine umpire. My rebuttal was, "Charlie, when they bring in a relief pitcher, he's allowed to make eight pitches, isn't that correct?" "Yes," he said. I said, "When they make a substitution of an infielder, the first baseman throws him some hard ground balls to loosen up his arm. Or in case of an injury to an outfielder, they let the replacement throw some practice throws to the other outfielders to warm his arm up, especially if he's been sitting on the bench. When you have a pinch runner put into the game, he stretches himself a little bit, and then runs down the right-field line, if he's on first base. I know you've seen it often. Why can't I warm up my pinch hitter? What have you got against pinch hitters? It's part of the game." Charlie said, "Well, they don't want it." Kauffman called me up in the office and asked me what was the problem with Rigney. I said, "He wants to use the batting cage to warm up his pinch hitters." He said, "What'd you say?" I said, "I told him to go to hell." He said, "You shouldn't be doing that."

I said, "Mr. Kauffman, you're in the pharmaceutical business. When you come up with a new product, do you let your competition have it?" He said, "No." I said, "Well, it's the same thing with the batting cage. That's why I told him to go to hell." He said, "I'll tell them the same thing." I don't know whether he did or not. I continued to do it, but I got in hot water. I was hardheaded, I guess. I came up with the innovative idea, and I didn't want to give it up. Now every new ballpark has got batting cages, either under the stands or somewhere there close, sometimes two for the home team and one for the visitors. I won the point, but I didn't win the battle.

In 1970 I got to manage against the great Ted Williams, who was manager of the Washington Senators. Ted was probably the exception of a great ballplayer being a manager. Ted was a good manager. Sometimes I thought he didn't like managing. But when he managed at Washington, he improved practically every guy on his ball club, especially the hitters. He made them way better than they had been previously. What more can you say about a manager when he does that? He was a good hitters' manager. They say pitching is 80 or 90 percent of the game. But the hitters have to get some runs too. I always felt that Ted was a very good manager. He was no pushover. I would have liked to seen him have a real good club, a contender. I bet they'd have run away with the pennant. Too bad he never got to manage the Red Sox.

I managed in two different big league settings, Chicago and Kansas City. Chicago probably had four or five newspapers in 1962, and Kansas City had one or two in 1970. The Chicago writers were kinder than the Kansas City ones. One day I made an announcement in Kansas City that I was going to use Ellie Rodriguez as my regular catcher. The very next day, I changed my decision, and I never did explain why. Oh, the writers cut me up, because they had written what I had first said. I had a very good reason, which I'm not going to mention here, for why I had to make the change. I didn't want to harm the ballplayer. Sometimes there were things that you didn't want the press to know about a player. But I really caught heck about that. They roasted me pretty good. As a manager, you have to take a lot of blame for all sorts of things. You're the lightning rod.

When the Topps people made a baseball card for my Kansas City manager year, they chose a photo that was taken after we had lost a doubleheader at Vancouver. I wasn't in a very good mood, and my face showed it. I thought, gee whiz. I talked to some of the Topps people and asked them why they couldn't get a better picture. They said, "Oh, we like this one." I get these cards sent to me in the mail from time to time, by fans seeking an autograph. That's flattering, but I still don't like that 1970 card. It now sells for $1.75 or so, but the original 1958 one goes for $25 on the memorabilia market

I made a couple of guys famous. If I had been unethical, if I'd been ruthless or dishonest, you would have never heard of Sparky Anderson. I was offered the job as the manager of the Cincinnati Reds by Bob Howsam, by telephone. I knew all the people at the Reds. But a day or so prior to that, I had just shaken hands and agreed to manage the Kansas City Royals. I had put the ball club together. I was there when the baby was born, so to speak. Now I'd be given the opportunity to manage the club, and maybe even if I had a rough time, they'd stick with me. But that didn't happen. If I'd had taken the Reds job, you'd have never heard of Sparky Anderson. But I didn't want to break my word or go back on my handshake. I felt I was a man of honor in doing that. Every year for many years, Sparky Anderson has sent me a Christmas card. I don't know whether it was because of our association or because I didn't take the job. Sparky would never have had those twenty-five or so seasons managing, or become the third all-time-winningest manager. Actually I even recommended him. I knew him when I was in Cincinnati and he was a manager in the organization. We worked together on the Reds' instructional manual. I liked Sparky, and when one of the Reds officials asked me who I'd recommend, I said, "Sparky Anderson." As it turned out, my judgment on him was great. Even though I regret not managing the Big Red Machine, I don't think anyone could have improved on the job that Sparky did with them.

In 1968, when we set up the Royals, they still played in Municipal Stadium in Kansas City. Cedric Tallis had an apartment there, and in the same building lived the man who was the designer of the new stadium in Kansas City. There was a lot of talk about building a domed stadium at that time. I had seen the Astrodome. I saw that thing being built. But this man, who was from HOK, the firm that eventually designed several stadiums, including Coors Field, was talking about a dome. The talk didn't go very far, but I recommended against a dome, because in Kansas City there'd be snow and rust, and the mechanism might hang up during the middle of a ball game. I told him to make the clubhouse big, because clubhouses were very small in many of the major league stadiums. I told him to put forty lockers in there. We had twenty-five players, of course, and then they'd bring up some, and then you had the coaches and the manager. I told him I wasn't in favor of Astroturf. It has a way of getting really hot, not like grass. I knew that I could get in trouble on that, because they'd pretty well set their minds on it. They were going to put some second-generation or third- or fourth-generation, I forget which, turf on the field. He showed me some tenth- or eleventh-generation turf, which was an improvement, but it wasn't going to be available for use anytime soon. I also mentioned to him that the seats down the lines weren't facing home plate, so they turned them toward home. Eventually they designed a very beautiful stadium, Kauffman Stadium, and thankfully, recently they went back to grass turf.

There were some lighthearted moments with the Royals. The year that I was coordinator of one of the practice fields at spring training for the Royals, a guy came by in a helicopter, set it down on our field, and asked me if I wanted a ride. I said, "Yes." So with my fungo bat and in my uniform, I got in there, strapped myself in, and we buzzed the field a little bit. But I saw that there wasn't a door on this helicopter, so I said, "Hey, no tricks." Because you look out that side door, where I was sitting, there was nothing but air. But then I got used to it, got to waving to the ballplayers. He gave me about a fifteen-minute ride. But we buzzed the practice field pretty good. I shouted at the guys to keep running, but they couldn't hear me over the roar.

They had a cow-milking contest in 1969. They wanted me to be in it. I was coaching. Galen Cisco was a pitcher on the team at that time. He had been a farm boy, so he knew all about milking. They wanted me to get in there. Heck, as a boy I had milked a cow, but not as many as some of these guys. I could milk one cow. They gave some of the guys dry cows. I think the players were afraid to do that to me, so they gave me a cow that was all right. But when they brought the bucket and they put it under the cow, they played a trick on me. I got to milking that cow. I had my head right there, and not paying any attention but milking like heck. I look down there, and the darn bucket was half full. What they had done was pour water in the bottom of the bucket. So I milked into the bucket with all that water. It looked like I had a full bucket of milk, but I didn't. They disqualified me for it. I had nothing to do with it. To this day, I don't know who did that to me.

When I was at Kansas City, we ran across a box of old Philadelphia Athletics contracts. The guy who was in charge of the stadium called me up one day, and said, "I want you to see something, Charlie." I said, "OK." This guy was always asking me to get him autographed baseballs. He took me upstairs to a storeroom and opened some boxes. He said, "Look there." They had some big three-by-three cardboard boxes. On the inside of the cardboard flap, it would say a year. These were contracts of the Philadelphia Athletics. This was in Kansas City after the A's had left for Oakland. I picked up some of them. I knew the story about when, in 1928, 1929, and 1930, Al

Simmons signed a three-year contract, which was unheard of then, for one hundred thousand dollars. I looked through them and found his contract. I saw all these contracts signed by Mr. Mack. I checked out the 1944 box and found a copy of my contract. The stadium guy offered me all of those contracts. There were also photographs. He said, "Charlie, why don't you take them? You played for them." I said, "Oh, I can't." He said, "Well, I won't charge you." I never did take them. But today, every once in a while, I'll ask somebody and they'll say, "Yeah, I've got a Mickey Cochrane contract signed," or "I've got an Al Simmons contract signed," or "I've got a Jimmie Foxx contract signed." I'd say, "Where did you get it?" I don't get an answer.

But there were also episodes that still leave a sour taste in my mouth. One time I got in trouble letting a player go. As I went along in my baseball career, I found out that the more you tried to explain, the deeper you got and the tougher it was. So I finally I came up with a stock method of doing it. I'd say, "Well, we're sending you out. You're not ready here, but you go down and you play, and I will be glad to have you on my club anytime, anywhere. But right now, I've made a decision, and you have to go down and play." Or if you released a player, you'd just say, "I enjoyed having you. I'm sorry." It was very brief, almost abrupt, and it went over great. But I had the task of telling Jerry Adair, a second baseman with the Royals, he was no longer wanted on the ball club. Jerry had a terrible habit of drinking too much beer. He would sit in the clubhouse after the ball game and drink a lot. The club felt that he wasn't a good influence on the younger players. I decided I didn't want the guy when he wasn't doing the job for us. We decided we were going to go with a younger guy. Jerry was past his prime. Cedric wouldn't tell him, so he called me and told me to do it. I said, "Well, I don't want to. I think that's management's job to tell him. If he wants to talk to me, fine. Then I can tell him why, but this is a front-office type of thing." Well, it didn't happen that way. We were leaving, going to Baltimore, and I couldn't get hold of Jerry before we left. When he got to the airport, I called him aside and told him that we were releasing him, to go to the front office. Boy, all hell broke loose. He criticized me something terrible. He disrupted the ball club completely. I almost lost control of the club because of that.

Another time I fined a few ballplayers and I made them pay. Moe Drabowsky called meetings with the pitchers about 3:00 or 4:00 in the morning. I fined them one hundred dollars each. They complained and went to Kauffman. He asked me about it. I said, "Send the money to the National Jewish Hospital in Denver." Kauffman said, "No, they've got enough money." He made me give the fines back. He said, "Or else," which was about as strong as you could get. I felt that would cost me control of the ball club. He waited until we won a doubleheader or something and made me hand the money back then. I didn't appreciate this. It undermined me as manager. I still regret giving that money back.

I had another chance to manage in Denver. Jim Burris was the general manager at Denver, and he called me. I was still scouting for Kansas City. Jim caught up with me at El Paso while I was there looking at some of the Double-A ballplayers. He called me and asked, "Charlie, would you be interested in managing again?" I said, "Well, I would be, but why?" He said, "I think you have to make a move there." I said, "Well, I'm kind of tied up. I made a commitment to the Royals on this, and I can't leave right here in the middle." But I could have had the Denver job again. I made a mistake with the Royals. I wanted a three-year contract as a coach. I was getting a little antsy about getting pension time. I needed five years. I knew all about the pension. It would be very good for an older guy like me who had spent all those years in different baseball positions. I was kind of anxious to get it, so I asked for a three-year contract.

I did an awful lot of things for the Royals, but I didn't stay around long enough to profit from them. I set the club going in the right direction. I put the firmness in the organization, and it paid off. The Royals carried on successfully after I left. Cedric was fired, and Lou Gorman took over as general manager. I can't say too much for old Louie. He talked a lot but didn't do much. He didn't know a ballplayer from a hole in the ground. But the Royals stayed in the first division, and I feel proud about that.

But I also feel that the Royals didn't stick with me long enough. Bob Lemon, who replaced me on the field in June 1970, turned out to be a pretty good manager. I didn't think he was a very good pitching coach, but he was a good manager. I had managed against him out in the Coast League. His Seattle ball club had beaten us in the final game of the championship. Cedric talked me into fulfilling my contract. For the rest of 1970 and 1971, I was a special assignment scout of sorts. Then I left and went to work with the Tigers again, in 1972. The Tigers took me back when they knew I was free. Jim Campbell offered me a contract, and I agreed. But looking back at the Royals, I'd hate to think that a bleeding ulcer was all the thanks I got for all my hard work and dedication. Perhaps Charlie Truitt hit it on the head when he told me once, "Charles, you work too hard and you're too honest."

ELEVEN

If This Is Tuesday, It Must Be Albuquerque

After I finished out my 1971 contract with the Royals, Jim Campbell of the Tigers invited me to come over as an advance scout. I suspect that Billy Martin, who was the Tigers manager, had something to do with the offer. For the next two years, I scouted for Detroit. In 1972 I did the advance scouting when the Tigers played the Oakland A's in the playoffs. I watched Bert Campaneris get mad a time or two. He threw a ball in the seats, and, man, he kind of blew his top. In the pregame meeting, Billy let me do some talking, and I said, "If you want to get him out of the lineup, just throw at his feet once. He'll do something rash, and they'll throw him out of the ball game." We threw the ball at him, and sure enough, Campaneris was furious. He threw the bat, and they suspended him. But we lost the playoffs. We lost the last game on the last pitch and the last out in the playoffs. I made the comment to Ernie Harwell, the Tigers announcer, that the game would be decided by one pitch, one hitter in the last inning. And that's the way it turned out. The A's beat us and went on to beat the Reds in the World Series.

At the end of the 1973 season, apparently I didn't fit the Tigers' plans anymore. Billy was no longer the manager. When Campbell heard I had a possible offer from the newly created Scouting Bureau, he suggested I take it. So Detroit and I parted company for a fourth time. I was the first guy hired by the Scouting Bureau. Jim Wilson, who had been a pitcher with the Red Sox and several other clubs, hired me and gave me a three-year contract. At that time, eighteen teams used the services of the Scouting Bureau. They all participated financially in the arrangement. The bureau had a network of scouts all over the country. I was the chief cross-checker. That was a very interesting job. When you made a report, it went to all eighteen teams with your name on it and your recommendations. You put your name on the line every time. When you work with general managers, the scouting group never puts its name on it. It's always the scout.

A cross-checker is a person who goes to see all the top prospects in the country. If a scout in the East, say in the Boston area, had a top prospect who he thought was great, but he wanted another opinion, that's where the cross-checker came in. The top cross-checker went and saw all the top players and rated them. Then, as the reports kept coming in, he'd check the reports against the ratings as he'd seen them. Then the clubs would make their number one selection, second round, third round, and so forth. It was a very tough job. You'd get to see a high school or college player, and you'd get to see him hit two times, three times, and maybe sometimes he'd get walked twice and swing a bat only once, but you had to make a money decision. It was one of the toughest and the most thankless jobs, but it was one of the most important in the organization.

Dale Murphy was a young guy up there in Oregon when I was a cross-checker for the Scouting Bureau. I happened to go up there and see Murphy in a high school game. He was a catcher. He threw the ball real well. He could run, and he had a tremendous arm, and I thought he'd make one hell of a first baseman or an outfielder. The first time he came up to bat, he hit a ball into left-center into the teeth of the wind, and it went about four hundred feet for a home run. Next time up, he hit a double. I saw him catch only four or five innings, because I had another assignment up in that area. But I considered I had seen enough of him. I made a report on him on the strength of two swings. I recommended a fifty-thousand-dollar bonus. I understand that I missed it by two or three thousand dollars. The Braves gave him fifty-two or fifty-three thousand dollars. I predicted that he would hit 30 to 40 home runs a year, and that he could play other positions. Everything I predicted about him came true. He won those Most Valuable Player Awards, and one day he'll go to Cooperstown. He didn't get 400 home runs. He finished with 398, but Al Kaline had 399, so Dale's in good company. When he played in Denver toward the end of his career, I made a copy of my scouting report on him and showed him that he was the number one guy I'd seen that year.

My old Vancouver shortstop Buddy Peterson, one of my favorite ballplayers, got me back during my Scouting Bureau days. I had fined him one hundred dollars when he played for Vancouver and he was one of the players who drove over to Seattle without getting permission. Years later, when I was Director of Player Procurement for the Royals, I hired Buddy, and he did a good job for us. When I moved over to the Scouting Bureau, I got Buddy hired there too. One time he had me come out to Sacramento, where he was living and working, to see some players he'd gotten lined up for me to check. So I went up there and spent about three days with him. He had a whole line of high school and college ballplayers for me to see. After we'd see a guy or a game, or before we were going to see a night game, Buddy and I would go out and have dinner. When the bill came, he would turn his head, and I'd pick it up and pay it. That went on for three days. Finally I said to him, "Hey, Buddy you're on an expense account. Why don't you pick up the tab for a change?" He said, "But, Chaz, you're the big guy. You've got the big expense account. Besides that, remember that hundred dollars you fined me?" I said, "Yeah." He took out his little notebook, looked at a page, and said, "The way I've got it figured, you still owe me $4.95." I said, "Delighted I could help."

When I was a cross-checker in 1974 and 1975, I traveled around quite a bit. After a while, the towns started to blur together. I'd see a player or two, have to evaluate them quickly, and write out my reports in detail. One time I got so tired I walked into a door. I got back down to the Bay Area after a busy scouting schedule. At the motel, I got up in the middle of the night and walked right into the edge of a door. I got a bloody nose out of that one. The travel schedule was hectic. For example, I went out to the Bay Meadows quarter horse track one night, and I was talking to D. Wayne Lukas, the famous horse trainer. Then I had to catch a 5:00 plane for St. Louis and rent a car to go to a little town in Illinois to see a ballplayer. It was raining so hard, they called the game. I didn't want to just twiddle my thumbs back at the motel. I asked for directions to a big horse ranch owned by Jake Bunn, the guy who got rich selling those coffeemakers. I drove out there, found him in an office in the barn, and introduced myself. He was a little doubtful, so I told him about my acquaintance with D. Wayne Lukas. Just at that time, the phone rang, and of all people it was D. Wayne! Bunn was doing a little horse business with him. While they were talking, Jake mentioned I was there. D. Wayne told him to put me on the phone. He said, "Charlie, what the hell are you doing there?" I told him I had had to check a ballplayer. He said, "But you just left here." That earned me some brownie points with both of these big horse guys.

Sometimes when I had to fly from Chicago to Los Angeles, we couldn't stop at Denver, but we'd fly over and I'd see my home down there. We have a little fifteen-acre place that we call the "Metro Ranch," northwest of Denver on Indiana Street. I'd be flying over on a crystal-clear day, scouting for the Scouting Bureau or later the Dodgers, and I'd look down and see Standley Lake, which is the reservoir for three or four communities there in west Denver. Then I could see Colfax Avenue, the street that goes east and west through the city. Then I'd pick up my little place about a hundred yards from Leyden Lake. I'd try to explain it to the flight attendants, but, of course, they couldn't see where I was talking about. But I could see it on a clear day.

As a scout, you had a lot of dead time, as we called it. I'd always get up early in the morning. Sometimes I'd get up at 4:00 and order a short breakfast, coffee and rolls, and while everything was fresh in my mind from the previous game, I would get all my scouting reports done. Then I'd have some time on my hands, so what I did often was search out some western art. This interest dated way back to when I was managing in the Pioneer League and we went into Great Falls, where they have a Charlie Russell museum. The Northern Hotel in Billings also had some Charlie Russell paintings. We would go into the Mint Saloon in Great Falls, where Charlie Russell hung out and would run up a bar bill. He would pay it off with some of his paintings or sketches. You could have bought a Charlie Russell ink sketch for five bucks at that time. When I asked a guy in the saloon what a couple ones I liked cost, he said, "A thousand dollars." I was only making five hundred dollars a month as a playing manager in the C league. But I became a Charlie Russell and western art buff.

Once I went to the Gilcrease Museum in Tulsa, and it was one of my most enjoyable times seeing all that western art. I was managing there, and I found the people all knew me. The sports fans had listened to me on the radio. They showed me all around the town. Boy, I enjoyed that. But perhaps one of the most interesting times was when I went to the Amon Carter Museum in Ft. Worth. I had a four-hour layover there on a connection, coming from Houston into Ft. Worth. I was going out west. I went to the Amon Carter Museum. It was early in the morning, about 8:00. I took a cab to the museum. I knocked on the door, but it wasn't open. Pretty soon a young lady came out and asked, "Yes?" I told her who I was and what I was doing and that I wanted to see the Amon Carter Museum and asked her if I could I see it. I turned on my best charm, and she said, "Well, do come in." So I did, and I said, "I want to see the artwork." She told me how they rotated the art due to moisture, putting one set on display for the people and the other sets downstairs in the vault room. She made me put on covers for my shoes so I wouldn't stir up the dust, and we went down there. What an amazing thing it was! I was like a kid in a toy store with all those works of western art. I was mostly interested in Charlie Russell. I kept looking at this one Charlie Russell painting, and I had a quizzical look on my face. The young lady stood there with a little grin, and she said, "What's the matter?" I said, "I'm looking at this Charlie

Russell painting." She said, "Well, what's wrong with it?" I said, "That's not an authentic Charlie Russell painting. That's a fake." She just laughed and said, "You are one of the very few people who would pick that out." It was a fake. They had it in the museum for comparison to some of the real Russell paintings. That pleased me very much, and she got quite a kick out of the fact that a baseball guy would know something about western art.

Another time, while I was in New York on one of my scouting trips, I thought I would go over to the Kennedy Art Gallery in the upper fifties off Broadway. I met the curator and introduced myself. I told him I was in baseball, and it turned out he was a Giants fan. We got to talking about baseball, and he was quite enthused. He said, "Charlie, I want to show you something." So he took me in the back room. There stood two bronze statues. I would say they were three feet high. One was a bronze of a ballplayer with a bat and the other a pitcher in his position of holding the man on. He bet me a cocktail and lunch if I could tell him who that hitter was. I took a look at it. This player was from before my time. But I looked at that and said, "'Shoeless Joe' Jackson." The curator almost fell over. He said, "How did you know that?" I said, "Well, I just know that's him." He asked, "Did you ever see him play?" I said, "No." He said, "Well, that's right. I owe you lunch. Well, let's bet another lunch." So he showed me the other bronze. It was of a pitcher. He said, "I got you now." I said, "Well, I don't know." He said, "Who is that?" Then I knew I had him again. I said, "That's Christy Mathewson." He said, "Oh, gosh!" So I got two free lunches, and we became friends. But the next time I came in, however, I found he had passed away.

I started becoming an autograph hound. I wanted to do something for my boys and my daughter, who were very western-oriented. I got some baseball covers and sent them to the Cowboy Artists of America. That was a select group of western artists, Brownell McGrew, Charlie Dye, and, oh, you name them. I sent some to the man who did the little buckaroo, the Indian friend, in the comic strip "Red Ryder." All the kids were crazy about "Red Ryder." In fact, I was wild about it myself. I asked him if he'd please autograph this baseball cover in his favorite western color. He had a museum in Pagosa Springs, Colorado. He wrote me back, "Why in the heck does a baseball man that does a lot of his own autographing want to get my autograph on a baseball cover?" My daughter has the collection of those covers now.

After the 1975 season, the Scouting Bureau released me. To this day, I have no idea why. Maybe it was a financial decision. Anyway, Al Campanis, the general manager of the Los Angeles Dodgers, found out I was loose and offered me a contract as an advance scout. Over the years, Al and I had had some conversations at meetings. He knew I had plenty of experience. I became his right-hand man for seven years. I was an advance scout. I scouted players in Mexico and the Caribbean as a special-assignment scout. I scouted the Dodgers farm system. And I became the first "eye-in-the-sky" scout. We went to the World Series three times while I was there, and in 1981, we beat the cursed Yankees. I got three World Series rings, and my wife, Helen, got similar necklace brooches.

When you think of the Dodgers in those years, you naturally think of Tommy Lasorda. Tommy deserves his place in the Hall of Fame. He has been the greatest ambassador for baseball, and he was a pretty good manager. He made some mistakes, but we all did. People talk about when he made a wrong move, like when he had his pitcher pitch to Jack Clark of the Cardinals in the 1985 playoffs, and they want to crucify him forever for that one move. I think Tommy's still replaying that one over in his mind. But, heck, Tommy managed pennant winners. We all made wrong calls if we managed long enough. There are some that I would like to forget too. They did right to put Tommy in the Hall of Fame. They should put some more of these guys who are still living, even coaching or managing or just retired from playing, in the Hall of Fame while they're living legends, walking testimonials for baseball. Don't make them wait five years or until the Veterans Committee gets around to selecting them.

Tommy Lasorda was a pitcher before he became a manager. I have always felt that a manager who was a pitcher had a tougher time than anybody else, because he had that tenacity, that aggressiveness, that determination, that stubbornness that pitchers must have. Pitchers don't want to come out of the ball game. When they don't want to come out and you leave them in, they get racked sometimes, pretty good. Tommy was always giving that pitcher another chance. He was living with that pitcher, but it would backfire on him. I saw it when I was with the Dodgers. He had a couple of good pitching coaches, Red Adams and Ron Perranoski. They stayed for many years, and they helped him out. Tommy became a good manager. He got the most out of the team. He had a way with the players. They might laugh at him, but he got what he wanted out of a player. I was very pleased for Tommy when he took the U.S. Olympic team and guided them to a gold medal in the Summer Olympics in Australia. He was perfect for the job.

Lasorda was a great friend to everyone. I don't think Tommy ever paid for more than a few meals. He had a lot of celebrity connections. In 1977 Frank Sinatra came through the dugout, and Tommy introduced me to him. Actually I had gone to a Sinatra concert, when he was with Tommy Dorsey, at the Pacific Ballroom in late 1940 or early 1941, in San Diego. I was standing offstage, and Frank came down during a break in the show. I said, "Hi, Frank." He said, "Hi, Kid." He asked me what I did, and I told him I was a baseball player. Thirty-some years later, in the Dodgers dugout, Frank remembered my name and thanked me for intervening with a couple of punks who were bothering him that night at the Pacific Ballroom. Another time Tommy grabbed me and said, "Let's go to Willie Crawford's birthday party." I got to meet Barbra Streisand, another of my favorite singers. Lasorda had a little too much to drink, and he almost killed us both driving back to the hotel.

Tommy was often the target of practical jokes. One time when we were in Cincinnati, I was having breakfast with him, when these two guys in white overalls, painters, with their caps pulled down on their head, showed up and started to paint where we were sitting. They put their ladders up right kind over the table, and they climbed up to paint the ceiling. Lasorda started calling for the maître d'. It was Jerry Reuss, the Dodgers pitcher, and that crazy outfielder Jay Johnstone in disguise. They must have paid the maître d' an awful lot. They got Tommy pretty good. But Tommy could take it.

Tommy could be a scrapper. I heard once about a fight he was in in Houston. I wasn't there. I just got it secondhand. Three guys came out and were going to say something, and Tommy fought them. Tommy told me once, "Charlie, always hit the guy in the middle. That's what I learned on the streets in Philadelphia." He was from nearby Norristown. He said, "Always get the guy in the middle. He's the ringleader. You get him, and the others are going to scatter for you." Tommy got in some scraps. In fact, he had some dandies when he was pitching.

Most people, however, don't know that at least twice I helped Tommy's career along. When Walt Alston retired, the Dodgers asked me what I thought of Lasorda as a possible major league manager. I recommended him. I told them, "Lasorda will be the best PR guy you can imagine. He's got a lot to learn as a manager. He'll be the exact opposite of Walt Alston. But he'll be the perfect fit." Tommy went on to prove my prediction right. He became a pretty good manager. But another time, the Dodgers were thinking of cutting him loose. He had crossed swords with Al Campanis. Al was furious with him. I said, "Calm down, Al. You can't do that to him. He's a Dodger through and through. He'll learn to be a better manager." Al was steaming, but he relented. Tommy probably doesn't know this, but basically I saved his bacon that day.

The Dodgers had some pretty good players during those years. Many of them came up through the farm system, especially the Albuquerque Dukes. Ron Cey was one of them. Cey was a bumblebee. He couldn't run, he couldn't field, and he couldn't throw. He had too little of this and that, but he didn't know that, so he went out and played in the big leagues for seventeen years. He looked terrible fielding, but somehow he got the job done. He looked terrible running, but he could hit like heck. He was a good clutch hitter. Lasorda gave him the name "Penguin." He walked like a penguin. Ron liked it, I guess.

I saw him first when I was working for the Tigers as a scout in 1972. I was sent to see some of the Triple-A clubs. I went into Albuquerque and made a report on that ball club. I can't quite remember all the players, but I had eleven or twelve ballplayers off that club as definite big league prospects. When Ed Katalinas, who was kind of the scouting director for the Tigers, got my reports, he called me up and asked, "Charlie, were you drinking when you made out these reports? Nobody's got this many prospects on a Triple-A club." I said, "Well, they have." They had Steve Yeager, Joe Ferguson, Cey, Davey Lopes, Tom Paciorek, Rick Rhoden, Doug Rau, Von Joshua, Charlie Hough, Greg Zahn, and Eddie Solomon. Steve Huntz, the shortstop, eventually went up and played a little bit with San Diego. He actually made the twelfth guy on that Albuquerque club to go to the majors. I had the pleasure of being right and being on the Dodgers with some of them. Years later Ed Katalinas saw me and said, "Charlie, you were right. Every one of them." It took Huntz a little longer to get up to the big leagues, but when he did, I called Katalinas and said, "That Albuquerque shortstop got to the big leagues." He said, "Who's that?" I said, "That's the twelfth guy that I scouted at Albuquerque." I told Al Campanis that story, and he said, "Well, you were right." It was a real good ball club.

Davey Lopes was a good ballplayer for the Dodgers. He was aggressive and could steal a base well. Along with Cey and Russell and Steve Garvey, he anchored the infield for several years. Now he's the Milwaukee Brewers manager. Steve Garvey, of course, was quite impressive. He was a superb hitter and a fine fielder, even though he wasn't the tallest guy in the world. He might get in the Hall of Fame some day. But he's certainly got some bad press for himself. We all thought he had political aspirations, but I remember one day, about the time when Steve was having problems with a paternity suit, Lasorda said, "It looks like he's trying to be the father of our country."

Bill Russell was one of my favorite ballplayers with the Dodgers. I had seen him, I think at Spokane, when he was playing outfield. But I had him down as a shortstop even then. Everybody would criticize him, because he'd make an error occasionally. But dang, he was on those pennant-winning Dodger ball clubs, and you can't win pennants without a good shortstop. If you don't have a good shortstop, forget about it. And Bill could hit some. He'd get a big hit every so often. He stayed eighteen years with the same team. He was a pretty good manager in Triple-A, but he had a rough time in his stint managing the Dodgers. I saw him a couple of years ago, and I said, "Hey, you're getting a little heavy." Maybe it was his jacket.

Willie Davis was a tremendous ballplayer. One time I asked him, "How fast are you?" He said, "I'm fast. I can run." He could. He could really fly. I told him, "I bet there's something that you can't do. You think you're that fast?" He said, "What's that?" He knew I was a scout. I said, "I bet you can't hit a fly ball in the air and cross second base before the guy catches it." He said, "I bet I can." I said, "Well, the next time you hit a fly ball, when you're in front or way behind in the ball game, try to see how high you can hit a fly ball and see if you can get to second before the guy gets it." I saw him try it three times, and he came within a step of doing it. Now it takes three point some seconds to get to first base, and another couple of seconds to get to second when you're running full speed, but you're making a turn, so you've got to hit the ball long and high. When I saw him later, either that same year or the next season, I said, "Willie, did you ever do it?" He said, "Yes, I did." I said, "When? Where? Tell me about it." He told me. I don't know if he did or not, but that's some kind of a feat.

Rick Monday was a pretty good day-by-day ballplayer. I think he was overshadowed by his claim to fame of taking away that American flag from a protester in a playoff game. He was a pretty good ballplayer. He hit that home run in 1981 to put us in the World Series. Mickey Hatcher was a free spirit, which is a good quality in a ballplayer, especially if he's producing. And what can you say about Jay Johnstone? He was a good player but completely unpredictable. The clubhouse wasn't safe when he was around. But you need guys like him and Hatcher to relax your ball club. Dusty Baker was a pretty good ballplayer for us with the Dodgers. He came over from Atlanta in a trade. Dusty got into some bad habits, but he got himself straightened out, and now he's a fine manager for the Giants. In the 1977 World Series, he misplayed a couple of balls in the outfield. He played too close against the Yankees. I think Bucky Dent or somebody hit a ball over his head for a three-base hit. I tried to get him to move back, but he wouldn't do it. He felt he knew how to play this guy. The next time I see Dusty, I'm going to ask him, "Why didn't you move back?!"

Kenny Landreaux was another guy I helped get for the Dodgers. Al

Campanis said we needed an outfielder, and he sent me to look at two or three guys in the American League. One was Fred Lynn of the Red Sox, and the other was Landreaux with the Twins. Every time I'd see him play, I never saw him do anything wrong. Lynn was in and out, was always hurting, wasn't in the lineup. When you're chasing for a pennant, you can't afford to lose the guy. So I was very strong on Landreaux. We got him at the Dodgers, and he did a tremendous job. He did everything and had power. He wasn't a pushover. If he had one bad habit, it was that he'd wander in the outfield. If you didn't watch him, he'd be wandering ten or fifteen feet out of position. You'd have to get him back over. Tommy Lasorda called him a "stargazer" or something like that and said Kenny was checking his passes in the upper deck and all those remarks. But I thought he was a good ballplayer.

Steve Sax came up with the Dodgers in 1981. He was a fine, aggressive player. But he had that terrible habit of throwing the ball away. Finally one day, after the Dodgers coaches had exhausted all their instruction on him, I told them, "I think I can break this guy in ten minutes." They said, "Well, if you're such a genius, go ahead." I had had a second baseman in the Sally League, Chris Sidaris, who also couldn't throw the ball to first base. I got him to improve a bit. So I was ready to try with Steve Sax. I said, "Heck, I can correct that in ten minutes." I did help him. I said, "Steve, when you take that ball out of the glove, take it as if you're standing next to a guy and you want to elbow him and just hit him in the elbow. Instead you're taking it directly out of the glove at that angle, way out there, and you're losing all control of it. You take that ball right out of that glove and just swing that elbow like you're elbowing a guy in the ribs, and then throw it." He corrected it, but every once in a while he'd go back to his original style, and he would lose the throws. It hurt his career overall.

I was involved in the trade that sent Glenn Burke from the Dodgers to Charlie Finley's Oakland A's for Billy North. Both Finley and Campanis thought that he got the better part of the deal, and that the other team got the worser part. There were rumors that North was on drugs. How much people knew yet about Burke being gay or even if that played a part in the decision, I don't know, but both clubs thought they got the best of the other. Burke was a tremendous prospect. He had one of the most muscular bodies we'd ever seen, and he had most of the tools to be a star. But he hurt his knee, and he was struggling with his sexual identity issues. He never did reach his potential. North was a real tough guy. He didn't take anything from anybody. He wasn't a fighter, but he didn't back down from anybody. He was like a steel spring. I'd want him on my side if there was a brawl.

Boog Powell, the big first baseman with the Orioles all those years, spent his last year with us at Los Angeles. I played a part in getting him over there. I said, "This guy can pinch-hit for you, can play part-time." But he was faced with a situation where the opposition usually walked him. They walked him so he didn't produce runs. He could still hit. He wasn't through, but every time he'd come up, he'd get a base on balls. They wouldn't give him anything good to hit.

Steve Yeager was all right with the Dodgers. He caught pretty regularly. He was a hard-nosed type of guy. He developed that throat protector after he got hit there. He was a good regular catcher. I liked Steve Yeager. He was a take-charge kind of guy. Joe Ferguson was also a good catcher. He was a big guy, one of that crop of Albuquerque players. Mike Scioscia was a pretty good catcher for the Dodgers. He had a weight problem, but he fought it pretty well. He was a pretty doggone good catcher. He could throw well, and he was a pretty fair hitter. Mike became known for his ability to block players off the plate in plays at home.

I was real glad to see Don Sutton get in the Hall of Fame. He was tremendously overlooked, slighted, if you will. This guy was a great money pitcher. I don't know that he ever had a sore arm. I don't know that he ever was bypassed in pitching rotation. I think he holds many records, or came close to many records, for pitching complete ball games. Perhaps he wasn't a twenty-five- or thirty-game winner, but he was a very consistent pitcher, a real money pitcher. He had a good sense of humor. I don't know if people understood him, but he was a class guy in every respect. If I were a manager and seeking a pitcher on my ball club, I would take Don Sutton anytime.

Eddie Robinson had been a pretty doggone good ballplayer, but I knew him better when he was an official and a scout with Baltimore and also as a general manager in Texas. One time Eddie asked me about Charlie Hough, the knuckleballer with the Dodgers. Charlie was having one heck of a time. The Dodgers fans were booing him when he would come in. The ball would get away from the catcher. Al said to me, "Charlie, find a trade for this guy; find a sale for him." I said, "All right. Where do you want me to start?" I was covering the American League. Al said, "Where are you going?" I said, "I'm going to Texas." He said, "Eddie Robinson mentioned something about Charlie. Talk to him." So I went and talked to Eddie, and he asked me about Charlie Hough. I think the price for him was twenty-five or thirty thousand dollars, which was a steal. Eddie said, "I know you always tell a man the truth; you don't lie to me. What about Hough?" I said, "If you've got a catcher that can handle a knuckle ball, you get this guy. This is what he'll do for you. He can start anytime. He can be a long reliever, and he can be a short reliever. But only if you've got a catcher who can catch that knuckle ball. Because if you don't, they'll run you out of town." Hough did a great job for Texas for many years after that. He lasted long and never gained an ounce. Gosh, he was a good pitcher. Every time Eddie would see me, he'd say, "You told me right about Charlie Hough." Eddie was a good official, and he was a good scout, a good baseball man. I saw Charlie one day in Detroit, and I said "Hey, you owe me a beer." He said, "Why?" "Do you know that I was directly responsible for you going from the Dodgers to Texas?" I asked. He said, "No." After I told him the story, he said, "Let's go." So I had a beer on him. I said, "Thanks." He said, "No, *thank you.*"

Doug Rau was a left-handed pitcher with the Dodgers. He had a sore arm when I saw him. He just never seemed to be right. Jerry Reuss was a fine pitcher, another free spirit trickster sort of guy. Burt Hooton was a very underrated pitcher. I think Lasorda gave him the nickname "Happy" because Burt supposedly never smiled. Al Downing was still on the squad. He was the pitcher Hank Aaron hit his 715th home run off of, but Al was no pushover. I first saw Rick Rhoden, the pitcher for the Dodgers, when he was at Albuquerque. Rick had a deformed leg. They'd sit up there in the stands in Albuquerque and say, "Oh, this guy he can't field. They'll bunt him to death." No sooner did somebody bunt than Rick bounced off the mound on that weak leg and threw the guy out. It never bothered him. He turned out to be a solid type of pitcher. Not only that, but he turned out to be a great golfer. That disability, if you want to call it that, didn't hurt him at all.

Dave Stewart was one good-looking pitcher, and I never could understand why the Dodgers traded him. He was a good competitor. He had a high-pitched voice, and I don't know whether they held that against him or not, but he was a tough batter and a good athlete. He was always in top condition. As it turned out, the Dodgers made a tremendous mistake letting him go. So did Texas and Philadelphia, because when he got to Oakland, Dave showed what a fierce pitcher he was.

I also scouted Rick Sutcliffe the same way I did Dale Murphy. I had to make a quick recommendation on him. I saw him as a pitcher and a first baseman in a high school league in a seven-inning game. I thought he would make an excellent hitter and first baseman, even had a double chance to make it. But he turned out to be a pretty good pitcher. A lot of people didn't like him because they called him a hooker. He'd hook his wrist back when he pitched. Some guys, like my old friend Al LaMacchia, said if you're a hooker, you can't pitch. I'd always kid Al when I'd see him by asking him if he'd seen any hookers recently. But Sutcliffe's performance put that theory to rest. He turned out to be one heck of a pitcher. He needed some advice early on. I watched him warming up in the bullpen in Albuquerque. I would usually watch the starting pitchers to see how they were that day, whether they had their control or were throwing all over the place. Rick was not concentrating on strikes. He was throwing maybe only five or six strikes during his warmups. Then he'd come in the game and get wild. Before he could settle down, he'd be out of the game. I took him aside and told him, "Throw strikes in the bullpen. Make every pitch good. Don't count on warming up in the game. Then it's too late." That helped turn him around, I believe.

When the Dodgers were thinking of bringing up Bob Welch, Campanis had me take a look at him. I'd seen him pitch already, and I made a good report on him. I was told to go down and bring him up. I did. Bob had a problem that he has since whipped. He loved his beer. I got on the plane coming from Albuquerque to Los Angeles, and he had a long sock with about five cans of beer in it. He carried it on the plane, and I thought, uh-oh. I didn't know that. But he eventually whipped his drinking and became a good pitcher. The confrontation between him and Reggie Jackson in the 1978 World Series stands out clearly in my memory. There was the great hitter battling, the young pitcher battling, neither one giving in. There was pitch after pitch. I don't know how many were fouled off before Welch finally struck him out. I'm glad I was able to witness that live. Bob Welch turned out to be an excellent pitcher for many years with the Dodgers and the Oakland A's.

One day in Cincinnati, Tom Niedenfuer, one of the Dodgers' pitchers, gave us a fright in the hotel. He had a seizure and passed out right on the mezzanine. I happened to be sitting down in the lobby and saw the commotion and went up there. He was turning blue. I reached into his mouth and straightened his tongue out and gave him some artificial respiration, which was about the only thing I knew. I turned him over on his stomach and brought him out of it. The trainer called me in and said, "What did you do?" I said, "I gave him artificial respiration." He said, "How?" I told them the old way that I learned first aid in the coal mines. He said, "Son, you might have saved his life. Did you take his tongue out?" I said, "Yeah, he was swollen." Nobody even thanked me for that. In fact, they got a little bit huffy with me, although the writers thought it was wonderful. I didn't need them to make a big deal about it, but a little bit of thanks would have been nice. Maybe they didn't want to advertise

Niedenfuer's problems. It scared the heck out of me. I thought there for a minute he wasn't going to show up, but he came around.

When I was scouting for the Dodgers in the early 1980s, they were about to send Orel Hershiser out. I'd seen him pitch. He was kind of scared or whatever, but he had a very good sinking fastball. That was his bread-and-butter pitch. I don't know what he did with it, whether it was a split-finger fastball or what it was, but he had a good sinker. He was always nibbling around the corners. Campanis and Lasorda were talking about sending him to Albuquerque. I told Al, "Heck, I can tell you in five minutes what this guy should do." Al said, "Well, when we have a meeting, we'll tell him." At the meeting, Al said, "Well, Orel, Charlie's got an idea he wants you to try." I said, "With your stuff, your good sinking fastball, all you have to do is throw the ball down the middle. It'll go out, or it'll go in. Throw your best stuff down the middle. Make it your best stuff. Stop that nibbling." And he did, and his next game he pitched a fine game. The Dodgers never did send him down. Orel turned out to be one heck of a good pitcher. He's been accused a time or two of doing something to the ball, but I don't think so. He was a fine young man.

As Al Campanis's right-hand man, I did a lot of special assignment scouting in Latin America. The Caribbean is a great source of talent. In Latin America, down in the Caribbean, the kids play everywhere. They don't stick to one position. They move around, and they'll find their niche sooner or later, but they remain pretty versatile. Some—like Bert Campaneris and Tito Fuentes and José Oquendo—could play eight or nine positions. The kids down there in the Dominican Republic are out playing ball at 5:00 in the morning. If there's daylight, they play. They play right though tropical showers. It doesn't matter. That's their way out of poverty; that's their way to financial success. There are no color barriers down there, no class barriers in baseball. If you want to play baseball, you can. You're going to see more and more Latino ballplayers, because it's an opportunity for them. It wouldn't surprise me someday to see a team made up completely of Latino players. Just the players' abilities, not their race, would decide the outcome of the game.

I never did go to Cuba to scout. I did go to Puerto Rico, the Dominican Republic, Venezuela, and Mexico for the Dodgers. The Dodgers were in the lead recruiting Dominican ballplayers. Other teams, like the Washington Senators, had access to the Cuban ballplayers until Fidel Castro came in and closed Cuba down. We tried one time to get in there, but it was closed up pretty tight. The other places were hotbeds of baseball, enough that we could get some fine players.

Vic Davalillo was playing in the Mexican League when Al assigned me to go see him. I covered the Mexican League and went down to Puerto Rico and the Dominican Republic. Al said, "Charlie, we need a left-handed pinch hitter." Somebody said something about Davalillo down in the Mexican League. Al said, "Go down there and take a look at him. Give me a report on him." I went down to Mexico, and I tried to find his club. It was Aguascalientes, I believe. I couldn't speak much Spanish, but I could get along because I was a baseball guy, and baseball guys wave their arms and make themselves understood. They had a big, black ballplayer by the name of White, who had been in the Negro Leagues. He could speak English. He told me where Vic was. I went up to this third-floor flat where he had a room. He had a cot there. He had a box with his suitcase on it and wine bottles all over. I said, "Uh-oh." I told him that I'd come down to take a look at him. He says, "Come on out." His club had gone over to another town. I said, "Are you going over?" He said, "Yes." I said, "Well, I'll see you there. I want to see you play." His brother Pompey was the manager of this club. The word got around that I was down there to look at Vic. Pompey asked me, "Now, Charlie, you're not fooling? Don't fool my brother." I said, "I won't. I'll tell you straight, but I'll tell you what I'd like you to do. I'd like you to give him a workout, let me see him. I want to see him run. I want to see him hit. I want to see him throw. And I want to see him play."

Vic Davalillo put on one of the darnedest exhibitions I'd ever seen. He went to left field and threw to second and home. He went to center field and threw to third and home. He did the same in right field. Then he got a first baseman's mitt and took infield practice. In batting practice, he put on a heck of a show. He hit the ball to left field, to center field, to right field. He hit the ball right through the box, everywhere. The only guy I'd seen do that was Paul Waner. Davalillo did the same thing. Then, in the game, with some competition, he hit a line drive to left field. He was a left-handed hitter. Vic also hit one through the box and one to right field. Then he tried to hit one out of the ballpark. It went a long way to right field but didn't reach the fence.

I made a heck of a recommendation on him. I called Campanis and said, "Al, this guy can help us." We were in the pennant chase. I asked Al, "Well, what do you give for him? I can't talk to these people in their language. What do you want me to give them?" He said, "Well, offer them $2,500 and tell the guy to call me." So I offered the business manager $2,500. Al made a side deal with him for a bonus above the $2,500. He got criticized by the press and various scouts, and I think he lost his job over that bonus. I was a guest at the business manager's home because I couldn't get a room at the hotel. They gave me their little child's bedroom, and I slept there. I negotiated the best I could in his language. He couldn't speak English very well, and I didn't know Spanish. But we got Davalillo. Vic came up to the Dodgers and became one hell of an asset. In fact, he got the base hit that won the playoffs against Philadelphia. He was a good ballplayer. Tommy Lasorda asked me one time, "Does Vic drink?" I played dumb and said, "I don't know." Finally, one day Tommy said, "You know, I never knew that he drank until I saw him sober." And I saw Pompey one time in the stadium, and he said, "Thank you." Vic played four years for the Dodgers, to go along with his earlier years with Cleveland, California, St. Louis, Pittsburgh, and Oakland.

I recommended Pedro Guerrero when I saw him in the Dominican Republic. I went down there for Al Campanis. A little later I said, "Al, I've seen your regular left fielder for ten years down here." Al already knew about him, so he came down to see him too. Pedro put on a pretty good show, and he was good. Pedro was a happy-go-lucky guy, maybe not serious enough. The Dodgers tried to make a third baseman out of him, but he couldn't play third. I thought maybe he might have been a better first baseman than anyplace else. In the outfield he was a walker, what we call a gardener. He was always moving. Candy Maldonado also was a tremendous prospect. I saw him in Puerto Rico. I saw him hit 2 home runs or two off the wall, I can't recall for sure. He had many skills but never did pan out for the Dodgers. Down there in the Dominican Republic, we also saw Tony Fernandez. He was very impressive at shortstop. On one play, he made a great catch of a little fly to center field over his shoulder, and then he forced the runner on third to go back. He kept cocking his arm while he was running in. I predicted he would play in the majors for a long time. He played quite a bit. Tony had an All-Star season for the Blue Jays a couple of years ago.

I had something to do with the Dodgers getting Fernando Valenzuela. I was assigned by Campanis to go down to Mexico and watch him pitch. Al wrote me a letter and said that one of his scouts, Carito Varona, had sent him a report on this young kid down there. He said he would send Mike Brito, a part-time scout with the Dodgers, with me. Brito is still taking credit for finding Fernando, but Carito Varona was the guy who actually found him. I've got the letter somewhere that proves that. We went down there, and I saw him. Valenzuela pitched a pretty good ball game. You could see he would be successful. He knew how to pitch. Everybody thought he was older than he was, but he was just a young guy. One game in Mexico City, he struck out ten guys and got fourteen ground ball outs. He knocked their big hitter down three times and then struck him out with three screwballs.

This young, moon-faced kid out there was fearless. I made a good report, and the Dodgers bought his contract. I still have the notes on the game I scouted him. I was very high on him. He had the makings of a good screwball. He didn't have a great curve, but it was a fairly decent one. Al asked for my input on the price, what I would give a high school or college prospect. I said, "Probably $75,000. But we're going to have to give him more than that." If my memory serves me right, they gave him $135,000 and sent him to the minor leagues.

The next time I saw Fernando was in San Antonio. Ron Perranoski was working with him. I recommended the Dodgers bring him up. I told Lasorda, "Don't be afraid to use him as a starter, as a long reliever, as a short relief man. Don't be afraid to use him. He'll do you a good job." And he did. I pride myself that I was correct. I couldn't miss on Fernando. He was great for Los Angeles, for the Latino people. Whenever he pitched, attendance was up ten to fifteen thousand more than usual. He was their hero. He wore his fame well. I understand that he built a home for his parents and gave them all the things that they never had down in Mexico, which is a great testimony to what a fine person he is. Valenzuela was fun-loving. He pretended he didn't understand English, but he knew it real well. We'd kid him about the meal money. "What are you doing with your meal money?" we'd ask, and he'd try to pretend he didn't understand what meal money was. But Fernando was a sharp young guy. He was very mature for his age, partly because he had been playing with the experienced older guys in Mexico.

How the Dodgers landed Bobby Castillo is a nice story. He lived within sight of Dodger Stadium in Los Angeles. The Dodgers turned him down when he asked for a tryout or was at a tryout camp. So he went down to Mexico to play for Monterrey in the winter league. Al Campanis told me one day, "I want you to go down and take a look at this kid, Castillo, that our scout down there, Carito Varona, says is a pretty good pitcher." Well, I went down to see Bobby, and I watched him pitch an eighteen-inning ball game and a one-hitter the game before. He was pitching this game, and for five innings he really looked good. He wasn't a very big guy, but he had a good curve ball and threw quick. He had the makings of a pretty good screwball. He was just a young guy. I recommended that we buy him.

I asked Al, "What're we going to give for him?" Campanis said, "We'll go to sixty thousand dollars, but see what you can do. That's your limit." I wasn't real familiar with the association of Mexican club officials down there. Mr. Cisneros, who later became the president of the Mexican winter league, was the business manager there. He was the guy I talked to, and they had the owner in there. I just came out point-blank and said, "We want Roberto Castillo. The Dodgers want him." They said, "OK." I said, "I'm not going to pull any punches. I'm going to tell you what we'll do." Cisneros said, "We'll listen." I said, "We'll give you sixty thousand for him. That's the purchase price. That's what I'm authorized to give." They thought about it. I said, "Now, this is a good price." When you showed a great interest in a ballplayer down there, they always were ready to haggle. Somewhere along the line, the Dodgers supposedly had shortchanged the club five thousand dollars, so they wanted sixty-five thousand. I said, "No." They started blaming me. I said, "Just a minute. I wasn't here. I didn't do that. This is what we will do. When I leave this office, we withdraw the offer." So I was going to play their game a little bit too. They went out and had a conversation and told me to go ahead and call Al Campanis. I picked up the phone and called Al in Los Angeles. I said, "Al, they're holding out for sixty-five thousand. They want that five thousand. I don't know a thing about the extra five thousand." He said, "No." I said, "OK." They came back in and said, "Did he give us the sixty-five thousand?" I told them Al said "no" to the extra five thousand dollars. They finally agreed to sixty thousand, we shook hands all around, and we wrote up the agreement. I put the document in the mail, and it took more than a few days getting there. I worried that it could have been lost in the mail. Al chewed me out a little bit. He said, "You're supposed to deliver that direct."

Castillo did a good job for the Dodgers. Bobby turned out to be a pretty good workmanlike pitcher. He was a very tenacious little guy. He wasn't a great pitcher, but he was an awful nice guy to have on the ball club. He was a good student who would learn what you told him. And as I expected, he came up with a pretty doggone good screwball. I got in a little bit of trouble with him and Valenzuela. It was my understanding that when a Mexican club sold a player to the major leagues, the Mexican club was supposed to pay the player 20 percent of the contract price. I told Castillo and Valenzuela that. They didn't know. The Mexican club owners weren't too happy with me.

The Dodger coaches were a pretty good bunch. Monty Basgall was a coach when I was the "spy in the sky," the eye in the sky, upstairs with a walkie-talkie. I'd relay the defense to Monty. We worked as a team for a few years. He was a nice guy and a very good infield coach too. He'd played three years with Pittsburgh. Red Adams was a pitching coach for the Dodgers when I worked for them as a special assignment scout and eye in the sky. Red was great. He was a good pitching coach, surprisingly, because he didn't have a great career in the major leagues. But he was a fine pitching coach, and he did a lot of good things for that ball club. He was there a long time.

Ron Perranoski, who was the Dodgers' pitching coach for quite a while, pitched for St. Paul in the American Association in 1960. When Bragan sent out that form letter asking managers to list top prospects on the other clubs in their leagues, I listed Ron Perranoski as a can't-miss major leaguer, as the best pitching prospect in the Association at that time. Perranoski went up and pitched for several teams over twelve years.

The great pinch hitter Manny Mota was the first base coach. He was a lot of fun and a positive influence on the Latino players. Over at third was Joey Amalfitano. I remembered Joey from the Pacific Coast League days, when he always seemed to be trying to pick up my signs. He was always cutting his eyes over me in the third base coach's box. Then he became a great coach. I think they should have a room at the Hall of Fame in Cooperstown for coaches. Joey Amalfitano should be one of the first inductees, right along with Frank Crosetti and Peanuts Lowrey and a few other guys.

If anybody wanted to duplicate the perfect ballpark, Dodger Stadium would be a candidate. I can't find many faults in the stadium except perhaps the outfield should have little corners out there, kind of octagonal. But it's a beautiful stadium. It was a very nice ballpark to play ball in. The parking facilities are magnificent. If you're in the upper deck in right field, you park in the upper deck, right-field section, down the right-field line. If you're in the box seats in the middle deck, you're parked on the right-field side or left-field side. Your parking is all close and adjacent to your seats. The box seats are the same way. The facility is pretty. When the game was over and you had fifty thousand people leaving Dodger Stadium, in thirty minutes it was cleaned out. Everybody was on their way to the freeways. The price of an outfield bleacher seat was two dollars for grownups and one dollar for children, so you could take a family of six for maybe eight or ten dollars. The concessions out there were reasonable. The Dodger Dogs were wonderful. The food in the press room was great. They had a wonderful press room where you were always welcome. That's one thing that a lot of ballparks have done. They always welcomed the baseball people in the stadiums to mingle with the press and some of their executive box seat holders.

Many times I saw fans leave Dodger Stadium to beat the metro area traffic. They came from all over the city of Los Angeles to attend the ball game, and I guess some of them had an hour to get home or some heavy traffic to get through. You could tell right quick when they were getting ready. But I also saw that in Tulsa in 1966. At 10:00 everybody would get up and leave, because they had to go to work and they wouldn't stay out late. It didn't matter whether we were way behind or way ahead in the game. The first time I saw that, I said, "What the heck are they leaving for? We're way out in front." Next time, we'd be way behind, and I said, "What?" Then I finally found out why they all left at 10:00.

The other stadiums of that era had their pluses and minuses, but the worst had to be Olympic Stadium in Montreal. I didn't like that stadium at all. I liked the old one, Jarry Park, better. That stadium seated only around twenty-five thousand people. One of the things that I admired about Jarry Park, and also Olympic Stadium, was the Royal Mounties, their police. Boy, there were no disturbances whatsoever in the ballpark. It amazed me. I saw a disturbance once at Jarry Park, but before you could turn around, there were five of these big, burly Mounties in blue coats. They surrounded this guy and escorted him out just very gently. He was in a circle of these five guys. He didn't say a word.

Regarding the eye-in-the-sky role I had with the Dodgers, Campanis came up with that idea. Football teams were already doing it. They had their scouts up in the booths giving information on the defense and so forth. I had been a player, a manager, a scout, a coach, everything, so why not an eye in the sky, or as I called it, a "spy in the sky"? I think I was the first one in baseball. I don't know if it had been used before. I had a walkie-talkie up there with me, and I would radio directions about the defense down to Monty Basgall. What I did was take a combination scouting report, with our scouting diagrams and everything, on the opposition and sit up in the press box and watch our outfielders and infielders. Sometimes a guy would wander or otherwise be out of position, so it was my responsibility to correct that. It worked very well. Sometimes too well, thought some of the other clubs. Occasionally they wouldn't let me sit in the press box. They'd reassign me to some lousy seat way out in the outfield.

We came into Cincinnati for a series, and before the game started, I was sitting back of home plate up near the press box. Then a guy came by and told me I couldn't sit there. I said, "Why not? I've been sitting here in every ballpark in the country." "Well, you can't sit here!" he said. I said, "By whose orders?" "Never mind!" he said. Well, I didn't want to fight with the guy, didn't want to make a fuss, so I said, "Well, where am I going to sit?" He said, "Anyplace you want to in the stadium, but you can't sit here!" The seats were all sold back of home plate, so I said, "Anyplace?" He said, "Yes." So I went up and sat in the upper third deck in center field, right back of the center fielder in the cheap seats, the ones that Bob Uecker would later make famous in television commercials. I figured that since I had been a center fielder, I could watch the game from there and get a sense of how to position the fielders. I could look right over the center fielder and second base and watch the pitcher and batter and, if necessary, walkie-talkie a message down to the Dodgers dugout. The seats were all turned up, like the cleaning crew does when they sweep and clean up. So I just started putting seats down to spell out "H-I" "I" "S-P-Y." Vin Scully, the Dodgers radio announcer, saw it and got the biggest kick out of that. He announced it on the radio, and there I was, sitting up there with a walkie-talkie, directing whatever I could.

It was a hot afternoon game following a night game. The crowd wasn't very big. The cleanup crew apparently hadn't gotten around to my section. A couple of feet away were the remains of a half-eaten ice cream bar someone had dropped the evening before. Naturally it drew a swarm of insects, a sizable cloud of gnats. Sooner or later, they started hanging around me. I began swatting at them with my clipboard or sheaf of scouting reports. This went on for some time, probably much of the game. I don't know why I didn't change seats. I guess I was determined not to let those bugs get the better of me. I kept swatting them, even when our batters were up. We went on to win three straight games, and I understand that the Reds were real upset with me. They thought I was stealing their signals out there and relaying them to our hitters with my vigorous gnat swattings. Hell, I was just swinging at the bugs.

One time when I was working for the Dodgers as a scout, I received a little bonus, $1,000, but after taking the taxes out, it was about $750.50. They gave it to me in a check, which was fine. At that time, we had a goat named Slugger on our ranch. I had always wanted a goat since I was a boy. He was a great companion on our ranch. Every morning when I went out to feed the horses or the cows, he would go along with me. He would walk on top of the fence. When I would do some woodchopping or sawing, he would be up on the woodpile, just looking at me and chewing. He would chew everything. If you left a pair of gloves around, he would chew them up. You had to be careful. That fall my wife wanted to go out to Reno to do a little gambling, to pull some slot machines. She had seen it one time and wanted to go. We sold a couple of horses and decided to take $1,000 of that money and put it together with the $750.50 bonus check and go out to Nevada. We'd drive out there and enjoy ourselves. So I said, "Go into town and get the checks cashed." She got one cashed but forgot the one from the Dodgers. I said, "Go on back in and get it." She came back, and we got to talking about this and that and getting ready. I said, "Do you want to go tomorrow?" She said, "Yes." I asked, "Did you get the check cashed?" She said, "Yes." She looked in her purse but couldn't find the $750.50. It was in a little brown envelope. I said, "Well, where is it?" We looked all through the pickup truck, the floor, in back of the seats, and on the ground. We retraced her steps. We still couldn't find the money. Helen got quite upset, but I said, "Forget it. We'll put more in there. It's gone." I went out to look some more, and I saw Slugger standing on the little house we built him. He was standing on top of his house chewing. I look at him chewing. I don't know why, but I went over close to him. I said, "Slugger, come here." He jumped down. He had a piece of that brown envelope in his mouth. I said, "Oh, no." I could see just a little bit of the green in the corner. I said, "Babe, Slugger chewed up the money." She wanted to kill him. She chased him every time she went out of the house. She would chase him all over the place with the broom. We postponed our trip for a couple of days. She had to go into town and get some groceries, because the kids were going to be there. She was headed for the car. I said, "Just a minute." I went over to this pile of green droppings and scooped up a couple handfuls. I said, "Hey, Babe, here's $75 for the groceries." Needless to say, I almost got it with the broom.

In 1977 and 1978, the Dodgers faced the Yankees in the World Series. On October 18, 1977, I was at Yankee Stadium when Reggie Jackson hit 3 home runs in one game. I was with the Dodgers, so naturally I was pretty glum. Three pitches, 3 home runs. Our reports on him were to not show a fastball, but if you have a fastball pitcher and that's his best pitch, then what are you going to do? He hit them off everybody that night. Burt Hooton wasn't a fastball pitcher, and Charlie Hough was a knuckleballer. Reggie put on quite a show. He wasn't much of a fielder, but he sure could hit that ball. What Lasorda said about Reggie that night you can't say in public. The next year, even though the Dodgers won the first two games, we lost again to New York. In 1981 it would turn out different.

Even though Reggie Jackson and George Steinbrenner were famous and powerful, occasionally I'd go round with them. During the 1981 World Series, I got to joking with Jackson down around the batting cage. He had massacred the Dodgers in the Series back in 1977 and 1978, but I loved the guy. He could rise to the challenge with the best of them, as if he were hearing some conductor waving the baton for a crescendo. That day I gave him a jab. He asked me if I had seen any better player than he was. "You know, you're not so hot, Reggie," I replied. "What do you mean?" he said. "Well, Reggie, you've struck out about two thousand times so far in your career. You get to the plate about five hundred times a year maybe. Hell, you haven't had a hit in *four* years!" He didn't know what to say to that.

George Steinbrenner deserves a better image. Sure, he wanted to win all the time, but he treated his people well, even those who left him or he let go. I think to this day, he continues to send a check to the widow of Cedric Tallis, his former general manager. But occasionally George could bug me, as in the 1981 World Series, when he assigned Birdie Tebbetts to sit next to me and jot down everything I said into the walkie-talkie. One time later, I bumped into Steinbrenner at a select horse sale in Lexington, Kentucky. We shared an interest in thoroughbreds, and it turned out we were staying at the same motel. At breakfast George saw me and motioned me over. We chatted a bit. Then I lit into him for a bad decision he had made previously. After the playoffs with Kansas City, he had fired his third base coach, Mike Ferraro, for sending a runner home who got tagged out at the plate. "George," I said to him, "that firing of Ferraro was unjust. The ball bounced back off the left-field wall to the outfielder just right, and he made a great relay to the shortstop, who made a tremendous one-hop peg to the plate. You can't blame a guy when it took three *perfect* plays to nail the runner." George didn't answer.

We neutralized Dave Winfield in the 1981 World Series with the Yankees. He got 1 hit for 23 at bats. I take a lot of credit for that development. I was the eye in the sky. I was also the coach in charge of the outfield defense. When Winfield came up the first time, there were a couple of guys on base. I was on the walkie-talkie with Monty Basgall. I had them move the outfielders back three separate times. Winfield was just standing there at the plate while we kept calling timeout and waving the white towels to position the outfielders. It was in Yankee Stadium with those big spacious power alleys, so we bunched the outfielders in. So when they start to pitch to him, I said, "Make him chase the ball." The Dodger pitchers threw some low pitches, and, man, did he go after them! He took that bait like nothing you'd ever seen. He chased those pitches in the dirt. He looked like he was killing worms. He chased them all over the ballpark, and we stopped him. When he finally got a base hit, he kissed first base. It was a deciding factor in the Series, stopping their big guy. Lou Piniella was their toughest out. My advice in my report said, "Don't let him beat you. Walk him. Don't let him beat you." When Lou would get walked, he'd really get red, what they call "the red ass." You didn't want him too riled up, because he was a tough hitter.

I don't know if George Steinbrenner knew what I did to Winfield, but he knew that I was up there doing that scouting. I was on the walkie-talkie directing the defense and everything, and the Dodgers had my reports, and I'd refresh them a little bit and watch the game from up there. Steinbrenner put Birdie Tebbetts right next to me, and he was writing down everything that I said on the walkie-talkie. He was working for the Yankees that year. Every once in a while, I'd turn off the walkie-talkie and make some nasty remarks, and poor Birdie had to write them all down. One time I turned it off and said, "Darn, Birdie, I got to go to the men's room. Is that all right?" When I got up to go to the men's room, he got up to follow me. I said, "You follow me in there, I'm going to hit you!" He said that his orders were to not let me out of his sight.

We also stymied Goose Gossage, who was enjoying a Hall of Fame career. When we played the Yankees and Gossage in the Series, I told Davey Lopes and a couple of our guys, "Make this guy wait. Make him wait. Don't let him bang on you." I'd been doing my scouting and eye-in-the-sky work, and I'd seen pitchers like him. Goose liked to get the ball and fire. So Davey would look down to the coach for a sign; then he'd step out and get the rosin bag and dust his hands and his bat. Then he would dust his shoes off. While he was doing all this, Gossage was out there fuming, wanting to throw the ball. The next thing I knew, it was ball one, ball two, and Goose just kept getting hotter. Davey did a great job. He unsettled Gossage. I don't know if everybody knew about that, but that's exactly what I would have done every time. But nobody did it, and Goose had that brilliant career. He became a surefire Hall of Famer.

The last game was incredibly exciting. Finally, when Bob Lemon took out Tommy John, I got so excited I yelled down to Lasorda, "We got them now, Tommy." And we did. I don't know whether I had the walkie-talkie on or not, but I was very excited. Lemon made the mistake of taking his best pitcher out of there too early. You could see that Tommy John didn't want to come out, but Bob took him out. Of course, that wasn't the only reason they lost, but it was a big part. I knew we had them then. What a wonderful feeling it was to beat the Yankees, to be World Champions! For me, there were some special warm feelings, because I had helped with my advice on Winfield and Gossage.

When I was with the Dodgers, I did a lot of advance scouting, making reports and such. I guess I was one of the first guys to travel with the club. In fact, I had a long conversation with Lee McPhail about advance scouting. He asked me what I thought an advance scout was worth to a big league ball club. I said the same thing as the coach. The guy could be worth 10 wins a season to a big league club, especially if he knew what he was doing. Clubs began to see the advantages. Now most clubs have advance scouts. You see them everywhere, and they do a good job. I still think a good advance scout is worth about 10 ball games.

I got to scout with some truly fine individuals during those years. Ben

Wade was the scouting director for the Dodgers. I knew Ben from our days in Vancouver when he pitched for us. Ben had pulled a leg, and it was really hurting bad. The club wanted to release him, but I wouldn't let them cut him loose. He was a hard worker, and I thought he'd come around. I got in bad with management on account of that. I thought they were being pretty cruel. I said, "Here's a guy who hurt himself, and now we're going to turn him loose." I wouldn't let them do that. Ben found out and always appreciated what I did for him. I got along with him fine. He was a pretty good guy.

Jerry Stephenson and I worked together with the Dodgers doing advance scouting for the World Series. He had been a bonus player with the Red Sox. He was a fun-loving pitcher. He dyed his hair green one time. I was afraid to mention that to him for fear that he might take a shot at me. But he was a good baseball man and a solid pitcher. It's terrible that the Dodgers let him go after he'd been with them so many years. Sometimes those things happen, but they're not very good when they happen to you. Jerry is one of my favorite people. I enjoyed working with him. His father was a tremendous scout for the Red Sox too. Jerry's son is currently a player in somebody's organization. It is quite a baseball family.

Dario Lodigiani was another scouting friend of mine. He had played for the Philadelphia A's and Chicago White Sox back in the 1930s and 1940s. We scouted together in Arizona, down in Scottsdale and Phoenix. One day he said to me, "Do you know anybody in the orange business?" We started talking about how much we loved oranges and grapefruit. I happened to become acquainted with a guy who ran a fruit packinghouse in that area. I knew the guy, and I would bring him some autographed baseballs. So I went over there and got about ten bags of citrus fruit—oranges, grapefruit—and brought them back to my room. I invited Dario over to my room. We were staying in the same hotel. He looked at me and wanted to know how I got stuff like this. I said, "Oh, I know somebody. You want some?" I gave him four or five sacks. Lodigiani was a fine person and a good scout too.

Earl Rapp was another of my favorite scouting guys. He played in the Pacific Coast League in the 1940s. I'd seen him play out there. He was a pretty good ballplayer, but he didn't play a long time on the major league level. I remember him very well because he had an interesting hobby. He carried a metal detector around with him when he scouted. I got to know him real well, and I saw him operating it. I said, "What the heck you looking for? You looking for guys with iron hands or some darned thing?" He'd laugh like heck. So one day, when we were in Boston, he took me with him to the parks or the Commons. We grabbed a cab to there. He had his metal detector with him. He started looking for coins, things in the park. I think we found about forty dollars' worth of coins in one park. Earl said, "I make more out of this than I do out of my meal money."

Ellis Clary was one of my favorite scouts. He played for Washington during World War II and then went on to scout for the Senators, I believe. One day he was scouting a ball game, and he had a heart attack. They called an ambulance, and he almost died. He was almost pronounced dead on arrival. As they were loading him in the ambulance, Ellis turned to one of his buddies and said, "Get the mileage." There he was, with a heart attack situation, and he's saying, "Get the mileage!" He would tell that story for years. Every time he comes through town, he calls me to find out how I am. I ask him where he's going, what he's doing. He's a big fan of Georgia football. He's from Valdosta, where their high school team has won a bunch of championships over the years. He always tells you about that. Ellis was a good ballplayer, very aggressive, very scrappy. I thought he'd fight at the drop of a hat. I guess that fighting spirit brought him through that trying time of the heart attack. "Get the mileage," he said.

As a scout, I got to meet some interesting characters, some of my favorite people. Bob Prince, the Pittsburgh Pirates announcer, was one. When I was scouting, he'd always see me either in the press room or sitting back of home plate, and he'd get me on his show the next day. Bob used to take his shirt off when it was hot, and he'd take his trousers off when it was real hot. He'd be up there in his shorts announcing the game. I was crazy about him as an announcer. I walked into his booth one time, at a game, and they were taking a short break in between innings. He turned around and saw me, and he said, "Here comes that goddamn Metro. He's going to freeload in the press box today. He's from Nanty-Glo. He's known the length and breadth of Nanty-Glo, Pennsylvania. He's famous back there. You know, there's only about three hundred people in Nanty-Glo." He was giving it to me but good. Then he says, "Now get the hell out of here." I was red in the face with embarrassment. I didn't know what to say. Then he turned around and started announcing the first hitter of the next inning. I didn't find out until the next inning that Bob had turned off the microphone, that he had been talking into a dead microphone. He did a pretty good job on me.

Another time, when I was scouting in St. Louis, Bob saw me and said, "You going swimming?" I said, "Yeah." The swimming pool was at the Chase Hotel. So we were swimming, having a good time. The game wasn't until that evening. Bob pointed to a window overlooking the pool and asked, "Hey! Anybody dive out of that second-story window?" I said, "Hell, no! Nobody can dive out of there!" He said, "I'll bet you ten bucks I can dive. . . . Bet you twenty dollars I can dive out of there." I said, "You're covered. You're going to dive out of there?" He said, "Yeah!" So up he went to the window and dove in the damn pool. I had to pay up. It was maybe five or ten feet from the building to the edge of the pool, but he did a beautiful dive. I found out he had been a champion college diver and tried out for the Olympics or something like that. He was very slender but athletic enough to be a diver. Bob was a delight.

The late Max Patkin, the great baseball clown, was one of my all-time favorite people. Max had been a pitcher, but like a lot of us, he never had all the abilities to become a big league pitcher, so he turned to being a comic. It seemed like every time I managed, he would put on his show, and I never got tired of it. My kids loved him. When they were growing up, they'd see Max and come home and imitate him. They wanted to know how he did all those things. I had a lot of nice experiences with Max. I was traveling as a scout in Texas, at El Paso. I had an old, beat-up Ford pickup truck that I used to take on trips because I could take my son Geoff and his friend Scott West with me. I had a brand-new engine and good tires on this truck. I always took it with me because I would make deals on things and bring them back in my truck. I saw Max at the ballpark. He said, "Hey, Charlie, where you going?" I said, "I'm going to Midland." He said, "Well, so am I. How you going?" I said, "Oh, I got a vehicle. Why don't you come with me, Max?" He said, "Well, OK." I said, "I've got an air-conditioned vehicle, pretty good." So early next morning, about 7:30, I picked him up at the motel where he was staying. The boys were in the back of the pickup truck inside their sleeping bags, snoozing. They'd been up all night swimming and everything, like teenagers. Max got in my truck and didn't say a word. We put his bags in the back and headed over the desert head for Midland. It was hot, about ninety to a hundred degrees. After about an hour, finally Max said, "Hey, Charlie, where's that air conditioning?" I said, "Right over there," pointing to the window. "Roll it down."

On that same trip, I got him worrying about how much gasoline we had. I had two tanks on the pickup truck. Max was watching the gas gauge on the thing, and he said, "Gee whiz, you better get some gas." I said, "Oh, no, we'll make it. Don't worry." But Max was worrying about it, especially when we were about thirty miles out of Midland and the engine started sputtering. I told him, "Well, we'll flip a coin to see who walks in and gets the gas when we run out." He didn't know that I had two tanks. So just to aggravate him I started chugging the engine. I said, "I think we'll make it." But I chugged that engine to the last moment, when I reached down and switched over to the other tank. I thought he was going to throw me out of the truck. Max was worried the whole time.

When we got to Midland, I told Max, "You don't have to pay for a room. We got two beds. Stay here and take your nap." He was going to leave after the game. So the boys had a water pistol fight in the room. Every time they hit Max, who had his shirt off, he'd jump up!

Another time, back when I was managing in the Pacific Coast League, Max was in San Diego to do his act while we were there. As the manager, I had a suite of rooms. I saw Max sitting around the lobby, and I said, "Hey Max, come on up. Where are you staying?" He said, "Right here." I asked, "Do you have a room yet? Come on up. I got a bedroom and a couch and everything. Come on up." So Max made me flip a coin to see who would get the bed. He won the toss. He'd sleep in the bed, and I had to sleep on the couch. Max laughed like heck. He was a total joy.

I had many a conversation with Al Rosen when he was a general manager at Houston and at San Francisco. We never could get one past him. He's a very shrewd judge of talent. You couldn't tell him anything that wasn't true. Al was a great horseman. He was very good friends with the people who owned the great racehorse Affirmed. Al and I talked about thoroughbred horses a lot because he had quite a bit of interest in Kentucky horses. We were looking at the same horse many times.

Another famous person I met in my baseball life was Richard Nixon. Every time I'd go out to California and go to the California Angels ballpark, I'd go into the press room. I walked in there one day, early, and over in the corner sat a man I knew. I said to myself, "I know him. I've seen him many a time." He looked up at me and said, "Hey, Charlie, come and sit here." I was stumped a little bit, but when I got there, I realized it was President Nixon. He was a great baseball fan. We talked about baseball. He asked me what I was doing and said, "I know all about you." He told me about my baseball career, you did this, you did that. He asked me how the pennant race was going to go. What a conversation! I was absolutely amazed at the knowledge he had about baseball. It was a most delightful time. I spent about an hour there. He wouldn't let me go. Finally I said, "I got to go to work and watch these guys." He said, "OK." He was a remarkable man, and what a memory he had on baseball! I never knew that. The only thing I regret is that I had a baseball in my pocket, and I should have had him sign it.

Speaking of guys in charge, though, I can't say I was wild about Commissioner Bowie Kuhn. Bowie had a lot of problems during his stay in office. I think he was continually fighting with somebody, somewhere, somehow.

I lost a lot of respect for the man when I happened to be down in Caracas, Venezuela, for the Caribbean Series and he was there as the commissioner of baseball. I don't know if he was lame-ducking or not, but he and Mrs. Kuhn were there. When he was introduced at this game, they booed him. They showed him that little respect. If I had been him, I'd have gotten up and walked out of there. And I might have said some very nasty words. I lost respect for him when he took that disrespect. I would never have taken that as a player, manager, or anything else, let alone the commissioner of American baseball.

In my scouting in those years, I had the pleasure of seeing some really fine talent. I saw André Dawson with Ellis Valentine and Warren Cromartie when they were playing for Denver. The Montreal Expos had a working agreement with the Bears. One day I was sitting with Charlie Fox, who was scouting for the Expos at that time. I said, "Charlie, you're working for Montreal?" He said, "Yes." I said, "You must have one hell of an outfield up there to leave these three guys down here. These three guys are big leaguers. You've got two guys that are going to be outstanding." They were Dawson and Valentine. And I said, "The guy in right field, Cromartie's not bad either." It wasn't long until they called them up and sent the other three outfielders down.

One time I was scouting the Cardinals farm club in Little Rock, and I saw one of the finest hitting exhibitions I'd ever seen. The shortstop, who was a switch hitter, had a great day at the plate. He hit a home run left-handed and then hit another one right-handed. He hit a triple left-handed, and he hit a triple right-handed. This was in a doubleheader. I believe he also hit three doubles and a single, or two doubles and two singles. In the field, he made every play perfectly, one of the best exhibitions of shortstopping by anyone. He came in on slow-hit ground balls and threw the guy out. He went over in the hole, fielded the ball, and threw the guy out. His name was Gary Templeton. If that guy had stayed on the right path, except that he strained his knees, he would have been in the Hall of Fame. He could do everything. He was fast, and he was the guy you dream you're going to find someday and sign him for your club. Later I ran across Bing Devine, who was the Cardinals' general manager at the time, and said, "Bing, I've seen one of the greatest darn ballplayers, greatest talents I've ever seen . . . an infielder." He said, "Who are you talking about?" I said, "Gary Templeton." He said, "You really think so." I said, "Yes. Wait'll you see him." They wouldn't believe me. Gary just didn't have his head on straight. The Cardinals traded him to San Diego for Ozzie Smith, so I guess they got the better of that deal.

Joe Torre has gone on to become a fine manager with the Yankees, guiding them to those World Championships recently. But I had the occasion to chew Joe out once. I don't know whether he's going to like this or not. He was with the Braves, and we came into Atlanta for a series when I was scouting for the Dodgers. I looked out to right field and there was Joe, sitting cross-legged in the outfield. The Braves didn't have a very good ball club. But I saw Joe lazing around like that, and it disappointed me. I don't know whether he was mad at management or what, but he was too good a ballplayer to be doing that. Not long after that, maybe even the next day, I just gave him heck. I just chewed him out. I said, "That's a disgraceful way of acting, a good ballplayer like you." He looked at me a little funny. I don't think he did it again.

Looking at the Alomar brothers, Roberto and Sandy Jr., these days, I remember a conversation I had with their father when I was a scout. Sandy was a pretty good regular ballplayer, a pretty good infielder. I saw him one time and kidded him when he was with Texas. I said, "Sandy, are you going to give your money back to the club?" He said, "Why?" I said, "How many times did you come up to bat when you were with Texas that one year?" I understood he was getting paid a pretty good salary. He had had twenty-nine at bats. I said, "How much is that, about two thousand dollars per time at bat?" He laughed and said, "Shhhh, don't tell nobody!"

As a scout, you see the game and its possibilities from many angles. One time when I was scouting the White Sox and sitting with Bill Veeck at Comiskey Park, I got a brainstorm looking at the tarp. I said, "Bill, why don't you sell space on that tarp for advertisements?" He said he had already thought of that. Bill said, "Charlie, you're the only guy who's ever mentioned that." I said, "Why don't you get that salt company with that girl with that umbrella that says when it rains, it pours?" There was no rule against that. Most of the tarps are plain green or blue, maybe light blue. But I'd want my advertising on a tarp, especially in a climate like Detroit or Chicago or Boston, where they get quite a bit of rain on occasion. Even if you brought the tarp out only five or six times a year, you'd still have ten, twenty, maybe forty thousand people seeing your advertising. Veeck said, "What do you think you'd get for that?" I said, "I'd charge them fifty thousand dollars a year for it." I understand that he did that, but then I never got back there to see it.

I haven't seen any fans go streaking nude on the field, but I saw that big-chested gal, Morganna, who was always running on the field and grabbing a player to kiss. They called her "The Kissing Bandit." I saw her quite often. She'd jump up and run out there and give the player a kiss. At first the players were shy and would kind of run. But after a while, heck, the guys all loved it. One time in Cincinnati, she ran out there toward Tommy Helms. She ran right out beyond the infield, and Tommy was the type of guy who wouldn't run from her. He just opened up his arms and said, "Come here, baby." She got Johnny Bench at first base once, when he was a runner. The game stopped, and I think John enjoyed that very much. She gave him a great big smooch. She did it at all sorts of stadiums. I don't know how she'd sneak in. They'd watch out for her at the gates, but she'd still somehow slip into the ballpark. She was outstanding. The ballplayers were really funny. I don't recall where it was, but one of the ballplayers took off his shirt out there in the field and helped her. But the fans booed one ballplayer because he ran from her. He might have been married.

In the late 1970s and early 1980s, there were some possibilities of major league teams moving to Denver. One of the Denver-area businesspeople who was very interested in getting a franchise was Marvin Davis. I was associated in a way with him here in Denver. I made a visit to him when I saw that he was interested. I introduced myself and told him what I was doing, that I was on the major league level, that I knew all the owners, and that I had a feel for the clubs that were in trouble. So he said, "Go on ahead and find out what's what out there with these clubs, and come back." During my travels, I would drop by his office. I knew his habits, that he would have his lunch in his office at 11:30. I would come in and tell the receptionist that I wanted to see Mr. Davis. She'd tell him I was there, and I would go in and chat with him.

We talked about the Pittsburgh club as a possibility. But I had talked to Joe Brown of the Pirates, and Joe had discouraged me. He told me the Pirates had a twenty-year lease they couldn't break. So Pittsburgh was out of the picture. Then we discussed Minneapolis. They were struggling a little bit in attendance. Calvin Griffith, the Twins owner, was interested, but he wanted his organization along with his people to be protected. The Twins were one of the last family-run operations in baseball. Calvin was a very generous guy, unlike the picture they used to paint of him. He took care of his people, of his ballplayers, who were all loyal. He was interested in the Denver option, but he feared he would be betraying the Twin Cities.

Another club that was pretty darn close to coming into Denver was the Baltimore Orioles. Jerry Hoffberger owned the Orioles as well as a national brewing company in the East, I believe. They weren't thinking about moving, but Jerry was getting ready to sell the club. There was no one in Baltimore who was that interested at the time. I talked to him about the status of the Orioles. I asked him if he would be interested in an outsider like Marvin Davis buying the club and moving it to Denver. He said, "Well, I can't stand in the way of that if I can't find anybody in Baltimore. At least I don't want to, but I have to look at it as a businessman." So I took that information back to Marvin Davis. Frank Cashen, who was working for Hoffberger, made a trip out here to research the situation, I understand. But then Jerry found a buyer, and they kept the club in Baltimore.

Then the White Sox were interested in shifting to Denver. They were having a very difficult time in Chicago. Bill DeWitt was chairman of the board or on the board of directors or something with the club. I knew Bill all the way back to my first contract with the St. Louis Browns. Bill was instrumental in my signing my first contract with the Browns. He called me from Florida and said, "Charlie, are you familiar with Marvin Davis?" I said, "Yes." He said, "Is he for real?" I said, "Oh, yes. Yes, he's for real." Bill said, "Well, we're interested in selling the White Sox." I said, "Well, tell me the particulars. Don't be pussyfooting about this. Set the price that you want for the ball club lock, stock, and barrel." He said, "I'm leaving here and going into Cincinnati and then up to Chicago. I'll talk to Bill Veeck." Then I got a call from Veeck, and he said, "Yes, we're interested." I said, "Well, what is the situation? What's the deal?" He said, "I want seventeen million dollars for the White Sox and I want it lock, stock, and barrel. We own the property." I didn't know that last part at the time. I went back and told Marvin Davis that Bill DeWitt said he'd sell the White Sox and that Bill Veeck called me and said they owed five million to the bank, they had a five-million tax carryover credit, and they wanted seventeen million for the ball club. I said, "That includes everything. By the way, Marvin, there's thirty-four acres of property, which includes the stadium, White Sox Park. Now his evaluation of the ballpark is way down there because it's dilapidated and they're going to have to build a new one one of these days. I don't know how long the current stadium will keep passing inspection." So things started moving. Marvin said he had his young lawyers working on it, and Veeck had his lawyers there. I may not have this accurate to the nickel and dime, but I understand Davis's lawyers tried to get the price down to sixteen million. But Bill Veeck said, "I didn't ask for eighteen million. I didn't say sixteen million. I said seventeen million." In conversation with Marvin Davis, I said, "The minute that you buy the White Sox and move to Denver, Charlie Finley will move the Oakland A's into Chicago, whether he gets permission or not. He will be your tenant." But the deal fell through. I'm not entirely clear why. I didn't hear all sides of the stories. But it was pretty close to happening. The White Sox would have been here in Denver and Charlie Finley's Oakland A's in Chicago.

As it turned out, I was the one who made a switch. After the 1981 World Series, I worked a deal to go over to Oakland. I needed a year of service credit to qualify for a pension. But I was also a little disenchanted with the Dodgers. Even though I got World Series rings for the three Series, the club didn't vote me a Series share, either losers' or winners'. Eventually I complained to Peter O'Malley and received $2,500 belatedly. The Dodgers did do something nice for the players' wives. They would let them make one trip with the club each season. I think they had two or three trips that they could choose from. The wives would go on the trip, and it was great. Most of them would want to go to New York or Chicago. The Dodgers had their own plane, which was quite luxurious. I thought it was very good for the players. I don't know whether clubs do that nowadays or not. The Dodgers did it, and I thought it was great. But in the 1977 and 1978 Series, we had to arrange for our own seats, and I had to get Al Campanis to agree to cover my wife's expenses coming out to the Series. I guess I expected better from the Dodgers, especially in light of my years of service as a scout, an eye in the sky, and Al's right-hand man in Latin America.

TWELVE

Billy Ball

In 1982 Billy Martin offered me the chance to coach for the Oakland A's. This would give me the year necessary to qualify for my major league pension. I was having a very difficult time. Billy's offer made life easier for us in our later years. It also got me back in uniform on the field. I was probably the oldest friend he had in baseball. I went back with Billy Martin to when he was just a kid at Oakland and Berkeley, and I was with the Oakland club in 1945. Then I had played and managed against him in the low minor leagues. I had kept in touch with him over the years, recommended him for a managerial job in Denver and later at Kansas City in 1970, and scouted for the Tigers when Billy managed them in the early 1970s.

I can't find anything bad to say about Billy Martin. Sure he got into scrapes. Heck, if some jerk said something to him, he'd belt him. Billy always told me to hit first and regret later. That was his philosophy. Don't get hit first. And he would; that's the way he fought. He came from that type of neighborhood, that environment, surrounded by bigger kids. You always had to fight your way. He carried his own weight. I can't say enough good things about Billy Martin. I don't care about his personal life, whether he drank or anything like that. I don't care about any of that. He was a good man, and he gave me a lot. He was the only guy who said, "I'll get you here on your pension, to qualify you." Some other guys had told me that, but they would run away from me when I'd approach them. When Billy offered me a job as a coach, he said, "I'm going to give you a salary coaching for me, but you're going to get one thousand dollars less than the lowest guy." The lowest guy was making a heck of a lot more than I dreamed of getting. My face dropped when I saw the figure he gave me. I said, "Oh, boy, this is great, if this is the lowest." That's what he did. He just put us one thousand dollars lower, but his coaches were well paid. I liked Billy immensely. In fact, I was crazy about him.

Many of the stories about him, I can say from my experience as his friend, are untrue or overexaggerated. Billy was the most gracious, most considerate baseball man I have ever met, in relation to the fans, to kids, to his players. He was very gracious and thoughtful. There were a lot of things to like about Billy. Most people don't know how considerate he was with other people. If he met you, no matter when it was, he'd remember you. He'd remember everything he told you or you told him. It was as if he had researched it. We were at the winter meetings in Houston one time quite a few years ago. My daughter, Elena, was with me. We went out with Billy. Whenever I'd run across him again, he'd ask how Elena was doing. He'd laugh like heck. At those winter meetings, she had a headache. They took her out dancing and everything else, and they kept her out all night, well into the morning. The next day we had these meetings, and she couldn't attend them. I don't think she was hungover, but it was pretty close.

I loved wearing cowboy boots. Heck, I was probably the first baseball guy who wore them all the time as a manager and a scout. Billy got interested in boots. I walked into the clubhouse in Scottsdale the year before I coached for Oakland, and I saw a pair of boots. They were nice brown alligator boots, with white leather on the front. I took a look at them and said, "Gosh, that's a good-looking pair of boots. Damn, what'd you pay for those, Billy? Where'd you get those?" He said, "I had them made." I said, "They're really nice." He said, "What size do you wear?" I said, "Nine." He said, "Try them on." So I took my old boots off and tried them on. He said, "They're yours." He gave me a pair of boots that probably cost $1,200 to $1,500 custom-made. You didn't dare say that you liked anything of his when he was around, because he'd give it to you. Once I went in a men's store with him. He was going to buy some shirts, and he said, "Charlie, what are you doing?" I said, "I'm looking at some leather jackets. These battle jacket–type things are nice." He said, "What size?" I said, "Forty-four." He said, "Will that one fit you? Try it on." So I tried it on. I went to hang it back up, but the clerk said, "Oh, no, sorry, sir, but that's yours." Billy had bought it for me. It was three hundred dollars. Not that money was everything, but he was that way.

I was in Boston early in the year covering a club for the Dodgers, when Billy was managing the Yankees. I was staying at the same hotel as the ballplayers, and he saw me there. He said, "Come on with me." I said, "Where are you going?" He said, "I'm going over to this store." We were staying at the Sheraton in Boston, I guess it was. So I went with him to this big department store. He said, "I want to get something for Helen's birthday." I said, "How do you know it's her birthday?" He said, "I know, I know." I never knew how he knew it was her birthday. It is May 15. So he insisted on buying her a present. I said, "Well, if you want to, but you'd better put a note on it." So he put a note on it saying, "To my favorite girlfriend. Don't treat Charlie too bad." He was thoughtful. I told him he didn't have to do that, but he wanted to.

Billy had quite a taste for history. He was a remarkable historian. He read quite a bit. He knew the Civil War as well as anybody I had ever met. He thought that Robert E. Lee was the greatest general in the history of the Civil War. I don't know if you could argue that point with him or not. I found a Civil War book about Robert E. Lee somewhere in a used bookstore, and I sent it to him. He really appreciated it. He never forgot when somebody did him a favor. He was extremely loyal.

Billy Martin was the most gracious baseball man I've ever seen with autographs for kids. He never turned down a kid no matter what the score was, whether he had a good day with the club, whether his club won or lost. He would always take time to give autographs. When the Oakland club came into New York, Billy would make you go get a couple dozen baseballs and then throw them to the kids. He was quite popular there.

Billy always insisted that the players get tipping money and tip the maids and the waitresses and cab drivers real well. He insisted that when you had breakfast, you had to tip. He'd check on that. He'd ask the women in the coffee shop. When we'd get up early and have breakfast, all the guys would sign the tab and pay it up at the end of the week. They'd put the room number down and put the tip down. The waitresses knew all the ballplayers who had breakfast there. Billy would check. He never forgot that he had grown up poor. Every day he wanted that done right. I'd see him tip big all the time. Of course, he had a massive expense account with the Yankees. When I was scouting for the Dodgers for the World Series, I'd come into town, and he would know I was there. He'd send a message up, saying he wanted to see me. So we'd go out, and he would treat those waiters real well, especially if they complimented him or the dinner was real special. He'd just give the whole amount to the waiters. He was very good at that. He wanted everybody treated royally, the maids, the waiters and waitresses, the flight attendants on the charter plane. He was a first-class guy in that respect.

Billy was a superb manager. He knew every move that was made, and he anticipated well. He was as fine a manager at calling a pitchout as I've ever seen. It always seemed like he knew what was coming. He knew what the guy in the other dugout was doing. Billy could read a pitcher real well. But I think one of his strongest abilities was that he knew when the other club was going to steal. He had a sixth sense about that. He'd call that pitchout and stop the other club dead in their tracks. He loved to control the game, and he did. He would maneuver with the best of them.

To watch Billy and Earl Weaver of the Baltimore Orioles managing in a ball game was something that you'd never forget. Billy, of course, would be telling jokes during the first five innings, and Earl would be over there smoking those cigarettes. He was a three-packer. Everybody was just having a good time, laughing and so forth. But as soon as that sixth inning came along, whoa, everything stopped. The jokes stopped, the cigarette smoking stopped, and the wheels started turning. They wound up every darn game that I saw them manage against each other with the best ballplayers in that situation facing one another, fielder, hitter, pitcher, pinch hitter, whatever. They had the ones who were right there at that particular time and let the players decide the game. They were a delight, and there's no question in my mind that Billy Martin should be in the Hall of Fame for his managing, as is Earl Weaver.

Billy was always an energetic leader as well as a constant fan favorite. When he managed the Minnesota Twins, they drew a lot of people. He went to Texas, and they drew a lot of people. He went to Kansas City, and they drew a lot of people and were winners. With the Yankees, he was a winner each time he managed them. His stint at Detroit was the same way. And he carried that on at Oakland. When Billy took over Oakland in 1980, the A's had just finished a horrible season, in 1979. He took them to second place and gave Kansas City a run for the division for a while. In 1981, during the strike-shortened year, he managed the A's into the split-season playoffs against the Yankees. He was a winner. If you could ever put a tag on a manager who fought his way up, Billy Martin was the man. He was a winner. Anytime Billy was without a job, he'd say, "I'll be back. I'll manage somewhere."

The biggest problem that I could see with Billy Martin was that everybody would try to tell him what to do. He made managing look so easy. It was so easy because he did everything right. I never saw him make a bad move, if I could be the judge of that, having managed many years myself. Everything he did was right, so he made it look easy. Everybody thought that they could do that too, so people started telling him what to do. After Billy had been with a team a couple years, some people wanted to tell him what to do. Billy Martin wanted to select the ballplayers, not let the general manager do it. They'd start interfering with his managing. When they interfered, it was like waving a red flag in front of him. That's when they'd come to a parting of the ways. I don't fault him for anything that he did. A lot of people would like to put a ring in their manager's nose, and Billy refused to have a ring put in his nose so they could pull him around and control him. He ran the club and ran it well. If there was any blame to be taken for anything, he would take the blame. He didn't pass the buck.

George Steinbrenner hired him five different times for the Yankees, and Billy was successful each time. Billy never talked much about Steinbrenner. After a blowup and everything else, he'd forget it. He hated some other managers that he managed against, but he never carried a grudge. He'd try to beat you to death on the field, but he didn't stay angry. Billy said that George treated him well. I believe maybe George Steinbrenner overstepped his bounds and tried to put a ring in Billy's nose, and you couldn't do that to Billy. He said it'd bother him too much sometimes when George would call him at 4:00 in the morning, when he was in New York or out on the road. But Billy once told me, "That SOB is just like I am. All he wants to do is win, and he doesn't care how." I think that was the finest compliment he could pay Steinbrenner. George was a fierce owner. I don't exactly buy his benevolence with Daryl Strawberry and Steve Howe and other guys who have been in trouble. He wanted to win all the time and probably overstepped his bounds at times with the manager, but I think they were a good pair. Billy and George were a good winning combination. Both had these winning complexes, these winning egos.

Billy Martin was the most intense, aggressive, focused ballplayer or manager I have ever seen in my life. Everything was based on winning, winning, winning. There were some guys Billy hated to manage against, because they were all showboats. Bill Rigney, for example, would put on a show and everything else. Billy always wanted to beat the heck out of him. Billy was a tough, demanding manager. He would get more out of a ballplayer than any manager I'd ever seen. Al Lopez got an awful lot out of his players. The year I coached for Al and the White Sox, I don't think we had an outfielder who hit over .250. But we made a run for the pennant. Al was superb. He was the quiet type. Billy was the opposite, but he still got his players to play to their abilities. He was fiery. He was intense and aggressive with umpires and opposing ball clubs, but he was very gentle with his own players, at least during the times I saw him. He was a baseball player's manager, but you had to play to the best of your ability. He took care of his players. He protected them. I never heard him get on or give a ballplayer heck in front of everybody, a style that I learned from him too late. I was the other side of that. I would be direct with a guy who made a mistake.

I told him right then and there so I wouldn't forget it or overlook it. Billy would just shake his head when a player would do something wrong, but then he'd give the coach an earful. Sometimes I felt sorry for the Oakland coaches. If a pitcher hung a curve ball to a hitter and the guy hit it a mile, he'd turn to Art Fowler and tell him, "Art, I want you to stop teaching those guys to hang that curve ball." If a guy was out of position and didn't play where he should in the infield, Billy would just give Clete Boyer heck. Billy was even competitive about what league he played or managed in. A lifelong American Leaguer, he used to look down on National Leaguers, such as when longtime Cardinal Enos Slaughter misplayed a drive by Jackie Robinson in the sixth game of the 1956 World Series. "You've got to get that National Leaguer out of left field," he supposedly told Casey Stengel.

It's no secret that Reggie Jackson and Billy didn't get along very well when they were with the Yankees. Reggie was quite a ballplayer, but he would loaf on a ground ball or a fly ball, and Billy didn't like anybody to loaf. He said you have to play up to the best of your ability. I've used that advice many times myself, even before Billy started managing. You play to the best of your ability. I'm not going to ask you for 110 or 120 percent, because you can't play 120 percent. You can play 100 percent, to the best of your ability. Reggie didn't. Reggie didn't make the plays. I think Reggie realizes it. I think if he had it back to do over again, he would have hustled more in the field. Billy took him out. Billy was fiery; he wanted to win. Reggie was an outstanding ballplayer, especially at the plate. Wow, he was a tough competitor at the plate. But Billy couldn't stand the fact that Reggie didn't charge the ball and get it back in to the infield faster. So he took him out. I've done that on occasion as a manager. I know a lot of managers who have done that. Some people say you show a ballplayer up when you do that, but I don't think so. The ballplayer does it to himself. What you do is try to get him to learn the lesson. You don't want it to happen again. Billy did that to Reggie, and Reggie didn't like it. I believe if they both had it to do over again, maybe they would have done it a little differently.

One time Billy started to give me heck. I'd been an outfielder, and Billy had been an infielder. I would do some positioning of outfielders. One game he looked out to left field and said, "Charlie, why are you moving him over that way?" I was moving Rickey Henderson over to left-center a little bit. I'd get his attention and motion him over three or four or five steps over. Billy questioned my judgment. He said, "These guys are going to hit the ball down the left-field line." I said, "No, they aren't going to hit the ball down the left-field line." I pointed to the flagpole, to the wind direction. The batter got hold of the pitch, and Rickey ran over to left-center and made a sliding, diving catch. Billy never said another word to me about it. That was a compliment.

Billy was a great student of the game. He was always asking questions, looking for new angles on how to win or manage better. He was always inquisitive, always wanting to know, why do you do this? Why do you do that? When I managed Bisbee in 1947, I'd come into Phoenix, where Billy was on the Phoenix club. We'd both talk about hitting all the time. I saw Billy many times while I was scouting and everything else. At the winter meetings we'd get together, and he'd ask me, "What makes a good manager?" I'd say, "Well, I believe what makes a good manager is the guy never was a star. An outstanding hitter or a pitcher doesn't know what goes through the average ballplayer's mind and what you have to do for an average ballplayer." He'd ask me, "Do you think I'm a good manager?" I'd say, "Billy, you're probably as good a manager as I've ever seen." He'd say, "You managed against Casey Stengel. Am I as good as Casey?" I said, "Yeah, Billy, and if you had the Yankee ball club that Casey had, you'd have won every year too." We discussed that all the time. Whenever Casey Stengel talked about Billy, tears would come into his eyes and everything. One night, in 1960 I think, when they were both still around, I ran across Casey. Regarding Billy, Casey said, "I loved that son of a gun" or words to that effect. Of all the things in Casey's life, the fact that he had to get rid of Billy from the Yankees hurt him the most.

Billy was what I call a bumblebee. He wasn't big enough to play ball like he did. He wasn't big enough, but he didn't know that. He couldn't hit, but he didn't know that. Every fielding play was an adventure to him, an exciting adventure. He couldn't field. He ran a little bit, but he couldn't run. He couldn't do anything but put it all together, and he was a winning ballplayer. Once I asked him about the great catch he made in the 1952 World Series, when he caught the ball right up at the pitcher's mound there. I said, "How in the heck did you know that?" He said, "I knew it. I sensed it. I made two steps in when the guy was swinging the bat. I was on the grass almost before the ball left the bat. I knew I had it." If he hadn't caught Jackie Robinson's pop-up, the game would have been over. He caught the ball and made the play. If you could ever pick out one play that won a World Series, his catch on Robinson's little pop fly in the infield would rank right up there.

But Billy Martin was very lonely in New York. When the Dodgers played the Yankees in the World Series in either 1977 or 1978, I had lunch with him the day before the Series started. I was surprised how lonely he was. I said, "Where are your coaches, Billy?" He said, "Oh, they don't come around."

Maybe they were leaving him to his own thoughts. We had a great time. I kidded him, "You're trying to get my sign, get our signs, aren't you?" He said, "No." I said, "Well, I'm going to get your signs." "No, you can't," he said. I think he had our signs pretty early in the Series, but we didn't get his.

What a practical joker Billy was! Billy had a great sense of humor. As a scout, I'd been used to taking a nap in the afternoon, because I did lot of night games. I would take a nap about 1:00, 1:30, thirty minutes or so, then go freshen up and go out to the game for the evening. I was an early riser. One Sunday while I was coaching in Oakland in 1982, I must have overexerted myself in warmups or something, because about midway through the game I got real drowsy on the bench. The sun was beating down, just catching a bit of the dugout. My chin started bumping on my chest. One of the worst things you can do in baseball is fall asleep on the bench. There I was, ex-manager, ex-player, ex-scout, asleep on the bench. I don't know how long I had dozed, but I began to feel some pain down around my feet. I woke up startled to see my shoes smoking. Somebody had given me a hotfoot! They put that bat rosin stuff on my shoes and laces and lit them. I looked down the bench, and nobody was looking at me. Everything was quiet, and Billy was standing in front there, and we were in the field. I leaped to my feet and cooled them off by putting each foot in the toilet water. "When I catch the son of a bitch who did this, I'll tear him in two," I roared. I looked up and down the bench for the telltale signs of complicity, but everyone looked at me like I was crazy. Then they started laughing at me. Finally I spotted Billy at the end of the dugout. He was fighting to choke back a laugh. I walked over to him and said, "Hey, Billy, we got some smart ass here on this club. Look what he did to my shoes." He said, "What?" I said, "Look at that. It burned them up. You ought to fine that smart ass a hundred dollars." Billy said, "Charlie, that smart ass is me." I'm not sure Billy did it. I think he was covering for Steve McCatty or one of the other pitchers who were always pulling stuff like that. I finally sat down, and I turned to Art Fowler and grumbled, "Art, I'll fine that so-and-so." He says, "You better not." Billy had that delightful sense of humor. Our club wasn't very good at Oakland. We were fourth that season, but fourth wasn't good enough for Billy. He didn't even like second. But Billy and the guys would have a lot of fun to keep the club relaxed.

Another time they did something to my favorite glove. A glove manufacturer had given it to me. Heck, they gave me quite a few, and I'd take them and give them to my boys at home. But I did have a favorite glove.

They called it a "pancake." I'd sit on it in the dugout. I'd sit on it, and when things were going a little bit tough, I would get up and try to relax the club. I'd tell them to get up there and just relax. Then I'd come back to my seat, and I'd notice my glove was missing. I'd start raising heck: "Where's my glove? Somebody's got my glove." Nobody would say a word. Finally I made everybody stand up, and one of the ballplayers would be sitting on my glove. I'd say, "I'm going to sit on your glove!" They'd all start laughing. It was a relaxing type of thing. I had it when I was coaching for Billy at Oakland. I was sitting there, and all of a sudden I looked out in front and there was a pile of dirt in front of the dugout on the step. They'd taken a couple of Popsicle sticks and built a cross. I was sitting and looking at that. Nobody was saying a word. Finally my curiosity got the best of me. I went over and pulled the dirt apart. They had buried my glove, my "pancake." The next time I lost track of my glove, I went into the restroom that we had alongside the dugout, and I saw they were trying to drown it! In the commode! They were trying to drown my glove. Then, when the season was about over, and we were in Kansas City, they tried to burn it. I looked down inside the dugout, and there was a glove on fire. They'd put rosin on my glove, and they were burning it. I had to put that one out. It ruined my glove. Then Billy told me to take the lineup up to the plate, because I had managed at Kansas City. I took the lineup up to the plate and came back and sat down. There was my glove in shreds! They had cut it up. I still have it, but they sure mutilated the thing. I threatened the guys' lives if I ever found out, and I said that I was going to tear their gloves up. Everybody was straight-faced. Nobody would tell who did it. I never found out. I kind of had an inkling who it was, but I'm still not sure.

One time we were having a beer at the bar in Toronto, and Billy got me good. I was sitting on the edge of one of those movable barstools. He walked over there and gave the barstool I was sitting on a kick, and I slid off of it. He went and got the security guard. I was sitting there, right flat on the floor where I had fallen off. Billy brought the security guy over and said, "This guy's drunk. Get him out of here." They were going to escort me out. I had to talk my way out of that.

I was probably the only guy who could ever call him "Coach." He hated to be called "Coach." He was "Number 1." He was the manager. I'd say, "Where you going, Coach? Can I go with you? Come on." "No," he'd say, "You can't go." I'd say, "Well, give me the money then. You're going to spend fifty dollars." He'd laugh like heck. But I could get to him with that "Coach" stuff. He'd say stop calling him "Coach." Nobody else would dare call him that. He wouldn't take that from anybody else. But because I knew

Billy Martin longer than anybody playing baseball, I could get away with it. During spring training the year I was coaching for Oakland, Billy had a trailer out in left field, where he'd hold press conferences and meetings with the coaches and everything. He also have a beer or drink after the workout. Frank Ciensczyk, the clubhouse guy, called out to me on the field one day. He said, "Hey, Charlie, here. Take care of these keys, and when Billy is ready, you go down there and you give him the keys." I said, "Come on. I don't want to take them." He said, "Go on. Take them." So I said, "OK," and put them in my back pocket. When the workout was over and Billy was doing something, I went into the clubhouse, took off my clothes, and showered. Ciensczyk came running in, shouting "Where's the keys?" I said, "Oh, my gosh, they're in my pocket, in my back pocket." I went and got the keys. He said, "Billy's out there fuming. He's mad." I said, "Did you tell him I did it?" Frank said, "Yeah, you were supposed to take care of them." So now I had to go down and face Billy. They were waiting for me. Billy was sitting back of his desk and having a drink of vodka. He was a vodka drinker. I looked at him and, boy, his face was dark and black. Frank came in. I said, "There's only one way. I'm going to tell the truth. Frank, you gave me a job to do and I fouled it up. You gave me a simple little job to do like this, taking care of these keys, and I couldn't do it. You can't depend on me, Frank. From now on, don't give me the keys. You can't depend on me." I looked over at Billy, and he was starting to laugh. I said, "Frank, no matter what, please don't ask me to keep the keys." I turned around to Billy and said, "Hey, Coach, can I have a drink?" He said, "You bet. Yes, you can." That relieved the tension. Afterward Clete Boyer said, "Metro, you get out of everything no matter what it is." Billy told that story on me many times to kid me.

Billy Martin should be in the Hall of Fame. Of course, he won't get to enjoy it, but I think wherever he is, he'll know, and I'll enjoy it with him. What's holding him back, I believe, is that he was very outspoken, very aggressive. Sometimes he'd give the sportswriters a good going-over. Billy wasn't very well-liked because he was so outspoken. You couldn't tell him anything; you couldn't criticize him. I heard sports page editors and sportswriters try to criticize him, and he just point-blank, with no diplomacy about him, told them, "You write your stories; I'll do the managing. You don't like it, you write your stories the way you want." But for a manager who won everywhere, there's no question in my mind that he should be in the Hall of Fame. When Billy went out there and kicked dirt on an umpire or really gave one heck, he always felt he was right about the call. He went to the full limit, he didn't slow down, and he didn't pull any punches. When I was down in the lower minors, working my way up in all the classifications, I would say to the umpires, "My players hustle. If they loaf, I get on them. So if you loaf, if you don't do your best for me, don't worry, I'll be out here." Billy was the same way. I heard him arguing one time with an umpire, and he said, "My players are hustling, and you're going to hustle." Boy, he lit into them. After a while, he'd question their ancestry, and they'd toss him from the game.

Billy was often in trouble, but many times it wasn't of his own making. Somebody would come up to him and say, "You're Billy the Kid" and start getting on him. He resented that. He didn't like that. I never heard him say a bad word to a fan, except when a fan got personal with him. One day in Oakland, some fan in the box seats right on the line started giving Billy heck. Billy was standing down at the end of the dugout, and the guy kept calling him all kinds of names. Boy, that triggered it. Billy went down and challenged him. The guy happened to be a deputy sheriff of one of the nearby counties. Billy just challenged him right there. Billy got in his share of scrapes, but there were times when he took the blame for somebody else. It hurt Billy too, because he wasn't the guy who started it. If the rumors are right, in one famous fight, Hank Bauer was the guy who belted the other guy, and Billy got blamed for it. Mickey Mantle and Whitey Ford were there at the club, along with Bauer and Billy. That fight put Billy in bad with George Weiss, the Yankees general manager. It broke Billy's heart to be sent away from the Yankees like that. Take also, for example, the famous fight Billy had with Jim Brewer. Cal McLish hit Brewer when he broke in on Billy over by first base. Cal told me so. But Billy took the blame for that. He covered up for Cal, who was his friend.

Billy was managing Texas the night in Cleveland in 1974 when they were selling beer for a nickel and a riot broke out. He had to pull his team off the field for their safety. He spoke of it just very briefly. He said, "Charlie, that's the closest I've ever been to riot that would turn into a massacre." That's all he'd say. I read about it, but I never did see it. I would have pulled my players off the field too. Luckily I never had to. I wouldn't let it get that far. But sometimes you couldn't help it. I've had teams that went out there, and everybody was swinging, two young ball clubs swinging at each other, and finally they got tired and quit. But there was never a situation when I felt that my players were in danger.

Billy took losses hard, especially when we had a lead. I saw him break up a clubhouse. Yeah, I saw him do everything to that place. We had a 5-run lead one game, which we blew. He didn't say anything, because he was furious at that time. The next night, we had a 6-run lead, and we blew that one. Oh, gosh, Billy just demolished the clubhouse. The shower doors and television set came down, and the phone came off the wire. Geez, he broke a lot of things up. By the next day Frank Ciensczyk, the clubhouse and equipment guy, had put the place back together. You'd have never known it had been completely demolished. Billy was just furious about the fact that he'd lost. The players didn't lose; he lost. He was the manager of the team, and he always felt responsible for a loss. Sure, the players didn't hit the ball or didn't make a good play or made the wrong pitch or something, but he lost. That's the way he took it.

Billy was a great host. In Baltimore he loved those soft-shell crabs. He'd get a couple of bushels on our breakaway day, and he'd always say, "If we win, we'll have crab." Well, we lost a game there, and Matt Keough, who had a pretty good sense of humor himself, came over to Billy after we'd blown the game and said, "I suppose we're not going to have any of your crab." Billy said, "No, you're not." But when we got off the plane, every guy would cadge a couple of crabs from him. He'd always give in. Billy was also a great chef. At spring training in Scottsdale at the team motel, he prepared a feast probably every doggone night. He cooked in a huge outdoor barbecue thing, two barrels long. He'd cook everything. They'd fly things in from all over the country, salmon, quail from Virginia, seafood and crab, and pheasant from Kansas. And he did the cooking. He was great with spaghetti and meatballs. He had that meatball pot cooking for what seemed like days. He was great at that, and he was a great host.

Billy was a great guy for entertaining. You didn't spend any meal money. Meals were always somewhere free. So one day in spring training in Arizona, I was bragging about the roll of money that I'd saved up, and Billy said, "Geez, Charlie, another week and you'll have more money than you got paid at Bisbee managing and playing." Then Billy said that we were going to this seafood place in Scottsdale, that he'd reserved it for us. We went there and, boy, what a feast! We had crab legs and shrimp, and we had this and we had that. There were about eight or nine of us, some minor league managers and scouts, maybe more than that. I was having a good time, boy, having a beer or two and everything. All of a sudden, about an hour later, I turned around and looked, and they were all gone, and I was sitting there by myself. A young kid brought over the bill to me. He said, "Here." I said, "What's this?" He said, "Billy said you're going to pay for it." It was about $180 or $200. The kid also said they had told him I was the best tipper on the club. I left him a $100 tip. I said, "When the guy asks you, and they're laughing about it, and they come back up here, you tell them about the tip I left and say, 'This is the standard.'" The next day Billy said, "How'd you like that place? " I said, "Great." I thought I would try to get back at him because they were all laughing at me. Art Fowler, Jackie Moore, George Mitterwald, and Clete Boyer were all snickering. I said, "You know something, nobody paid the tab. I didn't pay the tab. Nobody paid the tab." I said, "Thanks" and walked out of there. You could have heard a pin drop. I think somebody went by the restaurant and checked, so the joke was on them. But Billy laughed at that. Later Art Fowler said, "Thanks, big spender."

In 1968, Jim Burris, the general manager at Denver, called me and asked if I was interested in managing again, and I said I couldn't because I was committed to the Royals. He asked me who I would recommend. Without another word, I said, "Billy Martin. Get Billy. He will turn your club around." Jim said, "Do you really think so?" Jim became a Billy Martin booster. Billy came into Denver and turned that darn club around. They went from way down to way up, played way above .500. He had a way of doing that. I tried to get him the managerial job at Kansas City in 1970. I recommended we get him, that he would be perfect for the club. He was my first choice. I had seen him managing at Denver. But the Royals didn't want him for some reason they wouldn't say. They gave me the job instead. I had to explain the decision to Billy. I didn't tell him they didn't want him, that some of the bleeding hearts in the front office couldn't handle him and had decided against him. He was his own man.

Billy loved the West. He came out to the National Western Stock Show in Denver, and I sat with him a couple of times there. As part of his signing with Oakland, he had a home in the Black Hawk area of California, kind of up in the mountains a little bit. The club gave it to him, and they were going to pay for it for ten years or something of that nature, and at the end of the time, he could sell it. It was a magnificent home, swimming pool and all and acreage. After he was fired, I understand that he kept it for a while and then sold it, and they allowed him to keep the difference. I think he was living in Texas too. He loved Texas. He loved the West. He always wanted to own a ranch. I guess he did quite a bit of hunting too. He wanted to own a ranch in either Colorado or Wyoming. I told him about my sister in Montana, and he said Montana was great too.

I don't know if this is an old story or not. One time Billy Martin was hunting with Mickey Mantle in Texas. Mickey went up to the ranch owner to get permission, and the man told Mickey, "Do me a favor. I got an old horse that's ailing. I'd like to put him down, but I can't bring myself to do it. If you'll do it for me, you boys can hunt on my spread." Mickey agreed but didn't tell Billy. Mickey came around the barn, where Billy was standing, and said, "Son of a bitch won't let us hunt here." Then he picked up his gun and shot the horse. Billy took this as a cue and shot one of the rancher's cows. "Well, I shot one of his damn cows for that too," he said. Mantle was dumbfounded. "Billy, you just cost me the price of a cow."

When I called him just before the accident that took his life in 1989, his wife at that time, Jill, answered the phone. I said, "Jill?" She said, "Yes?" I said, "Can I speak with the coach?" She said, "The coach?" I said, "Yes. Turn around and tell him a man wants to speak with the coach." I could hear him in the background: "Who the hell is that?" She said, "Well, he wants to speak with the coach." He got on the phone, and I said, "Coach, how are you?" There was silence. He said, "Charlie, if you were here, I'd belt you one." I said, "That's why I said it, because I'm not there, Billy. I just want to wish you a happy holiday season. I've been thinking about you." He said, "How's Helen?" I said, "Fine." I said, "How are you liking your farm, your ranch there?" He said, "Oh, great, great." He really loved that. His death was just premature, too soon. But I know he's up there looking down and laughing at everything.

I never questioned him about his drinking. That was no business of mine. He'd never let anybody drive when he had a car in Oakland. He always drove. I don't know how to say this any other way, but Billy thought he was going to go quickly. He felt that he was going to die quickly. He told me that Mickey Mantle had had that same feeling, because his father and uncles had died early. I don't know what you call it, but Billy thought he was on something like a suicide mission in life. He was a fatalist. Every once in a while I'd be in my room scouting, and he'd give me a call and he'd say, "Hey, come on, meet me down here." I'd go over and we'd sit and talk. I think he had a bad ulcer or something. I don't think he had a bad heart. He was thin, and I didn't see him eat very much. We'd go out and order dinner, but he'd just kind of pick on his food. He must have had something that was holding him back. It's a tough grind being a big league ballplayer or a good big league manager. The demands on you are so great that so often you don't have time for yourself.

We had some fine coaches at Oakland in 1982. Billy had a good pitching coach in Art Fowler. They called him "The Old Hummer." He was a tremendous pitching coach. Just overlook Art Fowler's condition. He was big and heavy. But he was a master of pitching. When he was pitching for Billy in Denver, and even before that, he was always telling me that he wanted to go up with me when I became a big league manager. I said, "OK." But Billy beat me to it. When Art would be pitching in a ball game against my club, I'd keep talking to him, and he'd talk back to me while he was winding up. I'd say, "You get that little, that little jump, that little dab that you got, get it over the plate, and we'll show you." He'd say, "Yeah, well, let's see this guy hit this little dab." He'd have one wet. He'd have one loaded. Art will deny it, of course, but he was a master. He taught it well. You couldn't detect it. You couldn't find out how it was done. He was very loyal to Billy and did a great job for him. He let somebody else condition the pitchers, but he taught them how to pitch. He could bring a pitcher around. He wasn't given much credit for that pitching staff out there at Oakland when all those young guys came along and did such a great job.

Clete Boyer was the finest third base coach I'd seen in an awful long time. I guess you'd have to compare him with Frankie Crosetti, who was probably the greatest third base coach of all. Clete was superb. All the years that I saw him coaching while I was scouting and sitting on that bench with Oakland, I never saw him make a poor judgment call on base runners. He was absolutely the finest I'd ever seen in my time. I'd seen Crosetti some, but not as much as I saw Clete. I told him that once, but I think he thought I was joking with him. I recommended Clete as one of my choices to become the Oakland manager after Billy left, but they went with Steve Boros. Clete and I argued quite a bit about who was the best third baseman ever. I always told Clete he was right up there with Brooks, but I didn't tell Clete he was second. Recently Clete called me a big bullthrower, I think, because when they had big giveaways out at Oakland, I'd take all the girls out for lunch, and they'd give me any freebie stuff I wanted. One of the women, Pamela Pitts, has risen high in the A's organization. They'd give me the caps, the winter caps called toques, little duffel bags, buttons, and everything else. Clete and the other coaches couldn't get the stuff. I'd come back with a stack of things, and they'd wonder how I did it. Another time I bought a whole bunch of A's jackets and caps and sweatshirts, at cost, because I was an employee. I came back in the clubhouse, and Jackie Moore, who had a couple of kids, asked me for a couple of caps. I said, "Here, take three. I didn't pay for them." I even gave one to George Mitterwald, the bullpen coach, who used to needle me quite a bit. But I walked right by Clete and Art Fowler. I made them beg me for a hat or a jacket. I kept letting on that I got them for free.

Clete taught me how to save a little meal money while we were on the road. He was a late sleeper. He'd sleep in until about 11:30 on the day of a game. I didn't like to have a big meal right before a game, and neither did Clete. He talked me into meeting him for breakfast when he got up. We'd go have breakfast, a big one, that in New York would cost twenty or twenty-five dollars. But then after the game, we would just eat from the spread on the clubhouse table. I would tip the clubhouse guy twenty-five dollars for the whole series we were there, whether that was two, three, or four games. I didn't eat that much anyway. But we saved up some of our meal money that way. We spent it on other things, like going to a nightclub or taking in a late show. Jackie Moore became a very fine coach for Oakland and then later managed the club. I recommended him as a manager when I was coaching at Oakland, when they put Steve Boros in the job. They had some fine candidates for that position. I said, "There's the guy, make him your manager." Jackie had caught for me in the minor leagues. I thought he'd be a good change of pace from Billy. He was a good baseball guy. I also recommended Billy Williams, whom I had managed with the Cubs in 1962. We were in his corner when he was seeking a job as a hitting coach with Oakland. I highly recommended him, and he got the job. And I was instrumental in getting Eddie Mathews as a scout for the Oakland club when I was there. I gave him a very good recommendation. Billy Martin was crazy about Willy Horton. Billy had him working for the Oakland A's, when he managed out there. I thought Willy was a heck of a good ballplayer. He was a minor league hitting instructor out there. When Billy liked a guy, he'd always try to find a job for him. He did an awful lot of things like that that people don't know about.

We had some excellent players at Oakland in 1982, especially the pitchers. Some people claim that Billy took that great pitching staff that he had at Oakland in 1981 and wore out their arms by pitching them too much. I disagree with that totally. Those guys were geared to pitch every fourth or fifth day. Billy loved to keep his starters starting in rotation to get a good rotation. Nowadays, heck, a guy goes three innings and he's out of there, and they tell him he did a good job. The starting pitcher goes five innings, and they want to give him a Congressional Medal of Honor. Billy made all of those young pitchers wealthy men. He didn't overwork them. They pitched in rotation. Look at the record Al Lopez had with those pitchers in Cleveland when they won 111 games in 1954. Look at how many innings they pitched. Are we going to say that the pitchers today are softer than those Indians pitchers? Or that they were better then, or bigger, stronger men? The only difference I see is that the Cleveland pitchers were conditioned better then. In the early 1980s, Billy conditioned his ballplayers real well. They were ready to play. He pitched them in turn, and a lot of them didn't have those strong arms. But he made every one of those guys wealthy.

Matt Keough was one of those pitchers with the Oakland club. I knew his father, Marty. Matt had a pretty good year one year. In fact, I think he had two pretty good years back-to-back. Billy liked him. Matt was a good, young guy, but he had a terrible accident. A foul ball hit him in the head down in spring training down in Arizona. That just about ended his life, not only his career. He's scouting for somebody now, and he's a good one. Rick Langford was another one of those pitchers with Oakland who was a little short on stuff but great on moxie. He knew how to pitch to get the most out of his skills. Boy, he had a lot of determination. He was a likable guy. He'd give you a good effort every time he was out on the mound. Billy loved him. Steve McCatty did a good job for Billy. He was a good, tough competitor. He gave us what we called "a good day's work" on the mound. Tommy Underwood was a pretty good left-handed pitcher for us at Oakland. He went 10-6 that year. But Brian Kingman was a mystery to us at Oakland. He had good stuff but just couldn't win with it. He couldn't put it together. I think he had had some decent years somewhere along the line, but he just couldn't put it all together at Oakland. Billy told me once that Brian was the only ballplayer that he was frustrated with and couldn't help.

And then there was Mike Norris. Mike destroyed a very fine pitching career through his drug use. It was very sad. He was very talented. What a tremendous athlete he was. He had a good arm and everything going for him. It was one of the real tragedies of baseball for a guy like him to fall to the wayside. He was sort of a clown on the club. I did a little bit of everything that year for Oakland. I loved to hit to the outfielders, and they loved for me to hit to them. I'd work the pitchers for Art, and they loved that. I would work out hitting fungoes to the outfielders and pitchers. I'd keep the pitchers running back and forth. Some players like to clown around during batting and fielding practice, especially pitchers working out in the outfield. It is their way of relaxing. Norris would do that to me at Oakland. Mike would make the doggonedest plays out there. He'd run in on a fly ball and deliberately catch the ball just six inches above the ground. He'd do it on purpose. Then he'd catch one behind his back or spin around and catch a ball over his shoulder. Mike would catch the ball between his legs, behind his back, up over his ear, everywhere. It was funny, very humorous and relaxing. He was a quite the competitor. He never dropped the ball. That was the way he showed you his competitiveness.

I thought Oakland had one of the finest outfields in baseball at that time, with Rickey Henderson in left, Dwayne Murphy in center, and Tony Armas in right. Tony Armas was a fine ballplayer. He had a good arm, a real fine arm. He wasn't as fast as the other two, but he was a good, steady ballplayer. He went to Boston later on and eventually to the Angels. He had good power, and he could hit. He could do a little bit of everything, and he could do it pretty good, except he wasn't a very good runner. I think his son is now a pitcher in the big leagues.

Dwayne Murphy was a tremendous center fielder. In fact, if the ball was in the ballpark, he could catch it. If it was in the air, he wouldn't let it hit the ground. He could run like heck. He had some power, but he didn't quite make good contact. Dwayne struck out considerably more than he should have. But he was a great asset. I was the outfield coach, if you want to call it that, for Oakland. When Armas was in right field, Murphy was in center, and Henderson was in left, that was the easiest job I ever had. You never had to criticize them. They knew how to play. They all could throw well, they all could run, they all could field, and they all had power. If you had to rate those three guys overall, they'd be right up there with any combination of the major league outfielders. They never let a ball drop out there.

I was Rickey Henderson's outfield coach. But he didn't need much coaching. He was a good outfielder. I sat with a couple of scouts when he was with the A's organization in the minor leagues. He played for Ogden, I think, in the Pacific Coast League at the time. I was sitting there with this scout, who said, "Oh, he can't play. He's a left-handed thrower and a right-handed hitter. Those guys can't play." But all Rickey did was play like heck, a certainty for the Hall of Fame. He could field, run, throw. He had power. And he sure could steal bases. Somebody else who was scouting Rickey in the minors said, "Oh, he can't steal first base." I can't recall who that scout was, because if I did, I would really give him a good needling.

Rickey Henderson had very powerful legs. His legs took a pounding. That's why he didn't want to slide on his legs and would slide headfirst instead. He was always pulling his leg muscles. He was having a hard time. He was on the trainer's table all time. I'd say, "What in the heck are you doing on the table?" He'd say, "Charlie, I hurt." I'd say, "Did you pull them?" And he'd say, "No." He was just getting them rubbed up. One day he was on the rubbing table, and somebody asked, "How come he can run as fast as he can?" I said that he was built like a quarter horse, he's got real strong gaskins. In quarter horse talk, a colt or filly that had big, strong hind legs had gaskin muscles on the inside and big muscles on the outside. That's the way Rickey's legs are built. He has the big muscles on the outside of his legs, and on the inside he has the gaskin. Rickey asked me what I was talking about, what was a gaskin, so I showed him where it was. I got kidded about that the whole rest of the summer, even though half of the guys didn't know what a gaskin was.

Rickey Henderson had a contract with one of the shoe companies. I asked him, "Hey, Rick, what kind of money you getting from that shoe company?" He told me something like five or ten thousand dollars. I said, "Why don't you ask them for a million dollars?" I can't verify it, but I understand that he got a long-term contract for a million dollars. And then one day I asked him, "You like your mother?" He said, "Oh, yes." A lot of black ballplayers were raised by their mothers, not their fathers. I said, "Why don't you buy your mother a fur coat, a mink coat. Didn't she ever want a mink coat?" He said, "Oh, yeah." "Why don't you buy it for her? When you sign this contract for a million dollars or two or something like that, why don't you buy her a mink coat?" Next time I came in there as scout, I was up in the stands, and the game hadn't started yet, and I looked down below and there was a lady in a mink coat. Rickey saw me, and he brought his mother over. He said, "Mama, this is Charlie Metro." I said, "Well, it's about time you bought your mom a mink coat." He told her I was the one who had told him to. I told him to buy her a house and a car too. I'm sure he did, because he was crazy about his mom.

The year I was with Oakland, Rickey Henderson was breaking Lou Brock's season record for stolen bases. I used to joke that I taught him how to steal, but that would have been like a chicken teaching an eagle how to fly. He set the record finally and stole a few more for good measure. During the last series of the season, at Kansas City, I asked to be designated as the guy to pick up the stolen base as a souvenir for Rickey, because I had managed at Kansas City. Billy said, "You get the bag, because this is something." So Rickey stole one base and set the record again. I went out there and got the bag and brought it in. The last day, I think he stole two or three bases. Every time he stole a base I'd run out there, get the bag, and bring it in, but the groundskeeper would come around and get the base. So finally, the last one he stole, I kept for Rickey. I wouldn't give it to the groundskeeper. I gave it to Rickey. He gave me the bag, but I gave it to him. I said, "No, Rickey, you want to keep this." So he autographed it and put the date down and everything. Given the prices for memorabilia these days, I kind of wished I had kept it myself! I don't know whether he sold it or not. Recently I saw somewhere where the lineup card for the game in which he broke the record went for $4,800 or something like that.

Most of the other Oakland players were journeymen, but a few stand out in my memory. Mitchell Page was a delight. He and I would warm up. That was my claim to fame regarding Mitch. He was a part-time ballplayer. He could hit a home run every once in a while. He loved to play. Mitch had a career that started out really well, but then every year he declined from that. He had great ability. Some ballplayers reach their peak their first one or two years of their careers, and then from there it's all down. Some guys start out way up high, and then they sink. Not only do they not improve; they go the other way. They hang on for three or four years with the hopes of always retaining, or recovering, or regrouping what they had done at the first part of their career. Mitch was like that. Mitch should have been a fine, longtime ballplayer. I believe he got back in the game as either a coach for a major league club or as an instructor in the minor leagues.

Tony Phillips was a ballplayer at Oakland who was very much under-rated. He turned out to be a real good ballplayer. He did a lot of everything on the ball field and could play a lot of different positions. I think he had a little personal problem at one time, but he got straightened out. He became a very versatile ballplayer. Mike Heath was not much more than an ordinary catcher. He was what we call a complete red-ass ballplayer. Nothing ever satisfied him. No matter what he did at the plate, he was always mad at everything. But he could catch. He had a good arm. He could throw, and Billy liked him at Oakland. He wouldn't get a base hit, and he'd pout, and oh, gosh, he'd tear things up and everything. But he was a very good competitor.

I handled a couple of special duties for the A's those years. They were searching for someone to be their representative, a scout, a good man in the Dominican Republic. I suggested Juan Marichal, the longtime Giants pitcher. I was assigned to go down and talk to him. In the Dominican Republic, his reputation is tremendous. He's a national hero. I was having dinner with him one evening, and we were sitting with him and his wife in this very nice restaurant in Santo Domingo, and in walked the president of the Dominican Republic. If he wasn't the president, he was the highest official there. He came over, and Juan didn't stand up. The president recognized him and said, "No, you be seated." So we hired Juan, and he's done a fine job for them. I helped get him a higher salary. He named a low figure in the negotiations, but I urged him to go for a higher one. He helped Oakland start up a baseball school like the one the Dodgers had. I think he's still connected with the A's and has done some Spanish-language broadcasting for them.

Charlie Finley was one sharp guy. He was no longer the owner of the A's by the time I got there in 1982. He had gone through some major divorce problems and had sold the club to the Levi Strauss heirs in 1980. But when I was scouting in the 1970s, I had some dealings with him. If a scout was in town in Chicago, Charlie would find out. Somehow he'd find out where you were staying, and he'd have his secretary call you. Sure enough, they called me up one day when I was in Chicago, and I went over to his office.

He almost had me talked into working for him that day. I thought, holy smokes. What he would do is pick your brain. If you were not careful, you found yourself giving him a complete scouting report on every ballplayer in the country before you knew it. I caught myself in time, and I said, "Uh-oh." So finally I said, "Charlie, if you want me to give you a scouting report, hire me." We laughed about that. He was a good baseball man. Boy, he built those championship Athletics clubs about out of nothing.

But I have to set the record straight about one of Charlie's proposed innovations, the yellow baseball to improve visibility. Everybody thought that his idea of the yellow baseball was new. But I had seen it in the Middle Atlantic League in Johnstown, Pennsylvania. They played with a yellow baseball. And it met an untimely death at that time. The same thing happened to Charlie Finley and his yellow baseball. Apparently, it was too radical an idea. I also witnessed his experiment with starting each batter with a two-strike, three-ball count. I was watching in the stands. All you saw then was base on balls, base on balls, base on balls. It seemed like they were just loading the bases, forcing in runs. That was a short-lived idea too.

The first time I witnessed "the Wave" was in the Oakland-Alameda Coliseum. There was a guy there named Crazy Harry or something like that. He stripped to the waist and jumped up on the dugout and started "The Wave." He was chanting, "Bring them on." He got it started. Man, when you get forty-five or fifty thousand people pretty well packed into the stadium, that's one heck of a good show. I like that. In fact, I've done "the Wave" myself sitting in the stands. I love to participate. I see nothing wrong with it. But then it kind of dies down when the home team is not doing too well. So it takes care of itself.

And wouldn't you know that I got thrown out of a game as a coach in 1982? Richie Garcia was a good umpire, but that season I had a run-in with him that I didn't deserve. We were in Boston for a series, and I was sitting on the third step of the dugout. The sun was beating down real good, and I was sitting there with my arms up on the railing. I took my cap off, and I set it on the step. Well, all heck broke loose. Richie came running over and told me to put that cap back on. I didn't know what the heck he was talking about. I was scratching my head. He came over and made a big issue over the darn cap. I thought here I am, just a coach for Billy Martin, and I didn't want to be thrown out of the ball game. Heck, I was just a bench coach. This dispute went on, and Garcia threw me out. These days I suspect that Billy put him up to it because I wasn't fully dressed. I made some terrible remarks about him, because I did not have it coming. He was not one of my favorite guys, but he turned out to be a good umpire.

I was on the interviewing committee at Oakland when we interviewed candidates for the managerial position after Billy got fired. Hal Lanier was one. I told Hal that he would become a big league manager. He was well-prepared and became a pretty fair manager for the Astros later in the 1980s. But he had some health problem, which I can't recall, that limited him. I don't remember if it was asthma or something of that nature. I knew his father, Max, well. His father worked for me a little bit at Kansas City as a scout. Jim Leyland was another candidate who interviewed for the Oakland job when Steve Boros got it. I thought Jim presented himself very well. He was a good manager. He came up in the Detroit organization. But they didn't give him a chance. Detroit would bypass guys that they would nurse along in their farm system. I went through that with them. They were doing the same thing to Jim. Heck, he should have been the manager there before they got Sparky Anderson. Jim Leyland went on to prove he was a good manager with the Pirates, and he managed the Florida Marlins to a World Series championship. Then he put in a tough year with the Colorado Rockies. He was great with his ballplayers. He handled his players as well as anybody.

Jimy Williams was another candidate for the Oakland job. He was a pretty sharp young guy. He was not a bad manager, but he wasn't very well prepared when he had his interview, which is only natural. During an interview I had once, I wasn't very well prepared for the questions they asked me. He wasn't either, and I told him, "Be prepared the next time." He did, and he got the job. He went on to be a fine manager at Toronto and Boston. Guys like Dave Bristol and Jimy Williams weren't great ballplayers, but they became pretty good managers. I worked with Bill Rigney when he was an assistant to Roy Eisenhardt at the Oakland A's. He probably doesn't know this, but behind the scenes, I thought he should have been the manager after Billy Martin. I didn't openly push it. I wish I had said so in the meetings when we were talking about potential managers. I thought he should have been the guy. Where Billy was outgoing and feisty, Bill Rigney was kind of laid-back. He was not a bad manager, and he wasn't too bad a ballplayer either. He was a leader type of infielder, a captain of the infield, a take-charge sort of guy. I wish I'd pushed his candidacy further. Jim Fregosi was another possibility for the Oakland manager after Billy. Jim would've been a good one.

At the end of the 1982 season, Roy Eisenhardt asked me if I wanted a front-office job. I went to the 1982 World Series in St. Louis and Milwaukee as an Oakland A's representative. I told Roy, "I will call you every day at 10:00 A.M., unless I'm on an airplane at that time. I will not make any deals, but I will listen for any deals that could help the club." That's what I did. Every morning at 10:00, I'd call and have them put me through to Roy. Sandy Alderson, who was also in the A's front office, came to Milwaukee for a game, and we sat together. He was very much impressed with my efforts, how early I would get down to the field, talking to the managers and everybody else. Roy made me a jack-of-all-trades of sorts with the scouting department the next season.

So I went down to spring training in Phoenix as a scout. Steve Boros was the manager at that time, and Jackie Moore was still on the club. I'm a player counter. When I was scouting, I was a player counter. I'd count the players, and I'd look at them. The first time I'd see them, I'd say, "There's number eighteen. He's so-and-so." I'd look to see their physical qualities. So I counted all those players that day on the A's. I knew that there were about forty ballplayers who were invited that spring. There were four coaches and a manager, and then they had quite a few of the organization managers there. I counted them, but I couldn't account for all the players. I was twelve players short. I saw the coaches and the other personnel, but they were twelve players short. So I walked up on the field, and I said, "Hey, Jackie, where the heck are these players? You're supposed to have forty?" He made a motion with his thumb. I said, "Where?" He said, "There. Go in the visitors' clubhouse." So I went over to the visitors' clubhouse, and there they were. This was the second day of spring training. The sun was out, seventy-five or eighty degrees, down in Phoenix. It wasn't one of those eastern or northern cold countries where it would be snowing and still blizzarding. They were down there where the sun was shining at spring training, and they were all in the clubhouse. Ten of them were in there just pushing up weights and on those pulleys and everything else, riding on the bicycles and running on the treadmills. The one that got me was the bicycle. I never could understand where you used a bicycle on a play in baseball. Do you go around second base on a bicycle?

In 1983 I became a "Baseball Great." On August 12, the people in Vancouver invited me to the opening of British Columbia Place Stadium. Molson Breweries was sponsoring this event. They brought in a bunch of "Baseball Greats": Hank Aaron, Bob Feller, Monte Irvin, Lefty Gomez, Bob Lemon, Enos Slaughter, Luke Appling, Juan Marichal, Whitey Ford, Roger Maris, Bobby Thomson, Moose Skowron, Bill Mazeroski, Tony Oliva, Don Larsen, Charlie Silvera, George Bamberger, Rene Lachemann, Eli Grba, Ted

Bowsfield, Tony Muser, and me, Charlie Metro! This was an exhibition game, three innings or so, just enough to go around. Slaughter played as if it were his last game. I coached third and got a big round of applause.

As a scout for the A's, I got to see some good, upcoming talents, especially José Canseco. I saw him in Bend, Oregon, when I went up there to scout. This was in a rookie league. Canseco put on one of the dogdarnedest hitting exhibitions in batting practice I had ever seen. He *hit* those balls. He got up there and put a charge into the baseball. He hit a ball through the infield, a line drive right to the edge of the infield grass, and it took off, looking like it would skip halfway across the outfield. Gosh, he was powerful! He was just a tall gangly, skinny kid, real crude and green and rough, kind of like a diamond in the rough. You could see that he was going to be tremendous.

Roy Eisenhardt traded me back to the Dodgers as a scout for the 1984 season. I'm not quite sure why that happened or even how it happened. I heard about it from a scout before I got the official news from the front office. The Dodgers got mad at me when I left them in 1982, because I had worked for them for seven years, and I had been a solid worker in my field. In fact, I did pretty darn good working for them, but they got angry with me because I had to think of myself and my later years. During spring training in 1984, Al Campanis was very cool to me down at Dodgertown. So was Tommy Lasorda. Sometime before a game in Oakland in 1982 or 1983, I had been talking with the other coaches about our working conditions, which were pretty good because of Billy. I told them I hadn't been treated this well with the Dodgers. I told them I had been promised a coaching job, but they, particularly Tommy, had not offered me one. I didn't tell the press, but somehow it got in the papers. Tommy confronted me, but I told him it wasn't I who had leaked the information to the newspaper. By then it was pretty common knowledge anyway. I went ahead and did my job as an advance scout and spy in the sky. After the 1984 season, I read in the paper that all the Dodger scouts had been rehired, but it wasn't clear about me. I asked Al, "Am I coming back?" He was silent. I told him, "Tell me now, so if I'm not coming back here, I can go to the winter meetings and get hired with somebody else." But they didn't tell me until the winter meetings in Houston were nearly over. That forced me into retirement, because I couldn't locate a job that late. I guess the Dodgers took some revenge for my leaving them in 1982.

In 1985 I almost ended up with the Yankees again, the organization I'd broken in with as a playing manager in 1947. I had some contact with Woody Woodward, the Yankees general manager. Somebody with the Yanks was pretty impressed with my advance scouting abilities. Somehow the conversation got around to whether I would be available for the pennant stretch drive. The Yankees were still in the race at that point. I called up and offered my services as an advance scout against my old team the Dodgers. I said I'd do it for thirty-five thousand dollars. Woody said, "Thirty thousand." I said, "OK." I don't know if this got back to George Steinbrenner or he was behind the whole idea, but the Yankees faded and so did the offer. They faded badly just as I was going to come for the last month or five weeks of the season. But I would have enjoyed working with Steinbrenner. I didn't know it for sure, but retirement was on my doorstep, after forty-eight seasons in a baseball uniform or in the front office for one club or another.

THIRTEEN

Retirement? What Retirement?

Even though I retired in 1985, I've kept quite busy with a bunch of baseball-related projects and by following the Colorado Rockies since 1992. Retirement has also given me more time to enjoy my family. Two summers ago, we had a big family reunion in Red Lodge, Montana. Ninety relatives attended. It was an absolutely wonderful time. I passed out Sacajawea gold dollars to everybody as a remembrance, as well as wooden miniature bats with my 1939 autograph burned in and a "Metro Reunion Montana 2000" stamp on it. Our kids are doing quite well. Elena is the director of the Colorado Pork Council, and she was the only female on the Colorado Baseball Commission, which got the Rockies and Coors Field for Colorado. Bud (Charles Jr.) and Steve have a construction company back in Virginia, near Charlottesville. Geoff is a slot manager at a gambling casino in Black Hawk, Colorado. We have ten grandchildren and thirteen great-grandchildren. One of my granddaughters, Lakshmi Bertram, has published a book on waterbirthing, delivering babies underwater.

My wife, Helen, is a great baseball fan and a pretty good critic. But then every once in a while during my career, she'd dig me a little bit too much and I'd say, "Now, wait a while. Do I tell you how to cook?" She'd say, "You sure do." So I kept quiet. She didn't miss very many ball games. In fact, she'll tell you that during my managerial career in the minor leagues and everywhere, she saw more ball games than I did, because I was ejected out of so many. We celebrated on our sixtieth wedding anniversary in 2001. Many a baseball marriage lasts long and holds steady. You go through so many things together. Maybe in the absence, the heart grows fonder for somebody at home.

Some years ago, we visited Texarkana again. We took our daughter with us, showed her where we were married, where the boardinghouse had been but was no longer there, where the diner where we would eat was. By then it was a barbecue place, and we had barbecue, some of the greatest we've ever had. A black man was running it, and I told him about playing and living there in 1941, and he said, "You're going to have to have this on me." That was really nice. At Texarkana, we stayed overnight at the Holiday Inn. When I checked in, Helen and my daughter were outside in the car. The lady at the counter asked, "How many?" I said, "My wife and I and our baby girl." So she gave me the form to sign, and she took one look at me and asked, "How old is your baby girl?" I said, "Forty." She said, "Well, you got me there, but there'll be no charge. I've never had that pulled on me before." I said, "I didn't pull it on you, ma'am." She said, "Yes, you did." We got along great. She sent a basket of fruit to our room.

Out here in Colorado, I had visions of becoming a cattle baron. I should have known better, but baseball players and managers fancy themselves a whole lot of other things that they had best stay away from. When I was managing Denver in the early 1960s, we bought a home here, but we didn't like it. It was by the country club, but I wasn't much of a "country club" sort of guy. We bought a little fifteen-acre place instead, out of town on the edge of Arvada. We called it the "Grand Bar CM," and the kids loved that. I was going to become a cattle baron. Denver was a big hub for the western cattle industry and had a big livestock auction, where people bought and sold cattle. Having worked one winter with a couple of friends learning the cattle business, I decided that I was going to buy a couple of head, cows that were pregnant and going to have calves, and just learn that way. After studying and watching everybody working around those places, where they pen the cattle ready to go in the sale ring, I thought I was ready. A friend of mine told me, "Charlie, you're ready to buy a couple of head of cattle." I said, "OK." They give you a big whip, and you go in the pen and cut the cattle out. I walked into this pen and cut two head of cattle out and ran them down what they call the alley to the scales. Once those cattle are on the scale and weighed, they're yours. That's the procedure. I cut out two great big cows that looked like they were pregnant. They certainly looked that way.

At the scales, the weighmaster asked me my name. I said, "Metro, two cows!" They priced them at $145 apiece, 14.9 cents a pound or something like that. The weighmaster yelled out that information. The gate went up on the other side, and I looked in there. The two cows were weaving on their hooves. All of sudden, bang, down they go. Both those cows died right there of heart attacks. I had to pay $145 each for them. They were mine. Then I had to pay $10 apiece to have them taken to the slaughterhouse. The guy laughed at me and said, "Who'd you buy these from?" I told him, and he said, "That's the biggest thief in the stockyards." What the guy had done was give them a little hay sprinkled with salt. Then early in the morning, before anybody came out to the yard, he turned the water on and the cattle drank a lot, got bloated, and died. They had heart attacks, but they were a little old too. I kept that quiet for quite a while, but then the word got around. I took an unmerciful beating on that. I should have listened to my friend Eddie Newman when he told me, "Never invest in anything that'll spoil, rot, die, or need repair." I said, "Well, there's not much to that." Then he said, "And don't invest in the stock market." I said, "Well, what do you invest in?" He said, "Land." He owned twenty, thirty, or forty acres right in front of the gate of a big airbase that they used to fly planes to Alaska during the war. He was right. He turned that into an awful lot of money. That was the end of my cattle baron days.

Well, not exactly the end of them. I was scheduled to go down to spring training in Florida. Of course, my wife couldn't go down there. The kids were in school in Lakewood and Arvada. This was along about 1963 or 1964. I bought a load of cattle, twenty head, very nice Black Angus cattle. They were supposed to be with calves, but they weren't. I had bought a Black Angus bull for Christmas and given it to my wife, but I didn't tell her about the twenty head on order. I was doing a little scouting at that time. I left for spring training that February in a blinding snowstorm out of Denver. The next day, when I was in Florida, I got a call from Helen. She said, "What about these cattle?" I said, "What about them?" She said, "The man pulled up and said, 'Where do I put these cattle?' You bought these?" I said, "Yes." She said, "Well, what do I do with them?" I said, "Well, feed them," and I hung up. So she did. We came out of that one pretty well. We didn't make any money, but we came out of that with a pretty good experience. Except I got the silent treatment till I got back to Colorado.

The next summer, I decided we would breed the cows with the Black Angus bull. They were called "empty"—they weren't with calves. I told my son Steve to take some cattle chalk, a waxy kind of chalk for marking cattle, and mark the cows anytime he saw them breed. I said, "Now, anytime you see Methuselah, our bull, service one of these cows, you put an "X" on that cow." He said, "OK, Dad, OK." Then I was gone a couple of weeks on the road. When I came back and asked Steve how he did, he said, "Oh, fine, Dad." I said, "Well, let's go take a look." I went out and saw that there were chalk X's all over the place—on one cow. Methuselah had done a pretty good job, because the cows all became pregnant and had calves. But Steve had just put the marks on one cow!

Later we proceeded to nursing orphan calves. I bought about ten nurse cows to raise orphan calves. My wife loved to work with the animals. She would give the different shots that you have to give the baby calves. She called the cattle by name and everything. She would go up to the barn sales and auction houses and buy two-day-old calves, give them a shot, and put them in the back of an old car that I had. She would take the back seat out of the car, load the calves, and bring them to our ranch, then put three or four of them on one cow and raise them that way until they were big enough. Then she would package them all the same size, whether they were little bull calves or heifers, and sell them. She would get out there and bicker with the buyers. One particular guy, a doctor, wanted to buy some cattle, and she was asking ninety-five dollars a head at that time. They were about three months old. There were about six of them. Helen and the doctor were sitting on the corral fence, just bickering back and forth. Finally I came out and just kind of stood around being a spectator. The doctor said very strongly, "Well, I can buy all I want for sixty dollars a head, but you're asking ninety-five." Helen said, "Well, buy them all. You buy them." But he bought our cattle. It helped us through a tough period. I was scouting, gone all the time. Helen had a touch for this. She never knew anything about it before we started.

Then, from there, we went on to horses. In the off-seasons, we started raising racing quarter horses. Bish and Lucille Jenkins out at Idaho Falls had gotten us interested way back in 1956. I've always been very thankful because it gave my wife and me something to do in the off-seasons. My wife loved it. We bred the mares, and she loved to foal them out. She became doggone good at it. I would tell people that she would go out in the foaling barn about February 15, and I wouldn't see her until the grass came up. One time one of my scouting friends, Ellis Clary, came through Denver and called up to the house, which he did quite often to say hello. This particular time he called up, my wife and I were down at the corral or in the barn tending to the horses. My son Geoff answered the phone. Ellis asked him, "Is your dad there?" Geoff said, "Yeah." "Is your mom there?" He said, "Yeah." Ellis said, "Where's your dad?" Geoff said, "Oh, they're out in the corral breeding." We were breeding one of our mares with our stallion. I didn't heard the end of that from Ellis for twenty or more years!

I decided I would go into running quarter horses. We bought a couple of quarter horse mares, and then I wanted stallions. I found out about a stallion in California that belonged to Cecelia DeMille Harper, the film director Cecil B. DeMille's daughter, who was a tremendous horsewoman. She raised thoroughbred horses. She had a stallion named Dance Lesson, which I had found out was the fastest six-furlong horse in the history of racing. He held the world record for a six-furlong race at one minute, seven and two-fifths seconds. He was the fastest living three-furlong horse at thirty-two and a fifth seconds, a record he held for a while. Finally, after long negotiations, I bought him from her. She was a baseball fan. I was working for the Dodgers at the time. I'd go down and sit with her. It took me about a year and half to conclude the deal. One day I pestered her about buying the horse, and she said, "No." I told her, "Cecilia, this horse will never go hungry. He'll never be mistreated. And he will stay that way as long as I have him . . . till he dies." Apparently that impressed her. I met her in San Francisco for breakfast at 5:00 in the morning, and we finalized the deal. I paid on time and didn't pay an awful lot. She turned down a fabulous amount of money for him. Another time, I was in San Diego, and we had a day off. I went to the horse races in Del Mar. Bill Shoemaker was riding there. I sent in my Dodgers card and said, "I own 'Dance Lesson.'" Bill came out and sat with me for half an hour. He was riding later in the day. He sat there and told me about the horse. He said, "Charlie, he's the fastest horse I've ever ridden. If I had known, I would have broken every record there was for speed." I bought Dance Lesson, and he turned our lives around, just as Cecelia said he would. My only regret was that I didn't let her keep one dollar beyond the purchase price as good luck. I was quite superstitious. When the final payment came, I paid it, and the horse passed away. He gave us a bright outlook for many years, and we kept two daughters of his, twenty-some years each. One, Jetzsa Dance, we still have. A year or so ago, she foaled a filly, but the other daughter died. Even so, raising horses has been a great joy.

We had a lot of fun, both I and my family, with our horses, especially quarter horses. We met some wonderful people in the horse business. They were just as great in the quarter horse and the thoroughbred business as are the Hall of Famers in baseball. Bob Moore, of Oklahoma City, was a tremendous breeder. Walter Merrick, who was the dean of all quarter horse breeders, was what I would call the Babe Ruth of the quarter horse industry. He had some great champions. I had the pleasure of meeting two of the finest trainers in the industry, Blaine Schvaneveldt, who is still training quarter horses, and D. Wayne Lukas. He's one of the top trainers of all time now. He has been leading in earnings every year. Horses he has trained have won five Triple Crown races. Lukas would get San Francisco Bay mud and pack his racehorses' hooves every night before putting them to bed. He did that to make the hooves softer and also so that they wouldn't pick up pebbles or a tack or a nail or anything that could get lodged in their hooves. He'd pack them with that mud. Lukas would send the workers out to get the mud. Some of the Pacific Coast League umpires used that mud to rub the baseballs.

Of course, I can't overlook Brereton Jones, the former governor of Kentucky and owner of the Airdrie Stud Farm in Midway, Kentucky. I crossed some of my quarter horse mares with his thoroughbred stallions. I knew I would get along with him when I found out that he had been a shortstop in college. We talked about baseball. I also met Johnny Jones, who had a fine battery of stallions at a farm in Kentucky, and Allaire Dupont, who had shares in Northern Dancer. Louis Wolfson was a big man in the thoroughbred business. I got acquainted with him later on, when I got into the horse business. His brother Sam had owned the Jacksonville franchise in the Sally League. Sam was a wonderful person, just a typical fan. Another was Jerry Hoffberger, who owned the Baltimore Orioles. I bought a share in one of his stallions, the son of Northern Dancer's North Pole.

I was on the plane once coming from the East to Denver, coming home from one of my scouting trips. I was sitting up front in the first-class section, and this lady sat down next to me. She had the aisle seat, and I had the window seat. I was reading *The Sporting News*. She was reading the horse racing newspaper, the *Daily Racing Form*. I caught her looking over and reading my paper. She said, "By the way, sir, can I trade you for a minute?" I said, "Sure." So she gave me the horse racing form, and I gave her the baseball paper. She turned out to be Penny Tweedy, who owned Riva Ridge at that time. Riva Ridge was an outstanding racehorse. She told me, "Now we have a horse that you're going to be hearing a lot about. He's a two-year-old, and he's not quite ready." That was Secretariat. So I talked about the horses, and she talked about baseball. And what she told me was true because Secretariat turned out to be one of the greatest racehorses of all time.

Many years later, when I was really getting into the horse business, I was scouting a high school kid named Duane Henry up around Chesapeake City, Maryland. I'd heard the rumors about him and thought, well, I'll just go up there and look at him. I saw Duane warm up, but the game got rained out. I made a pretty good report on him. We didn't get him. I think Texas did. But while I was there, I heard that Northern Dancer was staying at a stud farm nearby. I wanted to see Northern Dancer, the famous thoroughbred horse, one of the great ones of all times. I decided to go over. I was going to try to talk the guy into breeding one of our quarter horse mares with Northern Dancer. That was unheard of, an insult to the thoroughbred horse people. I went to Winfield Farm, where Northern

Dancer was standing, and walked in the office. I said that I would like to see the top man. I couldn't remember his name, but I knew he was the farm manager. The woman there said, "What is your name?" I said, "Charlie Metro. I'm a baseball guy, but I have quarter horses, and I want to breed one of them with Northern Dancer." In a minute, a man popped his head out of the office and said, "Who?" I said, "Charlie Metro." He said, "Well, come on in here." I went in and sat down. He said, "What can I do for you?" I told him I wanted to breed one of my quarter horse mares with Northern Dancer as a test breed, which I was going to try and get for nothing. We got to talking, and he said, "You're not Charlie Metro." I had a gray mustache, and I was older. I said, "Yes, sir, I am." He said, "Do you remember me?" I said, "No. Where am I supposed to know you from? Give me an idea of where you're from." He said, "I was your batboy in Pocatello, Idaho, when you were manager of the Twin Falls Cowboys. You gave me that brand new baseball out of the bag." Back when I managed Twin Falls, we'd go into another town and they'd supply us with a batboy. They didn't pay them. These batboys just had the honor of being a batboy for the team. At the end of the ball game, you'd take the ball bag and tell them to reach in there and get a ball for themselves. They wouldn't take a good one; they would always take a dirty one. I would say, "No, no, get a good one." Once in a while, they would take one that was still in the box, a brand-new one. I would say, "Sure, you can have it." That was their pay. They loved that. Now here he was, the farm director at Winfield Stud Farm in Maryland. I tried to talk him into my breeding project, but I couldn't get him to budge. He said, "If something were to happen to Northern Dancer, like if your mare kicked him and hurt him, I'd have to shoot you."

At one time, Commissioner Landis would never let a player or manager own a horse. It was taboo to own a racehorse because of the association with gambling. *Betting* was a terrible word. But some of the finest people in baseball were horse owners. Bob Carpenter, the Phillies owner who was in the Dupont family, raised horses. Joan Payson, the owner of the Mets, was a big horse owner. George Steinbrenner owned horses. Of course, I guess the most famous one was John Galbreath of Pittsburgh. He had his farms back in Lexington and in Columbus, and he had some great horses. He had His Majesty and Ribot, the Ty Cobb of thoroughbreds, sire of Graustak. Ribot was a mean horse, but he was a winner, a great stallion. Bob Prince, the Pirates announcer, told Galbreath one time in the press room that I was a horseman. Galbreath said, "Well, come on over and join me." So we talked horses. He was married to a lady from the Firestone family, and she would talk about baseball all the time with me, when I talked about horses with

Mr. Galbreath, and then we'd get back to baseball. She was knowledgeable about horses and about baseball. Young Dan, his son, was a fine horseman too.

I visited their farms, both in Kentucky and up in Ohio. I had an experience at one of the farms that I love to tell about. I went down to one of the paddocks where there was a mare with a chestnut colt at her side. I was kind of new at this horse business. I looked at this mare, and she was a great big, gray, heavy-footed mare, like a work mare, like one of those Percheron draft horses. I thought, "What in the heck is that mare doing with a colt like that? Is this where the horse business is?" The black caretaker who was there saw the puzzled look on my face, and he said, "What's the matter?" I told him I was a baseball guy, and he was a baseball fan. He explained to me that the mare was a nurse mare. They had this thoroughbred colt nursing. The caretaker said, "You want to remember this little boy now." I said, "What's his name?" He said, "His Majesty." Well, His Majesty turned out to be a winner and a great sire. But I couldn't understand how this big, draggy mare had this fine, sleek colt.

I was lucky enough to get to the Kentucky Derby one year. It's always the first week in May, which was a problem for baseball guys because the season was in progress. The director of the Kentucky Derby was Lynn Stone, of Churchill Downs. He had played third base for me a little bit at Bisbee. He arranged for tickets for me. When I went there, I saw ten or so people from baseball, including Gabe Paul, Warren Giles, and the president of the National League, the man who owned the Cincinnati Reds, and the editor of the *Los Angeles Times*. There were quite a few of them there, and they all wanted to know what I was doing there. I told them, "The same as you're doing—you're playing hookey, and so am I." We had a lot fun. Having an outside interest in horses made those long scouting trips seem shorter.

I found that buying a yearling or a mare or breeding to a stallion was somewhat similar to scouting a ballplayer, especially if you're looking at records on the horses. You looked at the horse's confirmation, and you looked at a ballplayer's size. Then you looked at some of the horse's records, how he or she ran a race, and you looked at a ballplayer's running speed. Then you'd try to inquire of a trainer or whoever was around, "How does this horse run? Does he or she quit? Does he or she show a little extra breeding?" That was the same way you'd check out a ballplayer. You'd check his background, find out if he was a good student, find out what sort of family he came from. You'd check the pedigree of the horse, just as you would you check the pedigree of a player, his school, coach, family, and everything. There were some things that didn't compare, such as a ballplayer's hitting or fielding—there was nothing similar for a horse. But you could evaluate how he or she ran toward the end of a race, whether he or she gave up or not. I found it very similar. Guys used to laugh at me when I talked about the similarity between judging a horse and a ballplayer. Occasionally I laughed at them, because I had more fun with a horse sometimes than I did with a ballplayer.

One of the quarter horses that we bred was a stallion out of one of my good mares. I named him Six For Six. He won fifteen thousand dollars for us. I had great hopes for him, but he got hurt. He chipped an ankle, and I couldn't take him to the big All-American Quarter Horse Race in Ruidoso, New Mexico. The winner gets a million dollars. The tenth-place horse receives sixty thousand dollars, so it's a pretty lucrative race. I named him Six For Six after a hitting streak I had in 1943 when I was with the Detroit Tigers. When I told a friend of mine, Jack Tighe, he said, "Six For Six, Charlie? What do you mean? You never went six for six in your life." I said, "Yes, I did, Jack, in 1943. You were there with the Tigers when I was there. You should remember. One hit a month, for six months!" So, that was *my* six for six! But I also had a horse named Thirty-Six. That was my uniform number. He was a little quarter colt. He must have taken after his owner. I couldn't hit worth a damn, and this horse couldn't run worth a damn. I used to say he was a pretty good horse because it took eight horses to beat him. They'd all finish ahead of him, every time.

Along with owning our horses, one of the great pleasures of the past eight years has been watching the emergence of the Colorado Rockies. The attendance at Rockies games the first five seasons or so was phenomenal. Before the first season, the Rockies management said that they would be satisfied if they got a million and a half fans. I thought they were estimating low even then. When a group of owners, including Bill Giles and National League president Bill White, came out here to explore the possibilities of an expansion franchise, they asked me what I thought, because I had lived here in Denver all these years. I projected that they would draw two and a half million fans in their inaugural season at Mile High Stadium, with its seating capacity of some 79,000 or 80,000. I thought that on weekends they would have maybe 150,000 people. As it turned out, I was about a million and a half low at that. It was delightful to be wrong in that respect.

The Rockies have great fans here in Denver and in the region. I hope the club doesn't abuse them too much with outrageous concessions prices and parking rates. Those may seem like small, trivial things, but the repercussions will finally come. A family of four coming to the ball game can't always afford to spend a hundred dollars or more. The club will have to make some adjustments and give things back to the fans. The more the club does that, the better off they'll be. A good marketing program will certainly help. The Rockies have got a good organization. Chris Rice, who was my secretary when I was with Kansas City, became former general manager Bob Gebhard's secretary with the Rockies. She's retired now. There have been some good baseball people working for the club. I just hope the Rockies don't get fatheaded. There's a tendency to get fatheaded, to get overconfident and bullheaded—to lose a good ballplayer or two because of pride or ego. They don't want to give in or something. But I don't see anything dark in the Rockies' future. The fan base leveled off these past two years, but the Rockies didn't have very good teams either to keep the interest high. With a better team and good marketing, they may average thirty-five or forty thousand people per game, which would be fantastic.

I have high respect for Jerry McMorris, the major owner of the Rockies. Back in 1994, during the strike negotiations between the players' association and the owners, I felt very strongly that Jerry was the one bright light. I thought that maybe the union was getting a little out of hand, and maybe management was getting a little out of hand, and there had to be a happy medium. It's like an argument between husband and wife. If you want to stay together and live together, you'd better give a little here and a little there. Hardheadedness doesn't do you any good. McMorris would make one great commissioner. He has gotten his feet wet in the baseball business, and he shows far more intelligence than a lot of the other longtime baseball people. He also has a background of dealing in huge finances with his own trucking firm. He's very gracious, he's sharp, and he certainly knows what he's talking about. He'd be my ideal guy for the commissioner's job, although *my* endorsement would probably cost him the job. Whether he'd accept it or not, I don't know. He's not the type of guy who would play one side against the other. It would be great for baseball. I certainly hope they don't pick out a politician as commissioner.

The first ownership group of the Rockies got criticized something terrible. But they did some wonderful things. The organization can't help the background of some of the owners. Mickey Monus, unfortunately, just wasn't a good person. John Antonucci, however, did a lot of good things. His choices of purple, silver, and black for the uniform colors were great. The name "Rockies" wasn't greeted warmly, but I just think that it was just the greatest. The Rockies mountain chain encompasses a large part of the western United States from the Canadian border down to the Mexican one and as far west as the eastern side of the Sierras. In spite of what people say, Antonucci had a lot of class about him. He might have been abrupt and to the point at times, from what they say and what you read, but I think the club owes him a debt of gratitude. I don't know that he was in on any of those shady things Monus was involved with, but he set the groundwork for a wonderful organization. My hat's off to the guy.

Coors Field, here in Denver, is a magnificent stadium. It is the Taj Mahal of baseball. It has just about everything that you want in a baseball park. It has the latest in ballpark technology, all the modern things. They've got batting cages under the stands, even for the visiting club. The visitors' clubhouse is massive, big enough for fifty ballplayers. The one for the home club is even more luxurious. In fact, I don't know when the ballplayers are going to go out and play. They've got big television screens and saunas, and big seven- or eight-man whirlpools. They've got eating places, quick food in there and everything. I just don't know when they're going to get out on the ball field. The stadium is nearly perfect. There are only a few small things I can fault. The flagpole should be above the Rockpile in center field. I noticed once that when they played the National Anthem, and the ballplayers and the visitors stood up, they kept looking around for the flagpole and couldn't find it. They put it down somewhere back of the left-field foul line. The flagpole is supposed to be in center field in ballparks, so when you're out there you turn around and see which way the wind is blowing. Besides, it's the proper place for it. Another small fault is the foul poles. I still don't know why they make those foul poles that wide. Just an ordinary flagpole is good enough, and it doesn't obstruct the view for those fans sitting directly back of it. They've managed to remove most of the old poles that would hold up the roof in the old stadiums, but now they still have these foul poles blocking somebody's view. From a player's standpoint, I'd make the warning tracks twenty-four or twenty-five feet instead of what they are now, which doesn't give an outfielder enough time to adjust to the wall. Make it out of crushed rock so the outfielder can also feel it as well as hear it.

Outside the stadium, you see vendors selling peanuts and scorecards. I hope they never eliminate those guys. They shouldn't squash free enterprise like that. There's been a lot of scalping of tickets going on. I think that's another good sideline. A couple of guys got arrested for scalping, but I think that's great, because it's an indication the team is doing well when people want tickets badly enough to pay scalpers. I hope they don't discourage it too much. They've got all those memorabilia places around the stadium, the sporting goods shop, something for everybody. The club had better not antagonize them, because they're part of the culture, part of the scene, along with all those microbreweries and sports shops, dining and eating places, just a great variety. They have everything, as far as I'm concerned, everything but one thing—a World Championship.

You have to make room for parking at a stadium. That is going to become a thorn in the side for the Rockies at Coors Field. They need more parking. Less parking is fine in a place like Cincinnati, because there it's a five-minute walk from the hotel, from downtown. You can also park on the other side of town in Cincinnati. There are a lot of parking places there, and they're not terribly expensive. Parking would not be a problem if you made plans for it. But it can be a headache for a franchise. It was at the start of Busch Stadium in St. Louis, until they built a multitiered parking facility nearby.

Some clubs fly a flag when they win to let the fans outside the ballpark know. I'd like to see the Rockies do that at Coors Field. They could turn on a light, a bright purple light, when they won at home or on the road. That would generate some extra interest for the fans. I don't know if it'd cause any wrecks on I-25. Some people might gawk and look at the light instead of the road, but I think it's another thing that could be added to make it better for fans.

If some guy hits 5 home runs right here in Coors Field, if one of the Colorado Rockies hits 5 home runs here in one game, I'd give him a million dollars. He could have that as an incentive clause in his contract. I think that would add to the mystique of Coors Field. I don't think that you'd have an agreement with the opposing pitcher in that case. It would be legitimate. I think it'd be acceptable. It'd be a great promotion. Or I'd even like to see signs that read "Hit me and get this car" or "Hit me and win this pickup truck." A lot of ballparks have such signs. I think the fans would go crazy.

A couple of years ago at Coors Field, they put in a digital speed marquee sign that told the fans the speed of the previous pitch and what the pitch was. Putting the speed of the pitch up there was maybe encouraging a little bit of hanky-panky. They could say their pitcher was throwing ninety-five miles an hour when he wasn't. That would give the hitters a little advantage; they'd say, "Hey, this guy's only throwing eighty-five. I'll get ready for him." Maybe they could hit that pitcher. I don't see an awful lot of interest in that. Besides, you're getting just the gun. I've been sitting in a group of scouts who had those radar guns out, checking the speed of the pitcher. I'd see a scout turn up the gun, and I know darn well the pitcher wasn't throwing ninety miles an hour. The scout was trying to deceive everybody.

I'd like to talk a little bit about the Rockies organization. I'm pleased to have been here in Denver and watch the Rockies being born. I saw their first steps, and crawling, and walking. Having gone through putting together an expansion franchise with the Kansas City Royals and being more or less directly responsible for a lot of the choices in the setting up of the farm system and the scouting department, I think I'm pretty qualified to assess the Rockies on their success, or whatever you want to call it, in the first eight years. They've done pretty well in some spots. But I think that they lived too long with some players. They were waiting too long for them to arrive. For example, they should have sent out Roberto Mejia sooner than they did. They should have told him to go down to Triple-A and prove that he could play there and that if he developed, he'd be back up with the big league club. With others, the club should have admitted sooner it made a mistake. The pitcher David Nied, who was the first draft choice, milked his injuries for all they were worth. The Rockies leaned too long on guys like that. They're going to have to continue to upgrade the quality of the players. The Rockies are no longer considered an expansion team. They should be a contender each year, at least in their division. They've made some poor judgments on quite a few ballplayers, such as Bruce Hurst, Dale Murphy, Bret Saberhagen, and Billy Swift. They gave up some young ballplayers in that worthless trade with San Diego for Greg W. Harris. I think the Padres general manager got the better of them on that deal. It's common knowledge that there's been an awful lot of money dumped down the drain. It'll come back to haunt them.

The Rockies have had a fine scouting department. They've got a lot of good experienced people, which you need to have a good organization. About the only thing they're going to have to watch is to be a little more careful when they start making trades. They've been stung a time or two. Time will tell, for instance, whether letting Edgar Clemente go was a wise move. Maybe they need a professional scout or two to go out and look at the players more seriously. Some of this responsibility has to rest with the former general manager, who tried to do everything, who wouldn't listen to anybody, and who spent too much time on the field, in the clubhouse, and in the dugout. But the club has a different general manager, Dan O'Dowd, and a different manager, Buddy Bell, so perhaps the franchise has turned the corner. The new emphasis on speed is exciting, but you can't steal first base. You've got to have hitters first, especially in Coors Field.

The Rockies spent a lot of money on Daryl Kile as a free agent, but I think they mishandled him overall. He started off struggling in spring training. Well, that can happen. Some of his pitches weren't effective. His curve ball was probably not breaking as well down there in the desert air. He was probably a little anxious to produce. He should have been a doggone good pitcher, if they handled him correctly. Before the season, I predicted that Kile would rebound in St. Louis. I talked to the Cardinals pitching coach, Dave Duncan, and told him to get Kile to stop nibbling and start working faster, to get him to speed it up. Kile won 20 games in the 2000 season, with a 3.91 ERA, and could have been a candidate for Comeback Player of the Year.

Anytime another sports franchise in a team's city wins a championship, it puts pressure on the teams that haven't won one yet. When the Colorado Avalanche won the Stanley Cup in 1996 and 2001 and the Denver Broncos won the Super Bowl twice in 1998 and 1999, that put the heat on the Rockies. Even though the Rockies went to the playoffs in 1995 as the wild-card team, Bob Gebhard and the Rockies had to come up with a winner. And after Florida won the World Series in 1997, in their fifth year as a franchise, the Rockies could no longer hide behind the claim that they're an expansion team. They've had time, eight years now, to develop players in the farm system. I think the time has come to quit using the expansion thing as an alibi. They're a big league club. It's not going to be good enough to have a pretty good ball club. They've got to win the championship, the World Series, before they can be considered a great ball club.

The Rockies changed directions from their beginnings. They started out with young ballplayers, but then they switched to older ballplayers. A lot of young guys didn't turn out. We did that at Kansas City. The first year, we selected players on the free agency list. With the Royals, we selected ninety-six ballplayers, and out of those ninety-six, we came up with three who made the club. That's what you had to do. I explained this to Ewing Kauffman by saying, "I hope not, but we're liable to draft these ballplayers and not get one, and if we don't get one, you can fire me, because we got to have better talent hunters than that." I wish the Rockies would go back to the young ballplayers and scout them better and train them better at Triple-A.

A lot of people said the Rockies should have gotten rid of Dante Bichette sooner than they did. But I liked him a lot. Dante Bichette is my type of ballplayer. He's got a pixie disposition. He's got a delightful arrogance. He's a hardnosed type of ballplayer. Getting rid of him may turn out to be one of the biggest mistakes they ever make in the history of the franchise. Dante's exactly what you want. He'll play every day and produce. He did some dramatic things with the bat. He's got a good, pleasant personality. He kind of reminds me of Willie Mays, although he can't field like Willie. Dante can catch the ball, he can run, and he's a solid ballplayer. He's what I would call a franchise ballplayer. A few years ago, one of the Denver sportswriters wrote a column saying that Bichette couldn't win the MVP award, because he was only known here at Coors Field. Heck, if that's the case, then what about left field in Fenway Park? They've had some Most Valuable Players. What about right field in Tiger Stadium? A distance of 315 feet to the upper deck, 325 underneath. Al Kaline was an outstanding ballplayer there. There have been a lot of ballplayers who could hit in one park and couldn't hit in another. If you can hit at home, for your home fans, wonderful! I wouldn't care what he did, except as a manager, you'd like to have him produce some good numbers on the road too. I wouldn't criticize a guy because he's great at home. What if at one time you were classified as a center fielder, so you played center field? You weren't a general outfielder; you played a particular field. To ask Dante to go from right field after playing there years to a foreign field, over in left field, was tough on him. There are entirely different angles, differences in the way the ball comes off the batter's bat. Plus the stands might be a little bit different on that side of the park. He had to adjust while he was playing. And he had it rough at times. But, heck, having been a baseball scout, I was out there watching him. I took a look at Dante and compared him to the other thirteen left fielders in the National League, and he was right up in the top three. Not only that, but he had production that counted. He hit game-winning home runs, knocked in a bunch of runs, and hit for a good average. So he was doing all the offensive things to be a Most Valuable Player. Every guy will misplay a ball once in a while. Even Joe DiMaggio forgot how many were out one time and let a run score. I thought it was a terrible mistake, on management's part, to let Dante get away.

The Rockies should have played those two young guys, Todd Helton and Neifi Perez, every day in their rookie year. They're the future of the ball club. Heck, they've got all winter to rest. How was Helton going to learn to hit left-handed pitching if he didn't play? He was liable to be Rookie of the Year that season. Perez had a chance too. Why not play them every day? Throw them out there to the wolves. Let them experience tough pitchers. Let them know they're not going to get pansies out there, cream puffs every day. I've taken a hard approach to this, and it's worked! When I ran my pitchers the last day of the season, one of the hardest days that they worked all year, they were griping. I said, "You got all winter to rest up." I would have kept Andres Galarraga and Walt Weiss to bring along the young guys, although it's awful tough to argue against what Helton and Perez have done. Weiss was an excellent hitter in the eighth spot in the lineup. He got walks and gave the pitcher some needed rest. Helton is a very fine fielder, reminding me of Ferris Fain. My biggest gripe with Neifi is that he squats between pitches. It makes it look like he's worn-out or unfocused. I want to shoot him in the rump with a slingshot when he does that. They should also sharpen up Ben Petrick's catching skills. Put him in the batting cage every day for twenty or thirty minutes with all the gear on and have the pitching machine fire shots at his feet, to the left, to the right, until he gets better at blocking pitches. He also needs to work on his throws. He loops his arm instead of snapping it through. I wrote him a letter about this last year. I did similar routines with Gus Triandos way back at Twin Falls and made him into a catcher. Petrick can hit, and he has some power. The Rockies can't afford to waste his talents if they want him to be their catcher of the future.

I've been following the Rockies' minor league clubs a lot. It remains to be seen how well they're going to produce. But if I were on the parent club and I wasn't doing too well, I'd start worrying, because there's going to be a lot of guys who are going to be replaced, especially on the pitching staff. I don't think they're going to wait too long for some guys to come around. They gave up on Jamey Wright and unloaded him to the Brewers. Good organizations improve without spending an awful lot of money. It's going to take a lot of hard work to keep where they are. The Rockies have gained a lot of prestige, a good reputation, but they're going to have to hold it. I'd bring up all those good prospects to their Triple-A club and get rid of all the hangers-on. I'd put a pitching coach down there and a conditioning coach and a catching coach and an infield coach and an outfield coach. I'd put five or six coaches down there to stay with them a month. Give them a month of intensive game instruction, and when they're playing, keep a chart on them. Tell the young players, "This is what you didn't do right. This is where you've got to improve. This is what you've got to work on." What I'd also like to see is somebody from the Denver area or the suburbs, one of the schools—Arvada West, Thomas Jefferson, Cherry Creek, wherever—come out of there and be a homegrown player for the Rockies. John Burke was the closest, but they waited on him too long. Boy, I wish I were a boy again, so I could give it a shot!

There have been some pleasant surprises for the Rockies. Vinny Castilla was one that they didn't expect would do as well as he did. He was a diamond in the rough. They got rid of a very productive third baseman, Charlie Hayes. Whatever reason they had, the average fan doesn't know what entered into that. The Rockies got rid of a pretty good ballplayer. Hayes played like heck. They were fortunate to have another good replacement. They also had a nice surprise with Jason Bates, who was a valuable utility guy during the first few years. He fought his way up there. Eric Young was a good team player, a bumblebee, exciting and always hustling. Rockies fans will always remember his home run in the first game at Mile High Stadium in 1993 as a "glass of fine wine." Among the pitchers, Pedro Astacio could pitch on any starting rotation in the big leagues. The players hustled and played like heck those first few years. If they'd have kept that up, they'd never have had a bad year here. They just couldn't wait to get out there to play. You could see it and feel it in the air, and the players really liked it. They liked to play here.

It was fun watching the Blake Street Bombers belt out those home runs in 1995, when Larry Walker, Andres Galarraga, Vinny Castilla, and Dante Bichette each hit 30 or more, and then with Ellis Burks they did it again the next two seasons. I was with the Dodgers in 1977 when Ron Cey, Dusty Baker, Steve Garvey, and Reggie Smith became the first group of four to hit at least 30. It means that you've got four guys hitting pretty well. They build right off one another, try to not fade, not fall too far back. How many would they have hit in 1995, when they lost 18 games at the start of the season due to the carryover of the 1994 strike? Would they have all hit 40 home runs, which has never been done in major league history? Or would they have all hit 45? These guys are bigger and stronger. They swing a lighter bat, and they're pumping weights. They can hit them.

One time when Galarraga was still with the Rockies, I had the urge to call him. He was having a real rough time at the plate. I could see definitely that he was turning his hand loose before impact of the bat on the ball. I picked up the phone and called him in St. Louis and said, "Andres, you're turning your hand loose. You're missing the ball out there. Hold onto the bat until you make contact. And after you make contact, go ahead and do whatever you want. Turn it loose and head for first, or whatever. But you're turning it loose and the ball is outside and you're pulling away by four inches and you're missing the outside pitch." So what did he do? The first time he came up, he hit a double. He hit one up the alley, which was beautiful, and then he hit a shot through third base. Then he struck out one time at bat. He had two good swings, and then he went right back to turning that bat loose. On television you can watch it pretty well. The ball was outside. He missed the ball by four inches. It's very obvious. Why they haven't caught it, I don't know. This is an assessment, an observation that I've had over my lifetime of teaching hitters. I've taught some pretty good hitters. I didn't mess with them too much. I just took their swing and polished it up, like you'd do a diamond.

The turnover of coaches during the first three years of the Rockies bothered me a bit. Jerry Royster, Dwight Evans, and Amos Otis were there only a season or so. Ron Hassey was a pretty good third base coach. You should keep your coaching staff stable. I especially hated to see Don Zimmer go. He was as solid as a rock, and I'm sure he was a great help to Don Baylor, the manager. I hated to see him go. But it was his decision, and he did it with real class. As a player, he got the utmost out of his playing ability. He was a good manager. He got the most out of his ball club. When he had a club, you could say his club was going to be a contender up there in the first division. I saw many a game that he managed, but I don't think I ever saw one for which I could criticize him. I don't know why the press was after him a couple of times. He was a sound manager. He showed class when he walked off from the Rockies in midseason. I wish I could have talked to him. When he was quitting, I tried to get in touch with him but couldn't. Don Zimmer was one of my favorite people. He was a lover of horses. One year he was managing the Red Sox, and he was having a rough time with the ball club. I came into Boston, and I said, "Zim, forget everything. I'm your lucky charm." I told him I'd started raising quarter horses. I was there five days, and he won all five ball games. Zimmer wouldn't let me leave. He said, "You stay here." I said, "I have to go."

All I hear is alibis about the altitude here and the ball flying out of the ballpark in Denver. Yet the Rockies have scored more runs than just about anybody. I think that the altitude here is to their advantage. The pitchers should *love* to come in here and work with 5, 6, or 10 runs a game! Heck, who cares about earned run average. What counts is the big "W." Winning! Sure, it's great if they can win and have that great ERA too. If they would go nine innings, they would get some of those big wins, but they're not. The handling of the pitchers is pretty tough. I don't know why there have been so many moves. A pitcher gets a guy out and then the manager brings another guy in, even though the game situation doesn't require it.

Don Baylor wasn't very sharp as a manager at the start, but he was learning, through on-the-job training. I didn't see very much of Don when he was a player, but one thing was clear: he wasn't a very good fielder. I don't know whether he'd admit it or not, but he wasn't. Man, could he hit, though! He hit 338 home runs, and although he wasn't a great runner, he stole 285 bases. He wasn't what you'd consider a speed demon, but he had a great knack for stealing bases. When he managed, I thought he fooled around too much with his catchers. Joe Girardi was the best they had, but the Rockies lost him to the Yankees. Then came some journeymen and rookie catchers. Baylor should have taken his best catcher and let him catch. Let the other guys sit back. He jumbled his catchers, catching this guy one game, catching that guy the next game. I've seen it done, but with two experienced guys. At Detroit in the 1940s, Paul Richards caught Hal Newhouser and made him a great pitcher. Bob Swift caught Dizzy Trout and made him a great pitcher. They won almost sixty games between them one year. Richards was great with young pitchers. The Rockies have had a young pitching staff here. They need the best catchers they can get.

When Baylor was managing the Rockies, one spring training he had all the players run a seven-minute mile. I didn't quite agree with that. There's no play in baseball where you run a mile. Baseball is all sprints. I think the longest run for a regular ballplayer, a defensive ballplayer, is when a center fielder goes back or comes way in on a ball, or a left fielder or right fielder goes to the line. Those are the longest stretches. Now, if guy hits a triple, or even rarer, an inside-the-park home run, he's got to be able to run. But there's no play in baseball where you need to run a mile in seven minutes or whatever. I thought it was a publicity stunt, a show thing for spring training to let everybody look like they were working real hard.

This brings me to one of my biggest gripes about baseball today. I'm going to harp on this until the day I go to that natural grass diamond in the sky. I hate to be an old fuddy-duddy or an old-timer who's living in the past, but the conditioning programs are far inferior now. The players are not conditioned right. I'm absolutely appalled at the condition of the ballplayers today. They get out of the lineup at the least little thing—a rash, a small injury—as if they're going to be career-ending injuries. The disabled list grows every day. It's alarming. Heck, you want your best ballplayers, your gate attractions, to play every day. Why do you have some of your finest attractions on the ball club sitting out game after game? Look at Teddy Higuera, the former star pitcher for Milwaukee. He was out three years on the disabled list. It doesn't make sense. It's frightening. It's a tremendous financial drain to have a hundred or more ballplayers on a disabled list every day. Especially after the first month or two, at an average of a million or more dollars, you've got a hundred million or more dollars of salaries for ballplayers you're getting no production from. I think the disabled list is just a management excuse to keep control of the ballplayers. The general managers put the rule in there because it's an easy way of adjusting the roster and having more ballplayers available. If a guy has a little bit of a hangnail, he's on the disabled list, and they bring in a fresh guy. I don't know if that's a good idea or not.

Yet the clubs have the finest sports medicine facilities in the world today. Their clubhouses have saunas and whirlpools, and they even feed them right on the diet food. Some clubs in the 1980s and 1990s had stretch coaches and even ballerinas teaching certain movements to the players. Some of that is pretty good at times, but I think most of it is a showboat thing. I attribute a lot of the injuries today to the weight room. Many of these players look like they're in tremendous physical shape, but they're ripe for an injury. I'd like some trainer to tell me how all this modern training is conducive to keeping ballplayers in the lineup and playing. If somebody can give me a reason why all this current weightlifting and method of conditioning is so great, why do they have a hundred or more ballplayers on the disabled list each day throughout much of the season? Why all these sore hamstrings, charley horses, pulled muscles, and other injuries? And look at all the reconstructive operations! Isn't there anything in the way of preventive medicine in the training? Preventive training would prevent a lot of these injuries, and you'd see the top ballplayers, and even the other guys, playing more often. When I start seeing that there are only twenty or so guys, one from each club, on the disabled list, then I'll say that the current conditioning programs are good. Until then, I'm going to remain a doubter.

I was never a weights guy. If you do anything, you should run. There are some things a player can do to make himself stronger. Ted Williams had a gadget for strengthening his wrists and arms. He'd put two bricks on the end of a rope and tie the other end to a broom handle, and he'd roll that thing up one way and roll it down, then roll it up the other way. Red Schoendienst told me he did that too. I did that way back when I was a boy, even out of high school. I tried to strengthen up my wrists and my hands. I don't think a pitcher should lift weights, because his muscles should be fluid. A lot of the conditioning is not conducive to producing good baseball players. A hitter can pump iron and be strong in the shoulders and in the back. They do like weights and those strength things for their arms and their shoulders and their legs, which makes them stronger. But I can't see weights for pitchers. On and off, I've had some musclebound ballplayers who were lifting weights. Chris Sidaris, a second baseman for me at Montgomery, could hit a ton, but he couldn't throw the ball accurately to first base because he was musclebound.

From my observations over the years, every good pitcher I've ever seen had round, fat arms. They didn't have that muscular weightlifter's arms. Bobo Newsom, Virgil Trucks, Dizzy Trout, "Fat" Freddie Fitzsimmons, they all had those round, fat arms.

George Susce was the best conditioning coach I've ever seen. He was all over the ballpark, and he was dedicated to his job. He did everything that you would want on a baseball club. He was a good guy, just aggressive as heck, and positive. If I were to pattern myself after a coach who worked then, he'd be the one. He was a hard worker, strong as a bull. I don't know much about his playing career, but he was a wonderful guy to have on the ball club. He had the nickname "Good Kid." Everybody was "Good Kid" to him. He'd say, "Hi, Good Kid! How's it going, Good Kid?" I guess he didn't know your name.

Somebody, somewhere has sold a bill of goods to the baseball clubs. You've got to protect these players, they say. You don't have to do that at all. All you have to do is get them in good condition. If you get them in too fine a condition, which I've never heard of, give them a rest then. Put in the extra guys. There are some managers who know how to put their extra men in there, keeping them sharp as well as giving the regulars a rest. These days I see, at the start of the year, managers giving a guy a rest four days into the season. I can't imagine that happening when I played and managed. If you tried to take a ballplayer out four days into the season, he'd fight you. Temperatures are still cool then. Now, maybe they have so many outside activities that they don't have time to rest. But I can't imagine giving a guy a rest a week after the season starts and saving him for August or September. If a guy's a steady, regular player, you'd play him every day. He'd just go out of the lineup just once in a while. One guy once told me, "Play me every day." He wasn't in shape, wasn't ready, but he said, "Play me every day for three weeks, and I'll do a heck of a job for you." I told him, "If I play you every day, I may not be here three weeks." And that's exactly what happened. I got fired, partly because he wasn't doing the job. But still, I can't believe that they want to get a rest. A manager will take a guy out after catching four games. I can recall Harry Chiti joining my ball club in Denver. I had him catch 30 games in a row. He went from 210 pounds to about 185 in a hurry. You didn't want to get out of the lineup, and the manager didn't want to take you out. He'd force you to play. I had an occasion in Vancouver where Ron Hansen, the shortstop, was having a rough time batting, but he was playing every day. His batting average wasn't very good, but it didn't affect his fielding. So I said, "Ron, you've got two choices. You're going to make this decision. Do you want to play your way out of this slump, or do you want to rest?" He said, "I want to play my way out of this." That's the difference between then and now. Now they want out of the lineup.

There's something drastically wrong, and maybe someday the clubs will wake up to that and not be losing their fine ballplayers. There are some players who have played twenty years and for the most part avoided long injuries. Cal Ripken Jr., of course, comes to mind, as do Carlton Fisk and Robin Yount and George Brett. Were they blessed with anything special, or did they just condition themselves better to stay in shape? But they're the exceptions, not the rule. A ballplayer who's getting toward the twilight of his career has to work extra hard. It's just natural. You don't want to push yourself, but you have to train twice as hard, when you reach down toward the end. If he wants to play some more, he's got to work, instead of lazying around and maybe putting on a little extra weight.

Personally, as a player or playing manager, I had very few injuries. The only injuries we'd ever have on my teams would be when a guy got hit with a ground ball in the face, or got hit on the elbow or in the ribs with a pitch, or got a real bad bruise on the hand, or maybe twisted an ankle or broke a leg. Those were some things you couldn't keep from happening. But all these pulled hamstrings and all these operations on forearms I find inexcusable. Some guys say all these rotator cuff injuries occur because of the slider and the split-finger fastball. But they threw the slider many years ago and didn't have these injuries. I don't recall any rash of injuries when I was a player. When you had an injured player, he would stay right with the club. If you had a sprained ankle, they wrapped it and you played. There was a lot of competition then. With the Yankees, for example, manager Joe McCarthy would give you one mistake and then the next day you were gone, because they had a top minor league club in Newark that could have finished second in the American League. I can't remember whether there was a disabled list at that time or not, or whether you were just out of luck and had to carry a guy who was hurt. I don't remember seeing anybody sent out like that. He recovered right there on the club.

The whirlpools we used to have had just one big tub, maybe just big enough to sit in. They had a seat where you could sit and turn on the Jacuzzi-type thing. Two guys, if they had pulled leg muscles, could stand, one guy on one side and one on the other. You could only keep one or two guys in the tub. A pitcher could put his arm and shoulder all the way down. But now, good gosh, I understand you can walk in these hot tubs and whirlpools. Some of the clubs have got ones so large five players can walk into them. Back in my day, they wouldn't let a guy go into one of these hot baths or whirlpools before the game, because it would sap his strength. The heat would sap his energy. That's the first thing the trainer told me. He said, "Now, don't you get in that whirlpool before the game. You want to get in the whirlpool after the game. Because it will sap your strength."

Pitchers didn't ice up their arms as much back then. That came into vogue maybe ten or fifteen years ago. I've seen a pitcher take two towels and put them over his arm and let hot water beat on it. Then somewhere along the line, they said that cold water is better. These days, when you see an interview after the game, the pitcher usually has the ice bag on his elbow or shoulder. I don't know what that does. Nobody's ever explained that to me. One of these days, I'll ask somebody what that's supposed to do. I do know that if you get hit on the shins or on the foot or something and it starts swelling, you put the ice on it, and it'll take the swelling down. But I can't understand what that has to do with the arm. Pitchers would take cortisone shots and have to be careful, because the cortisone shot would dull the arm. If you had a torn muscle, you didn't know it and you just kept tearing it more. Shin splints were terrible, but you played anyway. You taped up, and you played. Players nowadays have those high-top baseball shoes, which can prevent you from turning your ankles. Turning an ankle was one of the major injuries in my day. Sometimes you could really bruise it, and it would swell up. But you played. You'd tape it up, and you'd play. They'd put some hot stuff on there. The trainer would have a bottle of alcohol, and he'd put wintergreen in it and mix them together to make some liniment, some fiery hot stuff. If you had a pulled muscle, he'd start putting it on and give you five minutes of rubbing and pat you, and that was it. That stuff would about burn through you. It would cure you in a hurry. Now you look at a trainer's room, and it looks like a medical clinic.

The trainers would keep a guy ready. Trainers would prevent those injuries. If they saw a guy who was a little lax in his training or his conditioning or not changing his sweatshirt when it was cold and he had sweated, they'd give him holy heck. They kept you playing. Lately it seems as if all the trainers want to get their names in the paper, telling them what's wrong with their pitching staff. A good trainer should have nothing to do, because his players are all in good condition. My trainer would come up to me and say, "Gee, Skip, I don't have anything to do." I would say, "Keep it that way! You're keeping those guys in the rotation. Keeping them healthy. I don't want you having to correct sore arms."

For the pitchers, the problem is the conditioning. If you take a look, 65 percent of the guys on the disabled list are pitchers. They've got everything wrong with their shoulders or their arms. I never heard of so many different types of injuries. It's simply because they're not conditioned for pitching. When you take a pitcher and put him in there in the summer heat, and he's going to throw 120, 130, 140 pitches or whatever, he is exerting all the strength he has for that many times. He's got to be in excellent, superb physical condition. His legs have got to carry that body and that arm. When the legs tire, then the strain is on the arm and the back and elsewhere. So they have to be superb physical specimens. It's not the fact that you've got to take ten pounds off a guy. If you run him enough, you get his legs in shape to carry whatever weight he is. You want his legs to carry that weight and carry it for 120 pitches or so. The point isn't about taking twenty pounds off a guy.

I asked Olympic runners, "How far do you run?" They said, "Fifty miles a day." I don't think ballplayers have to run fifty miles a day, but they do have to run. If they can't run on the field during a rainstorm, they certainly can run on a treadmill. Running is a lost art now in conditioning programs. They're just not doing it. I'm very critical about this lack of running, and I'll take on all comers in that argument. I was pretty demanding in my day. We all talk and laugh about it now, as we're older. When I see my former pitchers, they tell me how I used to run them and get them into condition. One of my pitchers accused me of running them until they were sterile, but I think he had seven or eight kids. So there's no truth to that rumor. But my pitchers at Vancouver pitched 12 straight complete ball games, and they won 11 out of 12. Everybody pitched nine innings. Some critics might say, "Ah, you old-timers are all alike." But the evidence is there.

The clubs also rush too many of the injured players through rehab assignments. Sometimes they give a pitcher only two or three games, maybe only seventy pitches. That's not enough. A pitcher should throw at least three or four games if he's on the rehab program. Three weeks is too rushed. All the evidence is there of rushing guys where they then fall back and lose a year. All you have to do is just use a little common sense and give them enough rehab starts, especially if they're young. An older guy maybe knows how to take care of himself a little bit better, and he can come around faster. But if you reinjure a young guy, you could ruin his career or even lose him for a year or two.

Another problem is the absence of pepper games. I had a discussion once with Ted Williams about the pepper game, and we both agreed that playing pepper was important in the conditioning of every player. Every movement that you make in a pepper game, whether you're swinging a bat or fielding the ball or throwing the ball or whatever, you would use in a professional baseball game. No matter what position you played—pitcher, infielder, outfielder, catcher—it didn't matter. But the pepper games are gone. They say it tears up the field or the walls or gets in the way of getting the game ready or could be dangerous to a fan. Even if that were true, it would still be worth putting every player through a pepper session every day.

Calisthenics are good. I wasn't too much of a wholehearted believer in calisthenics until I joined the Cardinals system to manage the Tulsa club. I was reluctant to see that they had a system of calisthenics, but they turned out to be absolutely superb. You would pump your legs to loosen up. You did the windmill on your arms. You bent the left hand to right toe, right hand to left toe. You put your hands on your hips and pulled your shoulders around. Everything that was done, you were using in baseball. The Cardinals had the finest calisthenics I've ever seen. I never did see a play in baseball where you lie down on your back, but you can do all your stretching standing up, which is how you play in the game, on your feet. This useless stuff is for show, I guess.

As a player, you have to get loosened up and stay loose during the game. That's why after a guy strikes out with nobody on base and less than two outs, the catcher snaps a hard throw to third. Then the third baseman will zip it over to second base, then over to short, maybe over to first, and then back to the pitcher, to keep their arms loose. Sometimes you don't get to loosen up enough, so you have to find any opportunity to do so. When I was a player in the minor leagues, I'd warm up my arm in center field. I'd get a ball from the bullpen and warm up with a bullpen pitcher. I had no patience with people who had no imagination. The results were great. They do it now in the big leagues, but they don't it as much as they should.

It's fine for pitchers to practice in the outfield, shagging flies and running around. They're catching the ball. They're handling the baseball. They're running after it. It's a lot of fun for them too. They get out there and make great plays. And you never know when you might have to use a pitcher at another position during a game. I had to play several pitchers at other positions in Montgomery. But everybody has got to practice. When I scout or watch games today, it disturbs me to go out and watch what some clubs do. They take outfield practice and make their throws, and some don't even make good throws. Some clubs don't even have guys throwing to the bases. I don't know why. Usually they're the last-place ball clubs. Executing plays real well is the net result of good practice. Practice is the answer to the whole thing. You can't turn ability on and off like a water faucet. You've got to practice, and practice right. That's the key to successful teaching. Good ball clubs do those things the majority of the time. Poor ball clubs don't execute, and you can see it. All you have to do is walk into the ballpark when you're scouting and you see all that. You can see a lackadaisical club.

I have mixed feelings about players playing winter ball. Some people say they're playing too many games, that they're risking injury down there in the Caribbean and Venezuela and Mexico, and that some of them are playing out of position. A couple of years ago, Neifi Perez, the shortstop for the Rockies, was on a team that had so many great infielders, he was playing third base. I think there ought to be a self-imposed rule against a guy who plays a full schedule—as a regular shortstop, regular catcher, regular outfielder—playing winter ball. Even though the fans want to see their national heroes down there, I don't think they should be playing.

They're jeopardizing the club that's paying their salaries, that has developed them and everything else. There's always the chance of an injury, because you play hard. You don't play lax. You give it everything you've got. Now, with a young ballplayer, it's a different story. A young outfielder or a young infielder can play a little bit down there. But in the case of Neifi, I believe that's a foolish thing for him to be playing second or third base in the winter leagues when all he has to do is hone his skills as a shortstop. He's got the makings of a truly outstanding shortstop. He shouldn't be playing a different position. But it's difficult for a player to turn down his country in the winter leagues.

In the off-season, your players, pitchers or whoever, can strengthen their arms with different exercises. Golf is good. It uses the arms, hitting those golf balls, and gets the legs walking. When I went to spring training as a player, I did an awful lot of running before I went to camp. I swung the bat as much as I could. A lot of the older baseball guys had good exercise routines. Al Simmons would go down to Hot Springs, Arkansas, a month before spring training started, put on a pair of great big lumberjack boots, and walk and jog for miles on those paths down there. Then he'd take those hot baths. It sure didn't hurt him. Joe DiMaggio had weights around his ankles, a pound or two that he could adjust or add more, and he would run around down there in spring training to strengthen his legs. Chopping wood with a double-headed axe is great for hitters. Every Hall of Famer I've met was always talking about how to strengthen your hands, your wrists, and your forearms. Some guys carry a rubber ball or tennis ball in their pocket and squeeze it all day long. A lot of them don't like those squeezing devices because they tighten up the wrong muscle in your hand. Plunging your arm into a barrel of rice, like Steve Carlton and Roger Clemens have done, is a fine conditioner for pitchers' arms. That strengthens everything. That makes all your fingers strong, all your muscles in your shoulder and arms, with no chance of hurting yourself, of busting a finger or pulling a muscle in your arm. It is tremendous. I don't know why every doggone pitcher doesn't copy these great pitchers.

There are plenty of good physical exercises you can do. I think at one time they wouldn't let you go swimming. Swimming was taboo. For what reason? Swimming is great for the legs, the arms, the back. But there are other things that you shouldn't do. Some daredevil things like flying recklessly or hang gliding can end a career real quickly. Kenny Hubbs and Thurman Munson sure found that out the hard way. Snowmobiling and skiing aren't all that great an idea either, as the examples of Carney Lansford and Jim Lonborg prove. Air conditioning and ceiling fans can cause problems too.

Occasionally one of my guys would get a real stiff neck. We had that quite often in the minor leagues. A pitcher would sleep with a fan on, which would stiffen his arm. After a while, the manager would tell him to sleep with a sweatshirt on. You'd come up with colds in your neck and your arm. Too much air conditioning will do that too. Some guys would take cortisone for their shoulders.

Regarding those dietary supplements, such as creatine and androstenione, that Mark McGwire got criticized for a couple of years ago, if they're sold over the counter at drug stores, I don't see anything wrong with that. Vitamins are in vogue now. I'm not in favor of those steroids that the National Football League guys want to take. They're just playing once a week, so they want to bulk up. But I thought it was a terrible thing to make a big fuss about what McGwire was taking. When I started playing, they would encourage you to eat red meat, prime rib and steaks of all kind. You had to be a meat eater. But now they're into vitamins and supplements.

One thing it's tough for a pitcher to ignore is a blister. The average fan probably doesn't understand how painful one is if it's on the pitching hand, on the end of a finger. It gets rubbed raw. Sandy Koufax retired because he had problems with a blister. His fastball and curve would wear everything off, and he just couldn't pitch. And the umpire won't let you put any tape on it. I've seen them try to tape a blister and douse it with iodine and try to cover it up as natural as the skin, and still the umps would see it. The hitters would see it too, so they'd make the pitcher take it off, especially if he was pitching well, to get him out of there.

At spring training, as a manager I had a definite conditioning and practice program. I'd line everybody up, five in a row at home plate, and have them run down the right-field line to the fence. I'd say, "Chaps, take your caps off. Get suntanned. Do whatever you want. But do the running and then walk to center field and then run down to the left-field line. Then walk in." We'd do that for ten, fifteen, twenty minutes. Everybody loosened up his legs. I'd say, "Kids, run fast, run slow, but don't pull any leg muscles." After that was over, we'd start warming up their arms, one on one. Catchers would throw with another catcher. Shortstops and second basemen threw together. Third basemen and first basemen practiced the long throws together. The outfielders threw together. All pitchers tossed together. We'd warm up the arms for ten or fifteen minutes. That was the routine that I had for about the first ten days.

Then we'd break up into groups and start taking a little infield practice about the third or fourth day. I'd have them play pepper games with one hitter, one fielder, one ball, one bat, loosening them up. They'd be making

all the motions, all the plays, working all the physical abilities that it takes
to play baseball, all the contortions of your body, backhand, forward, jump,
everything. This was all conducive to the one goal of getting the player in
condition to play baseball. I never had too many calisthenics at the start,
but then I went to about fifteen minutes later on. Then I'd mix it up. They
would take the infield, and the pitchers would warm up with catchers, and
we'd start batting practice and get in our running. Then we'd go through
all the fundamentals that I could think of: pitchers covering first, pitchers
fielding bunts, outfielders catching a lot of fly balls, infielders fielding a lot
of ground balls. For batting practice, I had a routine where you'd take five
swings and bunt one. Then that wasn't enough. So then you'd let a guy
take eight or ten swings and then bunt one toward third base, bunt one
toward first base. All these things were to get your ballplayers acclimated
to thinking baseball.

In warming up, if one guy dropped the ball, he had to run around the
other ballplayer. If a guy threw wildly, he'd have to run around the ballpark.
For the first four or five days, you'd see twenty guys running around the
ballpark. Then, as time went on, it would dwindle down to just five, then
finally only one, a hardheaded guy who thought it was childish to do it. He
would drop the ball deliberately. He would have to keep running. I did that
for several ballplayers, including Lou Piniella, until they got the message.
Then, at the end of the day, everybody would run, foul line to foul line. I
let the outfielders run together, and I'd let the infielders run together. Then
personally I would run the pitchers. They'd run by me, toss me the baseball.
I'd throw it a long way to them. They'd go from foul line to foul line.

Pitchers and catchers report early to spring training for a reason. The
clubs like to have the pitchers ready to start throwing batting practice as
soon as they can. So they give them a week to two weeks ahead of the
other players. They have the catchers because they need them to catch the
pitchers and warm them up. Nowadays March 1 is a compulsory reporting
date for the regular ballplayers, and then about the fifth day of spring
training they're supposedly ready to play. But as much as they say they're
ready, they're not. They always want to play themselves into shape. I don't
understand why they don't want to come down to spring training. It's the
most delightful time of the year. I don't think I ever heard of a guy from the
North Country, when he was in snow clear up to his knees, not liking spring
training when the rest of the team was down in sunny Florida or Arizona.
The first two or three weeks are fun, and then it gets serious. You're fighting
for a job, to impress the management and everybody, playing against good
competition. They all do that during the last ten days. The ideal timing for

spring training would be to arrive February 15 and then start your games about the third or fourth of March. That would give you two weeks or so to get everybody ready. Pitchers would have pitched every other day and warmed up every other day. Then they would throw in a couple of intersquad games and then be ready to go. I think you'd see better quality baseball.

We usually had one practice session, but then every once in a while we'd scatter the reporting time in the mornings, sometimes at 9:00, sometimes at 10:00, sometimes at 11:00. But most of the time, we'd have one long session. As spring training would progress, we'd have all our fundamentals and batting practice in the morning, then break for lunch and warm up and play ball games. We had so many ballplayers in camp that we had to have long sessions to see that everybody got a fair shake for evaluation.

The training table at spring training usually held a cup of soup and a small sandwich or something like that, very little. Compared to football, where they eat a lot, in baseball it was very sparse. There's an old saying that you can't do your best on a full stomach. The first time I heard that I kind of laughed, because I was young, and I always had an appetite. It was explained to me by a veteran manager and scout this way. He said, "When a cat eats, it always lies down and goes to sleep. You don't see a cat running around afterward." I learned you can't play on a full stomach real well. Most players could hold their food, but I did have a pitcher one time who every time we'd run, oh, gosh, he'd get sick. He couldn't run. It was tough trying to get him in shape. Finally I asked him if there was anything wrong. He said, "Oh, yes, Skip." I said, "What is it? What the heck's wrong with you?" He said, "My wife is pregnant, and she's having morning sickness." So he couldn't keep anything down. I said, "When's the best time for you to run?" He said, "The last thing during the day." I said, "OK."

I like to see players getting an extra advantage. I like seeing outfielders catch a few fly balls, throw from the outfield, and then take ten or fifteen minutes of infield practice. That helps them get a read of the ball off the bat. Everything is to the players' advantage if they know that. When you go into a strange ballpark, outfielders should go out to the fence and bounce the ball off the wall a little bit, in between rounds of hitting. In batting practice, a guy should bunt the ball down the third base side and one down the first base side, and then take all of the swings in the program. The last swing he takes while he's in the batting cage should be a fly ball, because he's asked many times during the course of a season to drive in a run from third base or to advance the runner from second to third base. It's very simple to do. You say, "Man on third . . . one out . . . BOOM . . . Let's see you drive him in." If he hits the ball well, sometimes it goes out of the park. I had hitters who weren't good hitters, but they would execute pretty well. You stand back of the cage and say, "The man's on second base, nobody out. . . . Advance him." So he'd hit the ball to the opposite field, or if he was a left-handed hitter, he'd pull the ball over this way and advance him. These are all things that contribute to a game, and maybe the average fan doesn't see, but the guy sitting in the dugout whose neck is on the line, the manager, knows when it's being done and when it isn't.

I'm very critical about infield practice because I've always wanted my infielders to practice just like they were in a game. In my infield, I had a definite routine. I would hit the first ball to the third baseman. He threw to first. Then to the shortstop the same way, and so on around the infield. Then after that, I hit the ball to the guy's left, and then to his right. Next we went to the double play. And when I got to the catcher, I'd roll the ball out to the third base side when he had to throw the ball to first. Then I'd roll the ball to the first base side, and he had to throw it to second or to third. Every once in a while, I'd bounce the ball on the plate, and the catcher would have to find and field the ball. While the ball was in the air, I'd yell, "First," "Second," or "Third," wherever I wanted him to throw it. That way, we were practicing everything. Oftentimes I would let the catcher take infield practice with the full gear on, especially with young guys starting out. I did it with Clint Courtney and Gus Triandos many times in the minor leagues. I did it with a lot of ballplayers starting out. As a catcher, you're throwing a guy out with the full gear and the mask on. You don't have time to take it off, so you practice with full gear.

With the outfield, you hit the left fielder a ground ball, straight at him, and let him throw to second base. Then you hit one down the line for him to field and throw to second base. That way, he was practicing fielding a ball hit down the line. Maybe he could cut if off and keep a runner from taking two bases. Then you hit a ground ball right at the left fielder for him to throw home. Everything was conducive to keeping the other team from scoring runs. You did the same routine with the center fielder. You hit him two balls, and he threw one to second base and one to third. Then you hit one a little bit to right-center, and he came in and threw the ball to third base. You have that ball hit often to the center fielder's left, toward right-center, in the game, and he's got to throw a runner out trying to go from first to third. You hit a fly ball out there and had him throw out a guy who was tagging up and trying to advance on a sacrifice fly. You did a similar pattern with the right fielder. Everything was done with the object of preventing runs, and you kept practicing so that they did it right. You had to do these things to be a good ball club. The players may not have agreed, and sometimes it was difficult to get it over to them. But the manager and the coaches sure knew what needed to happen. All they could do was shake their heads if the players didn't execute.

Some of the stuff you see these days is enough to give a longtime manager like me a heart attack! I saw a major league club, the Braves, in April or on May 1, not taking infield on a perfectly beautiful day in Los Angeles. They didn't take infield or outfield practice. It was a perfect day. The day was a Sunday, and the club had been there for two days. They didn't even take infield and outfield on those other days. Why not, I don't know. They couldn't have been tired. It was only April or May 1. They couldn't be needing to rest. They should have been out there in the sun. The Dodgers beat the hell out of them. You've got to practice the way you're going to play. If you don't practice well, you won't play well. You've got to warm up your arm, your legs, your swings, the things that you're going to use in a ball game. If you walk up to the plate cold, not having swung the bat first, you'd better be great enough to produce.

One year Dante Bichette came into camp weighing about 250 pounds. If he made a dive after a ball and it bounced out there in left field, he got a lot of criticism. But the weight helped his hitting. He was stronger. Sometimes a player can hurt his performance by taking off too much weight. Andres Galarraga took off a lot of weight for the 1995 season and kind of weakened himself. Some fans were down on him for losing too much weight. But he played hard and made great plays at first base. He was an anchor over there. Those infielders would make bad throws, and he'd come up with the ball. If I had my way, I'd just have let him play his way out of his slump. Find a spot for him. You don't put a batting champion on the bench and give him a rest. Let him work his way up, and he will.

From time to time, when you go to the ballpark, you see useless things that ballplayers are doing, things that have nothing whatsoever to do with playing the baseball game. One that always gets me is when, during batting practice, the catcher's got his full gear on and he goes to field bunts, and he stands on the infield, down the third base line, twenty feet in front of the plate. There is no play in a baseball game when that would happen. Why practice something that you're never going to use? It's not a position. If you want, you could set the catcher aside, and when the guy bunts, let him charge out, or even charge out from his catching position. There is value in executing that play. You're practicing a play that could come up in a game. But I've never seen a play in baseball in my lifetime where the catcher would field a bunt by standing out there when the pitch was being made. To me that's a useless play.

When you're managing or you're playing, you've got to be positive. You've got to think you're going to win every game if you're a pitcher. You've got to think that you're going to get a base hit every time you go up to the plate. When you're a manager, you've got fifteen, twenty, twenty-five guys, and you've got to always keep them positive, eliminate all the negative thoughts. Many years ago, I was fortunate enough to pick up a book called *The Magic of Believing* by Claude Bristol, a professor at Duke University, I think. I also read his other book, *TNT: The Power Within You*. I read those books, and I really went into this positive thinking stuff. In fact, the ballplayers kind of laughed at me. I wouldn't let anybody on the ball club say anything bad or negative about anything. I wanted everything positive. I got so involved in this that prior to a ball game, I would sit down and get my mind thinking positive. I'd sit there and think positive. Just for the heck of it, I'd play a game in which I'd put down what I thought the score would be in the ball game, knowing the opposition and knowing my own ball club. I'd put it on a piece of paper, seal it in an envelope, and put it in my pocket. When the game was over, I'd try to remember to look at the paper. I'd pick the correct scores for baseball games about a dozen times in a month. I was just absolutely positive about everything. I just figured that we were going to win, and we did. Somewhere along the line I lost track of it, and then it came back to me again. I didn't like to surround myself with negative people, such as we had with the Cubs. It was a very tiresome thing. I like to hear a guy say, "Yeah, I'm good," rather than cry about stuff.

I still do believe that great people have arrogance, not the distasteful or the unpopular arrogance, but the confidence kind. Willie Mays had a pixie arrogance. He played with the kids on the street. He was arrogant, and he was good. He was going to show it, and he wanted everybody to be good. That was a delightful arrogance. Stan Musial had a humorous arrogance. He'd laugh and kid with you and everything else, but if you'd throw him a fastball, he'd beat you. Joe DiMaggio had a graceful arrogance. Every move that he made was the arrogance of a beautiful swan. Mickey Mantle had a boyish arrogance. He played like heck. Pete Rose had an arrogance that bordered on overbearing arrogance. He created that image: "I'm Pete Rose, and I'm good, and I'm going to do anything." And he would! You think Bob Gibson didn't have arrogance? He knew he was going to get you out and you weren't going to hit him. Jim Bunning had arrogance. He'd brush you back; he'd come from the side and scare the devil out of you.

I put that down many times on my reports: "This guy's got an arrogance that I love." Johnny Bench had the arrogance of a giant oak tree, standing there in the hurricane or tornado, just standing majestically and defying that tornado to do anything. Tony Perez had a quiet arrogance, just like smooth water runs deep. Joe Morgan had that itchy positive, uncontrolled, energetic arrogance. Brooks Robinson was a magician with his glove, as if to say, "I can do any trick I want to with this glove." He performed time and time again. Red Schoendienst had the quiet, unassuming, laid-back, sleepy type of arrogance until it was his turn to do something, and he did it. Lou Boudreau was a college guy, and he had that college feeling about himself, like he was forever a college ballplayer. He managed that way too. He wasn't afraid to employ the Williams shift; he was going to stop Ted. It was beautiful. Lou Brock and Rickey Henderson had the base stealer's arrogance: "I can steal a base anytime I want. You can't throw me out." Al Kaline, in his quiet way, showed his confidence. He won a batting championship at an early age. Al carried himself well, as if he were the lead horse of a team. Orlando Cepeda had that bull-like arrogance that he was going to walk through that wall, that he was going to hit the ball regardless. Ted Williams, of course, had the utmost arrogance. Maybe they invented the word for him. The delightful part about it was he would produce to match his arrogance. He thought he was the greatest hitter, and he would produce. All the great ones had it. Arrogance is a wonderful thing. I don't say this in a critical manner. I say this as a delightful, complimentary way of describing a ballplayer.

The meek do not inherit the earth in baseball. I had a ballplayer once, a pitcher, who was very conscious of meekness. He studied and became a minister after his playing days were over. He had great stuff and should have played in the big leagues. He should have been a fine pitcher. He had all the things required of him, a strongly built physique, a good arm, and a good assortment of pitches. But he lacked one thing. He wouldn't pitch close to a hitter. He didn't want to hurt anybody, which is a fine trait generally, but in baseball you have to establish your territory, especially as a pitcher. He didn't have the aggressiveness of a Don Drysdale or a Bob Gibson or a Jim Bunning or an Early Wynn. They established who was the boss. This young guy wouldn't throw inside, and he had great stuff. He had a number one curve for the major leagues, as well as a number one fastball, and he had good control. He also had a nice change-up. He was a right-hander, yet he wouldn't brush a guy back. It was his downfall. He was meek. There's nothing wrong with that in its place, but there's no place for it in a pitcher.

I've always been a competitor, and I wanted guys on my team who were competitors too. Somebody said that there are only two places, first and everything else. I agree with that, and with Leo Durocher when he said, "They're good losers. Who wants a loser?" You've heard the phrase "Nice guys finish last" and all those things. When I was courting the gal that I married, there was a little competition. I didn't want to be second. I wanted to be first. I was going to beat the hell out of the guy who was my competition, if that's what it took to win. Yes, I suppose you can carry it too far, become obsessed with the idea, but that's the name of the game. And even if you're out of the pennant race, you can still at least look good losing. I had that losing ball club in Montgomery in 1953, but through seven innings, we played the living daylights out of those teams, and then their superior talent took over. I just wanted us to play. If they made a mistake, we could capitalize on it. You carry that creed over to everything. I got a good lesson in the horse business from Bish Jenkins. He said, "A good horse trader always gets a little to boot in the trade." He'll trade one horse for another and get twenty-five dollars more, or fifty or a hundred dollars. He always gets the boot. That's the way it is in baseball.

A couple of autumns ago, I had visions of making a comeback. I was talked into playing with this outfit where there were players of several age groups and some women playing too. Now mind you, I was seventy-nine years old at the time. I had visions of coming back and hitting the ball out of the ballpark. I couldn't run very well anymore, so they put in a rule that I thought was a heck of a good one. If I hit the ball, I had a designated runner standing right there by me, who would run for me. I picked out the youngest kid on the ball club. The catcher was sixty-nine years old. There was a professor playing third base and a mother playing second base. One team had a left-handed gal pitching. I had a great game against her. I "smoked" two shots through the middle that barely reached the outfield grass. The next time I came up, she hit me in the back of the leg! The catcher said to me, "Charlie, go on out there and wrestle her to the ground! She can't do that to you!" I said, "That'll look good, won't it?" I also got hit on the helmet. I ducked into a fastball. But I probably hit about .600 for the season, three times my lifetime big league batting average.

For years I helped out with baseball instruction clinics at a local college, Metropolitan State College, "Metro" for short. I joke with the kids that they named the college after me. Since 1991 I've been doing guest appearances and talks in a baseball history class at the college. And recently I took some batting practice and hit fungoes to the outfielders of the college baseball team. I challenged the college coach, Vince Porreco, to a long ball–hitting contest, but he declined. I guess he knew I would beat him handily.

A couple of years ago, I had maybe a dozen new fungo bats made by the bat maker SAM BAT out of Canadian maple from up in Ontario. Some were dark colored and some light. I designed the bats myself, forty-two inches long, with about an eighteen- to twenty-inch barrel. The only restrictions the company has are that the size of the bat has to be forty-two inches or shorter, and the barrel can't be wider than two and three-quarter inches, I believe, and it can't have a hole or cup any deeper than an inch drilled in the end of the bat. They have a winged bat logo on them. I understood that there were a few major league ballplayers, especially on the Toronto Blue Jays, using the bat. They say it lasts longer, and they get the good feel of the ball hitting the bat, better than they do with the ash or the hickory. I was going to use it in a fungo-hitting contest or a home run–hitting contest, if I ever got the chance to get my name drawn at Coors Field here during the 1998 All-Star Game contests. I wanted to be the oldest guy to hit a baseball for a home run. That summer I tried to win some All-Star Game tickets at a home run–hitting contest. I wanted to enter the contest where you take three swings and win that $10 million. So I practiced and went to another contest that was being held by Denver sports talk show host Irv Brown and his radio station. I missed the ball by a foot, both swings. There went my comeback right there!

The year the All-Star Game was in Denver, in 1998, I never knew I had so many friends. So many of my grandkids and their husbands and wives and friends, and just about everybody in the business, wanted tickets. I thought, "Oh, my gosh!" I didn't want to turn anybody down if I could help it, so I started contacting baseball people. I called Pat Gillick, who was with the Orioles. Pat had gone through my spring training camp out at Yuma, Arizona, and of course we've been friends for a long time. I called him, and he got me a whole bunch of tickets. Then I found out that they weren't enough. So I called Walt Jocketty at St. Louis and asked him if he had any. He said, "Yes." So he got me some tickets. Walt and I had been at Oakland together when he was in the farm department and I was scouting. We became good friends. I also called Bill Beck, who was a business manager with us at Kansas City, at Omaha, and later became traveling secretary with the Florida Marlins. He got me a few tickets. I filled out all my requests and even then was short. A couple of people I had to cut off. Otherwise it went very well.

I went to the Pacific Coast League's tenth annual reunion a few years ago in Los Angeles. I renewed acquaintances with guys who had played for me and played against me. Some told me how mean I was, and the others would say what a great manager I was. I saw Cece Carlucci, a very fine and popular umpire in the Coast League when I managed there. He became an entrepreneur, a restaurant owner, I believe. He also came up with a chest protector that's similar to the bulletproof protectors that the police wear. He designed them, and he's selling them. They're made of lightweight material. When you're prone to injury, when you get one right off the chest, it can hurt you. Apparently he's going to have good success with his invention. I saw Joe Stanka and Roger Bowman, two fine pitchers for Sacramento. Buddy Peterson, my shortstop at Vancouver, was there, as was Cuno Barragan, who was my catcher for a while with the Cubs. Chuck Stevens, who was director of the Professional Baseball Association for the minor leagues, was a major-domo. Paul Pettit was there too. I saw him when he was a pitcher, and he turned out to be a pretty good ballplayer and hitter. He became a highly successful high school or college coach, I can't remember which. Cliff Dapper, a catcher in the league, and Red Adams, a pitching coach for the Dodgers for many years, were there. I saw Herman Reich, a big strapping outfielder who I had played against in the winter league down when he was at Hermosillo and I was at Mazatlan in the Mexican League one winter. I had a lot of fun reminiscing with all those guys. But the fans were wonderful too. They enjoyed that reunion immensely. The gathering was wonderful. I hope to go again. It was terrific. The stories got longer, and the lies got bigger. There were an awful lot of stories, but most of them you just can't repeat.

There were autograph sessions, but there was no charging for autographs or anything like that. They had some baseball memorabilia that I'd never seen before. They had these laminated posters of various teams, including the 1943 Detroit Tigers, on which I was a defensive outfielder. One guy had a photo of me in an Oakland Oaks uniform with a young boy, showing him how to hold a bat. I was pleased, because they wanted thirty-five dollars for that one. It's a rare photo. It was sponsored by a bread company there in Oakland. I don't know whether it was Rainbo or Holsum or some other bread company. You bought a loaf of bread, and there were some cards in it. I already had one. My son Bud had found one back east at a card show. I asked him how much he paid for it, and he told me had to give twenty-four dollars. I told him I had a shoebox full, but I was just kidding.

Even to this day, I receive fan letters. I've gotten some wonderful things from the kids, and I wish I had kept them all. My prize letter was from a young guy, ten years old, who wrote me: "Dear Mr. Metro, [I] wish this finds you with good health and happiness, and would you please sign my bubble gum card or my cards, whatever. My grandfather saw you play and he says you were a great hitter." He underlined "great." That was pretty flattering, because my lifetime average was .193 in the big leagues. I would send replies to these types of letters, and if I had an extra picture of me lying around somewhere, I'd include it. A couple of years ago, I made a longtime friend, it seems, with a young guy in Cleveland. He sends me everything about the Indians. He sent me a Cleveland Indians cap. He sends me pictures and license stickers and everything else about the Indians. We have corresponded quite often. He wants to be a baseball scout, so I sent him a lot of scouting forms that I used and explained the system of rating. But I really enjoy the ones that say, "My grandfather saw you play." I don't charge for autographs, which is all right. Perhaps I don't charge those fans because I'm not that well-known. I'm not a Hall of Famer or a great ballplayer, locally or otherwise.

It's important to keep the kids interested in baseball. I've caught quite a few foul balls in the stands. In fact, I caught one at Coors Field. There was a little boy sitting in front of me, about five or six years old, and the ball hit up above us and came bouncing down the aisle. I was sitting in the end seat, and I turned around and there came the ball. I reached down and I caught it. The little boy had his hand out. I grabbed his hand and opened it up and put the ball in it. He was real proud. He shouted, "Mommy, Mommy, I got the ball!"

Every once in a while, I'll bump into some celebrity connected with baseball. Once we were up at a restaurant that a friend of ours ran in Minturn, Colorado. We were taking a shortcut across the Colorado mountains, and we stopped and went in. Bob Cherry, a former baseball player I had in camp at Boyes Hot Springs in the late 1940s, was the proprietor. He was one of the finest hitters I'd ever seen, but he spent time in the military, and when he came out, he had kind of lost the touch. We reminisced about that. But while we were there, who should walk in but "The Natural" himself, Robert Redford. Bob Redford and his wife were there. I had been in Buffalo and seen how they fixed that Buffalo ballpark for *The Natural*. When Bob Cherry introduced him to me to him, I said, "Hmm, high fastball hitter, likes the ball up." Redford got quite a kick out of that. The movie showed him swinging the bat pretty well. I said, "You're a pretty good hitter, Roy, but you can't play under an assumed name in the big leagues." He got a kick out of that too.

I've stayed quite busy with baseball stuff in my so-called retirement. A couple of years ago, I received a Pioneer Award for outstanding contributions to baseball in Colorado. I was very fortunate to be given the award. You get your name on the plaque. There were five of us inducted at Coors Field. It was quite an honor. I really enjoyed it. I had quite a few of the ushers root me on that night. I chat and visit with them every time I come for a game. They brought my wife and me down on the field by home plate. We were on the big Jumbotron. They gave a brief history of my baseball activities here in Colorado. I got a big plaque that says, "A Legend. Pioneer Award."

I joined the Rocky Mountain Chapter of SABR, the Society for American Baseball Research, and gave a speech for them on my career. I've been interviewed by several radio and television programs and even for a two hour video for a cable television arts channel. Local groups, such as a retirement home in nearby Westminster, ask me to speak from time to time. I also gave a talk at a museum in Golden, where they had quite a few items of baseball memorabilia. I lent them my Oakland A's uniform as well as a glove and a batting tee and a set of my hands from the Hitters' Hands series, which will be donated to the museum that's going to be at Coors Field. I got quite a kick out of the audience. I told all sorts of stories about my baseball career. A couple of the people in the audience were Chicago fans. They remembered me from my Cubs and White Sox days. Speaking of which, one day a while back, I was at the ballpark, and I was in the midst of a group of ladies, half of whom were Cubs fans and the other half White Sox fans. I kidded them quite a bit. I said, "Aaahhhh, the Cubs are no good," or "Aaaaahhhh, the White Sox are no good." But I was with both clubs. I've kept quite busy giving talks, going to the ballpark, and creating my own Hall of Fame, Hitters' Hands.

FOURTEEN

My Own Hall of Fame

A few years ago, about 1993, I got a phone call from a Denver-based sculptor named Raelee Frazier. She wanted to do a life-size bronze cast of my hands because a mutual friend with the Rockies had told her I had "great" baseball hands. At first I wasn't really interested. She called me again and again, maybe about five or six times. Finally I relented and said I would go down and get this over with. So I went down to her studio in downtown Denver, down off Colfax and Emerson, to find out what she had in mind. Once I got there, I walked into the studio and saw all these bronze things she was doing. She was doing mannequins for museums, doing buffalo and soldiers from the western Civil War. She doing quite a bit of things for museums back east. I saw a broomstick handle in a corner, and typical of a former baseball player, I picked it up and started to swing it like a bat. When I got into my hitting stance, Raelee said, "Stop. That's it! That's exactly what I'm looking for." I said, "What, with a bat?" She said, "Yes." She then proceeded to talk me into having a wax cast made of my hands gripped around a baseball bat.

I agreed, and she made a cast of my hands right then and there. I was surprised and pleased by how well they came out. They were actually lifelike casts of my hands. Then Raelee suggested that we expand the project to include casts of the hands of current major leaguers, but I reckoned that it would be difficult to get them interested right away. I supposed, instead, that it would be possible to get casts made of Hall of Fame hitters and sell the sculptures as lasting baseball memorabilia. "But who can contact Hall of Famers?" Raelee asked. "I can," I said, "I played with some of them, played against some of them, managed some of them, scouted a bunch of them. I can approach them about the idea." The more I thought about it, the more appropriate the idea seemed. After all, in baseball, players use their hands nearly all the time. Obviously pitchers, hitters, and fielders all use their hands, and even runners might have to use their hands sliding into a base. But the most important use of the hands is in hitting. The first thing I watched when I was a scout was to see if a guy had quick hands, strong hands, or whatever. The sculptures would preserve part of baseball history and make us some money.

The first guy we convinced was Ralph Kiner, who was broadcasting for the Mets. I talked to Ralph about it, showed him my set of hands, and he was interested. I said, "We would like to do your hands." He said, "OK." I picked him up at the hotel in my pickup truck, took him out to Raelee's studio, and made a cast of his hands. The next guy was Billy Williams of the Cubs, who I had managed and also was a bit responsible for getting a coaching job with Oakland. He is a wonderful guy, and so is Ralph. These Hall of Famers are all great guys. I talked Billy into doing it when I saw him in spring training and convinced him to come to the studio when the Cubs came in to play Colorado.

Thus the Hitters' Hands project was born. With Raelee's artistic abilities and my contacts with the former players, we felt it was worth a try. I secured an outside investor to get the ball rolling, and we began the campaign of convincing the players. I had built a good measure of trust and friendship with the players, and this greatly facilitated the efforts. Indeed Al Lopez's son, a lawyer, allowed his father to go ahead with the sculpture because my involvement with the project impressed him. The project started taking off. We traveled to where the ballplayer lived, or if he came into Denver with a ball club, we would sometimes arrange to get him to the studio. We would get permission from the player to use the model of the bat he actually used during his career. We'd get written permission to order bats from the Louisville Slugger people in Louisville, Kentucky. We would get each player's model of bat and put on it the date of the player's induction into the Hall of Fame. We had some twenty-two Hall of Famers under agreement to cast their hands.

So far we have cast the hands of Hall of Famers Richie Ashburn, Ernie Banks, Johnny Bench, Lou Boudreau, Lou Brock, Bobby Doerr, Monte Irvin, Al Kaline, George Kell, Harmon Killebrew, Ralph Kiner, Al Lopez, Eddie Mathews, Joe Morgan, Stan Musial, Pee Wee Reese, Brooks Robinson, Red Schoendienst, Duke Snider, Billy Williams, and Ted Williams. We hope to get those of Hank Aaron, Yogi Berra, and other Hall of Famers. We came close to obtaining casts with Bill Dickey and Johnny Mize, but they passed away before we could complete the arrangements, and we also missed out on Mickey Mantle and Joe DiMaggio. In addition to Hall of Famers, we've done casts of the hands of the great outfielder Minnie Minoso, current greats Andres Galarraga and Larry Walker and Tony Gwynn, and Negro League stars Buck O'Neil, Byron Johnson, Bobby Robinson, and Ted "Double Duty" Radcliffe. Recently we reached a tentative agreement with the Rockies' young superstar Todd Helton. We also figured out how to cast a pitcher's hand gripping a pitch, and to date we've done the hands of pitchers Goose Gossage, Ferguson Jenkins, and Bob Gibson. But it took us a while to figure out how to do it. We had Don Drysdale committed, as it turned out right before he died, but we didn't know how to cast the hands by the time Don came into town. We've even thought of casting the hands of famous baseball announcers with their hands on the microphone.

The process involves dipping the player's hands into a vat of hot wax. The player dips each hand, gripping a plaster model of the handle of his favorite bat, into the hot wax and then into cool water, then alternately back into the wax and the water until the impression is perfect. The wax doesn't hurt, but it surprises you at first. Occasionally there is a little bit of discomfort stripping the wax away from the hair on the hands and the wrists, but I remind the players that that's how women strip the hair off their legs! Through a sculpting technique called the "lost wax" method, Raelee then fashions a bronze cast of the hands. The wristbands are the color of the team's uniform most associated with the player. Then we attach the player's favorite model of bat, with his autograph on the bat head, to the hands by slimming down the part of the bat hidden behind the hands, sawing it in two, and reassembling it inside the bronze hands. Finally we mount the hands and bat on a walnut or oak home plate-shaped base, also with the player's signature, bat number, and date of induction lasered on it. Each limited edition sculpture, numbered one through thirty-six so far, comes with a certificate of authenticity signed by the player, Raelee, and me. Each sculpture takes about six weeks from start to finish. The sculptures are for sale to serious collectors and baseball buffs.

The finished hands have an amazing lifelike quality to them—so lifelike in fact that once Ted Williams was able to identify Ralph Kiner's hands without being told whose they were. We went to Orlando, Florida, to do Ted's hands. He was a little apprehensive, but we took the cast of Kiner's hands to show him what we were actually doing. I hid the name on the bat so he couldn't see who it was, except for the hands. I said, "Whose hands are these, Ted?" He took a look at them and stepped back and said, "Ralph Kiner." I said, "Holy smokes! How the heck did you know that?" I never realized how much attention they paid to the detail of how their fingers or knuckles were lined up or not lined up, where the thumb was. Ernie Banks's thumb, for example, is straight up. Clearly these great ballplayers paid attention to one another's hands and batting grips, even if only during spring training. Williams was a career American Leaguer and rarely saw the career National Leaguer Kiner! Ted was so impressed with the sculptures that he said, "Charlie, why didn't I think of that? Let's do it."

All of the players have been elated with the sculptures of their hands, and everyone involved has come to realize that these sculptures are not any old ordinary kind of baseball memorabilia but permanent reminders of the players' greatness and hitting styles. The detailing is so fine that you can just about take fingerprints off some of them. We have made every effort to ensure accuracy. When Stan Musial dipped his hand in the wax, apparently his top-hand thumb flexed upward and his wrist bent forward involuntarily. Musial noticed the error right away in the finished sculpture, so we redid Stan's hands. I saw Bobby Doerr a couple of years ago, and he said that his hands are fabulous. His wife has them displayed in their house, and everybody who comes by has to look at them, and they all marvel at them. He said that they are greatest thing that he has ever seen.

Harmon Killebrew came through here, and I picked him up at the hotel and took him out to the studio. He spent about half an hour looking at all these sculptures. We had about ten sets of the players' hands. He kept looking at their hands. He kept saying, "I'll be darned." He was amazed at their hands and the size. Galarraga and Johnny Bench had the biggest hands I had ever seen. I saw the size of Honus Wagner's hands when he was a coach for Pittsburgh during the war at Terre Haute. But Bench and Galarraga have got the biggest hands. Stan Musial, Al Kaline, and Ted Williams have hands like a surgeon, very fine, neat, expressive hands. I couldn't see the strength in them, but I could see the flexibility. Their hands were not big, but look at their records. Kaline was the youngest batting champion. Musial was the National League batting champion seven times. Williams had one of highest batting averages in modern times. All of these players had different grips on the bat. Ralph Kiner had his thumb straight up. George Kell hit like Ty Cobb, with his hands apart. Bobby Doerr had a choke hold on the bat. Lou Brock and Johnny Bench had their little fingers off the end of the bat.

We tried to get Joe DiMaggio to do his hands in bronze. I ran into him in Orlando and chatted with him about it. I said, "Joe, your hands—you caught a ball with your hands, you threw a ball with your hands. You were a superb outfielder, but, Joe, it was your hands that did it all." He kind of liked that, but he never agreed to do the hands. He, or his agent, demanded a fee of one million dollars for one set. Who would we get to purchase those? Then Joe died, so we lost all chance of landing him. This is very sad because his hands should have been preserved. We also lost the opportunity to get Mickey Mantle's, John Mize's, and Bill Dickey's hands. They, too, died before we could cast them.

Mostly we have sold sets of Hitters' Hands to private collectors, but eventually we hope to get more of them placed in museums. Already sets of Ted Williams's hands are on display in the Smithsonian Institution, the San Diego sports museum at Balboa Park, and Williams's own museum in Hernando, Florida. Steve Best, a *Rolling Stone, Men's Journal,* and *US* magazines executive, sponsored the sculpting of the hands of Negro League players O'Neil, Johnson, and Robinson, and Coors Brewing Company funded Radcliffe's hands. Eventually all four sculptures will be in the Negro League Museum in Kansas City—O'Neil's and Johnson's are already there. Jerry Colangelo, the owner of the Arizona Diamondbacks franchise, purchased three sets of hands—Musial's, Ted Williams's, and Banks's—for a museum at the new Bank One Ballpark in Phoenix. And Musial's hands are also at the Yamagata Trade Office in Japan. With good luck, we will get Cooperstown or even some state museums and sports museums very interested. During the All-Star Game summer in Denver, we had them on display at City Hall and the Embassy Suites hotel in Denver and at a museum in Golden, as well as at the Fan Fest center. We raffled off a set of Galarraga's hands in a contest in Denver for the fans. We also hope to persuade Hank Aaron, Willie Mays, Reggie Jackson, Yogi Berra, and Phil Rizzuto to agree to have their hands done someday, but some of these tremendous Hall of Famers get pestered all the time, so they're a little bit leery. Wouldn't it have been great if we could have had Babe Ruth, Ty Cobb, and other old Hall of Famers and seen their actual grips on their bats?

We are quite proud of the Hitters' Hands project. We operate the company out of my residence in Arvada and Raelee's studio, Highland Studio, in Denver. It's a great project, and it's keeping me young. I'm giving something back, as they say, back to baseball. Even if I don't make a dime out of it, I'm happy that we're perpetuating the memory of all these famous hitters for the young kids today to see what they looked like. But I need to make one thing clear: even though there are casts of my hands, I was just the guinea pig. I wasn't in the same category as the guys listed above. My lifetime major league batting average resembled my weight!

The Hitters' Hands project wasn't my first involving Hall of Famers. Quite a few years ago, I got the brainstorm of getting all the Hall of Famers living at that time to autograph some baseball covers, not baseballs but the unsewn covers that go over the centers and the wound-up yarn. I don't like to sit around. Two of my sons, Bud and Steve, were interested in the baseball players. Steve had been my batboy and clubhouse boy. My other son Geoff had been my batboy with the Royals down in spring training. One day I came up with the idea about the baseball covers. I had done some great favors for a sporting goods company, getting them uniform orders with the teams during my career, so I called a friend of mine with the Wilson Sporting Goods Company in Chicago and asked him for some covers. I said, "Just the covers, no printing, nothing on them." He asked me how many I wanted. I said, "Oh, maybe a hundred." He sent me over two hundred covers. Then I got the idea that I would send two covers to all of the living Hall of Famers. I got hold of their addresses. This turned into about a ten-year project on my part. During the time I was scouting and in between manager's jobs, I sent the covers to all the living Hall of Famers. They were very gracious, and I got two signed covers from each one. I sent them a stamped, self-addressed envelope to make it more convenient for the guys. Oh gosh, I got Waite Hoyt, Lefty Gomez, Ted Lyons, and Bill Terry, among many others. I got ninety living Hall of Famers over the course of the years. Only Hoyt Wilhelm refused. He was still mad at me for drafting him with the Royals and trading him to California. Then one year, my son Geoff was getting married and needed some money. He said, "Dad, do you think you can sell them?" So I tried a place or two, and word got around that I had these, and I received a call from a guy in New York, Barry Halper, who had probably the finest baseball memorabilia collection outside of Cooperstown. He wanted to know what I wanted for them, and I asked my son, and he said, "Well, I'm getting married. I'm going to need this, need that." So I priced them, and Barry bought one set. And about a year later he asked me if I'd be willing to sell the other set. There were only two in existence. Nobody in baseball ever had anything like that. So he bought the other set from my other son. I've got several other projects that I'm going to pursue, but I'm not going to tell anybody about them until I get done. I've got to be active, always thinking. If the big guy up there doesn't call me soon, I'm going to fulfill them.

In other chapters, I have talked about some of the great players, Hall of Famers I've seen, played with, managed, coached, and scouted. I'd like to talk about some of them a bit more and then make some comments about a few other Hall of Famers. I'd also like to make some recommendations about some players, managers, and other baseball men who should be in the Hall of Fame and how the hall should change its rules to allow some guys to get in sooner and widen its focus about who should be inducted.

When I was a kid, we heard all about some of the great players early in the century, such as Napoleon Lajoie and Honus Wagner. I would like to have seen them play. But they were dreams. You just dreamed of those guys. But with Babe Ruth and Gehrig and Foxx and Cochrane, it seems like those names were always rambling around in your mind. I was thrilled to be able to see them in person. Indeed I saw all the guys in the 500–home run club: Hank Aaron, Ruth, Willie Mays, Frank Robinson, Killebrew, Reggie Jackson, Mark McGwire, Barry Bonds, Mike Schmidt, Mantle, Foxx, Ted Williams, Willie McCovey, Eddie Mathews, Ernie Banks, Mel Ott, and Eddie Murray.

I saw Mel Ott when I was a young guy. I think he came from wherever he grew up right to the Giants and never played a game in a minor league. He was a tremendous hitter, a true Hall of Famer, who did everything. His credentials are just fabulous, 511 home runs. He had a good eye, and he hit with that foot way up in the air. I never did see Frankie Frisch, but I met him and stayed up talking with him one night with mutual friends of ours up in Connecticut. He talked baseball and he talked baseball. Good gosh, he was sharp, very aggressive and positive in his talking. It's no wonder he was a good manager. When you get older, you're not supposed to be that aggressive and talk that direct and that quick. But Frankie was that way. It was a wonderful evening for me.

They claimed that Ted Lyons was the strongest pitcher in baseball. They said that he could take a baseball and twist it in his hands and loosen up the cover. I'd never seen him do that, but the story is worth repeating. I didn't believe it when I first heard, but guys swear he could do it. He was in the service when I was up in the majors. I knew him a bit from spring training. Ted was a tremendous pitcher. He pitched for terrible clubs all of his career, twenty-one years with the White Sox. I don't think he was ever on a winning ball club. He pitched just about every Sunday. He was one of those Sunday pitchers for marquee match-ups. He also was a pretty good hitter and a fine person.

I had the pleasure of meeting Lefty Gomez at Sonoma Mission Inn at Boyes Hot Springs, California, when I had the Class C club in the Yankees organization. Lefty was the pitching instructor for the area east of the Mississippi, and he found himself in California. He was born and raised somewhere in that Northern California area, so they decided to send him out there to be close to home. He was a delight. My favorite memory about him is the story about the time he refused to pitch to Jimmie Foxx, "The Beast." Foxx was up with the bases loaded. Gomez was out there fidgeting around the mound and everything else but getting ready to pitch. Pretty soon the pitching coach came out and asked, "What's the matter with you?" Lefty said, "Nothing, nothing." So the coach walked back to the dugout, but Lefty still wouldn't throw it. Finally the coach came out again and said, "Lefty, what's the matter with you?" Gomez said, "You see who's hitting?" The coach said, "Yeah, Foxx, why don't you throw it?" Lefty said, "Maybe if I don't throw it, he'll get mad and go home." I think that's one of the most priceless ones I've ever heard.

Joe Medwick was the most positive ballplayer I've every met. I wondered why they wouldn't give these great ballplayers jobs in organizations. Even to this day, I wonder why clubs don't see the benefits they'll get from bringing in these former stars and the history they represent. Medwick was one of them. I don't know who I talked to, Walter Shannon or somebody, but I said, "Why don't you make Joe Medwick a roving hitting instructor, have him come down and talk to the kids?" They took my advice. Joe came down to Tulsa when I was there and instructed the players during the season. He'd walk around the clubhouse and say to each guy, "I've got you down for two hits," or "I've got you down for a long one," or "I've got you down for the big hit in the clutch," or "I've got you down for a great play." We had Hal Newhouser help out in the Baltimore system. It always puzzled me why the Tigers didn't call on him. At least they had Mickey Cochrane as a special instructor.

I bumped into Enos Slaughter at a couple of the card-signing shows that he attended. He was one of my all-time favorite guys, because of the way he hustled. He made that great run home to win the 1946 World Series against the Red Sox, but if you take a look at his stats, he played solid all his career. I asked him one time, "Enos, what was your first big league contract?" He told me it was for $1,500 a year, and he signed a two-year contract. That's when Branch Rickey was pretty tough with a buck. I understand that some of those guys—I don't know whether it was Enos or not—got $45 a month with the Cardinals in the minor leagues, down in the Class C league. But that was a standard, and if you wanted to play and there was no jobs at home, gee whiz, you'd play for nothing.

Ted Williams said that Johnny Mize was about as good a hitter as any man who ever put on a baseball uniform. Ted said he was tremendous. Mize agreed to have his hands cast in bronze for our Hitters' Hands project, but he passed away before I could get that done. He was a worthy choice for the Hall of Fame. Johnny played well for the Cardinals, Giants, and Yankees. At a time when the usual career didn't go beyond ten years, Johnny stuck around a long time as a real good pinch hitter. If you went beyond ten years with a ball club, they started thinking about getting rid of you, trading you off. Branch Rickey would do that—trade a ballplayer just before he started down in his career. But some players would fool the general managers, and Mize fooled them because he was an excellent pinch hitter.

Warren Spahn. What a competitor! How tough he was, holy smokes. I don't think he'd give his own mother a good pitch to hit. Geez, he was tough. He won a great number of his games after he was past thirty years old. Warren could hit too. He hit 35 home runs in his career. He was a nine-inning pitcher. I told him one day, "Warren, I know why you lasted as long as you did." He said, "Why?" Spahn owned a ranch in Hartshorne, I believe it was, in Oklahoma. I said, "I bet you I can tell you. You take your bags and you put them in the bedroom and you take off your dude clothes and put on those Levis and those boots and you go out there and you work on that ranch all winter long. The minute you put those cleats on for spring training, you're ready to go." He said, "Yup, Charlie, that was very accurate." That's why he pitched well into his forties. I hit against him in an old-timers' game, when I was managing Denver. I swung at that screwball he threw me, and I pulled both muscles, and then I got two charley horses running down to first. That's the last time I participated in an old-timers' game.

The late Pee Wee Reese was one of my all-time favorite guys. He worked for the Louisville Slugger Bat Company. He was always at the winter meetings. All the manufacturers of uniforms and equipment would gather. It was a really a wonderful atmosphere in the wintertime, usually the first week in December. Pee Wee was always there as an official associated with the bat company. Every once in a while, I'd walk into the display at the winter meetings, and he'd be there smoking a pipe. I'd say, "Hey, Harold." I always called him Harold. "Hey, Harold, what do you think Joe McCarthy would say?" Pee Wee's Dodgers had all those World Series battles with the Yankees. He would give me a certain four-letter word for where McCarthy could go. That went on for years. Pee Wee had a well-developed sense of humor. He was a great ballplayer. We got his hands in the Hitters' Hands series. He got his nickname as a marble shooter, and I always meant to challenge him. I understand he was a champion, but I wasn't too bad either in my time.

"The Scooter," Phil Rizzuto, was a true professional. He was on those great Yankees teams of the 1940s and 1950s. He played winning ball, did everything real well. Some people said his arm was weak for a shortstop, but he got the ball over there to first. Brooks Robinson didn't have a great arm either, yet you'd never fault him for that. Lou Boudreau didn't have a great arm, but Lou got that ball over there in a hurry. Lou always played a little shallow. So I wouldn't fault Rizzuto on that, if there's that much truth to it. Phil was the leader of the team, just like Pee Wee Reese was for Brooklyn. I don't know if the Yankees had a captain or not. Rizzuto played hard, and he was a deserving choice for the Hall of Fame. But I can't understand why it took them so long. Why won't they put the guys in the Hall of Fame now so they can enjoy it? The year they voted Rizzuto in, he was no better then than he had been ten years previously. Why make them wait the five years? What makes them better in five years' time? All it means is they're five years older.

I had the chance to ask a couple of Hall of Famers who was the toughest pitcher they faced, who gave them the most trouble. Ted Williams said immediately, "Two guys, Hoyt Wilhelm, with that knuckle ball." Ted would use strong words, a little on the profane side. He would say, "I couldn't hit that SOB. I'd walk up, move back, move away. I'd move in. That knuckle ball would dance all over the place. I had a hell of a time trying to hit it." I said, "Who was the other guy?" He said, "Ed Lopat." I said, "Ed Lopat! Ted, he couldn't break a plane of glass. I hit against him when he was down at Marshall in eastern Texas." Ted said, "You might have been able to hit him, but he drove me crazy. He could throw anything he wanted to, anywhere. He must have had forty different speeds on that ball." Ted Williams was a zone hitter. I haven't read his book on hitting yet, but I saw his articles in *Sports Illustrated*, where he talked about the strike zone. He said, "I hit the ball in the zone." He had such tremendous eyesight, just out of this world, so that it was no problem for him to look for a pitch in a zone.

And I asked Stan Musial the same question. I said, "Stan, anybody ever give you any trouble?" "Oh, Charlie, yes," he answered. I said, "Well, who?" I was anxious to find out, maybe some fireballer. He said, "Chris Short of the Phillies. He would wind up, he'd throw a leg, an elbow, a shoulder, and throw that little dab up there. He drove me crazy. He'd just throw it right here or right there. And Ken Raffensberger, another left-hander, who was with Cincinnati. He drove me crazy." I said, "Well, you never did say that in public, did you?" Stan said, "No." I said, "You mind if I repeat it sometime?" "Oh, no, it's all right. They can't get me out now," he said.

What can you say about Stan Musial that hasn't been said already? But he's funny. Stan's got a great sense of humor. He'd play on his mouth organ at the drop of a hat. He was a delight to watch play. Managing against him in the other dugout, you became a fan. You stopped being a manager for a moment; you wanted to see everything he did. Musial had that cocksure arrogance. He was tough in the clutch. There were times that I wished he'd caught the measles or the chickenpox so he wouldn't show up when we played the Cardinals. Musial was a good first baseman. He had hurt his arm as a pitcher and gone to the outfield, and later they switched him to first base. Few players had a longer career than he had. He kept himself in great shape. I heard that in his twentieth year, he was within two pounds of the same weight he played at when he was a rookie. I believe if he'd tried, he'd have been a 500 to 600 home run hitter. But Stan was a real team ballplayer. He thought more of winning than he did about his own statistics. Stan Musial represented the Cardinals with grace and dignity. He *was* the Cardinals.

Red Schoendienst, another Cardinal, was like a little red-headed kid going down a dusty road with a fishing pole and his dog and just minding his own business—but he's going fishing and he's got his dog with him, and he's going to catch those fish. Red played ball just like that, as if to say, "I'm going to make it, do my part, and we're going to win." He played a long time, nineteen years. Red was a fine everyday ballplayer. His handicap was an ailment of some sort in his lungs. But he was a good switch hitter and a good manager. He was real quiet and unassuming. It was an honor and a pleasure to know a guy like him. I would have liked to coach for him.

Ralph Kiner was a tremendous ballplayer, one of the premier power hitters, home run hitters, in the National League. In Forbes Field, they had a section called Kiner's Corner, where he would hit so many of his home runs. In 1947 he hit all those home runs for the Pirates, and even though I was down in Bisbee, I followed his chase of the record. Because I had lived up in that part of the country, I never lost my interest in Pittsburgh. For a while I thought, doggone, he's going to break or tie Ruth's record. I used to kid him that he quit too early in his career. I ran across him after he was done playing, when he was the general manager of San Diego. I said, "Ralph, why didn't you continue playing with that expansion team? My gosh, you'd have hit 600 home runs if you'd played a little longer." I never did find out why he quit so early. I think he was hurt or something. He became an extremely good broadcaster for the Mets, but every once in a while he'd make some crazy comment. It just doesn't come out the way he wants to say it. Every time I hear one of them, I laugh like heck. But he's an astute baseball man. He's not a court jester, but he's funny and he's good.

Richie Ashburn was another good nomination to the Hall of Fame. He was a real steady ballplayer. He played for the Phillies all those years and then with the expansion team Mets. He didn't have much power, but he was a good lead-off hitter and a fine center fielder. He took somewhat of a bum rap about his throwing arm, but he made up for it with his quickness. He could get to the ball quickly. I know quite a few ballplayers who did that, who didn't have much of an arm, so they got rid of the ball quickly. They'd also get a step or two charging ground balls, more quickly than anybody else would. Guys with the good arms would lie back, maybe trying to get the right hop, but Ashburn would charge the ball and get up there three, four, five steps closer to throw. That would disguise the fact that he didn't have a great arm, but he was accurate. He got a lot of walks, was very patient at the plate.

What can you say about Mickey Mantle except he was about the most awesome switch hitter who ever hit, that he could run faster than any ballplayer, and that he drove Casey Stengel crazy? Casey didn't want him bunting or stealing bases. Mickey would steal bases with those legs of his, and Casey would have a heart attack. You just wonder how good he would have been if he had had good legs. I used to run into him on occasion, at an autograph session here and there. We tried to get him for Hitters' Hands, but alcohol got him first. I was pulling for him. I knew him through Billy Martin. I was a great admirer of Mantle. I loved his arrogance, watching him laugh when he'd hit a ball and beat it out or take an extra base on an outfielder. I wanted him to live a full life, to whip his physical addiction, and to enjoy his family and his grandkids and everything.

Willie Mays. There's only one Willie Mays. Good gosh, what a ballplayer he was. You just loved to watch him play. He played with the exuberance and the excitement of a kid on a sandlot. He was a delightful ballplayer. Toward the end of his career, I thought he hung on maybe a couple of years too long. He should have stopped sooner, but I guess the money was starting to get better, salaries were starting to get a little bit better, and maybe he stayed on for that. He made that incredible catch in the 1954 World Series. He hit 660 home runs, but I'm sure if he'd played in a different type of ballpark than Candlestick Park, he'd have hit 800. Willie was an all-around player, one of those five-tool guys. He could steal a base, run, hit, throw, everything. But when I was managing the Cubs, I detected a slight flaw in Willie's playing. He wasn't throwing all that well, so I assumed he had a sore arm. I had my Cubs run on him quite a bit. But that's no big crime, because it happens to the best of them. Of all the ballplayers that you would ever want on a ball club, it would be Willie Mays. It's still very difficult to pick the greatest center fielder of the modern era, what with DiMaggio, Mantle, and Duke Snider there as well.

I remember quite a bit about Duke Snider, including Branch Rickey's teaching him how to hit. He was a great player, the Duke of Flatbush. Duke was a fun-loving type of guy, but he had an arrogance the way smooth water runs deep. He would rise to the occasion. And he *knew* he was going to rise to the occasion. Who was the best center fielder in New York in the 1950s, Mantle, Mays, or Snider? That debate will go on for a long time. Imagine them all in the same outfield. Managers dream about having such an outfield. I had a conversation with Duke when we were casting his hands for Hitters' Hands. He said that he would have to stand there with a bat in his hands, when the pitcher would be warming up, and watch the pitches and have to call each pitch as a strike or a ball. When I told him we'd done Pee Wee Reese's hands, Duke said, "Well, why didn't you do his 'pud'? He was a 'pud' guy." That means he was more of a fielder than a hitter. Duke said, "That little old pud! That would make a great thing. You didn't make him as a hitter, did you?" I said, "Oh, yes." Duke wanted me to rub that in to Pee Wee the next time I saw him.

The late Eddie Mathews was one tough guy. He played tough. He was arrogant in such a way as to say, "Listen, we're going to beat you; you're not going to beat me; you're not going to run over me." He played that way. I never saw it, just hearsay, but they say he tagged Frank Robinson pretty hard one time, and Frank got up and said something about how hard Eddie was tagging. The way I heard it, Eddie belted him one and said, "How do you like that tag?" He had the best short stroke of any hitter I guess I've ever seen. He just took the bat from here to there and—boom—that was all he needed. Eddie was very strong, and he played all the time. I imagine he played the full season almost every year. I was instrumental in getting Eddie a position with the Oakland A's when I was there. He grew up in Texarkana, where I had played minor league ball. I asked him if I was his hero when I was there. Anytime you meet a guy like that, he always says, "Oh, you were my hero when I was a kid." Eddie said, "Heck, I don't even remember you."

I asked Eddie, "You're not only a pretty good hitter, but a great hitter, and a great home run hitter. What guy gave you the most trouble?" He said, "That damn Marichal." I said, "Why?" He said, "He had about seven different pitches, seven or eight or ten. He got every one over. I never could figure him out, and he drove me crazy. He'd throw that little screw ball, and then he'd throw that slider, and then he'd throw that sinker, and then he'd throw four or five different change-up speeds on all of his pitches, and he had a hell of a curve. And he threw that foot way up there. You watched that foot go up, and you're not watching the ball. He drove me crazy."

Roberto Clemente was truly an all-around ballplayer. He could do everything. He was a tremendous fielder, probably one of the finest right fielders of all time. If you were to name three or four of the top right fielders, you'd have to put Clemente right there with them. He had the best arm I'd ever seen. At Forbes Field, he played that right-field wall like a magician, fielding the caroms and holding runners to singles. He was a national hero in Puerto Rico. He was going to join a club in 1965, when I was down there managing in San Juan, but then I left, so I didn't get to see him play in his home country. He'd come down and play some games. He was always in good shape. He was not the type of athlete to get out of condition. I think he could walk off the field after a full season and come back in spring training and pick up right where he left off. It's a terrible shame he died so young in that plane crash. He was in a class by himself.

Harmon Killebrew had difficulty getting started in his career. I think he was up and down several times with the Senators. In fact, I believe one year he was out of the organization. But he got straightened out and became one of the most feared right-handed hitters in baseball. Oh, tremendous! He was consistent, and he hit them a long way. Harmon was a big bull of a guy, thick through the chest, big broad shoulders, might have been a little bit musclebound. Killebrew was the Angus bull that was in charge of the whole herd. When he walked out on the field, it was as if to say, "I'm Harmon Killebrew. Get out of my way." I talked to him here not too many years ago. He was going over to Japan to get into a home run–hitting contest that they have over there in the Japanese leagues. I saw him after he came back, and I said, "Hey, Harmon, how did you do in that home run–hitting contest?" He said, "You know, they put the dead balls in for me to hit." Whether it was the truth or not, I don't know. But Harmon's a delight, a completely class guy. I kind of wish I could have had nine guys like him on the ball club.

Carl Yastrzemski was one of the topnotch players in the game. When I first saw Yaz, he was fooling around at shortstop. I believe he played shortstop in the low minors. I managed against him when he was at Minneapolis, the Red Sox farm club in the American Association. Man, he was a good hitter. And he turned out to be an outstanding left fielder. He could field the ball, charge the ball, and throw you out. He played that left-field wall at Fenway as well as anybody in the history of the Red Sox. He's a true Hall of Famer, and a Triple Crown winner too, one of the few guys to win that honor. In 1967 he carried the Red Sox on his back into the World Series, hitting something like .555 down the homestretch. He had a bit of a personality quirk, I guess. He was very quiet, kind of reserved. He was another guy that I would say had that good, competitive arrogance. I don't know if there are enough various adjectives for me to describe these guys, but he had competitive arrogance. He knew he was good. He knew he was a good hitter, and he showed it. Boy, I loved that. He had the walk, too, kind of a cocky walk. I would think that maybe Yaz might have been a pretty good manager.

Joe Morgan is another great Hall of Famer. He was a truly fine competitor. He played hard. He was a little guy, and they thought little guys couldn't play. But he was a giant when he had that bat in his hand. Joe was a natural-born leader and a very astute ballplayer. He was greatly underrated with Houston until he got over to Cincinnati with the Big Red Machine. I was instrumental in his going from Houston to Cincinnati. I was asked about it, and I said go make the trade. Years later, when we were doing his hands for Hitters' Hands, I told him about that. He said, "Thanks!" I said, "You're welcome." He said, "It's the best thing that happened." Houston wasn't exactly a good place for hitters. The ball didn't go out there. Morgan could do everything. He played in several All-Star Games. He hit home runs, 27 one year, 268 for his career, quite a few for a second baseman. He drove in runs and stole 689 bases. And what a fielder! If you had nine Joe Morgans on your ball club, you'd could sleepwalk through the season. He's a good television announcer. He analyzes things, he can predict plays, and he can be critical in a good way. He discusses the options a manager has and lets you decide.

Frank Robinson was another automatic Hall of Famer. He was a great ballplayer, a devastating hitter. I saw him in the minors, in an A league, and I saw him on the major league level. But I don't know whether he had enough managerial experience to be a successful manager. I think he was thrown into managing real quickly without much training. He's an intelligent guy. You have to be intelligent to be a good hitter like he was. I think if Frank had gone down and managed maybe one or two or three years, started out low, say in an A league and a Double-A league and a Triple-A league, and had some pretty good ballplayers, I think he would have been an outstanding manager. But he was a little overmatched because he didn't have experience, and he was learning on the job. That learning process in the big leagues is tough.

Willie McCovey played at Phoenix when I managed in the Coast League. He was a long, tall, lanky kid, who looked like the uniform hung on him. By the next year he came in there, he had grown. He was a murderous hitter. Willie hit balls out of their little Phoenix stadium regularly, and although they said it wasn't very far, he hit them over the light tower, and they were still going up when they cleared the tower. Man, I hated to see him coming up when the Cubs played the Giants. If there was a base to put him on where he wouldn't count, I'd always have him walked. He was a good choice for the Hall of Fame. His 521 home runs puts him in the 500–home run club. He was a good guy and a good ballplayer. He did everything well.

Orlando Cepeda deserved to get in the Hall of Fame, even if it took too long. I was involved in that trade that got him for the Cardinals from the Giants. Bob Howsam asked me about him, a general manager asking a scout for the appraisal. I said, "This guy will give you two of the best years you've ever seen. And then maybe you're going to have to trade him, because he kind of sloughs off a little bit, tapers off after the third year." Bob made the trade. Cepeda came over, became an MVP, and the Cardinals won the pennant with him. Some years later, they got back Ray Sadecki, who they traded to the Giants. So that was a pretty good trade by Bob Howsam. Cepeda's vote into the Hall of Fame was delayed by his arrest for drugs, but, heck, he lived it down and cleaned himself up. He hit .297 with a lot of RBI and 379 home runs. He was a pretty good fielder and a great clutch hitter too. Yeah, he was a threat at the plate. He'd battle you every at bat.

Tony Perez's induction into the Hall of Fame also was long overdue. Tony got a bad deal at Cincinnati as a manager. They released him too soon, before he had a chance. That was terrible. I can't forgive Marge Schott for that. I went through it at Kansas City. I know what it feels like. Tony was a man who dedicated his whole career to the club. He was outstanding not only as a ballplayer but as a citizen and a tremendous leader for the club. He was a great help to the organization with Latino ballplayers. They all looked up to him, and he guided them. Tony had the stats all along, 1,652 RBI, and although he hit only 279 home runs, that's not bad for playing all those years in a ballpark not exactly conducive to home run hitters.

I saw the late Willie Stargell play when I scouted the Pirates. He was a tremendous ballplayer, a Hall of Famer, no question, and a fine man too. Everything about him was classy. He had that trademark windmill thing he did with the bat, which probably intimidated a lot of pitchers. I had seen Jim Russell do that twirling motion too, but Willie got a bit more out of his, 475 home runs, and he'd put a charge into them, sometimes clear out of the ballpark.

I saw Bob Gibson pitch with the Cardinals. What a fast, strong pitcher he was even then! You could see that this guy was going to be a tremendous athlete. I've seen a few pitchers in my time who seemed to put every ounce of energy, every ounce of strength they had, into pitching. That's the way Bob Gibson impressed me. He could do everything. He was a tough competitor. This would be a tough question to answer, but if I had one game that I had to win, I believe Bob Gibson would be the guy that I would put out there. I mean this without slighting anybody. He's still a fierce competitor. I heard that at some fantasy camp a few years ago, some hotshot athlete fan came up, and Bob struck him out on three pitches and said, "Come back in fifteen years, and I'll strike you out again." I'm glad to see that he's back in baseball as a pitching coach.

Fergie Jenkins, gee, what a pitcher. He had great pitches. They gave him a little bum rap there toward the end of his career about the marijuana arrest, but he became a good pitching coach. Look at his record. He had a bunch of good years, with Cubs clubs that weren't very good either. He was tough. I'm delighted that he's back in the game, because he had some terrible things happen personally with the loss of people close to him. I wish him nothing but the best. I've associated with him a little bit in the horse business. He had a place down in Oklahoma—Guthrie, I believe it was. We talked horses with him several times.

Don Drysdale was a joy to watch. I would catch him pitching every once in a while at some ballpark. I saw him one time in Chicago. Boy, he intimidated me in the stands. And I saw him pitching again against the Giants. You could hear Willie Mays hollering because Drysdale said the inside of the plate was his, that if the batter encroached on that he's at his own mercy. I don't know if Drysdale would deliberately hit a guy. Don was a fine announcer for the Expos. He was very interested in the Hitters' Hands project, very interested in doing the pitchers' pitching hands in bronze. We were going to do it. Don sat discussing it with me for an hour and a half in the press room at Mile High Stadium. He said that the next time he came in with the Expos, we'd go ahead and try it. He was delighted about doing it. But I never saw him again. He died a few days before he was scheduled to be back in Denver. But he was one tough pitcher. If you had guys like him, you could coast.

Gaylord Perry definitely loaded up the pitches. He was one of the first cheaters, if you want to call it that. Or maybe I should call them magicians, because you never knew where it was coming from, how they got it. He threw quite a few of those spitters. He was a magician because you never could find the ball. He was a good pitcher, though, real tough, with 314 victories.

They didn't call Nolan Ryan "The Express" for nothing. He holds the record for the most strikeouts of all time. He pitched many years. Why can't young pitchers with great potential take a lesson from him? Here's a man who lasted all those years, well into his forties, and still pitched—and pitched well. I'm sure he had some aches and pain with his arm in his career, but how did he last that long? I'd like to have him write a book or pamphlet on his conditioning program. Let everybody in baseball read it. Nolan was on some clubs that weren't any good, so his career winning percentage seems lower than it should be. If you'd put Nolan Ryan on a Yankees ball club or a Cincinnati ball club, he might have won 30 ball games in a season. But even great pitchers lose games now and then, especially if they don't get run support. And a mediocre pitcher can give up a bunch of walks and hits and runs and still win because his team hit for him.

Mike Schmidt probably had one of the most solid batting stances I've seen in a long time. He made it into the Hall of Fame, deservingly so. He rates with the finest. In addition to being a great slugger, he was a great fielder too, one of the best ever at his position, right up there close to Brooks Robinson. Somewhere Schmidt picked up the rap that sometimes he wasn't a team player, that he just played for his stats, but I think that's a bum rap. I guess every ballplayer who ever put on a pair of spikes played for his stats on occasion. Some ballplayers were better when they played for themselves, and they contributed a heck of a lot to the ball game. I don't see how you can fault a guy who's playing for stats if he's up there trying to hit a home run maybe to make his home run total better. He's driving in runs and putting his team ahead.

I watched Robin Yount as he played with Milwaukee. He played his whole career with one ball club. He's an outstanding Hall of Fame guy. I was glad to see him go into the hall the first year he was eligible. He was a great team ballplayer, a great clutch ballplayer. He made the transition from shortstop to center field very successfully. He was just a fine all-around ballplayer.

The Hall of Fame's criteria and method of selecting players needs to be revised. I don't think players should campaign for induction. They should earn it. Some guys campaign for it so openly it's sort of embarrassing when they don't get in. They shouldn't make a former player wait for five years or longer when the Veterans Committee might pick him. They should induct some guys now, while they're still playing or managing. There are a lot of guys who should be in the Hall of Fame while they're still around. For example, Nellie Fox finally got in the Hall of Fame, but unfortunately he wasn't around to enjoy that. I think baseball is being a little old-fashioned there, failing to take advantage of these living legends. I've mentioned it a time or two in conversation with different baseball people, but never to one of the guys on the Veterans Committee. I've been asked several times about ballplayers, and I remarked on their qualifications for the Hall.

So I think they ought to restructure that and come up with some new rules or new guidelines for the Hall of Fame. They're missing a tremendous amount of goodwill. Playing for twenty years shouldn't be one of the big factors. Hitting shouldn't be the biggest criterion for the Hall of Fame.

Although I'm partial to hitters, I definitely believe that they should expand the Hall at Cooperstown and put in a division for the fielders too. Thus Bill Mazeroski deserved his selection to the Hall of Fame. There has to be a place for the great fielders, the guys who saved games with their gloves. Maz will always be remembered for the home run he hit to win the 1960 World Series, but his biggest contribution was his work at second base. Handling the double play can be as important as or more important than what the guy hits. And Mazeroski did it for seventeen years. Rocky Colavito might rate a look for Cooperstown on account of his defense, especially his throwing arm. Oh, what a rifle arm he had. Holy smoke!

Speaking of defense, Ozzie Smith probably invented the game of short-stop. When they called him "The Wizard of Oz," it was the perfect description of that guy. He made plays that you'd never seen before. I'm glad I wasn't the guy at San Diego who negotiated the trade with St. Louis and gave up Ozzie for Gary Templeton. Ozzie is going into the Hall of Fame one of these years, no question about it, with a glove. He's going to pave the way for more great defensive players.

As a scout and a manager and a player and a player evaluator for many years on the major league level, I consider Davey Concepcion of the Cincinnati Reds one of the finest shortstops who ever played. He's greatly underrated. He could do everything. He was outstanding as a fielder. He had a great arm and great range, played a long time, and wasn't a bad hitter. Davey hit .306 one year and .301 another. He had some power. Sure, he didn't hit as many home runs as Bench or Morgan or Perez did, but there have been very few great clubs that didn't have a great shortstop. If you don't have one, you've got a three-legged horse. A horse with three sound legs can run only as fast as that bad leg will permit. Oh, you might stumble through, if you've got four guys who can hit all those home runs. Concepcion was essential to the Big Red Machine. He should be in the Hall of Fame. In Venezuela he was and still is a national hero, right along with Luis Aparicio and Andres Galarraga. As a scout, I recommended him to the Dodgers. I told them that if they ever got a chance to make a trade for him, snap him up.

I think there ought to be room for specialists now in the Hall of Fame, especially the designated hitters and pinch hitters. There are quite a few of them. Manny Mota had the most career pinch hits, at one time, until somebody surpassed him. Jerry Lynch had a lot of pinch hits. Rusty Staub was a young guy when he came up with Houston and was an instant hit. He was a likable guy and a good ballplayer. He was a good pinch hitter and designated hitter and has some pretty strong credentials. Rusty played for twenty-three years. I would have to say that he should get strong consideration for the Hall of Fame, more so than what he's getting. He would be one of Houston's first guys in the Hall. They should take a good look at him.

Jimmy Reese probably won't get in the Hall of Fame, but there should be some special recognition there for his being the player and coach in uniform for the longest period of years. He spent more decades in uniform than any man in the history of baseball. He was the guy I was hoping to catch. Jimmy Reese was one of the truly fine men of baseball, a legend if ever I met one. He remembered everybody, and he was gracious to everybody. He was an absolute magician with a fungo bat. He could "throw" batting practice by hitting the ball with a fungo bat for a strike. He was absolutely remarkable and a joy and a delight. His other claim to fame was that when he was a young guy with the Yankees, he roomed with Babe Ruth or, stated better, with Babe's bags. I asked him once, "Hey, Jim, is that correct? Did you room with Babe?" He said, "Yeah, I had never seen him before." Somebody would get the bags up to the room, and Babe might check in briefly, and that's the last Jimmy would see of him that night. How true the stories are, I'm not sure, because as the years go by, they get bigger. But Jimmy said, "Yeah, I roomed with his bags."

I think they should take more ballplayers from the Latin American countries. In the same way that the Hall of Fame committee has voted for putting some Negro League baseball players in the Hall, they should consider some great Mexican League players who didn't play in the American major leagues. I have a couple of candidates right away. Mala Torres, whom I played with in Mazatlan in 1947, should be one. He never did play in the big leagues, but he was an outstanding ballplayer in Mexico in the winter and summer leagues down there. Moy Camacho is another one. I don't have the exact figures, but I believe he had 2,100 to 2,200 hits down there, as an infielder. I played against him many years ago too. Dennis Martinez, the Nicaraguan pitcher, pitched well into his forties and won a lot of ball games. He is a national hero in his home country and probably deserves a shot at Cooperstown. Dodgers pitcher Fernando Valenzuela should be in the Hall of Fame from the country of Mexico. If I were on the committee, I'd be the first one to vote for him. He was a big attraction for the fans, and he was a winning pitcher, a clutch pitcher, and everything that you'd want from a ballplayer. Aurelio Rodriguez, the longtime Tigers third baseman, was another pretty good ballplayer. He had an outstanding arm. He'd throw the ball on a line all the way from third to first, and it wouldn't dip a bit. Aurelio should be in the Mexican baseball hall of fame, if there is one, and maybe even in Cooperstown. He played seventeen years in the major leagues. He was a good, steady ballplayer all along. Andres Galarraga and Vinny Castilla, if they can put together some more years like the ones they had with the Rockies, might be good candidates down the road. And while they're at it, I think maybe some Japanese ballplayers should be in the Hall of Fame. Good gosh, Sadaharu Oh hit over 800 home runs! They say the fences weren't very far, but he hit them and nobody else did. Put him in the Hall!

Although I know I'll never get in the Hall of Fame as a manager, it has cheered me to see some more recent managers get inducted. As I mentioned earlier, it was totally appropriate for the Hall to choose Tommy Lasorda while he can still be an ambassador for baseball. Earl Weaver certainly deserved his induction too. As a manager who got tossed from a few ball games myself and scuffled with an umpire or two, I was happy to see them select Weaver. Earl was a banty rooster taking on the big rooster in the yard and running him off. Everybody remembers him for his feistiness, but Earl was a downright good manager too. Look at all those pennants he brought home to Baltimore. He handled Jim Palmer as fine as any manager ever handled a player, right into the Hall of Fame. Handling your ballplayers is a big job for managers, because you have all those different personalities, from different backgrounds and different educations. Earl was another one of those guys who never got a shot at the big leagues but who knew baseball and talent when he saw it.

I sat with Leo Durocher several times in my scouting travels. I ran into him once in Amarillo, Texas. What he was doing down there I don't know, but I ran into him. We spent an evening chatting together. I said, "Leo, you should be in the Hall of Fame." He said, "Well, Charlie, a lot of people think so, and I think I do too. I've done a lot for baseball, but if they put me in after I'm gone, I don't want it." Leo died before the Hall selected him in 1994. I also met up with him one year when he was managing the Cubs. He told me, "Charlie, you got to be tough with players. I would sooner be disliked by a player because I drove him to be a better ballplayer than be liked by him."

I was very pleased to see Sparky Anderson elected to the Hall of Fame. As I mentioned earlier, I was somewhat responsible for Sparky's getting the managing job at Cincinnati. He had his own style. He was called "Captain Hook" because he went out and got his pitchers out in a hurry. A manager who was a pitcher is prone to live the situation with his pitchers and will give them one more hitter. I felt that Lasorda was that way when he first started. But Tommy became an excellent manager. There's some controversy that Sparky had all those great players and they made him look real good as the manager. But Sparky had control of things. One thing that he did I thought was outstanding. He had three captains, Johnny Bench, Tony Perez, and Joe Morgan. They helped the manager out, especially when relating to other players in their racial groups. Sparky was a superb manager. When he had good talent, he won. When he didn't have good talent, he didn't win. He was one of the first guys to start platooning his players, and he made that a science. He knew how to handle the press. I think he became a little bit of an "I" man, but heck, how can you criticize him? He was very successful. He took teams in both leagues to World Championships. He was another guy who didn't play much in the major leagues but became an outstanding manager.

There still are a few other managers who deserve a place in the Hall of Fame. I mentioned earlier that Billy Martin should be in there. So should Whitey Herzog and Dick Williams. Whitey Herzog was one of the truly shrewd talent evaluators of baseball. He was very outspoken. It got him in trouble, I guess, in Kansas City. He didn't hit it off with Muriel Kauffman. He should have been there a long time. I kidded him about it after he left Kansas City and went to the Angels. I said, "Then you go out to California and you've got another woman, Mrs. Autry, telling you want to do. Whitey, you don't have a way with women, yet you've got two." He said, "Yeah, they're two of the wealthiest women in the business. Don't know a thing about baseball, but they want to tell you how to do your job." But he was a good manager in Kansas City, even though he was hogtied. Whitey had his mind set on what he wanted to do. He didn't take any interference from anybody in anything.

Dick Williams was a very aggressive manager. Boy, if you played for him, you had to do everything right. Williams was a very tough guy. As a player, he had somewhat limited abilities; he never could quite put it all together. But he was a competitor and a very intelligent man. He didn't fool around as a manager. He ran a tight ship. Sometimes ballplayers resent that even when you win and you make them better. I can't see why a ballplayer would feel that way, but some do. Dick Williams brought the ballplayers up a step or two and won with them. They should have known and appreciated that more. Dick should probably go into the Hall of Fame for the job he did with all those clubs. He was arrogant about it. He was good, he knew it, and he showed it. But he was a winner.

There have been a few good general managers put into the Hall of Fame. I never got to chat with Branch Rickey, but I listened to some of his oratory, some of his speeches at the major and minor league meetings. He really put it on. I saw him wring his cap and cry crocodile tears as he was describing something. He had that old cap, and he'd just wind that up. We called him "The Deacon," I guess because he wore that bow tie and that old hat. He could mesmerize you in speech. I met and associated with a lot of people who worked for Rickey, such as Al Campanis. I think Al tried to imitate him. Rickey's plan for a third major league, in the late 1950s, the Continental League, was a deciding factor, I believe, for Denver's getting the Broncos football team. And I believe Rickey was instrumental in Bob Howsam's getting the Cardinals general manager job. Branch was a good man, a great innovator, and a great teacher.

Lee MacPhail, a tremendous baseball man, has been inducted. He did a lot of everything in baseball. Of course, he's the son of Larry McPhail, and his young son, Andy, is general manager with the Chicago Cubs. Lee was an absolutely astute baseball man. He did a great job everyplace he had ever been. I worked kind of close to him when I managed Vancouver, and we had sort of an unofficial working agreement with Baltimore. We got a lot of their ballplayers out there. Lee was a fine choice for the Hall of Fame. Pat Gillick and John Schuerholz would also be strong candidates for the Hall as general managers.

They should also have a wing or a room for the great minor league general managers. A. Ray Smith, who I worked for at Tulsa, is typical of these grass-roots guys who should be considered and honored. He was a tremendous baseball guy. They shouldn't always have only the big leaguers in the Hall of Fame. But Bob Howsam should be in the Hall of Fame for his minor league accomplishments as well his service in the majors. I really enjoyed working for Bob. We stay in touch to this day, and I really enjoy going to the ball games with him. If you're an ex-manager, an ex-scout, an ex-baseball guy, you never lose your skill of watching the pitchers. Bob claimed that I was one of the best pitching scouts in the country. I knew pitchers very well. I've seen thousands of them, made thousands of moves with pitchers in my time. Bob built that great Big Red Machine dynasty of the 1970s that ranks up there with the greatest ball clubs of all time. Bob was extremely good at trades. He always got what he wanted. Very seldom did he give up anything that he didn't want to give up. He did it with shrewdness and knowledge and the good people that he had. He was a great believer in a good scouting system. To this day, I can't understand some of these organizations that keep crying about being small market

clubs and wanting welfare handed out to them. Heck, Cincinnati didn't
have a great amount of money or finances. When Bob went there, they
built a new stadium, Riverfront Stadium, and got out of the old ballpark.
He built an organization that nobody wanted to leave. They were loyal to
him. He treated his people well. It's a great injustice that Bob Howsam and
a lot of these tremendous baseball executives aren't in Cooperstown.

They've put several fine umpires in the Hall of Fame, but I think they're
missing at least one—Gus Donatelli. I've already talked about Augie's
playing career, time as a prisoner of war, and how he started umpiring.
But I want to reinforce here my belief that he should be in the Hall. He
was an excellent umpire. He umped all those years, took no guff from
anybody—even me—and developed that sort of crouching style when he
umped behind the plate. I called him "Gus." He said, "Call me Augie."
I said, "Oh, now you're a big league umpire, I can't call you Gus?" I am
starting a campaign right here and now to get Augie inducted into the Hall.

There's been a bunch of great announcers they've put in that special wing
in the Hall of Fame. I've talked about a couple I knew. I guess I could say
that I was also a very good friend of Harry Caray, the great sportscaster. We
met many times on the road, when I was scouting, when he was doing the
Cardinals games or the White Sox games. He worked a year out there with
Oakland and, of course, for a long time with the Cubs. I enjoyed him very
much. I thought that he and Steve Stone were an excellent combination.
I always thought that a former player and a nonplayer could make great
combinations. Harry was one of the top baseball announcers. He was great.
I even enjoyed his mispronouncing names. Out in Oakland, they tried to
program Harry, but that didn't work. You turn him loose, and he does a heck
of a job for you. Harry was very good with the White Sox too. I don't know
if there was something personal with the front office or what happened
to cause him to leave. The Cubs fans took to him immediately. They just
embraced him. They felt like they stole something from the White Sox.

But there are still some more players, old-timers and those who played
more recently, who are undeservedly missing from the Hall. Joe Gordon
is one. Joe was a tremendous clutch ballplayer. He always played to beat
you. He was a silent leader with his play-making abilities. He made the
impossible plays. Joe was an acrobat in college, and his athleticism always
showed on the field.

Jim Kaat maybe should go in the Hall of Fame. He had 283 wins. I guess
they're looking for guys who had 300 or more wins. But gee whiz, Dizzy
Dean didn't have 300, and who would argue against Diz's being in the Hall?
Kaat deserves definite consideration for the Hall. And he's young enough

now to be a really good ambassador for baseball. Dwight Evans is another guy who should get in. No one in the history of the Red Sox played right field as well as he did. He played a long time, hit pretty well, and had a cannon for an arm. Tony Oliva was a real good, solid ballplayer. He was one of the first guys that I saw who could swing at bad balls and hit them. I saw him in spring training before he came up, and I made a report on him. Somebody laughed at me on that and said that he'd never hit because he was a wild swinger. But Tony made contact a lot. He had a pretty good lifetime batting average at .304. Is he a Hall of Famer? He's pretty close, so they ought to give him consideration.

To this day, I believe that Roger Maris should be in the Hall of Fame. He hit a lot of other home runs, and he broke a longstanding record. He didn't do it cheaply. Maris held the single-season home run record longer than Ruth held it, all the way until Mark McGwire and Sammy Sosa broke it in 1998. He drove in a lot of runs and was the American League MVP two years in a row. I think I had something to do with Roger Maris's coming over the St. Louis Cardinals. Bob Howsam was the general manager of St. Louis at the time. I came out of New York, where the fans were booing Maris. I can't imagine why they would boo a ballplayer like him. He was a good player. He had a good arm. He always played hard and hustled, but I guess because he broke Ruth's record, they never forgave him. Bob asked me about Maris. I said, "Well, Bob, Maris is a great ballplayer. He does everything great, and he's not old. Can you get him?" He said, "Yes." I said, "Who do you have to give up for him?" Bob said, "Charlie Smith." I said, "Charlie Smith?" He said, "Yes." I said, "Well, make the trade." He said, "Yeah, Charlie, he's got a salary of seventy-five thousand dollars a year." I said, "Hell, Bob, nobody's got to know about the salary. You don't want to reveal the salary. Trade for him. That'll be one of the greatest trades you'll ever make." And it turned out to be. Roger Maris helped the Cardinals win two pennants.

Pete Rose was one of my favorite bumblebees. He couldn't run. He was the worst-looking runner I'd ever seen. He couldn't throw, and he couldn't field. He looked like he was swatting flies, and he couldn't hit home runs. At the plate, he'd get up there with that terrible-looking stance, humped over and everything else, he'd swing a bat, and he'd get a base hit. He had none of the tools individually. Yet he put it all together, and all he did was beat you, hitting, running, and stealing bases. He played like his pants were on fire all the time. He ran down to first on walks. Buddy Peterson did that for me at Vancouver, and then Pete Rose did it on the major league level. When they called him "Charlie Hustle," they meant it. He played outfield, third base, first base, and second base. He was always in the ball game. In my mind, Pete Rose should be in the Hall of Fame for his baseball abilities. Many former and current ballplayers have had problems. They've got to put him in the Hall of Fame on his baseball record. I don't know how good a manager Pete was, but I don't care about that. I don't know if he ever admitted gambling or not. There have always been some forms of gambling in baseball. Some players used to have a pool on who was going to get hits and who wasn't. With Rose, it's a matter of degree. If he did gamble on his own team while he was managing, then they should keep him out. But if he didn't, then put him in right away.

Eddie Murray and André Dawson should go into the Hall of Fame. Eddie's going to be rated with the top switch hitters in baseball. If I were to pick, I would rate him number two, right behind Mickey Mantle. I think Mantle was the greatest of them all, but Eddie's a pretty doggone close second. But he's got that rap that he wouldn't talk to the media. Somewhere along the line, I guess a writer wrote some unfair things or got on a ballplayer too much, and he just closed up. Eddie's one of them apparently. I saw it happen with Alex Johnson. California writers just gave him a terrible roasting, yet he won the batting championship. Maybe some writers want the player to give them a story, something sensational, and the guy has a bad day and doesn't feel like it. He's not in the mood. Some guys are just quiet. They don't like to talk. They let their bat and abilities do the talking. I saw André Dawson when he played the outfield with Ellis Valentine and Warren Cromartie in Denver, when the Bears had a working agreement with the Montreal Expos. Dawson was a tremendous talent. Wow! I would say he's pretty close to getting in the Hall of Fame. He's got over 400 home runs. He could do everything, steal bases, play the outfield well, all of it. And Goose Gossage has got to go into the Hall of Fame on his first try. Man, he made a lot of managers look good, I'll tell you. He was a rapid worker—give me the ball, bang, give me the ball, bang, give me the ball, bang. He's a surefire Hall of Famer.

Some current pitchers have a good chance at induction. If Roger Clemens continues to pitch as well as he has in the past, he has to be considered very strongly for the Hall of Fame. He's an overpowering pitcher. His postseason pitching this past year should reinforce his candidacy. He should have some successful years ahead of him if his arm holds up. Greg Maddux of the Braves will definitely go into the Hall. I think over the past few years he's been in a league of his own, a step above everybody. He looks like he's in a daze when he's pitching, but his concentration is fantastic. He knows what he's doing, and I think, if I were to say it as a manager watching pitchers, that he knows every pitch to every ballplayer in that lineup, what he's going to do and where he's going do it. And he does it, which makes him that good.

One guy who probably won't make the Hall of Fame, even though he hit over 400 home runs, is Dave Kingman. Everybody gave Kingman a bad time. He wasn't a graceful ballplayer, and he was a college guy. But some ballplayers don't want to be talked to. Some ballplayers are silent, like Charlie Gehringer; he'd say "hello" in the spring and "good-bye" in the fall. Kingman was kind of a private person, but, boy, he could hit those home runs. He was surly with the press. The press can get to you once in a while. I've had many a young writer ask me, after I'd pulled some outlandish play in a game that worked and we'd won the game, "What would you have done if it wouldn't have worked?" I believe that they would ask Kingman questions like that, and he would get a little disturbed with the reporters and just ignore them. But he could hit. He had 442 home runs. We should have had him in Kansas City. If only Lou Gorman hadn't called up Jack Schwartz at the Giants and said that we were going to take Kingman first! The Giants took him instead. So we lost him because our front office wanted to look good and tell everybody who we were going to pick.

Regarding Cal Ripken Jr., I hope he didn't become obsessed with the streak of consecutive games played. It wouldn't have been bad if he had finished second behind Gehrig. That's the only time that I feel I would have accepted second. What he did even before breaking the record was in itself a tremendous accomplishment. I was glad he didn't get hurt, that he broke the record, and then decided by himself when to give it up. But I worried whether or not he was still an asset to his team. Sometimes you just hate to say anything about a guy. Maybe he's not moving as well as he did, not covering as much ground as he used to. But in 1991, Cal hit 34 home runs, had 114 RBI, and led the league in fielding at shortstop, which wasn't bad for a guy his size. Eventually the Orioles moved him over to third base. As long as he can make the plays, then it doesn't harm the ball club. He's better at that than a lot of guys because of his experience. Put him in the Hall of Fame today. He's one of the best role models baseball has going for it. Showcase him to all the fans.

I'm going to end this chapter with a bit of controversy. I'm going to pick an all-time black team, an all-time Latino team, and an all-time white team. I don't mean this to be in any way racist. As I've said before, I've always looked at the ballplayer first and not his race. But just to generate a little hot stove talk, a little something for the baseball purist, here are my three teams. You can argue over these choices till the cows come home. These are all composed of guys who I saw play or manage. I'm probably going to get somebody upset at me, but here goes.

I'll start out with the all-time black team. Roy Campanella would be the catcher. Willie McCovey would be at first base. Joe Morgan would be at second base. Ernie Banks would be the shortstop. Bill Madlock would be the third baseman. In the outfield, I'd have Frank Robinson in left, Willie Mays in center, and Hank Aaron in right field. For starting pitchers, my staff would include Vida Blue, Bob Gibson, Dave Stewart, Doc Gooden, and Fergie Jenkins. Satchel Paige would be on this team too, because I saw him play. Lee Smith would be the reliever. The reserves—or, more accurately, the additional men—would be Frank White, Ozzie Smith, Reggie Jackson, Tony Gwynn, Eddie Murray, Billy Williams, Lou Brock, Willie Horton, Vada Pinson, Amos Otis, and Rickey Henderson. The manager would be Dusty Baker. That's my all-time black squad. I didn't pick them for left- or right-handed hitters. I picked them from the players that I have seen.

For the all-time Latino team, the catcher would be Pudge Rodriguez. Either Andres Galarraga or Tony Perez would be at first base. Rod Carew would be at second base. Davey Concepcion would be the shortstop. Aurelio Rodriguez would be at third base. In the outfield, Minny Minoso would be in left, Felipe Alou in center, and Roberto Clemente in right. The pitchers would be Fernando Valenzuela, Juan Marichal, Pedro Martinez, Dennis Martinez, Mike Cuellar, Camilo Pascual, Mike Garcia, and Luis Tiant. Tippy Martinez and Mariano Rivera would be the relievers. The additional players would be Roberto Alomar, Julian Javier, Luis Aparicio, Bert Campaneris, and Manny Mota. Either Al Lopez or Lou Piniella would be the manager.

For the all-white team, the catcher would be Johnny Bench. Stan Musial would be at first base. Bobby Doerr would be at second base. Lou Boudreau would be the shortstop. Brooks Robinson would hold down third base. In the outfield, Ted Williams would be in left, Joe DiMaggio in center, and Mickey Mantle in right, although you could just as easily switch DiMaggio and Mantle. The pitchers would be Steve Carlton, Bob Feller, Warren Spahn, Don Drysdale, Sandy Koufax, Hal Newhouser, and Jim Bunning. Hoyt Wilhelm and Goose Gossage would be the relievers. The additional players would include Babe Ruth, Lou Gehrig, Jimmie Foxx, Yogi Berra, Red Schoendienst, Eddie Mathews, Al Kaline, and Pete Rose. Billy Martin would be the manager.

So there are my three all-time teams. I hope they stir up some friendly arguments, and may the best team win in a playoff and seven-game World Series.

FIFTEEN

I Dream of Baseball

Baseball has been great for me. If I had to do it all over again, I'd want to live another fifty years in baseball. But the 1994 strike was devastating. It crushed me. I don't want to sound like an old fogey or anything, but I believe a lot of the players spoke out of turn. A lot of them didn't have to take those vicious stands and criticize management and the owners that much. Then they tried to make up with them. The damage seemed like it had been done. I can't understand why they criticize the owners. After all, they're the people who put up the money and earn the right to make profits. Look at the risk connected with a franchise. But the players keep crying and making alibis. I don't see why they don't sign a sliding scale agreement: we make money if you make money. If you don't make money, we don't make money. It'd be very interesting to see then how many ballplayers would take their strong stands. It's a great life for them. Look where many of them come from, all walks of life. They can really accomplish something with their God-given talents and some abilities that they have to hone and improve. It's hard for me to accept such strikes when I think about the time when the player didn't have anything to lean on except possibly his abilities and his words.

Don't get me wrong—I'm not against the players or the union. I was on the ground floor when they first started up a union in the 1940s. I donated $250 for the two or three years that I was up there in the big leagues. I had been a union steward in the coal mines. A lot of the older ballplayers became bitter about the recent high salaries. I don't know exactly who they were, but I know that there were around eight or ten ballplayers, Hall of Fame ballplayers, that the commissioner was subsidizing out of his office because they were destitute. It has always disturbed me that baseball didn't take care of its old ballplayers better. For example, for years Ernie Lombardi was the press box custodian out at San Francisco, with the Giants at Candlestick.

That's the only kind of job that he could get. It didn't seem right. They should have treated him better. Some of the old ballplayers today resent the fact that the ballplayers are making so much. I don't resent the fact that they make a lot. The only thing that ticks me off is when they get out of the lineup. Maybe I would too if I were making a million dollars and I didn't want to end my career on a injury note and get cut off. I pride myself on the fact that I did not become bitter or against the modern-day ballplayers.

The players today make some of the greatest plays you have ever seen as if they were everyday plays. Perhaps it's too bad that I'm so hardnosed and old-fashioned, but I would like to see those guys play all the time. I hate to come to a ballpark and not see the best players. I like to see them play, because they're good. These guys are bigger and stronger. They swing a lighter bat, and they're pumping weights. They can really hit those balls. The players are also faster. I see more great plays now in a week than I would have seen in a month when I was playing and managing. I don't mind saying that. You'd watch a major league game back in the 1940s, the 1950s, and the 1960s, and you wouldn't see a great play. If you were lucky, you'd see one maybe once a week on the major league level. Now you see great plays every doggone day. The players are leaving their feet and diving, and they're going up over the wall and making sliding catches and everything. In my days in the major leagues, I saw only one ballplayer leave his feet, and that was Doc Cramer. He would slide on his knee on the grass and make a play. He'd get in front of the ball so that if he didn't quite zero in on it in real well, he could reach out and get it. But now they do it all the time.

But the players still have some way to go to reconcile the fans after that 1994 strike. They've seen what damage they did to attendance in the first three years after the 1994 strike. I've always been conscious of attendance. As a manager in the lower leagues, you'd try to do things to stir up a little dispute, a little agitation, to bring fans out. But I don't know that you can have that now. I think fights are always going to happen, but they seem to bring out the worst in the fans. Players are going to have to start producing. The best way to win the fans back is to play like heck. Don't give a fan any reason to criticize you. Play hard. Play tough. Do less talking and more producing. The fans will come back if you do that. Look how they applaud a great play, a diving play. But notice how quiet they become when a star doesn't do anything or loafs. That's still the basics of being a ballplayer. Produce! If you don't get a base hit, make a good play. If you don't make a good play, make a good running catch. If you don't do that, back up a play. Just do all those things that a fan would like to see instead of hearing all the griping. There's too much talking. Ballplayers now have alibis for everything. Some ballplayers lead the league in alibis. A guy says, "I need my outs. I need my innings. I need my swings." The best way to get your swings in a game is to produce. The best way to get your innings is to produce. Do the job. Keep quiet. If you're good, you'll get paid. If you're not good, you're still being paid, but you won't get paid as much.

The ballplayers now have to let their abilities do the talking, especially since they've been getting these real high salaries. If they don't produce, they'll run some guys out of town, and they'll run them out of the next town. I've seen it happen. One of these high-priced players is not going to get much fan sympathy by holding out these days. Back when Hank Greenberg would hold out, they admired him, because Hank was representing the working-class guy. It was the same way with Joe DiMaggio, and later when Koufax and Drysdale held out together. Everybody was for them. Now, the ballplayers have mutilated the goose that's laying that golden egg. Just signing a few autographs is not going to do it. The fans expect the good players to play, just like if you go to a Broadway show, you want to see the star, not a substitute. When you go to a ballpark, you want to see the stars of both teams, and you want to see them performing well. They've got to give the fans their dollars' worth.

I have mixed feelings about incentives in contracts. When I played at Mayfield in 1939, the Merit Clothing Company offered a linen suit to each player if we won the pennant. At that time, a suit included two pairs of pants and no vest. We won the pennant, and all the guys got a suit out of it. I picked the two pants, the tweed suit. But I don't know that I buy the idea of incentives in the big leagues. After all, you're being paid to drive in a run; you're being paid to get some hits. The club will now give a guy an extra hundred thousand dollars for an incentive if he plays 140 games. That's supposed to make the guy a little more determined to stay in shape and get over the injury more quickly. I think today's players are a little prone to get out of lineups too easy, so maybe those incentives are OK. But you're being paid to drive in 100 runs, you're being paid to play 162 games. Some of the incentives are ridiculous. But I would agree with some sorts of incentives, such as if you break a team record, a World Series record, or a major league record. Maybe some guy would come along and 5 five home runs.

I wasn't thrilled to see Rupert Murdoch take over the Dodgers. He said that he's a very greedy person, that he's money hungry, and that would escalate the salaries. I hated to see the O'Malley family get out. The Dodgers have lost a lot of the luster they had when I worked for them. I thought maybe there'd be another heir coming along who would carry along the tradition of the Dodgers. But that wasn't the case, and the O'Malley family sold the franchise. It may upset the balance of clubs in that division. But money talks. You can almost buy a pennant there with a lot of money. Look at the Florida Marlins in 1997 and the Yankees over the past few years.

There should be no subsidization of the weaker clubs, though. There are always going to be some strong clubs and some weak clubs. Sometimes what mattered was how big the organization was, how many farm clubs they had. The Cardinals and the Yankees always had large farm systems, which helped them in pennant runs. I don't think there will be true parity in baseball. There's always a last-place team. There's always a fifth-place team. There's always a winner, and there's always a loser. I don't think they'll ever get to the point where everything is equal. Bowie Kuhn thought that he could bring that about. But you can't do it when there's competition. There's always going to be bad ball clubs, poor organizations, poor management, poor scouting. And those clubs that are successful have got the best talent hunters, the best scouts and player evaluators. The money thing seems to be a crutch, an excuse. Get a good scouting department. Unfortunately the thinking is that you don't need scouts. But you do need them. You can't just read the stats out of the newspaper and scout players. You have to know whether a guy can fit in with the chemistry of your ball club, whether or not he does things that aren't in the stats. Heck, I've had ballplayers whose averages you couldn't find, but they were among the top three important ballplayers on the club. There are those intangible things that you can't read in the figures, and that's where the scouts come in.

I like good management and good, hustling ball clubs. Sometimes I'm ashamed when I go and see a ball club just go through the motions. You look at the clubs and the standings on the first of June, and there they are, clubs 7, 8, 9, or 10 games out of first place and people don't go to see them. You have to win, or at least look good losing. When you had a last-place club in the minor leagues that was hustling and beat the heck out of the top club, it made it interesting. You have to be up there contending all the time. You don't have to always win the pennant, but you sure can always be tough for three-quarters of the season.

The "welfare" clubs should get out there and get a good organization and work harder than the next guy. It can be done, it's been done, and it can be done now, even in today's baseball climate. The Cardinals, for example, put good teams on the field for years despite having smaller payrolls. I don't think the more successful clubs should subsidize other clubs because of their weakness or their inability to have a good organization. Heck, the next thing you know, the pitchers will have to pitch the ball where the hitters want it and what pitch the hitter wants. You'll start hearing, "You can't throw me the curve ball. I want a fastball."

It will be interesting to see what they do about geographical realignment. I'm afraid that you may see some clubs go bankrupt with the way the costs are, the salaries and everything. They're going to have to recharge some cities. Maybe more teams will swap leagues like Milwaukee did. That might be something to consider along the line. It's going to stir up a lot of controversy. I shouldn't say this, because I don't feel that I've ever been a negative type of person, but I think it may be better to have a club fold before you see more expansion. I always feel badly when a club moves. I don't know if there are enough areas that will support those clubs that are having a rough time. There are some candidates. Vancouver, British Columbia, will be an excellent baseball city. They've got the population and the wealth. They've got an indoor stadium that could be very easily expanded. Buffalo would be a good, solid baseball city. Based on attendance, Buffalo could support a club if the salaries weren't completely out of line. The North Carolina area is a great untapped source for a ball club. The Memphis and Nashville areas are great too. Louisville may be too close to Cincinnati, but it's a solid baseball town. The nation's capital, however, may never get another team. Washington's ballpark is in a blighted area. Somebody said Washington wasn't a good baseball town because of the transient people, that the loyalties of the people that worked there were to their own home areas. I don't know if there's any truth to that or not.

Maybe the new commissioner will do something about these situations, when they finally get around to getting a new commissioner. I'd like to see baseball get a strong commissioner who will be acceptable to both management and the players and who will put the game above any individuals. That'd be great, but where they're going to find that person I don't know. I hope there's somebody somewhere who's qualified to do that. I'm not running. No, I'd be too tough.

Peter Ueberroth did some pretty good things for baseball. He brought major league marketing into the modern era, and he was very successful with that. Everybody in the major leagues, although I don't know if that includes coaches, trainers, and similar personnel, shares in the profits and products that are sold under the Major League Baseball logo. Gosh, it's been a tremendous amount of money for everybody. Ueberroth brought that marketing up to where it is today. So he left a great mark on the game. What type of commissioner was he? I think he was in over his head at times on baseball matters.

Bart Giamatti would have been a pretty good commissioner had he lived longer. He was probably too much of a fan, but it's better to have a fan as a commissioner than a general. Fay Vincent was overmatched, if anything, in the job. I don't think Bud Selig is a good commissioner. I think he's a fence-sitter. And I know Bud. He's an owner of a ball club, but because of that I don't think he can be effective. He tries to be fair, but he can't. I think he sits on the fence too much. He doesn't take a strong enough stand, doesn't face up to things.

From my standpoint as an old-line baseball guy, I don't care too much for salary arbitration. I think that it's always been said that the best ballplayers will always be paid well. The guys who aren't good are the guys who make the most noise, I guess. I think arbitration is like bringing somebody into your house right off the street to settle an argument between you and your wife. The rulings don't seem fair either way. Also the agents should be under the rule of the commissioner. They're part of baseball, and they should be under his supervision. This is not a blanket statement, but there are some people who are not very good agents. They're going to disrupt the outcome of pennant races and championships if they think their clients are dissatisfied. There are some good baseball agents, but those few who seem to be making the most rumble make me think they should be under the commissioner's rule.

One of the best things that ever happened for the players was when Marvin Miller became the union head. The owners had met their match in him. He was an excellent negotiator. He was tough, but he was fair. He didn't push beyond the realm of reason. In fact, more recently he made some comments that things had gotten out of hand. I was sorry when he retired. In fact, I thought he'd be a tremendous commissioner because he knew the business end, knew the owners, knew their ruses. Miller had the success of baseball in mind too. He was picking the players up out of the mud, not just raising the low salaries but improving everything. You can give him credit for the growth of the pension. He wasn't just for the players alone. He knew that the game overall had to be solid for the players. If baseball prospered, the players should prosper. I thought he was an excellent man. A lot of people might disagree with that.

I hate to see the players leaving the clubs that brought them up. I'd like to see more loyalty. I'd like to see them stay with the club. I liked the fact that Tony Gwynn stayed with San Diego all those years and that Kirby Puckett stayed with the Twins his whole career. I was glad to see Kirby get voted into the Hall of Fame recently. I'm still a boy at heart. I like my heroes. Babe Ruth was my hero, Joe DiMaggio was my hero, and I was a worshiper of Mantle and Musial and Ted Williams and Billy Williams and all those great guys. Maybe I'm nostalgic, maybe I'm an old-fashioned old-timer here, but I like my heroes to be a Dodger or a Cardinal or a Red Sox player or a Yankee or a Tiger for their entire careers, or at least most of it. Robin Yount stayed with Milwaukee the whole time, and it looks like Cal Ripken Jr. is going to end up his career with the Orioles. I like that. I know that the money is the big thing—it always will be—but I hate to see it.

It surprises me that many ballplayers today don't know much about the history of baseball or much about the former players. We knew *all* about the players, who Babe Ruth was, who Ty Cobb was. As I went along, I read and learned the history. I knew about the Pittsburgh Pirates when I was a young boy and about the Yankees, the great Yankees, who were way out there, a dream, a fantasy. Now the players don't even know the history of their own team. It's kind of surprising. Maybe it's the idea that money is the root of all evil, and that's the driving force behind it. We had a driving force too, but money was secondary.

Some of the recent innovations and restructurings in baseball leave me wondering. I don't like interleague baseball. It destroys all the arguments about which league is better and whose ballplayers are better. It has diluted the playoffs and World Series. The two clubs in the World Series may have already played each other, and one may have stomped the heck out of the other. They talk about how the big rivalry between, say, the Cubs and the White Sox drew a heck of a lot of people. They don't talk about the interleague games between the last-place clubs, which don't draw very well or aren't built on a longstanding rivalry. The good clubs will always draw, but the bad clubs won't. They say the interleague games have caused a big attendance increase, but I doubt those figures. I wish they'd be more honest about it and do a few other things instead to get the fans to come to the ballpark. They'll probably try split seasons after this interleague stuff doesn't draw the number of people that they want. But that would be a shame too, even though the minor leagues have done it. There are some great rivalries, and there have always been some exhibition games. Keep it that way. Instead of having only three days off for the All-Star Game, make it four or five, and if some clubs wanted to play the crosstown or cross-state rival, let them play two games or whatever. They'd get a tremendous draw, and each league would keep its own individuality.

The wild card for the playoffs is terrible. That's kind of like washing your feet with your socks on. It proves nothing and does nothing. I've had some conversations with some ballplayers who think that being a wild-card club is bragging about being mediocre. There's a lot of pride involved. I can't see a .500 club or one with a couple of wins above .500 getting in the World Series. I hope they never get to the point where they have to toss a coin to see who's the wild card. Furthermore, I don't like divisional play, those four- or five-club divisions. You take a look at the standings by the first of June, the middle of June, you've got a dozen clubs that are completely out of the race. They have no chance whatsoever. They used to laugh at the St. Louis Browns and say if they won the first game, they'd be leading the league, and that's the last time they'd lead it. There are clubs like that now. You would have more champions, divisional ones, but you also have more last-place clubs. Let the good organizations upgrade the whole thing. You're always going to have a last-place club whether there are four, five, or ten teams in the division. But I think the good organizations will be competitive longer.

In 1981, during that strike year, baseball had first- and second-half champions to try to smooth over what happened. I don't think it worked very well, even though my team, the Dodgers, got to the World Series and won it all. Cincinnati had the best overall record but didn't lead at the start of the strike or at the end of the season, so they got closed out of the playoffs. I don't believe that split seasons would work on a major league level. I saw them in the minor leagues, such as the Shaughnessy Playoffs. The first four teams would play. Then somewhere along the line, they decided to play a split season, to have the winner of the first half play the winner of the second half. In an eight-club league, one club would run away with the whole thing, and the fans would lose interest toward the second half. It worked out better in the minors because the parent clubs kept bringing players up or sending some down, so often the teams were quite different in the first and second halves. But I don't know that it would work on the major league level.

Speeding up the games isn't one of the biggest problems for baseball. I don't think the ball games are too long. I think a fan likes to sit there and get his or her money's worth. Some of the delays during televised games are for the commercials. How are you going to get around that? But they could do a few other things to speed it up, such as keeping the batter in the batter's box and cutting down the number of timeouts for base runners, such as when a guy slides into second base and he walks out to center field and dusts his pants off, or when a base runner gets on first base and calls time to see what the signs are. The batter should stay at home plate, not wander off halfway down the third base line to look at the third base coach, when the score is 8–0 against them. There's only one thing for him to do, and that's to try to start a rally. Maybe he's looking beyond him at the blonde up there in those box seats somewhere, but the hitters take too much time. I had the rule many years ago that I wanted my hitter to stand in the batter's box, with one foot out, and that's when I gave all the signs. That speeded it up, and, heck, we always were one jump ahead of the opposition by being ready. Some pitchers work slowly, but I think the hitters are more to blame.

The umpires are taking too much time with their delayed calls. The base umpires ought to be hustling. They stand out there with their hands in their pockets. Instead they should be saying, "Let's go, let's go, and play the game right." The umps could stop calling timeout every time a ball hits the dirt. Umpires shouldn't do that automatically. I would always say to the umpire, "Are you a watchdog for the hitters or what? Let them be alert to call time, to ask for another baseball." Outfielders and infielders should run on and off to and from their positions. I had a rule that they ran or trotted until they got to the foul line, and then they could walk to the dugout. But I would still allow the infielders and outfielders to warm up at the start of a half-inning. Pitchers should still get eight warmup tosses, if they want them, and they should still be allowed to make as many throws to first as they want to try to pick off a runner or keep him close. That's all part of the strategy of the game. Every once in a while, after three or four throws, the fans let you know that they don't want that. They give the guy a few boos if he throws over there seven or eight times. But a lot of times, the guy doesn't want to pitch to the guy at the plate. And I would still make the pitcher make four pitches for an intentional walk. Every once in a while, the pitcher will slip with his control and get a pitch close to the strike zone, and if the batter's alert, bang, he can get a base hit. That's action. If you want to speed up the game, put first base at ninety-three feet. You'll get outs more quickly. Or you could make a foul ball a third strike whether it's caught or not. Complaints about the length of the games are overstated. You never see fans, outside of a couple times, leave the ballpark when their home team is winning, say, 10–2, or even when they're losing by a similar score. They suffer with them, thinking that in the ninth inning, the home team is going to get 11 runs. It's one of the things that makes baseball wonderful.

While I'm thinking about it, let me say that the organizations overdo the pitch count these days. If you have watched as many pitchers as I have or another manager does over a career, you can tell when a guy's getting tired. You don't have to count the pitches. But by the same token, it's something that the sportswriters write about. It's greatly overemphasized now. In the minors, I had orders not to let a young guy pitch over seventy-five pitches, and that was a good thing. Even if he had a no-hitter going, I had to pull him. Once I didn't remove him. I let him get the next guy, and he struck the next guy out, but that took him four pitches over. I caught heck about it too. I've seen guys throw forty pitches in the first inning and by the second or third inning, sixty-five or seventy pitches, and you knew the guys weren't going to last. The complete game seems like a dinosaur now. It's a thing of the past. They now rely on long and short relievers. That's OK. Just bring in a fresh arm. But pitchers should be able to pitch. Heck, there have been some guys who pitched ten or fifteen innings. I saw a guy pitch nineteen innings in a ball game. Of course, he wasn't very good after that, but he wasn't a very good pitcher prior to that either. They're always afraid of ruining an arm. But if a guy's in good condition, you don't have to worry about it.

I'm not thrilled with old-timers' games. I like the old-timer meetings and reunions with the legends of the game. But it pains me to see them play. I'd hate to see the day when an old-timer, playing at age sixty-five, seventy, or even older, swings the bat, hits the ball, and because he has the same old instincts, comes charging out of the batter's box and has a heart attack. It would be a terrible catastrophe. I guess fans have mixed feelings. They want to see some of these players, especially the younger fans, because they're never going to get a chance to see them. But then other fans want to remember them when they were in their prime, not stumbling around. Remember them in your memory.

These senior league, Sunshine League–type arrangements like the ones down in Florida give me mixed thoughts. If an over-forty player builds up his conditioning, I think it's all right. Sometimes you can overdo it, though. They ought to have some good conditioning before they play. Maybe I'm getting to the age where I'm concerned about those things. Many of the guys at the fantasy camps are wonderful. Gee whiz, the thrill that they get out of it! One guy I talked to had two charley horses and he could hardly walk, but, boy, was he delighted. He said, "You know, I got this from hitting a single." He got charley horses in both legs, and he was still happy about that. This man frolicked on the hallowed ground of spring training. These players imitate the big leaguers instructing them. You can't put the competitive fire out in a ballplayer, in any athlete. I think the fantasy camps are great. They can't have enough of them.

I'm not sure I go along with an American "Dream Team" for the baseball competition in the Olympics. If I were in charge of an organization, I don't think I'd want to sacrifice a team, I wouldn't want to sacrifice my ballplayers right in the middle of a season or during a pennant race, so that they could go play for their home countries. Even if every organization has to send one player, it would be disruptive. During the Summer Olympics in Australia, it would have been right during a couple of hot divisional races. But it might be tough to tell some of these guys you can't get a gold medal, after they've seen Michael Jordan and all the other basketball players get theirs. For now, I think it's better they stick with amateurs or minor leaguers who aren't involved in pennant races.

Being named to the All-Star Game is one of the truly great honors that a player can have, American or National League. Anyone who's named to the All-Star team and tries to beg off for some insignificant reason is selfish. If the fans vote for these players or the manager names them as reserves, they should attend and play. It's a relaxed day, a fun day. Your league is trying to be better than the other league. And then, of course, they've got the home run–hitting contest. I think they should be forced to play or have a pretty doggone good reason why they can't. As for this idea of being tired or needing a rest, they can rest all winter as far as I'm concerned. The managers should try to get everybody into the game. When I managed an All-Star team, I said at a pregame meeting that I was going to try to get everybody into the game in some manner. On occasion, it just wouldn't work out that way. I'd leave a guy out, and I'd have to apologize to him. It's happened on the major league level too. Now they have a rule in the All-Star Game that you can bring a guy back in if your player's injured, which is fine. I wish they had had that in the minor leagues.

Regarding Little League, I think that they should muzzle the parents, because they do more harm than good. They should never let a parent be a coach. I went through that a little bit here in Denver many years ago when my son Steve was playing. I found out that parents should not be coaches, because they're going to make somebody mad every time. There's some danger to Little League, and I think that's the biggest one. I was in on the ground floor for Pee Wee Football organization in Montgomery way back in the early 1950s and was instrumental in setting up one of the rules. I don't know whether it has been changed or not, but I got a rule adopted that at the end of the quarter or the end of the half, whoever you were playing, your extra players should go in and play a couple of minutes. They would have a little game of their own. Your best ballplayers would play the biggest part of the game, but they all participated. I thought it was fair, and I thought they would do that in Little League too. A boy who goes out there to play should get a chance to play, at least maybe the last two innings of an official game. I don't want to discourage the kids. They should also keep score about who's winning. Some of these Little Leagues don't. I don't agree with that. I think you've got to teach young people to win too. Everything in life is about winning. When you're a businessperson, you want to be winning in your business. Winning, the big "W," is the main thing in life. Sure you can be obsessed, but for the most part it's for the good. And I think the clubs should be sponsored by businesses, and the kids shouldn't wear the uniforms of the major league clubs. Say a kid is playing for a team called the Marlins and the Florida Marlins are 17 games out of first place. That might not inspire the kid. Let the sponsors get their advertising and goodwill.

In recent years, Little League teams from Taiwan and the Philippines and Venezuela have won the Little League championships. Some of the kids one year may have been too old for their division. I think the organizations should come up with actual proof of age. I don't see why they just don't go to an honest ethical standard on that. I'm not sure the quality of American ballplayers is declining, so much as the kids in other countries have improved their level of play. If you go to the Dominican Republic, you see kids imitating the big leaguers and playing year-round. In the United States, the kids in the warm weather areas—California, Florida, Arizona, and Texas—are ahead of kids in the colder regions. But the Caribbean kids have even an extra advantage with that warm weather year-round.

I hope they never allow using aluminum bats in the major leagues, or in the minor leagues for that matter. I imagine the Little League, high schools, and college guys are going to keep using them, but I don't think you'll ever see an aluminum bat used in the major leagues. It's a deadly weapon. Some pitchers and maybe even some infielders would get killed or seriously injured. Maybe they might use them for exhibitions, such as home run–hitting contests, to see how far you could really hit a ball. Maybe they could hit it over the scoreboard at Coors Field. But I hope the fans are satisfied with all the home runs and hits being hit with wooden bats. If you get up close to the baseball these years, you'll hear it breathing. They're thumping inside, they're so alive. The balls are wound up tighter. I wonder where they're storing their balls. Are they storing them in a hot place or in a cold place? Put a baseball in the freezer, and you can't hit it out of the infield; if you put your baseballs under a hot concrete grandstand, where they will heat like in an oven, those balls will fly.

I've fooled around designing baseball bats myself. I made a bat with an oblong handle instead of the round handle. I had a discussion with Ted Williams about whether he ever thought a bat like that would be better because you'd get more accuracy. He said, "Why?" I said, "Well, Ted, if you look at tools like hammers, their handles are oblong. You take a hand axe or a sledgehammer, their handles are oblong. The same with a double-bitted axe. For accuracy of cut, the handle is oblong. Why not a bat? If you don't

need accuracy, like with a rake or a shovel, their handles can be round."
It got Ted thinking. In a conversation with Tony Gwynn when we were
making his Hitters' Hands cast, I brought it up again. He said, "Yeah, Ted
Williams mentioned that." You could have better accuracy with swinging
a bat with an oblong handle. There's no rule against it. Just the barrel of
the bat has to be round.

Some of the baseball broadcasters leave a lot to be desired. If they would
quit telling you about the weather two weeks ago somewhere, these play-
by-play announcers would have time to keep you informed about the game
and get in the commercials. Some overdo it; some underdo it. I'm being
critical of some announcers. They say too much about the weather. They
say too much about a game that happened two or three weeks ago. They
talk about things that are unimportant about the game, and they forget
to give the score. The great ones, such as Jack Buck, Harry Caray in his
prime, Ernie Harwell, Vin Scully, Jerry Coleman, Ralph Kiner, and some
other guys, all give you the score and they let you know what's happening
in the game. They don't tell you about so-and-so's mother-in-law visiting
the ballpark. Sure, people liked Dizzy Dean because he did tell you about
the fishing trips, but Dizzy would talk about things that he would tie into
the game. He'd say colorful things like "The guy slud into third base."
When he was criticized, he said, "All those teachers that can't say 'slud' ain't
making the money I am." Phil Rizzuto had a lot of stories and wisecracks.
He was a dandy. It was his trademark. But, basically, beyond that he stayed
right with the game, and you knew the score. He was such a Yankees fan,
naturally, such a homer, but you overlooked that. Jack Buck, in St. Louis,
was great. He'd say, "It's hit hard. Yep, it's a home run, and we got two runs
and the Cardinals are out ahead." I liked that. He was very low-key. Now, I
think many of them lack a lot of individual personality. They're all kind of
stereotyped. They say the same thing, shout and scream when somebody
hits a home run.

The quality of the umpires has improved greatly over the course of
the years. About the only thing that I don't like about the umpires is the
nonchalant attitude that some of them have. Sometimes plays come up, and
they get whipped on them. But the umpires are usually very knowledgeable.
They know what they're doing, and mostly they run a game pretty doggone
well. Sometimes they have rabbit ears and hear too much and are a little
quick on the trigger. The umpires have to be more consistent with their
strike zone calls. Sometimes they call it way too narrow, and other times they
keep widening the zone as the game goes on. That black part is extended
out another two or three inches. Baseball should assign the best umpires

for the playoffs and the World Series. Most often, the best teams make it there. The players and fans deserve the best umpires, not just the luck of the draw because of a rotation system. I know it's kind of like a fraternity thing among the umpires, but I don't agree with it.

The umpires wait too long to call a rainout. There may be too much money riding on the game for the clubs as well as rescheduling problems. I think they should wait long enough for a legal game, five and a half innings, if they can. But it can kill fans' interest, unless they're die-hards. I've seen fans out here at Coors Field sitting in the pouring rain, just enjoying the heck out of the experience. But ordinarily I think they wait too long. They should use a little more common sense about it. Instead of waiting an hour and a half or two hours, they should call it earlier. Otherwise it's like starting the game over again. By then 90 percent of the fans have gone home. You're better off to call the game and play a doubleheader, giving the fans a chance to see two games for the price of one. And you don't want the fans getting restless and drunk. I can't recall who, exactly, started the idea of stopping beer sales after the seventh inning, but it's not a bad idea. After the seventh inning, you should be done drinking beer, and people start to leave for home. I think it's more for the protection of the fans who are driving than anything else.

I'd like to see more emphasis on the team concept. As a manager, you always wanted to have a team that had chemistry. As Byron Johnson says, when he played with the Kansas City Monarchs, they could beat Bob Feller's All-Stars, because the Monarchs were a team and Feller's bunch was a collection of guys who hadn't jelled together yet as a team. There are a lot of situations in baseball when a player must sacrifice his own record, his own pride, and everything else to do something for the team, to win a game. That's something that you drive into the young guys. I can recall one guy I had who hit about .230 while everybody else was hitting .350, .320. The whole ball club hit with the exception of him, but every time he came up in a tough situation, he produced. We'd be getting spanked, the pitcher would be throwing us out of the ballpark, sawing off bats, and everything else. Finally we'd get a guy on base, and this player would come up and, bang, he'd hit one out. He was as valuable as the guys hitting .350. I let it be known that without him we couldn't do it. Every time he hit one, we made a big to-do, put a blue or red ribbon on his locker. He won the trophy. It's very difficult when you have a couple of so-called bad or misguided guys. If you can't straighten them out, like Al Lopez said, you have to get rid of them. Sometimes a guy just doesn't take care of himself. If a ballplayer drinks a lot of beer and so forth, if he doesn't take good care of himself, but he still gets out there and sweats every day, if he works hard and he produces, you might just stick with him.

I have some mixed feelings about those special days or nights they hold for players. There might be some resentment there because, after all, it takes a whole team to make you good too. I've had nights in my honor when we won the pennant. I was given a car. They gave me a shotgun and a pair of boots and a cowboy hat out in the West. I've had quite a few honors, but sometimes I think it gives a funny feeling to the rest of the team. You didn't do it alone as a player or even as a manager or coach. The whole team did it. I suppose it's all right to honor a guy for a great individual feat like Cal Ripken Jr.'s consecutive game streak. I think that sort of celebration is terrific.

I wonder if there isn't too much chatting between runners and first basemen and middle infielders. They're probably neighbors or friends from somewhere. Maybe they were on the same team. At one time, fraternizing, even talking to a ballplayer on the field at second base or first base, was taboo. You'd see them whispering, but managers didn't allow it. The rule has been lifted. Sometimes the talking is for a purpose. I know infielders on the defense who would engage a guy in conversation just to get his mind off the game situation, and they'd take advantage of him. They might double him off. Sometimes the second baseman will yell, "Two out. Two out" when there's only one. They hope to sucker the runner into running on anything. Sometimes I'd tell my players to find out who's mad at the manager over there. If one of my players had played with a guy the previous year or was from the same hometown or something, I'd say, "Listen, you go over there and find out what's up with that guy."

I would like to see players focus more on baseball in the clubhouse. The clubhouse belongs to the players, but they should be thinking more about the game. You didn't want a lot of things in the clubhouse that weren't pertaining to baseball. You wanted a pitcher who's going to talk about the hitters. You want the infielders to talk about how do you play it. They wouldn't allow food in the clubhouse, not even Cokes, no drinks or anything. All of a sudden, the Coke machines came in and then candy bars and so forth. Eventually they had luaus between doubleheaders and after the games. Now they sit around in the clubhouses watching television when they should be out watching the outfielders and infielders throw, seeing what kind of an arm the catcher has. Half the time, you don't see a ball club take infield practice. They're in the clubhouse playing cards. That's OK if it's during a rain delay and as long as you are talking about baseball.

I can recall we would dress in a clubhouse that was maybe twelve feet square. It had no restroom in it. The restrooms were outside, outhouses, really, in some of the smaller places. They had one showerhead over in the corner. I don't know why, but they only had one nail for your clothes. You had to hang all your clothes up on one nail. You had to wait your turn. The starting pitcher would always get the first shower, if he wanted it. The guys who didn't get a base hit that day would take the last showers. It was kind of a caste system, if you want to call it that. They didn't even have clubhouses at a lot of the ballparks in Class C and Class D. Even some of the parks in the Texas League, which was A level, didn't have a clubhouse. We'd dress at the hotel. You had to wash your own sweatshirt and sliding shorts and sweat socks. You had to take care of your own things. They didn't have clubhouse boys on the road in the lower leagues. You could tell the guys who weren't too neat. They'd wear the same sweat socks for two weeks.

But Coors Field has fifty lockers, all hardwood, all carpeted. They have television monitors and such everywhere. They've got a Jacuzzi and a hot tub and whirlpools and saunas. They just have everything. The visitors' clubhouse is massive for fifty ballplayers, and the home club's is even more lavish. They've got big television screens, saunas, and seven- or eight-person whirlpools. They've got all sorts of food. But I think it distracts the players from getting out on the field.

There are a lot of things Major League Baseball could do to make the game exciting and interesting for the fans. Fans like a lot of movement and action, such as the stolen base. I've had several ball clubs that could run and steal bases, and, boy, I ran them. I told them to go. The next thing you know, man, it caught fire. Even the guys who usually wouldn't steal a base or who weren't good base stealers would steal a base or two, and they'd be happy as they could be. It was as if they had done something that they were not supposed to do. Everybody on the team was running wild. I love that type of club. Good gosh, we'd run like heck. Then again, you shouldn't steal dumbly. You have to know the situation in the ball game, the time and the setting of the game, and your runner, the pitcher out there, the catcher, whether he can throw. You can run yourself out of more ball games than you'll win, if you're not careful.

I'd like to see the unrestricted hidden ball play come back into the game. I'd like to see the pitcher be allowed to be everywhere but on the rubber during the hidden ball play. I'd like to see him straddle the rubber while he doesn't have the ball. But if he gets on the rubber without the ball, it should be a balk. They can call that a balk.

Bunting in baseball, from the manager's standpoint, is a very important play. The manager is sitting there, maneuvering the game as it goes along.

He's trying to take control of the game. He doesn't want to manage the other club. He wants to manage his club and get it done right. The drag bunt is an offensive weapon to get a guy on base. Then the sacrifice bunt becomes very important. I always had a good bunter as a number two hitter, because you played for one run. But a lot of guys think there's nothing glamorous about a bunt. Everybody wants to swing and hit, naturally, and that's all right, but a well-executed bunt is a tremendous offensive weapon too. I used to have a surefire cure for the guy who didn't want to bunt. If a player didn't want to bunt and wouldn't put his heart and soul into executing the bunt and it would go foul, and then another one would go foul, I made him bunt on the third strike. No matter how many days and hours I spent teaching bunting, the most effective motivator I found was to make the ballplayer bunt on third strike. You'd be surprised how often that got their attention. I had almost a 100 percent rate of bunting successfully on the third strike. I've seen some excellent bunters in my time. Mickey Mantle and Rod Carew were two of the best. Hal Peck, whom I played with at Philadelphia, could really drop that ball down. He was a left-handed hitter. He slid both hands way up on the bat and just kind of used it as a little club. He had tremendous accuracy. He'd drop that ball down the third base line, and he'd be long gone. Bernie DeViveiros, who I've mentioned a few times, was an excellent teacher of bunting.

I loved the squeeze bunt. I called a squeeze bunt against Del Wilber when he was managing the Charleston club in the American Association. He'd been roasting me pretty good, some friendly jousting when I managed the club, and I said, "Well, I'll get back at you. You wait." I got him back in Charleston. I put the squeeze bunt on with nobody out, the bases loaded and three balls, no strikes on the hitter. That was just unheard of. Everybody was so shocked that the pitcher threw the ball into right field, and the bunter wound up at third base. We had 3 runs and a runner on third. So I put it on again, and the same thing happened. I put it on again about three times in a row and got 6 runs out of it. Then they waved a white flag of surrender in their dugout.

The squeeze bunt is a very good play, but you have to practice that. I used to stand back of the pitcher, and first I'd tell all the hitters, "You have to squeeze it, no matter what. If he throws at you, you got to squeeze it. You can't just say, 'Oh, he's throwing at me!' and run away. You have to squeeze the ball. If he throws it between your legs, you have to squeeze the ball." So I got that message over to the hitters. Then I went out to the pitchers, and I'd say, "Now, look, if somebody says, 'There he goes' and the guy's heading for home on the squeeze, there's only one thing you do. You have to throw the ball at the hitter. The best place to throw it is right at his knees. Because if you throw at his legs, he's going to jump out of the way and he can't bunt." I said, "You're not going to knock your own player down now, but you will in the game." And the base runner at third base can't give it away. He's got to run at the right time, not a second sooner. It's a good play. I did both the suicide squeeze and the safety squeeze. I enjoyed the suicide squeeze better than the safety one. If you had a pitcher up there bunting, you did the safety squeeze. I loved the suicide squeeze, and a lot of managers do. It shows a lot of daring on the part of the manager and the players.

Stealing home has become a lost art too. You rarely see it. The chances of its succeeding, I guess, are about 25 percent, not even 50 percent. Rod Carew was probably the best at it among the players I'd ever seen. I'll bet Billy Martin taught Rod Carew how to steal home. Billy was great at teaching that. It's an exciting play. Boy, the time it is really exciting is when it's the winning run or the tying run and it's late in the ball game, or a guy gets the idea he can steal and he does it on his own, or maybe you give him the sign. If he succeeds, you're a hero. If he doesn't, they're going to shoot you before you get to the dugout. I've called it several times. The runner's eyeballs get real wide. I'd say, "Go ahead. I'm going to tell them you went on your own." They'd laugh like heck. One time with Denver, Steve Boros stole home with two strikes on the hitter and two outs. I didn't give him the sign. He said, "I had a hell of a jump." I said, "Yeah, if he'd swung at that pitch inside, you'd be dead." He was right on top of the hitter. Thank God the pitch was way inside and the batter didn't swing. I thought we were going to lose a third baseman.

It's thrilling to see baseball expanding around the world. There have been several ballplayers who have come out of Australia, some pretty good ones. I don't know how they play out there. I had an opportunity many years ago to go over there for some clinics, but I didn't take it, and I still regret it. There are a lot of good athletes in Europe. What we ought to do in the wintertime is send clubs over there and spread the gospel of our baseball. Baseball will be a great peacemaker. The Caribbean, as I've said before based on my experience as a special assignment scout there, is a great source of talent. They've got their heroes down there. The language isn't even a big problem. When I played down in Mexico, I did very well with the Mexican ballplayers who couldn't speak English; I couldn't speak Spanish, but I communicated very well. Baseball sign language is universal. I wish they'd open up Cuba, because I'm sure there's a lot of talent there. It would take a little longer than just walking in there now and setting up a few teams, because the players that they have on the Cuban national team are well up in age. Every once in a while, age doesn't mean that much for a pitcher. You could get a guy who's twenty-six or twenty-seven, and he could come up and give you four or five years. But there are some good young ballplayers coming up.

I'm not sure about players from Asia. The main difficulty is that they're heroes in their own country and they hate to leave, but I think we could see a big flood of them playing in the United States in the future. Many years ago, somebody in Japan asked if I'd be interested in going there as a manager. They had a résumé on me. They felt that I was the type of guy for them, that I was tough and demanding but fair. When I broached the subject to my wife and kids, it didn't go over very well, so I just let it die. I kind of regret that. I would have loved to have gone over there. Will there ever be a "true" World Series? American teams playing Japanese teams or Latin American teams or European teams? Eventually, but I don't think the overall talent is there yet. Maybe if you had an All-Star team. I don't know how the logistics of travel and time would work in that. Maybe they could play the games during the winter in the warmer climates and the summers up in North America. Here in the United States, there could be more year-round play. I have always felt that there should be a Baseball Academy in Florida or Arizona, which plays three 90-game seasons during the course of the year that would prove whether certain ballplayers could play. You could develop them quicker, smooth them out, play three 90-game seasons in Florida or Arizona. Pitchers wouldn't complain about not getting enough innings. Hitters wouldn't complain about not getting enough at bats.

We could use some more stunts and promotions like the ones Bill Veeck used to feature. I saw one once where he had a guy with power batteries on his back, like Batman flying around on this machine, fly into the stadium and go around twice, once high and once low, before landing. That was one of the most thrilling things I believe I've ever seen at a ballpark. It was great. We need some promoters like Joe Engle down at Chattanooga, the Bill Veeck of his day in the minor leagues. He would have elephants parading and helicopters dropping money on the field and fan appreciation nights and a house giveaway and so forth. Oh, there were some dandy promotions and stunts. Somewhere I saw a players' diaper-changing contest to see who could do it the quickest. I think it was in the Appalachian League. They had three married guys, two from one club and one from the other. Their wives and kids were there. It was hilarious. It really went over well. As did the egg-tossing contests. They were very popular. You'd advertise them, and the fans would come out in droves. You'd get four ballplayers on the first or third base line and pair them with four other guys about ten feet into fair territory. They'd start tossing an egg back and forth, each time taking a step or two back when the guy caught the egg without breaking it. When they got about thirty feet or so, that's when the eggs would start breaking. But I saw them occasionally get almost to ninety feet! The pair of guys who were last to break their egg would win the prize. Usually it was ten or twenty bucks in the lower leagues. But then a couple of guys got wise. They had hard-boiled eggs! They wouldn't break, and those guys would win the contest easy.

I saw a greasy pig contest one time on the semipro or county level. It was the doggonedest thing I'd ever seen. They had this pig that they greased up with what we called axle grease, the regular grease that they used in cars, a good clear grease, almost like lard. Then they'd turn him loose. A guy would bring him out to the pitcher's mound in a wheelbarrow with a cage on it, then turn it over, letting the pig loose, and there he'd go! The players would get in a circle out there around the pitcher's mound, and then try to grab him. They couldn't hold him with all that grease on their hands. Somebody might grab him around the neck, and they'd call time and regrease the pig. I have never seen them catch it yet.

The rabbit-chasing contests were also a tremendous amount of fun. They'd get a crate of young rabbits and take them out on the pitcher's mound. Both ball clubs would circle around on the foul lines, and they'd turn the rabbits loose. Any guy who caught a rabbit would win a prize. They had first, second, and third prizes. It was one of the most hilarious things I've ever seen. Those rabbits would run like heck and head for the grandstand. The fans would get into the act and chase them back toward the field. You'd have guys diving for them every which way. It was a very enjoyable event for the fans.

So was donkey baseball. We played that game one time, and it was one of the funniest experiences I've ever had in baseball. Those donkeys wouldn't go anywhere you'd want them to go. They'd just stand there. You'd hit the ball and try to get him to go down to first base, but he'd head for the pitcher's mound. Every once in a while, they'd walk out and start grazing on the grass. I'd like to see it done on the big league level sometime. I'd love to see the big league ballplayers try to manage those donkeys.

There's no reason that with the right marketing and promotions, ball clubs, even some of these small-market clubs, can't draw a decent crowd. Bring back some of the old-time uniforms for a few games or exhibitions. I've really enjoyed that when the current teams have dressed up in 1940s or 1950s uniforms. Maybe they could even go back to the Cincinnati Red Stockings or the New York Highlanders just to show the fans what that looked like. I think it'd be great. Spruce up the stadium mascots. Some mascots are good, and some are not worth a darn. The guy at Philadelphia, the Philly Phanatic, is, I think, the funniest one. He's funny as heck when he goes around there with that big snozzle of his, kissing the umpire and all that. He's probably the best of all. I also loved the San Diego Chicken, but he got out of line, and he was doing things that weren't funny anymore. I can't say I care too much for Dinger at Coors Field.

Baseball should have more guys who can inject a sense of humor into the game. I used to enjoy guys like Bill Lee, the "Spaceman," or John Kruk. I heard all the stories about Lee, but he's a delightful guy. He's the type of guy you want on a ball club. He keeps your ball club loose and easy-going. He also keeps the fans interested. And he could produce, too, as a pitcher. Similarly Kruk didn't "look" like a ballplayer, but that's beside the point. He was tough, and he was a good model for the other players. And he made the fans chuckle. I think he made the classic statement, when he wasn't in the lineup one day, to Jim Fregosi, I believe it was, "Jim, if you don't play me, I'll take my ball and go home." And we need more guys like Max Patkin or Al Shacht, the Clown Prince of Baseball. I saw his act many times. We need somebody like them now to take the tension off some of the poor publicity baseball is getting. I wish somebody would come along that would have a little sense of humor and could produce too.

Baseball could also bring back the fathers and sons or fathers and daughters baseball games, like we used to have in the 1950s and 1960s. I don't know why they've eliminated those. I would imagine you would sure get some fans back to see the ballplayers with their kids out there, maybe even some of the mothers and the little tiny ones. They could have a contest to see whose kid crawls to first base the fastest. I think it's something that should be brought back. I don't think everything has to be new to be successful. You can dust off a lot of things, and they're still good. They should give all the mothers a rose on Mother's Day. They could have Easter egg hunts for the kids at the ballpark.

Maybe they should also bring back the club picnics. We used to have them in the minor leagues, and everybody connected with the ball club got involved. That was great for the fans. It made them feel like they were part of the family. The fans loved it. The club served hot dogs and Cokes, peanuts, typical ballpark fare. It was always good. Heck, a fan could pay a half a buck and get a hot dog and a Coke, meet the players and chat with them, and tell them how to play and how to hit and everything. Oh, it was great. Maybe they're a bit too sophisticated on the major league level to do that. The clubs don't have time for those things anymore.

Another thing that baseball has lost is the Knothole Gang. Branch Rickey was enthusiastic about that, because it would create future fans. I don't know why they won't have a Knothole Gang at Saturday games. Each Saturday they could bring in kids from different parts of the metro area to watch the game. I also believe the schools ought to close on Opening Day so the kids can see the game. The clubs or corporations should supply blocks of tickets, like they did when I hitchhiked to New York to see Babe Ruth at Yankee Stadium. They ought to do that again. Bob Howsam used to reward straight-A students at Denver by giving them free tickets. That was a fine promotion, fine marketing. I'll bet that a lot of those straight-A students are great baseball fans today. The clubs should keep rewarding kids and cultivating future fans.

Based on what I see at Coors Field, I'm glad to see more women at the games. They're coming back, and they're good baseball fans. I think baseball ought to do something to continue to attract more women to the parks. They used to have Ladies Day and charge a woman only fifty cents or a dollar admission. It was often on a Thursday afternoon. It was great. You'd look up there and all those ladies were there, very few men. They used to hold baseball clinics for the ladies. I'd go and talk to them and tell them all about the signs and what to look for. Then I'd forget to tell them that I'd change the signs in the game, and I'd confuse them when they'd come to the ballpark. I'd also speak to their clubs. Baseball should do all it can to get more women interested in the game.

Will there ever be a woman baseball player in the major leagues? I don't know, but I saw Babe Didrikson play. She was a tremendous athlete. She did everything well. I believe that if there's going to be a female athlete in the big leagues professionally, she'll be a pitcher. I don't know if a female athlete is going to be strong enough to be a position player. I just don't see where they have the physical stamina and strength on a regular basis for that. On the other hand, pitching would mean she'd have to exert herself every fourth or fifth day. I bet she'll be a left-hander. Don't get me wrong. I know there are some women who are tremendous athletes. Once I lost an arm-wrestling contest to a fishing woman in a bar, because she locked her wrist and threw my arm down. I had to buy her a drink. And I saw the All-American Girls' Professional Baseball League women trying out at Comiskey Park in 1943. They were real impressive. But we're probably going to see a female umpire before we see a female player. Even though

Pam Postema got a lot of static when she was umpiring, I think the time is coming for another female umpire.

I was rooting for Michael Jordan when he tried to make a professional career in baseball. Gee whiz, the White Sox would have drawn like heck, even on the road. He's a tremendous athlete. At first, I didn't think he was going to get very far. Then as time went on, I thought he might have a chance. But in his case, he just couldn't hit well enough. Ted Williams made the statement that if he had been able to talk with Jordan for a day, a half a day or something, that he felt he could have really made Jordan a pretty good hitter. Ted was a great teacher of hitting; he could get anybody to improve. But Michael Jordan didn't take that route. If he had spent a couple of days with Ted Williams, I believe he would have become a pretty good ballplayer. But they just threw him right in there, let him go up there and struggle against pitches he had never seen before. Hitting is 90 percent from the neck up, the great hitters will tell you. You start out with great physical abilities, but if you don't have it from the neck up, you're just a so-so guy. There was some resentment against Jordan on the part of career minor leaguers who had paid their dues. But they should have enjoyed one of the greatest basketball players of all time playing baseball. Maybe they should have been helping him somewhere along the line. I know I would have.

The Mark McGwire and Sammy Sosa home run race in 1998 was a shot in the arm for baseball. They were both great, and I was rooting for them both. I got to see McGwire in batting practice at Coors Field. It was about the most exciting thing I'd ever seen. The guy hit line drive shots that went out of the ballpark just like a bullet. He's amazing. He looks like a giant oak tree, with those massive arms. He's a delight. He hit a long drive that cleared the ballpark, clear out in left field. He hit a long, high drive into center, and he hit one off the backdrop. That's a pretty good shot. I don't think anybody else has hit it in batting practice, let alone during a game. McGwire hits the type of home run that you'd say, "How'd you like to be on that one, going home?" I never saw so many people around the batting cage. I think they kind of pester him, but I didn't see too many camera flashes. That kind of sets you back, that flashing in your eyes, even in your peripheral vision. It disrupts you and makes it pretty tough to focus again. I think they ought to leave him alone.

Home run derbies are great. I don't see why they don't have them more often, not only just before the All-Star Game. They used to have some sort of long ball–hitting contest between doubleheaders. They could hold one half an hour prior to the game. They could advertise it very well, get plenty of publicity on it. Maybe the losers would have to pay the winner's favorite charity. They could have other contests, like a field meet: catchers throwing to second base, runners circling the bases, running to first base, a fifty- or seventy-five-yard dash, fungo hitting. But the players are always leery about pulling their muscles. They feel that their swing will be altered, and they would be pressing. But I think they should enter the contest if only for the fans' sake. If they are in shape, they don't have to worry. There are a lot of things they could do without being too mercenary about everything.

Baseball can also help itself by constructing more new stadiums to attract more fans. I've already mentioned that I think Coors Field is the best place in the world to play and watch a game, but there are some fine new stadiums out there. I've got to admit that the Diamondbacks' stadium, Bank One Ballpark, has got to be one of the Taj Mahals of baseball at this time. It has everything that you could imagine and desire in a baseball park. The field itself is magnificent. The clubhouses and dugouts are great. The views from the stands from various places are great. All the seats are turned toward home plate. I saw only a couple of things that needed improvement. The batting cages under the stadium for the home team are beautiful, but the one for the visiting team is too narrow. A batter can hardly swing without hitting the netting. Maybe they could move the plate to one side, but that would cause the pitch to come in at a different angle. And in the cages, at least when I saw them a couple of years ago, the surface behind the batter was painted white, which would be dangerous to any pitcher pitching to a batter in the cage. Maybe they could have a screen in front of the pitcher. I made the recommendations at Coors Field that they paint the background green. Those are a couple of problems somebody overlooked. But otherwise it's a beautiful stadium. Jerry Colangelo and the Diamondbacks and people of Phoenix should be complimented on their fine structure.

They built a new stadium in Detroit, but it's different from the old Tiger Stadium. If they ever build another ballpark in Chicago for the Cubs, they should construct it exactly like Wrigley Field, maybe with the dimensions only a little different or something, and all up-to-date with the modern amenities. The same goes for Fenway Park. If they do build another stadium in Boston, they should keep Fenway as a museum. Maybe they should make it a theme park of sorts. They could charge people to come in and try to hit a ball over the left-field fence. But keep the new stadium as identical to Fenway as possible. Maybe they could increase the seating capacity some, but by all means keep it cozy, keep the fans near the field. Don't construct any more of those cookie-cutter stadiums like Veterans Stadium in Philadelphia or the ones in Cincinnati and Pittsburgh. I'm not very crazy about that kind of ballparks. They've got that Astroturf. I'm not too thrilled about the domed stadiums. They've built some for football, but I don't like them for baseball. The game is played better in the open air. Now with the technology, with the new method of drainage that they use, the field is cleaned off in thirty minutes, no matter how big a flood of water you have. In the South, in the warm country, a dome might make more sense. I don't think that you're going to see very many domes, unless they have that retractable roof, where you can close it if it's too hot or cold. That seems to have worked out very well in Toronto. But still, Cleveland's drawing very well at the new stadium, and it's an open-air one. I'm glad to see this present trend to open-air stadiums and grass fields. I love what they've done with Busch Stadium in St. Louis. I always loved scouting there, because you'd stay right at the hotel, right down the left-field line. You'd just fall out of bed and walk there. Everybody in baseball should take a page out of the Cardinals' book, the courtesies, the ushers and usherettes, and other ballpark personnel. At Busch Stadium, they're just fantastic.

Will we see baseball a hundred years from now? Yes, in a form we will. We may not recognize it. It might be more of a gladiator type of game. It might get more violent than it should. It could get to that point because we're losing sight now of what is right and what is wrong. Think of Daryl Strawberry these past few years. Good gosh, the bleeding hearts have given him chance after chance and paid him fabulous amounts of money. It looks like they're rewarding bad actions, bad behavior. Instead they worry too much about a player's chewing habits. I was a smoker. I smoked cigarettes, and then I quit. I didn't like what it was doing to me, and they weren't as tasty. So I just quit, many years ago, and I'm glad I did. But if a guy wants to chew, let him chew. If he wants to quit, let him quit. I think they have too much regimentation on what the players can and can't do. But if I were the groundskeeper, I wouldn't want them to chew and spit. It can get quite messy on artificial turf or in the dugout.

I think somewhere in the very near future we're going to see that baseball will be subsidized or financed by pay television. The playoffs and league championship series and the World Series will go worldwide, to a billion and a half or 2 billion television sets. The fact that more players from outside the United States are playing in the major leagues will increase the interest throughout the whole world. Let your mind wander about the dollar amounts possible in revenue.

Baseball's not just an excuse to drink beer. It's our national game, the National Pastime. It's our "country game." It seemed like when you were a kid, you found a pickup squad, you threw the bat, and you played on a sandlot or a vacant lot or field. The game was always in the country, out in little towns, the small schools, little mining towns, little country towns, farming towns, out in the open air. Then it became a city game, and the newspapers covered it and glorified it and marketed it and promoted it. Cities were identified with their team. A lot of immigrants were in the cities, and they started playing and watching the game. They loved it. And the country boys went into the city and played. They didn't want cricket, which was too leisurely and took too long. They were looking for action, and baseball gave them that action.

Baseball has been an escape for the workers, who fantasized themselves playing. Even at this stage, after I've gone through a whole career, I sit in the stands and visualize myself hitting. Every fan does the same thing. He can see himself making the great play in the outfield. He can see himself hitting that hard smash in the hole. He says, "Hey, but by the stroke of luck, if I hadn't gotten married, I'd be a big league ballplayer. If I didn't have to work at that darn job, I would be a big league baseball hero." That's part of the interest and glory of baseball. That's where the fantasy camps come in. They go down there, and they fantasize that they're a Don Drysdale or a Mickey Mantle. That's the beauty of it. But baseball also reflects our work. As I said before, whether it is the coal mine or the baseball diamond, you have to have teamwork to be successful. I have always loved how baseball combines individual skills and teamwork. When you're batting, you can't get help from anyone else. You can't have two people come up to swing the bat. Unlike in football, you can't have someone throw you a block. The pitcher's got to throw the ball himself. This is one of the beauties of the game. But teamwork is equally important. Starting a double play is an individual effort, but most of the time it takes at least two people to complete it.

Some people say baseball is like a machine, but it's more of an art form. It's a pitcher and a catcher working together to deceive the hitter, and the hitter tries to adjust to what the pitcher's doing. It's just like painting a picture. You make those moves, boom, boom, boom, till finally the result is either the pitcher gets you out or you hit the ball. It's like a finished product. The rules are really simpler in baseball. Without trying to get technical, you hit the ball, you run to first base, the next batter hits the ball, you go to third base if you can, and so forth. There's a little bit of a time element. You're on schedule: you hit at a certain time, you take infield at a certain time, and the umpires gather at home plate with the managers at a certain time.

Baseball did something for social mobility. I can vouch personally that it's a ticket out of the working class. If you were of foreign-born parents, and if you succeeded in something like baseball, then everybody, all the different ethnic groups and so forth, would say, "Well, gee whiz, he did this and he did that, and it's wonderful." If an Italian boy made good in baseball, gosh, he had all the Italian people rooting for him, just like most black people in America rooted for Jackie Robinson. In my own life, my father thought that baseball was wonderful. His support for my dreams helped me go a long way in realizing them.

One of the most wonderful things about baseball is that you're all equal. You start out equal. The greatest equalizer of all is that little round baseball. You can say anything you want about the conditions, about the fact that you're not doing this or that, but it boils down to you and that little round baseball. That little round thing comes out there toward you, and you've got to catch it, you've got to throw it, you've got to do everything with it. The pitcher, the guy who propels the baseball, is a little bit of a culprit, but that little round thing is going to equalize everything eventually. You either conquer that thing, or it conquers you. It's the greatest democratic equalizer in the world. It wouldn't surprise me to see a team that would have all white players and all black players or all Latino players, based on abilities, not on skin color.

Some historians say Americans like baseball because of all the numbers involved. Maybe so. Look at all the guys with those rotisserie leagues. They're true fans. I still like the statistical side of the game. Even to this day, the first thing I grab in the morning paper is the sports page. I check whether the game is going to be on that night, and then I check the box scores. I read the attendance figures. I see who got the hit, and I look down at the pitching staff to see what pitchers are doing. I don't have to read the account of the game, because I can read the line score and tell just about how the game went. Then I like to look at the averages, the figures like runs batted in. I like to see who is leading the hitting. I like to see at the start of the season that so-and-so is leading the league in such, and you know darn well that he's going to reach his level. I want to know why a guy is playing regularly when I can't find him when the weekend averages come out. That was part of my work too as a scout, always checking the lineups to see who's injured or slumping. Some of the managers use statistics quite a bit to get an advantage.

Certain statistics are overrated. A few years ago, they had those quality start and game-winning RBI statistics, which could be deceptive. Even the save statistic can be misleading. The save is fine, in itself, when you bring a guy in in a real tough spot, such as a jam with bases loaded and nobody out, and he gets the other side out. But if the reliever comes in when he's got, say, a four-run lead and gets a save, the real credit should go to the pitcher or pitchers who came in earlier. I think a lot of such saves are overrated. Perhaps they should have a degree of difficulty scale like in diving. Heck, if a guy comes in and gets the seventh-, eighth-, and ninth-place hitters out, the tail end of the batting order, and maybe a pinch hitter who's just been sitting on the bench for nine innings, it's a good job, but I don't think it has as much importance as a reliever who puts down the heart of the order with a 1-run lead. Fielding average can be misleading if a guy doesn't have much range, if he's a "postage stamp" player. Zeke Bonura was the best example of that. He couldn't move out of his tracks for a ball. And yet he never made an error. I think he fielded 1.000 one year. If the ball was hit right at him, he had to catch it in self-defense. Batting averages are not as deceptive. Sometimes somebody makes a big to-do about bunts and drag bunts. I think they're very clever plays, very good offensive plays.

The earned run average can be a deceptive statistic. I don't pay too much attention to it. You have to put that together with run support. I had a pitcher who went 15-3 or 15-4 and, good God, all of his wins were 12–9 and 14–11 and 15–10 and so forth. He never won a 2–1 ball game. He'd give up 8 or 9 bases on balls and 12 hits and a lot of runs, and then we'd squeak through at last. It would be one of those relaxing games, which I loved, where everybody was hitting, both sides, and you'd wind up in the last of the ninth with a fluke play getting you the winning run. I loved those games. You could go home and enjoy your dinner then.

Some statistics that you see are indeed meaningless. Then there are the things that meant the most to me, as a manager, that didn't show up in the statistics. I appreciated it when a guy advanced the base runner, or if an outfielder made a good cutoff throw and kept the runner from advancing a base. If a guy backed up a play and kept the winning run from scoring, or if a guy trailed another fielder down the right-field or left-field line and backed up a throw that might have gotten away from the first relay man or cutoff man—those sorts of things were very important to me. Those things don't show up in the statistics. I especially pay attention when a pitcher gets a guy out when he *has* to. Maybe he's been struggling and struggling, and all of a sudden the game is on the line, and he gets this one guy out in some manner. That's superb. Maybe somebody will mention it, but maybe not. You've got to look beyond the statistics sometimes. Continuing a rally, driving in a lead run, is very important, so I think the RBI statistic is pretty valid. The big RBI is the one that you have to drive in, that would keep you close or maybe even break the game wide open. On the other side, the men

left on base one is meaningful. I look at that one, and I scream. You look
at that a million times and ask why didn't he get a base hit, why didn't that
ball drop in? Left on base, that's the one that drives you crazy.

I'm also a little sad that fans don't keep score of the game anymore.
But the card now is not a scorecard—it's a magazine. The program is a
magazine, and it's got all those ads. You don't have time to look at it all.
The Cubs used to have an insert, just a scorecard, and a fan paid, I don't
know, a dime or a quarter or whatever it was for it. Now, they don't even
have the coaches' numbers or anything on these cards. They don't have all
the personnel there. They don't even tell you how to score. There are two or
three different ways people keep score. I think they ought to instruct fans
how to keep score. I'd see people all the time trying to keep score, and I'd
be looking over their shoulders and saying, "How'd you do that?" "Why?"
they'd ask. "What's that," I'd ask about one of their notations. Then I'd show
them how to mark the corners for base hit and put dots down for runs. But
truthfully I still don't know how to score. I look at it from a different angle,
the scouting angle. I'm looking at abilities from the manager's strategy. So
for scoring, I just put an R for a run, and half the time, I don't know if it's
F7 or F8 or 9 for a fly ball to the outfield. I couldn't be an official scorer. But
I don't know that I would want to, because I enjoy seeing the other parts
of the game.

For all its modern numbers, maybe baseball is not really a new game.
Maybe it repeats all sorts of ancient things. It's like a quest, where you go
out into dangerous territory and try to get home. People migrated from one
spot to another, and maybe migrated again and again. Baseball is a little bit
similar: you migrate from home plate to first to second to third and home
again. But somewhere along the line, there are obstacles, booby traps, and
there are only a couple of little safe spots, the bases. And the teamwork part
might go back all the way to warriors attacking a large animal, a mammoth,
to bring it down as a group. It was a group victory. One guy couldn't do it.
When I played and managed and coached and scouted, I was always aware
of the traditional aspects of the game, that this was something special, a
way of life.

Baseball is the only sport where you don't score with the ball. You don't
carry it across a line or put it through a hoop or a goal or whatever. If
anything, you try to avoid the ball. You try to hit it out of the ballpark. It's
unique in that sense. Another beauty of baseball is that you don't have to
worry that the game is going to be decided by a clock. You don't have to
go against time. Everything is not cut-and-dried. You can go five innings
without getting a base hit, and then all of a sudden you erupt. There's

nothing predictable about it. A club can come back from being way behind and win a game in the last time at bat, with the last hit. Oh, gosh, it's been done many a time. If you're a fan in the stands, you don't want to leave, because you're liable to miss something. I've been to thousands and thousands of games. Just when you think you've seen everything in baseball, you're going to see something else. Every time that you think it's cut-and-dried, something new comes up. For instance, I never thought I'd see a ball hit a pigeon, but I saw a ball hit a pigeon in a baseball game. I never thought I'd ever read about a guy throwing a baseball and killing a pigeon on a throw to the infield.

For all those reasons, I believe that baseball will last. It will be back every spring. Spring training was always my all-time favorite time of the year. You left the cold country and got down to Arizona or Florida. The sun would be shining, and it just made you feel so great, as if you were drinking from some fountain of youth. Everything was just alive, good, and exciting. Anytime I go to Arizona or Florida in the spring, I get that feeling. It's not spring fever; it's baseball fever. I've always had that fever in my blood. I wouldn't have had it any other way. I've always been safe by a mile.

Charlie Metro — Career Statistics

PLAYING CAREER—BATTING

Year	Team(s)/League	G	AB	R	H	2B	3B	HR	TB	SH	SB	BB	HB	RBI	SO	BA	SA
1937	Easton/Eastern Shore	23	74	12	15	2	0	1	19	NA	5	NA	NA	8	NA	.203	.270
1938	Pennington Gap/Appalachian	95	361	42	100	17	7	1	134	9	8	17	2	37	33	.277	.371
1939	Mayfield/Kitty	125	542	99	139	23	6	14	216	3	11	53	5	75	89	.256	.399
1940	Palestine/Texarkana/East Texas League	132	462	79	114	24	1	6	164	9	7	91	5	63	83	.247	.355
1941	Texarkana/Cotton States	138	527	110	151	30	9	20	259	2	12	71	0	96	103	.287	.491
1942	Beaumont/Texas	80	146	18	32	6	2	2	50	3	2	15	2	12	20	.210	.342
1943	Detroit/American	44	40	12	8	0	0	0	8	1	1	3	NA	2	6	.200	.200
1944	Detroit/American	38	78	8	15	0	1	0	17	1	1	3	NA	5	10	.192	.218
1944	Philadelphia/American	24	40	4	4	0	0	0	4	0	0	7	NA	1	6	.100	.100
1945	Philadelphia/American	65	200	18	42	10	1	3	63	4	1	23	NA	15	33	.210	.315
1945	Oakland/Pacific Coast	49	186	30	45	10	0	2	61	5	3	23	0	19	36	.242	.328
1946	Oakland/Seattle/Pacific Coast	110	330	37	68	15	0	4	95	6	3	29	0	25	45	.206	.288
1947	Bisbee/Arizona-Texas	125	451	131	148	37	8	20	261	4	13	92	4	121	46	.329	.588
1948	Twin Falls/Pioneer	127	482	102	169	32	1	22	269	2	9	09	1	116	54	.351	.558
1949	Twin Falls/Pioneer	102	361	110	111	24	2	17	190	3	4	115	4	73	38	.307	.526
1950	Montgomery/Southeastern	119	426	83	123	26	2	18	207	4	5	87	3	84	78	.289	.486
1951	Montgomery/South Atlantic	64	188	31	43	0	1	4	66	4	1	42	0	30	45	.229	.351
1952	Montgomery/South Atlantic	68	231	20	54	10	0	2	70	4	0	23	0	27	52	.234	.303
1953	Montgomery/South Atlantic			1	NA	NA	NA	NA	NA	NA	NA	NA	NA	NA	NA	.000	.000
	Major League Totals 1943–1945	171	358	42	69	10	2	3	92	6	3	36	NA	23	55	.193	.257
	Minor League Totals (totals do not include NAs) 1937–42, 1945–53	1,358	4,668	904	1,212	243	41	133	1,940	71	86	677	12	761	631	.260	.416

PLAYING CAREER—FIELDING

Year	Team(s)	POS	POB	A	E	DP	FPct.
1937	Easton	OF	42	1	0	NA	.1000
1938	Pennington Gap	OF	207	13	4	3	.982
1939	Mayfield	OF	265	21	13	3	.957
1940	Palestine/Texarkana	OF	306	21	8	1	.948
1941	Texarkana	OF	330	26	11	3	.970
1942	Beaumont	OF	7	1	0	1	1.000
		2B	44	41	3	11	.966
1943	Detroit	OF	28	0	1	0	.966
1944	Detroit/Philadelphia	OF	59	2	2	0	1.000
		2B	0	2	0	2	1.00
		3B	5	7	1	1	.923
1945	Philadelphia	OF	100	5	3	0	.972
1945	Oakland	OF	100	10	2	2	.982
1946	Oakland/Seattle	2B	69	46	8	4	.935
1947	Bisbee	3B	191	236	23	24	.949
1948	Twin Falls	3B	29	52	6	5	.931
		OF	216	20	7	3	.971
1949	Twin Falls	2B	64	61	3	17	.977
		3B	12	27	4	3	.907
		SS	61	92	22	18	.874
		OF	44	6	0	3	1.00
1950	Montgomery	2B	26	30	2	3	.986
		3B	44	79	9	3	.932
		OF	96	8	2	1	.981
1951	Montgomery	3B	16	28	1	1	.978
		OF	47	3	8	0	.862
1952	Montgomery	2B	47	56	2	12	.981
		3B	21	42	5	6	.926
Major League Totals							
1943–45			192	16	5	3	.977
Minor League Totals							
1937–42/1945–52			2,390	870	160	135	NA

MANAGERIAL CAREER

Year	Team	League	Level	Record	Place	Percentage
1947	Bisbee	Arizona-Texas	C	74-59	3rd	.556
1948	Twin Falls	Pioneer	C	75-51	2nd	.595
1949	Twin Falls	Pioneer	C	75-51	1st	.624
1950	Montgomery	Southeastern	B	77-54	3rd	.588
1951	Montgomery	South Atlantic	A	85-55	1st	.607
1952	Montgomery	South Atlantic	A	86-88	3rd	.558
1953	Montgomery	South Atlantic	A	50-90	8th	.357
1954	Durham	Carolina	B	70-68	4th	.507
1955	Augusta	South Atlantic	A	76-64	3rd	.543
1956	Charleston wv	American Association	AAA	5-17	8th	.227
1956	Terre Haute	Three-I	B	28-23	2nd	.549
1956	Idaho Falls	Pioneer	C	39-26	4th	.600
1957	Vancouver	Pacific Coast	AAA	97-70	2nd	.581
1958	Vancouver	Pacific Coast	AAA	79-73	3rd	.520
1959	Vancouver	Pacific Coast	AAA	82-69	2nd	.543
1960	Denver	American Association	AAA	88-66	1st	.571
1961	Denver	American Association	AAA	75-73	3rd	.507
1962	Chicago	National	Major	43-69	9th	.384
1966	Tulsa	Pacific Coast	AAA	85-62	1st	.578
1970	Kansas City	American	Major	19-33	4th	.365
Major League Totals						
1962, 1970				62-102		.378
Minor League Totals						
1947–61, 1966				1,249-1,035		.547

Index

Aaron, Hank, 171, 173–74, 244, 256, 264, 356, 400, 442, 445, 447, 468

Ackley, Fritz, 303–4

Adair, Jerry, 343

Adair, Jimmy, 203, 324

Adams, Bobby, 262

Adams, Red (clubhouse trainer at Oakland Oaks), 116

Adams, Red (pitching coach for Los Angeles Dodgers), 350, 362–63, 438

Adcock, Joe, 256, 264

African American ballplayers, xix, 17–18, 96, 151, 171–74, 201, 207, 236–37, 244, 251, 255, 260, 299–300, 334, 396, 467–68, 495

African American fans, 17–18, 42, 159–60

African American workers, 17–18, 63–64, 168

Agee, Tommy, 286

Aguirre, Hank, 258

Airdrie Stud Farm, 408

airplanes, 10–11, 51–52, 193, 246–47, 257, 303–4

Alabama Crimson Tide (football), 162

Alabama State University, xix, 172

Albuquerque Dukes, 352, 355–56

Alcaraz, Luis, 328

Alderson, Sandy, 400

Alexander, Hugh, 18

All-American Girls' Professional Baseball League, 103, 490–91

All-American Quarter Horse Race, 411

All-Star games or teams, 53–54, 84–85, 95, 123, 155, 170–71, 203, 220, 250, 256–57, 264–65, 298, 334, 437, 445, 455, 475, 479, 491

"all-time" teams, 467–68

Allentown Cards, 161

Alley, Gene, 324

Allison, Bob, 296

Alomar, Roberto, 374, 468

Alomar, Sandy, Jr., 374

Alomar, Sandy, Sr., 374

Alou, Felipe, 468

Alston, Walt, 268–69, 351

Altman, George, 252, 257, 265, 274

Altrock, Nick, 99

Alusik, George, 237–39

Alvarez, Ossie, 239

Amalfitano, Joey, 363

American Association, xvii, 47, 171, 192–93, 229, 242, 250, 363, 454, 501

American Eagle Squadron, 51–52, 69

American Football League, 189

American League, 143, 188, 193, 211–12, 314, 316–17, 327, 339, 383, 424, 465, 479, 499–501

Amon Carter Museum (Ft. Worth), 348

Amoros, Sandy, 240, 249
Anderson, George ("Sparky"), xv, 253, 311, 341, 399, 461–62
Anson, Adrian ("Cap"), 16
Antonucci, John, 412–13
Aparicio, Luis, 285, 459, 468
Appalachian League, 27, 31, 487, 499–500
Appling, Luke, 295–96, 400
Arizona Diamondbacks, xviii, 266, 445, 492
Arizona State University, 311
Arizona-Texas League, 124, 132, 138
Arkansas Travelers, 300, 373
Armas, Tony, 394–95
Army, 61
arrogance in players, 416, 434–36, 452–54
Ashburn, Richie, 442, 451
Ashford, Emmett, 211–12
Asian ballplayers, 487
Astacio, Pedro, 419
Astaire, Fred, 39
Astrodome (Houston), 252, 298, 312, 341, 371
Atlanta Braves, 320, 346, 353, 374, 466
Atlanta Crackers, 161, 164
Atwell, Toby, 208
Atz, Jake, Jr., 53–55
Atz, Jake, Sr., 54
Auburn Tigers (football), 162
Auburn University, 180
Augusta Tigers, 174, 184–85, 189–92, 194–95, 327
autographs: 66, 74–75, 112; on baseball covers, 445–46
Autry, Mrs. Gene, 462

Babich, Johnny, 115
Baker, Dusty, 353, 419, 468
Baker, Frank ("Home Run"), 17
Baker Bowl (Philadelphia), xviii
Balboa Park (San Diego), 445
Baldwin Locomotive Company, 97
ballparks. See stadiums

Baltimore Orioles, xvii, 70, 140–41, 200, 202–6, 209, 283–85, 300, 314, 317, 320, 322, 324–25, 328–30, 355, 375–76, 381, 408, 437, 448, 461, 463, 467, 475
Bamberger, George, 203–4, 207, 211, 223, 303, 400
Bamboo Room (Tiger Town), 182
Bank One Ballpark (Phoenix), 445, 492
Banks, Ernie, 251–54, 260, 265, 275, 442–43, 445, 447, 468
Barker, Cowboy, 29–30
Barker, Ray, 208–9
Barragan, Cuno, 258, 438
Bartirome, Tony, 230
baseball: as an ancient game or myth, 497; as an art form, 494; as a city game, 494; and comedy, 99, 113–14, 117–18, 181–82, 200, 211–12, 265, 371–72, 489; as a country game, 493–94; versus cricket, 223; history of, 16–17, 475; importance of, xiii–xv, 486, 493–98; and kids, 217–18, 439, 489–90; and race, xix, 151, 171–74, 201, 207, 236–37, 244, 290, 337, 495; and radio, 43 (see also broadcasters); as a religion, xiv; and social democracy, 495; and social mobility, xiv, 16, 494–95; and statistics, 495–97; and teamwork, 16, 482, 494; and television, 493; and time, 497–98; and work, 15–16; unique structural aspects of, 497–98
Baseball (PBS series), 260
Baseball Academy, 331–33, 487
baseball caps, 26, 80–81, 335, 398
baseball cards, 340–41
baseball equipment. See individuals terms
"Baseball Great," 400
Baseball magazine, 67
Baseball Professional Ballplayers' Association, 18
baseball shoes. See spikes
baseballs, 3, 8, 143–44, 149–50, 164–65, 217, 283, 447, 480; autographed, 71, 85, 97,

265; frozen, 127–28, 480; rubbing up of new, 283; yellow, 18, 398

base stealing, 145, 178, 257–58, 285, 300–301, 396, 484, 486

Basgall, Monty, 362, 364, 367

basketball, 162, 238, 287, 479

Bates, Charlie, 54

Bates, Jason, 418

bats, 1, 3, 53–54, 72–73, 79, 91, 125, 282, 470, 480–81

bat-sawing incident, 53–54

batting cages, xvii, 331, 339–40

batting tee, xvii, 12–13, 125, 132–33

Bauer, Hank, 204, 320, 388

Baumer, Jim, 239

Baumgartner, John, 177

Bay Meadows horse track, 347

Baylor, Don, 420

Beamon, Charlie, 201, 206–7

Bearden, Gene, 115

Bears Stadium, 307

Beaumont Exporters, 55–62, 142, 499–500

Beck, Bill, 437

Beck, Walter ("Boom-Boom"), 70, 437

beer: in the ballpark, 388, 482; breweries, 400, 445; Budweiser, 310; commercials about, 265; in the clubhouse, 191, 304, 310; Coors, 310

Bell, Buddy, 415

Bell, James ("Cool Papa"), 260

Bench, Johnny, xvii, 290, 311–13, 375, 435, 442, 444, 459, 462, 468

Berardino, John, 53

Berg, Moe, 99

Berra, Yogi, 182, 215, 249, 442, 445, 468

Berres, Ray, 281, 283

Berry, Charlie, xvii, 88, 339

Berry, "Jittery Joe," 92–93

Berry, Ken, 286

Bertell, Dick, 258, 263

Bertram, Lakshi (granddaughter), 403

Best, Steve, 445

Bichette, Dante, 142, 416–17, 419, 433

Biebel, Don, 277

Big Red Machine, xv, 341, 455, 459, 463

Biggs, Arky, 124

Bilbrey, John, 152

Billings Gazette, 149

Billings Mustangs, 149, 151, 153–54, 172, 314

biorhythms experiments, 278–79

bird-dogging. *See* scouting

Birmingham Barons, 238

Bisbee Yanks, xvi, 121–34, 137, 228, 384, 410, 450, 499–501

Black, Don, 93–94

Blackburn, Wayne, 182

Blake Street Bombers (Colorado Rockies), 419

Blue, Vida, 468

Bo's Burgers (Twin Falls), 155

boardinghouses, 24, 28, 152, 172, 403

Bob Feller's All-Stars, 482

Bonds, Barry, 447

Bonura, Zeke, 496

Boros, Steve, 233–34, 392–93, 399–400, 486

Borowy, Hank, 104

Boston Braves, 19, 282

Boston College, 237

Boston Patriots (football), 189

Boston Red Sox, 34, 41, 67, 87, 95, 98, 104, 171, 180, 184, 197, 200, 241, 280, 294, 322–23, 327, 334, 338, 340, 345, 354, 369, 399, 420, 448, 454, 465, 475

bottle caps as balls, xvii, 3

Boudreau, Lou, 245, 435, 442, 449–50, 468

Bowman, Roger, 438

Bowsfield, Ted, 400–401

box scores, xiii, 2, 16, 100

Boyer, Clete, 202–3, 383, 387, 390, 392–93

Boyes Hot Springs, 112, 138, 438, 447

Brace, George, 75

Bragan, Bobby, 318, 363

Braves Field (Boston), xviii

Breeding, Marv, 202

Brett, George, 337, 423

Brewer, Jim, 259, 269, 388
Brideweser, Jim, 209
Bridges, Tommy, 66, 70, 180
Briggs, Spike, 193–94
Briggs Stadium (Detroit), 73, 88, 102–3
Bristol, Claude, 434
Bristol, Dave, 314, 399
British Columbia Place Stadium (Vancouver), 400
Brito, Mike, 360
Brizendine, Colonel, 35–36
Brizendine, Maudie, 35–36
broadcasters, 481. *See also names of individual broadcasters*
Brock, Lou, 251–52, 255–56, 260, 265, 308, 396, 435, 442, 444, 468
Brooklyn Dodgers, 12, 19, 25–26, 107, 115, 200, 249, 274, 318, 449–50, 475
Brown, Irv, 437
Brown, Joe, 324, 328, 375
Brown, Joe E., 200
Brucker, Earle, 89
Buck, Charlie, 151
Buck, Cliff, 243
Buck, Jack, 481
Buffalo Bisons, 189, 312, 326
Buhl, Bob, 258–59
Bull Durham (movie) 38–39, 78, 185
Bullard, George, 187
Bullock, Helen Deane. *See* Metro, Helen Deane Bullock
Bunker, Wally, 326
Bunn, Jake, 347
Bunning, Jim, 193, 293, 434–35, 468
bunt: 96, 145, 208, 302; drag, 26, 30–31, 109; squeeze, 270, 280, 485–86
Burdette, Lew, 263
Burgess, Smoky, 283–84
Burgmeier, Tom, 327
Burke, Glenn, 354
Burke, John, 418
Burks, Ellis, 419
Burlington Bees, 186–87

Burns, Ken, 260
Burr, Raymond, 247
Burris, Jim, 344, 390
Busch, Ed, 95, 99, 105
Busch, Gussie, 305
Busch Stadium (St. Louis), 414, 493
Butler, Bill, 326
Butler, Dick, 168–69
Buxton, Ralph, 115
Bynon, Jim, 123, 129

California Angels, 238, 318, 328–29, 339, 360, 372, 446, 462
Camacho, Moy, 460
Cambria County Sports Hall of Fame, 203
Camilli, Dick, 186
Camilli, Dolph, 186
Campanella, Roy, 468
Campaneris, Bert, 345, 358, 468
Campanis, Al, 331, 349, 351–54, 357–62, 364, 377, 401, 463
Campanis, Jim, 325
Campbell, Jim, 180, 182, 227, 230–31, 344–45
Canadian Football League, 41
Canal Zone, 97
Candlestick Park (San Francisco), 452, 469
Canseco, José, 401
Canton Bulldogs (football), 180
Caraker, Sarge, 167–68
Caray, Harry, 464, 481
card-playing, 92, 111, 210, 483
The Cardinal Inn (Mayfield), 41
Cardwell, Don, 259, 263–64
career statistics, 495–97, 499, 500, 501
Carew, Rod, 468, 485–86
Caribbean Series, 373
Carlton, Steve, xvii, 300, 304–5, 428, 468
Carlucci, Cece, 437
Carnevale, Danny, 338
Carolina League, 186–87, 329, 501
Carpenter, Bob, 409
Carr, Whitey, 31

Casale, Jerry, 240
Cash, Norm, 235
Cashen, Frank, 376
Castilla, Vinny, 418, 461
Castillo, Roberto ("Bobby"), 361–62
Castro, Fidel, 358
Cater, Danny, 285
Caulfield, Jake, 105, 117
Ceccarelli, Art, 205–6
celebrities at the ballpark, 102, 117–18
Cepeda, Orlando, 266, 435
Cey, Ron "The Penguin," 352, 419
Chacon, Elio, 302
championships: Beaumont, 62; Denver, 234; Mayfield, 42; Montgomery, 164, 170; Tulsa, 300; Twin Falls, 154–55
Charleston Senators, 192–94, 197, 234, 485, 501
Cherry, Bob, 439
Chetkovich, Mitch, 115
Chicago Cubs, xv, 104, 151, 159, 181, 197, 223, 250–80, 283, 297, 327, 340, 393, 434, 438, 440, 442, 452, 455, 457, 461, 463–64, 475, 492, 497, 501
Chicago White Sox, xv, 19, 62, 66–67, 72, 95, 118, 161, 186, 195, 200, 202, 209, 280–99, 310, 322, 325, 329, 369, 375–76, 382, 440, 447, 464, 475, 491
Chiti, Harry, 423
Christopher, Lloyd, 93
Christopher, Russ, 93
Churchill Downs, 123, 410
Cicero, Joe, 95
Ciensczyk, Frank, 387, 389
Cincinnati Red Stockings, 489
Cincinnati Reds, xv, xvii, 43, 114, 153–54, 239, 250, 265, 267, 280, 293, 311–14, 316–17, 326, 333, 335, 341, 450, 455–56, 458–59, 461, 464, 476, 492
Cisco, Galen, 338, 342
Cisneros, Mr. (Mexican club business manager), 361–62
Clark, Jack, 350

Clary, Ellis, 370, 406
Clemens, Roger, 304, 428, 466
Clemente, Edgar, 415
Clemente, Roberto, 263, 453–54, 468
Clements, Bob, 154
Clements, Joe, 155–56
Clemmons, Lance, 325
Cleveland Indians, 85, 94–95, 100, 113–14, 118, 132, 188–89, 280, 282–83, 287, 326, 329, 360, 393, 439, 493
Clift, Harlond, 144
clothes, 71, 143–44, 314, 379, 471
clubhouse lawyers, 281
clubhouses, 103, 275–76, 310, 341, 389, 400, 413, 421, 483–84, 492
coaching career: with Chicago White Sox, xvii, 202, 281, 294, 382; with Oakland Athletics, xv, 197, 203, 377–99, 402, 453
coal mining, xiv, 13–15, 83
Coast Guard, 93, 98–99
Cobb, Bob, 150
Cobb, Herschel, 145–46
Cobb, Ty, 17, 144–46, 178, 444–45, 475
Cobb Field (Billings), 150
Cochrane, Mickey, 85, 91, 98, 144, 146–47, 180, 343, 447–48
Cohen, Sid, 127–28
Colangelo, Jerry, 445, 492
Colavito, Rocky, 459
Coleman, Jerry, 481
Coleman, Ray, 37
college baseball, 224, 311, 330, 332
"College of Coaches," xv, 250–51, 261–62, 318
Collins, Rip, 17
Colorado Avalanche (hockey), 416
Colorado Baseball Commission, 403
Colorado Pork Council, 403
Colorado Rockies, 139, 142, 197, 292, 324, 346, 399, 403, 411–21, 427, 461
Columbia Reds, 168–69, 171, 174
Columbus Cardinals, 168
Comellas, Jorge, 24

Comiskey Park (Chicago), 68, 103, 281, 284, 286, 294, 374, 490

Commissioner of baseball, 100, 412, 473–74. *See also names of individual commissioners*

Concepcion, Davey, 459, 468

conditioning, xv, 164–65, 183–84, 203–5, 207, 229, 288–89, 303, 308, 321, 326, 393, 400, 421–34

Conlan, Jocko, 277

Conners, Billy, 258

Connie Mack Day, 84–85

Consolidated Aircraft Corporation, 51–52

Consuegra, Sandy, 206–7

contest: cow-milking, 342; egg-tossing, 487–88; greased-pig, 488; home-run-hitting, 437, 479–80, 491–92; rabbit-chasing, 488; throwing, 137–38

Continental League, 463

Cook, Earl, 56–57

Cooney, Johnny, 282–83

Cooper, Bill, 310, 312

Coors Field (Denver), xiii, 341, 413–16, 420, 437, 439–40, 480, 482, 484, 489, 491–92

Corning Royals, 330–31

Cosman, Jim, 302

Cotton States League, xvi, 52, 324, 499–500

Country and Western music, 231, 247

Courtney, Clint ("Scrap Iron"), 121–25, 127–28, 134–36, 264, 432

Cousins, Bill, 278

Covington, Wes, 255, 258

Cowboy Artists of America, 349

Craft, Harry, 250, 274

Cramer, Roger ("Doc"), 66, 73, 76–77, 79–80, 83–84, 86, 101, 470

Crawford, Willie, 351

Crazy Harry (fan at Oakland), 398

cricket, 223

Cromartie, Warren, 373, 466

Crompton, Yitz, 97

Cronin, Joe, 211–12, 233, 338–39

Crosetti, Frank, 363, 392

Cruze, Bob, 174

Crosby, Bing, 118, 141, 146

Cuccinello, Tony, 282

Cuellar, Mike, 468

Culberson, Leon, 67

Cullenbine, Roy, 82

Cullop, Nick, 101

curfew and curfew violations, 39–41, 122, 176–78, 215, 230–31, 239

Curlee Clothing Company, 35

Daily Racing Form, 408

Dal Canton, Bruce, 325

Dallas-Ft. Worth Rangers, 229

dancing, 39–40, 147–48

Danville Leafs, 187–88

Dapper, Cliff, 438

Dark, Alvin, 271–72

Davalillo, Pompey, 359

Davalillo, Vic, 359–60

Davis, Marvin, 375–76

Davis, Spencer "Onion," 165, 167

Davis, Willie, 353

Dawson, André, 373, 466

Dean, Jay Hanna ("Dizzy"), 61, 264, 464, 481

Dean, Paul, 61

DeBusschere, Dave, 287

"Deep Freese" defense, 245

Del Mar race track, 407

Demeter, Steve, 186

Dent, Bucky, 353

Denver co, xvi, xvii, 98, 143, 217, 251, 260, 280, 294, 303, 316, 320, 347, 375, 408, 411, 414, 418, 437, 441–42, 457

Denver-area homes and ranch, xvi–xvii, 242, 347–48, 404

Denver Bears, xvii, xix, 109, 171, 189, 226–42, 244–50, 265, 300, 307, 331, 344, 373, 378, 390–91, 423, 449, 466, 486, 490, 501

Denver Broncos, 41, 234, 416, 463

Denver City Hall, 445

Denver club negotiations, 375–76

Detroit Tigers, xv–xvii, 25, 41, 47, 51, 55–
56, 64–84, 86, 88–90, 98–101, 122, 173,
176–81, 184, 189, 192–94, 200, 206, 227–
30, 234–38, 240–41, 245, 250, 253, 267,
295, 300, 315, 321, 326–28, 338, 344–45,
352, 378, 381, 399, 411, 420, 438, 448,
460, 475, 499–500

Deutsch, Dutch, 130

Devincenzi, Vic, 107, 118

Devine, Bing, 254, 373

Devine, Joe, xvi, 121, 124, 138–39, 141–42,
144, 148, 154

DeViveiros, Bernie, 179, 181–82, 485

DeWitt, Bill, 32–33, 250, 313, 376

Dickey, Bill, 7, 442, 445

Didrikson, Babe, 490

Dillon, Matt, 277

DiMaggio, Joe, xviii, 33, 102, 155, 197, 417,
434, 442, 444–45, 452, 468, 471

DiPietro, Bob, 223

Director of player procurement (Kansas
City Royals), xv, 70, 176, 211, 235, 237,
287, 310, 317–33, 336, 338, 346, 399, 412,
414, 416, 437, 447

diving, 42, 370–71

Dodger Stadium (Los Angeles), 197, 361,
363

Doerr, Bobby, 442, 444, 468

Donatelli, Augie or Gus, 21, 26, 278, 464

donkey baseball, 488

Donnelly, Ed, 240

Dorsey, Tommy, 351

Dougherty, Ed, 242

Downing, Al, 356

Drabowsky, Moe, 327, 343

Drago, Dick, 317, 326

Dressen, Chuck, 180

Drummond, Cal, 213

Drysdale, Don, 435, 443, 457, 468, 471,
494

Duncan, Dave, 416

Dunlap, Harry, 338

Dupont, Allaire, 408

Durante, Jimmy, 118

Durham, Joe, 201

Durham Bulls, 185–89, 192, 277, 501

Durkin, Harry, 186

Durocher, Leo, 436, 461

Dye, Charlie, 349

Dykes, Jimmy, 91

East Texas League, xvi, 44, 47–48, 51, 499–
500

Eastern League, 78, 274, 329

Eastern Shore League, xvi, 24, 499–500

Easton Browns, 24–25, 499–500

Ebbets Field (Brooklyn), 25–26

Eckert, Commissioner General William,
318–19

Edlund, Gene, 215–17

Eisenhardt, Roy, 399–401

Eisenhower, General Dwight, 266–67

ejections, 144, 149, 159, 177–78, 247, 307,
398–99, 404

Elliott, Bob, 250

Ellsworth, Dick, 259, 269

Elston, Don, 259

employment (other than baseball), 13–15,
25, 43, 44–46, 51, 55, 62–64, 136–37, 146,
156, 82–83, 162, 225

Engle, Joe, 487

Engle, Rip, 1

Enright, Jim, 253–54

Enright, Morey, 149–50

Erautt, Eddie, 207

Erautt, Joe, 56, 58

Eskenberry, Jim, 139, 141

Estalella, Bobby, 87, 96, 99, 172

Estrada, Chuck, 204–5

European ballplayers, 486–87

Evans, Dwight, 197, 419, 465

Evans, Frank, 334

Evansville Bees, 194

Evers, Hoot, 55, 57, 59, 66

exhibition games: Annapolis MD, 97; Bainbridge MD, 97; Camp Leonard Wood MO, 97; Camp Polk LA, 61, 97; Curtis Bay MD, 93, 97; Great Lakes Naval Base IL, 97; Montgomery AL, 89, 171; Norfolk VA, 97–98; Tulsa OK, 307–8; Utica NY, 78

expansion or relocations of franchises, 473

"eye-in-the-sky," xv, 350, 362, 364–65, 367, 377

Fain, Ferris, 417

Fan Fest, 445

fans: gifts from, 483; letters from, 438–39; promotions for, 48, 112, 148, 170, 342, 414, 479–80, 487–92

fathers and sons/fathers and daughters ball games, 489

Fayetteville Highlanders, 187

Feller, "Rapid Robert," 98–99, 400, 468, 482

female ballplayers. See All-American Girls' Professional Baseball League

fences, 37–38, 98, 101, 112, 214, 270, 314–15

fencing, 163

Fenway Park (Boston), 67, 87, 101–2, 106, 294, 417, 492

Ferguson, Joe, 352, 355

Ferguson, John, 306

Fernandez, Tony, 360

Ferrarese, Don, 206–7, 214

Ferraro, Mike, 367

Ferrell, Rick, 79, 227

Ferrick, Tom, 333

Field of Dreams (movie), xv

fights, 124–25, 130, 152–53, 160, 232–33, 264, 299–300, 302, 351, 378, 388, 453, 470

Filchock, Frank, 41

fines, 40–41, 155, 169, 176–77, 255, 299, 303–4, 307, 309–10, 343–44, 346–47, 385

Finkelstein, Willie, 162

Finley, Charlie, 354, 376, 397–98

Finnegan, Frank, 123, 130

Fiore, Mike, 329

Fisher, Eddie, 282, 287

fishing, 144, 196, 451

Fisk, Carlton, 423

Fitzgerald, John, 312

Fitzmorris, Al, 325–26

Fitzsimmons, "Fat" Freddie, 422

Fleitas, Angel, 165

Flores, Jesse, 94

Florida Marlins, 399, 437, 472, 479

Fond du Lac Panthers, 157, 274

food: 24–25; at the Astrodome, 298–99; in the clubhouse, 275–76, 310, 483–84; Dodger Dogs, 363; at Tiger Town, 230. *See also* The South: food of

football, 41, 54, 140, 162–63, 165, 172, 180, 185, 189, 234, 272, 307, 416, 479

Forbes Field (Pittsburgh), xiii, 17, 263, 276–77, 451, 454

Ford, "Tennessee Ernie," 14

Ford, Whitey, 327, 388, 400

Fortes, Manulo, 133, 137

Foul Ball Club (Tulsa), 305–6

Fournier, Jack, 19–23, 26

Fowler, Art, 383, 385, 390–92, 394

Fox, Charlie, 373

Fox, John, Jr., 27

Fox, Nellie, 282, 458

Foxx, Jimmie, 24, 84, 91, 343, 447–48, 468

Foy, Joe, 317, 322–24

fraternization, 41, 299, 483

Frazier, Joe, 214

Frazier, Raelee, xviii, 441–43, 445

Freak incidents, 30, 99, 101, 130–31, 151, 184–85, 189–90, 223, 295

Freeman, Mark, 215

Freese, George, 245

Fregosi, Jim, 399, 489

Fricano, Marion, 223

Friend, Owen, 214, 220

Frisch, Frank, 447

Fritz, Paul, 194

Fuentes, Tito, 358
Funderburk, Dutch, 34, 44

Gable, Clark, 245
Galarraga, Andres, 417, 419, 433, 443–45, 459, 461, 468
Galbreath, Dan, 410
Galbreath, John, 82, 409–10
Gallagher's (Cleveland), 294
gambling, 155, 466
The Game of the Week (CBS show), 264
Garcia, Mike, 468
Garcia, Richie, 398
Gardella, Danny, 41, 134
Garrison, Ford, 95
Garvey, Steve, 352, 419
Gas House Gang (St. Louis Cardinals), 190
Gassaway, Charlie, 94, 105
Gebhard, Bob, 412, 416
Gehrig, Lou, 7, 447, 467–68
Gehringer, Charlie, 467
Gentry, Rufe, 70
Geraghty, Ben, 171
Gerkin, Steve, 94
Gerl, Bernie, 158
Giamatti, Commissioner Bart, 473–74
Gibson, Bob, 434–35, 443, 456–57, 468
Gibson, Josh, 17, 260
Gilcrease Museum (Tulsa), 348
Giles, Bill, 411
Giles, Warren, 410
Gilhousen, Rosie, 333, 336–37
Gillespie, Bob, 56
Gillick, Pat, 222, 437, 463
Gilliland, G. E., 32
Gilmore Field (Hollywood), 53, 112, 117
Gilson, Harold, 300, 308–9
Girardi, Joe, 420
Gladding, Fred, 240
gloves, 3, 31, 122–23, 385–86
Goldsman, Ben, 163–64
Goldsmith, Ralph, 27, 29, 31, 33

golf, 119–20, 143, 179, 218, 252, 287, 356, 428
Gomez, Lefty, 85, 400, 446–48
Gooden, Dwight ("Doc"), 468
Gordon, Joe, 119, 214–15, 230, 315, 320–21, 337, 464
Gorman, Lou, 317, 320, 322, 327–28, 330–32, 344, 467
Gorsica, John, 66, 70–71
Gossage, Goose, 368, 443, 466, 468
Grand Bar CM (Metro Ranch), 404
Grant, Margaret (Marge) Moreskonich (sister), 16
graphology profiles of 1962 National League managers, 266–75
Gray, Pete, 86
"Gray Goose" (airplane), 193
Grba, Eli, 400
Greco, Dick, 165–67, 170
Green, Lenny, 201–2
Green Bay Packers (football), 163
Greenberg, Hank, 18, 66, 72, 81–82, 100, 471
Greenberg, Joe, 18
Greensboro Pirates, 187–88
Grich, Bobby, 330
Griffith, Calvin, 375
Griffith, Clark, 84
Griffith Stadium (Washington), 79, 103
Grimm, Charlie, 279
Groth, Johnny, 98
groundskeepers, 167–68, 215–17, 308
Grove, Robert Moses "Lefty," 85
Grzenda, Joe, 240
Guerra, Fermin "Mike," 24
Guerrero, Pedro, 360
guns, 29–30, 50, 81, 99, 134, 152, 259, 483
Gustin, John, 16
Gutteridge, Don, 282
Gwynn, Tony, 443, 468, 474, 481
Gyselman, Dick, 153

Haak, Howie, 328

Haas, Mule, 91
Hackney, Sara, 53
Hadacol Caravan, 170
Haefner, Mickey, 104
Hafey, Tom, 115
Hall of Fame, 79, 255–56, 268, 277–78, 287–88, 296, 300, 305, 313, 320–21, 346, 350, 355, 373, 381, 387, 395, 442, 445–46, 448, 450–51, 456, 458–67
Hall of Fame game, 1944, 78–79, 304–5
Haller, Bill, 212, 242
Haller, Tom, 242
Halper, Barry, 446
Hankins, Jay, 334
Hansen, Ron, 202, 282–83, 285, 423
Haraway, Frank, 235
Harnicher, Frank, 294
Harnicher, Shorty, 294
Harrah, Toby, 330
Harris, Greg W., 415
Harris, Lum, 221
Harrisburg Senators, 175
Hart, Bill, 109
Hart, Schaffner, and Marx, 71
Harwell, Ernie, 345, 481
Hassey, Ron, 419
Hatcher, Mickey, 353
Hawaii Islanders, 308
Hayes, Charlie, 418
Hayes, Frankie, 95
Healy, Fran, 329–30
Heath, Mike, 397
Heath, Tommy, 216
hecklers, 54, 115, 222, 245–46
Hedlund, Mike, 326
Hedrick, Joe, 162
Heffner, Don, 53
Heilmann, Harry, 73–74
Heisley Coal Company, 12
Heisley Row, 12
Held, Mel, 206–7
Helms, Tommy, 375
Helton, Todd, 417, 443

Henderson, Rickey, 383–84, 394–96, 435, 468
Henderson Oilers, 54
Henley Field, 182
Henrich, Tommy, 332–33
Henry, Duane, 408
Henshaw, Roy, 70
Herbert, Ray, 287
Herman, Billy, 332–33
Hernandez, Jackie, 317–18, 325
Hershiser, Orel, 358
Herzog, Whitey, 462
Higbe, Kirby, 164, 167, 191
Higgins, Mike ("Pinky"), 66, 72–73, 76–77, 98
Higgins, Roger, 168
Highland Studio (Denver), 445
Higuera, Teddy, 421
Hitchcock, Billy, 180
Hitters' Hands project, xviii, 282, 440–45, 449, 452–53, 455, 457, 481
hitting exhibitions, 17, 61, 73–74, 90–91, 195, 327, 359, 373
Hoak, Don, 263
Hobbie, Glen, 259
Hodges, Gil, 273–74
Hoerner, Joe, 299–300
Hoffberger, Jerry, 375–76, 408
Hofheinz, Judge Roy, 249, 298–99
Holland, John, 250, 261–62, 279
Hollywood ballpark. See Gilmore Field
Hollywood Stars, 117, 201
home runs, 8, 24, 30, 40, 53, 59, 78–79, 98, 100, 101, 102, 104, 130–31, 135–36, 151, 153, 167, 170, 214, 223, 233–34, 238, 256, 264, 285, 301–2, 327, 353, 356, 418, 461, 465, 479–80, 491–92
Homestead Grays, 17
Hooton, Burt ("Happy"), 356, 366
Hoover, Joe, 72
Hope, Bob, 118
Horlen, Joe, 287
Hornsby, Rogers, 61–62, 142, 279

horseback riding, 196
horseracing, 92, 347, 367, 372, 395, 420. *See also* racehorses
Horton, Willie, 241, 393, 468
Hostetler, Chuck, 72
Hough, Charlie, 352, 355–56, 366
Houk, Ralph, 234
Houston Astros, 325, 455, 460
Houston Buffaloes, 61, 245
Houston Colt .45s, 250, 252–53, 274
Houtteman, Art, 206
Howard, Bruce, 287
Howe, Steve, 382
Howe, Warren, 123
Howsam, Bob, xvii, 227, 240–41, 244, 246, 300, 305, 310–14, 317, 335, 341, 456, 463–65, 490
Hoyt, Waite, 446
Hubbs, Kenny, 251–52, 257, 428
Hudlin, Willis, 159–60
Hughes, Jim, 249
Hundley, Floyd, 37
hunting, 63–64, 71, 80–81, 96, 133, 146, 151–52, 259
Huntz, Steve, 352
Hurst, Bruce, 415
Husky, Ferlin, 231
Hussey, Jack, 187
Huston, Gordie, 47
Hutchinson, Freddie, 264–65, 267–68

Idaho Falls ID, xvi, 227, 237, 406
Idaho Falls Russets, 115, 154, 195–99, 501
Igoe, Mary Minnick (sister), 6, 100
Illinois Institute of Technology, 278–79
Indianapolis Indians, 286–87, 306, 310
injuries, 99, 154, 189–90, 196, 203, 208, 314–15, 357–58, 421–22, 424, 478. *See also* Metro, Charlie: injuries of
insects: cockroaches, 55; gnats, 365; mosquitoes, 166
interleague play, 475
International League, 170, 312

investments, 224–25, 297–98, 338–39
Investors Syndicate of Canada, 225
Iowa Cubs, 302
Irvin, Monte, 400, 442

Jackson, Reggie, 74, 357, 366, 381, 445, 447, 468
Jackson, "Shoeless Joe," xv, 349
Jackson Generals, 41
Jackson Mississippians, 159–60
Jacksonville Tars, 170–71, 173, 408
Jacobs, "Doc," 24
Jacobs, Ray, 145, 152
jail, 6, 135–36, 244
Jarry Park (Montreal), 364
Jaster, Larry, 303
Javier, Julian, 468
Jefferson County Bank (Lakewood), 242
Jenkins, Bish, 196–97, 199, 406, 436
Jenkins, Ferguson, 443, 457, 468
Jenkins, Lucille, 196–97, 199, 406
Jenners PA, 1, 3, 5, 8–11
Jennings, Ted, 109
Jessel, George, 118
Jewish-American ballplayers, 96
Jocketty, Walt, 437
John, Tommy, 282–83, 287–88, 368
Johnson, Alex, 300–301, 466
Johnson, Bill, 165
Johnson, Bob (Seattle Rainiers), 119
Johnson, Bob (Kansas City Royals), 324–25
Johnson, Byron, 443, 445, 482
Johnson, Connie, 201, 207
Johnson, Syl, 144
Johnson, Walter, 33
Johnstone, Jay, 351, 353
Johnstown PA, xv, 1, 15, 18–23
Johnstown Flood, 1889, 19
Johnstown Johnnies, 18
Jones, Governor Brereton, 408
Jones, J. W., 165
Jones, Johnny, 408

Jones, Keith, 189
Jones, "Puddin'head," 165
Jones, Red, 100
Jordan, Michael, 479, 491
Jorgensen, John "Spider," 200–201, 221–22, 228
Joshua, Von, 352
Juarez Indios, 131
jujitsu, 52
Jurges, Billy, 332

Kaat, Jim, 464–65
Kaline, Al, 314, 346, 417, 435, 442, 444, 468
Kansas City Blues, 284
Kansas City Athletics, 250, 320
Kansas City Monarchs, xix, 251, 260, 482
Kansas City Royals: xv, 70, 119, 176, 211, 226, 235, 237, 283, 287, 310, 315–44, 367, 378, 381, 390, 396, 399, 412, 414, 416, 437, 446, 456, 462, 501; expansion draft for, 317–19, 322–23, 325–30, 467
Katalinas, Ed, 352
Kauffman, Ewing, 315, 319, 322, 331–32, 335–40, 416
Kauffman, Muriel, 320, 338, 462
Kauffman Stadium (Kansas City), 342
Keane, Johnny, 272–73
Keefe, Dave, 96
Keeneland horse sales (Lexington), 264
Kell, George, 88, 95, 99, 442, 444
Kelly, Michael "King," 116
Kelly, Pat, 329
Kelly, Tom, 140
Kennedy, John F., 237, 248
Kennedy Art Gallery (New York), 349
Kentucky Derby, 123, 410
Keough, Joe, 329
Keough, Marty, 214, 329, 393
Keough, Matt, 329, 389, 393–94
Kernek, George, 300, 302, 307
Kerner, Nick, 243
Kile, Daryl, 415–16
Killebrew, Harmon, 442, 444, 447, 454

Kinder, Ellis, 41
Kiner, Ralph, 442–44, 451, 481
Kiner's Corner (Forbes Field), 451
King, Martin Luther, Jr., xix, 173
Kingman, Brian, 394
Kingman, Dave, 320, 467
Kingsport Royals, 331
Kinney Jerry, 319–20
Kirby, Gene, 264
Kirkpatrick, Ed, 318, 328–29
Kissel, George, 181
Kitty League, xvi, 32–34, 41, 51, 499–500
Klann, Fritz, 35, 39–40
Klein, Lou, 251
Kluttz, Clyde, 29
Knuyper, Bennie, 34
Koonce, Cal, 259
Korcheck, Steve, 332
Koslo, Dave, 41
Koufax, Sandy, 262–63, 429, 468, 471
Kovach, George, 48
Krichell, Paul, 25
Kruk, John, 489
Kuenn, Harvey, 241
Kuhel, Joe, 68
Kuhn, Commissioner Bowie, 372–73, 472
Kurowsky, Whitey, 161–62

labor violence, 15, 29
Laboy, Coco, 300, 302
Labosh, Ann, 13
Lachemann, Rene, 400
Ladies Day, 490
Lady Marines, 75
Lajoie, Napoleon, 446
Lake, Eddie, 67
Lakewood Country Club, 242
LaMacchia, Al, 165, 356–57
Lamont, Helen, 13
Lamour, Dorothy, 118, 136
Landes, Stan, 212–13
Landis, Jim, 282, 286

Landis, Commissioner Kenesaw Mountain, 83, 89, 409
Landreaux, Kenny, 353–54
Landrum, Don, 257–58
Lanfersieck, Edward "Red," 34, 38–40
Langford, Rick, 394
Lanier, Hal, 399
Lanier, Max, 134, 334–35, 399
Lansford, Carney, 428
Larsen, Don, 400
LaRue, Bubbles, 248
Lasorda, Tommy, xv, 350, 352, 354, 358, 360–61, 366, 401, 461–62
Latino ballplayers, xix, 24, 84, 96, 124, 137–38, 160, 172, 207, 299, 358–63, 460–61, 467–68, 486–87, 495
Lavagetto, Cookie, 25–26
Lazzeri, Tony, 7
League Park (Cleveland), 103
Lee, Bill ("Spaceman"), 489
Lee Bears. See Pennington Gap Lee Bears
Leishman, Eddie, 124, 138, 142, 148
Leland Hotel (Detroit), 76, 81–82
LeMay, Dick, 302–3
Lemon, Bob, 300, 338, 344, 368, 400
Leonard, Dutch, 104
Levi Strauss, 397
Leyden Lake, 348
Leyland, Jim, 399
Lindquist, Carl, 165
Lipon, John, 55–57, 59
Little League baseball, 479–80
Litwhiler, Danny, 181
livestock: bull, 405; cattle, 404–6; goat, 365–66
Locker, Bob, 287
Lodigiani, Dario, 369
Loeser, Dick, 160
Lolich, Mickey, 229, 315
Lombardi, Ernie, 53, 140, 469–70
Lombardi, Vic, 210
Lombardi, Vince, 162–63
Lonborg, Jim, 428

Lopat, Eddie, 51, 327, 450
Lopes, Davey, 352, 368
Lopez, Al, xv, 185, 202, 281–82, 284–87, 293, 382, 393, 442, 468
Los Angeles Angels (Pacific Coast League), 112, 116
Los Angeles Dodgers, xv, 53, 259, 262, 268–69, 274, 282, 290, 313, 323, 328, 331, 347, 349–52, 354–55, 357, 360–65, 367–69, 374, 377, 379–80, 384, 401, 407, 419, 438, 460, 471–72, 475–76
Los Angeles Times, 410
Louisiana State University, 272
Louisville Colonels, 171, 233–35, 240, 249
Louisville Slugger Company, 442, 449
Lowrey, Peanuts, 363
Loyning, Pauline Moreskonich (sister), 16
Lucadello, Johnny, 18
Lucchesi, Frank, 123, 128
Lukas, D. Wayne, 347, 407
Lujack, Johnny, 27
Lujack, Stan, 27
Lupien, Tony, 180–81
Lynch, Jerry, 459
Lynn, Fred, 354
Lyons, Hillman, 123, 131
Lyons, Ted, 66, 195, 446–47

Mack, Connie, xv–xvi, 84–100, 105, 107–8, 118, 171, 343
Mack III, Connie, 85
Mack, Earl, 88
Macon Peaches, 190
MacPhail, Andy, 463
MacPhail, Larry, 97, 463
MacPhail, Lee, 314, 318, 368, 463
Maddux, Greg, 466–67
Madlock, Bill, 468
The Magic of Believing, 434
Maglie, Sal, 134
Mahaffey, Art, 303
Majeski, Hank, 98

Major League Scouting Bureau, xv, 104, 176, 334, 345–47, 349

Maldonado, Candy, 360

Maltzberger, Gordon, 62

managerial career: Augusta Tigers, xvi, 174, 184, 189–92, 327, 501; Bisbee Yanks, xvi, 121–34, 138, 228, 383, 410, 451, 501; Charleston Senators, xvi, 192–94, 197, 234, 501; Chicago Cubs, xv, 151, 197, 250–80, 283, 297, 340, 393, 434, 438, 440, 442, 452, 501; Denver Bears, xvii, 109, 171, 189, 226–42, 244–50, 300, 307, 344, 423, 449, 501; Durham Bulls, xvi, 185–89, 192, 501; Idaho Falls Russets, xvi, 195–99, 237, 501; Kansas City Royals, xv, 283, 323–24, 337–41, 344, 390, 396, 456, 501; Montgomery Grays, xvii, 158, 163–85, 189–90, 192, 197, 199, 234, 300, 312, 316, 422, 427, 436, 501; Montgomery Rebels, xvi, 89, 157–62, 501; San Juan, Puerto Rico, winter league club, 299, 454; Terre Haute Huts, xvi, 194–95, 237, 244, 501; Tulsa Oilers, xvii, 260, 283, 300–312, 326, 426, 448, 463, 501; Twin Falls Cowboys, xvi, 115, 138–56, 274, 278, 409, 418, 501; Vancouver Mounties, xvi, 114, 131, 185, 188, 198–25, 228, 250, 267, 284, 300, 303, 316–17, 321, 324, 327, 340, 344, 346, 369, 423, 426, 438, 455, 463, 465, 501

managerial style, 61, 88–89, 110–11, 122, 131–32, 134, 140, 145–47, 153–55, 167, 177–79, 181, 186–87, 191–94, 196, 198, 202, 204, 206, 209–10, 213, 220, 224, 229, 232–34, 237–38, 244–45, 252, 254–56, 260–61, 265–75, 279, 303, 306–7, 309–10, 322–23, 329, 343, 383, 419, 423, 429–30, 434, 452, 485–86

Mann, Earl, 161

Mantilla, Felix, 171

Mantle, Mickey, xviii, 126, 197, 273, 314, 319–20, 388, 390–91, 434, 442, 445, 452–53, 468, 474, 485, 494

March Field, 52

Mariana, Nick, 150

Marichal, Juan, 397, 400, 453, 468

Maris, Roger, 302, 400, 465

Marlowe, Dick, 206

Marshall, Mike, 328

Marshall, Jim, 210

Marshall Tigers, 49, 51

Martin, Babe, 115

Martin, Billy, xv–xvi, 115–16, 124–26, 127, 320, 345, 378–94, 397–99, 401, 462, 468, 485

Martin, Freddie, 261

Martin, Hershel, 115

Martin, J. C., 287

Martin, Morrie, 207

Martin, Pepper, 190–91

Martinez, Buck, 325, 329

Martinez, Dennis, 460

Martinez, Pedro, 468

Martinez, Tippy, 468

Maruca, Bob, 139

Marx Brothers, 118

mascots, 489

Mathews, Eddie, 266, 270, 297, 393, 442, 447, 453, 468

Mathewson, Christy, 349

Matlack, Jon, 324

Mattick, Bobby, 153

Mauch, Gene, 270–71, 288, 293

Mayberry, John, 325

Mayfield KY, 51–53, 55, 63, 80, 85, 97, 106, 120, 157, 251

Mayfield Browns or Brownies, xvi, 33–42, 77, 134, 471, 499–500

Mayo, Eddie, 72

Mays, Willie, 416, 434, 445, 447, 452–53, 457, 468

Mazeroski, Bill, 140, 400, 459

McAulifee, Dick, 241

McCarthy, Joe, 96, 224, 424, 449

McCatty, Steve, 385, 394

McCovey, Willie, 447, 455–56, 468

McCraw, Tommy, 286

McDaniel, Jim, 234, 237

McDermott, Mickey, 334

McDougald, Gil, 129, 141–43, 153

McDowell, Banks, 165

McGee, Frank, 162

McGhee, Bill, 92, 95

McGowan, Bill, 67, 79, 98–101

McGrew, Brownell, 349

McGwire, Mark, 429, 447, 465, 491

McHale, John, 173, 180, 193–95

McKeon, Jack, 329

McKnight, Jim, 262

McLaren, Bill, 56

McLish, Cal, 335, 388

McMorris, Jerry, 412

McQuinn, George, 77

McReynolds, Dale, 333–34

Medwick, Joe ("Ducky"), 17, 179, 448

Mejia, Roberto, 415

memorabilia: 71, 85, 97, 265, 438, 282, 341, 349, 396, 440–46; photographs, 75, 153, 498. *See also* baseballs: autographed; Hitters' Hands project

Memorial Stadium (Baltimore), 327

Men's Journal, 445

Merit Clothing Company, 35, 42, 471

Merkle, Fred, 17

Merrick, Walter, 407

Mesner, Steve, 266

Metkovich, George ("Catfish"), 41, 213–14

Metro, Charles ("Bud"), Jr. (son), 5, 118, 138, 190–91, 199, 242–43, 251, 330, 403, 438, 445

Metro, Charlie: as altar boy, 5–6; as basketball player or referee, 18, 82, 162; birth of, 1; boyhood of, 1–11; change of name of, 2; children of, 157–58, 163, 196, 199, 251 (*see also individual children's names*); comeback of, 436; courtship with Helen Deane Bullock, 36–37, 43–46, 52; defensive abilities of, xix, 24, 26, 38, 47–48, 54, 57, 59, 87, 98, 102, 126, 137, 153, 165–

66; family of, 403 (*see also individual family names*); first major league hit by, 74; fondness for Western art of, 348–49; as football player or referee, 23, 82, 162; and gardening chores, 5; injuries of, 15, 26, 52, 57, 64, 148, 152–53, 161, 337, 344, 449; mispronunciation of name of, 54, 119; as national cross checker, xv, 345–49; playing Santa Claus, 43–44, 163; school baseball played by, 8; school problems of, 8–9; teenage years of, 11–23; tobacco-chewing incident of, 67; town team baseball played by, 3–4, 11–13, 18; Ukrainian heritage of, xvii, xix, 1, 12, 27, 55, 119, 172; ventriloquism of, 266; watermelon stealing by, 50; wedding of, xvi, 52–53

Metro, Elena (daughter), 57, 62–63, 76, 90, 118, 138, 199, 203, 242, 251, 379, 403

Metro, Geoff (son), 137, 242, 251, 299, 371–72, 403, 406, 446

Metro, Helen Deane Bullock (wife), xvi, 36–37, 43–44, 52–53, 55–56, 76, 133–34, 138, 146, 158, 161, 171, 175, 188–89, 194, 196, 199–200, 225, 227–28, 242, 251, 294, 307, 350, 365–66, 377, 380, 391, 403–6, 440

Metro (Moreskonich), Jim (brother), 26

Metro (Moreskonich), Joe (brother), 16, 26

Metro (Moreskonich), John (brother), 16, 175–76, 333–34

Metro, Steve (son), 5, 114, 190–91, 199–200, 217, 242, 251, 299, 405, 445–46, 479; named after Steve O'Neill, 55, 171

Metro Ranch, 347

Metropolitan State College (of Denver), 436

Mexican League, 34, 41, 134, 335, 358, 438, 460

Michigan State University, 189

Mickelson, Ed, 158–59

Middle Atlantic League, 18, 398

Mile High Stadium (Denver), 171, 411, 418, 457

Milks, Marvin, 143–44, 474

Miller, Abe ("Payday"), 47–50

Miller, Hack, 71

Miller, Ray, 204

Mills, Art, 78

Milwaukee Braves, 124, 194, 207, 249, 255–56, 258, 263–64, 266, 269–70, 277, 280, 297

Milwaukee Brewers, 204, 241, 325, 352, 400, 418, 421, 458, 473, 475

Minneapolis Millers, 47, 454

Minnesota Twins, 282, 317, 329, 354, 375, 381

Minor League Professional Baseball Association, 186, 438

Minoso, Minnie, 442, 468

Mitterwald, George, 390, 392

Mize, Johnny, 445, 448

Mizell, "Vinegar Bend," 158

Monday, Rick, 353

Monroe, Vaughn, 128

Montgomery Grays, 163–85, 190, 192, 197, 199, 234, 300, 312, 316, 422, 427, 436, 499–501

Montgomery home fire, 173, 227–28

Montgomery Rebels (Cardinals' farm club), 157–62, 499–501

Montgomery Rebels (Red Sox' farm club), 171

Montreal Expos, 302, 320, 373, 457, 466

Monus, Mickey, 412–13

Moody, "Buns," 13

Moore, Anse, 55, 57

Moore, Bob, 407

Moore, Eddie, 151, 172

Moore, Jackie, 390, 392–93

Mooty, Jake, 70

Morehead, Dave, 327

Moreskonich, Charlie. See Metro, Charlie

Moreskonich, Metro (father), 1–2, 5, 11, 12–14, 16, 18, 22, 100, 187, 220

Moreskonich, Pauline (mother), 1, 4–5, 14, 22–23

Morgan, Joe, 442, 455, 459, 462, 468

Morganna, "The Kissing Bandit," 374–75

Moriarty, George, 178–79

Morjoseph, Joe, 33–34, 38

Morningside College, 334

Morrison, Lennie, 165

Morton, Bubba, xix, 237, 244

Moss, Les, 306–7, 310–11

Most Valuable Player award, 346, 417, 456, 465

Mota, Manny, 363, 459, 468

Motley, Don, 334

Mueller, Les, 90

Mullen, Pat, 181–82

Mungo, Van Lingle, 26

Municipal Stadium (Cleveland), 295

Municipal Stadium (Kansas City), 327, 335, 339, 341

Munson, Thurman, 428

Murcer, Bobby, 319–20

Murdoch, Rupert, 471

Murdock, Mel, 230

Murphy, Dale, 346, 356, 415

Murphy, Dwayne, 394–95

Murray, Eddie, 447, 466, 468

Murtaugh, Danny, 271

Musburger, Brent, 294, 307

Muser, Tony, 401

Musial, Stan, 80, 137, 263–64, 305, 311, 434, 442, 444–45, 450–51, 468, 474

Nacchio, Joe, 97

Nanty-Glo PA, xiv, 1, 6, 11–13, 17, 19, 31, 52, 189, 278, 370

National Football League, 429

National Jewish Hospital (Denver), 343–44

National League, 193, 251, 254, 262, 265, 267, 278, 288, 383, 410–11, 417, 451, 479

National Western Stock Show (Denver), 390

Native American ballplayers, 42, 72, 81, 119

The Natural (movie), 439
Navy, 97–98, 319
Negro Leagues, 17–18, 201, 207, 334, 358, 443, 445, 460
Negro Leagues Museum, 207, 334, 445
Nelson, Chet, 228
Nelson, Roger, 322
Nettles, Graig, 202
Neville, Ernie, 186
New York Daily News, 298
New York Giants, 41, 60, 78–79, 107, 186–88, 447–48
New York Highlanders, 489
New York Knicks (basketball), 287
New York Mets, xvi, 251, 265, 273–75, 323–24, 409, 442, 451
New York Yankees, xv, xvii, 1, 6, 12, 19, 23, 25, 43, 51, 82, 91, 95–96, 101, 104, 107, 121–22, 124–26, 138–42, 145, 147–48, 152, 155, 157, 179, 182, 200, 202, 209, 234, 274, 282, 284, 293, 312, 318–21, 323, 350, 353, 366–68, 374, 379, 381–82, 384, 388, 401–2, 420, 424, 448–50, 458, 460, 472, 475, 481
Newcombe, Don, 333
Newhouser, Hal, 66, 68–69, 71, 180, 420, 448, 468
Newman, Eddie, 150–51, 233, 279, 405
Newsom, Bobo, 91–92, 422
Nicholson, Dave, 221, 286–87
"nickel curve." *See* pitches: slider
Nied, David, 415
Niedenfuer, Tom, 357–58
Niehoff, Bert, 161
Nieman, Bob, 221
Niggeling, Johnny, 104
night baseball, 28–29, 38, 207, 308
Nischwitz, Ron, 240
Nixon, Richard M., 372
Noah, Charlie, 1391–40
Norman, Bill, 180
Norris, Mike, 394
North, Billy, 354

Northern Dancer, 408–9
Northey, Ron, 329
Northey, Scott, 329
Northrup, Jim, 228–29, 241
Novikoff, Lou ("The Mad Russian"), 119

Oakland Athletics (or A's), xv, 197, 203, 342, 345, 354, 356–57, 360, 376–401, 437, 440, 442, 453, 464
Oakland Emeryville ballpark, 112
Oakland Oaks, xvi, 94–95, 105–19, 124, 267, 378, 438, 499–500
Oakland-Alameda Coliseum, 398
Oana, Hank ("Prince"), 72
O'Brien (Catholic priest), 106–7
Oceak, Frank, 277
O'Doul, Lefty, 108–9, 222
O'Dowd, Dan, 415
Ogden A's, 395
Ogden Reds, 153–54
Oh, Sadaharu, 461
Oklahoma City '89ers, 193
Oklahoma City Indians, 51, 60
Old-Timers' games, 296, 449, 478
Oliva, Tony, 401, 465
Oliver, Bob, 317, 329
Olympic Stadium (Montreal), 364
Olympics baseball, 478–79
Omaha Royals, 287, 325, 329, 437
O'Malley, Peter, 377
O'Malley family, 471–72
"On the Wings of a Snow White Dove" (song), 231
O'Neil, Buck, xix, 251, 260, 262, 443, 445
O'Neill, Steve, xv–xvi, 55, 57, 59, 61–62, 64, 66–67, 69–71, 74, 76–80, 88, 100, 171
Oquendo, José, 358
Orengo, Joe, 72
Osborne, Bo, 185, 234–35, 239, 331
Otis, Amos, 324, 419, 468
O'Toole, Danny, 136–37
Ott, Mel, 447

Outlaw, Jimmy, 66

The Outlaw (movie), 112

Overmire, Stubby, 56–57, 59, 66, 69–70, 81, 88, 193, 327

Owen, Marv, 17, 179, 265

Owens, Mickey, 134

Pacific Coast League, xvi, 87, 93, 105–6, 108, 111–12, 114, 150, 153, 179, 185, 188, 197, 199–200, 204, 211, 213, 220, 223, 228–29, 250, 257–58, 261, 267, 296, 308, 311, 317, 320, 363, 370, 372, 395, 408, 437–38, 455, 499–501

Paciorek, Tom, 352

Paepke, Dennis, 329

Page, Mitchell, 396–97

Pagliaroni, Jim, 207–8

Paige, Satchel, 17, 260, 468

Palestine Pals, 44–46, 499–500

Palica, Erv, 205, 207, 218

Palmer, Jim, 218, 327–28, 461

Parks, Jack, 164–65

Pasadena Junior College, 224

Pascual, Camilo, 468

Pasquel, Jorge, 134

Patek, Freddie, 318, 324–23

Patkin, Max, 371–72, 489

Paul, Gabe, 410

Pavlesic, Dave, 309–10

Payson, Joan, 409

Peck, Hal, 87, 96, 485

Pee Wee Football, 479

Pehanick, Al, 240

Pelekoudas, Chris, 213

Peña, Orlando, 328

Penn State University, 1, 23

pennants. *See* championships

Penner, Ken, 158

Pennington Gap ballpark, 28

Pennington Gap Lee Bears, 26–31, 499–500

Pennsylvania, xiv, 5, 25, 32, 83, 132–33, 189, 220

Pensacola Pilots, 160–61

Pension matters, xix, 281

pepper games, xv, 26, 321, 426, 429–30

Perez, Neifi, 417, 427–28

Perez, Tony, 435, 456, 459, 462, 468

Perkowski, Harry, 240

Perranoski, Ron, 350, 361, 363

Perry, Earl, 136

Perry, Gaylord, 457

Pesky, Johnny, 241–42

Peters, Gary, 282, 287

Peterson, Buddy, 201, 210–11, 334, 346–47, 438, 465

Peterson, Wayne, 123

Petrick, Ben, 418

Pettit, Paul, 438

Pfeil, Bobby, 309

Philadelphia Athletics (or A's), xv–xvii, 25, 51, 69, 71, 84–107, 115, 119, 171–72, 228, 342, 485, 499–500

Philadelphia Phillies, 42, 70, 128, 239, 258, 270, 275, 288, 293, 305, 325, 356, 409, 450–51, 489

Phillips, Tony, 397

Phoenix Giants, 188, 223, 257, 455

Phoenix Senators, 124–27, 384

Piché, Ron, 302

pick-up baseball games, 2–3, 493–94

Pickett, Charlie, 127

Pierce, Billy, 72

ping-pong, 136

Piniella, Lou, 322–24, 367, 430, 468

Pinson, Vada, 220, 468

Pioneer Award, 439–40

Pioneer League, 115, 139, 144, 152–54, 195, 199, 314, 348

Pipgras, George, 101

pitch-charting, 68–69, 89, 205

pitch counts, 477–78

pitches: curve ball, 24, 26, 57, 70, 88, 90–91, 103–4, 139, 142, 148, 180, 204–5, 383; knuckle ball, 104, 115, 141, 164, 259, 287, 355–56, 450; slider, 91, 115; spitball and other illegal pitches, 70, 115, 214, 263, 392, 457

pitching, 57–59, 160–61

pitching machine, 182–83, 331

Pitts, Pamela, 392

Pittsburgh Pirates, 1, 17–18, 66, 82–83, 118, 140–41, 151, 154, 195, 208, 263, 271, 276–78, 283, 296, 324, 326–28, 360, 362, 375, 399, 409, 444, 451, 475

Pizarro, Juan, 282, 287

players' abilities, 470

players' habits, 493

players' loyalties, 474–75

playing career: with Beaumont Exporters, xvi, 55–62, 165, 499–500; with Bisbee Yanks, xvi, 121–33, 138, 499–500; with Detroit Tigers, xv–xvi, 25, 41, 51, 64–84, 99–101, 200, 206, 228, 295, 411, 438, 499–500; with Easton Browns, xv–xvi, 24–25, 499–500; with Mayfield Browns (or Brownies), xvi, 33–43, 471, 499–500; in Mazatlan, Mexico, 133–38, 438, 460; with Montgomery Grays, 158, 163–85, 499–500; with Montgomery Rebels, 157–62, 499–500; with Oakland Oaks, xvi, 107–19, 267, 378, 499–500; with Palestine Pals, xvi, 44–46, 499–500; with Pennington Gap Lee Bears, xvi, 26–31, 499–500; with Philadelphia Athletics, xv–xvi, 25, 51, 69, 71, 84–107, 119, 172, 228, 485, 499–500; with Seattle Rainiers, xvi, 116, 118–21, 499–500; with Texarkana Liners, xvi, 47–55, 243, 324, 453, 499–500; with Twin Falls Cowboys, 138–56, 196, 499–500

playoff restructuring, 475–76

Pocatello Cardinals, 155

Point Stadium (Johnstown), 19–22

Pokel, James, 187

pole vaulting, 9, 243, 244, 330

polo grounds, 256

Polich, Joe, 141

Popowski, Eddie, 187

Porreco, Vince, 436

Porter, J. W., 116

Portland Beavers, 179, 323

position (on field): catching, 57, 71–72; first base, 87, 118; second base, 57, 86–87, 141, 165–66; shortstop, 57, 134–35, 137; third base, 87, 109, 126, 137, 148, 166

Postema, Pam, 491

potato race, 148

Powell, John "Boog," 355

Powers, Captain (Montgomery police chief), 176

Powis, Carl, 218

practical jokes, 76–77, 113–14, 182, 230–32, 247–48, 277, 284, 342, 351, 353, 385–86, 389–90

Price, Jackie, 113–14

Prince, Bob, 370–71, 409

Propst, Jim, 124

Puckett, Kirby, 474

Queen Elizabeth Park (Vancouver), 15, 214, 223

Quinn, Bob, 325

racehorses, 82, 264, 372, 406–7, 408, 409, 411

racial integration, xix, 96, 151, 171–74, 201, 244

racial segregation, 220

Rapp, Earl, 369–70

Rapp, Vern, 241, 246–47

Rau, Doug, 352, 356

Rawlings Sporting Goods Company, 160, 302

Reader's Digest, 51

Red River Ordnance Plant, 55

"Red Ryder" (comic strip), 349

Redford, Robert, 439

Reese, Harold "Pee Wee," 442, 449–50, 453

Reese, Jimmy, 460

Regan, Phil ("The Vulture"), 232, 240

Reich, Herman, 438

Reichardt, Rick, 285–86

Renna, Bill, 140, 224

retirement: xvii–xviii, 403, 439–40; pension matters of, xix, 378

reunion: xviii, 478; at Mayfield High School, 43; with Metro family, 403; with Pacific Coast League, 437

Reuss, Jerry, 351, 356

Rhoden, Rick, 352, 356

Rhodes, Dusty, 188

Rice, Chris, 412

Rice, Sam, 17

Rice University, 54

Richards, Paul, 66–67, 71–72, 121, 167, 200, 202–3, 205–6, 209, 221, 252, 420–21

Ricketts, Dave, 300, 302

Rickey, Branch, xix, 448, 452, 463, 490

Riebe, Harvey, 56, 58

Riesgo, Arnie, 160

Rigney, Bill, 339, 382, 399

Ripken, Cal, Jr., 423, 467, 475

Ripley's Believe It or Not, 47

Rivera, Jim, 161

Rivera, Mariano, 468

Riverfront Stadium (Cincinnati), 464

Rizzuto, Phil, 141, 445, 449, 481

Roarke, Mike, 233, 237–38

Robello, Tony, 313, 335

Robinson, Bobby, 443, 445

Robinson, Brooks, 202–3, 216, 435, 442, 449, 458, 468

Robinson, Eddie, 355–56

Robinson, Floyd, 221, 286

Robinson, Frank, 171, 174, 244, 327, 447, 453, 455, 468

Robinson, Jackie, xix, 96, 151, 383–84, 495

Rocky Mountain Chapter (SABR), 440

Rocky Mountain News, 228

Rodgers, Bob ("Buck"), 238

Rodgers, André, 223, 251, 257, 263

Rodriguez, Aurelio, 460–61, 468

Rodriguez, Ellie, 329, 340

Rodriguez, Ivan "Pudge," 468

Rolling Stone (magazine), 445

Rooker, Jim, 317, 319, 326–27

Rookie of the Year, 142, 205, 323

Roosevelt, President Franklin, 65

Root, Charlie, 153

Rosar, Buddy, 95

Rose, Pete, 210, 434, 465–66, 468

Rosen, Al, 372

Rosenthal, Larry, 94–96

Ross, Cliff, 153

Ross, Don, 72

Rowe, Schoolboy, 179

Royster, Jerry, 419

Ruby, Jack, 248

Ruel, Muddy, 177

rule books, 212–13

running, 9–10, 18, 32, 66–67, 87, 183–86, 204, 207, 224, 229, 303, 322, 330, 421, 424–25, 428

Russell, Bill, 352–53

Russell, Charlie, 348–49

Russell, Glen, 112

Russell, Jane, 112

Russell, Jim, 33, 39–40, 42, 83, 456

Ruth, George Herman ("Babe"): xvii, 1, 6–8, 84, 91, 108, 153, 282, 302, 445, 447, 451, 460, 465, 468, 474–75, 490; visit with, by Metro, 6–8, 490

"Ruth Beer," 3

Ryan, Connie, 213

Ryan, Nolan, 457–58

Saberhagen, Bret, 415

SABR. *See* Society for American Baseball Research

Sacramento Solons, 216, 266, 438

Sadecki, Ray, 456

Sady, Jim, 186, 188

St. Louis Browns, xv, 18, 21, 23, 26, 31–33, 41, 44, 46, 52, 74, 77, 85–86, 103, 115,

125, 130, 134, 144, 159, 165, 282, 338, 376, 476

St. Louis Cardinals, xvii, 17, 19, 81, 103, 122, 157–59, 161, 169, 179, 181, 190–91, 229, 254–55, 257, 263, 272, 282, 293, 300–302, 304–9, 311, 315, 324, 335, 337, 350, 360, 373, 381, 400, 415, 426–27, 437, 448, 451, 456, 459, 463–65, 472, 475, 481, 493

St. Paul Saints (American Association), 245, 363

salary matters, xix, 81–82, 111, 114–15, 198–99, 250, 313–14, 333–34, 336, 342–43, 358–62, 397, 465, 469–71, 474. *See also* salary negotiations

salary negotiations: xvii; with Cincinnati Reds, 198; with Detroit Tigers, 64–65, 82; with Kansas City Athletics, 250; with Kansas City Royals, 317, 344; with Los Angeles Dodgers, 377; with New York Yankees, 402; with Oakland A's, 378–79; with Oakland Oaks, 107; with Philadelphia Athletics, 84–85, 343; with Seattle Rainiers, 118; with St. Louis Browns, 22–23, 31–33; with Vancouver Mounties, 198; with Washington Senators, 84

Salisbury Indians, 24

Sally League, 163, 170–72, 174, 177–78, 185, 312, 354, 408, 499–501

Salt Lake City Bees, 151–52

Samaklis, Charlie, 164

Samuel, Amado, 249

San Antonio Missions, 138, 165, 200

San Diego Chicken, 489

San Diego Padres (Pacific Coast League), 210, 213, 304, 451

San Diego Padres (National League), 352, 415, 459, 474

Sanford, Ron, 193

San Francisco Giants, 237, 266, 269, 271, 320, 349, 353, 372, 397, 455–56, 467, 469

San Francisco Seals, 72, 108–9, 152, 214–15, 320–21

San Juan, Puerto Rico, winter league club, 299, 454

Santa Clara College, 140, 224

Santee, Wes, 322

Santo, Ron, 251–52, 255–57, 275

Sarna, Tom, 189–90

Savage, Ted, 300–301

Sawyer, Eddie, 330

Sax, Steve, 354

scalpers (ticket), 413

Scalzi, Frank, 18

Scarsella, Les, 114–15

Schaal, Paul, 328

Schacht, Al, 99, 489

Scheffing, Bob, 241, 250

Scheib, Carl, 94–95

Schmidt, Mike, 447, 458

Schoals, Leo ("Muscle"), 51

Schoendienst, Red, 80, 305, 307, 422, 435, 442, 451, 468

Schott, Marge, 456

Schroeder, Bruce, 139

Schuerholz, John, 320, 463

Schultz, Barney, 259–60

Schultz, Joe, 338

Schuster, Bill, 116–17

Schvaneveldt, Blaine, 407

Schwartz, Jack, 467

Schweinbrenner (coal mine superintendent), 12

Scioscia, Mike, 355

scoring games, 497

Scott, Bill, 34

Scouting: advance, 290–91, 293–94, 350, 368–69, 401–2; bird-dogging, 335–37; Latin American, xv, 350, 358–63, 373, 377, 397; by other scouts, 144, 197, 288–94, 311, 330, 415; racial designations on reports of, xix, 290, 337; strategies, 288–94

Scouting Bureau. *See* Major League Scouting Bureau

scouting career: with Chicago White Sox, xvii, 62, 280–99, 322, 440; with Cincinnati Reds, xvii, 311–14; with Detroit Tigers, 344–45, 352, 378; with Kansas City Royals, 333–37, 344; with Los Angeles Dodgers, xv, 137, 159, 349–62, 365, 368–77, 379–80, 401, 419; with Major League Scouting Bureau, xv, 345–49; with Oakland Athletics, 400–401, 437

Scully, Vin, 313, 365

Seattle Angels, 300, 302

Seattle Mariners, 322

Seattle Pilots, 143–44, 316, 323, 328, 338

Seattle Rainiers, xvi, 87, 116, 118–21, 150, 153, 215, 223, 225, 267, 344

Segrist, Kal, 209

Selig, Commissioner Bud, 474

Senior League baseball, 478

Sewell, Rip, 83

Seyfried, Gordy, 240

Shannon, Walter, 158, 448

Shantz, Bobby, 171

Shaughnessy, Frank, 170

Shaughnessy Playoffs, 170, 476

shaving in the clubhouse, 218, 275

Shaw, Bob, 185–86, 189, 277

Sheehan, Tom, 237

Sheehy, Earl, 118, 120–21

Shepard, Larry, 314

Shetrone, Barry, 209, 220

Shibe Park (Philadelphia), 84, 91, 95, 99, 103–4, 270

Shoemaker, Bill, 407

Shore, Ray, 313–14

Short, Chris, 450

Short, Ed, 280, 283, 285, 288–90, 299

Shreveport Sports, 47, 57, 62, 164

Sidaris, Chris, 174–75, 354, 422

Siebert, Dick, 92, 94–95

signs, 37, 55–58, 154, 159, 166–67, 180, 197, 207–8, 213–15, 236, 264, 269, 275, 277, 302, 385, 486

Silvera, Charlie, 400

Silvers, Phil, 117–18

Simmons, Al, 85–87, 90–91, 94, 342–43, 428

Sinatra, Frank, 350–51

"Sixteen Tons" (song), 13

Skaff, Frank, 329

Skelly Field (Tulsa), 307–8

Skowron, Bill ("Moose"), 282, 284, 400

Slaughter, Enos, 241, 383, 400–401, 448

sliding, 67, 179

small-market franchises, xix, 463–64, 472–73, 488

Smith, A. Ray, 305–8, 310–11, 463

Smith, Charlie, 465

Smith, Hal, 140

Smith, Lee, 468

Smith, Mayo, 198, 250

Smith, Ozzie, 373, 459, 468

Smith, Reggie, 419

Snider, Duke, 442, 452–53

Soares, Joe, 152–53

Society for American Baseball Research (SABR), 440

Solomon, Eddie, 352

Somerset County Coal League, 1

Sommers, Bill, 101

Soriano, Dewey, 242, 307

Sosa, Sammy, 465, 491

The South: 158, 173, 244, 294; food of, 27, 28, 35, 64, 294, 404; racial issues in, xix, 42, 173; religion in, 27; women of, 27–28, 158

South Atlantic League. *See* Sally League

Southeast Conference (football), 162

Southeastern League, 89, 157, 159, 161, 499–501

Southern League, 62, 71, 164

Spahn, Warren, 257–58, 296, 449, 468

Speaker, Tris, 17

speeding up ball games, 476–77

spikes, 3

Spinelli, Tony, 7

Splittorff, Paul, 334

Spokane bus crash, 171

Spokane Indians, 352

The Sporting News, 16, 18, 177, 408

The Sporting News Guide, 302

Sports Illustrated, 450

Sportsman's Park (St. Louis), 74, 103, 264

sportswriters, 340

spring training, 52, 55, 62, 64–66, 82, 93, 104–5, 110–11, 112–13, 120, 138, 142, 147, 151, 158, 163, 178–84, 190, 192, 201, 215, 220–21, 228–32, 235, 238, 241–42, 260, 297, 309, 321–22, 337, 342, 387, 389, 400–401, 405, 428–29, 430–31, 437, 442, 449, 498

"spy-in-the-sky." *See* "eye-in-the-sky"

stadiums, xviii, 202, 341–42, 492–93. *See also individual stadium names*

Stallard, Tracy, 300, 302–3, 306, 326

Stan and Biggies (St. Louis), 265

Stanka, Joe, 438

Stanky, Eddie, 234–35

Stanley, Mickey, 229, 240–41

Stanley Cup, 416

Stargell, Willie, 33, 456

Starr, Bart, 162–63

statistics. *See* baseball: and statistics; career statistics

Staub, Rusty, 459–60

Steinbrenner, George, 366–67, 382, 401–2, 409

Steiner, Mel, 213

Stengel, Charles Dillon ("Casey"), xvi, 107–11, 113, 118, 124, 183, 209, 265, 267, 273–74, 383–84, 452

"Stengelese," 108

Stephens, Vern, 34–37, 39–42, 77–78, 134

Stephenson, Jerry, 369

Sternweiss, Snuffy, 282

Stevens, Chuck, 18, 117, 438

Stewart, Dave, 356, 468

Stock, Wes, 205

Stone, Lynn, 123, 410

Stone, Steve, 464

Stone's Drug Store (Mayfield), 36–37

Stovall, Ann Moreskonich (sister), 16, 147, 315, 390

Strader, Red, 141

Strawberry, Daryl, 382, 493

Streisand, Barbra, 351

strikeouts, 287

strike: in 1981, xiii, 476; in 1994, xiii, 469–70

Stuart, Dick ("Dr. Strangeglove"), 296–97

"Stubby" (local coal miner and baseball player), 15

Style Mart clothes. *See* Merit Clothing Company

Summer Olympics 2000, 350, 478–79

Sunday restrictions on ball games, 215–16, 218

sunglasses, 68, 95, 186–87, 255

Super Bowl, 416

superstitions, 42, 131, 159–60

Susce, George, 422–23

Sutcliffe, Rick, 356–57

Sutton, Don, 355

"Swanee" (song), 129

Sweet Lou, 323

Swift, Billy, 415

Swift, Bob, 71, 420

swimming, 39, 49, 428

Tabor, Jim, 67

"Take Me Out to the Ball Game" (song), xiv

Tallis, Cedric, 184–85, 198, 200–202, 208, 210, 217–20, 225–26, 315–17, 320, 323, 325, 328, 335, 338, 341, 343–44, 367

tampering, accused of, 318–19

Tappe, Elvin, 251, 261

Tasby, Willie, 209–10

Tate, Bennie, 33, 38, 40–41, 43

Taylor, Bill, 188

Taylor, Hawk, 328
Taylor, Joe, 201, 211
Taylor, Sammy, 258
teamwork. *See* baseball: and teamwork
Tebbetts, Birdie, 269–70, 275, 280, 367–68
Ted Williams Museum, 218
Temple, Johnny, 154–55
Templeton, Gary, 373, 459
Terre Haute Huts, 194–95, 237, 244, 501
Terry, Bill, 178, 446
Texarkana Liners, 47–55, 243, 324, 499–500
Texas League, xvi, 47, 51, 55, 59–62, 142, 164, 241, 279, 484
Texas Rangers, 128, 355–56, 374, 381, 388, 408
Texas Tech University, 209
Thacker, Moe, 258
Thompson, Tommy, 151
Thomson, Bobby, 400
Three Rivers Stadium (Pittsburgh), 17
Three-I League, 194, 501
Thrift, Syd, 330, 332–33
Throneberry, "Marvelous Marv," 265
throwing problems: of catchers, 147–48, 189, 330; of fielders, 174–75, 354, 422
Thurston, Hollis ("Sloppy"), 289, 293–94
Tiant, Luis, 468
Tiger Stadium (Detroit), 417, 492
Tiger Town, 178–84, 228, 230–31, 241, 265, 267
Tighe, Jack, 180, 327, 411
Timken Company, 315
Tincup, Ben, 42
TNT: The Power Within You, 434
Tolan, Bobby, 300–301, 307
Torgeson, Earl, 119–20
Toronto Argonauts (football), 165
Toronto Blue Jays, 153, 325, 360, 399, 437
Torre, Joe, 374
Torres, Mala, 137–38, 460
Trail of the Lonesome Pine, 27
trainers, 26, 424–25

training camp at Belleville IL, 32–33, 52
trap wall, 179, 265–66
travel: by airplane, 223–24, 227; by army tank, 61; by automobile, 97, 120, 137–38, 141, 157, 195, 199–200, 227, 371; by bus, 28, 60, 128–31, 135–36, 152; by subway, 6; by steamers, 76; by train, 60, 75–76, 79–80, 106–7, 111–14, 135
Traynor, Pie, 17
Tresh, Mike, 67
Triandos, Gus, 140–41, 143, 145, 147–48, 418, 432
tricks at ball games, 30, 38–39, 79, 116–17, 164–65, 168, 215–17, 277, 308, 484
Trout, Dizzy, 66, 68–71, 76–78, 90, 180, 420, 422
Trucks, Virgil ("Fire"), 66, 69–70, 422
Truitt, Charlie, 316, 320, 336–38, 344
tryouts: with Brooklyn Dodgers, 25–26; with New York Yankees, 25; with St. Louis Browns, xv, 18–23, 26, 278
Tucker, Thurman, 68
Tucson Cowboys, 132
Tulsa Oilers (Pacific Coast League), xvii, 260, 283, 300–312, 326, 426, 448, 463, 501
Tulsa Oilers (Texas League), 59
Turner, Jim, 104
turquoise, 127
Tuskegee Institute (AL), xix, 172
Tweedy, Penny, 408
twenty-four-inning game, 89–90
Twin Falls ID, xvi, 138–39, 152–53, 155–57, 197, 418
Twin Falls Cowboys, 138–56, 196, 274, 278, 409, 499–501

Ueberroth, Commissioner Peter, 473
Uecker, Bob, 249, 364
umpires, 21, 100–101, 143–44, 148–51, 159–61, 175–76, 178, 190, 211–14, 247–48, 275, 277, 284, 299, 307, 387–88, 398,

408, 438, 464, 476, 481–82, 491. *See also names of individual umpires*
unidentified flying object, 150
uniforms, 60, 117, 128, 160, 184, 190–91, 214, 304, 320, 412, 440, 484, 488–89
Union, players': 474; activities of, 82–83, 369; steward of, 469
United States Olympic [baseball] team, 350
University of Arizona, 311
University of California at Los Angeles, 140, 224
University of Colorado, 243
University of Southern California, 140, 224
University of Wisconsin, 285
University of Wyoming, 243, 330
Unser, Al, 71
Unser, Del, 71
US (magazine), 445

Valentine, Ellis, 373, 466
Valenzuela, Fernando, xv, 124, 360–62, 460, 468
Valenzuela, Joe, 124, 130
Vancouver Mounties, 23, 70, 114, 131, 185, 188, 198–225, 228, 250, 267, 284, 300, 303, 316–17, 321, 324, 327, 334, 340, 344, 346, 369, 423, 426, 438, 455, 463, 465, 501
Varona, Carito, 360–61
Vaughan, Arky, 17
Veal, Coot, 234, 238
Veeck, Bill, 113–14, 288, 294, 298, 374, 376, 487
Ventura Yankees, 278
Venzon, Tony, 21–22
Vernon, Mickey, 25
Veterans Committee, 350, 458
Veterans Stadium (Philadelphia), 492
Victoria Rosebuds, 241
Villanova College, 25
Vincent, Commissioner Fay, 474

Virgil, Ozzie, xix, 234, 237, 244–45
Voiselle, Bill, 60
Vosmik, Joe, 132

Wade, Ben, 368–69
Wagner, Honus, 66, 83, 444, 446
Wakefield, Dick, 55–57, 66–67, 73, 82
Walker, Harry ("The Hat"), 157
Walker, Larry, 419, 443
Walker, Rube, 260–61
Walsingham, Bill, 157
Waner, Lloyd, 17
Waner, Paul, 17, 194–95
Ward, Pete, 282–85
Warden, Jon, 327
Washington, Vernon George, 58–59
Washington Senators (1901–60), 24–25, 33, 68, 84, 104, 332, 358, 370, 454
Washington Senators (1961–71), 330, 337
Wasiack, Stan, 195
waterbirthing, 403
water episodes, 38–39, 48–49, 78, 128
waterskiing, 185
The wave, 398
weather events: floods, 65, 128–29; fog, 246–47; heat, 53, 60, 129, 169; hurricane, 299; rainstorms, 28, 48, 78, 112, 154–55, 193, 201–2, 210, 248–49, 482; sandstorm, 120; sleet/snowstorms, 65–66, 138–39, 155, 405; tornado, 46–47, 169–70
Weaver, Earl, 381, 461
Webster, Bob, 152
weights, 422
Weiss, George, 388
Weiss, Walt, 417
Welch, Bob, 357
Welters, Frank, 201
Werle, Bill, 210
Wert, Don, 235–36
Wert, Jim, 123
Wessing, Joe, 56

West, Scott, 371–72
Western League, 158, 228
West Texas State College, 209
Weyerhauser Lumber Company, 140
Whitaker, Steve, 323
White, Bill, xix, 290, 337, 411
White, Charlie, 201, 207–8
White, Ernie, 168–69
White, Frank, 468
White, Hal, 66, 69–70, 78
White, Jo-Jo, 118–20
Whitlow, Colonel Robert, 279
Wickert, Bill, 278
Wilber, Del, 485
wild card playoff teams, 475–76
Wilhelm, Hoyt, 141, 282–83, 285, 287, 318, 446, 450, 468
Williams, Billy, 251–52, 254–55, 265, 274, 393, 442, 468, 474
Williams, Bud, 35–36, 38–40
Williams, Claude ("Bob"), 49–51, 243
Williams, Dick, 462
Williams, Hank, 170–74
Williams, Jimy, 399
Williams, Merlyn, 23, 242–43
Williams, Ted, xviii, 34, 51, 73, 101–2, 194, 235, 287, 340, 422, 435, 442–45, 447–48, 450, 468, 474, 480–81, 491
Williams, Walt, 300–301
"Williams Shift," 245
Willie's Sports Palace (Montgomery), 162
Wills, Maury, 269, 307
Wilson, Earl, 171
Wilson, Grady, 165
Wilson, Jim, 104, 345
Wilson, Rube, 250
Wilson Sporting Goods Company, 446
Winfield, Dave, 367–68
Winfield Stud Farm (Maryland), 408
winter baseball, 51, 133–38, 299, 361, 427–28

Wise, Hugh, 41–42
Wolff, Roger, 104
Wolfson, Louis, 408
Wolfson, Sam, 408
women at the ballpark, 220–21, 248, 276–77, 294–95, 440, 476, 489–90
women in the clubhouse, 222, 248
women's softball, 42–43
Wood, Jake, xix, 236, 244
Wood, J. P., 54–55, 59, 66, 73–75
Woodeschick, Hal, 192
Woodling, Gene, 108
Woodrine, Ken, 17
Woodward, Woody, 401–2
World Series: 1932, 153; 1935, 179; 1939, 43; 1945, 66; 1946, 241, 448; 1949, 155; 1952, 384; 1954, 188–89, 452; 1955, 249; 1956, 383; 1959, 282, 294; 1960, 140, 459; 1968, 229, 240, 315; 1977, 353, 366, 377, 384; 1978, 357, 366, 377, 384; 1981, xv, 350, 353, 366–67, 377, 476; 1982, 400
World War II: 47, 65, 106, 123, 150, 266, 278, 370, 405; exhibition games during, 97–98; restrictions on gasoline and travel during, 65, 97; ballplayers during, 69
Wright, Glenn, 144
Wright, Jamey, 418
Wrigley, Philip K., xv, 89, 251, 254, 262, 276, 278–80
Wrigley Field (Chicago), 102, 254, 256–57, 262, 264, 276, 492
Wynn, Early, 282, 288, 435
Wytucki, Gabby, 174

Yankee Stadium, xiii, 6–7, 25, 87, 91, 95, 97, 102, 104, 366, 490
Yastrzemski, Carl, 454–55
Yeager, Steve, 352, 355
Yellowstone National Park, 142
Yewcic, Tom, 189
York, Rudy, 66, 72, 79–81
York, Tony, 120

Yorkitis, John ("Snorkey"), 12
Young, Dick, 298–99
Young, Eric, 418
Younker, Hal, 210
Younkin, Katherine or Kay Moreskonich
    (sister), 16, 315
Yount, Robin, 423, 458, 475

Youth CCC (Civilian Conservation Corps),
    11

Zahn, Greg, 352
Zeller, Jack, 64–65, 82–83
Zimmer, Don, 419–20
Zimmerman, Jerry, 207–8

"One of the best baseball minds that I've ever known."—**Buck O'Neil**, *Baseball Hall of Fame's Veterans' Committee*. "Charlie was a master at running the game and getting the most out of all the players. . . . The most important lesson I learned from Charlie was that baseball was a serious business and when you get to the park every day it's your job. So get serious!"—**Brooks Robinson**, *winner of sixteen consecutive Gold Glove Awards*. "[Charlie] was very demanding, and he insisted that we play hard every day."—**Lou Piniella**, *Seattle Mariners manager*. "He was a good, hard-nosed manager."—**Billy Williams**, *Chicago Cubs coach*.

Charlie Metro's career runs the gamut of the specialties found in baseball—player, coach, manager, scout, inventor. Metro has lived baseball at every level from the Great Depression to today's multimillion dollar contracts. One of a kind, Metro's life mirrors the astounding changes in the game as well as in the nation. Metro's tale is full of heart and a wealth of anecdotes, the result of a fascinating life and a true love of the game.

Charlie Metro was born Charles Moreskonich in Nanty-Glo, Pennsylvania, in 1919. He played in the major leagues from 1943 to 1945 with the Detroit Tigers and

the Philadelphia Athletics. He managed for parts of two seasons, with the 1962 Cubs and the 1970 Kansas City A's. He also coached the 1965 Chicago White Sox and the 1982 Oakland Athletics. Although he had far longer service in the minor leagues, he will probably be best remembered as one of the great scouts and teachers in baseball history.

Charlie, coaching with the Oakland A's, 1982.

Tom Altherr is a professor of history at the Metropolitan State College of Denver. He is a coauthor of *Sports in North America: A Documentary History*.

University of Nebraska Press
Lincoln NE 68588-0255

www.nebraskapress.unl.edu

ISBN 0-8032-8281-8 $29.95

9 780803 282810   90000

DATE DUE

GAYLORD			PRINTED IN U.S.A.